The Sociology of Religion

A Substantive and Transdisciplinary Approach

To the faculty at St. Xavier High School, Cincinnati, Ohio, who intensified my interest in religion and inspired my sojourn on the meaning of life. My education at St. Xavier set the foundation of my personal and professional perspective that builds on science, humanities, and religious studies. This book is a waypoint, and I thank St. X for the embarkation.

The Sociology of Religion

A Substantive and Transdisciplinary Approach

George Lundskow

Grand Valley State University

PINE FORGE PRESS
An Imprint of Sage Publications, Inc.
Los Angeles • London • New Delhi • Singapore

For information:

Pine Forge Press
A SAGE Publications Company
2455 Teller Road
Thousand Oaks, California 91320
E-mail: order@sagepub.com

SAGE Publications India Pvt. Ltd.
B 1/I 1 Mohan Cooperative Industrial Area
Mathura Road, New Delhi 110 044
India

SAGE Publications Ltd.
1 Oliver's Yard
55 City Road
London EC1Y 1SP
United Kingdom

SAGE Publications Asia-Pacific Pte. Ltd.
33 Pekin Street #02-01
Far East Square
Singapore 048763

Printed in the United States of America.

Library of Congress Cataloging-in-Publication Data

Lundskow, George N., 1964-
The sociology of religion: a substantive and transdisciplinary approach/George Lundskow.
    p. cm.
Includes bibliographical references and index.
ISBN 978-1-4129-3721-4 (pbk.)
    1. Religion and sociology. I. Title.

BL60.L86 2008
306.6—dc22   2008008551

This book is printed on acid-free paper.

08   09   10   11   12   10   9   8   7   6   5   4   3   2   1

Acquisitions Editor:	Benjamin Penner
Editorial Assistant:	Nancy Scrofano
Production Editor:	Karen Wiley
Copy Editor:	Teresa Herlinger
Proofreader:	Jenifer Kooiman
Typesetter:	C&M Digitals (P) Ltd.
Indexer:	Sheila Bodell
Cover Designer:	Gail Buschman
Marketing Manager:	Jennifer Reed Banando

Table of Contents

Preface

Religion has always intrigued me, and although my personal beliefs have at times been uncertain and inconsistent, I have always accepted two basic sociological principles: that people require community, and that they require meaning. Historically, religion has been the mediator between the individual and a sense of transcendence. The existential crisis of modern times—the loss of meaning—defies history, and perhaps the essence of human existence. Modernity's bargain, as Adam Seligman calls it, trades individuality for everything else, but is such an absolute notion of individual potential we witness today actually viable without the solidarity of social life? Anomie, alienation, ennui, and other characteristic feelings of modernity are not just concepts, but disruptions of human existence that not only threaten fulfillment, but also increase the possibility of radical and desperate attempts to reclaim the transcendent. Terrorism and war both require a population willing to carry out the orders of outside authority, and people who feel lost and alone all too easily become willing fodder for aspirations of destruction.

Yet this book concerns itself significantly with the everyday, the way in which religion plays out in the daily lives of regular people. Although the events of grand achievement and tragic cataclysm stand out powerfully, we should remember as sociologists that most people most of the time live in the mundane world, where routine commitment to family, school, and work defines our lives. In our routines, we often find the small degrees of satisfaction that cumulatively enable us to rise and face or even to cherish a new day. Yet isolation and purposelessness reside in the routine as well, and here, in daily life, we seek the solace of religion as earnestly as we seek a paycheck or the loving embrace of family. People without religion in some form (deistic or not) succumb to existential decrepitude through unrequited emotions and forlorn dreams no less often than people without home, friends, and productive purpose.

This textbook addresses religion on multiple levels as a guide to the sociology of religion, but also to render religion as something worth studying, and as something that holds wondrous and provocative interest independently of college courses and formal education. The study of religion need not be sterile. After all, aren't we studying, among other things, how people in different times and places have sought the meaning of life, and sought to comprehend the only universal and absolute fact of life, which is death? The study of religion also includes the study of ironic opposition, that people in pursuit of what's right often commit the greatest good, and sometimes the greatest evil. Religious feeling animates both the ideals of emancipation and the depravity of conquest. As Zoroastrians believe, good and evil often stand in balance; human action decides the outcome.

In this spirit, let us broaden sociology to include insight from other disciplines. Let us also maintain an objective perspective and at the same time sensitivity to the subtleties of being and becoming. In short, let us be clear, factual, insightful, and worthwhile. Let's not waste our time in trivialities, and instead seek nothing less than enlightenment.

George N. Lundskow
Grand Rapids, Michigan

Introduction

The great sociologist Edward Shils (1980) once said that "the hard fact of existence is that any serious truth is terribly difficult to discover." Not for the nonchalant intellect or the casual observer, "it requires an exceptional curiosity, capacious memory, powerful intelligence, and great imagination as well as stamina and self-discipline beyond the ordinary allotment to human beings." As if this weren't enough, the search for truth also requires "the discipline of a tradition; it requires the acceptance of an inheritance of knowledge; the reception and assimilation require strenuous exertion" (p. 414). With this in mind, this book is not the end of debate, but the beginning. Far from providing a final word or an all-inclusive and definitive treatise, I hope to inspire the reader to look further, to think more deeply, and to offer up all the Shilsian effort that is required of those who seek enlightenment.

In the study of religion, the knowledge, the intellectual traditions, and the substantive content of religions around the world are vast and nearly timeless. Those who would study religion as Shils calls us must possess greater and deeper knowledge, and greater stamina, discipline, curiosity, intellect, and imagination, than other fields require. Ancient in history, religion seems at once like a grand monument to humanity's greatest aspirations and an edifice to our profoundest horrors. From religion rises hope, liberation, and purpose, but also cruelty, war, and destruction. What is sociology to something so vast and vital?

Sociology is the scientific study of society, which includes individuals, groups, and especially the relationship between them. Groups can be as large as nations, or even today, the global world, or they can be of a smaller scale such as work groups, schools, and the family, or smaller still in the form of friendship networks or even a few individuals, or the relationship of one individual to the surrounding world. Groups can be anonymous and formal entities, such as large institutions like a major research university, less anonymous and more casual such as a small liberal arts college, or personal and intimate such as the dyad of a romantic couple.

In all cases, though, a sociologist uses a scientific approach. In essence, this is conceptually quite simple: logic (theory) + evidence (observation) yields insight. Theory is a systematic application of logic, a conceptual explanation in combination with systematic observation of the real world. This combination yields insight—knowledge of the word that also reveals why things are the way they are. The scientific approach offers both great potential and certain limitations.

The limitation most relevant to the study of religion is that science cannot answer perhaps the most important question of all, as the noted sociologist Max Weber ([1919] 1958) argued: "What should we do and how should we live? That science cannot answer this question is indisputable" (p. 129). However, what we *can* answer are questions such as these: Why do religions rise and fall in popularity? Why does the same set of beliefs inspire peace and love, as well as violence and terrorism? Why does the same set of beliefs inspire service to others and self-sacrifice, but also condemnation of others and self-centeredness? Why do people need religion in the first place? What needs does religion satisfy? Science in general, and the sociological approach in particular, can speak to these and many more important questions, even if alone it cannot tell us the meaning of life.

Sociology studies the interaction of people and groups, the interaction of belief and practice. Through a variety of methods and perspectives, we will see sociology applied to all manner of belief and practice, from the mundane to the extreme, the everyday to the bizarre. Religion is an ancient institution, and to understand it, we must become ancient as well.

Yet religion thrives today and, like society, changes with the times. Thus, we must also be contemporary; we must know the new facts early; we must be in the real world as it emerges. Perhaps a sociologist must even be "cool." In any event, this book calls upon students to think creatively, critically, and realistically, to get in the world rather than stand on the sidelines.

Colleges and universities teach numerous courses about religion, as the study of religion is inherently interdisciplinary. Spread out across diverse disciplines, including sociology, anthropology, political science, psychology, history, literature, religious studies, theology, and divinity, some are introductory courses, and many are upper level. Most departments offer only one or two courses. Yet religion has been a central, substantive area in sociology since its founding in the nineteenth century.

Thus, any sociological textbook of religion must also move beyond disciplinary boundaries, but I contend it must furthermore transcend even interdisciplinary conceptions. So, how does one offer a textbook that draws from a wide variety of disciplines, without favoring one and offending the others, and still retain a specifically sociological perspective?

The answer is that the text must be more than simply a collection of ideas and theories from various disciplines, or a sociological literature review, and instead build a substantive approach that informs students about the real world. In a word, this text presents a *transdisciplinary* approach, which incorporates existing disciplinary knowledge and perspective into a new, substantive, and issue-centered perspective. Yet far from losing sociology in the mix, it places sociology as the universal social science—in this case, focused on religion. Why exclude interesting, timely, and relevant material from other disciplines? It does not. This text merely incorporates all relevant material into the sociological perspective.

Moreover, the text emphasizes factual knowledge that various disciplines have acquired, with sociology as the interpretive framework. More than just a factual reference, the text narrative attempts to discuss how analytical concepts may be applied. With concepts thus placed in a real-life context, students can critically develop their own analysis.

The substantive approach examines religion as it actually exists in all its forms, including belief, ritual, daily living, identity, institutions, social movements, social control, and social change. Within these broad categories, the book devotes particular chapters to important historical moments and movements, leaders, and various individual religions that have shaped the contemporary form and effect of religion in the world today. Most texts use real-life examples only superficially to illustrate concepts. My approach is the opposite—students will learn the facts of religion in its great diversity, all the most interesting and compelling beliefs and practices, and then learn relevant concepts that can be used to explain empirical observations. The book thus follows the logic of actual research—investigate and then analyze—rather than an abstract classroom approach.

Let me also introduce a more radical concept into the sociological study of religion. Following sociologist Douglas Porpora in his revolutionary *Landscapes of the Soul* (2001), I want students of this text to connect sociology, religion, social issues, and the meaning of life. In *The Sociological Imagination* ([1959] 2000), C. Wright Mills attacked sociology for betraying its potential. For Mills, sociology offered a vision, based in science and intellect on one side in combination with morality and justice on the other. Mills indicted sociology for betraying this vision. Its crimes? See the listing in the sidebar.

> ### The Crimes of Mediocre Sociology
>
> 1. Theory so "grand" and abstract that it lacks all relevance to the real world
>
> 2. Empiricism (especially quantitative) so minutely and technically focused that it also lacks all relevance to the real world
>
> 3. Devotion to institutions of power, namely governments and corporations that buy out sociology and direct it to often exploitative or even malevolent agendas
>
> 4. Careerism—people who use it as a vehicle to promote themselves

In place of what he sees as misguided and cowardly conformist failings, Mills calls upon us to embrace the *sociological imagination*—a type of vision that unites science with social justice—boldly and morally. We must establish the conviction, through science and humanity, that we are right in our understanding of human relations, and that the world can be made better through this understanding. For Mills, compassion and objective science must work together so that each improves and tempers the other. I write this book in the same spirit. As we study religion, we should certainly call upon sociology as a science in order to clearly and accurately learn about and analyze what people think and do as they practice religion. Yet at the same time, we must be able to sociologically imagine beyond the empirical and the theoretical, and remember that religion, from whatever intellectual perspective, pertains to matters of ultimate importance—the meaning of life.

We face all manner of distractions in the contemporary world, among which are education, career, and consumption. Do we learn in class today, exchange knowledge and ideas in order to become more enlightened and thus a better person and a more conscientious citizen? Or do we pay money and consume our degree? The Eastern religions call such distractions *Avidya,* a state of preoccupation over small and ultimately meaningless things. Instead, let us approach sociology as something more noble than a set of theoretical frameworks and technical methodological precision, and religion as more than just another intellectual curiosity or worse, an "object of study." Instead, let us inquire into the past, present, and future ways that people have, do, and may yet approach the existential issues of life. As we proceed, we may yet fulfill the promise of sociology that Mills envisioned, and someday contribute to a better society.

In my view, the most successful scholars who study religion—from founders like Max Weber and Emile Durkheim, to present-day scholars like Douglas Porpora, Elaine Pagels, Stephen Prothero, and Sarah Pike—all have the ability to understand religious belief, feeling, and devotion alongside critical scientific insight. In other words, they have a sense of the profound and the uncanny, yet they can also critically evaluate religion, and in their work they move back and forth between the uncanny ecstasy of religion, and the critical precision of science.

To achieve excellence in this field, you must develop this skill as well. The ability to analyze data, by itself, is insufficient to understand religion, because religion is not primarily about objective (observable and measurable) truth but rather about ontological truth. That is, it is about the truth that derives from experience and emotion—the truth of the nature of existence. As a science, sociology has long stared suspiciously at religion, perhaps not as strongly as the natural sciences, but throughout its history, sociology and religion have been discordant. This textbook follows sociologist Douglas Porpora's (2001) lead, in that it is both a book about the sociology of religion as well as a kind of religious sociology—a bold move, to be sure. Yet if the Catholic Church can accept the theory of evolution without caveats or conditions, as Pope John Paul II did in 1997, then perhaps sociology can learn something from religion as well. If you feel that I am trying to convert you to Catholicism (or indeed any version of Christianity or other religion), please read my short biography that accompanies this book. Let me close with an anecdote from a movie, based on a book by physicist and philosopher Carl Sagan.

In the book *Contact*, by Sagan ([1985] 1997), as well as the movie based on it, which stars Jodie Foster as Ellie Arroway, a scientist, and Matthew McConaughey as Palmer Joss, a theologian, the two characters discuss major issues, including the meaning of life. Palmer Joss represents a religious perspective, and Arroway a scientific one. The story centers on an alien intelligence that sends plans for how to build a ship that will travel vast distances in space by creating a dimensional portal. Arroway is eventually chosen to be the rider. When the mission seems to fail, Arroway testifies before an investigation committee that in fact she did travel to a far-off planet, even though the ship appeared to simply drop through the portal in a matter of seconds. What appears to be only seconds to an outside observer was in fact about 16 hours for the person inside the craft, because of the dimensional shift. Needless to say, the court and the public find it difficult to believe Arroway for want of concrete evidence. They have only her testimony. As Joss and Arroway are leaving the courthouse, a reporter asks Joss if he believes her. He responds that "although she and I are bound by different covenants, we do share something in common—we both seek the truth. Yes, I do believe her."

This book seeks the truth, cognizant that different types of truth exist and from different perspectives. It calls students to develop a mature, serious, and sensitive intellect, but also a perception of knowledge and insight as something greater than themselves. To understand religion, to really understand what it means to the devout, one must imagine a much greater and more important world and expanse of being than mundane facts can convey. I do not for a moment suggest we discard rational observation, but facts and methods without perspective are empty motions and pointless shards. We must imagine a greater sociology. Let's not dwell on the minute nor the vast abstractions of society; the petty and meaningless concerns of busy pointlessness. As the poet e. e. cummings ([1926] 1994) wrote, "pity this busy monster, manunkind, not/ . . . [L]isten, there's a hell/of a good universe next door; let's go."

CHAPTER **1**

Theory

Introduction: Sociological Theory and Religion

As a scientific discipline, sociology offers certain types of insight, and excludes others. One of the most common errors regarding science in general, both in the natural and the social sciences, is to align scientific theory with political orientations. This conflates two different things. Science attempts to understand the world, and while this always involves a bias of perspective, it is not the same as a political orientation that seeks to control social institutions and exert decision-making power. Although science can provide insight upon which political platforms may be based, science as a means of generating knowledge and insight, whether natural or social science, is not a political platform. It is an analytical system, not a system of management and political control. In our effort to understand religion, sociology studies religion critically, but at the same time cannot draw conclusions about the merit of particular religious belief or practice. As with any science, critical analysis, using logic and evidence, constitutes the basis of knowledge, not the political agenda that scientific knowledge may inform. In this sense, so-called conservative theories such as functionalism and rational choice are no less critical of conventional notions than leftist or so-called radical theories, such as Marxism or feminism.

Sociology as we know it today began as an attempt to apply scientific principles of logic and evidence to modern society. In particular, scholars sought to understand modern society in order to understand and hopefully alleviate its social problems. For sociologists, modern society begins with the rise of the industrial era, in the early 1800s. However, historians would point out that the basic elements of modernism emerged during the Renaissance, which we can date from the fall of Constantinople in 1453. Many scholars, artists, statesmen, and religious leaders—in essence, most of the intelligentsia and creative classes of the Byzantine civilization—fled to the West, mostly to Italy after 1453, and contributed their talents and energy to the Italian city-states, which rose as the founders of the Renaissance. From 1453 to the beginning of the Enlightenment around 1700, all the decisive elements of modernism emerged. Most importantly, science and math developed sufficiently to allow for rationalization—which means to make something systematic and predictable. This would eventually affect all spheres of life, including religion.

Thus, sociology has long held a Western focus, given its origins as a science devoted to understanding modernity as it arose first in the West. This differs from a Western bias, a prejudiced and ethnocentric notion that the West serves as the standard for all things, that the West is the best and everything else fails by comparison. The study of Western modernism defined much of sociology, its approach and concepts, and developed most extensively in Germany, France, and the United States. Still today, the vast majority of sociological research and theory comes from these three countries. However, nothing prevents sociology from expanding and adjusting concepts so they apply meaningfully to non-Western religion. The goal is to understand, not to judge, the essential quality of one religion over and against another.

Still, sociology does not just study social phenomena; it also organizes such phenomena conceptually and actively draws conclusions. These conclusions create an order to our understanding of reality, and in this way, sociology is not a neutral observer. We seek to create order using scientific research methods and conceptualization. We apply theoretical frameworks in order to interpret data.

However, we do not seek to make normative, that is, to make value judgments about, what is right or wrong, what is on the right path spiritually, or what is misguided. Nevertheless, a sociologist does argue about right and wrong in terms of logic, evidence, and analysis. As a science, sociology cannot discuss what is true or not true about the nature of God or what sorts of thoughts and behavior God may or may not approve of, but we can discuss and prove or disprove what any given religion or understanding of God represents in a social context. That is, given the time and place in which we observe particular practices or beliefs, we can discern what they reveal about the people and the society that uphold them. Sociological validity stands on observable evidence and the logic of theory.

This chapter examines sociological theory relevant to the study of religion. Later chapters will occasionally expand on theory, but focus more on empirical observations about religion.

Death and the Meaning of Life

In order to understand religion today, one must also understand its counterpart—spirituality. While religious practitioners often view themselves as spiritual, it makes good sociological sense to distinguish between these concepts. Indeed, empirical research confirms that religion and spirituality are in actual practice two different things (see Table 1.1). Dictionaries are often not very useful in scientific endeavors, because they typically convey conventional, pedestrian usage, not scientific conceptualization. In sociology, religion is not simply a definition, but an analytical concept.

What is religion? In a recent book, Paul Heelas and Linda Woodhead (2005) define religion as a more or less fixed institution that exists independently from the people who attend its services, volunteer for its projects, and serve in its administrative offices. As an institution, a religion teaches particular beliefs and practices, and expects new and continuing members to conform to its institutional requirements. Religion premises a common good and higher authority, both of which supersede the individual (p. 14). Furthermore, religions consist of congregations—groups of believers who assemble consistently to celebrate their faith and perform necessary rituals. Sometimes a central authority or organizational bureaucracy unites the various congregations, but just as often does not. Some religions are significantly centralized, such as Catholicism in Rome (Vatican City) or Southern Baptism (the Southern Baptist Convention). Others, such as Islam and Hinduism, have no formal centralized authority or organizational bureaucracy. Nevertheless, all of these religions and others evidence common-good ethics (at least for their own members) and devotion to a higher entity that possesses transcendent power, wisdom, love, and other attributes otherwise beyond human capacity.

A related and often confusing concept is spirituality. This concept refers to a much broader sense of connection between the individual and the surrounding world. It exists as a feeling, rather than as an observable pattern of behavior or set of beliefs. Decisively, spirituality emphasizes individual and subjective feeling and experience rather than devotion to external, collective, and superior beliefs, rites, and deities. Heelas and Woodhead (2005) identify this as a holistic approach that privileges personal and subjective emotions and experiences as more valid than formally established creeds or churches. In holistic spirituality, the individual is free to construct personal beliefs, and choose freely from any source material to invent a personal blend to suit individual needs and tastes. Moreover, spirituality of this sort and religion often compete against each other, and empirical research shows that "the congregational domain and holistic milieu constitute two largely separate and distinct worlds (Heelas and Woodhead 2005:32). This conflict occurs because religion consists of institutional structures that maintain consistency across generations. We could say that religions serve communities. In contrast, spirituality consists of individuals who, even when they join together in groups, retain a highly personalized set of beliefs and practices. We could say that spirituality serves individuals.

Does this mean that religious congregations neutralize individuality? In some ways, yes, particularly regarding the essential beliefs and practices of the religion. For example, it is difficult to be Catholic if one does not recognize the authority of the Pope in religious matters, or if one does not accept the Nicene Creed as valid. In other ways, however, religious congregants are free to maintain their individuality. For example, Catholics are free to dress as they want, hold divergent political views, and disagree about interpretations of the Bible. In Wahhabism, a strict version of Islam enforced by the government (an institution) in Saudi Arabia, religious beliefs dictate manner of dress, especially for women, who are forbidden to appear in public with their head uncovered. In any case, it is the institutional structure and collectively oriented beliefs that define religion, not the strictness or comprehensiveness of belief. Some religions govern most of life, others only certain aspects of life.

Similarly, the individualistic nature of spirituality usually includes some commonalities. For example, most spiritual systems, such as New Age, Theosophy, and

Table 1.1 Religion and Spirituality

Religion	Spirituality
Common-Good Ethics—The needs of the community override the needs of the few, or the one	**Individual Ethics**—Beliefs and values serve the personal needs of the individual
Common-Good Morality—The institution decides right and wrong	**Individual Morality**—The individual decides right and wrong
Institutional Autonomy—Religion exists trans-generationally and independently of personal control	**Personal Autonomy**—Spirituality exists within and for each individual
Institutional Hegemony—Exists externally to and coercive of the individual; responds to historical change, not personal decisions	**Personal Hegemony**—Personal freedom of choice; responds to personal feeling and choices

Swedenborgianism, share beliefs of balance, that harmony arises from the proper balance of energy (Ellwood 1995; E. Taylor 1995). Individual innovation often draws from widely diverse sources, and people share ideas quite extensively. Just as religious congregants retain many personal characteristics, so spiritualists share certain ideas despite their personalized beliefs.

While both religion and spirituality have degrees of individuality and degrees of collectivity, religion is premised overall on collective continuance, whereas spirituality is premised on individual autonomy. In religion, the community is the measure of all things; in spirituality, the individual is the measure of all things. A religion requires collective commitment but may allow individuality. In spirituality, an individual may choose collective commitment or not. This book will use the term *religion* broadly and often encompass what technically should be called spirituality, unless otherwise noted. As with the issue of faith, much of the sociology of religion applies equally to spirituality.

Overall, both religion and spirituality share something in common—a leap of faith. In other words, both depend, at an essential level, on faith—that which *cannot be proven or disproven* but is accepted as true. The emphasis here is that faith *cannot* be proven, which differs from something that *is not yet* proven, but could possibly be proven through empirical means. To make this distinction, Max Weber often quoted Tertullian (Quintus Septimius Florens Tertullianus, 155–230 CE), who in defense of early Christianity said, "Credo non quod, sed quia absurdum" or in translation, "I believe nothing except that which is absurd." At some point, all religions define themselves through articles of faith, not proof. Although religion need not necessarily be in conflict with other ways of knowing, such as science, religion goes beyond the observable world to which science is limited. From Tertullian to Weber to present-day theorists and many in between, faith often contrasts with logic and reason, and thus in comparison appears "absurd" if a person privileges logic over faith. At the same time, some faith-based explanations appear absurd if applied to issues of observation and logic.

In the long-standing faith versus reason dichotomy, no resolution is possible, nor even any discourse as each side premises its knowledge on entirely different and contrary grounds. However, as Stephen Jay Gould (2002) (a biologist by training) argued throughout his career, each form of knowledge speaks to a different sphere of knowledge; faith and reason are both accurate because they address essentially different aspects of existence. While this view definitely makes progress, this textbook, as argued in the introduction, proceeds with the assumption that we have not yet learned either to decisively separate or combine faith and reason. While I agree that Gould's position works effectively most of the time, students should consider the full range of human knowledge and use it to develop their own insight. The way in which pieces fit together may yet require a wholly new approach.

For now, let us remain in established theory.

The Place of Religion in Society

The words at the end of this sentence, among the most famous in all of the English language, describe the existential conundrum of humanity—"to be or not to be. . . ." To live or not to live, and if to live, how and why? For what purpose? And what of death, that "undiscover'd country from whose bourn no traveler returns"? We thus face an existential crisis that, as Hamlet realizes, has no automatic answer, no decisively true and certain solution. We have instead only feelings and intellect that, with effort, may produce a sense of conviction (a sense of faith) that we have discovered the meaning of life, and how to live it correctly. Throughout human history, religion has spoken to such existential uncertainties, and to the extent we hear its words and enact its rituals, religion successfully instills meaning where otherwise we would face only an infinite void of despair.

To be, or not to be: that is the question . . .

To die: to sleep; No more; and by a sleep to say we end

The heart-ache and the thousand natural shocks

That flesh is heir to, 'tis a consummation

Devoutly to be wish'd. To die, to sleep;

To sleep: perchance to dream: ay, there's the rub;

For in that sleep of death what dreams may come

When we have shuffled off this mortal coil,

Must give us pause: there's the respect

That makes calamity of so long life. . . .

But that the dread of something after death,

The undiscover'd country from whose bourn

No traveler returns, puzzles the will

And makes us rather bear those ills we have

Than fly to others that we know not of.

—William Shakespeare, *Hamlet*

We can embrace Shakespeare, and many others, who express the essence of human existence with great eloquence and passion. However, such is not our purpose as sociologists. There are other ways to understand the human condition, and through science, we may understand in ways that differ from the poet's moving passages, but perhaps, by the end of this book, prove no less powerful.

In his now classic *The Sacred Canopy* ([1967] 1990), the sociologist Peter Berger identifies the vital existential questions—questions that define the meaning of life—that underlie all of human existence. Berger poses four great questions:

Peter Berger's Four Existential Imperatives

Who am I?

Why am I here?

How should I live?

What happens when I die?

For Berger, these questions define the uncertainty of human existence, and religion serves to answer these questions at some collective level. To be effective, they must be shared answers acknowledged among a population of people yet which each individual accepts willingly; they cannot be forced onto people. Furthermore, the revealed religions face an additional pressing issue—the problem of *theodicy.* The revealed religions are those that hold that God has a revealed purpose for all people, and that we are moving inexorably toward some final moment, whether Armageddon—the final battle between good and evil—or salvation, or possibly both. Theodicy is the issue that arises thus: If God is good and cares about us, why does evil exist? Furthermore, if God is omniscient (all-knowing) and omnipotent (all-powerful), then again, why does evil exist? In the earlier mystery religions, theodicy was not an issue, because God (or the gods) offered no particular plan, and no particular end point to history. The mysteries were revealed only to a select few, usually only after grueling initiation rituals or by the merit of one's birth.

Finally, Berger concludes that in responding to the four great existential questions, and to the issue of theodicy, religion provides a *nomos,* a coherent system of meaning that connects the individual to society and to a sense of purpose above and beyond the empirical and temporal realm (see Figure 1.1). Meaning must be universal and eternal, but also relevant to real moments in life, especially the existential moments of birth, life, and death.

Thus, religion is a set of beliefs that connect the individual to a community, and in turn to a sense of being or purpose that transcends the individual and the mundane. In this way, people reassure themselves, through collective belief, that life is more than a series of events that ends in death, but part of something eternal, something important, something that assures the individual a place in this world, and in some larger scheme of being.

Religion is thus crucial for the long-term survival of any community, because it not only justifies the particular values and lifestyle of a community, but

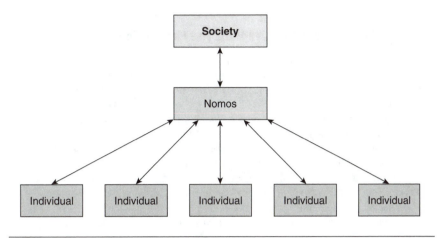

Figure 1.1   Role of the Nomos

reinforces purpose and meaning, and thus connects the present with the past and future. Religious beliefs are thus the collective totality of social beliefs, which, precisely because they are collective and derived from social, not individual existence, appear to the individual as eternal and transcendent truths, as something outside of and beyond the individual, and which must empower the individual as an active member of the very same community. Thus humans create a feeling of the supernatural, of spiritual connections beyond what can be directly observed.

Berger identifies the central aspect of spirituality, deistic or not, as its ability to construct and maintain a nomos—a belief system that explains the meaning of life. This nomos arises specifically from actual social relations as well as visions of society as it ought to be. Without a nomos, a society falls into alienation and *anomie* (a sense of being without values that meaningfully explain life and therefore place meaningful moral regulation on conduct), which produces diverse and extensive social problems. For example, Native Americans continued to live after Europeans destroyed their civilizations, but they lived as strangers in a homeland that was now a strange land, stripped of political power as well as cultural and personal identity.

Yet a firmly accepted nomos builds societies and can hold a social group together despite intolerance and persecution. Numerous historical examples exist: Christians under ancient Rome; the Jews in the diaspora after 70 CE until the 20th century; African Americans during the civil rights struggle, the same aforementioned Native Americans who rediscovered their cultural heritage—all of which united with a specifically religious nomos.

In this way, transcendent beliefs (faith) function affirmingly only to the extent they embody material conditions and promote realization of the self in conjunction with social interests. This means two things: First, the nomos as mediator between the individual and society functions in both directions, as both a top-down system of control and a bottom-up expression of real-life hopes and aspirations of real people. Second, social conflict becomes relevant, as we will see among the classical era theorists.

> ### Ibn Khaldun (1332–1406): The First Sociologist
>
> Born in Tunis, Khaldun spent much of his professional life in Granada, Spain, and Alexandria, Egypt. Extensively educated, he wrote numerous histories and an autobiography. He also wrote a decisively sociological treatise, 400 years before sociology existed as such.
>
> Rarely studied in the West, we may legitimately call Ibn Khaldun the first sociologist. Although the name "sociology" comes from Auguste Comte (1798–1857), Khaldun actually created many of the basic concepts of the field. In his brilliant work, *The Muqaddimah*, he coins concepts such as social force, social fact, group solidarity, and theories of material and ideological conflict, especially urban versus desert life, and the conflict of hierarchy based on economic and cultural domination. He also analyzes the decline of great civilizations. In all of this, religion plays a vital role in various ways. This is required reading for any serious student of social theory.

Berger draws significantly from three of the founders of sociology—Émile Durkheim, Karl Marx, and Max Weber. All three of these scholars studied, and were influenced by, modernity. Modernity is both a time period and a concept. As a time period, it refers to the rise of capitalism and rational (systematic) social organization, which begins to define society around 1500, becomes predominant around 1800, and continues today. As an analytical concept, this process of rational organization changed over time nearly all of society, including economics; government; education; knowledge; culture; and of course, religion. Regarding religion, the force of rationalization not only changed religion, but changed the way we look at it. Rationalized knowledge (in the form of science) allowed people like Neils Bohr and Marie Curie to study the natural world, and their contemporaries such as Marx, Durkheim, and Weber to study other less tangible but no less real aspects of existence, such as religious devotion and beliefs (see Figure 1.2). Science enabled them to study religion in all its aspects as objective phenomena, and in so doing separate it from other forms of knowledge, especially from faith.

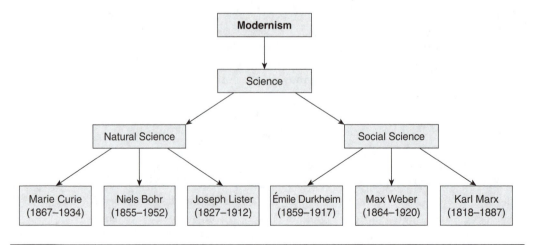

Figure 1.2   Basic Branches of Science and Example Contributors

Classical Theory

In all of sociology, the works of three famous foundational scholars of the field—Karl Marx, Max Weber, and Émile Durkheim—are perhaps the most extensively misunderstood. In this section, we will cover their major works most relevant to religion by examining the primary texts rather than the secondary literature.

All three felt that science could be applied to social issues in the same way scientists had already applied it to the natural world. During their lives in the 19th and early 20th centuries, social science in general was a fledgling field, and no clear lines of demarcation had yet developed. Thus, Weber, for example, freely moves between history, social psychology, and what we might recognize today as sociology proper. Marx similarly combined philosophy, history, and economics. All three integrated whatever fields and insight they found relevant to the task at hand, and the task was to understand the massive social change and upheaval that the transition to modernity wrought. In this effort, they viewed their work in decisively moral terms, believing that clarity and accuracy matter, and that truthful insight is a moral obligation. For all three theorists, as we will see, one of the first and most significant casualties of modernity was religion. Once modernity seized control of the world, nothing would be the same anymore, especially not religion.

Émile Durkheim

Émile Durkheim (1859–1917) argues that religion must provide a "collective effervescence" that celebrates the ideal social order of society. Whatever people believe is the correct and proper way to live, the established religion of that society will portray this order in the ultimate idealized form, as a divine order. The gods, or the one God, have ordained that we live as we already live. Faith in the divine is really then faith in human society, that in order to attain meaning and salvation, one must attain the right type and extent of social integration. Durkheim identified four forms of incorrect or insufficient socialization: egoism—integration is too weak; altruism—integration is too strong; anomie—integration is of a dysfunctional type that fails to regulate the individual; and fatalism—integration is a dysfunctional type that overregulates the individual. Of the four types, Durkheim argued that anomie would prove most relevant to religion in modern times. As religion loses its ability to create existential meaning, people become *anomic* (without a nomos). In this condition, people have no reason to regulate their desires, especially in the realm of economics and acquisition. Durkheim uses anomie in this sense, and not in the general sense of normlessness. The anomic person specifically lacks a sense of meaning and purpose, but may have other norms and values. As Durkheim argues, anomie is found most intensely in successful business executives, who have a powerful normative standard—making money and enjoying the thrill of power—but who lack a sense of meaning. In essence, Durkheim argues that money can buy property and thrills, but not happiness (see Durkheim [1897] 1951:247–250 and 253–257).

Today, we may think of this as consumerism, the idea that we work and spend and consume, always looking for the better deal, the bigger house, the bigger car, the bigger paycheck, the plasma TV, the surround sound stereo system. With natural desires, such as food, there are natural limits in that a person can only eat so much (although advertising and food companies always seek to expand our eating capacity). In contrast, socially created desires are essentially unlimited: there is always more money, more fame, more power, and more property to acquire, more thrills to experience. There is no natural limit to how much of these things we can accumulate. As of this writing, for example, the billionaire financier Kirk Kerkorian (b. 1917), at age 90, seeks to add more millions to his approximately $15 *billion* in personal assets (Kroll and Fass 2007) by attempting to raid and dismantle Chrysler, General Motors, and other companies. How much money is enough?

Without a meaningful nomos, people lack a value system to set limits, and thus lose themselves in the endless and inherently unsatisfiable pursuit of bigger, better, and more of everything subtle and gross that modern society can offer for sale. In this social environment, even people become objects for consumption, and eventually all objects lose their flavor, importance, and ability to fascinate. People eventually find themselves surrounded by meaningless objects in a meaningless world. In its most extreme forms, anomie results in suicide, as a person faces feelings of exhaustion and hopelessness. The thrill is gone, and life feels empty.

Modernity thus differs significantly from earlier forms of society. In earlier forms, mechanical solidarity held society together by connecting people directly to each other. For Durkheim, mechanical solidarity meant the unity of sameness, that each person held more or less the same skills and significance as everyone else. The division of labor was generalized to the extent that each person, having similar skills, performs the same tasks in the community. Although some simple division of labor exists in such societies, especially a gender division of labor in that women do certain things and men do certain different things, all the women and all the men respectively do the same things. Mechanical solidarity promotes communal living, as no person possesses anything unique or different in terms of skills, knowledge, or property that could serve as a basis for domination.

As Margaret Mead ([1928] 2001) found in traditional Samoa, for example, or as Herbert Spencer ([1862] 2004) found among the Teutons in ancient Germany, claims to leadership depend on freely sharing skills and resources, not using resources for personal gain over and against others. Whether a peaceful society like traditional Samoa, or a war-and-plunder society like the Teutons, they both rely on mechanical solidarity, and thus a person claims the mantle of leadership based on sharing or achievement that benefits the collective rather than personal good. Homogeneity holds the community together. Religion reflects this homogeneity, makes sacred everything that maintains the mechanical solidarity, and makes profane everything that disrupts the cohesion of similarity.

In contrast, modern society dissolves mechanical solidarity because it converts individuals into specialists, each with a different position and function in society. The more modernism advances, the more specialized and therefore increasingly dissimilar people become. Just as mechanical solidarity produces sameness, a simple division of labor, so specialization produces difference and a complex division of labor. Yet people still depend on other people, and people must still cooperate with each other, even more so as they become more specialized. Whereas the mechanical person possesses various skills, including a complete set of survival skills, the modern form of organization, which Durkheim refers to as organic solidarity, produces specialized parts, each of which depends vitally on the whole. As an individual, each person is only an incomplete part. As a whole, the various diverse parts come together in unison and constitute a society that is, in terms of its functions, far more complex than is possible in the mechanical form. But if everyone performs within various and diverse groups, each with its own requirements of skills, education, training, experience, and organization, how can people function as a unified whole? What brings all the various specialized parts together as a functioning organism?

Durkheim argues that on one level, economic interests provide a type of unity. However, he also argues that by themselves, economic interests, which manifest as laws, trade agreements, legal contracts, monetary exchanges, and the production of goods and services, only establish the relationship of people to objects, but not people to other people. This is a crucial problem in modern society, which elevates organic specialization to the highest degree. As Durkheim ([1893] 1984) writes, this kind of relationship "links things directly to persons, but not persons with one another. . . . Consequently, since it is only through the mediation of persons to things that people are integrated into society, the solidarity that arises from this integration is wholly negative" (p. 73). In other words, economic ties connect people through the objects that people seek to buy and sell, but this means solidarity is negative (passive) in the sense that it creates order, but only one of convenience. There is no positive (as in active) unity, or as Durkheim states it, there is "no cooperation, no consensus" on what is right and wrong, no solidarity between people, only momentary order based on mutual convenience. Economic ties, although vital to any society, cannot by themselves produce active *moral* cooperation and commitment to other people and to society. Especially in modern times, economic interests alone produce only intense self-centeredness and profound disconnection from other people.

Although modern society is decisively organic, some ancient civilizations developed organic solidarity as well. For example, in ancient Greece and Rome, religion served the main integrative function. Although not completely separated from class and status, Roman civilization developed a complex division of labor and relied on technical expertise of engineers, judges, governors, educators, and administrators of all types. A merchant and craftworking class also arose that created new opportunities for individual advancement. Religion permeated Roman society, and the rich pantheon of deities, each committed to particular locations, trades, ethnic groups, status groups, and many other unique groups, integrated Rome's diversity into a more or less cooperative unity.

Although Roman society was clearly hierarchical, and elites often exploited the lower classes ruthlessly, religion nevertheless created positive (active) integration in the sense that it compelled individuals to serve interests beyond their own personal ones. These social interests could include the Roman state, the city, one's peers, family, or any combination of commitments that transcended the individual. In short, people did not like every aspect of Roman society and conflict frequently occurred, but they accepted it overall as a meaningful order to life overall and thus respected and served that order.

The early Christians serve as a useful example to illustrate Roman social morality. The contemporary scholar Robert Louis Wilken (2003) argues that the Romans did not hate the Christians, but rather distrusted them because they shunned all social activity that involved the pagan gods, which was nearly everything. This not only separated Christians from pagan religion, but from Roman society, which religion permeated and integrated. To intentionally reject the gods was to unintentionally reject the order of Roman society. As the great Roman statesman Cicero (Marcus Tullius Cicero, 106–43 BCE) wrote, "the disappearance of piety towards the gods will entail the disappearance of loyalty and social union among men as well, and of justice itself—the highest of all virtues" (Cicero [c. 40 BCE] 1960).

Marcus Tullius Cicero (106–43 BCE)

The man known to us as Cicero wrote on many topics, including religion. One of the most effective politicians and orators in Rome, he cherished and celebrated the Republic as many would celebrate religious devotion, and indeed, Cicero connected public service and democracy to true religious faith. He could not prove that democracy was a divine form of government, but he believed it nevertheless. His faith would cost him his life. Although offered power in the emerging imperial system, Cicero refused to compromise his devotion to democracy and justice under the law. Marcus Antonius (Mark Antony) ordered him assassinated, and Cicero's alleged final words were, "There is nothing proper about what you are doing, soldier, but do try to kill me properly" (Cassius Dio, *Roman History*).

In Durkheim's first book, *The Division of Labor in Society* (his dissertation; [1893] 1984), he proposes no institution to remedy the fractured relations of modern times. He concludes only that economics alone cannot positively integrate people, and to the extent we rely on economic interdependence, we create only anomic relations, that is, mutually beneficial relations that have no meaning beyond the transaction of the current purchase, or the momentary relations of working conditions.

In order to further understand the social problems of modern society, Durkheim empirically developed a sociological framework in *Suicide: A Study in Sociology* ([1897] 1951). He offers four famous concepts to explain different types of suicide—egoistic, altruistic, anomic, and fatalistic (see Figure 1.3).

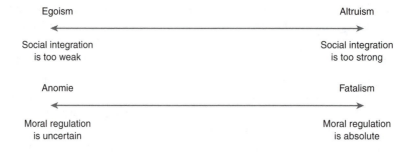

Figure 1.3   Durkheim's Problems of Social Integration

All derive from problems with social integration, although in different ways. For Durkheim, suicide includes all self-destructive behavior, such as substance abuse, and willingly joining the military to kill and be killed. Later in the book, he identifies homicide and suicide as identical, except that in the former the object to kill is external, whereas with suicide, the object is oneself. With this in mind, Durkheim examines the impact of various social institutions, including, family, education, and religion. In the case of religion, he rejects the notion that differences in beliefs explain the frequency of suicide. He observes that statistically, of the three religions common in Europe—Judaism, Catholicism, and Protestantism—Jews are lowest in frequency, then Catholics, with Protestants being the highest. Both Catholicism and Protestantism condemn suicide strongly. However, there is no official proscription against suicide in Judaism.

So why are the Jews the lowest in suicide frequency, when they don't even prohibit suicide as a sin? Durkheim ([1897] 1951) argues that

> the beneficial influence of religion is therefore not due to the special nature of religious conceptions. If religion protects man against the desire for self-destruction, it is not that it preaches the respect for his own person . . . but because it is a society. . . . The more numerous and strong these collective states of mind are, the stronger the integration of the religious community, and also the greater its preservative value. The details of dogmas and rites are secondary. The essential thing is that they are capable of supporting a sufficiently intense collective life. (p. 170)

Of the three religions, Protestantism allows the greatest individual investigation of scripture and requires the fewest obligatory observations. As a result, people are freer to explore their faith, and indeed, as we will see in the next chapter, Protestantism in the United States develops nearly unlimited variations. Yet this freedom also diminishes the regulatory power of religion, or in other words, it integrates the individual less powerfully into the collective identity. People may thus stray into egoism, where they become isolated both emotionally and socially. This isolation produces depression and despair.

Conversely, altruism results when the individual loses his or her individual identity completely in favor of the collectivity. In this case, the individual must be willing to do anything for the group, even if this means death. Sometimes it means killing oneself; sometimes killing others; or as we will see with religious terrorists, sometimes both together. In altruism, the individual life becomes inconsequential—only the group matters.

Often described as normlessness, anomie refers more exactly to a lack of meaningfully regulating normative values—in other words, the lack of a meaningful morality. Durkheim sees this type of dysfunction as most common in modern times. In order to open new markets and to increase consumption, modern capitalism must simultaneously break down personal inhibitions and social prohibitions—anything that might restrict consumption and infringe on profit. People must feel free to indulge in every vice, all manner of consumption, all types of new sensations and thrills. All three classical theorists in this chapter agree that, although desires may differ from one person to the next, the one desire all modern people share is that they want more—of anything and everything.

Durkheim observes that animals seek what their instinct tells them to seek—food, reproduction, and so on. Their needs have clear boundaries of satisfaction, and they do not obsess over what they don't have. They more or less automatically tend toward equilibrium in life, because their satisfaction is directly connected to and proportionate to their needs, the limits of which nature sets for them (although one of my cats definitely eats too much, and the other is quite insatiable for affection. That's what living with humans does to an otherwise noble animal.) However,

> this is not the case with man, because most of his needs are not dependent on his body or not to the same degree. . . . How to determine the quantity of well-being, comfort or luxury legitimately to be craved by a human being? Nothing appears in man's organic nature nor in his psychological constitution which sets a limit to such tendencies. . . . Human nature is basically the same in all men, in its essential qualities. It is not human nature which can assign the limits necessary to our needs. They are thus unlimited so far as they depend on the individual alone. (Durkheim [1897] 1951:247)

As social animals, we suffer no inherent regulation to our desires, and thus they are inherently unlimited. Those things of a social nature, such as money, fame, thrills, and power, are inherently unlimited; we can only eat so much food, but there is always more money, fame, and power to accumulate. Only society can set a limit on socially created desires, which it has done historically through religion. Although a higher class may enjoy a much better standard of living, with far more luxuries, religion has provided a meaningful justification for the established social order, and meaningful limits on what a person could or could not do. As Durkheim notes, the need is to establish meaningful and legitimate limits on desires, not just formal limits. People must find satisfaction, not just barriers.

The special problem in modern society, which capitalist values rule, is that "unlimited desires are insatiable by definition, and insatiability is rightly considered a sign of morbidity. Being unlimited . . . they cannot be quenched. Inextinguishable thirst is constantly renewed torture" (Durkheim [1897] 1951:247). Such people find themselves in a state of perpetual unhappiness, and "a thirst arises for novelties, unfamiliar pleasures, nameless sensations, all of which lose their savor once known" (p. 256). Hence their separation increases, and even the slightest decrease becomes an intolerable cataclysm. People want it all, and they want it now. They want more, and the more they seek, the less satisfaction they find. This produces feelings of desperation, despair, and self-destruction. Unfortunately, Durkheim feels that "religion has actually lost most of its power" to meaningfully regulate. In the absence of religion, modern capitalist society has in its place sanctified unlimited desires, "and by sanctifying them this apotheosis of well-being has placed them above all human law. Their restraint seems like a sort of sacrilege" (p. 255). Money and profit are the new gods.

The inverse of anomie is fatalism, where moral control so completely and absolutely governs life that it chokes off all longing and hope. Fatalism "is the suicide derived from excessive regulation, that of persons with futures pitilessly blocked and passions violently choked by oppressive discipline" (Durkheim [1897] 1951:276). In history, we often find that people will bear great burdens in the present if they feel that the future will be better, if not for themselves then at least for their children. To the extent religion can instill a sense of a better future, that is, a sense of hope, it successfully mitigates the effects of fatalism. As we will see in subsequent chapters, people will tolerate very little and more readily violate the established social order if they believe that the future will not be better, that is, if they lose a sense of hope.

Durkheim also addressed religion specifically in *Elementary Forms of the Religious Life* ([1915] 1965). Whatever its doctrines, any particular religion must be able to create a meaningful social order and instill this order within the individual. Not only must the religion celebrate the present, the collective effervescence mentioned earlier, but it must also instill a sense of something larger that transcends the individual. Usually, this is the divine, the eternal, that which specifically cannot be observed directly.

The Soul

The concept of a soul exists in many different religions and cultures.

Christianity, Islam, and **Judaism—the three monotheist religions,** derive from the same Abrahamic tradition, and their beliefs about the soul are highly similar. The soul exists separately from the body, and although it abides within the mortal body for a while, its existence is eternal. This concept derives most directly from Socrates (in Plato). The **ancient Greeks** also believed in an afterlife, although its quality varied greatly depending on one's mortal life.

Hindu beliefs also vary greatly, but many believe that the *Jiva, Atman*, and *Purusha* are aspects of the divine that reside within each person. As in Christianity, it is eternal and indestructible.

Animistic religions are found throughout Africa, especially Zambia, the Democratic Republic of the Congo, Gabon, and the Republic of Guinea Bissau; throughout Southeast Asia, especially Indonesia, Japan, Laos, Myanmar, and Papua New Guinea; as well as among Native Americans and Europeans in premodern times. They believe that life essence (anima) permeates all things, and often this essence develops a consciousness that not only transcends but also resides in the individual. Particular people, animals, plants, rocks, and so on are born, live, and die, but the animistic essence of life is eternal.

When religious people feel a rush of excitement, when they feel that God is near or within them, when they feel a power and intensity of belief, commitment, and the sanctity of moral regulation, they are not, as sociologists sometimes conclude, succumbing to an illusion. Religious devotion is not deception. Rather, Durkheim ([1915] 1965) says, "We can say that the believer is not deceived when he believes in the existence of a moral power upon which he depends and from which he perceives all that is best in himself" (p. 257). Yet let us remember that Durkheim seeks a sociological understanding of religion. Sociologically, he argues that this power exists and it is real, but it is not God the person worships: "it is society." However crude or sophisticated the imagery and beliefs of a religion may be, behind them "there is a concrete and living reality . . . [that] translates everything essential about life and the relations to be explained: for it is an eternal truth that outside of us there exists something greater than us, with which we enter into communion" (p. 257). God is society, or at least society in an idealized form.

Furthermore, religion not only regulates behavior through morality, but also shapes and defines people. It makes us into something, into what society requires that we become in order to live within its parameters, and in order to serve the collective order. It does this symbolically and metaphorically, through rituals, sacraments, and scripture. Religion shapes people at the highest or eternal level of understanding, yet since society must consist of people, this collective and transcendent sense can only exist if real people feel it and believe it. In religious conception, the transcendent aspect of ourselves is the soul.

Sociologically, Durkheim interprets the soul as a social construct, as something that exists both separately from and within the individual. The soul has a dualistic nature in which one part is essentially impersonal and serves the collective interest of the group. Yet people are at the same time individuals, and the soul consequently has a second aspect, an earthly aspect tied to and in accordance with each individual body, and it is therefore also personal. The soul is eternal, but lives at least for a time in individual bodies, and thus we are all one people and members of society, yet also individuals. Both the collectivity and the individual are sacred.

Expressed more sociologically, "a person is not merely a single subject distinguished from all the others. It is rather a being to which is attributed a relative autonomy in relation to the environment with which it is most immediately in contact" (Durkheim [1915] 1965:306). Furthermore, the belief in a soul allows a person to meaningfully integrate personal experiences and thoughts with that of society, and this frees the individual from isolation and the inherent natural limits on life—that is, we all die. In order to make sense of life and death, we must oppose individual and natural frailty with collective and social strength.

Yet consistent with his earlier analysis in *Suicide*, Durkheim distinguishes individuality as a quality of being from *individuation*, a process by which a person becomes dissimilar from other people. Individuality is simply the ability to think and feel as a particular person, whereas individuation disconnects a person from collective meaning and generates anomie. As Durkheim ([1915] 1965) writes, "passion individuates, yet it also enslaves. Our sensations are essentially individual; yet we are more personal the more we are able to think and act with social concepts" (p. 308). In other words, thoughts can be shared through concepts, but passion can only be felt at the individual level, which makes it antisocial. For Durkheim, religion is a civilizing force because it elevates the intellect over passion. Even the passion of ecstatic rites occurs within socially defined parameters. Use of hallucinogenic substances, for example, or overt sexual displays; flagellation; or sacrifices, whether animal or human, do not promote a loss of control, but rather, place the passions under religious, and thus social, regulation.

Overall then, Durkheim argues that religion must establish boundaries: on one side those things crucial for the health and well-being of the community—the sacred; on the other side those things that are inherently detrimental to the community—the profane. There can also be a third area, the mundane, which is a kind of neutral territory or gray area that is neither essential nor detrimental inherently. Let us be clear, though, that Durkheim offers a sociological perspective, not a theological one. For Durkheim, evil and profane are not synonymous. Rather, the profane addresses whatever is both threatening to and outside of society. Evil may be both outside and part of society. As Durkheim ([1915] 1965) explains,

> Things are arbitrarily simplified when religion is seen only on its idealistic side. In its way, religion is realistic. There is no physical or moral ugliness, there are no vices or evils that do not have a special divinity. There are gods of theft and trickery, of lust and war, of sickness and death. Even Christianity itself, however so high the ideal of which it has made divinity to be, has been obliged to give the spirit of evil a place in its mythology. Satan is an essential piece of the Christian system; even if he is an impure being, he is not a profane one. The anti-god is still a god, inferior and subordinated, it is true, but nevertheless endowed with extended powers. . . . Thus religion, far from ignoring the real society and making abstraction of it, is in its image; it reflects all its aspects, even the most vulgar and the most repulsive. (p. 468)

In this passage, Durkheim clarifies that religion reflects all aspects of society, not only the idealistic or most desirable parts. In this sense, he says, religion is realistic. Yet it must always extend the possibility of hope, no matter how powerful the negative aspects may appear. The positive must always triumph, if not now then in a vision of the future, or else life would be impossible.

Religion does, however, idealize society, in the sense that it immortalizes the structure and conflicts of the present. It projects the present back into prehistory, and extends it forward into eternity. Just as society is immortal, in that it precedes and outlives the individual and therefore transcends the mundane, so religion similarly surpasses the moment. In its representation of both good and evil, religion encompasses the individual and makes us part of something larger and more important, and thereby makes our lives more important. Religion brings about "a state of effervescence which changes the condition of psychological activity." When a person embraces the beliefs and practices of one's religion, "a man does not recognize himself; he feels transformed and consequently he transforms the environment which surrounds him" (Durkheim [1915] 1965:468–469). Religion not only connects people to society and to each other, but it also inspires and empowers people to achievement in this reality. Far more than just a collection of absurd ideas and abstract faith as Tertullian suggested, Durkheim sees a powerful social and material basis behind the ideas of religion.

Yet this is not a crude materialism, meaning that religious ideals are more than just a straightforward representation of material conditions. Ideals are also real when people think them and behave accordingly. Although no idea can survive long if people do not affirm it in practice, neither can material relations endure when they lose legitimacy and especially when they lose a moral foundation. Durkheim sees religious beliefs as a kind of theory about the meaning of life, and just like a scientific theory, it must be understandable, and it must have practical application with discernable effects.

Although Karl Marx predated Durkheim, we will consider his work next, because he adds an additional dimension to the sociology of religion that follows logically from Durkheim.

Karl Marx (1818–1887)

One of the most misunderstood people in history, Marx was never the rabid revolutionary that later self-identified Marxists and anti-Marxists would portray him as. True, Marx sometimes wrote quite incendiary tracts against capitalism, and he did participate in the Revolution of 1848, but the vast majority of his work is very dense and scholarly. Marx seriously and carefully considers the nuances of modern capitalist society, regarding its impact on economic relations and the well-being of humanity, including spiritual well-being.

Very similar to Durkheim, Marx accepts that established religion legitimates the established order of society. However, this is only one type of religion for Marx, an oppressive type. The other is a revolutionary type.

In the oppressive type, religion not only legitimates the established order of society, but in doing so, legitimates the domination and exploitation of one class over and against the others. A *class* is determined by the relationship to the means of production, or, in other words, whether a person owns income-producing property or not. Those who own income-producing property therefore become the ruling class, because they own the property that produces livelihood. Other classes may be salaried types with considerable job autonomy, such as professionals (doctors, lawyers, professors, engineers) or wage earners with much less autonomy, such as factory workers or service employees, like cable TV installers or FedEx drivers. Either way, these people do not own income-producing property, and must therefore sell their ability to work to the owners. They do not work for themselves, but for the owners, who pay them only part of the value they create. Marx calls this economic or class exploitation. For example, when factory workers produce cars, they don't get paid the full value of the cars they produce, but only a part of the value. The company keeps the rest in the form of profit.

This is how Marx sees capitalism, or any system based on economic, that is, class inequality. In this context, religion legitimates the class order. It teaches people not only to accept, but also to celebrate their subordination and exploitation. It teaches people that their place is correct and proper, whether owner or worker. In other words, Marx argues that oppressive religion teaches people how to bear their burdens in life, not how to overthrow them. Whether in monotheistic Christianity, Judaism, and Islam, or in polytheistic Hinduism or ancient paganism, or in atheistic Buddhism and Shintoism, or in many other religions, oppressive forms maintain the established social order.

In contrast, revolutionary religion legitimates challenging, changing, or replacing the established social order when it no longer serves the interests of the people. To adapt a phrase from Abraham Lincoln, revolutionary religion is "by the people and for the people," whereas oppressive religion is by and for the elite. In simplest terms, think of the difference as top-down religion (oppressive) versus bottom-up (revolutionary) religion.

Let us look at Marx more closely. His thoughts on religion appear throughout his work, but especially in the earlier work. Economics always occupied a central place for Marx, but never separately from existential concerns. Humans need more than just material satisfaction; they also need spiritual sustenance, something to make life worth living. In the *Economic and Philosophic Manuscripts* ([1844] 1978b), Marx sees a direct connection between the issues of philosophy and the issues of economics. From philosophy, Marx draws existential concerns about the essence of existence and the meaning of life, which determine our emotional and spiritual satisfaction. From economics, Marx draws issues of production and material satisfaction. Marx finds existential and material concerns interconnected and both equally vital for human life. Modern society can no longer harmonize the facts of daily living and economic activity with spiritual needs. As Marx writes, "with the increasing value of the world of things, of commodities, proceeds in direct proportion the devaluation of the world of men" (p. 71). This basic observation arguably underlies all of Marx's theory, including his views on religion. Capitalism cherishes the commodity—the product that is produced for sale—above all other concerns. The more important commodities become, the less important our humanity becomes. The commodity-driven society, the capitalist society, creates an inherent separation between people and what Marx calls our "species-being," or in other words, all the things that define what it means to be human.

Nature endows some of these uniquely human characteristics, and society some others. Capitalism separates people from both their natural essence and their social essence, and transforms an essentially social species into isolated individuals, separate from nature and from each other. Although humans in capitalism continue to interact for economic purposes (namely, work and consumption), the commodity relationship negates the deeper, spiritual experiences. In other words, capitalism estranges or alienates (Marx uses both words, *entfremdung* and *verfremdung,* respectively in German) humans from "external nature and our spiritual essence, our human being" (Marx [1844] 1978b:77). We become estranged or alienated from ourselves, from other people, from nature, from work, from everything that is important and necessary for a meaningful life, including alienation from God. Just as other people, the natural world, work, and even our bodies appear as something separate from us, as something entirely external to us, so we also see the alienated God as something external, as something that commands us from above, whose interests stand over and against our own interests as people. God becomes the taskmaster, the overbearing and unknowable boss whom we must serve without question, or who appears disconnected from real life. Thus begins Marx's critique of alienated religion, the necessary outcome in a society that places profits over people.

In the *Theses on Feuerbach* ([1845]1978c), Marx critiqued the theoretical atheist Ludwig Feuerbach (1804–1872) who wrote a book called *Das Wesen des Christentums* (*The Essence of Christianity*), in which Feuerbach argues that Christianity has become nothing more than a set of fixed beliefs and empty rituals. It has long since departed from the main course of history. He also argued a subjectivist position that God must arise from within, not as an imposition from some remote above-and-beyond abstraction. Marx does not contest these points. Rather, Marx argues that because Feuerbach relies on a subjective interpretation of religion, and thus endows it with a subjective essence, he fails to see the fundamentally social essence of religion. Whatever form religion takes, it is essentially social in origin, not subjective. Marx writes that "Feuerbach resolves the religious essence into the human essence. But the individual essence is no abstraction inherent in each single individual. In its reality, it is the ensemble of social relations" and furthermore that "Feuerbach . . . does not see that religion is itself a social product " (p. 145). If capitalism produces alienated social relations, then religion, as a product of social relations, also takes on an alienated form. Yet religion need not take an alienated form.

A common misconception about Marx's theory of religion stems from one famous passage from an introductory essay intended for inclusion in a much larger critique of Hegel's (Georg Wilhelm Friedrich von Hegel, 1770–1831), *Philosophy of Right.* The often-quoted phrase that religion "is the opium of the people" (Marx [1844] 1978a:54) refers to religion in capitalist society specifically, not to religion in general. As with any quote from any writer, context is decisive. If we consider the full context of Marx's comments, we will see an important qualification, namely, that Marx draws a distinction between otherworldly religion, which is oppressive because it directs people to an ideal vision based on a nonexistent god, and the possibility of an alternative, this-worldly religion that arises from actual lived experience, and correspondingly offers emancipatory potential to the extent it validates the lives of oppressed people and leads a revolutionary sentiment to overthrow oppressive conditions of this world. Marx saw religion as both a specific and general theory of the world ([1844] 1978a:53) that maintains social order through morals, customs, rituals, and belief about how the world ought to be. It connects the individual to established social order, and furthermore, justifies the established order as sacred and therefore inviolate. To rebel against society is to rebel against the divine.

From a materialist standpoint, present-day religion reflects an inverted social order, in which those who own property or hold title stand over those who work and actually build society. Since conscious realization of this inversion is intolerable to any hierarchy, religion places the Truth of existence beyond the grasp of real people, and into the hands of a supreme and unreachable being, into the hands of God, whose earthly representation is the church, or more generally in sociological terms, religion. Since religion, like any other institution, is naturally a socially constructed entity, the "struggle against religion is, therefore, indirectly a struggle against that world whose spiritual aroma is religion" (Marx [1844] 1978a:54). Thus, the struggle is against religion that supports—or fails to challenge—the established order of and suffering in this world. To the extent religious devotion is a form of compensatory satisfaction, Marx maintains that "religious suffering is at the same time an expression of real suffering and a protest against real suffering" (p. 54). It is thus not simply a drug (an opium) or a diversion, but a type of insurance against popular discontent, and at the same time, an expression of the very same discontent and suffering.

However much oppressive religion may disempower or pacify the masses, it also embodies their discontent. Class hierarchy cannot justify itself; it requires some other transcendent legitimization, whether God, Nature, the Nation, or some other higher power. However, Marx believes this condition cannot persist indefinitely as real-life suffering increases.

Despite the potential of religion to thwart political, economic, legal, and social change in general, religion nevertheless corresponds directly to real dissatisfaction, to real suffering that arises from the inequality of life:

> Religion is the sigh of the oppressed creature, the sentiment of a heartless world, and the soul of soulless conditions. . . . The abolition of the illusory happiness of men, is a demand for their real happiness. The call to abandon their illusions is a call to abandon the conditions which require illusions. (Marx [1844] 1978a:54)

The crucial point then follows that the task of the revolutionary is, "once the other-world of truth has vanished, to establish the truth of this world," and furthermore, to "unmask human self-alienation in its secular form now that it has been unmasked in its sacred form" (Marx [1844] 1978a:54). Marx addresses the criticism of religion toward those religious institutions that mask the suffering of this world, that maintain the oppression of this world for the sake of a supposed truth from the "other world" when in reality, the ruling class projects its legitimacy through religion in order to maintain its material advantage.

Rather than a general broadside and universal condemnation, Marx's attack on religion seems particularly focused in that he criticizes the role of religion within particular social contexts, with particular social ramifications. He does not condemn all religion simply for being religious. For Marx, religion becomes oppressive to the extent that it presents a universal and eternal truth over which an omnipotent and implacable Divinity presides. In this context, humans can only submit to such formidable power, and in turn, people can only submit to the authority of the real world. In this way, idealism dominates social life, such that real lives of real people become irrelevant. Instead, Marx advocates a materialist religion based on conditions in the real world, as opposed to ideal religion based on the prerogatives of nonexistent deities.

In modern society, religion shields the secular relations of capitalism from critical scrutiny, so that morality and the meaning of life appear entirely separate from economic issues, especially economic injustice. Yet for Marx, they are all social and species issues, all essential to human physical and spiritual well-being; they cannot be conveniently separated.

Max Weber (1864–1920)

On the assertion that economics as the basis of material fulfillment and religion as the basis of spiritual fulfillment are inextricably connected and fundamentally social, Weber entirely agrees with Marx. Regarding the *Protestant Ethic* book in particular (discussed in this section), some sociologists see Weber as an idealist, compared to Marx the materialist. Supposedly, Weber argues that values and ideas lead to social change. Regarding the power of ideas, Weber ([1905] 2002) clearly states that all of the values and ideas associated with modern society acquired their present-day significance as a result of the connection to the capitalist organization of work. . . . Hence, all of these new ideas would never have significantly influenced the social structure and all the problems associated with it specific to the modern West. Exact calculation, the foundation for every-thing else, is possible only on the basis of formally free labor. (pp. 156–157)

Like Marx, Weber sees a material basis to all of the definitive aspects of modern society.

Weber developed a type of applied sociology that looks at religion both as an institution of social order and as one of social change. In his lifetime, he published two great works on religion: *The Protestant Ethic and the Spirit of Capitalism* ([1905] 2002), and *Ancient Judaism* ([1919] 1967)—the last work shortly before he died. In both, Weber studies the conflict between forces of order, and forces of change. In the *Protestant Ethic*, Weber argues that, in order for modern society to develop, forces of rationalization transformed the old, traditional forms of religion into a strict code of conduct for daily life in the form of asceticism (Puritanism). In *Ancient Judaism*, Weber examines the impact of charismatic authority on social change, which almost always appears in a religious form.

One of the greatest misunderstandings about Weber's theory is that most of his concepts are ideal types. As the name suggests, the ideal type is a purified concept that includes all the elements that Weber considers decisive (*entscheidend*) and elim-inates all the elements that are related but not essential. Weber distills the ideal-type concept from real-type observations, but the ideal type does not exist in a pure form. Rather, Weber uses it as a basis of comparison, as a touchstone to analyze the extent to which any given real case fits the ideal-type concept. All of his most famous con-cepts, whether they pertain to religion or not, are ideal types. Unfortunately, many sociologists assume that Weber intends the ideal type to be a real type, which is clearly not the case if one actually reads Weber.

For example, one of his most controversial concepts (ideal types) is the ascetic Protestant, which we will consider in detail below. Basically, Weber argues that in the 1500s, a new religious type emerged, which he calls Protestant asceticism, also known simply as asceticism or Puritanism. Among other things, this includes a denial of pleasure, and a new attitude toward work, a work ethic that commends hard work and condemns laziness. Endless work becomes a moral requirement and nonproductive free time a great sin. Weber clearly states that ascetic Protestantism is an analytical tool, and not a literal description of real beliefs and practices. He iden-tifies four main branches of asceticism, with Calvinism as first and most important. The three others are Pietism, Methodism, and the various sects that developed out of the Baptist movement. Each of these denominations actually includes many sects—for example, Calvinism includes the Dutch Reformed Church, English Puritanism, and Presbyterianism.

Perhaps the most important sociological point is that "none of these carriers of ascetic Protestantism were absolutely separate from any of the others, and the dis-tinction in comparison to the non-ascetic churches of the Reformation cannot be strictly maintained" (Weber [1905] 2002:53). In other words, these are analytical concepts as much as real religious distinctions. Various elements of asceticism, as discussed below, are found throughout the different ascetic denominations, but none of the real denominations exhibits all the aspects of asceticism in a pure form. Moreover, the nonascetic denominations include some elements of asceticism, but they are sufficiently different to warrant a different conceptual categorization. Even traditional Catholicism requires some ascetic practices, such as no meat on Friday and giving up certain luxuries during Lent. The vast majority of the time, however, Catholicism relegated Puritanism to the monasteries, where particular individuals devoted their lives to austerity in order to approach God in a pure and uncorrupted form at all times. The general masses instead lived in a cycle of sin and redemption, regularly enjoying the pleasures of life and atoning for them at the appropriate times. Weber thus sees the Catholic Church as the embodiment of traditional society—a society that does things as they have always been done.

As such, the Catholic Church involved mystical beliefs and rites, such as transubstantiation (the belief that the bread and wine of the Eucharist transform into the body and blood of Christ). Catholicism also involved various traditional celebrations throughout the year, which coincided with changing seasons, and which the church had often assimilated from earlier pagan festivals. The Christmas tree for Saxon pagans represented light and life awaiting rebirth in the darkness of winter, and Easter eggs and rabbits for Celtic pagans represented fertility, as well as the celebration of Easter, which represented life emerging from winter. Halloween and Day of the Dead also correspond to pagan beliefs that the veil between this world and the next is thinnest in late autumn, a time of dying, when nature goes dormant. These examples, and many others, speak to the mystery of life, death, and the afterlife.

Table 1.2   Traditionalism Versus Rational Asceticism

Traditionalism	Rational Asceticism
Cycle of Life—People live in ongoing sin and redemption; sin is forgivable.	**Constant Vigilance**—Sin must be consciously avoided at all times; sins only accumulate.
Eudaemonism—People live as they are accustomed, neither seeking pleasure nor avoiding it, but living as familiar and comfortable.	**Puritanism**—Pleasure of any kind must be consciously avoided at all times. Work in the calling is the only moral behavior.
Forgiving and Loving God—God loves everyone and it is never too late to atone for transgressions. God favors the meek; to whom more is given, more is expected.	**Harsh and Judgmental God**—God detests the weak and lazy. God favors the strong and bold; all must work hard whether blessed with gifts or not.
Salvation Through Christ—Jesus died for everyone willing to strive toward righteousness.	**Salvation Through Predestination**—Only the predestined are saved, all others are damned, and no action can change one's outcome.

The Protestant Ethic and the Spirit of Capitalism

In *The Protestant Ethic,* Weber examines the rise of ascetic (Puritanical) Protestantism in the 1500s–1700s. Through this period, Weber sees ascetic Protestantism as a force of rationalization in European religion. Ascetics included various particular denominations, such as Baptists, Methodists, Pietists, Quakers, and most importantly, Calvinists. John Calvin (1509–1564) introduced two notions that Weber argues reshaped the ethics of Western civilization, and in so doing contributed to the development of full modernity. On the road to modernity, Protestantism introduced *rationalization* into daily life, which in this sense means to make something calculable and predictable, to make something systematic, to demystify something. As Weber terms it, it means the disenchantment of the world. It made everyday life systematic in order to fulfill the word of God.

In order to live a life pleasing God and to systematically avoid sin, Weber identifies a new ethic, which he calls the "Protestant work ethic." Work becomes far more than a means of survival, or even a means to fulfill the obligations into which a person is born. For Calvin and other versions of asceticism, work becomes the means to salvation. One should work hard not just because one's livelihood depends on it, but because the soul depends on it. With this in mind, a person must studiously and consistently pursue a calling, not just from time to time, but constantly and systematically. A person must live free from sin in the calling at all times. Asceticism as the manifestation of the rationalization of life not only transforms work, but every moment of every day into a matter of ultimate importance. Of course, this means that a person must give up luxuries of all types, even though through hard work the individual may earn a lot of money. A person must save money or reinvest it in business, not spend it on luxuries.

For Weber, though, the importance of asceticism is not the beliefs as such, but rather, that asceticism represents a rationalization of religion and of society. Ascetic Protestantism has the effect of demystifying Western Christianity, and as its work ethic became increasingly mainstream, it shaped work and life in general into a form that emphasizes and rewards efficiency and diligence. It eliminated mysteries such as transubstantiation and the magic of confession, and replaced them with systematic behavior.

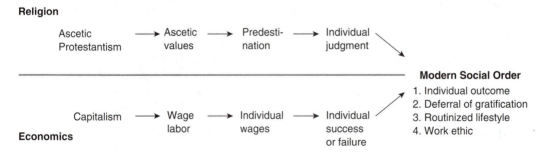

Figure 1.4   The Elective Affinity of Asceticism and Capitalism

As the illustration in Figure 1.4 shows, the rationalization of life occurred in two different and initially separate spheres, in economics and in religion. For Weber, the Catholic Church represented traditionalism, the value system that people should live as they have always lived, that life is an ongoing cycle of seasons, of celebrations, of sin and redemption. In contrast, ascetic Protestantism introduced the rationalization of life, that every moment must serve a purpose, and that purpose is to serve God's will. Asceticism follows from predestination and the calling. The calling refers to the belief that God calls everyone to serve some purpose, to fulfill some part of God's plan. This plan remains known only to God, and people must obey, not question, and not shirk the responsibilities of the calling. Secondly, predestination teaches that since God is all-knowing (omniscient), He has already decided whom He will save and whom He will damn to hell. There is no way to change this. No priest can intervene, and neither can another person, community, or god. For the Calvinists and their English branch, the Puritans, Jesus died only for the elect, not for everyone. Each person thus stands entirely alone before a harsh and unforgiving God.

Yet God requires that all people obey Him, and since no one knows who belongs to the elect, everyone must live a moral life that pleases God at all times. In ascetic Protestantism, sins are cumulative; they cannot be forgiven or atoned for as in Catholicism. Thus, a person must live an ascetic life, that is, a life that denies all ease and pleasure. In traditional Christianity, Weber sees instead a eudaemonistic ethic— that people merely live the easiest life possible, not a hedonistic life, which is the pursuit of pleasure. Asceticism, also referred to as Puritanism, requires that people avoid any kind of gratification, even emotional gratification. Emotional release such as crying, or displays of joy and sorrow, confer pleasure; it feels good to release pent-up emotions. People should sleep on boards, for example, because a mattress confers unnecessary comfort, and people should not eat meat, because big steaks with a nice rind of fat taste good. Boiled vegetables and legumes, free of spice and devoid of flavor, suffice to provide adequate nutrients to live. People require only nutritious, not savory foods. The current popular belief that a firm, hard mattress is healthier than a soft mattress is more religious than medical; soft mattresses are sinful pleasures. Notice that from a medical standpoint, people with back problems use a soft, memory foam mattress that conforms to the contours of the body. In short, traditionalism teaches that wine is proof that God wants us to be happy; asceticism teaches that wine is proof that the devil is in the world. Matters of style and taste, as well as recreational activity, interfere with a moral life, a life focused solely on fulfilling God's will.

How can a person avoid pleasure at all times? In traditional Catholicism, they can't. The Church expected people to confess their sins and atone for their wrongs periodically, and then the cycle of sin and redemption starts over. Basically, the medieval and Renaissance Church divided the entire year into days of feast, and days of fast—days of pleasure, and days of atonement. Yet for the ascetics, a life free from sin at all times was required. How to avoid pleasure at all times?

One word: work. Although not an end in itself, work provides the means to avoid sinful thoughts and actions. If one focuses solely on work, then one will not drift off into sin. As the old sayings go, "Idle hands are the devil's workshop," and

"Early to bed and early to rise." Work is a morally neutral activity, neither devout nor sinful in itself, but pleasing to God if the person works in the calling. In that case, work becomes an obligation; it is not a means of atonement, but rather, the basic activity that God requires of all people, for even the damned are called to fulfill some divine purpose.

Everyone must work, whether saved or damned, and none may know whether they are saved or damned. This ethic began in the ascetic Protestant sects in the 1500s, but by the 1600s, it had become a generalized religious ethic, and by the 1700s, a generalized—and secular—social ethic. Weber quotes Benjamin Franklin from the 1700s, and argues that Franklin sees ascetic hard work no longer as a religious value, but as a utilitarian social value. One should be thrifty with money, for example, because it makes practical sense to save for a rainy day, or one should be honest in order to build a solid reputation, because a solid reputation furthers one's career. Nowhere does Franklin mention God's will. For Weber, Franklin served as an example that the values of asceticism, namely dedication to work, had lost their particularly religious association, and had become a generalized and secular social ethic. In other words, it had become the value system of modern capitalist society (see Figure 1.5). The notion that one should work hard and that each person bears sole responsibility for his or her own outcome in life no longer involves God and salvation in the next life, but rather material success or failure in this life.

Religion thus contributes directly to the rise of the modern capitalist order, by providing its value system and by justifying the destruction of traditional obligations. No longer could or should people depend on their village or community for assistance, or for joy. Each person now stood alone, individually responsible for personal success or failure. The emerging wage system separated people from their traditional social role and placed them, as individuals, among other individuals. Puritanism transformed work into a conscious choice, rather than a traditional obligation. Whether a farmer, blacksmith, cooper (barrel-maker), fletcher (arrow-maker), tanner, fuller (felt-maker), or any other tradesperson, a man followed the path of his forebears, not his own choices. In traditionalism, people were born into their roles, and although most people lived at a relatively low socioeconomic level,

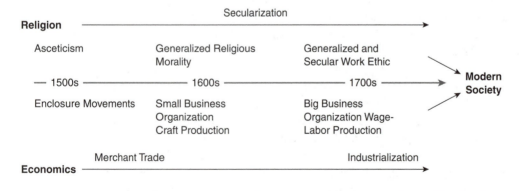

Figure 1.5   Rationalization of Social Values and Economics

and the unsystematic nature of production often proved unreliable, traditional society had one great advantage—existential certainty. No one doubted his or her place in this life, or the next. Should a person stumble occasionally, the church and the community were there to help and comfort them.

In modern capitalism, Weber argues that the work ethic contributed to the destruction of the traditional communities, including the church congregations. Although it freed people from often oppressive traditional obligations, and enabled the peasant to rise above the misfortune of birth, it also introduced a great problem—existential uncertainty. The ramification of this is that despite worldly success in terms of money, fame, power, and property, people are cast adrift. In this regard, Weber ([1905] 2002) describes a very bleak social and psychological landscape:

> The Puritan wanted to be a person with a vocational calling; today we are forced to be. . . . Tied to the technical and economic conditions at the foundation of mechanical and machine production, this cosmos today determines the style of life of all individuals born into it. . . . This pulsating mechanism does so with overwhelming force. Perhaps it will continue to do so until the last ton of fossil fuel has burned to ashes. According to Baxter, the concern for material goods should lie upon the shoulders like a "lightweight coat that could be tossed off at any given time." Yet fate allowed a steel-hard casing to be forged from this coat. (p. 123)

In an old translation, Talcott Parsons renders *stahlhartes Gehäuse* as "iron cage" rather than the more exact "steel-hard casing" in this translation by Weber scholar Stephen Kalberg. In defense of Parsons, I would say that his translation is more poetic compared to Kalberg's, which is more technical.

Perhaps the most misunderstood concept in sociology, Weber describes the "concern for material goods" as a "steel-hard casing" (or iron cage). Material goods, or what Marx termed commodities, govern our lives and encase us inescapably. Material goods, once a light cloak that could be thrown off nonchalantly, have become a steel-hard casing. The market and commodities, rather than religion, rule us now. By the way, many sociologists believe that "steel-hard casing" or "iron cage" refers to bureaucracy. This begs the question, Does that interpretation make sense in the context of religion and economics?

Weber ([1905] 2002) continues, saying that capitalism no longer requires the devotion that asceticism generates, because capitalism has become self-sustaining. As he elaborates,

> The pursuit of gain, in the region where it has become most completely unchained and stripped of its religious-ethical meaning, the United States, tends to be associated with purely competitive passions. Frequently, these passions directly imprint this pursuit with the character of a sporting contest. (p. 124)

In colloquial terms, whoever dies with the most toys wins. Unfortunately, we fail to realize the vacancy of our petty little lives, pathetically devoted to buying things. Weber ([1905] 2002) concludes that "No one any longer knows who will live in this steel-hard casing and whether entirely new prophets or a mighty rebirth of ancient ideas and ideals" will occur (p. 124). That is, new leaders may introduce new religious zeal, or on the other hand we might rediscover and cherish the ideas and values of old. Or we might just as likely become rigid and frozen in time, forever dedicated to the commodity system, "with a sort of rigidly compelled sense of self-importance . . . narrow specialists without mind, pleasure-seekers without heart; in its conceit, this nothingness imagines it has climbed to a level of humanity never before attained" (p. 124).

The modern world is a great nothingness, a great cultural and spiritual wasteland that consists of mindless and heartless consumers, forever dedicated to making and spending money in pursuit of mindless pleasures.

However, Weber sees another powerful force in history, which one usually encounters in a religious context—charisma.

Charisma

Weber borrows the concept of charisma from Rudolf Sohm, and it refers to the belief that a person or thing possesses supernatural, transcendent powers. For Weber, charisma never really exists; it is only a belief, but to the extent that people accept the belief and act accordingly, they endow the person or thing with absolute power, the power of a god. In his book *Ancient Judaism* ([1919] 1967), Weber studies the prophets of the Old Testament, and sees them as a charismatic force that challenges established Hebrew law and traditions. Their claim to authority is *charismatic,* that God has endowed them with a special message and chosen them specifically to deliver it. If people accept a charismatic claim as valid, then that claim overrides all established authority, because God overrides all human establishments.

Overall, Weber concludes that charisma is an unpredictable and dangerous force, because it relies entirely on feeling and emotion. Moreover, it derives its power from intensity of emotion, and usually involves intense love of one thing, such as God, and intense hatred of another thing, the great Evil. Whereas rational decision making and behavior change the world through observation and logical planning, charisma changes the world through emotional intensity and devotion, the results of which can be unpredictable. Rationality seeks measured material change, whereas charisma seeks unrestrained idealistic change and emotional gratification.

The real, material world will only change so much and only so far; reality has inherent limits. What limits can there be to something like emotional gratification?

In the unfinished manuscript that we know today as *Economy and Society,* Weber (1978) sees rationality as "structures of everyday life" that revolve around the economy. That is, both "are concerned with normal want satisfaction" (Vol. 2, p. 1111) which in this context means material satisfaction—food, shelter, and security, for example. Those things that fall outside of rationality find fulfillment in an entirely different manner, that is, "on a charismatic basis" (p. 1111). Sometimes, people attempt to fulfill very real material necessities, such as food, shelter, and security, through irrational means, through charismatic means. This occurs especially in times of social turmoil and uncertainty.

As recent research shows, this often takes the form of rapid social change that causes people to reconsider values that seemed to be eternal. Especially after the collapse of the Soviet Union, Laquer (1996) finds a sudden upsurge in neofascist and reactionary clerical membership. Similarly, Lamy (1996) finds an upsurge in specifically American millennialism and doomsday cults. However, both researchers point out that contemporary groups typically reshuffle the ideology and myths from earlier times, in an attempt to interpret the rapid social and political changes of the present day. For example, Satan is no longer threatening the United States in the form of the Soviet Union, but now through vast networks of satanic cults is converting teenagers to gang life, drug use, violence, and destruction of the family (Victor 1993). We are now one step closer to the apocalypse as Satan brings the battle closer to home (Lamy, 1996). Although rock music, especially heavy metal, has long been thought of as "evil" and the cause of delinquency (Verden, Dunleavy, and Powers 1989), it becomes literally the "sounds of Satan" for some in the face of job loss and political change (Weinstein 1991, 2000).

When social problems intensify, Weber sees two primary responses: on the one hand reason, and on the other hand faith—the basis of charisma. Each, however, defines the problem and works for solutions in entirely different ways. Reason "alters the situations of life and hence its problems" (Weber 1978, Vol. 1:245) which means that reason attempts to rectify the causes of the problem by making some concrete change in society based on empirical observation and analysis. In direct contrast, charisma does not address the causes of social problems through empirical analysis, but rather seeks "a subjective or internal reorientation . . . in a radical alteration of the central attitudes and directions of action with a completely new orientation" (p. 245). More specifically, "charisma, in its most potent forms, disrupts rational rule as well as tradition altogether and overturns notions of sanctity." Charismatic authority plays on the emotions and beliefs of people; as Weber (1978) says, "it enforces the inner subjection to the unprecedented and absolutely unique" power which is charisma (Vol. 2, p. 1117). Essentially, "the power of charisma rests upon the belief in revelation and heroes" (p. 1116). As such, it attempts to alleviate social problems through magical means, and those who claim leadership or the ability to correct social problems on the basis of charisma, claim this power of magic or divine endowment (see Figure 1.6).

In summary, reason defines the problem and seeks solutions based on logic and observation. Charisma defines problems based on emotion; it creates "change" by changing the way people interpret the problem. As Weber argues, charisma appeals to inner emotion and psychic disposition. Thus, its ability to actually manage daily affairs and solve social problems is incidental. As God says to the villager in *The Good Woman of Szechuan,* by Bertolt Brecht ([1943] 1999), the neighboring village flooded because the dam was not maintained properly, not because the people failed to pray hard enough.

To the extent people accept charismatic claims, they have given up on reason as a means to deal with problems, and instead hope for deliverance through some sort of magical powers or divine grace, even though "pure charisma is specifically foreign to practical considerations" (Weber 1978, Vol. 2, p. 244). For Weber, charisma,

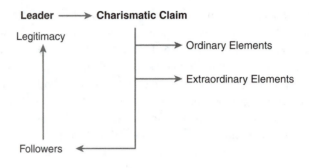

Figure 1.6   Formation of Charismatic Authority and Identity

magic, divine grace, and the like simply do not exist as such, but instead all ideas and attributes, "whether religious, artistic, ethical, scientific, or whatever else" (p. 1116), derive from social origins, both psychological and structural.

Weber clearly argues for a socially based perspective that establishes charisma as a social process, as an ongoing relationship between the holder of charisma and the people. The specific characteristics that people perceive as signs of charisma, and also the social role of charisma, both depend entirely on the sociohistorical context. If charisma does not exist in reality and depends entirely on public acknowledgment, the recognition of charismatic power is always tentative. Weber (1978) defines charismatic authority thus:

> The term charisma will be applied to a certain quality of an individual personality by virtue of which he is treated as endowed with supernatural, superhuman, or at least specifically exceptional powers or qualities. These as such are not accessible to the ordinary person, but are regarded as of divine origin or as exemplary, and on the basis of them the individual concerned is treated as a "leader." (Vol. 1, p. 241)

The exact attributes that a person must possess who would claim leadership on this basis depends on the specific circumstances. For example, Weber (1978) writes that such a person "gains and retains it solely by proving his powers in practice. He must work miracles, if he wants to be a prophet. He must perform heroic deeds, if he wants to be a warlord" (Vol. 2, p. 1114). To be more exact, a person must do things that are perceived as charismatic, that is, perceived as supernatural or superhuman. However, despite any other achievements, one particular requirement overrides all others. Weber says that "most of all, his divine mission must prove itself by bringing well-being to his faithful followers; if they do not fare well, he obviously is not the god-sent master" (p. 1114). This latter aspect proves crucial for Napoleon, for example, because it is exactly what he promised for the people of France, but could never actually deliver. Despite certain gains, he led France to endless war and ultimate collapse. The same is true for Hitler, for Mussolini, for Idi Amin, for Pol Pot, for Juan Peron, and other national leaders. On a smaller scale, cult leaders like Charles Manson, Shoko Asahara, Marshall Applewhite, Jim Jones, David Koresh, and others claimed divine being, and all led their followers into death. Some held a specifically religious position, and some held secular offices, but all claimed direct divine appointment from God or other supernatural power, such as Nature or Destiny.

Consequently, failure to provide well-being for the followers causes support for the charismatic claimant to fall away and likewise the status as leader. Clearly, Weber sees the public in a very active role; the people must acclaim the charismatic qualities within the claimant and in so doing project the status as leader. The masses continue to play an active role throughout the claimant's tenure as leader. Charisma only exists if and to the extent that people acknowledge it. In other words, leaders do not seize power; people hand it to them through submission. Charisma always comes from the people and is never a quality that the leader actually possesses, since gods and magic (for Weber) do not really exist. Although different people certainly have different abilities, and some people have highly unique ones, we are all only human.

If the public acknowledges the charismatic claim as valid, they must likewise bow down in subservience. Acknowledgment means deference regarding the issue of leadership and authority. For Weber (1978), the individual's charisma in no way actually flows from some supernatural source, but rather "what is alone important is how the individual is actually regarded by those subject to charismatic authority" and most importantly that "it is recognition on the part of those subject to authority which is decisive for the validity of charisma" (Vol. 1, p. 242). If the followers or believers acknowledge the claim, "it is the duty of those subject to charismatic authority . . . to act accordingly" (p. 242). So long as the public recognition (acclaim) of the person as charismatic continues, this "mere fact of recognizing the personal mission of a charismatic master establishes his power" (Vol. 2, p. 1115). To acclaim charismatic endowment inherently means "the surrender of the faithful to the extraordinary and unheard-of" (p. 1115) to which all tradition and regulation is irrelevant, except that it must bring well-being to the followers. In any case, recognition and subservience inextricably occur simultaneously through an ongoing process of claim and acclaim.

Of Priests and Prophets—Establishment Versus Charisma

Thus, Weber elaborates in *Ancient Judaism* about two essential forms of religion. One is the religion of the establishment, the religion of priests, who in some official capacity ensure that people observe the established tradition of the ruling religion, and that people do not stray from the official doctrine. The other form of religion is that of the prophets who, under the aegis of charismatic authority, deliver messages that overturn one or more aspects of the established religion. Weber explores this distinction empirically, using ancient Judaism as a historical example, although it is not limited to Judaism.

Ancient Judaism differs in many ways from Judaism today. In particular, a body of priests officiated over the religion in the Temple of Solomon in Jerusalem. Highly educated, these priests also wielded considerable political power and served the interests of the King of Israel. Alongside the priests, an oracular, that is, a charismatic tradition of prophetic seers existed outside the purview of the priests. The priests served God, known as Yahweh, or often written as YHWH because the exact vowels are unknown. The priests guarded God's secret rites and dominated all official discourse about God and scripture. Yet their political position and service to the king discredited their religious authority for much of the common population, who embraced instead the prophetic tradition in Judaism. We see examples of both in Judeo-Christian-Islamic scripture, also known as Abrahamic scripture. Of course, "the priests sought to monopolize the regular management of Yahwe worship and all related activities" (Weber [1919] 1967:168). As part of the established order, they would tolerate no dissention. Yet as we will see, the prophets were often beyond their physical and spiritual reach.

Jewish and other Semitic people (such as Arabs) migrated into the Middle East and Egypt particularly sometime before 1700 BCE, when a reliable historical record begins and by which time the Jews were well established. Prior to this time, the Jews were apparently a nomadic people. The Jews were also enslaved in Egypt as the Old Testament depicts, but why and for how long is still uncertain historically. In any case, Jewish kingdoms and city-states were established around 1200 BCE, and eventually these consolidated into one kingdom under David, the first King. Solomon succeeded his father as king around 965 BCE. His successor, Rehoboam, ruled badly, and in 926 BCE the kingdom divided into the Kingdom of Israel in the north and the Kingdom of Judea in the south, both located more or less, but also larger than, where we find modern Israel today.

The Jews subsequently fought many wars against many adversaries, losing most. The only significant building the Jews built was the Temple of Solomon around 940 BCE, which the Babylonians under Nebuchadnezzar II destroyed in 587 BCE. In 586, the Babylonians took many Jews as slaves, and many others fled to Egypt and Persia, in what is now called the First Great Diaspora. After the Persians defeated the Babylonians, the Persian King Cyrus the Great allowed the Jews to rebuild the temple, which they completed around 515 BCE. Two prophets, Haggai and Zechariah, competed with two priests, Nehemiah and Ezra, for spiritual control of the new Jewish state. In Weber's view, they claimed legitimacy based on two entirely different traditions, one prophetic and revolutionary, the other priestly and based on social order.

Eventually, Alexander the Great defeated the Persians and granted the Jews greater political freedom, which thus vindicateed the prophetic claim to authority that emphasized change and renewal. However, Alexander died in 323 BCE, and numerous states conquered and reconquered Israel over the next several decades. The Roman general Pompey (Gaius Pompeius Magnus) conquered Israel for Rome in 63 BCE. In 6 CE, the Emperor Augustus (Gaius Octavius Caesar Augustus) made Israel a province under a governor, known as a procurator, the title that Pontius Pilate held. The Jews rebelled in 66 CE, and the new Emperor Vespasian sent his son, Titus Vespasianus, to suppress it. He completed his task in 70 CE, which culminated with the destruction of the Temple of Solomon in 70 CE. Much of the population again dispersed throughout Europe and the Middle East in the Second Great Diaspora.

The destruction of the temple meant the demise of the priests, who never reestablished themselves, but it also meant the destruction of an independent prophetic tradition. After 70 CE, Judaism became rabbinical, that is, the rabbis united the priestly and prophetic traditions that define Judaism today. The rabbis represent a harmony between forces of change and forces of order in that after 70 CE, the Jews required both in order to survive. As a pariah people, they could not afford internal division and strife. They would face considerable hostility and persecution wherever they sought solace. In their diasporic wanderings around Europe and the Middle East, the Jews required order to maintain the coherence of their communities, as well as a coherent means to manage the constant change that diaspora entails, as different communities of Jews formed in different lands amidst varying conditions and customs.

Weber examines such history (although this is a very brief synopsis) and draws conclusions about the basis of religious legitimacy, and this is one of Weber's contributions to sociology. The prophets, as charismatic figures, claimed authority directly from God, through spontaneous revelation. The prophet spoke "under the influence of spontaneous inspiration wherever and whenever this inspiration might strike. . . . [T]he predominant concern of the prophet was the destiny of the state and the people. This concern always assumed the form of emotional invectives against the overlords. It is here that the demagogue appeared for the first time in the records of history" (Weber [1919] 1967:269). With the history of the Jews in mind, they had a lot to be concerned about. It is the history of wars, enslavement, exile, and finally, total domination. The Jews would not reestablish a homeland until modern times in 1947. The nearly constant social turmoil produced a long history of prophets who spoke out against the various "overlords," both Jewish and non-Jewish.

At the same time, "the holders of power faced these powerful demagogues with fear, wrath, or indifference as the situation warranted" (Weber [1919] 1967:271). They might try to win them over, or just as often, outlaw and if necessary, execute them. Like Durkheim, Weber does not attempt to assess whether God actually speaks through priests or prophets, but instead seeks a sociological explanation. Weber argues that many prophets likely succeeded in their message because they accurately assessed the political situation of their day, and thus their advice to submit or rebel, as appropriate, proved the correct and beneficial course of action. Sometimes, though, prophetic advice proves disastrous. For example, in 66 CE, a group called the Essenes, a millennial and prophetic group that practiced a militant and austere version of Judaism, likely inspired the Jewish uprising against Rome, which led to ruin in 70 CE, as described above. Such outcomes usually explain why a movement disappears into history. It is not the content of the beliefs (austerity is a common prescription for problems) but rather, measurable success or failure.

Overall, the prophet thinks and acts independently, and usually speaks in terms of generalized rather than specific outcomes. Prophets focus mostly on moral issues, not concrete political or military strategy. Yet their moral focus does not pertain to specific rules or prohibitions, but rather, to the overall orientation an individual and community has to God. In other words, the decisive concern for the prophet was faith. This signified "the unconditional trust in Yahwe's omnipotence and the sincerity of his word and conviction in its fulfillment despite all external probabilities to the contrary" (Weber [1919] 1967:318). With this in mind, the rebellion of 66 CE becomes more intelligible. Historical accounts clearly show that the power of Rome over the Jews was considerable, if not obviously indomitable—from a rational perspective. The priests of the temple did everything they could to prevent the uprising, including turning over agitators, especially prophets, to the Roman authorities. The priests likely saw Jesus as one such prophetic agitator. In any case, the Essenes prophetically called upon the Jews to wield religious faith against Roman swords. The outcome was never in doubt. For this reason, Weber sees the prophets, and charismatic leaders in general, as dangerous. Recall his earlier conceptualization that charisma attempts to reshape the world through inner transformation and conviction, not through rational analysis of external conditions.

The rise of rabbinical Judaism marks the end of the Jewish prophetic tradition, but prophesy transferred to the emerging religion of Christianity. Weber sees this as entirely predictable, given that no official Christian hierarchy existed for nearly 300 years. Christianity spread initially through voluntary individuals and friendship networks, such that each person became a self-proclaimed authority. Scripture records Paul as one who defined Christianity to a great extent, but in his own day, he was one of many. However, the prophetic tradition in Christianity, as we will see in later chapters, introduced a new element, the concept of the eternal evil adversary.

This creates one of the most problematic aspects of religion, love of the righteous and hatred of the wicked—both unrelenting and absolute. In turn, this often leads to hostility toward those people whom the leader identifies as evil, and this sometimes leads to individual persecution, mass persecution, and even genocide. Such became the preoccupation of sociologists during and after the World War II period.

Middle Sociology: World War II and Its Aftermath

In 1941, German social psychologist Erich Fromm (1900–1980) published the first book he ever wrote in English, *Escape From Freedom*. He introduced the concept of *authoritarianism* to the English-speaking world, which eventually inspired hundreds of studies in many different contexts. Although this book and the concept of authoritarianism spoke initially to the rise of Hitler and totalitarianism generally, Fromm and many others would quickly and extensively apply the concept to religion. Authoritarianism means the desire to submit to anyone or anything perceived as stronger or superior, and simultaneously the desire to dominate anyone or anything perceived as weaker or inferior. Since this desire depends on feelings rather than actual assessment of strength and weakness, ability or incompetence, authoritarianism relates closely to Weber's concept of charisma, as explained above.

Applied to religion specifically, Fromm sees a conflict in the West, expressed through the Judeo-Christian tradition, as an ongoing battle between empowerment and capitulation. Through a series of books, namely, *Man for Himself* (1947), *The Sane Society* (1955), and *The Anatomy of Human Destructiveness* ([1973] 1994), Fromm argues that modern society substitutes efficiency process and object-desire for all other possible connections between people, and in the process, we regard each other as mere objects, devoid of humanity and spiritual significance. In so doing, we diminish our own lives to the point of becoming a thing, in that we are each nothing more than a commodity that has value only so long as there is demand in the social marketplace. As a living commodity, we seek what makes any other commodity valuable—demand. Thus, people seek attention more than anything else, more than, for example, enlightenment or a record of accomplishment. Fromm ([1941] 1994) observes that "in the course of modern history the authority of the church has been replaced by that of the State, that of the State by that of conscience, and in our era, the latter has been replaced by the anonymous authority of common sense and public opinion" (p. 252). For those who do not acquire attention, three main outcomes become likely—narcissism, destructiveness, and necrophilia (see sidebar).

Likewise, religion becomes a product for consumption on Sunday, with little meaning elsewhere. It becomes no more than a means of gaining personal satisfaction. Religion thus becomes an irrelevant set of ideas in the form of beliefs, and an empty set of motions in the form of rituals. In *You Shall Be as Gods* (1966), Fromm argues that Judeo-Christian scripture teaches both empowerment, the progressive message, and domination and capitulation, the reactionary and authoritarian message. In a larger sense, he contends that this translates into genuine

---

Erich Fromm: Outcomes of Modern Isolation

Narcissism—Contrary to popular usage, this is not self-love and a secure sense of self, but rather self-loathing and intense insecurity. It develops in a person who has no accomplishments, no knowledge, and no love to give. Rather than learn and achieve, the narcissist demands attention and acclaim anyway, simply for existing.

Sadistic Destructiveness—Sometimes insecurity of the self generates aggression, a desire to destroy, either literally or symbolically, anyone who enjoys life or anything that represents joy or fulfillment. This is more than jealousy, but an intense hatred of one's own self and one's own life. This person seeks to dominate, and the ability to destroy is the ultimate expression of control.

Necrophilia—Not simply a love of death, this type of person hates anything alive, anything that signifies passion and humanity. More than a love of corpses, the necrophiliac loves anything cold and mechanical, such as inanimate objects over people, or procedure over purpose.

---

religion that, like Marx argues, empowers people to live genuinely meaningful lives and in the process, develop their own abilities and insight in cooperation with others. On the reactionary side, scripture legitimates the strong over the weak, severe punishment rather than forgiveness of sin, and the annihilation of evil—in whatever form—even if this means annihilating entire races or religions.

Research and theory thus continued in the area of authority and especially charismatic authority. Levi-Strauss (1971), Lowenthal and Guterman ([1949] 1970), Mazlish (1990), and Willner (1984) show that exaltation of the leader and demonization of the enemy occur through a specific and predictable social process. If the public withdraws support, the leader, or prophet, or warlord, or whatever falls from grace and loses divine status. The role of the agitator, or in other words the charismatic claimsmaker, is crucial as a focal point for a submissive public to project its emotional longings. Charisma is exaltation of the in-group, a type of mythological conception of the leader, who is the supreme representative of the in-group. It is also the damnation of the out-group, the mythological conception of the people who are the eternal enemy of the in-group.

Franz Neumann ([1944] 1966) in the detailed and sophisticated *Behemoth: The Structure and Practice of National Socialism*, sought to understand how one of the most socially and technologically advanced countries in the world (Germany) could embrace a reactionary and superstitious force like Nazism. To understand this cataclysmic historical turn, scholars such as Massing (1949) in *Rehearsal for Destruction* and Horkheimer ([1936] 1995) in "Egoism and Freedom Movements: On the Anthropology of the Bourgeois Era," studied cultural history, discovering that the foundations of Nazism developed over time, and did not just suddenly appear during a period of hardship.

Certainly, political-economic factors shape the type and availability of life opportunities (or lack thereof) and determine the type and presence of social controls, yet only people can have thoughts, hold values, practice religion, love, hate, or decide to follow orders or not. This is a fundamental principle in sociology, that for example, "Nazism is a psychological problem, but the psychological problems themselves have to be understood as being molded by socioeconomic factors; Nazism is an economic and political problem, but the hold it has over a whole people has to be understood on psychological grounds" (Fromm [1941] 1994:206). Thus, any explanation of human attitudes and actual behavior must focus on how people interpret, react to, and behave according to structural influences.

In this regard, several detailed empirical studies soon followed, including one Fromm conducted in 1936, but which was not published in any language until 1984 (in English translation), which surveyed and interviewed social and political attitudes in Weimar Germany, and the period of 1929–1947 includes at least 15 lesser studies (Stone, Lederer, and Christie, 1993). Following Fromm's initial theory, Lowenthal and Guterman ([1949] 1970) found that ideological themes "directly reflect the audience's predispositions" (p. 5). The agitator does not manipulate the audience from the outside, in the sense of brainwashing them, but rather appeals to psychological attitudes that are already present. Extremist ideology provides a framework that shapes preexisting but inchoate feelings and gives them a fixed and certain foundation.

Extremist ideology in the authoritarian form supplies a sense of certainty not by identifying specific grievances and problems, but rather by "destroying all rational guideposts," which leaves "on one end the subjective feeling of dissatisfaction and on the other the personal enemy held responsible for it" (Lowenthal and Guterman [1949] 1970:6–7). This simplistic worldview creates a hierarchy in which the insecure person finds solace through order—a higher power or purpose to which one submits, and an enemy to dominate and persecute. Although seemingly unrelated on the surface, hatred of the poor, often expressed as consternation against welfare recipients, and the consistently high prevalence of rape and other expressions of misogyny pervade contemporary politics and culture. If one looks even slightly below the surface, however, the actual similarity among racism, misogyny, nationalism, radical identity movements, and hate crimes, not to mention the still more virulent forms of hatred—persecutions and genocide—becomes clear. They all share a belief in some great Enemy of supernatural proportions that is everywhere yet nowhere. It is the cause of our problems and permeates everything contrary to whatever "we" believe in, yet remains so diabolically surreptitious it eludes all attempts to peacefully, and rationally, remove it.

In the late 1940s, researchers at the University of California, Berkeley, conducted over 1,000 interviews and collected vast amounts of quantitative data to study the issue of authority in a democratic society, namely, in the United States. Religion was a key variable. Theodor Adorno, a contemporary of Erich Fromm, developed the theoretical conclusions for these studies, known as the Berkeley Studies, and published them in 1950 in a book called *The Authoritarian Personality*. The theory has several variables, which the team argues apply to many forms of human social interaction, including religion.

This study inspired an entire generation of social psychologists, who tested for authoritarianism in nearly every conceivable social context—in churches, at work, in schools, on sports teams, in fraternities and sororities, in the family, and in many other contexts. From 1950 to 1974 alone, the study of authoritarianism generated over 750 separate studies. Both the theoretical and methodological innovations (in terms of quantitative data collection, use of Likert-type measures, and regression analysis) greatly expanded the prominence and influence of sociology throughout the 1950s–1970s.

The Landmark Berkeley Findings 1–3

Essential Authoritarian Character

Conventionalism means a rigid adherence to what the person perceives as conventional values; whether such values actually predominate in society, and thus constitute the typical or mainstream values, is not really the issue. Rather, "adherence to conventional values is determined by contemporary external social pressure. . . . [I]t is based upon the individual's adherence to the standards of the collective powers with which he, for the time being, is identified" (Adorno et al. [1950] 1982:159). The person identifies with and thereby submits to powers they deem superior and proper, rather than "a mere acceptance of conventional values" (p. 159).

Authoritarian submission is the "desire for a strong leader" (Adorno et al. [1950] 1982:160). Authoritarian submission to a leader occurs not as a rational evaluation of the leader's goals and likely ability to accomplish them, but as "an exaggerated, all-out, emotional need to submit" (p. 160). The authoritarian personality submits only to what he or she feels is superior and more powerful.

Authoritarian aggression results from a displacement of resentment and frustration, which the condition of submission produces. Authoritarian submission creates an inherent contradiction in the individual's personality, and thus "the authoritarian *must*, out of an inner necessity, turn his aggression against outgroups" (Adorno et al. [1950] 1982:162). Because the person cannot challenge the authority to which he or she submits, the individual can only vent frustration and aggression against a constructed, stereotyped out-group, which is itself a negative counterpart and immoral abomination that threatens to contaminate the sanctity of one's own pure and sacred in-group (Levinson [1950] 1982:98–100). In order to lessen the anxiety and tension that submission to the in-group leader creates, the authoritarian is driven by psychological contradictions and compulsions "to see immoral attributes [in the out-group], whether this has a basis in fact or not" (Adorno et al. [1950] 1982:162).

Recent research from Altemeyer (1997) and Hunsberger (1995) confirms the relationship between commitment to fundamentalist religious ideals and intolerance and aggression. In a different study, Hunsberger (1996) found that fundamentalism determines authoritarian submission and aggression among Jews, Hindus, and Moslems as well as among Christians. Stone et al. (1993) applied the concepts anew to contemporary cases, and discovered that authoritarianism ebbs and flows depending on broader social conditions. Meloen (1999) studied authoritarianism through global comparative studies, and found it strongest in countries undergoing rapid social change, whether the change is generally for better or for worse. If society changes suddenly, even positive change can increase authoritarian tendencies if change disconnects people from sources of meaning, especially religion. We will return to the theory of authoritarianism in later chapters.

Berkeley Findings 4–6

Typical Additional Character Elements

Anti-intraception is a fear of sensitive, introspective, gentle emotions. This individual fears sensitive emotions because it might lead him or her "to think the wrong thoughts, or realize pangs of guilt, unrequited feelings, emotional emptiness, and so on" (Adorno et al. [1950] 1982:164). The most important effect is "a devaluation of the human and an overvaluation of the physical object. . . . [H]uman beings are looked upon as if they were physical objects to be coldly manipulated—even while physical objects, now vested with emotional appeal, are treated with loving care" (p. 164). Inanimate objects are emotionally safe because they possess only the feelings projected onto them.

Superstition and stereotypy become the means by which a person replaces his or her own feelings with fixed external impositions. Superstition, or the belief in "mystical or fantastic external determinants of the individual fate, and stereotypy, the disposition to think in rigid categories" (Adorno et al. [1950] 1982:165), are both systems of belief that stand above and beyond the individual's ability to fully understand, question, or change. Both superstition and stereotypy "indicate a tendency to shift responsibility from within the individual onto outside forces beyond one's control," and most importantly this shift occurs in "a nonrealistic way by making the individual fate dependent on fantastic factors" (p. 165). Thus, the individual bears no responsibility for his or her actions. Superstition and stereotypy depend on irrational and subconscious insecurities rather than a shrewd analysis of actual social conditions.

Power and toughness is the tendency to view all human relations as power relations in dichotomous categories with an underlying power dimension: good–bad, strong–weak, leader–follower, superior–inferior, and so on. The obsession with power and toughness "contains elements that are essentially contradictory. . . . One solution which such an individual often achieves is that of alignment with power-figures, an arrangement by which he is able to gratify both his need for power and his need to submit" (Adorno et al. [1950] 1982:166–167). This type of person typically seeks reassurance by joining anonymously with some general movement and ideology that emphasizes in-group superiority based on simple and crude factors, such as race or language, which also allows the authoritarian to condemn others who do not belong.

Yet the research that the Berkeley Studies prompted for the most part emphasized the psychological side of the social-psychological equation. Studies that originated at other institutions and that dealt with a different issue—race and racism—extended a critical approach to U.S. society and to religion. Race and religion together have shaped many of the historically transformative movements in the United States.

Berkeley Findings 7–9

Typical Additional Elements

Destructiveness and cynicism express undifferentiated hostility that results when the individual has "numerous externally imposed restrictions upon the satisfaction of his needs" and who thus harbors "strong underlying aggressive impulses" (Adorno et al. [1950] 1982:168). The authoritarian translates abstract social forces into personified out-groups. Almost any group may become the enemy, whether Jews, blacks, gays, feminists, liberals, welfare cheats, communists, and nonbelievers of many types, any and all of which constitute the evil, immoral, or viciously corrupt foundations of all our problems, and thus in the eyes of authoritarians, these people, these evil and perverse creatures, must be eliminated.

Projectivity is the means by which the authoritarian creates the mythical enemy and endows them with all the negative, unholy, and abominable characteristics that purportedly make up their essence. "The suppressed impulses of the authoritarian character tend to be projected onto other people who are then blamed out of hand" (Adorno et al. [1950] 1982:169) for all the problems of society.

Sex measures suspicion and hostility regarding sexual activity, and furthermore the belief in such phenomena as "wild erotic excesses, plots and conspiracies, and danger from natural catastrophes" (Adorno et al. [1950] 1982:169) as indicators that the world is full of dangerous and unfathomable passions beyond human perception or control. This justifies constant suspicion and the compulsion to seek out, condemn, and destroy evil in all its guises. A person becomes preoccupied with sexual perversity because of "a general tendency to distort reality through projection, but sexual content would hardly be projected unless the subject had impulses of this same kind that were unconscious and strongly active" (p. 170). In other words, projection often takes a specifically sexual form because of one's own repressed sexual desires and the frustration they create.

Race: The Great Religious Divider in the United States

Sunday church services are the most racially segregated institutions in the United States, more than neighborhoods, work, education, or any other aspect of American life. Of course, this is not incidental, but developed consistently and congruently with racism throughout the history of the United States. As we will see in the next chapter, race and religion configured many of the contemporary issues of civil rights and justice in the United States. In terms of race relations, religion has worked both progressively and oppressively, in more or less equal measure.

On the oppressive side, the racial segregation of American churches began around 1830, by which time significant numbers of black people, some free but mostly slave, had converted to Christianity. Yet segregation was not initially so absolute. In the late 1700s and early 1800s, black people attended the same churches as whites, but occupied separate pews (Emerson and Smith 2000). Segregation by church took place over time, but mostly occurred after the Civil War and continued well into the 20th century, and despite the Civil Rights Act of 1964, remains mostly in place today. Sociologically, churches like neighborhoods remain racially segregated because of social networks, demographic differences, and personal and institutional racism. Overall, people worship where they live and socialize with their local cohorts. Racialization in religion reflects the racialization of all aspects of social life in the United States, including work, housing, consumer patterns, and culture (Emerson and Smith 2000).

Although racist beliefs partly result from a lack of knowledge and experience, racism results much more from a complex interaction of social and psychological factors. Regarding political economy and social culture, that is, regarding structural factors in society, much research indicates that modern capitalism has underdeveloped black communities in particular (Gans 1996; W. J. Wilson 1997) and disenfranchised blacks from the mainstream economy (Bates 1997; Marable 1999). This disenfranchisement overlaps race and class, and not only disadvantages blacks, but positions them as a "an industrial reserve army," available to serve as scab labor or more generally as a labor pool available to work for even lower wages and benefits than their tentatively employed white counterparts (Kasarda 1990; Marable 1999). As a series of recent studies finds, however, the United States increasingly "warehouses" the nation's poor in prisons (Herivel and Wright 2003). As the studies show, mass incarceration of ethnic minority and poor populations has broken poor families as much as economic uncertainty, and has fractured religious communities among the poor as well, given that large segments of the current generation are in prison. As William Julius Wilson (1997) finds, public policy often actively maintains an economically desperate ethnic underclass, and as Massey and Denton (1998) find, urban renewal rarely benefits the urban poor. Instead, it pushes them aside to make room for upper-income real estate and businesses.

Thus, the sometimes-held notion that blacks are a threat to employed whites is to some extent genuine, although this conflict is the result of structural class relations within capitalism, and not something that blacks would willingly assume. Quite the contrary; in fact, lower-class blacks typically espouse mainstream values—hard work and education (Kelley 1996), both of which express strong belief in the current economic system, and that people should not expect special privileges. If anything, white workers have become far more cynical about the value of dedicated, honest work than blacks and other minorities (Roediger 1999). The point is that race often becomes a matter of conflict because of its associated overlap with class and economic survival. Therefore, simply telling people that racism is an ignorant attitude and that race has no relevance is, however unintentionally, also saying that class and economic concerns do not matter in life. The concerns about race overlay very real material interests that people cannot simply forget.

Beginning with Adorno et al. ([1950] 1982) in social science, and Sartre ([1948] 1995) in philosophy, numerous scholars have pointed to the notion of the racial out-group or the demonized racial Other as fundamental to authoritarian racism and ethnocentrism. Many scholars have rediscovered this approach, such as Langmuir (1990a, 1990b) with the concept of chimera, and Noël ([1989] 1994), who characterizes the oppressed as a "stigmatized abstraction" (pp. 109–110). Dinnerstein (1994) shows how important such abstractions are for maintaining an overall social climate of racial suspicion and sometimes hostility. Regarding the overall social climate, in which authoritarian racism can take various forms, Forbes (1985) finds strong correlation between ethnocentrism and nationalism, in which general authoritarian attitudes serve as a foundation.

Early contributions include Bettelheim and Janowitz (1950), who examine two predominant expressions of racism in the United States, namely anti-Semitic and antiblack racism. They find that, in general, racism exists as external social pressures, but crucially, this requires a framework of internalized values that predispose the individual to accept certain ideas or course of action, and to reject others. However, and this is decisive, the tendency to perceive the world in dualistic terms typifies the authoritarian disposition toward many issues, and thus people who believe in racist stereotypes often uncritically accept other dualistic oppositions, such as good versus bad, honest versus dishonest, or strong versus weak, with little room for anything in between.

People who hold racist and other intolerant attitudes are not ignorant, in the sense of being uninformed individuals. Indeed, Aho (1990) shows that racist-right extremists in Idaho are above average in formal educational level attained. They are in fact thoroughly integrated into the dominant values of society. At the same time, and this is crucial, their basic orientation predisposes them to attitudes that deliver high levels of emotional satisfaction through absolutist views, often coupled with behavior directed as a sort of moral crusade.

Lower-class blacks and whites face many of the same structural inequalities and systematic exploitation as cheap and transient labor forces. As capitalism and nationalism developed in the United States, racism developed as a means to "withdraw the dominant group's sympathy from an 'inferior race,' to facilitate its exploitation," initially through slavery and sharecropping, and presently as "a surplus labor pool" such that "a permanent underclass of blacks is created" (Marable [1984] 2007:72–73). In fact, history shows that wealthy whites consciously excluded blacks from the best wage opportunities immediately after the Civil War, so that impoverished whites would not need to compete with, nor join with, impoverished blacks (Fredrickson 1983:209). This policy was quite effective, such that by the turn of the century, Northern labor unions sometimes attempted to rally white workers against the supposed threat of "mechanical Negro labor" as an aspect of class consciousness in the overall struggle against capitalist oppression (Fredrickson 1983:222–223). As the historical data in Allen (1994), Fredrickson (2002), and Vaughan (1995) shows, racism systematically excludes blacks from a central role in the modern economy, and simultaneously becomes an aspect of white culture that provides economically insecure whites with an emotional pacifier and a feeling of superiority over blacks, coupled with a supposed solidarity with more prosperous whites. Hence the influence of a political economy begins to shape emotional attitudes.

The importance of feeling in the face of unfavorable material conditions leads to important questions: What if factual knowledge, in this case regarding race, means little or nothing to a person? How is it that some people prefer a prejudiced, or in general a superstitious view of the world over and against verifiable fact or even personal experience? What if a person responds overwhelmingly to emotionally potent belief or ideology, rather than rational analysis? This suggests that various attitudes of domination, such as authoritarianism, racism, ethnocentrism, and sexism, are related. As we will see throughout the book, religion can either amplify or mollify these sentiments.

Wieviorka (1995) captures the central point about authoritarianism and its racist manifestation. That is, he argues that racism in Western culture depends on perception, which develops from material encounters and interests. In other words, "racism was formed, even before it received its present name, out of the encounter with the Other—most often a dominated Other" (p. 5), which acquired a status opposite that of the ruling race. Just as the ruling and superior race embodies everything good, wholesome, proper, strong, perseverant, and so on, the Other embodies everything evil, vile, foul, weak, corrupt, lazy, and so forth. In the same way that many feminists beginning with Simone de Beauvoir discuss women as the Second Sex, as the Other, in the way they have been historically treated, so racism similarly positions the racial Other as the out-group, forever different from and inferior to the in-group. These views did not suddenly appear, nor result from the work of individual agitators, but developed over time in conjunction with political-economic conditions. Eventually, the myth becomes deeply rooted, almost as an automatic impulse or a belief about the essential "truth" of our times.

It is important to remember that such discrimination is not always conscious, nor is it always institutional. As Essed's (1990) interview data shows, racism may be passive (apathetic inaction, and thus support) confirmation of dominant values, or individual, whereby particular business managers, for example, hold racist attitudes and practice discriminatory hiring, while others in the same business do not. Nevertheless, Essed concludes that whatever the form, the underlying principle remains constant, that racism occurs to the extent individuals internalize dominant values—whether norms, interests, customs, religion, or other values (p. 32)—exalt the in-group, and demonize the out-group. Later research (Essed and Goldberg 2001) confirms that the systematic demonization of blackness continues. This includes not only black people, but a person of any color perceived to have "black" attributes or behave as a black sympathizer.

Whatever group becomes the demonized Other, religion often encodes in terms of an evil Other, an evil enemy. This evil enemy designation may be placed on a real group or an imaginary group, but either way, the enemy acquires an unreal and impossible stigma—they become an evil with allegedly supernatural powers.

The Evil Enemy

Given the holocaust in Europe, in which Nazi Germany murdered about 6 million Jews and 6 million others, the issue of the great Enemy, the great Satan, and similar beliefs occupied much of the study of religion in the post–World War II period, and arguably, remain highly relevant today. Maurice Samuel in *The Great Hatred* ([1940] 1988) sees absolute hate as the mirror of absolute love. In this sense, absolute love can only apply to those who are exactly like ourselves, and those who directly threaten this ideal of perfection can be nothing other than the great Evil. Just as the believer must absolutely support and submit to the great Love, they must simultaneously attack and destroy the great Evil.

Jean Paul Sartre in *Anti-Semite and Jew* ([1948] 1995) conceptualizes the Enemy, in this case the Jew, as a mythical creation, such that "if the Jew did not exist, the anti-Semite would invent him." As contemporary social historian Gavin Langmuir (1990a, 1990b) elaborates at length, the evil Enemy is a chimera, a mythical creature that consists of a goat, snake, and lion. Separately, these are all real animals, but when combined into a single beast, it is mythical and impossible. Such is the nature of the great evil Enemy, which is fiendishly clever but also ignorant and inferior, rich yet dependent on welfare, everywhere yet nowhere specifically.

> The great enemy of truth is very often not the lie—deliberate, contrived, and dishonest—but the myth—persistent, persuasive, and unrealistic.
>
> —John F. Kennedy
>
> Mass movements can rise and spread without a belief in God, but never without belief in a devil.
>
> —Eric Hoffer, 1951

Even though national anti-Semitism has somewhat waned, it is "not, of course, that any magic spell suddenly stopped people from hating the Jews. But the ill will remains in an unfocused state" (Finkielkraut [1980] 1997:147) so that other groups may, if structural factors develop appropriately, occupy pariah status. Indeed, the current president of Iran, Mahmoud Ahmedinejad, often rails against Israel and the Jews as a Great Evil that must be eradicated. Agitators can also foment belief in imaginary enemies, and even lead a sort of crusade. However, neither structural turmoil alone nor the cajoling of singular individuals produces authoritarian racism unless it provokes an emotional response in members of the population, and specifically, feelings of fear that arise from insecurity. Emotionalism is inherently unstable, and therefore unreliable as a political force, but so long as structural inequality, prejudice, oppression, violence, and lack of economic opportunities persists, authoritarian tendencies will persist, often just below the surface. Thus,

> racist ideology couldn't keep its hands off the wreckage of Nazism. Universally rejected in public, it now shows its face only in private, with a violence that's frightening nonetheless. We've become used to this dichotomy: while politicians speak the language of justice and equality, it's left to individuals to express their brutal antipathies or racial prejudice. (Finkielkraut 1997:148)

So although open racism may not play to political advantage, racism still exists as long as material and emotional insecurity exist, so that at times politicians can use code words such as "welfare mothers" for inner-city black women, which plays on unspoken racial prejudice. The racism of which Finkielkraut speaks appeared as a response to the flooding of New Orleans in 2005 from Hurricane Katrina—the belief that the predominantly black population simply reaped the outcome of their own lazy and immoral lifestyle. For example, commentators such as Hal Lindsey and Charles Colson (2005, "Religious Conservatives Claim Katrina Was God's

Omen") attributed the destruction to the wrath of God, as a warning that cataclysm in other cities would be coming if we don't remove the moral rot from our midst. Why New Orleans first? Finkielkraut would say that, since New Orleans was 80% black, the derogatory remarks about the city and its people carry an implied racist element (they are expendable), not an explicit element. But overt racism is not necessary if such sentiment is already widespread.

Such attitudes waver in and out of public discourse, and gain greater acceptance as social problems increase, especially in the absence of substantive public discourse and open exchange of information (Chomsky 1989, 1991; Parenti 1994). Not everyone believes the Big Lie all at once, totally, and for all time.

Research shows that attitudes among whites toward blacks, for example, are often ambivalent, or more accurately, passively racist. In practice, the majority of whites in the United States favor the idea of racial equality, but simultaneously oppose concrete practices, such as blacks moving into their neighborhood, or interracial marriage. Kovel ([1970] 1984) thus specifies a distinction between "aversive" racism, and "dominative" racism. The aversive racist is the classic liberal, or in other words someone who is 10 degrees left of center in good times, and 10 degrees right of center if the issue effects the individual personally. Expressed in a more technical way, aversive racists may overreact and amplify their positive behavior in ways that would reaffirm their egalitarian convictions and their apparently nonracist attitudes, but as social and personal insecurity increases, the underlying negative portions of their attitudes are expressed with varying degrees of force, but always in a rationalized way. The aversive racist retains passively a belief in imaginary characteristics about the out-group, and regards these beliefs as fundamental and inviolate principles, however much the person may consciously sympathize with the plight of the out-group.

As social conditions change, the path from sympathy to blame and hatred often proves quite short. The passive racist, who feels smug with a sense of superior contempt for lesser people, is transformed by the right conditions into a fearful, insecure, and active racist who views the racial enemy with "fear, convulsive horror . . . and vast delusions of persecution." What was initially a "conviction of superiority" transforms into "a cringing inferiority complex and a haunting, unremitting fear" (Samuel [1940] 1988:17) such that hatred acquires a new appeal and virulence as feelings of insecurity and vulnerability increase.

Although real people bear the brunt of mythical hatred, it is not real Jews, for example, that the anti-Semite hates, but the mythical image or "chimera" of Jewishness (Langmuir 1990a, 1990b). It is not the real welfare recipient—the harmless mother who receives governmental support for an average of 16 months—but the fictitious, vile, and foul creature that refuses to work, and supposedly prefers to parasitically live off the hard work of others while reproducing future generations of lazy, and oftentimes criminal, miscreants.

As Lowenthal and Guterman ([1949] 1970) note in *Prophets of Deceit: A Study of the Techniques of the American Agitator,* extremist ideology does not build an objective argument, but rather concentrates the follower's dissatisfaction "through a fantastic and extraordinary image, which is an enlargement of the audience's own projections" (p. 9). Extremism provides an image upon which the audience can focus its hate and negative energy. Although the agitator may often use extravagant and even wildly fantastic imagery, the causal relationships between the enemy and one's own problems are always "facile, simple, and final, like daydreams" (p. 9). The appeal thus lies not in factual analysis of grievances, but rather in satisfying emotional longings for a sense of certainty, and being an outlet for the emotions of frustration.

Lowenthal and Guterman ([1949] 1970) contend that extremist visions appeal primarily to the "malaise which pervades all modern life" that "is a consequence of the depersonalization and permanent insecurity of modern life" (pp. 16–17). Since malaise results from deeply seated psychological dissatisfaction, unfulfilled emotions, and a fundamental lack of self-esteem, ideological extremism can shift focus from one issue to another, with no particular logical connection except the underlying enemy and the evil it imposes. Complex theories about economic change, for example, whereby social forces are beyond the control of any one person, do not seem as real or as the immediate emotional reactions of those who feels trapped perpetually by social forces they do not understand. Thus, extremist themes appeal to such a person because they relate real-life conditions to abstract and independent forces, "which exist prior to the articulation of any particular issue . . . and continue to exist after it" (Lowenthal and Guterman, p.16). Thus, once again the overall vision and the implied causal relations between one's problems in life and the eternal enemy are far more important than the face value of particular grievances. On the surface, extremist ideology appears to be the ravings of an irrational or vicious malcontent on the rampage about anything and everything. However, at the psychological level, extremist rhetoric is "consistent, meaningful, and significantly related to the social world" (Lowenthal and Guterman, p. 140) in the minds of the followers. Extremist ideology speaks a kind of code language that the authoritarian understands as clear, direct, and satisfying.

Women as Other

Simone de Beauvoir originated the concept of the Other, which corresponds to similar concepts mentioned earlier, such as "chimera" and the "out-group." At the same time as the Other constitutes opposition, it also "is necessary to the Good" (de Beauvoir [1952] 1989:143) because without its opposite, the Good (the in-group) has no basis for comparison. Yet the Other lacks its own creative ability, and thus at certain times in history becomes a demon in our midst, which we must annihilate. When the hatred of the Other applies to women in particular, we may call it misogyny.

As de Beauvoir ([1952] 1989) also argues, "woman is not the only Other" (p. 143) in history, nor even in any given society, but the particular out-group depends on the dominant culture's values that focus emotional reaction on a given group at a particular time and place. For example, Sanday (1990) finds in her study of fraternities that women constitute the status of object when present physically, and constitute an abstract Other in a fraternity culture that represents an idealized external threat to group identity and cohesion. As Sanday argues, the impact of this is very real, because for the brothers it transforms rape from an act of violence to an act of male bonding in which the woman serves only as a vehicle for heterosexual men to emotionally bond with each other. In a broader study, Sanday (1997) finds that the general public, women as well as men, see women's bodies as objects, such that the woman herself is expected to relinquish control upon demand, especially for sex and childbearing.

This particular act of male bonding through rape and the general objectification of women signify a relation of superiority and inferiority, which is itself the product of but also a predisposition of misogynist attitudes in general. Sanday (1990) argues that fraternal identity typically revolves around highly idealized male virtues of control, power, and aggression, with a corresponding and equally essential negatively idealized notion of femininity (and women), which embody all the undesirable qualities the fraternity supposedly extrudes from itself.

For much of human history, women have played a secondary and often a submissive role in religion. In some cases, they are viewed as inherently inferior, even evil. However, we should not conclude that women are entirely subordinate in religion, past or present. On the contrary, as we will see in the next chapter, women have been quite important in religious history, and as will be clear in Chapter 7 about neopaganism and neofundamentalism, women are quite active in examples of two very different religions.

All of the aforementioned forms of the Other—whether based on race, gender, or religion—find renewed expression in some religious movements. As we will see in later chapters, the notion of an evil enemy configures various belief systems and often becomes the center of debate both within and between religions. We should seriously consider if Eric Hoffer is correct, that religion can exist without a belief in a god, but never without belief in the devil.

Religion After World War II

Not summer's bloom lies ahead of us, but a polar night of icy darkness and hardness. . . . When this night shall have slowly receded, who of those among us for whom Spring has finally returned will still be alive? And what will have become of all of you by then? Will you be bitter and banalistic? Will you simply and dully accept whatever form of domination claims authority over you? Or will the third and by no means the least likely possibility be your lot: mystic flight from reality. . . . In every one of these cases, I shall draw the conclusion that they have not measured up to their own doings. They have not measured up to the world as it really is in its everyday routine. (Weber [1918] 1958:128)

Max Weber made this chilling prediction shortly after the end of World War I, and he did not live to see the rise of Hitler and the destruction of World War II. Yet Weber seems especially prescient, in that modern society has lost its traditions, especially its religion, and replaced it only with the vacancy of material accumulation. But Weber by no means stands alone. Sociologists such as Theodor Adorno, Max Horkheimer, Herbert Marcuse, and Walter Benjamin on the left, Thorsten Veblen in the middle, and Oswald Spengler on the right all argue that modern religion had become a façade that means nothing by itself, and most importantly, conceals the fact that it means nothing. Religion had not disappeared, but it had changed form. As the standard of living rose dramatically after World War II, economics alone could no longer explain dissatisfaction. Sociology turned to culture, and religion again became a primary focus.

The classical theorists—Weber, Marx, and Durkheim (as well as others)—informed a new generation of sociology, which coalesced around two theoretical frameworks, functionalism and critical theory. Although usually utilized by competing political interests, as theories they are not as incompatible as many sociologists sometimes conventionally regard them. If we separate theory from political agenda, they share certain attributes in common. For the sake of clarity, I will focus on so-called critical perspectives here, and functionalism will be covered in Chapter 4. The reader should keep in mind, however, that the names and many prior associations regarding these names are often misleading. A critical perspective, which means to question conventional and superficial understanding, may or may not be found in any theoretical perspective; Marxism can be just as dogmatic as functionalism, and functionalism, as we will see in Chapter 4, can be critical as well. For now, let's return to the unfolding of theory as applied to religion.

Using sociology, critics of both left and right political orientation challenged the triumph of modernity and the process of rationalization. On the right, Oswald Spengler argued in his sophisticated *Decline of the West* ([1918] 1991) that Western civilization had lost the emotional power, and therefore the meaning, of its religious fervor. Spengler argued that modern rationalization had stripped religion of its intensity, and thus it now lacked the power to define cultural and racial identity, in which people find the meaning of life. For Spengler, meaning derives from blood and soil, an argument Nazi party philosopher Alfred Rosenberg promulgated. In the center, Thorsten Veblen earlier put forth a theory in *The Leisure Class* ([1899] 1994), which John Kenneth Galbraith later extended in *The Affluent Society* ([1958] 1998), that predicted religion would fade away in favor of bland, meaningless leisure.

As we know today, commercials, pageants, MTV videos, movies, and our culture in general remind us that superficial physical qualities are most important, and are defined within very narrow parameters of body size, dress, even attitude and topics of discussion. Romance becomes a means to acquire an object, and "the difference between people is reduced to a merely quantitative difference of being more or less successful, attractive, and hence valuable" (Fromm [1947] 1990:73). Self-esteem becomes dependent on whether a person can sell himself or herself in the market. The familiar term that bars are often "meat markets" illustrates the point. Overall, the marketing character strives to become what it thinks others want it to be; it defers its own goals, interest, and desires, both in career and personal relationships, to what will sell.

Galbraith and Veblen may reach similar conclusions, but their reasons are different. For Veblen, religion loses out to a type of corruption, in that people become fascinated with the easy life, a leisurely life, which has no particular highs or lows, and thus no need for great thought, emotion, or struggle, and therefore little need for religion. Galbraith agrees, except he feels that greater, more pressing problems will occupy our time, problems such as greater and greater wealth inequality, pollution, poverty, crime, and various other social problems that we face today. People will thus focus on the practical issues of the day, rather than the abstract affairs of religion, which he predicts will appear increasingly abstract and distant compared to real-life social problems. We can see today that neither perspective is accurate. Religion has endured, in its traditional forms, in innovative new forms, and in forms that, at least on the surface, do not appear religious. We will address these forms in later chapters.

In the World War II period and its aftermath, most social scientists agreed, whether on the left or the right, that religion as it had existed in history was on the way out. It would prove increasingly irrelevant to modern life, fade away in the face of ease and moral corruption, or fracture into innumerable and ultimately personal variations. Daniel Bell in the *Cultural Contradictions of Capitalism* ([1976] 1996) argues the latter, and recent empirical studies support this view. Following the classical theorists, Bell argues that

> the force of religion does not derive from any utilitarian quality (of self-interest or individual need); religion is not a social contract. . . . The power of religion derives from the fact that . . . it was the means of gathering together, in one overpowering vessel, the sense of the sacred—that which is set apart as the collective conscience of the people. (p. 154)

From a sociological perspective, religion serves to justify the social relations that constitute people's lives, and thus "to say then that 'God is dead' is, in effect, to say that the social bonds have snapped and that society is dead" (Bell, [1976] 1996: 155). All the theorists of the last 150 years we have examined, despite certain differences in intellectual and political orientation, agree that society depends on religion to legitimate the social order, and thereby to endow life, and death, with meaning.

As the famous sociologist Robert Merton (1910–2003) observes, religion has historically reinforced the existing society and at certain crucial times motivated people to radically challenge the existing society. Sociologists must therefore acknowledge that "systems of religion *do* affect behavior, that they are not merely epiphenomena but partially independent determinants of behavior" (Merton [1949] 1967:44). In other words, religion exists as an institution that endures independently of any given moment, and which exerts its own agenda (like all institutions). As Merton continues, "it makes a difference if people do or do not accept a particular religion" (p. 44), just as it makes a difference if people do or do not kill each other. In religion as in anything else, extremism tends to arise from the uncertainty of social disorder, when as Bell says social relations have snapped.

It would be a serious misunderstanding to conclude that religious extremism occurs only in so-called primitive or backward areas of the world, or perhaps only among small cultic groups, or in countries suffering from the most massive social change, such as Germany between the wars, or Eastern Europe after the collapse of the Soviet Union, or the Middle East today. Although significant social change typically prefigures the rise of extremism, the desire to submit and dominate, to relinquish rational thought and embrace charismatic fantasy, can occur at an everyday level, woven into the everyday practices of living. Similarly, a sort of everyday tendency toward irrationalism can become manifest if the right catalyst appears to focus emotional longings in some coherent way. The outcome need not be devastating, nor involve mass and brutal persecutions.

As an example, Willner (1984) records that an Indonesian worker believed that the Indonesian language was the most widely spoken language in the world after English:

> Probing disclosed that the basis for his belief was someone's assurance that Sukarno [the Indonesian leader] had said this in one of his speeches. If Sukarno had said it, he stubbornly repeated, it must be true. It became clear that the only way we could have shaken his conviction would have been to persuade him that Sukarno had not made such a statement. (pp. 25–26)

Similarly, people generally trusted Ronald Reagan as president of the United States (1980–1988), who retained *personal* approval and therefore legitimacy as leader, despite very low *job* approval. As Reagan's job performance rating plummeted to only 35% approval in January 1983 (which corresponded to double-digit unemployment), his personal approval rating remained in the 60%–70% range (Heertsgaard 1988:152). Thus, if Reagan or his appointed representatives announced that steps were being taken to solve America's problems, the problems must lie elsewhere, somewhere separate from Reagan himself. Although he was president, he was not of the political ilk, but a crusader who, in times of need, steps forward to wield the sword of righteousness.

Theory and Religion Today

Overall, the closer our narrative comes to the present day, the more we discover that religion becomes increasingly personal, and less institutional and collective. Believers see in Reagan whatever they want to see, and likewise in their perception of God. People see what they want to see, not what tradition, family, or society teaches. Although people still worship together, often in large numbers as we will see later with megachurches, they are mostly a crowd, not a coherent religious community. As a recent sociological study of youth and religion reveals, the vast majority of youth (12–24) as well as their parents, see God and/or Jesus as a personal helper, who answers prayers to accomplish whatever the individual desires, rather than seeing the individual as conforming to what God requires, or in sociological terms, what the community desires. Religion, whether explicitly religious or a kind of deified secularism, becomes increasingly commodified as modern society advances, such that religion subsumes as a form of conspicuous consumption. As Thorsten Veblen ([1899] 1994) writes, "persons engaged in conspicuous consumption not only derive gratification from the direct consumption but also from the heightened status reflected in the attitudes and opinions of others who observe their consumption" (p. 84). Today, we routinely see public declarations of piety, conspicuous professions of faith, which Veblen sees as a kind of consumption, a proclamation of loyalty to a particular brand. We now have three types of society, and each type configures religion according to the social relations that dominate each respective type.

The three charts below show the differences between *gemeinschaft* religion, *gesellschaft* religion, and the most contemporary version, which we may call individualistic or *consumerist* religion.

In the gemeinschaft, a German term from Ferdinand Toennies ([1887] 2001) usually translated as "community," the individual (the self) exists as an instance of the collective elements of the community (see Figure 1.7). It has no independent aspect. Similarly, the various institutions are always part of the larger collective, and here we refer to a church, in that a true gemeinschaft, such as a clan or tribe, has only one religious belief. Everyone believes and practices the same religion, in the same way, according to the same traditions. Overall, tradition governs all aspects of society. The forces of tradition—rituals, customs, obligations, status of birth and so on—leave little if any room for personal choice. People are born into and live within strong ties, forged by family, clan, religion, and other immutable facts of birth. Some term this a *community*, which emphasizes the close-knit and homogeneous nature of relationships.

In the gesellschaft, also from Toennies, usually translated as "society," each institution, as well as the individual, exists in both a public and private aspect (see Figure 1.8). No one person or group controls the entire society, and both individuals and groups have aspects of their lives that are separate from the society (private). Yet no one is entirely private or separate; everyone belongs or participates simultaneously as a private individual but also as a member of an association that the collective rules of society govern. The gesellschaft is a pluralistic society that recognizes and safeguards differences and also routinizes means of respectful interaction in terms of religion, ethnicity, and whatever else. Individuals form weak ties and enjoy a certain amount of choice unbound, at least formally, by the facts of their birth. They are called weak ties precisely because individuals may move between institutions, such as change religious membership. Thus a *society*, and in particular a modern society, consists of numerous but weak ties that emphasize the rationally

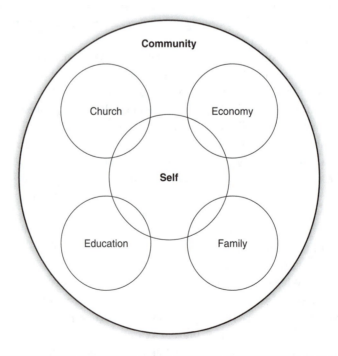

Figure 1.7 Gemeinschaft

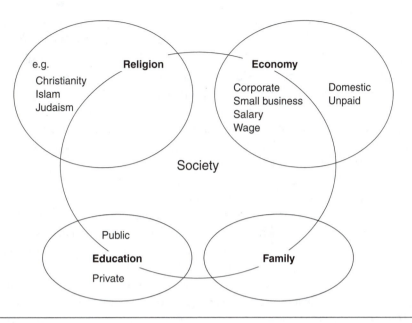

Figure 1.8   Gesellschaft

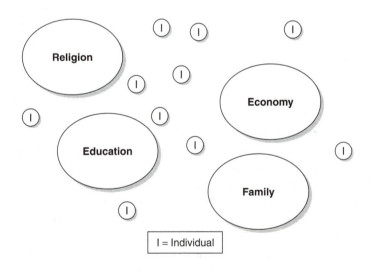

Figure 1.9   Consumerist Society

managed and pluralistic, heterogeneous nature of relationships. Collective coherence still exists, but typically by choice and convenience.

The consumerist type (from Erich Fromm) lacks any coherent collective aspects. Institutions and individuals have no particular relationship to each other, and people and groups change their relationship as desired or as particular conditions require (see Figure 1.9). Few particular or universal obligations exist, and people have rights, responsibilities, and privileges based on what they are able to purchase, whether with money or other means of exchange. Religion thus becomes entirely a matter of personal choice, no more or less rigorous, public, or obdurate than the individual desires. People form only loose ties (Florida, 2004), which allows them to move easily from one set of relations to another. Some call this a *postmodern* condition, in which the social ceases to exist altogether and all relations become a matter of negotiation between ad hoc groups of individuals. This emphasizes the random and ever-changing nature of relationships. Without consistent institutional affiliation, each individual conspicuously declares allegiance to any given religion in order to adjust his or her status. As Fredric Jameson (1991) argues, personality becomes a collection of clothes, cars, music, and whatever else may be consumed conspicuously.

The rise of one type does not automatically or immediately cause the others to disappear. They often exist simultaneously, and perhaps in perpetuity. In that case, conflict arises based on different expectations of what life and religion should be like. Some people expect religion, for example, to consist of close ties through familial, neighborhood, or friendship networks, in which each person must make certain commitments to church and faith, for the good of the collective. This often requires that the individual defer personal gratification in some way so as to benefit the collective. In contrast, the postmodern person expects to readily move in and out of collective religious practice, as convenient, and to maintain such beliefs and values as the individual finds most comforting. God and the group serve the individual, rather than the reverse. In this context, contemporary scholars see the decline of the community (Antonio 1999; Florida 2004) for all but wealthy people who can buy community like any other commodity, or people willing to defer payment and benefits in favor of location and lifestyle.

In an attempt to regain strong ties, the sociologist Robert Antonio argues that highly cohesive and exclusionary tribes will arise, centered on class or religion or both, and this will only increase social conflict. The tribe has one belief, one lifestyle, and one people. Choice is irrelevant. Tribalism in this context thus refers to a system in which society breaks down into discrete groups, or tribes, each battling against all for power and resources.

Whether strong, weak, postmodern, or tribal, this means sociologically that importance moves away from the content of beliefs, away from the particulars of belief, and moves toward the type of relationship people and groups have to each other. In other words, the sociological perspective, while it does not dismiss the importance of beliefs, instead concentrates on social relations. As the classical theorists argue, neither the individual nor religion exists in a vacuum, but rather as part of a historical process, as part of a larger social context. Even in the postmodern case, people do still engage in social relationships, even if loosely and randomly. The very loose and random nature is itself significant. Modern society detaches people from traditional moorings and sets them free and alone in an ever-larger world, in which today the forces of globalization connect and combine once disparate cultures and traditions. In so doing, globalization also severs the individual from particularity, so that he or she is no longer bound to time and place. The individual becomes free, but also universal and alone—forever facing the vicissitudes of fate without the comfort of community. The greatest challenge today, perhaps, is to live in the immense global world, and yet retain the uniqueness of time and place from which we derive friendship, love, and meaning—in both life and death.

CHAPTER 2

A Sociological History of Religion

Section I. Religion in Premodern Times

Introduction

In this chapter, we will explore a brief history of religion, from a sociological perspective. This differs somewhat from a historical perspective, in that a sociologist seeks to explain change through theoretical frameworks, whereas a historian seeks primarily to chronicle events in their proper sequence. Although the historical project is essential to a sociological history, the sociologist uses theory to establish causal links and to develop a critical analysis. Thus, events that a historian requires to fill in sequential gaps may be of little significance to the sociologist, for whom events are important to the extent they contribute to social stability or social change.

In contrast to historians, who tend to date movements based on events particular to that movement, as sociologists we should think in terms of convergence and divergence. Dates become important not when some particular thing happens, but when social forces with different origins converge at a particular time, and when thereafter they concur as a new social force that moves society toward a different future. Conversely, events also become sociologically important when they cause divergence, when elements of society break apart or competing trends develop. Like any social phenomenon, religion depends on its context—the time and place in which it exists. Most contemporary religions have ancient origins, and we must become ancient ourselves in order to understand the social forces that created them and changed them over time.

The Dawn of Religion

For the vast majority of human existence, religion has been almost entirely traditional, which means people practiced it as their community always practiced it, as far back as anyone can remember. Tradition is the legitimating force. In its earliest form, religion was animistic, meaning that people attributed living, sometimes cognitive qualities to forces of nature. The natural world consisted of living entities, including animals and plants, but also rivers, groves, rocks, and forces such as the sun, wind, rain, and so on. In animism, everything possesses a life force, or what Durkheim calls *mana.* This life force animates all of existence. Most deities, when present, are anthropomorphized manifestations of nature. One of the earliest is the general type known as the *ouroboros* (Image 2.1), a self-devouring serpent or other creature that represents the ongoing cycle of death and rebirth. Found in numerous cultures from Asia, across Europe, and in the Americas, a variation would be the serpent mound, which depicts a serpent devouring an egg (also a symbol of life) (Image 2.2). Although not as old as sites or relics in Europe and Asia, it portrays a

Image 2.1   The Ouroboros

Image 2.2   The Serpent Mound

Source: Ohio Division of Travel and Tourism.

similar theme that death and life are intimately connected and necessary components of an ongoing cycle.

Other early symbols include mother-goddess and fertility deities. We see the Venus of Willendorf (the village where it was discovered), which dates from the Pleistocene era, roughly 20,000 BCE (Image 2.3). It is the earliest known depicted sacred form. The characterization of nature, often depicted as a feminine but abstract deity, is intended perhaps to represent a kind of everywoman, a universal feminine, or perhaps to represent an individual named deity. Since masculine and pantheon gods would supersede the feminine deities before the rise of the historical period, we cannot know the exact meaning of ouroboros and other earth figures. Many argue that the ouroboros represents a universal feminine, that the feminine corresponds to the timeless and eternal aspects of existence, such as the earth. The sun and moon rise and set, and the moon goes through phases, but the earth remains constant and, from a human perspective, unchanging. In contrast to the eternal feminine, the masculine then corresponds to all that is transient, all that lives, dies, and is born again.

Although it is extremely difficult to confirm or reject such an interpretive theory, let us consider some argument and evidence. Marianne Weber (1907) in *Ehefrau und Mutter in der Rechtsentwicklung* (translation: *Wife and Mother in the Development of Rights*) argues that woman-centered societies should in some times and places be called matrifocal rather than matriarchal, because social organization does not employ a hierarchy. Rather, society centers on matrilineal descent and the authority of elders who have earned their status through practical knowledge in child care, farming, storing, gathering, and other communal tasks of livelihood. If accurate, as Weber and others below will argue, then the Goddess would be the manifestation of collective, nonhierarchical virtues directed toward the practical sustenance of the community and the celebration of life.

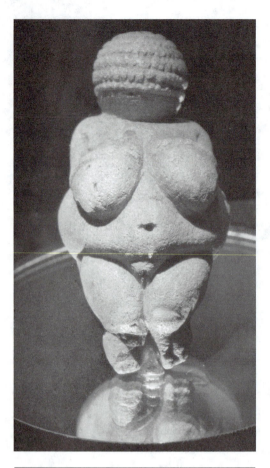

Image 2.3 Venus of Willendorf

Source: Matthias Kabel.

This is a complex issue that involves arguments and evidence from many disciplines, including archaeology, anthropology, history, and sociology, and the evidence includes art, weapons, fabrics, pottery, ruins, symbols, and technology. For example, people who have only kilns can make pottery (often of advanced technique), but they cannot make metal weapons and armor. They could make stone tools, which double as weapons, but this often does not leave clear artifacts. Metallurgy requires forges, which are purpose-built and cannot double as pottery or bake ovens. Yet Stone Age people clearly fought battles, and could butcher each other quite effectively without metal implements. The earliest known artistic representations of human culture date from the Upper Paleolithic era (30,000–10,000 BCE).

Riane Eisler in *The Chalice and the Blade* (1988) reviews existing archaeological evidence, including cave art, pottery, and burial accoutrements. She notes that male scholars from the nineteenth century imposed several assumptions on archaeological finds, especially cave art. Early anthropologists assumed that men did all the cave art beginning with the earliest known examples from the Upper Paleolithic era, but there is no evidence for this exclusivity. Eisler observes that, for example, in pre-sent-day cave painting cultures, such as the Vedda in Sri Lanka, "it is in fact the women, not the men, who do the rock painting" (Eisler 1988:3). Further, the Paleolithic cave paintings in Europe depict animals, which anthropologists assumed were depictions of some Great Hunt, which they further assumed was the primary male occupation. Eisler points out that in most such paintings, we find nothing to clearly indicate the depiction of a hunt. As in the example in Image 2.4, we see only animals.

Other sites, such as Bhimbetka in India, contain many cave paintings from the same Paleolithic era, and they depict a wide range of activities. Some clearly depict hunting, but many other activities are shown as well, including group dances, and one clearly depicts a female mother-goddess deity (Kamat 2006) with milk issuing from her breasts, which creates growing plants where it hits the ground.

The vast majority of Paleolithic paintings, which range from France through central Europe all the way to the Ural mountains in eastern Russia and to India, mostly portray animals without a human presence, with nothing to indicate their meaning, who painted them, and why. It is likely that Paleolithic men and women venerated these animals, but we cannot know the content of their beliefs with certainty.

Image 2.4   Paleolithic Cave Painting in France

By the Neolithic period (10,000–3000 BCE), the greatest number of figurines were clearly female, with features such as large breasts, a womb, engorged vulva, pregnant belly, and feminine curves (Gimbutas 2001:41). Usually exaggerated, the features celebrate uniquely female characteristics, and their ubiquity suggests a considerable degree of importance. Archaeological evidence shows that women took part in early religious temple activities in this period, but there is no evidence that men did (Gimbutas 2001:98). In conclusion, Gimbutas argues that overall, the many female figurines and temple carvings indicate that women were associated with and revered as the keepers of the "tomb and the womb" (pp. 70–71)—the most sacred moments in life—the beginning and the end. However, evidence also suggests that Neolithic societies practiced the familiar gender division of labor, and Gimbutas does not dispute that women performed the gathering, storing, and preparation of grains and other staple plants, and the raising of children. She also accepts that men tended livestock and/or hunted. We should realize, however, that at this time, there is no evidence to suggest that men enjoyed any greater status or power compared to women, but rather, it appears that Neolithic communities valued both types of work. Indeed, they blended the sacred closely with everyday life, such that their temples "sanctified everyday activity" and not "abstruse, arcane rituals." With this in mind, "women's work took on sacred meaning" (Gimbutas 2001:98) as central activities that all communities required for survival.

Given the later historical forms of female sects in the Greco-Roman world (Angus [1928] 1975; Burkert 2005; M. Meyer [1987] 1999; Turcan 1989), we may confidently but still critically continue with the likely possibility that feminine deities and women played a far more important and valued role in religion than feminine aspects and women play in the historical period, including today. Indeed, the classical anthropologist J. G. Fraser in the landmark *The Golden Bough* (Fraser and Fraser [1890] 1994) suspected as much through his interpretation of mythology, but in his day he possessed no concrete evidence. In fact, his mere suggestion that female deities and women once held a central position in prehistoric religion so offended scholars in the late 19th and early 20th centuries that the publisher purged such passages (and others about the crucifixion of Christ) in the 1922 edition (R. Fraser 1994:ix). Other notable nineteenth-century scholars, such as Johann Bachofen, Robert Briffault, and Edward Hartland, also held that prehistoric societies were "matrilineal, matriarchal, and even polyandrous," meaning they had more than one male intimate partner—the inverse of polygamous (M. Stone 1978:33).

By the time Merlin Stone wrote in 1978, contemporary comparative anthropology provided relatively strong evidence that

> though cause and effect between matrilineal descent, high female status, and the veneration of the Goddess are often confused . . . repeated evidence attests that the religion of the Goddess and a female kinship system were closely intertwined in many parts of the Near East. (p. 58)

Around 4000–3000 BCE, mysterious tribes from the north and east invaded the Near East. Their male gods and patriarchal society of war conquered the matrifocal and agrarian societies, and replaced the Goddess with violent and brutal male deities. Evidence and diverse scholarship allows Stone (1978) to connect these Stone Age invaders with the later "barbarians" known to the ancient Mediterranean civilizations. Violent, nomadic, and warlike patriarchal tribes arrived in the Near East and the Mediterranean periodically over several thousand years (pp. 66–67), and each brings a fresh infusion of patriarchal dominance and exaltation of the warrior. The patriarchal warrior tribes descended first on India, where mythology and archaeological evidence converge to reveal a story and artifacts of male warriors conquering and then dominating female deities (pp. 72–73). Merlin Stone cites many anthropologists, historians, and linguists to piece together a complete picture of dramatic social change that began around 4000 BCE in India and spread westward. Linguistical analysis reveals a correspondence between values of hierarchy and domination with the emergence of male warrior gods or heroes bringing light, fire, or lightning to the people they conquer. In contrast, the settled Goddess worshippers valued stability and harmony, and celebrated earth and water as divine (pp. 75–76), as the essential elements of growth in a farming culture. Not only did patriarchal society usher in male gods, but it brought a social order premised on war and conquest as well.

Cave art and artifacts seem to support the Gimbutas-Stone thesis, at least in terms of timing. Transition to male-centered activities, especially hunting and warfare, appears first in India and then gradually moves westward. If the thesis is correct, then we would expect an Eastern society such as India to exhibit patriarchal characteristics first, before the invaders press farther west into Europe and the Mediterranean. Decisively masculinist and patriarchal art appears in the Late Neolithic period in Europe, compared to the Middle Neolithic in India.

Sociologically, we can argue with some assurance that Goddess worship and matrifocal social order existed where people practiced a settled economy of agriculture and livestock. We find that male gods of light and fire and patriarchal social order existed where people lived nomadically and relied on hunting and the spoils of war to survive. The Mother-Goddess of this-worldly sacredness gives way to the male sky gods of otherworldly sacredness.

The fate of the Goddess depends on the exact culture. She retained greater reverence in Greek culture, even to the extent that the city of Athens bears the name of a goddess—both the Goddess and the city in Greek are called "Athena." Many other Greek goddesses retained significant importance, such as Artemis, Aphrodite, and Hera.

Jean Markale (1999) argues that goddess-worshipping cultures also celebrated a vital aspect of life—sexuality. Fertility rituals occupied central aspects of goddess religions, and many artifacts depict highly sexualized female forms (Gimbutas 2001; Markale 1999). As patriarchy superseded matriarchy, sacred female sexuality was relegated to either sacred virginity, or vilified as the castrating beast—the Whore. The virgin represents the imprisoned female, tamed and controlled, while the whore represents the Other, the wild and untamed enemy. Female symbols of life and regeneration became symbols of evil, and the material earth subordinated to the light of the heavens (Sjoo and Mor 1987:288–289). In this view, patriarchy transforms the life-centered religion of the Goddess into evil and filth, in favor of the transcendent-centered religion of the sky gods.

In simplest sociological terms, idealism replaces materialism, such that virtue becomes not the reverence of life, but the reverence of superiority. Sjoo and Mor (1987) go so far as to argue that patriarchal religions are archaeologically and historically based on domination, and that their transcendent gods are inherently superior and often aggressive. Worldly life becomes something to transcend, a mere stopover on the route to something better, and often a test of worthiness for transcendence. In contrast, matrifocal religions are based on equality and celebration of actual living, and the idea that this life is the point of existence—or as Bruce Springsteen sings in "Promised Land" from his album *Darkness on the Edge of Town*, "It ain't no sin to be glad you're alive." Returning to one of J. G. Fraser's most controversial hypotheses, was Jesus crucified because he advocated a return to the values of the Goddess—peace and love?

Greek mythology demonstrates a typical transition from feminine universalism to masculinist pantheons. That is, the ouroboros and Mother-Goddess decline in confrontation with individual named deities, which are all part of a polytheistic pantheon—a collection of all the gods and goddesses, such as the Greek Olympians.

Image 2.5   Greek Gaia

In all known pantheons, however, such as the ancient Greco-Roman and ancient and contemporary Hinduism, the greatest deities are masculine. Feminine forces do not disappear, but neither do they occupy what was likely a former universal prominence. Some theorize that this corresponds to a shift from prehistoric matrilineal and egalitarian cultures to patriarchal and hierarchical culture, but again, this is debatable. As more evidence emerges, however, mostly through feminist scholarship, the likelihood improves.

In the case of Greek mythology as an example, the earth mother, in the form of Gaia (from an ancient representation) (Image 2.5), has a counterpart in the form of Ouranos, god of the sky. Myths, though not literal, tell stories of absolute truth in that although the events of the story may or may not be literally true, they convey a universal truth about human existence. In this case, Ouranos and Gaia, which represent all that is transitional and all that is constant, respectively, give birth to several offspring, the Titans. Each Titan represents a particular aspect of nature. For example, Chronos, the eldest of the Titans, represents time (his name is the root of chronograph, chronology, etc.); Hyperion, the sun; Eos, the moon; and many others. In each case, the equal and balanced existence that Ouranos and Gaia represented now becomes an existence of particular and distinct forces: time, the sun, the moon, and so forth. The Titans are not yet fully anthropomorphic, but still maintain a quality of infinitude and force of nature. Yet they are discrete forces, no longer one and continuous with Gaia and Ouranos. Other cultures have similar associations, as among the much older Sumerians, for example, and among the Celts, both of whom are not Indo-European.

Gilgamesh (Image 2.6) who may or may not have been an actual historical king and son of Enmerkar from c. 3500 BCE, fights various battles and faces various trials and tribulations, until he joins with Enkidu, a wildman, who together with help from the sun god Shamash slay Humbaba, a giant who guards a grove of cedar trees. Humbaba and his ilk are equivalent to the Titans of the Greeks. After more adventures, the goddess Ishtar, also known as Inanna, attempts to seduce Gilgamesh, who refuses her, and she convinces Anu, her father and sky-god, equivalent to Zeus, to punish Gilgamesh for his insolence. Anu sends the Bull of Heaven, which Gilgamesh and Enkidu kill, but as a result of the battle, Enkidu also dies. Numerous

Image 2.6   Gilgamesh—a Babylonian Mythical Hero

ancient Babylonian stone artifacts depict this primordial battle and subsequent fate for offending the gods: although a hero among mortals, Gilgamesh earns the eternal wrath of the sky-gods and suffers torment by bulls in the afterlife.

In the case of the Celts, the Titans are known as the Formorii, who are great giants from the sea, and who become misshapen monsters in later versions of Celtic mythology. The mythical ancestors of the Celts in the British Isles, known as the Tuatha Dé Danann—the people of the goddess Dana— arrive later and overthrow the Formorii. Dana was an earth-mother deity, equivalent to Gaia. Among the Tuatha Dé Danann, the various individual gods are found throughout Celtic culture, and among the most important are Lugh, god of light (equivalent to Apollo), and Dagda, father of the gods (equivalent to Zeus). The relationship between the Tuatha and humans is complex; suffice it to say that they fought each other, but also coexisted and sometimes produced mixed offspring (the named heroes of legend) until the Tuatha decided to leave the earth for the underworld. Humans still depend vitally on the Tuatha for food, favorable weather, healthy children, and many other things. The celebration of Samhain (pronounced SOW-en) is the Celtic New Year on October 31 or November 1, when mortals may communicate with those in the underworld, such as the Tuatha Dé Danann, and with the dead.

In Greek mythology, the Titans give birth to the gods and goddesses of Olympus, who overthrow their father, Chronos, and establish themselves as the new masters of existence. The Olympians are fully anthropomorphized, far from the raw and primal forces of nature. They are each in turn the embodiment of human virtues and ideals, for example, Zeus—power; Athena—self-control and intelligence; Aphrodite—beauty. Zeus appears in Image 2.7 with Thetis (a minor water goddess) in a painting by Jean-Auguste-Dominique Ingres (1811).

Both the historian and the sociologist could fill in many more details, but each of a different type. The historian seeks all the details to complete the story and to complete the descriptions of each deity. The sociologist seeks to explain what the myths tell us about the social change that the mythical narrative represents.

From a sociological perspective then, the first transition from Gaia/Ouranos to the Titans portrays two decisive aspects. First, society began to move economically

Image 2.7   Zeus and Thetis

from nomadic hunter-gatherers to a more stable, agrarian existence. Yet this is not a return to the Stone Age matrifocal society. Rather, this transition and its attendant religious beliefs reflect a new orientation to the natural world in that humans are no longer continuous with nature, but rather, are able to intentionally utilize the environment according to human design. Thus, the transcendent realm reflects this new orientation, with a greater specialization of supreme beings. The sky is no longer simply Ouranos the father, but the sun, the air, the wind, the moon, and so on are separate beings with unique attributes. The proper understanding of each brings greater reward, just as the proper understanding of wind, rain, temperature, and seasons brings greater yield in farming. Similarly, the earth is no longer simply Gaia, but different soils, climates, terrain, and so on. A clear understanding of increasingly diverse factors contributes to greater success both in this world, and in relationship to the divine.

The second major change is that both the father and the mother, both Ouranos and Gaia, become less and less omnipresent and omnipotent, as changing social forces divide them into constituent parts. The natural world appears less and less universal, timeless, and mysterious, and more and more knowable and controllable. However, the Titans are still more or less equal to each other. Although they each have unique attributes, characteristics, and abilities, none is greater than or has command authority over the others. This nonhierarchical differentiation would change. In all the aforementioned examples, the Greeks, the Celts, and the Sumerians, the Titans or giants become destructive, threatening forces that stand in opposition to civilization and its greater social order. No longer at the mercy of natural forces, humans embrace deities who, while far from compliant, may be appeased and, significantly, may thus actively change human conditions. The Titans are not approachable nor do they interact with humans. Once the Titans are overthrown and the society they represent superseded by more advanced civilization, the Titans become a kind of celestial criminal, forever imprisoned (frozen in ice) in the case of the Norse cultures, or reinterpreted as monsters in the case of the Celts and the Sumerians. Compared to the pantheonic gods, and the more advanced social order they reflect, the giants are brutal and primitive, the last remnants of an earlier and more primitive society and level of existence.

Numerous demographic changes brought new people with new customs and beliefs into the Mediterranean world, which enacted concurrent social change.

Originally populated by goddess-oriented agrarian communitarians, warlike and patriarchal peoples now entered the Mediterranean world. Their entrance, both peaceful and conflictual, changed Euro-Mediterranean culture such that the new pantheon of anthropomorphized gods corresponded to their patriarchal and hierarchical social structure. Over time, their pantheon replaced the Titans, a transformation that mythology explains as a great cosmic battle in which Zeus, leader and most powerful of the Olympians, overthrows the Titans. His father, Chronos, attempts to swallow Zeus and his siblings, but eventually, they emerge from Chronos and overthrow the Titans, and subsequently establish themselves as the new lords of existence. Zeus claims the sky, Poseidon the seas, and Hades the underworld. Although there are numerous goddesses as well, and some of them, such as Athena, wield considerable power, none of the female deities have command authority over any aspect of existence.

This religious change, like the transition from Ouranos/Gaia to the Titans, reflects corresponding social changes. Many argue that prior to the arrival of the pantheonic gods, Indo-European society was basically agrarian, peaceful, and centered on a harmony with nature. In such a social formation, ouroboros, earth-centered deities—in particular, mother-goddess deities—represented the social values of cooperation and harmony. In other words, society was (1) cooperative rather than hierarchical, and (2) matrifocal rather than patriarchal. Women served as the center of knowledge and nurturing. The notion of domination and power arrived with the male-dominated warrior societies, from somewhere beyond the Steppes, most likely from central Asia. This depiction of pre-pantheonic society has some evidence and perhaps a reasonable degree of validity, but not beyond all doubt. While human civilization from India to the British Isles in fact does become increasingly hierarchical, we do not know whether the pre-pantheonic societies were matrifocal, or if so, whether male warrior bands coexisted with them.

Also, a few matriarchies do exist today. See Peggy Sanday's (2004) *Women at the Center: Life in a Modern Matriarchy* for a detailed empirical study of a modern-day matriarchal society among the Minangkabau— one of the largest ethnic groups in Indonesia, on the island of Sumatra.

It is clear, however, that by the time we have historical records, two things are certain. First, Euro-Mediterranean societies are decidedly patriarchal as well as hierarchical. Whether they were different at some point prior is the subject of debate, as discussed above. When the historical period begins in Egypt and the Near East around 800 BCE, all historical societies are decisively patriarchal and hierarchical. The first term means not only rule by men, but rule by male-centered values. Men enjoy automatic status and privilege over and against women and children. Such societies often bar women from power, both formally and informally. In cases where women obtain power, such as Maatkare Hatshepsut (late 1500s–1482 BCE), one of the most successful and powerful Egyptian pharaohs, and considerably later Elizabeth I of Britain (1533–1603 CE) (Image 2.8), and Catherine the Great (1729–1796 CE), Empress of Russia (Image 2.9), the female leaders were all known for their iron hand of authority and masculine demeanor. All were excellent rulers who greatly expanded the power and glory of their empires, but they lived austerely and produced no children. In short, the few women rulers in history suppressed their femininity in order to conform to the masculine ideal. It should be noted that the images of Hatshepsut as pharaoh were all defaced or destroyed within a few years of her death.

Image 2.8   Elizabeth I of England

Image 2.9   Catherine the Great

Second, hierarchy means that certain types of people, in this case not simply men but men of the ruling class, wield command and status authority over other people and aspects of society.

As these changes occur, a greater differentiation of labor also occurs, such that people become increasingly specialized in their trades and roles in society. By the time Athens reach its zenith around 450 BCE, it exhibited a complex division of labor, with many classes from slaves at the bottom to various strata of patricians at the top. Each class further subdivided into various groups, with the freemen—those who hold neither title nor land—composed of merchants and craftworkers such as armorers, weaponsmiths, coopers (barrel-makers), fletchers (arrow-makers), and many others. This pattern of the complex division of labor developed throughout Europe and the Asian continents. As the divisions of labor became more complex, so too did the gods become more complex to reflect the social change they mirrored. Eventually, gods became associated with particular trades, such as Hermes, messenger of the gods, associated with trade, and Athena, with knowledge and education.

Polytheism

This brings us to the first religious age of recorded history—polytheism. As the term indicates, such beliefs celebrate the existence of many gods. In places where people celebrated many gods, they usually did so in cults, which is not to be confused with the contemporary application of the word. The term *cult* when applied in the ancient context refers to an exclusive group dedicated to one particular deity. Usually, the concept of a pantheon—the complete collection of deities—existed only in large cities with extensive trade contact and population migration. Through trade and migration, people introduced and shared beliefs and customs from various different and often far-off locales. Isis, for example, originated in Egypt, but eventually found devotees throughout the Greco-Roman world.

Outside of such major cities as Rome, Athens, Delhi, and Shanghai, the vast majority of people worshipped only a few deities, often only one. Initially, before the rise of trade and open travel, people lived intensely local lives, in small villages where everyone looked the same, spoke the same language, lived the same lifestyle, had more or less the same quality of life, and worshipped the same one deity. One local religion, Judaism, would eventually produce a local figure of relatively little note—Jesus—who would, 300 years or so after his death, inspire a religion that changed the world—Christianity. What became a world-transformative force started as a local variation (a cult) in Judaism. We will consider that development later.

For now, it is important to note the difference between urban and rural life in ancient times. Each locale with its local god or goddess contrasted sharply with the great cosmopolitan cities, a contrast we might still recognize today. However, even the most remote town today has access to the greater world through modern technology, which obviously did not exist in ancient times. Thus, polytheism existed as a vast assortment of local deities, particular to and reflective of local beliefs, traditions, and ways of life. One locale in Asia Minor created the cult of Cybele, a variant of the earth-mother theme, although modified to stand as the patroness of grain production. As civilization encompassed the land and people of Asia Minor, Cybele joined her many comrades throughout the Greco-Roman world. Likewise, warrior gods such as Ares likely arrived with primitive, warlike nomads from the Black Sea area, but by the time the historical record begins in Greece around 600 BCE, Ares is already well established as a prominent fixture in Greek mythology.

In polytheism, more gods are always possible and admissible, with only the occasional exception. One would be in Livy, one of Rome's greatest historians, who tells that in 186 BCE, a woman named Hispala Faecenia, a prostitute, informed the consul (two

---

Mithraism

Many religions besides Christianity that increased in popularity during the tumultuous years 300–476 CE in the Roman Empire promised salvation through a savior sent by God to redeem humanity. Among these was Mithraism, based on the figure of Mithra the bull-slayer. The epithet suggests that Mithraism began as a local tribal belief, likely based on the life of an outstanding individual.

The earliest references to the Mithra cult date from 1380 BCE, in a treaty between Subbiluliuma, King of the Hittites, and Mativaza, King of the Mitanni (Turcan [1989] 2000:196)—both Persian peoples. With origins thus in Persia, Mithraism spread across Asia Minor, and arrived in Rome sometime in the mid–first century CE.

As human civilization advanced and perception of the cosmos grew in size and complexity, the gods likewise matured from local tribal peculiarities into grander and more powerful deities. Once impressive, the ability to slay a bull no longer was enough to suggest godhood. As Mithraism spread westward, Mithra transformed from a hero into a divine redeemer, whose life now showed the path to salvation. Sacred sites remained in caves, called grottos, the setting of Mithra's original bull sacrifice. The cult remained a mystery faith, although some argue that in fact toward the end of the Western Empire in 476 CE, it more closely resembled the revealed religions of Judaism and Christianity (M. Meyer [1987] 1999; J. Smith 1990) with devotional rituals of redemption open to the public and the seeking of converts.

consuls shared the highest executive office) Spurius Postumius Alburius that one of her customers, Publius Aebutius—a man of equestrian rank—had told her stories of the rites of Bacchus, a cult in Rome. These rites included orgies, and most appallingly, human sacrifice. The consul ordered a praetor (a high-ranking judge) to conduct an investigation, which yielded several suspects whom the consul called in for questioning. However, the suspects either fled or committed suicide, which the consul interpreted as an admission of guilt. He ordered the cult disbanded and its temple destroyed. Any assets were to be given to the poor (Livius [c. 12 CE] 2002).

There are many interesting aspects to this story, but for our purposes, note that religion falls under the jurisdiction of the state. Also note that people cannot break the law (in this case, by performing human sacrifice) for religious purposes. Even the lowest members of Roman society (such as prostitutes) have rights, and not even the noble classes are above the law. In general though, all the various cults were free to practice as they saw fit, as long as they upheld the law, without interference from the state or public outcry against infidels or sinners. Rome and other polytheistic societies fought many wars, but never over religion.

Inclusive Monotheism

More changes were on the way. The Mediterranean world engaged extensively with the Near East, in particular with Persia. Ancient itself, Persia was for most of its history polytheistic, but sometime between 1400 and 1000 BCE, a man of noble birth named Zarathustra (Zoroaster to the Greeks) introduced a novel concept—monotheism. In this version, which we now know as Zoroastrianism, it's not that there is only one god, but there is definitely only one *good* god, and one evil god. They each have lesser minions who serve them, and the sides are distinct—pure good versus pure evil. The god of pure good is called Ahura Mazda, the one of pure evil is called Ahriman, and earth is their battleground. Each requires human adherents to gain ground against the other, until the final battle when fire will consume the earth. This imagery might seem familiar—pure good versus pure evil that confront each other with their armies at a final battle in which the world ends. Moreover, Ahura Mazda takes fire and light as his symbols, and Ahriman takes darkness and cold. Good and Light versus Evil and Darkness. As this dichotomous theology might suggest, Zoroastrianism became exclusive, while Mithraism and others remained inclusive; that is, they accepted the validity of other monotheisms on the assumption that they all worshipped the one true god. Known by different names and manifested in different forms, inclusive monotheism accepts diverse approaches through different languages, cultures, and traditions. Henotheism is another term for inclusive monotheism.

Also, monotheism introduced a second vital change—the revealed faith. In ancient polytheism, existence goes through cyclical change, such as birth, life, death, rebirth, and so forth. Social customs follow the seasons and various other natural and timeless rhythms. These are mystery religions, that is, the gods intervene in the world, but as they please and without any larger plan or purpose. In contrast, monotheisms teach that the One God has one plan for all humanity. Although the details vary from one version to another, all work from the undeniable premise that God cares about us, and God has a plan. Every event that occurs and every life that enters and leaves the world does so according to God's plan. God reveals this plan, or at least elements of it, through signs, scripture, and other means that the faithful can understand. In short, there is a purpose to everything, which the faithful can understand—God willing.

Although Zoroastrianism was founded in Persia (now Iran), it migrated westward, went through a few permutations along the way (Riley 2003), and impacted Western religion through Judaism specifically, and Greco-Roman culture generally.

Judaism, influenced by the Zoroastrian binary that emphasized the good-versus-evil orientation, exalted Yahweh, the supreme God of the Jews, and demonized all others, especially feminine fertility deities such as Lilith (Image 2.10) and Jezebel, who were earth-mother types common in the Middle East, and originally celebrated among the Jews as well. These and all others (although fertility deities represented evil more than others—Jezebel became a whore and Lilith the Great Castrator who steals men's seed in the night) became evil demons, minions of the

Table 2.1   Polytheism and Monotheism Compared

Polytheism	Monotheism
Cyclical—Society celebrates and patterns natural cycles, especially the seasons, as well as phases of the sun, the moon, and other astronomical objects.	**Linear**—Existence begins and concludes at particular points. Individual events begin and end as ordained by God. At some point, God's plan is fulfilled and existence will end.
Pluralistic—Recognizes a wide range of ever-more-diverse deities, forces, and powers. Each represents a facet of life, and often a particular culture in which the entity originated.	**Monistic**—Belief that there is only one true God (has two forms): **Henotheistic** versions accept the legitimacy of other faiths, so long as they worship what is believed to be the one God. **Exclusive** versions allow for only one approach to the one god.
Mystery—Time passes, but existence continues without end, and without a larger sense of purpose. Knowledge of the divine (the mysteries) accords only to a select few.	**Revealed**—God has a purpose for everything, and it is knowable to all who practice the appropriate faith.
Deities have a range of qualities, personality traits, individual history, and variable interests in human affairs, which ranges from extensive to none. Humans can influence their interest and actions, through both supplication and offense.	**The One God** is eternal, without beginning or end, and is constant in purpose and interest. Although capable of reward and punishment, God's commitment to humanity never wavers.

Image 2.10   Lilith, an Earth–Mother Deity

One Great Evil. Judaism also incorporated the imagery of light and dark. As the spirit of Zoroastrianism spread further west, it morphed into Essenism—a variation of Judaism—and influenced Mithraism—a hero cult that later rivaled Christianity as a religion of salvation. The Essenes, with whom Jesus perhaps had contact or of which he may even have been a member, viewed the entire world as evil, and sought to separate themselves from it until such time as the battle to reclaim the earth from evil arrived.

This moment, they believed arrived, in 70 CE, when they fomented a rebellion against Roman control of Jerusalem. The Romans utterly crushed the rebellion, however, and under the command of the future emperor, Titus Flavius Sabinus Vespasianus, destroyed the Temple of Solomon, the most sacred building in Judaism. As noted in Chapter 1, this also meant the destruction of the priests in Judaism, who had never reformed, and whom the rabbis subsequently replaced. The Romans also destroyed the Essenes, but not before their apocalyptic message worked its way into Judaism, especially into the emerging cult we now know as Christianity.

As mentioned, Mithraism also arose at this time, and rivaled Christianity as one of the first monotheisms in the West. Unlike Christianity, however, Mithraism was an inclusive monotheism. Mithra (also from Persia) was not a god himself, but a great hero, God's only son, who was conceived to show humans, through example, how to live and how to fight evil. Among the primary attributes were physical health, cleanliness, sexual abstention (except in marriage), and actively confronting evil whenever it appears. Mithraists built sacred shrines called grottos, which as the name suggests were usually underground, built into hillsides to commemorate where Mithra was born, the poor son of migrant goat herders, and where he died fighting evil. We know little else about the beliefs of Mithraism (M. Meyer [1987] 1999). In Image 2.11, we see an underground temple from Ostia (the port city for ancient Rome), built in the third century CE. While obviously not a natural cave, the temple maintains the underground and cave-like atmosphere typical of traditional Mithraic temples. Known as the Mithraeum, it is the best preserved of Mithra temples.

Image 2.11 Ostia Mithraeum

Source: Michelle Touton.

Here again we see syncretic elements. Mithra is of divine creation but born to human parents of lowly status who, as nomadic shepherds, lack even a particular locality. Mithra is sent to show people how to live, and that God has revealed a plan for humanity. Mithraism, Zoroastrianism, and later Christianity are examples of revealed religions, those that involve a plan with definite stages and a definite conclusion, in contrast to the mystery religions in which existence is ongoing but also indefinite. In this regard, Mithraism constitutes an intermediate form, in that it is inclusively monotheistic but not entirely revealed like Zoroastrianism or Christianity. As far as we know today, it involved no final battle.

Another syncretic element is the concept of divine or virgin birth. Although we do not know if Mithra was immaculately conceived, we know that Christians hold this belief about Jesus, as did the Romans about the founders of Rome, Romulus and Remus. Livy tells us that Romulus and Remus were immaculately conceived around 771 BCE by the vestal virgin Rhea Silvia, sired by Mars, the god of war (Titus Livius [c. 12 CE] 2002). See the full discussion of this story and possible connections to Christianity in Lewis and Reinhold (1966:52–53). As a vestal virgin, Rhea Silvia could not raise the children, despite the fact that her virginity was not compromised, and she set the twins adrift on the Tiber River, similar to the way the infant Moses was of noble birth and set adrift on the river. For Romulus and Remus, Mars sent a she-wolf to raise them, the wolf being his patron animal. They were eventually taken in by a shepherd named Faustulus, who, with his wife

Deus Sol Invictus

Another important monotheistic tradition was that of Deus Sol Invictus—the Unconquered Sun God. While its origins are obscure, it rose to prominence during the third century CE alongside Zoroastrianism, Christianity, and Mithraism. Indeed, it was a collective holiday for several faiths of Eastern origin (including perhaps Christianity) for all of which the sun played a central role. The date of this celebration is telling—December 25.

Like Christianity in the fourth century when the Emperor Constantine became a champion of the faith, so Deus Sol Invictus was elevated by Elagabalus to a dominant position. As emperor, Elagabalus also ruled as the high priest of Sol Invictus. Although he reigned for only 4 years (218–222 CE), his successors continued the celebration of Sol Invictus as Dies Natalis Solis Invicti, or Birthday of the Unconquered Sun, which remained a part of official state religion until 390, when Theodosius I banned pagan religions. Still, the Day of the Sun (Sunday) remains the holy day of rest and reverence in Christian culture. For a further discussion, see the *Catholic Encyclopaedia*, Vol. 3 (1908).

Acca Larentia, taught them human speech and raised them to adulthood. Like Mithra and Jesus, these children of apparently low but actually noble or divine and virginal birth go on to accomplish great things. Just as Cain killed Abel, Romulus kills Remus and becomes sole king of Rome and its celebrated founder.

The issue is not whether the Romans were right or wrong (note that Livy relates this story as a myth, not as fact) or whether the story of Jesus is true or not, but rather, what this tells us about religion. Clearly, many elements of religious stories are shared throughout the ages. Even the story of Romulus and Remus, Michael Grant ([1962] 1995) finds, goes back to much earlier times, most likely back through prehistory to the earliest forms of ancestor worship in the age of the Ouranos/Gaia traditions. Indeed, this story in one version or another may have come from Egypt and originated perhaps in 2000 BCE or earlier. In essence, these stories show how humans, chosen or inspired by the divine, overcome all adversity and accomplish great things. They also show how syncretic culture really is—that each group's members work with material already present and adapt various elements to represent their own time, place, and beliefs.

Exclusive Monotheism

As the first monotheism, Zoroastrianism was also the first *exclusive* monotheism, based on the life and teaching of Zoroaster, also known by his Persian name, Zarathustra, who lived sometime between 1400 and 1000 BCE (Boyce [1979] 2001). That is, there is one good and correct god, and all others are myths, or evil. Furthermore, there is one correct way to worship this god, one correct way to live, and one correct set of beliefs. The will of God appears in sacred texts, such as the Bible or the Quran. In the West and Middle East, Christianity would become the dominant exclusive monotheism until the arrival of Islam around 650 CE and continuing to the present. If we use Islam as an example, we find typical exclusively monotheistic beliefs. There are several essential beliefs that all Muslims share, as noted above, and five pillars of faith that define Sunni and related (such as Sufi) practices. Of all the sects of Islam, only Shia does not proclaim the five pillars.

But let us backtrack a bit. Christianity, Mithraism, other monotheisms, and all the pagan cults, none preeminent over the others, coexisted until 313 CE, when the

Roman emperor Constantine officially recognized and legitimated Christianity through the Edict of Milan. Although he didn't covert from Mithraism himself until his deathbed, 313 marks a decisive turning point, when the power of the Roman state not only legitimates Christianity, but makes it attractive as a means of political advancement. From this point on, paganism endures for centuries more (some argue until the present day) but always in decline against the relentless advance of Christianity, and later and in other parts of the world, Islam. The monotheisms triumph.

Constantine claimed that he saw a vision of the cross the night before the battle of the Milvian Bridge, October 28, 312 CE. Constantine defeats his rival, and becomes sole emperor of Rome, a triumph he attributes to the Christian God. Let us assume that Constantine is sincere, even though in every other way he behaved with cunning ruthlessness like all successful Roman emperors. Let us ask not about his sincerity, but as sociologists, about the social forces that contributed to the success of Christianity.

How could he reverse hundreds of years of Roman polytheism, and the complex society that practiced it? The answer is that society was already changing, that the Rome of Constantine was not the Rome of the first emperor Augustus 300 years earlier. There were several key social changes that had occurred and continued to occur during the reign of Constantine, changes to which Christianity ably corresponded, and thus, over time, proved more relevant to real life than the ancient pagan ways. The gods of Olympus passed because the society to which they corresponded had passed.

First, the imperial period (which began with Augustus in 27 BCE) increasingly consolidated power in the hands of the

---

Essential Beliefs of Islam: A Typical Exclusive Monotheism

Belief in God (*Allah* in Arabic simply means "God"), the only one worthy of all worship

Belief in all the prophets and messengers (sent by God)

Belief in the books sent by God

Belief in the angels

Belief in the Day of Judgment (*Qiyamah*) and in the Resurrection

Belief in Destiny (Fate), *Qadaa* and *Qadar* in Arabic. This does not mean one is predetermined to act or live a certain life. God has given humans free will to act and make decisions. Rather, it means that God has a plan, and everyone is part of that plan.

Five Pillars of Islam

1. **Shahadah** (literally the testament). "There is no God but God, and Muhammad is his prophet (or messenger)."

   In Arabic: ﺍﻟﺮﺳﻮﻝ ﻣﺤﻤﺪ ﻃﻠﻠ ﺍﻻ ﺍﻟﻪ ﺍﻻ (reads right to left). In Arabic, "Allah" means God; it is not the name of a particular god.

   Romanized: "lā ilāh illā-llāh; muẖammadun rasūlu-llāh."

2. **Salah** (prayer). All Muslims should face Mecca and pray five times a day:
   Between dawn and sunrise (Fajr)
   After midday (Dhuhr)
   Midway between midday and sunset (Asr)
   Right after sunset (Maghrib)
   Approximately one hour after sunset (Isha'a)

3. **Zakah** (almsgiving to the poor).

4. **Sawm** (fasting).

5. **Hajj** (pilgrimage). All Muslims that have the financial and physical means to perform hajj are required to do so at least once in their lifetimes. The pilgrimage to Mecca can only be performed during the Islamic month of Dhul Hijja. Anyone who is Muslim can perform the hajj, regardless of where they are from.

emperor. This consolidation included, especially, bureaucratic consolidation that governed the production and distribution of vital goods and services, including food, wine, and military protection. Although the Romans never had a criminal law enforcement system, the emperor replaced the Republican system of consuls, who constituted an executive function, and the praetors, who constituted a judicial function with imperial bureaucrats. The emperors also installed bureaucrats in place of *qaestors,* who served as public accountants, and *aediles,* who governed food and entertainment. In the republican period (509–27 BCE), all these positions were elected, and often, this meant that popular, rather than technically competent, people filled these positions. Although these positions remained in the imperial period, they became purely honorary. In their place, the emperors installed a professional bureaucratic administration, filled by experts according to ability. Although emperors might in certain periods change frequently, the bureaucrats stayed in place because their positions depended on expertise, not on political loyalty.

As power and administration centralized, the emperor became the ruling god on earth, which emperors after Constantine formalized as "divine right," a concept that ruled the West throughout the Middle Ages after the fall of the Roman Empire in the West. It also ruled the Eastern continuation of the empire, which we know today as the Byzantine Empire. The concept of one God corresponded neatly with the concept of one earthly leader as His chosen representative and, of course, chosen earthly authority. The structure of society had changed from a conglomeration of provincial enclaves, each devoted to particular deities amidst a pantheon of deities, and transformed into a formalized and centralized administrative apparatus. To people now living in such a society, the many gods no longer resonated with the reality of their lives. Instead, the one God, ruler and creator of all without peer, resonated more directly with a society now ruled by the one Emperor, lord of all things and without peer.

Second, Constantine himself played an active and decisive role. Prior to his acceptance, Christianity competed with many other innovative religions, such as the aforementioned Mithraism. There were also innovative versions of the cult of Isis, and others of which, because they did not succeed as Christianity did, we have little knowledge. Constantine provided vital and powerful support for this new religion, which, after 312 CE especially, gained converts quickly. Now associated with power, converting to Christianity opened new political doors for aspiring people from nearly all classes, and promoted shifting power alignments in the empire. As the old priests lost influence, the new Christian priests and bishops ascended to ever-greater influence and wealth. Changes in tax laws, property rights, and other legal developments contributed to a Christian power, and thus the religion became attractive as a means to social ascent in a society which offered very little social mobility.

The third key social change was that the empire faced many threats, from plague, famine, drought, and especially from barbarian invasions. As Rodney Stark (1997) shows, numerous and ongoing crises throughout the period of 300–476 CE disrupted traditional Greco-Roman order and its associated polytheism. Yet the rise of monotheism was a long and complex process.

Transition From Paganism to Christianity

The fact remains that Christianity did supersede paganism. We often assume, or like to think, that people make informed, rational choices, and this is what rational choice as a formal theory in sociology argues. But did paganism die, as rational choice theory predicts any inferior product supposedly would in a competitive market? Sociologist Rodney Stark (1997) states that paganism "toppled over dead" (p. 94) once and for all in the crisis years 300–476 CE. Other research suggests that this is not true. In fact, it prospered outside the major cities of Rome, Antioch, and Constantinople for several hundred years. Indeed, as we will see, paganism did not decisively disappear, but in fact continued quite influentially through the Middle Ages and the Renaissance, perhaps even into modern times. As we have already seen, Christianity is not wholly original and independent, but in fact has been greatly influenced by and has blended with paganism.

As wars, invasions, plagues, droughts, famines, and infanticide depleted the population of the Roman Empire, especially of women, the empire became increasingly unable to tend to the very same and ongoing social problems (Stark 1997: 58–160). However, let us remember the time and place, and especially the social order of Greco-Roman society in the late empire period. Recent attempts to forge ancient motivations into contemporary values go something like this: Chaos in general and plague in particular affected everyone, contemporary rational choice theory argues, but it was the Christians, compared to the pagans, who offered both spiritual and physical solace to the suffering and dying. Christianity was thus a superior product.

> **Orthodoxy, Eastern Orthodoxy, and Catholicism**
>
> When speaking about the history of Christianity, let us clarify terminology. In the first 300 years of Christianity, many different visions and versions coexisted, each particular to a certain region, and sometimes to particular towns or even particular individual leaders. No standards existed regarding belief or ritual.
>
> The Council of Nicaea in 325 CE, which created the first version of the Nicene Creed, and other subsequent councils contributed to the development of official doctrine and celebration of the mass. This official version became known as the Orthodox Church, or Orthodoxy. This Orthodoxy regarded other versions of Christianity as rivals, and in conjunction with Roman state power, sought to suppress the more popular rivals, such as Arianism and Nestorianism. After the Great Schism of 1054, Orthodoxy and the Orthodox Church came to refer only to the Eastern Church, also known as the Byzantine Church and the Greek Church. The Western Church is known as the Roman Catholic Church, or Catholicism.

According to Rodney Stark (1997), the personal cost was high, in that all Christians must both tend to the ill and suffering in order to receive help themselves in this world and to receive salvation in the next. Stark concludes that first, the Christians "deeply impressed" the pagans (p. 165) with their martyrs, who sacrificed themselves for the cause of Christianity and their belief in the loving God. Unfortunately, there is no evidence for this. As we see from Lucian of Samosata (below), people often saw Christians as pitiful fools. Also, as correspondence between Pliny (Gaius Plinius Caecilius Secundus, 63–113 CE) and Emperor Trajan shows, the policy toward Christians was no different than toward anyone else. Christian monotheism was not illegal nor was it widely persecuted; the Romans prosecuted religious irreverence toward the gods only if it suggested disloyalty to the state (Wilken 2003). Christianity neither especially impressed people, nor drew special attention from authorities.

Second, Stark (1997) notes that Christianity supposedly offered rewards in the form of relief from suffering, and a very valuable compensator (something that is not the reward itself, but indicative of a favored condition)—immortality. Those unwilling to serve the poor and suffering are thus denied the benefits—rewards or compensators. The particular combination of costs and benefits we may group together as a Christian way of life (pp. 168–170). The Christian way of life meant service to the general community of Christians, and in times of crisis, service to everyone in need, which typically involved great self-sacrifice in exchange for the compensator of salvation. Stark argues that, in time of crisis, Christianity offered far more to people compared to paganism that outweighed the higher costs of membership.

However, no uniquely Christian character emerged for at least the first 600 years, except that both pagan and early Christian writers agreed that the only uniquely Christian characteristic was sexual asceticism (Pagels 1989:58). All other characteristics, such as charity, were at best practiced inconsistently, and many early Christians argued that asceticism was fine for beginners and simpletons, but the greatest rival to early Christian Orthodoxy, the Gnostics, rejected asceticism in favor of higher spiritual accomplishment (Pagels 1989:60). Indeed, it appears that two different and competing Christian traditions developed as early as the mid–second century—one known as Orthodoxy and one as Gnosticism. Both relied on scripture.

Orthodoxy, the version of the emerging hierarchy of bishops, priests, and deacons, followed the scriptural tradition that traced back to the Twelve Apostles, the tradition that we know today as the New Testament. The Gnostics, in contrast, relied on accounts outside the Twelve, especially texts attributed to Mary Magdalene, Thomas, James (brother of Jesus), and Paul (also in the New Testament but not an apostle). Orthodox leaders, such as Tertullian (155–230 CE), Priest of Carthage, and Irenaeus (130–202 CE), Bishop of Lugdunum in Gaul, aggressively attacked and persecuted the Gnostics, whom they condemned as heretics. Only those who traced their doctrine and authority to the Twelve Apostles were legitimate. Orthodoxy successfully suppressed the Gnostics, such that they disappeared from the historical record, except as depicted in Orthodox attacks, until the discovery of the Nag Hammadi in 1945, a collection of Gnostic gospels and other writings (Pagels 1979). In the crisis period of which Stark speaks, each side rivaled the other in terms of membership, with Orthodoxy dominant in the West and Gnosticism in the East. Orthodoxy eventually triumphed by applying its formal hierarchical power against the egalitarian Gnostics, who eschewed all authority. Despite Constantine's attempt to unite Christian theology in a way acceptable to all sides at the Council of Nicaea in 325, widespread sectarian disagreement and often violent hostility intensified as more of the empire accepted diverse versions of Christianity (see Pagels 1989:98–126).

As a result, the notion of Christian charity, for example, as a consistently defining feature does not appear until late in the Renaissance period or even into the eighteenth century (Waite 2003). Care of the poor and downtrodden, although present inconsistently in earlier times, is a uniquely modern Christian mission.

Furthermore, the supposed Christian ethic of self-sacrifice as part of the ascetic lifestyle did not impress the ancients, but rather, drew mostly amusement, as Lucian of Samosata ([c. 170 CE] 2001) describes:

The poor Christian wretches have convinced themselves, first and foremost, that that they are going to be immortal and live for all time, in consequence of which they despise death and even willingly give themselves into custody, most of them. Furthermore, their first lawgiver [Jesus] persuaded them that they are all brothers of one another . . . by worshipping that crucified sophist himself and living under his laws. (p. 15)

Yet Lucian ([c. 170 CE] 2001) does not admire their brotherhood and selflessness; on the contrary,

Therefore they despise all things indiscriminately and consider all things common property, receiving their doctrines of faith without any evidence. So if any charlatan and trickster, able to profit by occasions, comes among them, he quickly acquires sudden wealth by imposing upon these simple folk. (p. 15)

In addition to Lucian's testimony, and contrary to popular belief, the Romans persecuted Christians very irregularly, having killed only a few hundred people, not thousands, over roughly 300 years of time (Frend 1965:413). Moreover, patricians like Constantine the Great experienced neither stigma nor sacrifice after October 28, 312 CE (battle of the Milvian Bridge) when he accepted Christianity as legitimate. If anything, his move toward Christianity only solidified his political power. It would seem that unscrupulous free-riders could readily exploit early Christians.

We know that Christianity triumphed, but we must avoid "the quite crude error of supposing the now familiar outline to have been already clear in the Fourth Century" (MacMullen 1981:136). If Christianity offered some special reward that would motivate great personal risk, it was not charity for the poor and succor for the sick and lonely. Barraclough (1976), for example, shows that sincerity in Christian devotion for centuries often amounted to "the untaught, wandering prophet, naked and dirty, who appears often to have been regarded as a prophet simply because he was an unbalanced lunatic" (p. 24). Indeed, it was the ease of membership, rather than the trials and tribulations, that appealed to ruling elites who could convert easily, yet make a strong political statement in the process.

Comparatively, the personal cost to join any number of pagan cults was often much higher. For any particular cult, initiation might require castration, self-flagellation, poisoning, lacerations, serving others in humility, or any number of combinations that often endured for days or even weeks (Turcan 1996). After initiation, ancient cults required regular demonstration of devotion, which typically involved repeated trials as well as monetary contributions. Again, Christianity was in practice simply one of many sects that exacted some form of commitment and offered certain rewards in return, no greater or substantially different from the others.

We will return to a more likely motivation later (politics), but for now, evidence argues against Stark's (1997) further assumption that the Great Conversion of 313 CE (the year Constantine legalized Christianity) meant a decisive death for paganism. As mentioned in the introduction to this book, sociology like all the other sciences uses theory and evidence to adjudicate between accurate and inaccurate explanations. In this case, rational choice theory does not seem to have the support of evidence. But then, what did happen to paganism?

What Happened to Paganism?

In reality, it is difficult to overestimate the enduring influence of pre-Christian (i.e., pagan) beliefs and practices. Despite "laws against sacrifices, seizures of idols by the state, and so back through the crowded chronicles of violence to suppress paganism . . . [t]he pagans survived, unterrified" (MacMullen 1981:134). Many communities beyond the major cities in the late empire period—Rome, Antioch, and Constantinople—refused to convert to Christianity, even when threatened with death and even when death was delivered. Even as late as the Byzantine emperor Justinian (527–565 CE), for example, this successful warlord and devout Christian conquered the southern half of the Italian peninsula to discover the people had retained many pagan practices, including polytheism, and still celebrated many pagan holidays. He executed or starved out thousands to force conversion to Christianity, to little avail. Similarly, he and his successors never converted the communities of the African Mediterranean coast; they retained many pagan beliefs and practices well into the 1300s, long after even the Muslim conquest of the area, although the Muslim method of rule was far more civilized and did not require conversion to Islam.

Ramsay MacMullen (1997) documents numerous pagan towns and communities well into the 800s CE, especially in Spain, rural Italy, and nearly all of North Africa (pp. 74–77). Despite the best efforts of Roman and Byzantine emperors and their bishops, priests, and lay people to eradicate pagan cults, they endured. In fact, the ongoing pressure and frequent violence to crush paganism only increased its fervor. On numerous occasions, the

---

Mardi Gras

There are no other celebrations like Mardi Gras in the United States. French for "Fat Tuesday," Mardi Gras began in New Orleans in the early 1800s as haphazard street festivals. In order to rein in overzealous revelers, the city recognized officially registered Krewes (official organizers of the parade and ball for Carnival), the first of which was The Mistick Krewe of Comus in 1857.

Beginning 2 weeks before Lent, which starts on Ash Wednesday (46 days before Easter), Mardi Gras celebrates the medieval Catholic practice of "farewell to the flesh," or *carnelevare* in Latin Vulgate. Originally, Mardi Gras followed the Catholic celebration of Candlemas, also practiced in the Orthodox Church as Hypapante tou Kyriou (Coming of the Lord—set as February 14), the lighting of sacred candles to celebrate the presentation of Christ in the Temple (the Purification). Christianity assimilated this holiday from the pagan Imbolc, a Celtic fire festival to celebrate the return of spring.

Although the vast majority of tourists who attend Mardi Gras are oblivious, Krewes still acknowledge the medieval and pagan origins of the festival. For example, The Krewe of Rex, founded in 1872, has always paraded the symbolic sacrificial White Bull float (Image 2.12), the Boeuf Gras.

Image 2.12   The Boeuf Gras

Source: Krewe of Rex, New Orleans.

local populace organized and resisted pressure and even military campaigns to defend their pagan cults. Where rational choice theory predicts its easy disappearance, paganism continued.

Furthermore, recent evidence now shows conclusively that paganism actually survived, if diminished, throughout the Middle Ages, in nearly all parts of Europe if not elsewhere (Hutton 1991, 1999). The most popular rites and festivals were incorporated into Christianity, but also existed alongside of and, as far as church leaders were concerned, in opposition to Christianity. For example, the Kalends, a celebration common to nearly all of pagan Europe and the Middle East (MacMullen 1997:39), continued into the 700s if not later. Indeed, Saint Boniface (born Winfrid of Devon, England, 672–754 CE) reported in 742 "the annual parading, singing, shouting, and loaded banquet tables in the open squares in Rome around St. Peter's Cathedral on the traditional date follows the pagan custom" (cited in MacMullen 1997:37). The Kalends are preserved today in festivals such as Mardi Gras in New Orleans and Carnival in Rio de Janeiro. Although paganism lost its organizational structure, it assimilated into Christian culture as folk medicine, herbology, and wise women and cunning men skilled in the arcane and often very practical arts of midwifery and animal husbandry.

Many places celebrated the solstices, equinoxes, and other times of the seasons perhaps to modern times. Even in the vehemently Christian Byzantine Empire, celebrations such as the Maiouma (month-long nude bathing) in spring to celebrate the return of warm weather continued until at least the early 600s. Clearly, pagan culture lived well beyond the demise of pagan Rome, and shaped the cultural development of Christianity from its beginnings as an ascetic cult into the ostentatious pageantry and embrace of life it had become by the time of the Renaissance. Indeed, the Renaissance—the Rebirth—was a rebirth of the ancient pagan arts and sciences, architecture, sculpture, and philosophy. For our purposes, this demonstrates that the relationship between paganism and Christianity was not an either/or proposition. Various and often competing priorities would eventually lead to a Christian Europe, yes, but along numerous and changing paths. Clearly, more than just rational calculation of gain and loss was in play.

Rural areas beyond Mediterranean Europe accepted Christianity only nominally and blended it with many traditional pagan and folk beliefs and practices, including animal husbandry and farming (Kieckhefer 1989), herbology and medieval medicine (Barstow 1994), and trade guilds (Hutton 1999). Whether threatened with forced conversion or allowed to live peacefully, people held fast to deeply held paganism, both as a belief and as a tradition. If paganism was instrumentally irrational because it meant censure from office in both the East and West, confiscation of land and title, or death, it certainly proved its worth for much of the population in terms of emotional commitment. Using Bell's framework introduced earlier, the bonds of pagan society had not snapped, and hence its religious expression continued.

Did Christianity introduce certain beliefs that readily distinguished it from paganism? The answer is, not decisively. Notions of heaven, for example, the ultimate reward in Christianity, derived from various pagan sources, and continued to evolve in the Christian era, and thus no distinctly Christian notion of the afterlife exists separately from other religious cultures or the ongoing effect of time and place (McDannell and Lang 2001). As Riley (2001) indicates, historians have long since rejected the "Israel-alone" model (p. 5) in favor of syncretic explanations that Christianity formed from a synthesis of Judaism with Greco-Roman, Syrian, and Persian paganism. Both the pagan origins and effects of time and place on Christian thought, art, and literature are well documented, as for example in a general perspective in the classic texts by Edward Gibbon ([1776] 1993) and in detail by Seznec ([1953] 1995) concerning the Renaissance period, which beyond artistic rebirth contributed to a new sense of humanism that Christianity has accepted only intermittently.

Even the most cherished aspects of Christian belief, such as the creation story, were adapted from paganism in both symbolism and morality (Pagels 1989). The very conflict between light and dark, good and evil, God and Satan, derives from various pagan and non-Western sources (Messadié 1996), especially from Zoroastrianism (Boyce [1979] 2001; Nigosian 1993; Riley 2001) which itself had assimilated many other traditions and thus changed over time, as well as produced schismatic sects, such as Manichaeanism (Stoyanov 2000), that in turn exerted influence in the West. Even the Cain versus Abel story derives from the ancient Roman myth about how Romulus, who founded Rome, slew his brother Remus to become sole ruler of the Latins. As we have seen, Romulus and Remus were twins, whose parents were the god Mars and the mortal Rhea Silvia, a vestal virgin. The Christian version parallels the divine paternity and virgin maternity, with the difference that Romulus becomes a hero in the Roman version, compared to Cain the apostate in the Christian one.

Thus, the development of and transition to Christianity were not a seamless linear series of events. Conversion to Christianity offered elevation in social status, imperial appointments, money, land, and power as rewards. None of this, however, made significant inroads in many areas for several hundred years. Even after 312 CE when Constantine initiated a future Christian monopoly based on the Orthodox view, and later emperors actively suppressed a free religious market, paganism endured.

Crucially, Christianity blended with both Roman politics and culture, with great variations from one locale to another, which often led to bitter conflict among Christians. Indeed, the split between East and West after the fall of Rome in 476 CE followed every possible fissure: political, economic, cultural, linguistic, and of course, religious (Angold 2001:38–48).

Christians of various types, as represented in

> ### Decline and Fall of the Roman Empire, by Edward Gibbon (1737–1794)
>
> In three volumes, this work constitutes the first major Western attempt to recreate the history of Rome, 300–1453 CE. Working from ancient and medieval sources, Gibbon achieves tremendous detail and clarity of thought. At the same time, he writes with a passion characteristic of the Enlightenment age in which he lived. At the time, Gibbon lacked evidence from archaeology, so in addition to written sources, Gibbon traveled to various sites from the ancient world. In an effort to envision all aspects of ancient life, he spent considerable time walking the forum in Rome, imagining common life of the period, as well as respectfully musing about the discussions between priests on the meaning of life while walking amidst the ruins of ancient temples. This intuitive approach, similar to Max Weber's *verstehen* sociology, seeks to understand people and their lives from within, to see and feel as the subject feels. Although Gibbon's work has certain flaws, it stands as a valuable and definitive scholarly achievement that still surpasses most scholars on the decline and fall of Rome.

Table 2.2, struggled both alongside and against each other (Pagels 1979), but also alongside and against pagans and later, Muslims. Despite elite efforts on all sides to achieve theological purity, and observable trends that distinguished East and West generally, the various religions of the era influenced each other syncretically. In all the major expressions of social life, such as art and culture (Soucek 1997; Tabbaa 1986; Thomas 1997; Thomson 1978; Vryonis 1985, 1997), economics and politics (Angold 2001; Nicol [1972] 1993; Norwich 1995; Runciman 1990), and religion (Cunningham 2002), East, West, Christianity, paganism, and Islam each shaped the others. This blending is not a modern recreation of the past, but in fact a process recognized in medieval times as well, as for example in *The Alexiad,* by Anna Comnena ([1120] 1969).

Thus it seems impossible to argue that Christianity somehow represented a unique and totally new system of belief, morality, or practice. Although some Roman cults were definitely elite institutions (especially the emperor cults), many also appealed to and attracted the masses, as Turcan (1996) shows regarding the cults of Mithra and Isis, for

Table 2.2 Early Christian Sects and Beliefs

Sect	Decisive Beliefs
Orthodox (Catholic)—Before the Great Schism of 1054, Orthodox refers to the official church, which the imperial government supported throughout the empire. After 1054, "Orthodox" refers only to the Eastern or Byzantine church, and "Catholic" only to the Western or Roman Catholic church.	Religious hierarchy based on the relationship between Jesus and the Twelve Apostles; Nicene Creed defines official beliefs; the one Holy and Apostolic Church is founded by the Apostle Peter.
Gnosticism—Local enclaves with local customs and diverse beliefs; egalitarian and often communal	Religious equality based on both Apostolic and non-Apostolic scripture and Hellenistic philosophy; all true believers should seek individual understanding of belief.
Monophysite—e.g., Arianism, founded by Arius of Alexandria, c. 256–336 CE	Jesus was all divine, with no human attributes—of one nature—but a separate and lesser god compared to God the Father.
Duophysite—e.g., Nestorianism, founded by Nestorius of Syria, c. 400–451 CE; the Syriac Church; the Antiocene Orthodox Church	Jesus was equally God and human—of two natures, which, however, exist entirely separately—the soul is divine, the body human.
Triphysite—Catholicism, Eastern Orthodoxy	The Trinity: the One God exists equally as father, son, and holy spirit—of three natures.

example, which embraced charity and the concept of everlasting life for its members (M. Meyer [1987] 1999). These cults offered a sense of meaning and belonging to the many displaced people in the major cities of the late Roman Empire (Turcan 1996:26). In this context, Christianity was one of many cults offering succor in this world and redemption in the next, provided that followers appeased the relevant god(s).

Let us consider a more thorough sociological analysis of this time period, certainly one of the most important in the history of the world. The eventual dominance that Christianity achieved not only shaped European history, but gave rise to Islam, and over the centuries entered into all corners of the world.

The Role of Class

As Angus ([1928] 1975) noted long ago, the main benefit of Christianity after Constantine's acclamation was consistent with ancient pre-Christian practice; in the ancient world, "the attitude of that age toward authority was altogether different from that of the present day. The tendency of the age was to seek authority and rest in it" (p. 298). Through its attachment to the ruling classes in the Roman Empire, Christianity gained newfound authority and thus attracted members on that basis. Far from a popular movement that rationally broke with the past, Christianity arose to dominance in the traditional Roman manner—association with power.

Wealthy and powerful Romans had a much higher survivability in times of crisis (Chadwick [1967] 1993; MacMullen 1997) because they isolated themselves in vast estates, far from the squalid and diseased urban areas, especially after they were overrun and plundered by barbarians. Indeed, early Christianity consisted mostly of patricians, not freemen or slaves (Dale Martin 1990). As Dale Martin shows, the metaphorical use of "slavery" in early Christianity applied to spiritual, not worldly relations, and thus imposed no particular constraints or obligations on the elite converts.

It is difficult to imagine that Christians from the patrician class would directly give of themselves to alleviate the suffering of a member of the lower classes simply because their new religion dictated so. Clearly, this did not happen in Christian Byzantium (Norwich 1989), the direct descendent of Christian Rome—they called themselves Ρωμαιοι (the Romans)—which maintained for over 1,100 years (May 11, 330–May 29, 1453 CE) the same economic class and social status structure as ancient Rome. Although the Byzantine Empire maintained certain social institutions for the poor, such as an orphanage in Constantinople, a communal system of grain distribution, and a pension for soldiers' widows (Norwich 1992), the concept of *personal* sacrifice for the poor, or the notion we think of today as *personally* ministering to the needy, was unknown.

As the first Christian emperor (reigned 312–337 CE), Constantine the Great neither practiced nor encouraged anything even remotely approaching Christian charity and self-sacrifice. He and his successors, going all the way through the Byzantine period (476–1453 CE), wielded Christianity in typically Roman fashion—as a calculated instrument of control. Christianity survived and prospered because the ruling class upheld it, not because it ministered to the poor, plagued, and downtrodden masses. Rome and Byzantium survived for a collective 2,100 years or so because the class structure survived, and the ruling class used its wealth and power to raise new armies or buy the loyalty of neighboring rulers, and at the same time used its military power to crush popular movements that threatened class privilege. In fact, the entire Byzantine period, the first and longest lived Christian empire, endured numerous internal battles, all of which pitted one elite group against another; there were no popular uprisings (Nicol [1972] 1993; Norwich 1995) in the name of religion. Elites invoked Christianity in the service of empire, and not to mitigate deprivation and oppression.

The elevation of Christianity as the new official religion of the empire meant the political and economic demise of pagan temples and the priestly class (Stark 1997:199), especially after its ascendance in the Byzantine Empire. Yet Christianity did not prosper as a grassroots movement, but moved significantly beyond the ruling class only after Constantine decriminalized Christianity with the Edict of Milan in 313, and embraced it officially at the Council of Nicaea in 325. Like Constantine, subsequent emperors realized the political utility of Christianity, as it now served as a loyalty test not to the one God, but to the emperor (Chadwick [1967] 1993). Constantine's successors, namely Constantine II, Constantius II, Constans, Valentinian, Valens, and Gratian, all used Christianity like a bludgeon against political opponents, but not against opponents of Christianity specifically; they left pagan temples intact and priests alive. Not until Theodosius I in 392 does the emperor appear to hold Christianity as a goal in itself (Norwich 1989), and not again until Justinian in the 500s. Although some subsequent emperors were personally pious, politics usually subsumed their piety.

Far from showing Christian charity, late Roman and subsequent Byzantine emperors crushed peasant rebellions as ruthlessly as their pagan Roman predecessors crushed slave rebellions and barbarian uprisings. Even for the adherents from the lower classes, Christianity maintained the familiar social structure of Greco-Roman society in metaphorical terms (Dale Martin 1990) even as it broke from other cultural traditions, namely, paganism. Still, Byzantium maintained the Hellenistic aspects of ancient society (Runciman 1987), and after the fall of Constantinople in 1453, intellectual refugees carried Hellenism back to the West and reintegrated it with Christianity to inspire the Renaissance (Runciman 1990).

The Role of Culture

Traditional celebrations in particular, especially when practiced in the face of persecution, indicate a deeper and more profound orientation to life than instrumental rationality. To sing, dance, laugh, feast, bathe nude, and in general, to enjoy being alive, indicates a happiness and gratification in being human and alive in *this* world. In contrast to the dour and ascetic early Christian theologians (Pagels 1989), the pagan communities cherished life in this world, and through their celebrations, expressed contentment with life and the worldview that legitimated the social order, which sociologically is the celebration of idealized community (P. Berger [1967] 1990; Durkheim ([1912] 1995), as the various theorists argued in Chapter 1. If the temples were the domain of the priests, the larger pagan culture they represented was certainly the domain of popular participation in mass festivals (Ryan 1999). Although we do not know exactly what common people believed, they liked it enough to celebrate it several times a year.

Beyond celebrations, evidence now suggests that natural philosophy, or what we now know as science, was associated with pagan mysteries from the fifth century to the Renaissance (MacMullen 1997) and thus continued in the Middle Ages as magic or other arcane art. In the witch persecutions of 1450–1650 (Trevor-Roper 1969), the people typically persecuted were primarily unmarried or widowed women in cottage businesses, such as beer, bread, butter making, spinning, weaving, healing, and midwifery (Barstow 1994)—all traditional roles for women. The healing/midwifery practitioners in particular were known as "wise women," who some now believe possessed ancient knowledge associated with what medieval society understood as natural magic, itself a product of non-Christian, pagan mystery-cult traditions

(Kieckhefer 1998, 1989). Also persecuted were "cunning men" whose skills pertained to animal husbandry and crop production—traditional roles for peasant men. Despite the fact that witch hunters translated the ancient practices into Christian imagery of Satan and Evil, the practices of pre-Christian knowledge and the associated class and gender roles remained from ancient times.

Thus, paganism as a cultural tradition, whether viewed positively or negatively, involved many cultural practices beyond a set of beliefs. Advanced natural and philosophical knowledge was, even several hundred years later, viewed as pagan (and often interpreted as anti-Christian). Conceptual and practical knowledge, art, and joy of living were also embodied as pagan, not as Christian traditions (Comnena [1120] 1969; Hutton 1999). Whatever belief a person may subscribe to during a crisis, these are only momentary associations, compared to their ongoing beliefs during routine times, which reflect their history and social location—the traditions of their class and culture—the foundations of any society.

Class and Culture Convergence: Engines of Religious Change

To understand the rise of Christianity, let us recall Peter Berger, who observes that spirituality, and the religious institutions that arise from it, are always an attempt to create meaning, an attempt to arrange the realities of life into a coherent unity with purpose and meaning. Chief among these realities is death. Regardless of how we live, we all die, and through spirituality, people seek to create meaning, and thereby emotional comfort, in order to live and, of course, to face death with some degree of reassurance. As long as death remains, as Shakespeare ([c. 1601] 1963) said, "the undiscovered country from whose bourn no traveler returns," and which "puzzles the will" (*Hamlet,* III, I:79–80), so people will need spirituality in one form or another to make sense of the ultimate reality of life, which is death. Without a sense of meaning, the fact of death would render life absurd.

Similarly, Walter Benjamin ([1927] 1999) noted that socialism "would never have entered the world if its proponents had sought only to excite the enthusiasm of the working class for a better order of things. . . . Marx understood how to interest the workers in a social order which would both benefit them and appear to them as just" (p. 395). Although socialism is a modern concept, the point applies to the ancient and medieval world under discussion, in that commitment to something new requires a sense of justice. That is, people will not commit to major changes in life just because it is abstractly rational. Although Christianity presented opportunities for the ruling class, the many practices and routines that included paganism remained just and meaningful for the masses, based on their logic of affect and tradition.

In other words, the rise of Christianity is relatively straightforward once one understands the social forces of class and culture. As the legitimating belief system of the ruling class, Christianity served to enforce both elite submission to higher elites, and submission of the lower classes to the elite classes. Christianity only spread through the lower classes to the extent that it assimilated or only gradually permeated established traditions and thus reflected and reinforced the reality of commoner life. Christianity required several hundred years to rise to popular social dominance beyond its initial political dominance.

The Medieval Period (476–1453 CE)

The Roman Empire in the West collapsed, at least by conventional understanding, in 476 CE, when invading barbarians forced the last emperor, Romulus Agustulus, to flee the city. In traditional texts, the old empire was gone, and a new (and Christian) empire would rise from the ashes, Phoenix-like, to take its place in world history. There are two main problems with this view.

First, the Western empire did not so much fall as it became poor. Taking advantage of the empire's inability to maintain its armies, administration, roads, bridges, commerce, and law, barbarians rampaged throughout its territories and eventually sacked Rome itself, for the first time in 410 CE when the Vandal king, Alaric, seized and looted Rome by sea (hence the origin of the term *vandal*ism). However, barbarians had been settling inside the empire for centuries, and many of Rome's greatest defenders, such as the general Vegetius (Publius Flavius Vegetius Renatus), were educated men from barbarian backgrounds. The great emperors Hadrian and Trajan, as well as Constantine himself, for example, were of barbarian descent, and not Roman at all. Depleted of wealth and inundated with diverse barbarian cultures, the Western empire became impoverished and chaotic, as the barbarians culturally mixed with the Latins and other Roman peoples. The result was not a collapse in the sense that the old Roman civilization simply disappeared, but rather a transition—tumultuous and often violent, but a transition nevertheless—which incorporated the old society with newly introduced elements. Even Christianity was an import, which arose amongst the Jews, who themselves were never fully assimilated into the empire.

The second problem with this traditional view is that the Eastern half of the empire—now known as the Byzantine Empire—remained intact and indeed increased in power and wealth as the center of civilization moved from Rome to Constantinople. In 949, Luidprand, a Western bishop, journeyed to Constantinople on behalf of the German emperor, Otto I. When he arrived in Constantinople (present-day Istanbul), there occurred what today we would call a culture clash. In his writings, Luidprand tells us that the Roman emperor (the Byzantines called themselves Ρωμαιοι, Romans), Constantine Porphyrogenitos (born to the purple), descended from the ceiling seated upon an immense throne made of gold, silver, and precious gems. As he alighted, hundreds of birds made of gold began singing, each according to its type, and immense lions made of wood and sheathed in gold roared as their great maws opened and their tails swished, all by way of some unseen mechanical ingenuity (Norwich 1992). Numerous servants and slaves attended the emperor at all times, and he wore robes of silk with gold and silver thread interwoven. Indeed, all the men and women of the court wore the finest fabrics and most intricate jewelry (Vryonis 1997). Nobles paraded around in the public places in litters carried by slaves, with all manner of attendants, courtesans, advisors, and eunuchs ready to serve. The city itself featured numerous public baths, each perfumed with rare and exotic oils and spices, into which spilled fountains and waterfalls. The people bathed at least once a day, and often spent considerable amounts of time in the baths, discussing daily affairs, playing games, and reading. Statues, many from the pagan era, stood throughout the city, and nearly everywhere one's gaze fell, some new expression of artistry and opulence delighted the eye.

In contrast, Luidprand, one of the most educated and sophisticated men of the West, wore coarse brown robes, and almost never bathed. He ate with his bare, unwashed hands, whereas his Byzantine hosts ate with cutlery, favoring as Luidprand describes it, a three-pronged instrument for which Luidprand had no word, but which we today know as the fork. In addition to public baths, the Byzantines supported public education, a pension system, retirement homes, and formal bureaucratic management (Norwich 1992). The West lacked even the concept of such things. The vast majority of people in the West, including the nobles, were completely illiterate, as well as unrefined, unwashed, boorish, and crude. The new society in the West was based almost entirely on fighting, and therefore, warlords reigned supreme. Their power depended on land holding, on feudal estates in the countryside, which each lord ruled more or less autonomously. This was the Christian society of the West.

The Empire in the East had not fallen. Although Byzantine territory included many non-Greeks, their bureaucratic administration assimilated the great many culturally dissimilar peoples and managed land, people, money, and armies with precision. Courts administered a consistent and universal law, which allowed for peaceful resolution of disputes compared to the West, where fighting determined justice. Although Byzantium carried on many Roman traditions, they were now a strongly Christian empire, but of a remarkably different type from the West. In the great cities of the Byzantine Empire, namely Constantinople, Antioch, Trebizond, Nicaea, and for a time, Jerusalem, most people were at least basically literate, and the municipal governments supported an educated class of philosophers and theologians. The previously mentioned Constantine VII Porphyrogenitos himself was highly educated and knowledgeable of philosophy and history. The bureaucratic system they had inherited from the old empire remained, which the Byzantines perfected. The military in particular used professional, highly trained and disciplined soldiers. This organization allowed the Byzantines to win many battles against much larger opposing armies. The entire social network of rational taxation, administration, education, pensions, care of orphans and the elderly, and systematic management of food supplies all contributed a much greater stability and quality to life than existed or was even possible in the West.

These outstanding differences divided the two halves of the empire, Europe and the Near East, into two very different societies which, despite the fact that they were both Christian, were not really compatible with each other. This social incompatibility led to political incompatibility, which led to religious incompatibility, which led to the two great socially significant moments for our study of the sociology of religion in the Middle Ages. One is the Great Schism, and the other is the Crusades.

Schism and Crusades

The Crusades and Their Outcomes

The First, 1095–1101—Successful, militarily; discussed in detail in this chapter

The Second, 1145–1147—Led by King Louis VII of France; major military defeat

The Third, 1188–1192—Led by Philip Augustus, Frederick I Barbarossa, German Emperor, and Richard Coeur-de-Lion, King of England; major military defeat

The Fourth, 1204—Led by Boniface of Montferrat, sought to conquer Egypt and Jerusalem but took Constantinople instead

Children's Crusade, 1212—Led in two groups by Nicholas, a shepherd, and Stephen de Cloyes, a young boy. The latter claimed the power to perform miracles, and visions from God telling him that only children could conquer the armies of Islam. They led approximately 35,000 young people and children in total, most of whom died or were sold into slavery before leaving Europe. None reached the Levant.

The Fifth, 1217—Led by Leopold VI of Austria, Andrew II of Hungary, John of Brienne, King of Jerusalem, Hugh I of Cyprus, and Prince Bohemund IV of Antioch, sought to conquer Egypt; major military defeat

The Sixth, 1228-1229—Led by Frederick II, uses diplomacy rather than force to gain Nazareth, Sidon, Jaffa, Bethlehem, and all of Jerusalem except the Dome of the Rock

The Seventh, 1248-1254—Led by King Louis IX of France; major military defeat

The Eighth and Ninth, 1270—Also under Louis IX, much of the army dies of disease on the way from Northern Africa to Jerusalem. Prince Edward of England arrives with reinforcements (the Ninth) and wins a few battles around Jerusalem, but returns to England to become King. Acre falls in 1291, the last of the crusader states in the Levant.

Like the societies of which they were a part, the Eastern and Western churches differed as well. There were numerous issues on which each side could not compromise. These issues included the authority of the Pope, orthodoxy in the East, the depiction of holy images, and Monophysite (Eastern) versus the Duophysite (Western) views. The official schism occurred in 1054, but as argued, the differences were as much social as theological. The Eastern Church upheld the concept of orthodoxy in religious services, and Monophysite beliefs, that Christ was of one essence (all divine) rather than of two (divine and human in combination). All of this corresponds directly to the ancient and also formally hierarchical structure of Byzantine society. In 1054, the West had no central political authority, and much of its history had been lost or thoroughly blended with new influences from various and diverse barbaric tribes. Their art and literature barely existed at all, and as mentioned, very few people had any formal education. The churches thus divided, as their respective societies were already divided and developing along different paths. They would gradually find common theological ground in the concept of the trinity (the dominant belief today), which declares that God exists simultaneously as the father, son, and holy spirit, but this took centuries to find widespread acceptance. In the meantime, conflict ensued.

The Crusades followed. Although they are known for unleashing vast pain and hardship on the Islamic world, they pillaged and plundered the Byzantines as well, and even their Western Christian compatriots. Western Christendom, standing amidst ignorance, poverty, and a culture premised almost entirely on fighting and warfare, proved perfect for this new thing—a holy war.

The First Crusade started in 1095, and it is commonly held that eight or nine (as some historians separate the eighth into two parts) total crusades took place. Whichever number we choose from the historians, as sociologists we should note a great difference between the First Crusade and those that followed.

The First Crusade began when two great leaders, the emperor of Byzantium, Alexios I Comnenos (1048–1118 CE, Byzantine emperor after 1081), and the Western Pope, Urban II, confronted different but ultimately intertwined problems. Alexios, who inherited a weakened military that had been resoundingly defeated at the fateful Battle of Manzikert under his predecessor, Romanus IV Diogenes, now himself confronted the very same Seljuk Turks, themselves only recently converted to Islam. Urban II also inherited issues from his predecessor, Gregory VII, who envisioned a great reconquest of Jerusalem, as well as a great thrashing of Muslims, pagans, infidels, and other nonbelievers in general. So as fate would arrange, Alexios sent a letter in 1095 requesting to incorporate 500 or so professional Western knights to bolster the Byzantine military. Thus, Urban II saw his chance: our Eastern Christian brethren had requested assistance (Runciman 1987). Urban II prepared to send far more than 500 professional knights. By 1097, the army of the First Crusade would number nearly 80,000, including knights and peasants.

The Pope sent out the call at the Council of Clermont, and the people answered. With the call *Deus vult!* (God wills it!), anyone, royal or commoner, who "took up the cross" would be granted absolution of all sins and automatic entry into heaven, whether they died in battle or just along the way. As events unfolded over the next several years, and eventually over nearly 200 years, the cry *Deus vult!* would be used to justify acts of courage, as well as atrocities.

The First Crusade consisted of essentially two parts. The People's Crusade, led by Peter the Hermit and Walter the Penniless, departed first, in 1096. Spurred on by faith alone, these peasants had no weapons other than farm implements and no martial training. About 40,000 strong, they came mostly from France and Germany. While still in Germany, crusaders led by Count Emicho decided to annihilate Jews first, against the direct orders of the Holy Roman Emperor Henry IV. Emicho's crusaders attacked and utterly annihilated several Jewish communities in Cologne, Speyer, Mainz, and Worms. Bishops Ruthard of Mainz and Johann of Speyer attempted to thwart the crusaders, who nevertheless succeeded in killing every last man, woman, and child. As far as these peasants were concerned, the Jews had killed Christ, and the Jews alive in their time were therefore children of Satan.

This belief leads us to an important sociological point: The peasants of the people's crusade seem to have been inspired entirely by faith. They ignored both the orders of the Emperor, and those of the Bishops. Maurice Samuel ([1940] 1988) calls this type of faith a Great Hatred, a belief that some people represent pure evil and can only be evil for all time. This evil enemy must be furiously opposed and destroyed; there can be no tolerance or mercy for the Evil Ones. The army of knights that would follow seems to have shared this belief as well. Sociologically, the evil enemy is the Other—not just a person or group that is different, but one that is perceived to be the exact opposite in existential terms. As we saw in the previous chapter, the Other is everything evil, vile, corrupt, and in all ways the enemy of everything we hold to be good, righteous, and pure. The Evil Other cannot be reasoned with; it can only be destroyed. Thus, the Jews in central Europe became the first victims of the First Crusade, the first Evil Other the holy warriors annihilated.

Eventually, the People's Crusade reached Constantinople, raping and pillaging along the entire way. Much to the horror of Alexios Comnenos, this was not the professional army of knights he requested. They were in every way incompatible with the well-ordered and disciplined Byzantine military, and with Byzantine society in general. Alexios agreed to ferry this mass of unwashed and superstitious peasants across the Bosporus and into Seljuk territory. Upon their arrival in Asia Minor, the People's Crusade killed every person they could find, almost all of whom were actually Christian. Eventually, the Seljuk army arrived and annihilated the peasants.

By this time, in 1096, the army of knights sent by Urban II was ready to depart. They had taken some time to argue over who would lead this army of nearly 80,000, and exactly how to divide up conquered territory. Being illiterate and with no formal authority structure, they argued for nearly a year. Like their peasant counterparts, the army of knights eventually arrived in Constantinople, in 1097. Some arrived by land, some by sea, and Baldwin of Boulogne by shipwreck. The Byzantine coast guard rescued him and he lived at court by the grace of the Emperor until his compatriots arrived. Once assembled, Alexios found them equally distasteful and impossible to manage as the peasants, and thus regretted to inform the crusaders that he and his army would not join them. However, he will ferry them across the Bosporus if they will do two things: (1) swear fealty to him, and (2) turn over any lands they conquer to Byzantium. In no position to argue, they accepted.

The crusaders, after much hardship and fighting, reached Jerusalem in 1099. To their dismay, the city consisted of three neighborhoods: one Jewish, one Christian, and one Muslim. The three groups lived together quite harmoniously, and indeed this harmony and cooperation had made the city quite wealthy. The crusaders eventually gained entrance to the city and slaughtered the population, regardless of age, sex, or religion (Runciman 1987). They also burned and looted. The crusaders herded the Muslims into the Dome of the Rock, a mosque that stands where Muslims believe Muhammad ascended into heaven, and where the Temple of Solomon used to stand before Titus Vespasianus destroyed it in 70 CE. The crusaders slaughtered every last Muslim inside. This atrocity inspired Muslims to rename it the Al-Aqsa Mosque, or Mosque of the Martyrs. Thus ended the First Crusade, in an orgy of blood and fire.

The crusaders established the kingdom of Jerusalem, with Godfrey of Bouillon as the first king. He refused the title of king, and instead adopted Advocatus Sancti Sepulchri, or Defender of the Holy Sepulchre. He died a year later, and Baldwin, his brother, ascended the throne as Baldwin I, King of Jerusalem. He aggressively expanded the kingdom, and he introduced a new economic system based on the model of the Italian city-states. With merchants and fleets from Genoa, Venice, Florence, and Pisa, the kingdom of Jerusalem became an urban and trade-based economy, much like the Byzantine Empire and the surrounding Islamic principalities, and quite unlike the feudal system of Western Europe. Descendants of the First Crusade who were born and raised in the kingdom of Jerusalem learned Greek and Arabic, adopted many Eastern customs such as regular bathing and emphasis on literate education, and in general acquired a much more refined sense of politics, culture, and courtly conduct.

Sociologically, we should note certain elements. First, religion by itself was not sufficient to unify the Christian world. Culture plays a decisive role as well, such that the Byzantines found themselves much more culturally akin to the Arab world, despite the fact that the Arabs were Islamic. Both cultures emphasized education, art, literature, science, and personal sophistication in all matters. A Byzantine noble was expected to be a poet and scholar with refined tastes as well as a warrior, all values that the Arabs cherished as well. The Western nobles sharply contrasted with this far more complex and ancient culture, which the Byzantines and Arabs shared, both greatly influenced by ancient Greece, Rome, and Persia.

Second, although Jerusalem was segregated by religion, with respective Jewish, Christian, and Islamic areas, the peoples lived more or less amicably and cooperatively. The Jews handled money lending and finances, the Muslims provided military protection and administration, and the Christians provided merchant transport. In this case, we see that in the early period, there was no inherent battle between these religions, but rather, various social and economic factors enabled them to live together quite cooperatively. Indeed, this cooperation led to a cultural unity among the three neighborhoods that resembled the similarity that the Byzantine and Arab civilizations shared. Their unity arose not from religious debate and discussion of ideas about faith, but through the practices necessary to maintain economic activity and management of a community. Although each respective set of religious beliefs remained important to in-group identity, their mutual cooperation and prosperity depended on a socially shared common ground, founded on material activity—economics and the necessity of practical management.

Also, the descendants of the First Crusade assimilated into Middle Eastern culture, and this culture transcended the particular religions, whether Christian, Jewish, or Muslim. Although conflict continued between the crusader states and the indigenous Muslim states, subsequent crusades brought more Europeans who proved increasingly incompatible with the culture of the Middle Eastern Christians, and this conflict created organizational and political problems. Despite a periodic influx of soldiers from the West as later iterations of crusades arrived, they did as much harm as good in terms of maintaining the crusader states.

The Crusades continued through several more iterations, each progressively more professionalized and institutionalized. After the First Crusade, no longer would great masses of peasants and undisciplined knights take the field. Rather, professional armies with clear political and territorial goals replaced the mass rabble. The more institutionalized the Crusades became, the less central religious goals seemed to be. In fact, the Fourth Crusade, initially intended to retake Jerusalem, which had reverted to Arab control, decided to sack and occupy Constantinople instead—a fellow Christian city. In 1204, the city fell to the Fourth Crusade in another orgy of destruction and slaughter that rivaled the taking of Jerusalem in bloody fervor. Not only did the crusaders carry off Constantinople's vast treasures in precious metals, gems, and art, but they also destroyed the Great Library, an immense depository of ancient manuscripts, including many Christian documents, possibly original copies of the Gospels, and other biblical texts, as well as a picture of Jesus painted by Saint Luke. As Runciman (1990) says, the Crusades were basically a Western barbarian invasion and sacking of the great civilizations of the East.

The Western occupiers established the Latin Empire in Constantinople, and crowned Baldwin IX, the Count of Flanders, as the first emperor. Although the Greek Byzantines, relegated to the Empire of Nicaea, recaptured the city in 1261 under Michael VIII Paleologos, the city and the empire it ruled never regained its former power, territory, or majesty, reduced now to Constantinople, Nicaea, and the immediate surrounding provinces. The empire fell to the Turks in 1453, marking the end of the Middle Ages and the end of the Roman Byzantine empire. It also marked the ascension of the West.

Early Modern Period

Economic power had been shifting to the West over the last couple of centuries, and the fall of Constantinople to the Muslim Ottomans (Turks), though shocking to many in the West, including the Pope, was also not surprising. Once the richest city in the world, Constantinople was the last stronghold of an ancient but ultimately inflexible Roman civilization. In its place, a rejuvenated Rome and its Catholic Church stood alongside an increasingly dynamic and powerful Western civilization. As the West rose, the East, and the Muslim world, declined. Although Islamic civilization reached its zenith in the early 1500s (recall Ibn Khaldun's contributions from Chapter 1), the West developed more dynamically by creating a civil sphere separate from the church. Ironically, the formerly barbarian West surpassed the once vastly more prosperous and civilized East by reducing the influence of the Church to purely religious affairs. This did not happen overnight, however.

After the fall of Constantinople, its most accomplished scholars, philosophers, artists, and theologians fled west, mostly to the prosperous Italian city-states. In conjunction with the rise of merchant capitalism, the Byzantine Greeks from the East quickly elevated intellectual activity, and contributed significantly to the Renaissance. Through the Byzantine intellectual and professional refugees, the West rediscovered ancient art and philosophy, which they eventually surpassed with new fields of medicine, architecture, and what later became modern science. No less than other areas of intellectual and cultural life, religion underwent changes as well.

Martin Luther (1483–1546) initiated what we know today as Protestantism when he challenged the Catholic hierarchy over various doctrinal issues and practices. Shortly after Luther, numerous others broke with the Catholic Church. Most of these schismatics articulated an ascetic doctrine, which as we saw in the previous chapter, introduced a rational, that is, systematic code of conduct for daily living, and this rationalization of daily life became central to the emerging modern order. Principal among the Protestant reformers, John Calvin (1509–1564) developed the most rigorous and encompassing doctrine, which demanded the greatest commitment to a sin-free life through endless hard work. Other ascetics included Pietists, Methodists, and Baptists, all of whom to varying degrees advocated denial of earthly pleasure and tireless endeavors to avoid a life of sin and displeasure to God. Calvinism spread throughout Europe, and many local congregations in turn broke from the Calvinist church, including Presbyterians, Puritans, and Congregationalists.

In 1618, the Calvinist Friedrich V (also written as Frederick) became King of Bohemia, an area that constitutes most of the Czech Republic today. Bohemia, split between Calvinists and Lutherans, was officially part of the Austrian Empire, which the Catholic Habsburg dynasty ruled. Bohemia fought with Austria, ostensibly over concerns that the new Austrian emperor Ferdinand II would reverse the policy of religious tolerance that his predecessor Rudolf II had implemented, but the larger issue was clearly Austrian political hegemony, regardless of religious issues. The Habsburgs ruled an empire that consisted of many ethnic groups, languages, and versions of Christianity. If any one group such as the Bohemians should secure independence, others might follow.

Although Austria defeated the Bohemian rebels in 3 months, the ensuing war would last 30 years. It would draw in France and Spain on the side of the Catholics, and Denmark, Sweden, Flanders (now Belgium and the Netherlands), and England on the side of the Protestants. Far from coordinated alliances, each country sought territory and various sovereign rights over and against the others, such that sides formed and dissolved every few years as each battled all. After 30 years and frequent side-switching, a combined Danish, Swedish, French, and Flemish army defeated the main Austrian army at Zusmarshausen in 1647, which produced the Peace of Westphalia in 1648. Europe was devastated. The ideals of the Renaissance would eventually lead to the Enlightenment and subsequently to the modern world we know today. Yet during the time of the Thirty Years' War, the devastation introduced a new element to Christianity, which we glimpsed during the First Crusade, but which would now intensify as armies rampaged across Europe and religious institutions fell into chaos and splintered into competing denominations. Mass persecution of an evil enemy returned.

The Witch Craze

The Thirty Years' War itself, with the concurrent forces of combat, forced enlistment, slaughters, and widespread pillaging, was not the entire extent of the devastation. Mass persecutions, far more malignant and obdurate, emerged from the tumult. As early as 800 CE, the recently crowned Emperor Charlemagne declared that witches did not exist, and he would tolerate no talk of witch hunts (Trevor-Roper 1969). By 1450, however, with Europe increasingly tumultuous as social forces transformed medieval society into modern society, a witch craze emerged.

Two Dominican monks, Jacob Sprenger and Heinrich Kramer, in 1486 wrote a book called the *Malleus Maleficarum,* usually translated as *The Hammer of Witches;* however, a better translation would be *The Hammer of Evildoers.* Although no church, Catholic or Protestant, ever officially adopted

> ### Excerpt From the
> ### *Malleus Maleficarum*
>
> But the natural reason is that she is more carnal than a man, as is clear from her many carnal abominations. And it should be noted that there was a defect in the formation of the first woman, since she was formed from a bent rib, that is, a rib of the breast, which is bent as it were in a contrary direction to a man. And since through this defect she is an imperfect animal, she always deceives.... To conclude. All witchcraft comes from carnal lust, which is in women insatiable. (Sprenger and Kramer [1486] 2000:264–265, 274)

this book, it nevertheless served as a guide for the discovery, torture, prosecution, and execution of witches. Moreover, it reveals late-medieval attitudes about women, namely, that they are inherently evil in nature. In contrast, men may have sinful desires, but created as they are in the image of God, have inherently good natures. The *Malleus* elaborates in grim and gruesome detail about the inherent evilness of women, as in the sidebar excerpt on why a woman is inherently evil.

The authors provide an extensive list of evil characteristics, some of which are physical—body, voice, stance, gaze—and some of which are behavioral, especially ambition. More than anything else, a woman's desire to achieve more than the station of her birth demonstrates collusion with Satan. Nearly everything about a woman's body is seen as evil, and all behavior is sinful except for quiet passivity. Above all, carnal lust, which "in women is insatiable," drives them to all manner of "abominations." Clearly, Sprenger and Kramer had a misogynistic view of women, far beyond the common attitudes of the day.

Of course, not all women faced persecution equally. The vast majority of victims were middle-aged or elderly, widowed or never married, childless, and somehow economically independent. A typically nightmarish depiction of a witch and warlock attending a satanic sabbath (Hans Baldung Grien, 1508) is shown in Image 2.13. Grien and other artists possessed an imagination no less vivid than Sprenger and Kramer's lurid details of feminine depravity.

Many women accused of witchcraft earned a living through conventional domestic labor, such as baking, brewing, or tailoring, but also medicine, herbology, and especially midwifery. Yet how could a lone woman earn a living, perhaps even prosper, without a man? In retrospect, the answer is clear. They availed themselves of this relatively new thing called a market. They sold their bread, beer, herbs, and services as commodities, for which they received money. This capitalist relationship of buying and selling in an open marketplace is readily understood today, but in the mid-1400s, most economic activity still occurred through traditional networks, with little separation between producer and consumer. Through extended families, people produced whatever they needed and consumed their own produce. Women who were on their own survived the only way they could; landless, without a husband, children, or other means of support, they sold their goods and services to whoever wanted to buy them, and in the process, conducted a typical capitalist exchange. To common people with no awareness of anonymous market relations, this new type of livelihood appeared mysterious, and evil. How could a lone woman survive, even prosper, unless she made a pact with Satan?

Capitalism thus provided opportunity for women who otherwise would have had few if any prospects. At the same time, the forces of capitalism placed traditional European society of self-sufficient agrarian communities into conflict with emerging capitalist communities centered in growing cities, which economically squeezed the peasants, who joined the side of the nobles and became a reactionary force opposed to capitalism (Moore [1966] 1993). Capitalism and urbanization displaced the peasants and changed the way in which people

Image 2.13   Hans Baldung Grien Witch Sabbath

produced and obtained the necessities of life. It also created new wealth, independent of the feudal estates, which nobles dominated. A new capitalist class emerged with competing economic and political interests. In combination with war, plagues, famines, floods, and Protestantism, European society cleaved along political, economic, religious, and gender fault lines that shook apart the established order. Amidst this increasing uncertainty, people found satisfaction in one simple explanation—demonic witchcraft.

When confronted with pure evil, as people in the years 1450–1650 believed they were, every good person must be prepared to do anything and everything to defeat it. We do not know for sure how many women (and men) were tortured and executed for witchcraft, but a reasonable estimate stands around 300,000. In some villages, church authorities (both Catholic and Protestant) executed entire female populations, including all female children.

Yet the witch persecutions did not affect all of Europe equally (see Table 2.3). It was most intense in France and Germany, least intense in England and Russia, and nonexistent in Italy. This presents an interesting sociological question: Why did some countries escape the intensity of witch persecutions? The answer seems to be related to the breadth and magnitude of social change. At the time, Russia, an Eastern Orthodox country, was quite backward and superstitious compared to Western Europe. One might expect Russia to produce the most zealous witch persecutions, yet they did not. Russia experienced none of the social upheaval that plagued the West, especially France and Germany. Although primitive and oppressive, Russia was stable; life was certain in terms of daily routine and one's life course.

In contrast, France and Germany experienced the greatest upheaval through ongoing plagues, famines, and wars. Moreover, the intruding forces of capitalism challenged the firmly entrenched feudal system of rural agrarian estates and the power they granted the reigning nobles. Although capitalism advanced further and

Table 2.3   Areas of Europe and Witch Persecutions, 1450–1650

Location	Outcome
France, Germany (States of the Holy Roman Empire)	Rapid social change, numerous Protestant sects, wars, plagues, and famines create fear, moral crisis, and mass persecution.
England	Gradual social change creates relatively minimal persecution.
Italian City-States	Consistent economic prosperity and consistent moral (Church) authority insulates against mass persecution.
Russia	Primitive but unchanging traditional society insulates against mass persecution.
Spain	Initiated to persecute Jews and Muslims, the Inquisition broadens its mandate to all manner of evildoers, including witches.

faster in England, the feudal system was only a continental import, which never rooted as firmly nor defined English society so decisively. Comparatively, England proved more flexible, and although not without witch persecutions, they numbered in the hundreds, not tens of thousands. The battles between competing religions, economics, and ways of life raged primarily in Germany and France. Spain faced real-life political, military, and religious adversaries in the Islamic Moors, but as the Inquisition intensified, it acquired some degree of imaginary-evil persecution as well, but the focus was on Muslims and Jews.

As sociologists, we have seen repeatedly that no one person, book, event, or thought causes social change, wars, or movements. Rather, widespread and intersecting changes in the type of social relations in European society produced social upheaval that people at the time failed to understand. These forces included emerging capitalism, free classes independent of noble hegemony, free cities, independent women, revolutionary religious movements, and early science. In section II of this chapter, we examine what such revolutionary changes wrought in society and in religion. Suddenly, the universe seemed to change into something much more vast and no less mysterious, despite the advances of science. As the universe expanded, so did the Divine. Just as the ancient hero Mithra started as a bull-slayer and culminated as an omnipresent deity, so the Enlightenment and industrialization changes the concept of Jesus, but in an opposite way. Mithra started locally as hardly more than a very skilled and brave but still very human role model. As Mithra traversed the ever-expanding Roman world, he transcended his locality and mortality to become an omnipresent and immortal deity.

In contrast, as industrial capitalism drew the farthest reaches of the world closer, yet also rendered human relations ever more impersonal in the process, so in reaction, Jesus (and salvation) became ever more intensely personal, as we will see.

Social values changed as well, with quite dramatic impact. One of the most important changes was the work ethic, which itself transforms even as it influences Western culture, especially in the United States. Our narrative now stands at the dawn of fully modern society.

Rise and Transformation of the Work Ethic

The English merchants and settlers initiated a Protestant culture that has shaped American culture ever since. One of the primary relations is one of economic culture, and the work ethic stands as perhaps the most tenacious contribution to American culture generally. In his famous thesis, Max Weber ([1920] 2002) argued that the work ethic was not simply a moral value that people held up as such, but rather an entire way of life that carried moral implications and upon which rested one's salvation. Gradually, as it spread in conjunction with a rising capitalist system, this way of life lost its specifically Protestant and religious association such that everyone born into modern society today must submit to a system that demands long work days and commitment to self-reliance within the capitalist order.

Thus, the work ethic grew in proportion to other facets of life and came to dominate them. It reshaped the family into nuclear units in which personal happiness and family became merely aspects of work and career. The work ethic and nuclear family division of labor reached perhaps its high point in the 1950s, epitomized in *Father Knows Best, Leave It to Beaver,* and many other television shows of the period that depict Dad as a wage-earner, and Mom as a stay-at-home wife who defers to Dad's authority. Even by the late 1960s and early 1970s, the same model still resonated with Americans in *The Brady Bunch.* Mom's unpaid domestic labor maintained Dad as the financial provider, and allowed businesses to get two workers while only paying one. As Stephanie Coontz (2000) in *The Way We Never Were* demonstrates empirically, however, this nuclear family existed more commonly as an ideal than as reality for the majority of the population. Indeed, even in the newly emerging phenomenon known as the suburbs, 1950s' households contained far more dissatisfaction than 1950s' television portrayed.

The 1960s and 1970s challenged many of the conventions of American life—religious life no less than family and politics. Many new divisions emerged within established religions, and religious innovators imported mysticism from the East, especially from Buddhism and Hinduism. New religious and spiritual groups arose in the cities, and many established alternative communities on farms in rural areas. Strongest in the period 1960–1975, according to Timothy Miller (1999), alternative religious communities appear frequently in U.S. history, typically in reaction to great social change. The 1880s–1890s saw the rise of Hutterites, Shakers, Millerites, and many others in reaction to the radically transformative impact of industrialization, and alternative communities arose again in the 1930s during the Great Depression. As Miller argues, the alternative religious movements of the 1960s were relatively tame compared to the apocalypticism that permeated American religion in the late nineteenth century.

In the 1980s, career eclipsed religion and the family, things one could dispense with altogether. Consumer capitalism smashed the morality that defines both religion and the family as institutions. In movies such as *The Big Chill,* the characters revel in their pursuit of money; even drug dealing is acceptable if it supports an ostentatious lifestyle. Appearing in 1983, the film portrays characters who are friends from the 1960s, all former activists who have reunited in the present day for the funeral of one of their cohort. In this film, families amount to little more than a strategic partnership or a one-night stand to produce an offspring, which two characters do apparently because it is the cheapest and quickest way to acquire a baby. As the movie develops, we see that all the characters have sold out their 1960s values that opposed U.S. militarism, consumer culture, and class exploitation. We also learn that the deceased character was the only one who retained his counterculture values and never applied himself to making big money; he killed himself. The message? Only fools cling to moral values. As the movie tells us, those who do not pursue career and profit face personal ruin, despair, and suicide.

In the course of the twentieth century, then, the work ethic transforms from hardworking asceticism that is pleasing to God, as we saw in Chapter 1, into an ethic of personal accumulation. The 1990s appeared to mitigate this lust for money, softening financier Gordon Gecko's famous 1980s declaration in the film *Wall Street* that "greed is good." Yet the 1990s did not fully reverse the ethic of individual accumulation, but mitigated it somewhat into something that more closely resembled Luther's traditionalism. Max Weber sees in Luther a directive that people should live according to their ordained station in life, that "everyone should abide by his living and let the godless run after gain.... The pursuit of material gain beyond personal needs appears as a symptom of a lack of grace, and since it can apparently only be attained at the expense of others, directly reprehensible" (Weber [1920] 1958:83–84). Economic gain is thus not an end in itself as it was for the 1980s' yuppies, but rather a necessary outcome of modern circumstances—the reign of consumer capitalism.

Unlike Calvin, who taught that enjoyment of earthly pleasures was sinful, and thus later ascetics invested their gains back into the business, Luther neither glorified nor condemned earthly delights. Instead, people indulged them according to their station in life. Unlike both Luther and Calvin, as well as myriad other religious leaders, reformers, and everyday practitioners, life in the early twenty-first century involves many competing moral claims, but one need not belong to a moral community at all. The ancients understood divergent moral communities, as we have seen, but they never envisioned an individual existence entirely outside of some moral community or another. Perhaps this supersedes other religious development in the twenty-first century—people increasingly live with no collectively shared moral foundation at all. This condition of moral anomie, closely tied to the decline of collective religious influence, will appear consistently throughout this book.

In section II of this chapter, let us consider the United States as an example of religious transformation amidst the spread of modernity.

Table 2.4   Premodern Versus Modern Society

Premodern	Modern
Feudalism—Self-contained economic estates (fiefdoms)	**Capitalism**—Interdependent systems of production and markets
Noble Privilege—Certain elites, by fate of birth, inherently receive special status above the law.	**Universal or Common Law**—A systematic law that applies equally to everyone
Traditional Obligation—Marriage, work, lifestyle, religion, and other major factors of life are governed by traditional obligations, and thus people bear collective responsibility.	**Personal Choice**—Individuals are free to make choices regarding the major factors of life, and thus bear individual responsibility.
Religious Dogma—Official and fixed dogma stands as the only explanation for life, both sacred and mundane.	**Science**—Open and critical inquiry strives for ever-improved knowledge about observable phenomena.
Certainty Without Opportunity—Rigid and closed society offers certainty about life and one's place in it.	**Opportunity Without Certainty**—One's outcome depends on one's achievements, with failure a distinct possibility.

Section II. Religion in Modern Times

Modern Times

Sociologists usually say "modernity" in reference to the modern historical period and the social conditions that define it, and we say "modernism" in reference to value systems and perspectives that actively promote modernity as a preferred way of life. Although the United States arguably becomes the greatest and most clearly distilled example of modernity and proponent of modernism, neither originated there.

After the English Civil War, fought on and off between 1642 and 1651, the first modern capitalist society emerged. Holland and the Italian city-states had prospered through merchant capitalism in the late Middle Ages, but now in England there arose a version of capitalism that depended on rational calculation and systematic production, not simply on trade. A particular relationship arose between owner and worker, and a new class—a wage-earning class—emerged as the counterpart to the owners, also known as capitalists. Although a king still formally ruled the country, the power of parliament steadily increased, as the capitalist class demanded greater autonomy. Democracy likewise emerged in its modern form, complementary to a capitalist system that depended on formally free labor, free exchange of goods, free and open education, and the free circulation of new ideas. The merchant economies could prosper quite well under a noble or some other nondemocratic system, but for modern capitalism to function, it required a much more open society in general beyond what most monarchies could tolerate. Modernity requires far greater individual freedom, the free exchange of ideas, open travel, innovation, advanced education, and liberation from stifling and often religious traditions. The English Civil War represented a transfer of political power from the old feudal and merchant system to the new, rationalized capitalist system.

This transfer of power and the rise of a rationalized way of life, especially as it migrated to the Americas and, in particular, to what became the United States, transformed religion faster and more extensively than ever in history, at least since the rise of monotheism in ancient times. These wholesale changes coincided with and mutually reinforced broader social changes, as we will see. Just as religion has changed according to social changes in various areas of society, so this relationship continues today. As the early contributors to sociology, Marx, Durkheim, and Weber, argued, religion always represents society and social order in an idealized form—sometimes the established social order and sometimes a future order. Like any idea, it only develops and makes sense in conjunction with other social forces and institutions.

In general, we will see that as the American economy and territory expanded after the Revolutionary War, the issue arose of whether and to what extent individual volition plays a role in salvation, now known as the First Great Awakening. Next, the Second Great Awakening corresponded to a drive to instill a sense of purpose and the importance of individual choice as crucial for salvation. Third, the issue of slavery divided evangelicals into pro- and antislavery camps, which unified progressive and reactionary forces across denominational lines. Fourth, the rise of industrialism created new urban centers with new urban problems, and evangelicalism divided again on class issues. Some embraced the social gospel as crucial to save oneself and others, while reactionary forces embraced religious notions that corresponded to class ethics that those on top have worked harder, lived a cleaner life, and thus deserve greater success. Fifth, evangelicalism divided between fundamentalist and modernist views; the former rejected modern science, education, welfare, and other social programs, whereas modernists accepted science as a different and also valid form of knowledge than scripture.

In North America, European powers founded colonies in the late 1600 and early 1700s after capitalism was clearly ascendant in England and France. Although Spain established colonies and trade routes nearly 100 years earlier, they developed mostly plantation systems, called *cabildos,* or semifeudal estates, which we will revisit in a later chapter. England controlled 13 modern mercantile colonies in North America, and France controlled mainly Quebec and various Caribbean islands. England and France were, in simplest terms, numbers one and two, respectively, in terms of modern economic development. Thus, North America developed without the baggage of feudal history and traditions and with the benefit of emerging democracies in England, then France after 1789. Yet like in Europe, war would provide the catalyst for large-scale religious change.

As is well-known, different religious groups founded or significantly contributed to the growth of each of the original 13 American colonies. The pilgrims in Plymouth, Massachusetts, most famously, were Puritans, practicing a version of Calvinism, who fled to the New World after being persecuted in England. Roger Williams founded Providence, later part of Rhode Island, as a haven for Baptists whom, like Williams himself, the Puritans had persecuted in Massachusetts. Anglicans, another name for members of the Church of England, settled the first colonies in Virginia, and Dutch Calvinists settled New Amsterdam, later named New York. Although Catholics founded the first European colony in North America at St. Augustine, Florida, their influence remained minimal for political and economic reasons. As a Spanish possession, the colony was often in conflict with its northern neighbors, who despite their differences, were consistently against Spain and decidedly anti-Catholic. Initially a collection of disparate colonies with various religious sentiments and national allegiances, the original thirteen would eventually unite under the Declaration of Independence and subsequently the U.S. Constitution.

Since the first Protestant settlement at Jamestown, Virginia, in 1607, religious practice had for many become staid and uninspiring. The spirit of the times inspired the First Great Awakening, which emphasized that religious practice should include genuine emotional commitment, that faith and practice should inspire the individual, that devotion to God and Christ should be passionate. Going through the motions without heartfelt enthusiasm no longer sufficed. This became the first significant interdenominational movement in the United States. Just as the secular Declaration of Independence and the Constitution united the colonies politically, so the First Great Awakening united them religiously.

This movement persevered from 1720 to 1781, before and during the American Revolution. As sociologists, we can meaningfully mark the end at 1781—the end of the Revolutionary War. Victory in 1781 brought a feeling of possibility, a sense that the future was wide open, and these new "Americans" could make of it what they desired. The Second Great Awakening began at this time and continued until the end of the Civil War in 1865, following the convergence and concurrence logic of sociology. Victory against a foreign oppressor in the Revolutionary War and later, the rise of the emancipation movement and expansion westward, inspired the concept of *free will* in religious commitment—the idea that we are free to make of life and faith what we want, and others should enjoy this freedom as well.

Vital Religious Experience and Personal Volition: The First and Second Great Awakenings

The Great Awakenings mark the emergence of uniquely American evangelical communities (Kidd 2007), which were primarily, up to this point, steeped in Calvin's ascetic denial of feeling, and rigid submission to inevitable predestination. The Awakenings introduced, as I will cover in more detail, modifications to the calling that did not negate the Calvinist version, but rather mutated it into a uniquely American form.

Among the most notable proponents of the First Great Awakening was the English preacher George Whitefield, who became the leader of Calvinistic Methodism. Other important figures included Theodorus Frelinghuysen, a Dutch Reformed minister of New Brunswick, New Jersey, and Gilbert Tennent, a Presbyterian minister in the same town. They were joined in their common preaching effort by Jonathan Edwards of Northampton, Massachusetts, who provided a strong intellectual defense of the new emphasis on personal religious experience. Together with many other clergymen who shared a heritage of Calvinistic doctrine, these men stressed the importance of vital religious experience as the cornerstone of effective religious life (Bushman [1970] 1989; Swift 1998). The Great Awakening was very much a reaction to the stifling controls of puritanical codes, which had so characterized early Calvinist and American Puritan congregations. Prior to the First Awakening, evangelical scholars and preachers taught what amounted to strategies for coping within an oppressive emotional system (Noll 2004; Tracy 1989); they taught their congregations how to bear the burdens of this world and forge ahead without satisfaction. For the supporters of the Great Awakening, religious experience should be passionate, not passive; it should exhilarate, not stultify.

Of course, many opposed the passionate nature of the Great Awakening and condemned it as the devil's work. Nevertheless, it revived many congregations and won many new converts to evangelicalism, especially among blacks and Catholics (Swift 1998). Freed of some of its doctrinal oppressiveness, evangelicalism enjoyed new appeal among a new generation of Americans.

The leaders of the Great Awakening were radicals in the sense that they challenged the established order, which stressed a repression of feeling and denial of contentment. Given the close affiliation of religion with everyday life, it is perhaps not surprising that many of the most ardent supporters of the Great Awakening sought broader changes in American life and eventually lent their voice to the American Revolution, also based on their religious convictions (Hatch 1989). We will not explore this connection any further, except to point out that civil life has from the beginning been connected either directly to religious doctrine, or secondarily, though still powerfully, through cultural values that began in religious doctrine. As argued, one central issue has been, and still is, how a godly person should live and compose himself or herself in accordance with religious belief yet still meet the challenges and requirements of an imperfect world.

The rapid social change of the Revolutionary War period only renewed controversy in religious circles when the war ended. Riding in on the last battle of the war in 1781, the Second Great Awakening swept the country. Evangelicals such as Charles G. Finney emphasized free will, divine forgiveness for all, and the need of each person to freely accept or reject salvation. Whereas the First Great Awakening drew on Calvinist theology and was very much a movement within Calvinism (that also produced the breakaway Presbyterians), the Second drew from Arminianism (named for Jacobus Arminius, 1560–1609), which admitted human decision making into the salvation process. In contrast to the early Calvinists who believed firmly in absolute predestination, the Second Awakening emphasized the role of free will, that humans are free to choose, and these decisions determine whether a person follows God's path or not. The Second Awakening shared with the First an emphasis on personal experience, passionate commitment, and ongoing spiritual renewal.

But the Second Awakening brought another component to the forefront of American evangelical life and faith. Most importantly, America began the process of modern industrialization, which, although it would not become the predominant mode of social life until after World War II, transformed American evangelicalism. As the first industrial working class appeared in American cities at the height of the Second Awakening (1820–1850), evangelicalism won many converts and renewed support among the working class (Schultz 1994), and in general, evangelicals of the Second Awakening swept across America, in close conjunction with the rise of a modern market economic form (Sellers 1991). As modern society spread, the new awakening that represented its values spread with it—the priority of individual moral choice.

Consistent with its evangelical foundation, the Second Awakening provided the moral justification for formally free labor, an essential precondition for the rise of capitalism. As Weber ([1920] 1958) observed long ago, "the attainment of repentance under certain circumstances involved an emotional struggle of such intensity as to lead to the most terrible ecstasies" (p. 140). Thus, emotional conversion, in the sense of being born again, constituted the very essence of Methodism and in general the spirit of the Second Awakening, which the Baptists have retained so remarkably today. But more important than the emotionalism and charismatic ecstasies, the emphasis on personal choice as crucial for salvation offers "ethical justification for the modern division of labor" (Weber [1920] 1958:163). God will lead the elect to higher and higher stations, if the individual follows the opportunities each step of the way. Although the calling was nothing new by this time, the fact that people (men mainly, at this time) could rise above the station of their birth through a series of moral choices was new, and corresponded directly with the structural shift to formally free labor that capitalism promotes and requires.

Thus, the Second Awakening introduced a new morality even as capitalism introduced new class relations. Each justified the other, or as Weber would say, they shared an elective affinity. Like early sixteenth-century Protestant theologians, those of the Second Awakening were not concerned with economic affairs as such. Instead, they focused on how to live a godly life, and thus regarded the predominant economic system as an established fact; it was not the point of scrutiny itself. The morality they developed coincided implicitly, though not purposely, with the predominant economic system in which people must live and work. Both capitalism and the Second Awakening emphasized individual free will and personal choice as the key to spiritual salvation on one hand, and social improvement on the other. These developments were progressive to the extent they created greater social mobility and the liberating belief that personal actions matter on Judgment Day. If salvation were contestable to an extent, then perhaps so were social relations.

But other ramifications of this new collusion and the social form it introduced in the emerging modern society were less than liberating. As noted in Chapter 1, Max Weber describes modern society as a "steel-hard casing" (or iron cage, in the Parsons translation) of class relations, endless economic acquisition, and commodities. The Second Great Awakening ushered in a modern social form, which set in place the basis of ongoing conflict to the present day. Issues of freedom as they relate to personal choice (and thus salvation) combined with issues of social justice (within capitalism) and the possibility of earthly fulfillment and a godly way of life become the primary questions. The Second Awakening set into practice what Weber highlighted in theory—a steel-hard casing premised on a fusion of religious morality and capitalist material necessity.

Ernst Troeltsch ([1912] 1960) identifies the crucial difference between the Calvinist and Lutheran ethic as being that Calvinism strives to remain active, to accomplish more, and in all cases to keep busy and stay focused on career, work, and

---

Ernst Troeltsch (1865–1923)

Like his close friend Max Weber, Troeltsch held little regard for disciplinary boundaries. Drawing freely from history, philosophy, sociology, and theology, he wrote two major works that are well worth reading today: *Social Teaching of the Christian Churches* and *Religion in History*. Although Troeltsch was devoutly Lutheran and Weber resolutely atheist, they shared many perspectives, especially the view that religious beliefs must correlate with material reality, and just as important, material reality must revolve around higher ideals. Both also agreed that such ideals are only "higher" in the sense that people perceive them as transcendent truths; they may lack nobility. Selfish accumulation can be a higher ideal as well as magnanimous generosity. Troeltsch's work deserves far more attention than it currently receives.

enterprise. In contrast, the Lutheran ethic "is inclined to endure existing conditions humbly and patiently . . . [I]ts passivity involved the habit of falling back upon whatever happened to be dominant at the time" (pp. 573–574). Furthermore, the Lutheran ethic legitimates no particular form of government or social system, whereas the ethic of Calvinism supports (though not intentionally) a system of free labor, private property, and personal acquisition—capitalism. Based on a core doctrine of predestination, the Calvinist enters fully into the world, and attempts to transform it, through his individual actions, into an expression of Divine Will (p. 588). In contrast, the Lutheran ethic looks to the inner emotional state of the individual, to "a constantly renewed effort to maintain intact the purity and stability of a faith which is independent of works or merit. Hence all emphasis is placed upon cultivation of the emotional life of the individual" (p. 588).

In his insightful *Social Teaching of the Christian Churches,* Ernst Troeltsch ([1912] 1960) concludes that the Calvinist ascetic ethic compels people to "a life of unceasing, penetrating, and formative labor" (p. 589) as a mere tool of God to express His will, and likewise the Calvinist remains emotionally truncated and narrowly focused on practical means and strategies to increase productivity. Similar to Weber's social-psychological argument, Troeltsch's work points to the same opposition, that ironically, the more the Calvinist engages in the world, and the more benefits that accrue from that ceaseless activity, the more the Calvinist rejects the world and renounces its pleasures. The work itself is satisfaction. In contrast, the Lutheran neither contemplates nor much engages in the world, but rather lives according to the circumstances at hand, and seeks satisfaction through personal and internal spiritual growth, intellectual sophistication, and emotional complexity, all of which the Calvinist regards with suspicion.

In the early days of Protestantism, then, the work ethic as the core of daily life provided a moral system and collective will to resist and ultimately overthrow oppressive medieval and feudal traditions. The work ethic was an emancipatory force of social change, and it contributed to the rise of greater individual autonomy and the possibility for a higher social standard of living. Of course, the rise of capitalism, with which the work ethic became associated, introduced powerful new inequality, as well as, in its purer forms, alienation and dissatisfaction.

I should emphasize again that neither Lutheran traditionalism nor Calvinist work-asceticism spread through American culture as such, not even as the Protestant work ethic. Rather, religious ethics developed and spread in close affiliation with social changes, and thus became, early on, social ethics as much as distinctly religious ethics associated with particular denominations. In the Second Awakening, personal choice in spiritual matters and larger issues of civil freedom could not avoid the obvious fact that millions of people were held in bondage as slaves—the literal property of the owner. Amid the fervor and enthusiasm of the Second Awakening was the issue of slavery. Were slaves not human as well? Should they not have equal opportunity to fulfill their role in God's plan? In a larger sense, if a person does not have socially and spiritually predetermined obligations, how then should he or she navigate to salvation?

Religion and American Culture:
Slavery and Its Aftermath

Although both the First and Second Great Awakenings corresponded to changes in American society generally, slavery would divide evangelicals not only theologically, but also politically, morally, ethically, geographically, and in nearly every other way. It also brought devout evangelicals into political action—on both sides. By the time the Civil War began, the largest evangelical church—the Baptists—had already argued for and against slavery, and after bitter theological clashes, divided into a Northern sect that opposed slavery, and a Southern sect that not only tolerated but also openly advocated slavery. Baptists would play a central role in American society in the Civil War era, and much of their role evolved from their history.

After founding a Baptist colony in Rhode Island in 1639, by 1700 the Baptists had gained their greatest influence in the middle colonies, especially in Pennsylvania and New Jersey (Ammerman 1990). Less than 30 years since its establishment in America, the midcolony variety had already developed a unique theology called "particular" Baptism that differed from the Rhode Island version. Particular Baptism held that only certain people are predestined for salvation, and this view proliferated in the middle colonies over and against general Baptism (that anyone can be born again and saved), such that each side regarded the other as a heresy.

This division amounts to far more than an interesting theological disagreement, because it introduced into Baptism a kind of spiritual superiority over and against the initial founding principles of the Baptist faith and the spirit of the Second Awakening. In other words, slavery brought a shift to Baptist theology that had previously emphasized the "general" salvation of anyone who opened his or her heart to the Lord. In particularism, only the elect, which could also be interpreted as an elite, created a theological separation between those for whom the possibility of salvation was available, and those whom God had preselected for damnation, a fate which no earthly condition or human effort could change. In practical application, this allowed white Southerners, and slave owners in particular, to justify their position as one of God's chosen and likewise justify the continued enslavement of blacks, whom God had denied the divine spark. Thus, the association of divine providence with slavery and other forms of social inequality began early, not only in terms of class exploitation, but in America in terms of cultural values as well, predicated on race.

When the Southern Baptist Convention (SBC) was born in 1845, it officially adopted a modified version of "particular" Baptism, in that only those who were born again would be saved, and only from among those to whom God offers the possibility of salvation. Furthermore, Southern Baptists reflected popular notions of the day and codified them into a belief of white spiritual superiority that not only accorded whites the opportunity for salvation (and denied it to others), but also promoted a "manifest destiny"—that the godly way of life, embodied in white people, especially those of high social status, should determine the destiny of America.

Charles Hodge holds a central position in history because of his education at an elite school (Princeton) and his intellectual yet popular views in which he legitimated white superiority through religious values. His leadership, which influenced many ministers at a local level (Hewitt 1991), provided a theological and scholarly cover for racist sentiment. Hodge emphasized "the enduring power of sin" and in manner and custom "personified social conservatives in the South" (Hewitt 1991:88). Hodge's preoccupation with sin and temptation led him to condemn most forms of social unrest, as well as any form of social change that challenged established and conventional routines. Although responding to the issue of slavery pertinent to his day, Hodge also represented an antimodernist, anticapitalist thinker who supported the Old South. Hodge rejected universal suffrage and advocated slavery as a natural and divine order.

Most significant, perhaps, Hodge argued that "the person and the soul are completely passive," whereas God is the only active force. For this reason, "sinners are by themselves unable to perform any holy act," (quoted in Hewitt 1991:56) and "real" people of God therefore accept their fate rather than try to make their fate.

For Hodge, people can only submit to God, and if God wanted to change the social order, He would do so. According to Hodge (1866), "God approves certain individuals and predestines them for eternal life. The ground of this choice is His own sovereign pleasure; the end to which the elect are predestined is company to Jesus Christ" (p. 459). Hodge exemplifies the attempt to reinstate predestination as an element of modern Baptist belief and justification for the social dominance of one group over others. For Hodge, predestination not only determines the fate of one's soul, but also establishes the social order of this world. In this view, predestination applies to entire groups at a time, rather than person by person. The entire black race was predestined for servitude in this life and damnation in the next.

At the same time, evangelicals who preached and led the Second Great Awakening joined with the emancipation movement on the Northern side. Charles Finney, for example, advocated "the freedom of the human will at the expense of divine sovereignty" (quoted in Hewitt 1991:88)—a bold statement in any day. Even more directly, a number of Finney's disciples, such as Theodore Dwight Weld and Arthur and Lewis Tappan, joined the abolitionist movement and called upon all good pastors to fight slavery as part of their regular gospel sermon and all good people to fight against slavery in their daily lives. Still more forcefully, William Lloyd Garrison, a Northern Presbyterian, harshly attacked any church or congregation that would not denounce slavery. His abolitionism rested squarely on deeply felt religious beliefs (Swift 1998:132). His aggressive and at times vitriolic attacks on parishes that remained silent on the slavery issue earned him widespread public notoriety and many political enemies.

Far from challenging God, however, Finney sought to understand freedom of choice as something ordained by God and thus a component of divine will. On a theological level, Finney and Hodge could not be more opposite. Both sought to create a sense of certainty in the midst of sweeping social change and a Civil War. Both sought to establish social order based on divine will. However, Hodge saw divine will as an absolute law; Finney, on the other hand, saw divine will unfolding through active, thoughtful, conscious engagement with all aspects of life. Finney also continued the evangelical tradition that sought to unify all people under God. Hodge instead looked inward, putting forth that chosen status depended on essential racial characteristics. Southern versions of evangelical churches no longer spread the word, and in effect could not properly be called evangelical because salvation depended on essence, not conversion. Indeed, the major denominations split over the political issue of slavery, and the spiritual issue of the elect.

Whereas Finney preached that everyone could make moral choices to shape their fate, this doctrine also held that no one was inherently better or worse in God's eyes; each person had to walk his or her path based on the choices that individual made. Hodge and the conservative contingent he represented in the South reverted to the older predestination doctrines, with the notion of Anglo-Saxon superiority. Congregations, and the promise of salvation they offered, were now open only to the true people of God—whites.

As a result, the major denominations formally split apart, based on the spiritual issue of human agency and the political issue of slavery. Presbyterianism split in 1857, into the New School sect (in the North) and the Old School sect (in the South). As mentioned earlier, the Northern and Southern Baptists effectively divided in 1840, and the Southern Baptist Convention officially formed in 1845 (Swift 1998:133). Although the SBC officially held no position on slavery and maintained that it was a civil matter outside the affairs of religion, their first president, William B. Johnson, declared "the South is now free to promote slavery" (quoted in Swift 1998:133).

The South seceded from the Union, leaving the Northern states, predominantly over the issue of slavery. Behind this one issue, however, we find several important sociological factors. First, industrialization advanced in the North, transforming its major cities from relatively small ports on the Atlantic seaboard into ever-larger metropolitan powerhouses, with increasing cultural diversity, economic opportunity, and wealth. In the rural areas, where most of the population still resided, most people lived on small but viable family-owned farms. Together with small business owners and professionals such as doctors, lawyers, accountants, teachers, and engineers in the cities, these family farmers constituted a growing middle class in the North. In the North, a merchant class centered on Chestnut Street in Philadelphia and an emerging industrial (modern capitalist) class centered on Wall Street in New York City controlled Northern politics. Gradually, the middle-class farmers and professionals gained political influence as well, especially during the Civil War.

In the South, very little industrial or merchant activity developed. A few very wealthy families, known as *physiocrats*, owned vast plantations, worked by black slaves. Most white people lived in rural areas, as in the North, but under very different conditions. Namely, they worked as tenant farmers and sharecroppers who rented the land from the plantation owners, in contrast to Northern farmers who owned their own farms. This system in the South ensured the continuous impoverishment of the majority of the white population. The South lacked a middle class almost entirely, and thus consisted of a few extremely wealthy families, a multitude of impoverished land renters, and slaves. Ironically, even as Protestantism promoted the work ethic of capitalism in the North, and thus implicitly capitalism as a system of economic organization in general, the Southern variants became an economically reactionary force that supported the plantation system and the social class structure that constituted it. This turning point is crucial in the history of American evangelicalism, and correspondingly in American culture, because it was "no longer outcast dissidents fighting for the rights of minorities" (Ammerman 1990:43) but now represented the faith of a white and wealthy elite of plantation owners, who resisted social change that threatened their position.

In this socioeconomic context, the issue of slavery became the catalyst. Baptism (and the other denominations that broke along Northern and Southern lines) thus reflected the society that created it. Northern Baptism and other free denominations contributed most of the officers to the Union army—educated men who, inspired by their religious beliefs, volunteered for service to fight against the evils of slavery. Northern farmers also opposed slavery, and although not as quick to volunteer, embraced antislavery denominations as well, especially Northern Baptism, Episcopalianism, Methodism, Unitarian/Universalism, and Quakerism. Whatever their exact religious background, Northerners viewed slavery as a great evil that conflicted with their religious beliefs, which coincided with notions of a free and democratic society. Religion in the South became much more monolithic and coincided with the notion of tradition and elitist hierarchy.

In contrast, why did poor Southern farmers fight so tenaciously for a society that oppressed them nearly as much as slaves? Scholars and others have debated this quite intensely. Let me suggest a sociological answer. Southern culture included a strong sense of honor and loyalty between social superiors and their minions—in this case, between land owners and renters. This sense derived from the personal contact between the rich and poor, over generations going back to the original colonies. Whereas the North outgrew this relationship in favor of increasingly impersonal market capitalism and later, wage labor, the South retained it. Poor whites lived only slightly better than slaves, but they were technically free, and as such identified with the wealthy white owners, with whom they also shared a religious and patrimonial bond. On Sundays, rich and poor worshipped together.

The bond between rich and poor was thus heartfelt and long-standing, despite the tremendous disparity in quality of life. This bond, sanctified through religion, inspired poor white men to defend their home territory, way of life, and wealthy high-status patron against the Yankees, whom they perceived as outsiders and invaders. We may conclude sociologically that poor Southern whites were not deluded, stupid, or insane, but rather, were committed to their social institutions, at the center of which stood the church. Poor whites were not so much proslavery, because they owned no slaves, but rather were pro-South, of which plantations and slavery were dominant institutions.

Moreover, men in the South typically revered virility and honor over and against humility, discipline, and benevolence (Swift 1998:81). Although evangelicals, following the teaching of the Second Great Awakening, denounced displays of manly violence and posturing, such as fighting, dueling, gambling, and drinking contests (Swift 1998), the advent of the Civil War invoked manly honor and bold courage, which diminished the impact of evangelical ministers and teachers. Evangelicals stressed humble personal character above all else, but this represented a direct challenge to established male marshal identity, and furthermore seemed inappropriate during an impending war. Evangelical tolerance, charity, and humility would find minimal acceptance among men in the South who now faced a "manly" challenge on the battlefield (see Table 2.5).

Thus, the dominant male culture of the time reflected the lives of the wealthy few, and included complex yet unspoken rules of interaction. Men were expected to show a "tasteful" and sophisticated combination of "generosity, physical force, courage, conspicuous consumption, education, a bit of hedonism, and paternalism" (Swift 1998:131) in order to maintain social esteem. Poor white men had little hope of any of these, and thus relied on vague notions of honor and paternalism, premised heavily on a belief in superiority over blacks, to maintain their self-respect.

After the Civil War, industrial capitalism grew tremendously in the North, and with it, the bastions and sources of its power: factories, cities, the urban working class, banking, and the bourgeoisie. The apparent opportunity that industrial growth offered to Europeans attracted many immigrants, as is well-known, but many in the North as well as the South were imbued with notions of cultural, racial, or religious superiority, and immigration meant not only ethnic mixing, but an influx of Catholics from culturally diverse areas: Italy, Ireland, Poland, and southern Germany.

Table 2.5   Northern States Compared to Southern States on the Eve of the U.S. Civil War

	Northern States	Southern States
Economy	Family farms, small business, and emerging industry. Most people are self-employed owners or wage workers. Banking system serves all levels of economic development.	Sharecroppers, tenant farmers, and slaves. Most people are dependent on wealthy owners and pay high rent. Slaves have zero opportunity.
Culture	Diverse immigration settled in particular states, counties, and towns	Monolithic dominance of Anglo-American customs
Religion	Mix of traditional churches and grassroots innovation	Baptists dominate.
Overall	Economic dynamism promotes social mobility. Clearly developed civil society allows for pluralistic prosperity, with broad standard-of-living increases.	Upper-class dominance of economics, politics, and religion allows for little social mobility and produces social stagnation and low standard of living, except for a very small wealthy elite.

Rapid industrial growth also brought a rapid growth in the discoveries of science and the desire to explain the world according to science instead of religion. The clash between modernism and fundamentalism began. More than a point of doctrinal disagreement (although this by itself inspired considerable militancy), the spirit of the Second Awakening, as its enthusiasts encountered the squalid living conditions in the industrial cities, called forth a social gospel that clashed with nativist beliefs based on race and doctrinal purity. Science, religion, democracy, justice, opportunity, and freedom collided over the next several decades. To understand this collision, let us examine the further developments in American evangelicalism.

American Evangelicalism

As the social historian Christine Leigh Heyrman (1997) concludes, "Evangelicalism's complex beginnings in the early South would probably claim the curiosity of only a small circle of historians were it not for the fact that this legacy now shapes the character of conservative Protestant churches in every region of the United States" (p. 256). Moreover, the evangelical churches greatly de-emphasize formal ritual, and conservative or otherwise, contemporary American Protestantism manifests the influence of doctrinally sparse, ritually minimal influences in favor of personal belief and individual commitment.

Origins

Evangelicalism, the largest Christian type in North America, descends both institutionally and culturally from the Protestant Reformation in Europe. Protestants only just secured their existence in Europe when they began to settle North America, and consequently the religion, and its many sects that would appear, was far from solidified. The "protesting" and rebellious nature of Protestantism makes it especially prone to ongoing revision and the formation of breakaway factions, such that the religion continually evolves as divisions occur.

Baptists are an offshoot of the earlier Anabaptists, which Conrad Grebel founded on January 21, 1525, in Zürich, Switzerland. Their newfound faith led them to immediate and serious conflict with established Catholic authorities, so the Anabaptists mostly fled to England. Once there, they developed into the Puritan Independents, also known as Congregationalists. Now in conflict with the established Church of England and the crown—where Henry VIII had only just separated the Church of England from Rome with the Act of Supremacy in 1534—the Congregationalist Puritans fled to Holland, and then some went back to England in 1611, where they founded the first Baptist congregation. As soon as possible, they left for North America, where Roger Williams founded the first Baptist congregation in America (1639) as well as the colony of Rhode Island. Meanwhile, those Puritans who stayed in England played a critical role in the English Civil War, fought intermittently from 1642–1651. At a decisive battle at Oxford on June 24, 1646, the

parliamentary forces, also known as roundheads, defeated the Royalists, also known as cavaliers. With this victory, the Puritans became highly influential political leaders.

Although Scottish Presbyterians initially held most of the formal political power immediately after the war, the Puritan leader Oliver Cromwell commanded the army, and consequently was able to assert Puritan influence. However, the constant fighting among Protestant groups allowed a royalist army with strong Scottish support to reestablish the monarchy in 1660, and from that time forward, English puritans would never again hold power as a group. Unwilling to rejoin the Church of England, they became known as Nonconformists.

During the same period, some Puritans journeyed to America, where they established colonies in New England in 1620, the first at Plymouth in Massachusetts. As mentioned, the Baptists joined them in New England shortly thereafter in 1639 in Rhode Island, and the two colonies coexisted peacefully as both predicated their faith on Calvinist principles. However, Roger Williams, in decisive contrast to almost every other religious and political leader of his day, and for many decades afterward, believed that Native Americans were no less human than Europeans. He lived for extended periods of time with Native American tribes, learned their language and customs, and encouraged others (without much success) to do the same. Williams believed that Native Americans could accept the Gospel yet still retain their indigenous beliefs.

Thus, even from the earliest days, American evangelicalism was by no means a seamless unity (Wolffe 2007). Roger Williams, though a radical in his own day, constitutes a significant break in evangelicalism. Though he adhered to strict Calvinist morality as part of his devout religious faith, he also held to a kind of humanism and respected the rights of all people—not just to live, but to retain their own customs even after conversion. Although fundamentalism as such would not emerge until the early twentieth century, Williams represents a more tolerant element in a period characterized by absolute notions of faith, when principles of religion were not a topic for doubt or discussion, at least not within the same congregation. Williams promoted tolerance, not as a break with his faith, but as an expression of his devotion—a form of evangelical faith that would reemerge to fight against slavery in the nineteenth century. Like his later devout successors, Williams's faith inspired both his adherence to Calvinist asceticism and its strict codes of behavior on one hand and universal tolerance on the other.

Although both early Baptists and Puritans based their theology on Calvinist principles, especially predestination and ascetic denial of worldly pleasure, the differences became more salient than the similarities. Specifically, the Baptists, in cooperation with the Methodists, would lead the First and Second Great Awakenings that transformed American evangelical thought and life. This period of revival would inspire many people to fight against slavery as a result of their religious convictions. Yet the doctrine of predestination and the idea of the select—that only a few who were preordained by God would receive salvation—remained stronger in the more rigid and closed Congregationalist communities. With the additional influence of certain British imports, this early and nuanced division would lead to later decisive divisions within evangelicalism, as we will see below.

At this stage in American history, the Baptists played a progressive role. Unlike the closed communities of the Puritans and the Anglicans—renamed Episcopals during the Revolutionary War—the Baptists welcomed new revivals, and as evangelicals, always sought new converts. In the upcoming First and Second Awakenings, Baptism acquired the revival spirit and emphasis on personal conversion that identify it today. In fact as we will see, the unyielding fundamentalist orientation that characterizes Southern Baptism in particular today is the product not of initial doctrine, but of later social change that reshaped religion in its own image. Specifically, the institution of slavery and the political-economic power struggle that appeared in the Civil War separated North from South in religion and culture as well as politics, as we have seen.

In addition to religious refugees, among the first European settlers in North America were Dutch merchants (who settled New Amsterdam) and later, English merchants and colonists, who occupied New Amsterdam and changed the name to New York. Since that time, American Protestantism has descended primarily from the English and Baptist side rather than the Dutch side, with closer ties to the Puritans. This influence has been ongoing for much of American history, and many developments that seem particularly American are in fact imported contributions from England.

Evangelicals in the early colonies struggled with apparently contradictory codes of behavior as men and women in a wilderness area on one hand, and proper Christians on the other. Evangelical beliefs called upon the devout to become "self-denying, will-less, subject and submissive, humble and meek, chaste and pure" (Greven [1977] 1988:125) servants of Christ. However, the demands of colonial life on the frontier created stress between these religious ideals, and the need for a vigorous social life and to expand the community for basic survival (Sweeney 2005). The Puritan Cotton Mather wrote numerous tracts that address this very situation, which shows that the colonists were themselves aware of the inconsistency.

Still, Mather could not resolve the issue himself, and he wrote extensively about the "thorough vileness" of sex, yet fathered many children himself. Greven ([1977] 1988) thus concludes that sexual guilt, tied to an ideal of submission to Christ, severely divided evangelical male identity. This reinforced the notion that the body is dirty, with a strong propensity for indulgence and corruption. Both men and women sought to overcome this condition by denying sexual pleasure entirely (p. 141). However, this required a denial of the emotions that accompany sexual attraction and sensation. Early evangelicals had to separate passion from love, which would have cultural repercussions later as the First Great Awakening endorsed emotional experience as vital and necessary for religious life. In 1655, Cotton Mather's father, Increase Mather, writes that, through awareness and expression of love and passion he developed a "tender conscience" (quoted in Greven 1977:141) that made him a better father and member of the community. Whatever other forms of denial and abstinence the Puritans may have inflicted on themselves, they did not separate "manly" and "womanly" emotions, nor did they believe that women should be the only source of emotional succor for children.

Only later did masculine and feminine emotions become constructed so opposingly as we now know them.

However, Coontz (2000) shows that not only did men and women contribute equally to the material sustenance of the family and community, but men also contributed emotional sustenance to their children. For example, Cotton Mather and other Puritans remark how children seek the emotional comfort of both parents. Not until the "bastardy" laws of 1834 and subsequent rulings, combined with religious and economic changes, did women become the nearly exclusive emotional provider (Coontz 2000:62–63).

As American society developed, the quest for purity and the denial of sensual stimulation characterized American Protestantism throughout the 1700s and 1800s (Curtis 1991; Rosman 1984). Theological arguments often centered on what type of physical sensation was sinful and what type or quantity was overindulgent. During this period, the changing laws and the attitudes they reflected further isolated women as the domestic worker, child-raiser, and sole emotional comfort for children. As we have seen already, female sexuality was also suspect, and hence itself became an object to be controlled. Women must be demure and deferential. In contrast, the ideal male should be strong in both mind and body, and coolly rational. This separation led to a new masculine ideal that favored strength, certainty, assertiveness, and control—especially in public. Although writers did not explore the issues of masculinity, femininity, and identity in sociological terms until the early 1900s, I suggest, however speculatively, that gender identity was a problem from the beginning of Protestantism in America. If it were not problematic, why did so many writers address the issue theologically? Why has the "proper" gender ideal been a recurring debate within evangelicalism? From a sociological perspective, I suggest that bifurcated gender identity is inherently problematic in this context, given the decisive break between evangelical devotion to high ideals, and the difficulty of living up to those ideals in reality. The highest spiritual life is transcendent, yet people must live in the mundane world. That is, it is not so easy to be purely masculine, or purely feminine. The stricter the code, the more often transgressions will occur.

The demands on early Protestants were difficult, both physically and mentally. As the colonies and later the nation expanded, so evangelicalism expanded. Living on an expanding frontier after the Civil War, evangelicals faced many hardships, and their comparatively severe religious morality offered little sanctuary or certainty. As time passed, the frontiers stabilized and the South reintegrated into the United States and its modern economy. Once a bastion of rugged, individual, rural self-reliance and Southern white superiority, evangelicalism at the end of the nineteenth century moved into the cities where industrialization created immense wealth next to immense poverty. As the United States moved westward and the natural frontier ended at the close of the nineteenth century, a new urban frontier emerged in the cities of the industrial revolution. Ministers and others of religious devotion now ventured into the forbidden cities amidst the soot, steam, and fire of working-class neighborhoods.

The Rise of Progressivism and Fundamentalism

As modern social relations developed, and as industry grew and science advanced, American religion on one hand supported modernity as progressivism, and on the other hand attempted to stall if not completely reject modernity as fundamentalism. Progressive people of faith from this era (1865–1939) believed that science could assist with the realization of perfectionism—that the Second Coming would happen when people were able to make the world as God intended it to be. This required an end to poverty, war, injustice, and all the other things that man-made society had created. Only then would God's grace shine down, and the moment of rapture would be at hand. Success in ending slavery was just the beginning, but it proved that moral, progressive religion could lead to progressive change. Just as slavery divided American religion prior to the Civil War, so modernity divided American religion in subsequent years, from the end of the Civil War (1865) until the start of World War II (1939). From the end of the Civil War to the first decade of the twentieth century, promodern and antimodern sides drifted further apart (Curtis 1991)—one looking to the future, and one looking to the past.

Far from seeing it as a challenge to religion, progressives looked to the future and believed that science could provide humanity with the knowledge necessary to fix social problems, and industry with the means to build a better society. Religion tells us where to go, and science tells us how to get there. Both could thereby assist in the attainment of heaven on earth. Science, like anything man-made, could be applied either for good or evil, and as the Second Awakening proponents taught, people must make their own moral choices.

In contrast, there arose a counterforce that rejected modern "progress." Fundamentalists rejected everything modern, especially science, and argued that America should return to its premodern heritage and small-town life centered on the local parish. They favored absolute gender roles, and they promoted scripture as the only valid source of knowledge. Fundamentalism as such emerged around 1900, not as a rebirth of the past, but as a particular interpretation of the past that idealized austere (and difficult) colonial life and the supposed glories of close-knit but highly restrictive small-town agricultural life. Fundamentalism was thus born in the United States in the first two decades of the twentieth century as a reaction specifically to modern society. Many pastors, as well as lay people, were upset that science had moved into the classroom and seemed to so decisively guide political policy. Moreover, modern life uprooted people from their small-town life, thrust them into cities, and brought many different ethnic groups, cultures, and religions together. At the same time, modernity left people in rural areas suddenly impoverished, small towns depopulated, and family farms ruined.

In reaction, conservative Protestant leaders developed the belief that the end of time was approaching, that modernism represented the final dispensation or time of trial for men, after which the apocalypse would occur. To save true Christian souls, preachers such as Harry Parsons (a Presbyterian) in 1879 and his disciple Samuel Andrews (a Congregationalist) in 1898 called for a return to scripture, a return to what they termed "biblical fundamentalism," based on a literal reading of the Bible (Wolffe 2007). Using apocalyptic imagery from the Bible that seemed to correspond to events of the day (such as the Franco-Prussian War, the rise of a new Sodom—New York City—and other urban areas with diverse ethnic populations), these early fundamentalists attracted white Protestants who believed (to some extent correctly) that their exclusive moral grip on the nation was waning, and modern industrial society and a new industrial working class were replacing the agrarian pastoral world they idealized. Deeply imbued with religious feeling that corresponded to their sense of social location, they viewed these changes as signs that Satan was taking over, and therefore inferior, degenerate, and immoral people were swelling the population.

More successful than most, Dwight L. Moody systematized the form of the fundamentalist revival that is still the model for mass evangelical revivals today (Fuller 1995:124). Many others followed, and all shared the hallmarks that distinguish fundamentalism today: moral perfectionism and antisecularism. Most of the "enemies" fundamentalists name throughout the twentieth century are typically modern and secular—evolution, science, humanism, communism, and pluralism, to name a few. With the core doctrine in place, there remained only the task to provide a formal and routinized fundamentalist interpretation of scripture, which appeared as the *Scofield Reference Bible* in 1909. The first edition sold nearly 5 million copies, and the reissue in 1967 sold another 5 million (Fuller 1995:127). Variations on the Scofield version have been in print ever since. Although Scofield claims no original insight, the actual biblical text is heavily edited and replete with copious explanatory margin notes. Since 1967 and the proliferation of television, fundamentalism has become primarily an audiovisual faith, with many preachers vying for the loyalty of the faithful, including Jimmy Swaggert, Oral Roberts, Pat Robertson, Jerry Falwell, Bob Jones, and many others. In addition to television, megachurches rely on jumbo screens and sophisticated multimedia systems to reach the large congregations gathered in huge, arena-like sanctuaries.

Thus, to summarize, two sides to basic religious questions formed. Modernists hold that scientific discoveries are all part of God's truth—just another way for humans, endowed with God-given intellect, to understand God's plan. Science is a corollary to the scripture; it is the product of the ability to reason that God gave us. Modernists tend to favor liberal political views, and often subscribe to a social gospel, that spreading the Word is not enough; Christians must work to improve the world, to work for peace, justice, equality, and harmony. Fundamentalists, on the other hand, believe that the Bible contains literal truth, that each passage is a whole and complete truth. Whatever contradictions we may see are merely human perceptions or our failure to understand God's divine plan (Heyrman 1997). Fundamentalists typically hold to a conservative political view and conventional notions of gender roles (Marty and Appleby 1992). They also overwhelmingly interpret political issues in moral terms, and moral or immoral behavior as the outcome of inherent good or evil in a person, not just a good or bad choice (Morone 2003).

Even before the Civil War, before the split between Northern and Southern Baptists over slavery, and the emerging conflict between modernists and fundamentalists, a crisis had developed in masculine identity. Also connected to emerging capitalist class relations and the demands of a capitalist system of employment, masculine identity faltered as the old conventions fell to capitalist intrusions. What new ideals could replace the old and survive in the new world? Ready to provide a new model was "muscular Christianity"—an obscure movement at first, but one that gained widespread popularity both in England, where it originated, and in the United States, where it furthered a new Christian masculinity more in line with capitalist class relations.

Religion and the Rise of Modern Manhood

T. C. Sanders coined the term "muscular Christianity" in 1857 to describe a new Christian ethic and lifestyle in a book he reviewed called *Two Years Ago,* written by Charles Kingsley (cited in Donald Hall 1994:7). Kingsley and others, such as J. M. Ludlow and F. D. Maurice, contemporaries and all Protestant ministers, wrote novels in which the main characters triumph over seemingly impossible adversaries and insurmountable obstacles through two broadly drawn and simply stated principles: (1) physical strength and purity, and (2) devotion to Christ. The first attribute was a necessary precursor to receiving Christ's guidance—a sound body and a sound mind. For the latter, a man must continually practice physical purity, cleanliness, and in general maintain a high level of physical fitness. Only after attaining physical purity could a man hope to receive spiritual purity, which only God can grant.

Physical purity had always been an aspect of Christian morality, from the earliest days in the Roman Empire (Meeks 1993), and actually predated Christianity in Judaism and many pagan religions. In British Victorianism, however, it became more than a temporary abstinence associated with particular religious rites. Whereas ongoing religious abstinence or other bodily discipline applied only to priests for both early Christians and pagans, ongoing physical discipline and self-denial became an integral part of everyday Victorian morality.

As Max Weber ([1905] 2002) observed in Chapter 1, asceticism, from which the Victorian ethic descended, rose to prominence in Western culture through various Protestant sects, including Calvinism, Methodism, Pietism, and numerous versions of Baptism. Asceticism was a natural corollary to a work ethic, and each is an aspect of the other. Despite theological differences, Weber concludes that for the purpose of understanding the control that a social morality exerts over the individual, we can treat ascetic Protestantism as a single whole. That is, the ascetic moral virtue that became part of everyday social behavior was present and in the same form in various Protestant sects, even though the sects differed in other ways. Thus, we may speak of a single Protestant work ethic. Converting Weber's theory into a series of testable hypotheses, the contemporary scholar Jere Cohen (2002) corroborates Weber's argument.

Thus, by the Victorian era, the specifically Protestant work ethic and its moral companion, asceticism, was no longer a uniquely Protestant or even a religious virtue, but had now become a generalized cultural virtue. As came to be generalized socially, it became an everyday practice and an obligation for everyone who would live a proper and moral life, something that each person must observe daily. No longer the responsibility of an elite priestly caste or a rite of a particular religious ceremony, asceticism became the standard of daily life and work. With this in mind, exactly how one should live a clean and pure physical life, and what constituted such a life, became the focus of debate, both among religious and secular scholars.

British evangelical churches expanded the range of permissible activity to include physical exertion for the purpose of improving one's body and mind. As early as 1810, British evangelicals regarded bodily exercise and physical recreation as pleasing to God, and by the 1830s, many congregations conducted outdoor excursions and sports days (Rosman 1984:124). The muscular Christian movement that followed in the 1840s stood as a fully crystallized version of healthy Christian living and a step into the modern era. Muscular Christianity joined the medical discoveries of the day with traditional beliefs in order to address the problem of certainty in salvation that had troubled Protestants from the beginning. With each major economic or cultural shift, Protestant denominations have struggled to define themselves in response to changing social environments and in accordance with their beliefs, history, and tradition (Luidens 1993; Weeks 1993).

In an attempt to specify the principles of healthy masculinity in relationship to religious and social life (which were often indiscernibly blended) Kingsley, writing in the 1850s, "reconstituted masculinity as a private, partially disclosed, substitute of self" (Rosen 1994:19). In accordance with his Protestant faith, the founder of muscular Christianity created a masculine image fairly close to the so-called strong, silent type, a man who reveals little about his personal feelings and dedicates himself to work, family, and accomplishment yet without fanfare or self-serving promotion. Devoted to his faith, he knows that God will see his good works and recognize the true faith in his heart. He therefore requires no worldly recognition or adulation.

Muscular Christianity and the Victorian ethics it reflected differ sharply from Catholic ethics and Protestant traditionalism. For Kingsley, purity and the quest for redemption is not a cycle, but more of a linear climb toward perfection. In fact, this particular version of physical purity (asceticism) as an indicator of moral virtue was associated so distinctly with Protestantism that it became a central theme in mid–nineteenth-century anti-Catholicism (Wolffe 1994:183–187) and contributed later to the notion of moral perfectionism among twentieth-century fundamentalists.

Yet Kingsley does not promote asceticism as a Protestant virtue and end in itself, nor in the usual sense of self-denial and deferral of gratification. Kingsley moved asceticism entirely into the business world as a utilitarianism and basically an attitude of rational sensibility. For other areas of life, Kingsley allowed for sensual satisfaction, but within definite bounds that he justifies both on a religious basis and a scientific one. In Kingsley's view, God created man and woman as separate sexes, each with naturally endowed and complementary characteristics, and therefore wholesome living must revive and maintain the "physical realities that God created" (Fasick 1994:92). For Kingsley, God created the world and everything in it, but He also created nature as a complex system, an all-encompassing entity in itself, and to the extent humans are the product of this natural world, the natural laws of human existence can be observed and confirmed through scientific methods to instruct people how to live. Kingsley thus embraces a modernist view of religion that allows for the discoveries and validity of science, yet these discoveries are merely recognition of a divinely created natural order acquired through scientific observation and expressed in clear scientific terms that humans can understand. Although Kingsley remained a firm believer, his acceptance of science as an ally of religion earned him many enemies, and furthered a fundamentalist versus modernist debate that continues to the present day.

Kingsley drew on the medical science of his day, as well as Darwin's theory of evolution, to conclude that the present-day male (and female) are the end result of both God-given essence and evolutionary biology—a combined product of both God and Nature. Man and woman were created—and evolved—to complement each other, such that "they could only achieve a mutually beneficial union by retaining the distinctive features of the respective sexes" (Fasick 1994:93), or they would fall into both an unnatural and ungodly state.

How then should people live in a godly and natural manner? If moral purity as the key to godly living depends on abstinence from earthly pleasure, as many conservative evangelicals believed, Kingsley wondered how we reconcile ourselves to natural drives, especially the sex drive? He believed that sexual desire, as a natural part of human biology and part of God's plan, should be satisfied, not denied, but only in a godly manner—that is, within marriage. Perhaps needless to say, Kingsley approved only of heterosexual marriage and sexual activity, because it maintained the difference of the sexes that God and nature had ordained. However, Kingsley's view of heaven is far from a desexualized and dispassionate Puritanism, and is no longer a vague notion of eternal happiness or land of abundance in contrast to a worldly life (for most people before modern times) of degrees of deprivation. Paradise for Kingsley meant men and women together in physical perfection engaging in "uninterrupted sexual intercourse" (quoted in Chitty 1976:81). Not to be confused with any prurient sexual desire, Kingsley envisioned physical and moral perfection as the end result of lifelong devotion to Christ. However, he remained unclear what "devotion to Christ" means in everyday life beyond general notions of physical strength and health. To understand the ethics of the period, we must now turn to his contemporaries who articulated a more specific vision.

Among the most influential and widely read muscular Christians of mid–nineteenth-century Britain, F. D. Maurice also led the Christian Socialist movement and, unlike Kingsley, accepted and promoted the term muscular Christianity (Pennington 1994:133). Maurice and others in the movement merged conveniently with a concurrent secular emphasis on masculine identity and expression through sports. Like today, late nineteenth-century Britain had professional athletes and saw the emergence of sports as a spectator pastime, but earlier in the nineteenth century, athletic participation was almost universally amateur, with many untrained players casually taking part. As this fascination with sports grew and athletics became a central pastime, so also the virtues of athletics reinforced the dominant values of the society that created them: physical strength and training, quiet dedication, and a sense of fair play. On the athletic field, the values of modern society—hard work, individual responsibility, and the notion that practice of both led to an appropriate and deserved fate, that is, victory and honor for the virtuous, defeat for the less virtuous—reinforced the legitimacy of the social order that built the stadiums and turned leagues into a system of owners, supervisors (coaches), and workers (players).

In England at the time, rugby was the first popular spectator sport for which primarily middle-class men trained and played to escape the routine of their office jobs in law, accounting, banking, and so on. Yet rugby surpassed the call to moral virtue and became additionally a symbol for masculine and national identity (Chandler and Nauright 1996). In America, football superseded rugby as a test of masculine virtue, and for preachers like Billy Sunday (discussed below) at the beginning of the twentieth century in America and Bill McCartney (former University of Colorado football coach and founder of the Promise Keepers) at the end, football and sports in general provided a model for moral virtue and masculine identity.

But modern sports are more than a symbolic touchstone from which to learn moral lessons. They also reflect a specifically modern class structure and the expectations and obligations of each person in society, depending on one's class position. Although the class distinctions of modern sports may appear obscure now, they were readily recognizable in the nineteenth century. The middle-class Londoners who founded the game of rugby battled for control of league rules and boundaries with far more wealthy industrialists from northern England (Martens 1996:32–33). Eventually, small business owners from London who both played on and sponsored teams, which they promoted as more legitimate athletic contests, compared to the teams owned by industrialists, who hired men from the working class to play. The industrialists managed their teams like they did their commercial enterprises. Owners hired managers who hired coaches and players who worked for wages, unlike the player-sponsors on the middle-class teams.

Ultimately, the industrialists formed separate and exclusive leagues, the owners of which sheltered themselves in private clubs or estates, and built ever-larger stadiums with increased ticket revenues. Soon, the modern division of labor superseded the player-sponsor arrangement that typified middle-class teams, just as the industrial model of big capital replaced small businesses in other spheres of the economy (Martens 1996:37). As industry moved into colonial possessions, the owners took their sports teams and rivalries with them, such that colonial teams played teams from the core nation, and the games acquired often overt nationalist and at times racial importance (Wee 1994). Thus, the origins of muscular Christianity tied in with economic and political expansion of the modern industrial system and cultural changes it wrought. With old chivalric customs fading with the last remnants of feudal society, the new bourgeoisie class set its own standards of virtue and manhood even as it reorganized economic life.

Since its inception, English muscular Christianity showed only tentative allegiance to English nationalism (Wee 1994), even as popular culture of the day closely associated sports with God and country. In general, muscular Christian leaders favored socialism over capitalism as the model for modern economic organization

Christian Identity refers specifically to people and congregations who believe that the white race is the true descendent of the biblical Israelites. All other races are considered inferior infidels or children of the devil—especially Jews and their willing dupes, black people. Christian Identity includes millennial groups as well as white supremacist groups. For a more complete explanation, see Barkun (1997) and Aho (1990).

This belief underlies nearly all of the contemporary racist groups in the United States and Europe, such as the Ku Klux Klan, Aryan Nations, and the various skinhead groups. Their symbols display their racist-religious orientation. For example, when six Confederate soldiers formed the Ku Klux Klan in 1865, they invented the Klan Cross, shown here, in which the white cross stands for white Christianity and the drop of blood stands for the blood that Jesus shed to save white people only. Another common symbol is taken from ancient Norse mythology, the rune of life. Originally representative of Yggdrasil, the tree of life, white supremacists have endowed it with racist meaning.

Also, the medieval crosses of the Knights Templar (shown here) and of the Knights Hospitaller (white cross on a black background), also known as the Knights of St. John, have been transformed into a racist symbol. Nazi Germany took symbols from Eastern religions, notably the swastika from Hinduism (a symbol of life, as here in the sunwheel), which they added to the geometric Zoroastrian faravahar (a guardian spirit) to create the infamous Nazi eagle, the symbol of Nazi Germany.

Ku Klux
Klan
Cross

Rune of
LIfe

Knights
Templar

Hindu

Faravahar

Nazi Eagle

Religious symbols (except Faravahar) provided courtesy of the Anti-Defamation League.

(Donald Hall 1994). Yet this situation would change as muscular Christianity journeyed to America, a trip it made alongside another British import to America—British-Israelism, the precursor to the contemporary Christian Identity movement.

When British-Israelism and muscular Christianity arrived in America, they found a nation in turmoil. In England, each appealed to a particular economic class and cultural group—muscular Christianity to progressives, mostly from the professional middle class and the wealthy, and British-Israelism to the petty-bourgeoisie and poor farmers. In America, one aspect common to both British-Israelism and muscular Christianity became the salient issue among both factions of the clashing Protestants—the notion of purity. Where British-Israelism emphasized racial purity, muscular Christianity emphasized physical-moral purity. In the American South, racial purity (and white superiority) appealed to an embattled white aristocracy and an impoverished white tenant farmer class on the verge of a civil war. The South turned away from the muscular Christian emphasis on physical perfection and humble character, leaving only the notions of purity and identity joined as one. Whereas British muscular Christianity stood for purposeful accomplishment, that a person had to put forth effort to achieve a character and demeanor pleasing to God, Southerners saw purity and identity as a God-given essence. This formed the basis for the post-war appeal of British-Israelism, and the eventual rise of violent racism, Christian Identity, the Ku Klux Klan, and neo-Nazi movements.

The British imports fomented the increasing distance and growing conflict between a more universalist and modernist Protestantism as it resided in the North, and the racial-regionalist (rather than racial-nationalist) version that developed in the South. Not surprisingly, the notion of racial purity as a corollary to spiritual purity and superiority found widespread acceptance in the slave-owning South, and regionalism found greater appeal in the South than in the immigrant cities of the industrial North. As the Civil War approached, Northern and Southern Protestantism became more and more clearly demarcated (Gauvreau 1994). The South on the eve of the

Civil War was as eager to retain its traditional way of life as the immigrants and the industrialists who employed them were eager to leave tradition behind.

During the war, Southern culture changed little, though it would change drastically after the defeat. With all the old pillars of Southern society destroyed, white men now faced a world of free blacks, and an industrial North that seemed to embody, among other things, an inversion of the proper social order. In the two decades after the Civil War, notions of white supremacy began to coalesce, based initially on British-Israelism. Although British-Israelism peaked in England in the 1920s with only 5,000 members (Barkun 1997:15), figures such as C. A. L. Totten found a much wider audience in the United States. Though not a promoter of British-Israelism as such, Totten used it as the basis of his own version of white supremacy. This belief had great impact on a young evangelist, Charles Fox Parham, who on January 1, 1901, would claim that people in his congregation began speaking in tongues at several revivals, and this was a direct communication from God. He shortly thereafter founded the Pentecostal movement (Barkun 1997:20). Pentecostalism grew rapidly in the South and the Midwest, and gained another influential supporter in the form of J. H. Allen, who transferred the key belief of white supremacy into Midwestern Methodism (Barkun 1997:21). At this point, however, white supremacy was primarily a belief that Anglo-American whites would fulfill crucial sections of biblical prophesy. It had not yet acquired the persecutionary virulence of later versions, especially in the 1920s when the Klan reached the height of its national prominence, and again in the 1960s during the civil rights movement.

Nevertheless, the fact that white supremacy became a central organizing theme in the early days of two major evangelical groups is important. The issue of segregation after the Civil War, and slavery before the war, created divisions among evangelicals, and eventually disempowered evangelicalism during the civil rights struggle of the 1960s, and only recently are evangelicals in general drawing together against racist beliefs. Indeed, the Southern Baptist Convention, the single largest evangelical organization, did not renounce slavery or segregation until 1995 (Newman 2001). Prior to the 1990s, evangelicals would often travel in other, less tolerant directions.

With the appearance of Reuben F. Sawyer in 1921, American evangelicalism in the South and the Southwest moved closer to the Ku Klux Klan. Klan rhetoric at this time emphasized both hatred of blacks, the focus of the first wave of Klan activity immediately after the Civil War, which Sawyer and others now joined with strong anti-Semitism and the need to preserve white culture in addition to what they saw as the genetic purity of the white race.

Meanwhile in the North, the progressive modernist descendants of the Second Awakening focused on the conditions of the working class. Pastors like Washington Gladden preached that "sport, glee, and fun" provided greater satisfaction than hard work, and people should pursue both in equal measure (Curtis 1991:37). Others, such as Mary Eliza McDowell, avidly supported labor strikes and the expansion of health care and sanitation (Curtis 1991:162–163). Her efforts represented a definite shift away from ascetic and otherworldly orthodox Protestantism to a social gospel committed to collective social improvements. Those who support the social gospel, a theology founded primarily by Walter Raushenbusch (1861–1918), who identified himself as a "Christian Socialist" (Fuller 1995), often worked in labor movements and aid-to-the-poor assistance programs, and in general took a pacifist position on war.

Rauschenbusch believed that Christians must work to improve society generally, and to save souls by saving society, upon which we all depend. This direction gained strength particularly after the Civil War, and continues in progressive Protestantism today. Evangelicals in the North and the Midwest incorporated the theology of Charles Finney and other more progressive-minded ministers (Wolffe 2007). The goal was to spread the Gospel through collective social interaction, and a unity of body, mind, character, and faith, which taken together constitutes a *vital*, rather than a submissive or aloof, orientation to the world.

Arising from a concern for the working class, many Christians dedicated to the social gospel joined the temperance movement, and supported prohibition legislation. As Gusfield ([1963] 1986) shows, the movement consisted of many diverse interests, including the expected fundamentalists and religious zealots who saw alcohol as the devil's juice and therefore supported prohibition on moral grounds. But the movement also included social gospel advocates who saw alcohol as a destructive social influence, and early feminists who saw how men beat their wives and children after heavy drinking, and thus supported prohibition because of the actual harm to which alcohol contributed. Although many people supported the temperance movement for religious reasons, only some were no-fun zealots; the movement brought modernist and old-school evangelicals together, although temporarily and only on this issue.

Muscular Christianity, evangelicalism generally, and the work ethic coalesced in various preachers, many of whom became political figures as well. One of the most important was Billy Sunday (1862–1935). Born Wilhelm Sontag in Ames, Iowa, to German immigrant farmers, he anglicized his name and eventually became a highly paid professional baseball player with the Boston Beaneaters. Baseball players were known for prodigious drinking, and Sunday was the king. One night in 1887, Sunday staggered out of a bar after a victory against the Chicago White Stockings, and into the Pacific Garden Mission in Chicago. Although he wasn't saved until the next week, Sunday gave up booze and baseball to become a YMCA pastor, then a traveling preacher (Bruns 1992).

By the time Billy Sunday appeared as a preacher around 1900, an American ethic of moral living, personal health, success, virility, and even national loyalty—a combination of stimulating experience and faith—already defined a vital Christian life. Industrial capitalism was securely established by 1900, and it brought a new challenge to personal happiness. As capitalism provided security for more of the population (although labor struggles were bitter and violent), middle-class evangelicals felt a new challenge to their faith—routinization. Like capitalist mass production and the workday, religious observance, once an opportunity to socialize and celebrate, more and more became the tedium of routine.

By the early twentieth century, the original form of muscular Christianity had run its course, such that Sunday's version retained only the emphasis on purity and a simplistic sense of masculine toughness. Gone were the concerns about social justice, sexual satisfaction, and favorable attitudes toward socialism. Sunday was the first representative of an American Christian manhood, one that associated

Christian manhood with servitude to the nation and nationalistic exclusion. Sunday preached against the evils of alcohol and supported the temperance movement, which eventually brought about prohibition. Sunday also preached a masculine identity that he felt was appropriate and necessary for a Christian man, and specifically a working-class man. He hoped his vernacular style would appeal to workers who marched off to the factories every day to work with equipment they didn't own, and to make things they couldn't afford. How could a man be a man when he spends his day shackled to a machine and subservient to the boss's orders? Although he borrowed the name muscular Christianity from the earlier British movement, and related it to physical prowess and accomplishments in sports and a general dedication to success, Sunday advocated at once a passionate display of masculine emotion, as well as submission to higher powers—God and the social order. Although Sunday had been a professional baseball player, he used sports not as an endeavor in which the common man could perfect his manhood, but as a model of moral virtue from which the common man should learn important lessons.

For Sunday, real men of God did not conceal their intensity or downplay their accomplishments with calm reserve. Instead, as one observer described Sunday's movement,

> This was no dainty, sissified, lily-livered piety the crowd was hearing. This was hard-muscled, pickaxed religion, a religion from the gut, tough and resilient. Prayer here was a manly duty; faith was mountain moving, galvanic. There was power in reverence, energy in belief. The tough guys were on the right side. This was no place for weak-kneed, four-flushing boozers and sin-soaked infidels. (Bruns 1992:15–16)

Sunday was the most boisterous of many preachers who joined the Men and Religion Forward movement founded by Harry W. Arnold and Fred B. Smith in 1911. These men felt that religion had lost its passion, and that it lacked a manly sense of virtue and power. Unless evangelical congregations could rediscover what Religion Forward saw as the manliness of Christ, Christianity would continue to lose men to temptation and sin. Sunday prayed that the "Lord save us from off-handed, flabby-cheeked, brittle-boned, weak-kneed, thin-skinned, pliable, plastic, spineless, effeminate, sissified three-karat Christianity" (Sunday [1912] 1992). For the men in Religion Forward, activity, not contemplation, were the marks of a true Christian man.

Like the religious changes that preceded it, Religion Forward both reflected and reacted to larger social change, but unlike the social gospel movement, Religion Forward taught men to look inward, to change their orientation to the world, not to challenge the social reality. Sunday lamented the unsanitary and often dangerous conditions that many workers faced, yet he encouraged them to be "real" men in their hearts and in the eyes of God. For Sunday, real men did not need unions or other crutches.

With the Civil War well in the past, Christian men now faced a society with rapidly developing factions. Urbanization increased alongside industrialization. Farmers who lost their farms moved to the cities for factory jobs, willing to work for low wages, and immigrants poured in from Europe, willing to work for even lower wages. Both groups left their traditions behind with the familiar surroundings of their places of birth as they moved into the squalor of the industrial cities. Despite the emphasis that Sunday and others in Religion Forward devoted to the working men in the factories, few working-class men answered their call.

Notions of ideal manhood developed alongside and under the influence of political and social issues. In modern times, the secular world intertwines so thoroughly that church leaders who so desire must make special efforts to separate their congregations from social issues. As Shibley (1996) has shown, changes in church attendance away from conventional churches toward a kind of emotional revival style are best explained by a reaction to contemporary life. Perceived moral relativism is only one symptom of a much larger cultural ambiguity, in which symbols have multiple and conflicting meanings. As a result, Shibley finds that churches that use a casual style punctuated with emotional outbursts appeal more strongly to younger converts who dislike and distrust formal, routinized, and in general what they see as "old-fashioned" services.

But this type of trend has happened before, as American society shifted from a primarily agrarian, rural economy to a modern and urban industrial economy. As the economy shifted and people moved to the cities, so an identity crisis developed as cultures merged or faded. Muscular Christianity emerged precisely as a reaction to the advances of industrial capitalism and its attendant culture over and against agrarian villages and extended families.

The growing divide between urban and rural populations intensified after the Civil War, and especially during the waves of immigration that followed in the latter half of the nineteenth century. Immigrants to the United States from southern Germany, Poland, Ireland, and Italy increased the ranks of Catholicism in what was a predominantly Protestant nation. Furthermore, they established their own ethnic enclaves in the large cities, with their own language and culture. This culture included, among other things, alcohol. Without wine, beer, whiskey, and scotch, life does not seem to go as well. Far more than alcohol, this cultural infusion of language, history, hope, and religion prompted a nativist backlash, the belief that the United States was and always should be a white, Protestant nation. Even in the North, changing demographics changed attitudes, such that by the late 1800s, following a farming crisis of rapid price drops for agricultural produce that bankrupted many family farms, formerly antislavery sentiment shifted to anti-immigrant sentiment.

And so it was that the temperance movement to ban the sale of alcohol was rural, anti-immigrant, and anti-Catholic. We should note, however, that secular interests joined the movement as well. Socialists saw alcohol as the "opium of the people," in the words of Marx—a means for big business to dull the senses of the working class and keep them docile. Intellectuals such as Jack London condemned alcohol because of his own addiction. Nevertheless, nativist religious sentiments provided the strongest inspiration and greatest number of activists. Prominent temperance leaders included Carrie Nation, William E. "Pussyfoot" Johnson, and Billy Sunday.

Sunday quickly became a champion of the temperance movement, as well as an advocate of muscular Christianity, as we have seen. One of his most popular sermons was the "booze" sermon:

Alcohol is nothing but despicable, traitorous, left-wing sewage . . . a menace whose red flag is dyed with the blood of women and children. It is hell soaked through and through, and the saloon from which the devil's pawns purvey their poison will take the shirt off the back of the shivering man. It will take the coffin from under the dead. It will take the milk from the breast of the poor mother who is the wife of the drinking man. It will take the crust of bread from the hands of the hungry child. It cares for nothing but itself, for dirty profits. It will keep your boys out of college. It will make your daughter a prostitute. It will bury your wife in the potter's field. It will send you to hell. . . . Alcohol withers the corpuscles, rots the tissues of the body, turns the stomach into a vile cesspool and paralyzes nerves. . . . Throw off your slavery! Act you men of God! In the name of your pure mother, in the name of all that is good and noble, fight the ogre before the saloons and their left-wing communist red devils send the husbands and sons of this country home maudlin, brutish, devilish, vomiting, stinking, bear-eyed, bloated-faced drunkards! (quoted in Bruns 1992:167)

Sunday was a fiery, passionate speaker who combined nativist sentiments with conservative patriotic politics. Alcohol was not only evil; it was anti-American. Regarding the content of his sermons and their style, Sunday became the standard for conservative evangelical (born-again) ministers.

Conservative movements constituted only one side of American religion. Just as conservative religion allied itself with conservative and anti-immigrant nativist politics, so the progressive side of religion joined with progressive political movements.

Progressivism

Like the temperance movement and the conservative evangelical movement, the Progressive movement was interdenominational and included secular supporters as well. Also like the conservative version, women played a prominent role. Famous activists include Jane Addams (1860–1935), founder of American social work, and Ida Tarbell (1857–1944), a journalist who exposed the political manipulation that big business exerted, especially Standard Oil. Charlotte Perkins Gilman (1860–1935), now considered to be a founder of feminist social theory, worked for women's suffrage.

Prominent religious leaders included Congregationalist Horace Bushnell and Anglican Frederick W. Robertson. Walter Rauschenbusch perhaps most concisely captured the essence of the religious side of the Progressive Era, the social gospel movement, for which he argued that "Christianity is in its nature revolutionary" and that the kingdom of God "is not a matter of getting individuals to heaven, but of transforming the life on earth into the harmony of heaven." To this end, Rauschenbusch established a mission in Hell's Kitchen, one of the most depressed and violent neighborhoods in New York City. The goal was not to convert people to the Word, but to eliminate poverty (Sweeney 2005). Rauschenbusch joined with socialists and labor leaders to fight capitalist exploitation of workers.

The conservative side of evangelicalism in the form of the prohibition movement effectively disbanded after achieving the Eighteenth Amendment to the Constitution, which banned the manufacture, sale, and transportation (but not possession) of alcohol and ushered in prohibition. The progressive side continued through the 1920s. After the stock market crash of 1929 and the entrenchment of the Great Depression, government agencies under FDR's New Deal took over much of the poverty relief that progressive religious groups formerly endeavored to provide. Moreover, many progressive initiatives, like their conservative counterparts, succeeded, including women's right to vote, public education, and labor and antitrust laws.

American Innovation:
The Democratization of Religion

One of the most significant innovations that American society has contributed to religion is its democratization. Far more than just a technical, analytical concept, this kind of democratization covers belief, practice, lifestyle, and attitudes. Three important factors allowed for democratization in general and religion specifically. First, through quality public education, the vast majority of the public became literate, and for the first time in history, common people could read important documents for themselves, including scripture. Second, the larger context of a free and democratic society certainly plays a role, but these social conditions only create the possibility of expanded religious freedom. Third, the First Amendment to the U.S. Constitution states, "Congress shall make no law respecting an establishment of religion, or prohibiting the free exercise thereof; or abridging the freedom of speech, or of the press; or the right of the people peaceably to assemble, and to petition the government for a redress of grievances." (See Image 2.14.)

In its entirety, the First Amendment freed people from traditional religious obligation, and through free expression and assembly, to create new denominations, and to seek redress from persecution. Furthermore, mass literacy beginning in the nineteenth century allowed common people to read the Bible and theological texts for the first time. This social environment greatly expanded the range of religious possibility. Today, we know these social forces as the democratization of religion (Ahlstrom 1972).

These forces in the United States have produced a wide variety of innovations in Christianity and other faiths. In Europe and elsewhere, most governments still recognize one religion, and often only one version of that one religion, as official. In Saudi Arabia, for example, not only does the government enforce one religion, Islam, but moreover, only one version of it—Wahhabism. This particular version is a type of fundamentalism, which reads sacred texts literally and accepts them as inerrant.

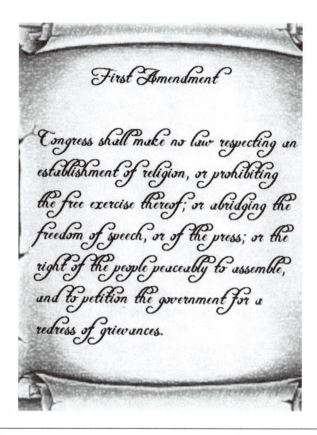

Image 2.14   The First Amendment to the U.S. Constitution

In the United States, fundamentalism coincided with the rise of modern science, and constitutes one of the most clearly American innovations in Christianity. The most famous conflict rages still, or perhaps especially today, over evolution versus creationism (see Table 2.6). Although often promoted as a competing theory, creationism and its variant, intelligent design, are not scientific theories. The belief that scripture reveals the creation of the earth to have occurred approximately 6,000 years ago, which James Ussher (1581–1656) calculated as 4004 BCE, is not in any way compatible with the current scientific theories that the earth is 6–8 billion years old. The related belief that an intelligent designer, namely God, is the only way to explain the apparent sophistication of life, is also not scientific, because it is not in any way testable; it can neither be confirmed nor denied through observable evidence.

Creationism also posits explanations for other questions, such as the diversity of geological formations. For science, topology forms as a result of complex and interactive natural forces, such as wind, rain, erosion, plate tectonics, volcanic activity, glaciation, and other such processes. Creationism explains geological formations as the result of Noah's flood, as told in the book of Genesis.

Table 2.6   Popular Views on the Origin of Humans

Statement	Percentage That Agree
God created human beings pretty much in their present form at one time within the last 10,000 years or so.	45%
Human beings have developed over millions of years from less advanced forms of life, but God guided this process.	37%
Human beings have developed over millions of years from less advanced forms of life, but God had no part in this process.	12%

Source: Gallup Poll, February 19–21, 2005.

The greatest conflict rages over the origin of species, especially the human species. Not only has science proved that the earth is not the center of the solar system, but in 1858, a joint paper published by Charles Darwin and Alfred Russell Wallace argued that the human species, like all others, evolved over time, in response to the changes in the natural environment. This directly contradicts the story of creation in Genesis, for people who read the Bible literally. Fundamentalism arose as a movement to counter the claims of science.

The first public battle of political and social significance concerning this issue is known as the Scopes Monkey Trial of 1925, in which John Scopes, a biology teacher, was tried for teaching evolution at a high school in Tennessee, where evolution was officially banned by the Butler Act. For both sides, Scopes's guilt, which was apparent, was not the issue. Rather, both sought to fight in a public domain over who would control the content of public school curricula—religious leaders or scholars. Ostensibly about science and religion, the trial was also about who should wield power in public education. This aspect still exists today.

Since 1925, science has amassed extensive evidence in support of evolution, not only for the human species, but for many others as well. Yet creationism enjoys strong public support, as recent poll results show.

Although a slight majority (49% to 45%) accept the concept of evolution, the majority also believe that God plays a decisive role, whether they accept evolution or not. Only a small minority accept a purely scientific view. This introduces a difficult question regarding religion and education in a democratic society: To what extent should school course content reflect public opinion, compared to the position of experts?

Fundamentalism in the United States is thus not a new development, but gained its name and most of its doctrine from the *Scofield Reference Bible,* published in 1909 by Cyrus I. Scofield. In this work, Scofield presents an annotated version of the King James Bible that connects contemporary and future events with biblical prophecy. In this process, Scofield develops the essential doctrine of what we now call fundamentalism: biblical inerrancy, belief in miracles, and dispensations. The first point holds that the Bible is word for word complete and correct, and must be read at literal face value, not through higher interpretation. Dispensations refers to the belief that God has ordained specific worldly periods or governances, and will yet ordain a rapture, at which moment the true people of God will ascend into heaven. The unproven and the wicked will remain on earth to face the end times and the battle of Armageddon, the final battle between good and evil.

Although these ideas existed prior to the Scofield Bible, his work suggested scholarly support for popular beliefs, and presented them in writing. As a result of mass education and mass printing, millions have read his book. This focused the resulting fundamentalist movement, which still vies for power at various levels of U.S. society, from national politics to state governments to local school boards. Since 1909, the movement has widened its perspective and now attacks many aspects of modernity, of which science represents the most obvious target. Yet modernism also includes secularism, and an emphasis on reason, rather than religion, as the primary guide to living and government. Modernism acknowledges a pluralistic acceptance of diversity, including religious diversity. As we have seen with prohibition, religion often becomes a cover for other grievances or prejudices, such as the anti-immigrant attitudes of nativists. As we will see in a later chapter, attacks on science and other aspects of modernism are not so much about whether competing religious views are correct about, for example, the origins of humans, but more about power and control.

Democratization of religion allowed common people to develop their own beliefs and to organize new perspectives and denominations, often independently of educated theologians or clergy. The free movement of people in and out of faiths has produced a religious marketplace in which churches vie for membership with no inherent advantage in terms of employment or government that characterizes nearly every other nation past and present. The United States has become in the process a tremendously diverse and religious population. In the absence of compulsion, American religion thrives more vibrantly than in most countries. Contrary to popular assumption, church, mosque, or temple attendance is highest in the more liberal countries, and lowest in the more strictly religious countries that allow only one official faith or one version of that faith. The democratization of religion and the generally free and open culture of the United States without an official state religion produced great diversity within Christianity.

The Twentieth Century

At the end of the nineteenth century, evangelicals in the United States faced more than economic restructuring. The new industrialism brought with it a new emphasis on science that seemed to overturn religious doctrine every day. The Scopes Monkey trial of 1925 was perhaps the most famous confrontation between creationism and evolution, between religious doctrine and modern science.

Moreover, the race issue once again intensified as black people challenged racial beliefs and institutional barriers that had been codified into legal practice in the South (and elsewhere). Literacy tests, special fees, inconvenient polling sites, terrorist violence, and various other means all discouraged or prevented blacks from voting in many areas. Not until the Voting Rights Act of 1965 did blacks finally receive governmental guarantee of the right to vote, yet this was only the beginning, as many counties in the South failed to comply. Southern churches faced a major rift as the civil rights struggle gained momentum. Martin Luther King was an accomplished preacher, and he used scripture to rally people around the cause of civil rights, even as his opposition cited scripture to deny civil rights. King's group, the Southern Christian Leadership Conference, would eventually gather together diverse mainline evangelical denominations, yet retain its original evangelical character.

These two issues—fundamentalism versus modernism and integration versus racial separatism—divided the nation throughout the 1960s. Toward the end of the decade, the Vietnam War became a third major issue that still further separated the forces of progressivism and orthodoxy, and a fourth issue divided churches—the Cold War. Central to all of these issues were themes that religion had addressed since the First and Second Awakenings: human rights (later civil rights), the emancipation of oppressed people, the role of moral choice, the role of emotion and personal experience, and the proper path to salvation. Many churches, parishes, and individuals joined larger social and political alliances, and by the 1970s, any possibility of "American" or "Christian" unification had become all but impossible. Orthodox and reactionary forces sought political power and influence in the 1950s and 1960s, both as a reaction to a perceived aggression against true believers by the federal government (in the form of the Civil Rights Act and a secular scientific curriculum) and as an active means to reestablish a true Christian society (Ammerman 1990:70–71).

To be sure, conservative Christian organizing took up a combination of religious devotion and secular politics amidst the social turmoil after World War II. As the Cold War descended on the United States, so American Protestantism in its orthodox forms confirmed that the Soviet Union, China and the Yellow Menace, and Communist Subversion were all enemies of the true Christian man and his family. The American Council of Christian Churches, led by the Reverend Carl McIntire, joined with Senator Joseph McCarthy, and continued after McCarthy's fall to organize anticommunist groups in local parishes (Wilcox 1992:71). Another notable movement of the period was the Christian Anti-Communist Crusade, founded by Fred Schwartz in 1952. The organization doubled its revenue every year until 1961, and then faded quickly after Barry Goldwater, with whom the Crusade was closely allied, lost the 1964 presidential race (Wilcox 1992:71).

In the political turmoil of the 1960s, the issue of manhood once again appeared. Progressive forces challenged the three pillars that conservative Christian men had based their sense of manhood on for a generation: God, Nation, and (patriarchal) Family. And some held to a fourth pillar: racial superiority. Although by the mid-twentieth century many blacks were evangelicals, racism strongly and absolutely divided congregations.

David Duke was a member of the American Nazi Party in the 1960s, and the Imperial Wizard of the Knights of the Ku Klux Klan in the 1970s. After that, he founded the National Association for the Advancement of White People. In the Louisiana 1990 and 1992 senatorial and gubernatorial races, respectively, Duke insisted that he had put his racist past behind him, that these were "indiscretions of his youth," and ran as a Republican in both races. His Democratic opponent in the 1990 senatorial race was J. Bennet Johnston, a strong supporter of big oil and petrochemicals. Duke rallied a fusion of racism and populism, but lost 53%–44%. In the 1992 gubernatorial race, he faced Edwin Edwards, a multiterm former governor indicted three times for but never convicted of corruption. Edwards won 61%–39%. As a resident of New Orleans at the time, I often saw anti-Duke bumper stickers such as "No Dukes," "Vote for the Crook," and "Elect David Dork: Führer." Duke's support came mostly from rural areas.

We have now reached a point in our discussion where we must turn our attention to social forces beyond the individual culture or nation-state, and toward the forces of globalization. Like anything else today, globalization affects religion in profound ways. Chapter 9 considers globalization in greater detail. For now, let us complete our history of religion in the United States.

Civil Rights and the Vietnam War

Like the official Southern Baptist Convention doctrine of the Civil War period, most Old School and "traditional" evangelical denominations remained silent on the race issue during the civil rights struggle of the 1960s. Likewise, they initially remained silent about the war in Vietnam, and later, when the war became a major public issue after 1966, they still remained silent or even spoke out in support of the war as a stand against the rapacious spread of communism. In contrast, American Baptists (an offshoot of the older Northern Baptists), and many mainline Protestants, sided with the secular left against the Vietnam War (Quinley 1974) and similarly sided with the left on welfare, opposed the death penalty, and joined the call for civil rights (Wald 1987; Wolffe 2007). In my research on the Promise Keepers in 1997 (Lundskow 2002), two of my respondents who were in their 20s in the 1960s commented that they were disappointed that their congregation (both are Southern Baptist) did not speak out in support of Martin Luther King. One man said, "It's a shame we didn't realize at the time how vital his mission was to men of God. It's 30 years later and we are just realizing that."

At the time, many of the fundamentalist congregations viewed Martin Luther King, John F. Kennedy, and of course more radical leaders such as Malcolm X as evidence of a mostly covert anti-Christian alliance. They believed that Kennedy, as a Catholic, was using his position to further the cause in cahoots with militant black leaders who sought not only to seize power, but surrender the United States to communism (Roof and McKinney 1987). As a result, many mainline Protestants viewed fundamentalists as ignorant, uneducated rustics susceptible to the most outlandish stories. More recent history further demonstrates an increasing distrust (and dislike) between divergent evangelical groups. In particular, many Southern Baptist leaders, and the Convention in general, failed to condemn David Duke (see sidebar) in the 1990 senate race and the 1992 gubernatorial race in Louisiana. Moderate evangelicals are also troubled by the close alliance between Pat Robertson, the Christian Coalition, and close ideological affiliation (if not organizational affiliation) with racist groups like the Christian Identity (Noll and Kellstedt 1995). Still more recently, this discomfiture with the religious right and its organizations such as the Family Research Council, Focus on the Family, and various "creation studies" colleges threatens to break apart American churches again, including Catholic and mainline as well as evangelical churches (Greeley and Hout 2006; C. Smith 2002).

By the 1970s, Southern Baptism projected a distinctly fundamentalist religious vision combined with a conservative political agenda, propelled by a core faith of "inerrancy" that the Bible is absolute and without error. Fundamentalists gained control of the Convention in 1969, and the Moral Majority emerged in 1979 as a projection of fundamentalist power in the Convention to carry fundamentalism into politics, where political power could be used to elect favorable candidates and influence policy decisions in accordance with fundamentalist religious beliefs. As memory of the civil rights movement faded and the women's movement in support of the Equal Rights Amendment failed to achieve ratification and the movement fractured into diverse agendas, the country moved to the right as the 1970s ended.

Fundamentalist Resurgence

As a reaction to progressive cultural change, the Moral Majority was founded in June 1979 by Jerry Falwell, Jerry Kennedy, Charles Stanley, Tim LaHaye, and Greg Dixon (Georgianna 1989:26). As officially stated, the Moral Majority sought to "formulate nonpartisan political organization to promote morality in public life and to combat legislation that favored the legalization of immorality" (Falwell 1981:188). Legalized immorality included abortion rights, homosexuality, secular education, and all types of sexual activity outside of (heterosexual) marriage. Jerry Falwell, in particular, quickly gained national media attention and shortly thereafter, the attentive ear of President Ronald Reagan. The Falwell–Reagan program called for, among other things, the basic fundamentalist principles envisioned after the fundamentalists took control of the SBC: education based on creationism and the superiority of Christian culture over non-Christian and non-Western culture, prayer in public schools, enforcement of obscenity and antigay (sodomy) laws, and a legal system based on biblical justice (Georgianna 1989:40). The last point about biblical justice usually meant "an eye for an eye," that the death penalty should be used more readily and for a wider range of crimes, including rape, and the (it was hoped, soon-to-be outlawed) practice of abortion.

The rise of the Moral Majority followed from severe discontent among conservative Southern Baptists, which also found an audience among conservatives in other evangelical denominations. These conservatives used long-standing church networks to organize a political constituency on a local and regional basis that quickly unified into a national constituency around their political champion. However, Ronald Reagan in 1980 was not the first such champion.

Rather, Jimmy Carter first rallied conservative and fundamentalist evangelicals in 1976. Carter often spoke of his Southern Baptist convictions, and this resonated with both liberal and conservative Baptists. As his presidency continued, conservatives realized that, although Carter often expressed his views in religious terms and professed his personal commitment to faith, and was a Southern farmer as opposed to a Northern politician, many of his policies, especially regarding abortion, demonstrated a liberal tendency that displeased them. In 1980, most evangelicals turned to Reagan, whom they saw as a far more credible supporter of (conservative) Christian beliefs (even though he was Catholic).

The Reagan presidency, in close cooperation with Falwell and other fundamentalist leaders, postured the United States as a sacred and holy country and as the spiritual enemy of the "Evil Empire," the Soviet Union. The Moral Majority published a report that condemned the Soviet Union for "breaking up families according to a Communist division of labor" and "torturing and killing people for practicing their religious beliefs" (Snowball 1991:155). The report further condemned Europe and more or less the rest of the world as a threatening place filled with godless and immoral people who would strike down any true Christian who would not join their wicked ways. In this way, the Moral Majority merely perpetuated familiar Christian themes, most of which were descended from the antimodernist doctrine of the 1920s, the anti-integration doctrine that opposed racial integration in the South (the roots of which reach back to the Civil War), and white ethnic regionalism. Thus, the Moral Majority was really the last campaign in a series to construct and then attack what it saw as insidious communism, feminism, integration, and secularism.

Moral Majority membership rose dramatically between 1979 and 1984, then plummeted toward the end of 1984 after Reagan won reelection, and dropped off still more in 1985. The Moral Majority officially ended at 10 AM on January 6, 1986, with an announcement from Jerry Falwell that they had accomplished all their goals (Snowball 1991:151). Two years later, George H. W. Bush succeeded Reagan as president, but by no means did he retain cohesive conservative support, especially among religious conservatives. Jerry Falwell officially and publicly resigned from political life in 1989, as he said to devote his time and energy full-time to his ministry in Lynchburg, Virginia. He would return to public life in 2001, just after the September 11 terrorist attacks.

In retrospect, the direct influence of the Christian right within American evangelicalism was relatively short, although in that time, from 1979–1988, the movement readjusted the parameters of debate on social issues from a pluralistic center to a religious-right position, which includes an attack on welfare recipients, whom the right characterizes as lazy and therefore moral violators. Films of the period reflected a new conservative culture, such as *An Officer and a Gentleman,* in which the son of a hard-drinking enlisted man becomes a navy officer and rescues a working-class girl from the depressing and hopeless routine of factory life. In another film that extols the revival of a militaristic spirit as well as the virtues of conservative politics and "might makes right," Tom Cruise portrays a navy pilot in *Top Gun* who, based solely on his will to achieve, defeats a nameless, faceless enemy. Conservative entrepreneurs such as Donald Trump became highly regarded authorities on social problems, and career political commentators like William Bennett in his book for children, *The Book of Virtues,* provided an authoritative moral voice of abstinence, deferral of pleasure, the virtues of hard work without complaining, and unquestioning respect for authority.

As the eighties came to a close, evangelicals witnessed the end of the Soviet Union, which in earlier decades and for Ronald Reagan had been a primary "godless" enemy, and thus a useful rallying cry for the religious right. At the same time, middle-class evangelicals found themselves the victims of corporate downsizing, with early retirements, diminished opportunities for promotion, and decreasing autonomy. The disappearance of the Moral Majority left a void within conservative evangelicalism, and what they saw as two major social problems remained—abortion and homosexuality.

Religion After the Cold War

The Moral Majority included both a cultural component and a political component. Organizations like the Promise Keepers inherited the cultural aspect, and the Christian Coalition the political aspect. In 1989, just 3 years after the Moral Majority disbanded, Pat Robertson founded the Christian Coalition, and less than a year later in 1990, Bill McCartney founded the Promise Keepers. Both claimed the void in evangelical national organization left by the dissolution of the Moral Majority. However, the Christian Coalition from the beginning organized as a political action group. The Promise Keepers, in contrast, organized officially as a men's ministry, and one that specifically and carefully avoided political affiliation or involvement. With substantially different points of focus, the two groups appealed to different interests and constituencies. A common error, often found in the mass media, assumes that all evangelicals are alike and hold more or less interchangeable beliefs. As the preceding historical narrative and current research shows (see Greeley and Hout 2006; C. Smith 2002), evangelicalism and conservative Christianity are a diverse contingent, full of disagreement and differing goals.

With the fall of the Soviet Union and the end of the Cold War, muscular Christianity would find renewed vigor, carried to the public this time by the former football coach Bill McCartney and his Promise Keepers organization. Even before the dissolution of the Soviet Union and the collapse of the Berlin Wall, Smart (1987:224) correctly predicted a clash of theological counterpoints in American Protestantism as the Cold War thawed. Moreover, economic restructuring in the 1980s and 1990s meant decreasing promotion and autonomy for many middle-level executives and other professionals. As Peter Berger (1992) argues, the fall of the Soviet Union has opened the door to a more pluralistic value system, as a kind of marketplace of identities, values, beliefs, and lifestyles in the absence of an overriding national identity premised on the destruction of an archenemy. In the same way, Linda Kintz (1997) sees the contemporary evangelical movement as a product in a marketplace, and one that modifies itself to suit changing preferences. I would go one step further, to suggest that the new forms of evangelical churches proffer highly general notions of Christian theology and leave the details to each individual. Although the United States never held anything close to a value consensus during the Cold War, the presence of a perceived omnipresent threat relegated struggles for civil rights, urban improvement, women's rights, education, environmental concerns, and nearly everything other than military production to a second level or lower priority.

With the end of the Cold War, pluralism has become "not merely a fact of the external social environment" (P. Berger 1992:67) in that there are indeed people of different beliefs and lifestyles out there, but it "also impinges on human consciousness . . . not just as something external . . . but as an internal reality, a set of options present in the mind" (P. Berger 1992:67). Even though a person might reject certain options, they still reside in the mind because they reside in social life and culture. With many diverse religious beliefs from the very beginning in the Thirteen Colonies (Loewen 1995), American Protestantism has always faced challenges not only from denominational conflict, but also from ongoing social change. As we have seen, muscular Christianity changed as history unfolded to reflect broad economic and cultural change. As religion and society changed, so too did masculine identity.

Protestantism in the United States has always involved a struggle for identity. After the First and Second Great Awakenings, slavery, anti-Catholicism, anti-immigrant platforms, and various attitudes toward poverty and war have created wide rifts in American evangelicalism. At times, evangelicals have generally stood with progressive forces that sought to expand democratic culture and politics, sought to alleviate poverty, and stood against war and oppression. At other times, evangelicals have sided with the rich and powerful, with conservative interests who resisted any changes to slave society, and more recently, even minimal aid to the poor. Contrary to popular belief, evangelicals have been not only conservative, but also progressive in their collective history. Religious devotion inspired abolitionists to fight slavery, sometimes at great risk to themselves. Religious ideals were also a motivating force behind anti-Catholic nativism, racism, and aggressive policies against Irish and Italian immigrants.

The Promise Keepers and other revival movements at the end of the twentieth century were neither the first nor the only evangelical organizations to answer the call for identity, certainty, and unity in a rapidly changing economic, political, and cultural environment. Yet the PK was the most successful (see sidebar) and represented a progressive change in an otherwise strongly conservative evangelical culture (Bartkowski 2004; Lundskow 2002). Far from crude patriarchs who seek to ruthlessly oppress women, the appeal of the Promise Keepers resides in their poetic and symbolically complex articulation of Christian manhood. As Bartkowski describes, the Promise Keepers are "reducible to neither logical reasoning . . . nor emotional release" (p. 58), but instead follow the principle of loose essentialism, which posits "predispositional differences between men and women while portraying these differences as malleable and unfolding. . . . [It] gives men license to change over the life course and to find points of overlap with women—such that men are capable of discovering their 'feminine side'" (p. 61). Seeking a

---

The Promise Keepers (PK) began on March 20, 1990, while the University of Colorado football coach Bill McCartney, known generally as *Coach* among PK enthusiasts, and his friend Dave Wardell, the University of Colorado athletic director, were on a 3-hour car ride to attend a meeting of the Fellowship for Christian Athletes. The first conference, as the mass rallies are called, happened in July of 1991 in the University of Colorado basketball arena, with 4,200 men in attendance. By 1992, they attracted 52,000 to a conference at Folsom Field, the football stadium at the University of Colorado. By 1996, they drew 1.1 million men to stadiums around the United States, 800,000 in 1997, and an additional 700,000–1 million that year to the mall in Washington, D.C., for their special event—Stand in the Gap. As of this writing (2008), the PK conferences draw typically 35,000–50,000 a year. The revivalist nature of the PK likely explains their rapid rise and decline, in that revival inherently inspires an intensity that is difficult to maintain.

As a Christian ministry, the Promise Keepers follow a long history of revival in the United States, beginning with the First and Second Great Awakenings in the eighteenth and nineteenth centuries, the progressive period of the early twentieth century, and the contemporary evangelical (born again) movement. From the beginning, the PK has maintained a minimal administration, and it carries little cash over from one conference season to the next. The Promise Keepers are not a membership organization, but an interfaith dialogue group that coordinates events open to all men. The conferences include music, drama, humor, multimedia presentations, and sermons.

Nondenominational and nonpolitical, the Promise Keepers seek to energize and unite men of all faiths and races through the Seven Promises. The Seven Promises emphasize devotion to Jesus; obedience to scripture and God's call to service; vital relationships with men through friendship networks; and purity in thought, word, and deed. Moreover, the PK asks men to actively participate in their family and in their church, and to reach beyond racial and denominational barriers in order to work toward biblical unity.

balance between traditional gender roles and masculine identity codes, the PK poeticizes male gender identity, and through this symbolic and often lofty language, the PK men feel empowered and permitted to explore a more dynamic and far less strict male identity and marriage relationship than previously found in American evangelicalism.

This 1990s' approach differs considerably from the 1970s' approach that the Moral Majority pursued. The Moral Majority emerged as a call to arms against domestic moral permissiveness and pluralism. The movement rejected rationalism, scientific and secular education, and lifestyle diversity in favor of a unified fundamentalist interpretation of scripture (Smart 1987:225). They created a bifurcation between decent and moral people of God who work hard within the established economic order, and other types, namely the immoral people who promote hedonism and individualism to the point of "anything goes" godlessness. Thus, American fundamentalism is not completely antimodern as conventional wisdom maintains (see, for example, Watson 1997:13). Rather, the movement rejects only the progressive social achievements of modernism, but still embraces the modern capitalist system and its attendant social order—that is, its class and power structure.

A further difference is that the Promise Keepers and others in the 1990s advocated what they term "racial reconciliation." Men of all races must become united under God, and not just in tolerance of each other, but in active appreciation. Second, whereas the Christian Coalition and its recent successors name many enemies—welfare cheats, liberals, gays, the media elite, the intellectual elite, abortionists, and many others—the Promise Keepers focus on self-improvement and devotion to a just life in Jesus. Their enemy exists internally, as weaknesses in individual men and all men; the PK teaches that men should work toward moral perfection, but also recognize that they will always fall short. Overall, the PK seeks unity among all "good" men, regardless of faith, color, creed, or class. Although perhaps naïve, it reflects Bill McCartney's nonconspiratorial and generally positive identity based on exaltation of the in-group, rather than condemnation of some supposed enemy.

In contrast, Christian Coalition founder Pat Robertson, in his book *The New World Order,* argues that an international commission has for decades manipulated governments and the world economy to enrich itself. When the time is right, this commission will overthrow the United States (as it is the last stronghold of Christianity) and establish the New World Order under the Antichrist (Robertson 1991). This notion of the impending emergence of the Antichrist has been a common theme in American fundamentalism since 1900 (Fuller 1995; Morone 2003), and Robertson is a theological descendent of M. L. Moody and Billy Sunday, who routinized imagery and doctrine of omnipresent and absolute evil, and tied the struggle against it to monetary donations and a mass ministry.

Not only does Robertson name the enemies cited above, but he also posits an enemy of international scale that pulls the strings from behind the scenes. He refers to them as "the Rothschilds" and "the Germans" and "European capital." Many scholars interpret these phrases, which many people before Robertson have used, such as Father Coughlin in the 1930s, as euphemisms for "Jews" (Conn 1992; Heilbrunn 1995). Furthermore, some argue that Robertson betrays not only an anti-Semitic disposition (Boston 1996:127–130), but also, like Coughlin, a belief that Jews run an international conspiracy that seeks to enslave the world (Lind 1995; Worrell 2005). Robertson's vision seems on the verge of hallucination. In a more rational tone, Pat Buchanan (2007) articulates a similar message. The enemies have somewhat different names, but the overall point remains that hidden enemies from without and from within seek to undermine our sovereignty and destroy our way of life.

Attack on supposed evil enemies has taken increasingly active forms. Although antigay sentiment has long simmered in American social culture, the extent of grassroots activism among evangelical women on this issue is perhaps surprising. Where the Moral Majority and mainline evangelical groups have not been able to mobilize women as political activists (nor have they necessarily tried), the issue of gay rights unexpectedly found conservative women ready, willing, and able to fight an antigay crusade (Diamond 1998; Herman 1997). Phyllis Schlafly and Anita Bryant of the 1960s and 1970s, long-standing antigay activists, found new company in the late 1980s with first-time activists operating at a local level, and others such as Beverly LaHaye and Jeannette Beeson who began at a local level and soon founded national organizations, the most prominent of which is Concerned Women for America.

Collectively, the Christian right contributed to significant political victories at a local and state level in the 1992 elections with a constituency that voted a pre-dictable bloc (Rozell and Wilcox 1995), although they were less successful at the national level (until the election of George W. Bush in 2000). Christian conserva-tives who contributed important votes to Ronald Reagan in 1980 and 1984 did not rally behind George H. W. Bush in 1992 or Bob Dole in 1996. Apparently, Christian-right supporters did not acclaim either candidate as a true representative of their values. This suggests that simply claiming the appropriate values or promising to uphold moral decency was inadequate, as neither appeared authentic. Fundamentalists have always emphasized personal moral righteousness (Obenhaus 1963:54), and therefore believers must recognize some quality they accept as an indicator of moral purity incarnate, which is to say, a charismatic supernatural attribute, as they did with Reagan (Lundskow 1998).

Pat Robertson and the Christian Coalition retrieved the support of conservative and fundamentalist evangelicals, especially of Southern religious conservatives, the stronghold of Jerry Falwell. However, the unyielding political and social agenda has remained in Christian-conservative sentiment, if not in overt rhetoric. The Moral Majority and its successor, the Christian Coalition, carried a perceived "redneck" stigma, partly through affiliation with televangelists and partly because most funda-mentalists are lower-middle-class and poor rural whites (Smidt et al. 1996). Moreover, fundamentalism, which often correlates with conservative political agen-das and a preference for charismatic candidates (Guth et al. 1996b), further decreased the legitimacy of the conservative religious political movement with better educated middle-class evangelicals, mainline Protestants, and of course Catholics and seculars.

Thus, the religious right carried two significant stigmas—associations with low socioeconomic status and excessively aggressive moral platforms—that rendered its political movements at least distasteful, if not objectionable, to middle-class, educated Christians and those who considered themselves "more aware" and sophisticated than lower-class fundamentalists who preferred simple dogmatic clarity. As comparative studies show, evangelical Christians were divided on major issues at the end of the 1980s. For example, the progressive Just Life organization backed pro-life candidates, but only if they "also took a liberal stance on social justice issues, rejected the death-penalty, and held a strong anti-militarism stance" (Guth et al. 1996a:67). This differed significantly from the highly conservative Focus on the Family, founded and led by James Dobson, and the militant Operation Rescue, headed by Randall Terry. Other allied groups include Americans for the Republic, who work closely with the Christian Coalition on both antiabortion and pro–death penalty campaigns, and the Concerned Women for America, who support antiabortion campaigns as well as initiatives to legislate a return to traditional domestic lifestyles for women (Guth et al. 1996a) and legislation that denies gay rights. All of these groups adhere strictly to antiabortion, pro–death penalty, antiwelfare platforms.

In contrast, the antiabortion group Just Life also opposed the death penalty, and called for reduced military spending and reduced U.S. military involvement worldwide (Guth et al. 1996a). This brought it into association with groups like Bread for the World, founded by Lutheran pastor Arthur Simon, the brother of the late U.S. senator Paul Simon. The organization sought to feed the poor, both at home and abroad, and called for Washington to divert military spending toward social concerns. Bread for the World called for the eventual dissolution of political boundaries, which they see as dividing the natural and divine unity of all people, in sharp contrast to conservative evangelical groups that advocate definite boundaries between Christian and non-Christian countries. Bread for the World and many other mainline and liberal religious groups draw their constituency and donations from the middle- to upper-middle class in the Northeast and Midwest, whereas the conservative Christian groups draw their support primarily from the South and the West (Guth et al. 1996a:68).

Many middle-class Protestants, even those with fundamentalist religious beliefs, dislike the perceived backwoods character of fundamentalist activist organizations, as well as the often affiliated charismatic and "blind faith" beliefs. Bread for the World and Just Life have a preponderance of professionals in education, law, medicine, and the clergy with a significant concentration in major metropolitan areas. Importantly, however, women constitute the majority of membership in the conservative groups and, like Beverly LaHaye, hold leadership positions in Christian-right activist groups that address women's issues (Guth et al. 1996a).

Although Jerry Falwell sought a diverse coalition of conservatives, regardless of religious denomination, the Moral Majority remained almost totally white, with all-white leadership (Wilcox 1992:41), and like Focus on the Family today, with all-male leadership (Alexander-Moegerle 1997). Not all evangelicals support a conservative agenda generally, even if they agree on some issues, such as abortion. Many liberal evangelical congregations were active in Democrat George McGovern's presidential campaign in 1972 (Wilcox 1989), and many are outspoken liberal feminists (Wilcox and Cook 1989). In closer retrospect, it becomes clear that a particular branch of evangelicals, the Southern Baptist Convention, ruled the Moral Majority and set its agenda, which mobilized conservative and fundamentalist evangelicals on the political front.

Despite the fact that Bill Clinton has always been a devout Southern Baptist, as president (1992–2000) he closed the White House door to the religious right. However, far-right evangelicals continued to organize, especially at the local level (M. Taylor 2005). During the 1990s, the religious right built a voting machine that returned many favorable politicians to office, and handed the U.S. Senate to the Republicans. Notable religious-right senators include Rick Santorum (Pennsylvania—lost in 2006), Sam Brownback (Kansas), and James Inhofe and Don Nickles, both of Oklahoma. All favor Christian Dominionism, a movement we will examine in greater detail in a later chapter. With the arrival of George W. Bush as president, a resurgent religious right once again commanded political clout nationally and shaped educational policy, in particular locally. On April 24, 2005, several local, state, and national politicians, including Senate Majority Leader Bill Frist (Tennessee), joined the religious-right leadership for Justice Sunday. This nationwide multimedia event proclaimed the latest political agenda and denounced the usual litany of "liberal" causes that allegedly undermine the United States, including abortion, supposed "coddling" of terrorists, gay rights, and criticism of President Bush (Wilcox and Larson 2006).

Religion Today and in the Near Future

The noted Harvard author Diana Eck (2002) claims that the United States is the most religiously diverse nation in the world. As sociologists of religion Christian Smith and Melinda Denton (2005) retort, "that simply is not true" (p. 32). In fact, the percentages of religious affiliation have changed little in roughly the last 100 years, with only minor percentages of non-Christian faith (see Figure 2.1). If we break it down further, we see that Protestants hold a clear majority, with Catholics a strong second, and all others present at very minimal levels (see Figure 2.2). We should note that nonbelievers constitute a sizeable minority, larger than many religious denominations. Also, youth (ages 13–25) differ somewhat from their parents in their religious affiliation, but not greatly.

Despite their general predominance, we should also note that Protestants are a very diverse group, as shown in the graph of Protestant denominations in Figure 2.3.

Although Baptists constitute the single largest group, they are far from a majority, and 33 denominations altogether register on the survey of Protestant denominations. We could break down the Baptists still further into Southern, Northern, and American congregations.

Today, most conservative congregations draw characteristics from Southern Baptism and what Shibley (1996) calls Southern-style evangelicalism. American and Northern congregations hold comparatively more liberal social and political views. However, regardless of their specific affiliation, one characteristic distinguishes Baptism from other Protestant sects, from the earliest days of the seventeenth century to the present. The Baptists believe that the Word of God is a living spirit and power, and that it exists "not as a written document, but as the force of the Holy Spirit working in daily life, which speaks directly to any individual who is

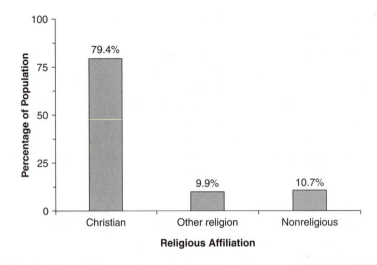

Figure 2.1   Religious Affiliation in the United States

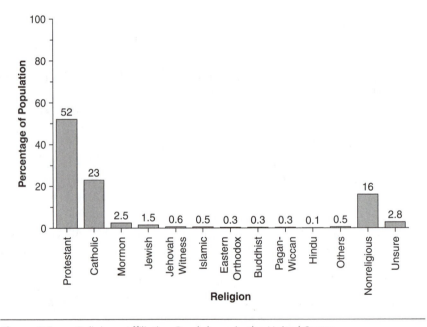

Figure 2.2   Religious Affiliation Breakdown in the United States

willing to hear" (Weber [1905] 1998:146). Although Baptism shares attributes with other sects, such as the calling with Calvinism (now more commonly known as Presbyterianism), they are unique to exclaim the continuance of revelation, that God works in each person individually and differently. Anyone can receive this holy grace, provided he or she is willing to be born again. The Baptists "carried out the most radical devaluation of all sacraments" (Weber [1905] 1998:147), compared to the other Protestants. In this way, Baptists far more than the others emphasized the daily renewal of one's commitment to Christ, since the person could not rely on the

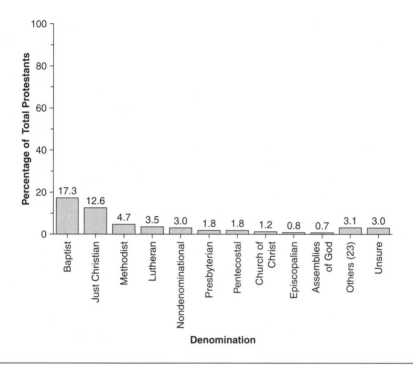

Figure 2.3   Protestant Denominations in the United States

church as an institution nor on the supernatural power of sacraments and ritual. This emphasis on personal salvation and personal testimony in the form of public declarations of piety greatly shapes the practice of religion in the United States today, across many Protestant and other denominations. The Bible remains a vital source of inspiration, but this inspiration arises from personal feeling, not necessarily from accurate knowledge of scriptural content or context. Still, fundamentalists have moderated their views somewhat regarding their orientation to modern society overall, and try to "steer a middle course" as they see it, "neither withdrawing from the world nor becoming fully absorbed in it" (Carroll and Roof 1993:15).

In many parts of the world, religion still seems to be a vital social force that continues to shape society and world events. In the Middle East, in the United States, and elsewhere, religion remains a dynamic and sometimes controversial force that sometimes progressively confronts social problems, at other times serves the interests of social control and domination, and at other times creates conflict and sometimes violence. Christianity, Islam, Judaism, Hinduism, and other religions, both in the United States and around the world, seem as central to social life and personal identity as ever.

Or are they? Scholars in sociology and other disciplines argue this very point. On one side, we find the dynamic model, in which scholars such as Stephen Prothero and Amanda Porterfield argue that the numerous and ongoing changes in religion, especially in free and democratic countries like the United States, demonstrate the dynamic power of religion to change with the times, yet powerfully remain central to social life. On the other side, we find the secularization model, in which sociologists like Steve Bruce, Douglas Porpora, and Thomas Frank contend that overt and often public declarations of faith demonstrate the diminishing power of religion rather than its intensification. The more strongly people assert religion and faith into politics, the greater the desperation and weaker foundation it betrays. They need the power of the state to legitimate and enforce their beliefs.

The dynamic model argues that religion has always changed as history unfolds, and it always will. As we have seen, religion must remain relevant to social life, to the actual lived experiences of real people in the real world. The more detached it becomes, the more purely idealistic, the less it regulates and eventually, the less it really means to people in their daily lives. In short, it becomes merely an exercise on Sunday or some other holy day. The secularization model predicts that the forces of modernism continue to relegate religion to the background, to an increasingly recreational or luxury role—either way, it becomes optional. Let us consider these two postulates in greater detail, because this debate, which connects to debates in theory about religion, shapes much of sociological discourse about religion today.

In *American Jesus,* Stephen Prothero (2003) traces the development of Jesus from ancient prophet all the way to the many different images of Jesus today. Prothero sees Jesus as a national icon in the United States, which different groups shape according to their own particular preferences. He is the hero of the oppressed for some, the ultimate radical and populist who always places humanity over business and profit, people over politics and guns. For others, he is the judge, jury, and executioner who rewards the righteous and punishes the wicked with swift and perfect justice. Moreover, Jesus no longer resides exclusively in the Christian domain, but influences and is in turn influenced by Islam, Buddhism, and other Eastern religions both in the United States, and as far away as China, Korea, and Southeast Asia. Jesus has thus become a global icon. As Prothero argues, he is the bodhisattva, the enlightened one to Buddhists, the eternal truth to Taoists, and an incarnation of Lord Krishna to Hindus. Jesus has become Proteus, the ancient Greek god who had no form of his own, but could assume any form (Prothero 2003:290–291). In the dynamic view, Jesus exemplifies the eternal power of religion to transform in conjunction with social change, and thus continue to influence human thought and action. Jesus and religion remain very much alive and powerful.

In contrast, the secularization model contends that as modernism advances, as it disenchants the world as Max Weber described, it reduces religion to images without meaning, ritual without content, and services without relevance. Religion loses it ability to integrate people into a community with a clear moral identity, and as Weber argued in the previous chapter, religion gives way to rationality; there is no room for gods anymore. As Steve Bruce (2002) argues, the fact that Jesus and other religious leaders and their institutional doctrines become increasingly malleable demonstrates their fading power. Religious doctrine that once imposed moral control over people, and in the process set boundaries on behavior and also instilled a collective identity, reduces to ever more individualized and personal moral codes. Eventually, even individual moral codes diminish into individual preferences and personal feelings, at which point religion holds no power over the individual at all, either to enforce moral regulation or maintain collective identity.

The most rapidly growing denominations today, the charismatic sects, allow the greatest degree of personalization and thus, for Bruce (1990), most strongly prove the secularization thesis, that "as the West becomes more secular, those people who wish to remain religious will increasingly be found embracing the highly individualistic and consumerist spirituality" (p. 178). Like good consumers, people will see their religion in terms of "value" and "choice" and personal satisfaction. Akin to Bruce's position, Thomas Frank (2000) argues that such illusions neglect the fact that "the logic of business is coercion, monopoly, and the destruction of the weak, not 'choice' or 'service' or universal affluence" (p. 87). The business model seems incompatible, in fact anathema, to the institutional role that religion has historically played—that of building community. As Durkheim argued, and as Frank emphasizes, business seeks profit, power, and domination, not community. If the business model does take over religion, Frank argues that the leadership will demand "the simple faith of childhood," just as corporations ask for consumer trust without accountability, and once in power, the masters will "counsel the rest of us to become as little children" (p. 87) who happily and naïvely accept whatever they want us to consume.

As we will see in a later chapter, the business model has already risen prominently among the charismatic denominations who determine religious authenticity based on the power of individual emotional commitment, as perceived by the individual. The more strongly a person believes his or her feelings about Jesus, God, and whatever else are authentic, the more intensely the person feels that they are real, then the more real they are in fact. In this context, doctrine disappears entirely, but then, so does community. McBain (1997) calls this "inverted narcissism"—the individual celebrates the self as the one and only member of the community; each person lives in a community of one, and all these individuals collect themselves together for Sunday services.

As C. Smith and Denton (2005) conclude in their large-scale empirical study of American youth today, the vast majority find meaning in religion, and the majority say that their faith is important or very important. However, Smith and Denton also conclude that youth conceive of religion as "moralistic therapeutic deism," a personal self-help device that provides moral guidance and some concept of God, but only on an individual basis. This is in contrast to earlier times, when religion, as part of tradition, regulated individual behavior by socializing the individual into a community, and as a member of a community, the person acquired collective responsibilities that at the same time suppressed excessive individualism. As Durkheim recognized a century ago, religion has long since lost this power, and in its place, we learn from Smith and Denton that

> American youth, like American adults, are nearly without exception profoundly individualistic, instinctively presuming autonomous, individual self-direction to be a universal human norm and life goal. Thoroughgoing is not a contested orthodoxy for teenagers. It is an invisible and pervasive doxa, that is, an unrecognized, unquestioned, invisible premise or presupposition. (p. 143)

This extreme and total individualism effects religion as much as anything else, and it drives the assumptions and logic of moralistic therapeutic deism. One's notion of and relationship to God are purely individualistic, and furthermore, God serves the individual, who is free to call upon God whenever desired and free to send God away whenever convenient. From this perspective, a person may call upon God, for example, to make that person more attractive to a romantic interest, but then be free to send God away while making out with that romantic object. The individual may call upon God for therapeutic comfort when the romantic relationship collapses, but then send God away when engaged in underage drinking. Far from an all-powerful being who shapes all of existence, God becomes whatever particular thing the individual wants, on a completely personal and idiosyncratic level.

The analysis shows that youth today perceive God according to the following profile:

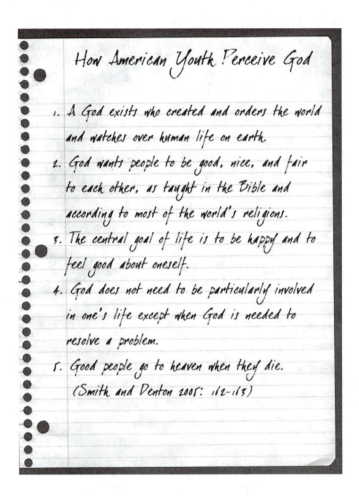

How American Youth Perceive God

1. A God exists who created and orders the world and watches over human life on earth.

2. God wants people to be good, nice, and fair to each other, as taught in the Bible and according to most of the world's religions.

3. The central goal of life is to be happy and to feel good about oneself.

4. God does not need to be particularly involved in one's life except when God is needed to resolve a problem.

5. Good people go to heaven when they die.
(Smith and Denton 2005: 162–163)

Notice that nowhere does this necessitate community membership or commitment of any kind, and that instead it reinforces total individualism. This corresponds to the consumerist economic system in which we live, in that people may choose what to believe according to personal need, and may freely accept or reject whatever level of commitment and self-sacrifice they find convenient, including no group commitment at all. The social bonds have snapped.

The secularization model also predicts that, rather than devolving into a great multitude of individual interpretations and feelings, some people will embrace a kind of opposite—fanaticism. Rather than an intensely personal religion, they embrace an intensely external religion that demands absolute submission. In this case, the individual ceases to exist and becomes a mouthpiece that spouts dogmatic rhetoric. Either way—absolute individualism or absolute submission—religion becomes an abstraction, either hopelessly large and impersonal, or absurdly small and only personal. Religion no longer mediates between the individual and society. It no longer meaningfully integrates the individual with a larger purpose, whether we adhere to society or a sense of the divine, but rather validates meaning at the individual level—but only for the individual. What is true for me becomes irrelevant for someone else. Or it serves the interests of some person or group in power, and leaves nothing for the negated individual.

As Bell ([1976] 1996) predicted, the death of religion is the death of society; we live as a collection of disparate individuals, not as meaningfully integrated social actors. Have we reached the great nullity that Weber predicted?

Yet C. Smith and Denton's (2005) recent empirical analysis of religion among 14- to 25-year-olds in the United States also shows that religious devotion does saliently affect actual behavior. Youth tend to drink alcohol and do drugs less, engage less in risky sexual behavior, study more, and generally develop greater psychological health the more devoutly they subscribe to a religion, whether liberal or conservative (pp. 222–227). As the authors interpret their findings, using both statistical and ethnographic methods, they discover that peers exert the greatest influence on youth, and that if peers are religious, any given 13- to 25-year-old will conform to one's peer's religious expectations. If this means no alcohol, then the person won't drink. However, if the peers drink and blow off school and engage in promiscuous sex, then any given youth will behave similarly, once again according to peer expectations. Their study suggests that religion today has minimal independent power to shape attitudes and behavior. It requires peer reinforcement and integration with school, and especially with leisure activities.

We may also consider a third perspective, one that acknowledges both the dynamic and the secularization perspectives. Sociologist Douglas Porpora (2001) argues that people will always require religion as the primary means of understanding the supernatural and the transcendent. Whether individual or social, people need to have meaning in life. Of course, meaning becomes strongest when shared. We require other people to recognize and in the process validate our individual existence. How sure can any one person be of his or her beliefs over time if no one else accepts those beliefs as valid? Porpora, as a sociologist, argues that we require social validation, even if the reference group is relatively small. But also as a sociologist, he inquires about social meaning and the loss of collectively shared moral space. That is, there must be a moral space in which all people hold and respect in others the same basic rights and responsibilities, which is necessary for a pluralistic, free, and democratic society. Moral meaning underlies all issues of justice in society.

To meaningfully guide thought and action, religion must mediate between the individual and society. It must make us into a certain type of person with certain

---

Dominant Trends in Religion Today

1. Third Awakening Theory—People are reviving established religion with new feeling.

2. Secularization Model—Religion has become a consumer commodity devoid of meaning.

3. Revolutionary Model—People are creating new and meaningful forms of religion with both oppressive and emancipatory potential.

Each of these theories has evidence for and against it. Which is correct? Perhaps it is too early to tell. They all use the same evidence, but using different theories, they draw different conclusions. This issue requires more empirical research to answer, and it is possible that all three are correct because all three are occurring simultaneously. If so, it would mean that society is becoming trifurcated—breaking apart in three competing directions. This would likely increase social conflict unless one supersedes the others or some fourth way emerges to reconcile them.

---

boundaries and privileges both for ourselves and for others, but it must also allow the development of individuality. Moral values must mediate, not dictate. As Porpora (2001) expresses the concept, "it is one thing to believe in God" at an individual level, which the overwhelming majority of people in the world do, but "it is another thing for that belief to be operative in our lives" (pp. 96–97). In order to be operative, it must connect, not in some practical or convenient way, but in a cosmic way. As Porpora sees it, being, meaning, and morality all coincide, and what we most require is a moral vision located in being, in the fact that we exist, and that we exist in an impossibly expansive universe. If science has revealed that the earth is 6–8 billion years old, and that the universe contains billions of galaxies, each with billions of stars and planets, then how do we fit into such vast and timeless proportions? How can our little ideas and petty accomplishments mean anything in that context? Certainly, if science can show us the truth of our littleness surrounded by such bigness, does it not therefore call forth religion ever more strongly?

We live today in a social context where the issues of our existence matter less than sports, entertainment, and of course, money. Commercial capitalism dominates our world, defines it, and excludes all else that interferes with the accumulation of profit. If Big Brother in Orwell's *1984* was a totalitarian government that sought to eliminate all passions except the love of Big Brother, then today Big Brother has become the corporation. As Porpora (2001) writes,

> as long as we are free to buy as much as we want of whatever we want at the lowest price, we are happy. We cease to notice that the real choices—what is made by whom, where, and how—are no longer up to us. Seduced into civic mindlessness, we accept what we are served. McWorld is a reign in which we are encouraged to identify our very souls with market segments. (p. 309)

Clearly, Porpora makes a materialist argument, and asserts that economic interests dominate even our spiritual lives, that even our souls become a commodity. What has become of human dignity if we devote our mind, body, and soul to the market? The Sanskrit concept of *avidya,* used throughout Hindu texts, refers to a concern with superficialities that prevents us from seeing life in a deeper and more meaningful way. Porpora (2001) thus argues that "McWorld is a social order that thrives on avidya. . . . McWorld produces surplus avidya" (p. 309). Porpora, who in the end blends sociology with religious sentiment, concludes that if we believe that we have a higher purpose, that we exist to achieve something worthy of God, then religion must break free of McWorld, which debases everything it assimilates and degrades human dignity and higher potential. For Porpora, the authentic religions of the future will be those that challenge consumerism.

Overall, then, scholars see three dominant trends in religion today. One is the Third Awakening, the idea that a new and profound revival is under way within established religion. A second view is the secularization model, that the apparent awakening is really a last dying gasp, as religion passes into the realm of commodities and superficial fashion with no particular hold over daily life, and no power to integrate people meaningfully into society. The third we might call a revolutionary model, in which religion actively seeks to overthrow oppressive social conditions in favor of deeper and more meaningful human relationships, fueled by a belief in a higher purpose. Let us also face the other side of the revolutionary thesis, that new, more brutally oppressive forms of religion will appear. In the chapters that follow, we will focus mostly on the present day, with the goal to accumulate sufficient knowledge and theoretical perspective to evaluate the veracity of these three perspectives. As students, you may arrive at your own analytical conclusions about religion today, a fourth perspective.

CHAPTER **3**

Superstition
and the Supernatural

Introduction

Not everything that involves divine, transcendent, or otherworldly forces properly falls into the category of religion. However, sociologists and other scholars often study these groups, beliefs, and movements as part of the study of religion. Indeed, it depends greatly on how we define the material.

In Chapter 1, we considered a conceptualization of religion as compared to spirituality. As mentioned, sociologists often do not make this distinction unless there is substantive reason to do so. Since we are interested in social relationships, whether in the form of large and international organizations or small and local friendship groups, the doctrine matters less than observable behavior or measured attitudes. One finds social relations within spiritual movements as well as in religious institutions. Even in the case of Neopaganism, which has the least centralized organizational structure and no particular scripture, and other religions such as Hinduism, Buddhism, and Islam, which have no formal organizational structure and various scriptural texts that vary by sect, all nevertheless are part of or relate to an identifiable institutional and cultural tradition. Although spirituality posits the individual at the center compared to religion, which posits the institution, both connect the individual to a larger community and sense of purpose. In both cases, the system of belief and practice legitimates one's sense of self and one's life. Religion and spirituality are thus both social phenomena, although in different ways.

Even an almost purely spiritual movement like Neopaganism, for example, exists through local, regional, and national organizations, even if they have no formal connection to each other, or don't even know that particular organizations exist. Solitary practitioners peruse the Internet for a sense of social solidarity (Beall 2005) and discover a larger community through festivals, niche retail stores, and friendship networks (Pike 2001, 2004). From a sociological perspective, such connections unite otherwise independent individuals and groups as part of a larger movement, culture, or institution. Remember, sociology does not just study social phenomena; it also organizes them conceptually and actively draws conclusions. These conclusions create an order to our understanding of reality, and in this way, sociologists are not neutral observers. We seek to create order using scientific research methods and conceptualization. A lack of formal organization does not automatically diminish a movement's vitality or authenticity. Through concepts, sociologists often see the world differently from the people they study.

Therefore, some beliefs and practices that the enthusiasts themselves may regard as religious (or spiritual), we as sociologists should more accurately regard as something else, and that something else is the subject of this chapter. For those things that do not fit conceptually into religion as an institution or spirituality as a popularly constructed culture, we will use the more general concept of the supernatural, or as some would say, superstition. Since the latter usually conveys negative connotations, let us clearly conceptualize it.

Some people would simply say that religion and superstition are the same thing. A closely related view would be that the one true religion is ordained by the divine, while all others are false claims, that is, superstition (see Table 3.1). The first view contrasts religion/superstition with reason and rationality. Superstition and religion rely on sentiment and irrationality to create explanations for observable occurrences and therefore constitute a form of ignorance—see, for example, Hitchens (2007) for biting wit and Dawkins (2008) for bitter venom on the subject. Some people who take this perspective are, by necessity, atheists (from *a,* meaning without, and *theos,* meaning God); they reject the notion of God. Some others are instead agnostic (without *gnosis*—higher knowledge); they have no knowledge or

Table 3.1   Religion and Superstition: Conceptual Clarification

Religion	*Superstition*
Shared Beliefs and Values—Social recognition validates faith and morality	**Idiosyncratic Beliefs and Values**—Meaningful only to the individual; does not connect the individual to a larger community
Shared Way of Life—Socially shared values (morals) shape behavior	**Personal Life Choices**—Independent of social standards or expectations
Shared Meaning—Beliefs and lifestyle mitigate existential uncertainty	**Personal Meaning**—Existential uncertainty remains because beliefs and lifestyle change according to personal vicissitude and perspective; lacks social consistency and stability
Social Identity—Individual as part of social reality	**Solitary Identity**—Individual stands alone
Life Validation—Legitimates engagement with the world	**Life Negation**—Legitimates hiding from the world

belief about the divine. As we have seen thus far, religion involves far more than just a set of beliefs about God, which by themselves may be in fact very complex and extremely erudite. Like nearly anything, religion can also take a simplistic and ignorant form, but this is not inherent nor is it typical, as the vast amount of religious scholarship and theology from around the world attests. The implication that superstition as a form of ignorance equates with religion is misleading and does not really make sense conceptually. The second view, that superstition refers to anything that is not the believer's one true and correct faith, is an argument beyond sociology. Science cannot discern the ultimate truth about the divine, but we can discern the observable social truths of religion.

It should be readily apparent to the serious student of religion, whether a believer in a god(s) or not, that religion and superstition are really two very different phenomena. In simplest sociological terms, both seek to address the existential questions that Peter Berger identified in Chapter 1. The difference is that religion creates community and connects the individual to that community; superstition does not. Its beliefs and way of life, no matter how sophisticated, are entirely personal. The debate over religion versus superstition is far from new—it goes back to ancient times.

Superstition

Let us go back to ancient times and explore a conceptualization of superstition that offers both conceptual clarity and scholarly utility. For this, we go back centuries to one of the greatest scholars of the ancient world, and indeed one of the greatest of all time—Plutarch (Mestrius Plutarchus, 46–127 CE).

Born in Chaeronea in the Greek province of Boetia in central Greece, Plutarch inherited considerable wealth (his full name means "Mestrius the rich"), which enabled him to travel much of the ancient Greco-Roman world. Plutarch studied at the greatest libraries throughout the Mediterranean, and he wrote extensively on a variety of topics. His work shows considerable literary quality, and his histories provide a detailed narrative of events as well as keenly analytical portraits of famous ancient personages. In addition to his fully researched and referenced histories, Plutarch wrote a number of essays on topics as wide-ranging as friendship, politics, love (of various types), travel, and of course, religion. His biographers, both in his time and later, portray him as a very intelligent, careful scholar, but also as a very engaging person of friendly disposition. Using his money to full benefit, he studied with the greatest minds of his time, and he also cultivated a very noble and sophisticated but never arrogant disposition.

Moreover, he was a very devoutly religious person, and was initiated into the secret mysteries of the Temple of Apollo in Delphi, one of the greatest religious centers of the ancient Mediterranean. As the senior of two priests, he was responsible for facilitating the auguries made by the Pythia (or High Python Priestess) of the Oracle. This position conferred great social status and influence. Correspondingly, he maintained a very active social life and produced a vast body of written work. His *Parallel Lives* pairs one famous Greek and one famous Roman, in order to examine the similarities and strengths of Greek and Roman culture as well as the failings of both. In other words, his works are not pure histories and definitely not simply praises for famous people, but rather, they are critically insightful and analytical works that use a comparative method.

In his essay "On Superstition," Plutarch provides us with a very useful and meaningful differentiation of religion compared to superstition, one which resonates with contemporary scholars. As Durkheim argues, religion celebrates community and shared meaning. Not only does religion maintain order, but it also inspires people to a higher order, both in terms of understanding and in actual living. Important things like truth and justice are never perfect, but they can be better tomorrow than they are today. Religion reassures us that such higher purposes are in fact important; whether it be the polytheism of Plutarch or the monotheisms that dominate today, the divine inspires us to improvement.

For Plutarch, superstition is not religion at all, but its negation. Citing Heraclitus, Plutarch ([c. 100 CE] 2002) argues that

> people awake enjoy a world in common . . . but the superstitious man enjoys no world in common with the rest of mankind; for neither when awake does he use his intelligence, nor when asleep is he freed from his agitation, but his reasoning power is sunk in dreams, his fears ever wakeful, and there is no escape or removal. (p. 463)

Plutarch mentions several despots, all of whom inflicted harsh judgment and severe restrictions on life, but none of whom enjoyed the absolute control over people as does superstition. With superstition, compared to the human despot, "there is no escape, no running away, no chance to revolt (Plutarch [c. 100 CE] 2002:465). With religion, the gods provide knowledge and the intelligence to discern truth from falsehood, virtue from depravity. As Plutarch states, the religious person "looks to find reason in himself and in his surroundings." Religion thus enables a person to live actively and meaningfully. It connects the individual to other people and to the larger world. In contrast, superstition disables a person. Social conditions and events that we might understand through observation and insight become unfathomable. As Plutarch writes, "in the estimation of the superstitious man, every indisposition of his body, loss of property, deaths of children, or mishaps and failures in public are classed as afflictions of God or attacks of an evil spirit" (p. 475) rather than the outcome of one's own actions or forces in society. We will see examples of both misclassifications, that people who embrace superstition embrace a kind of magic and mysticism. It reduces people to the haphazard whims of unknowable forces.

As a result, superstitious people fear every moment and every event, no matter how apparently momentary and trivial. They interpret everything as a sign, as a portent of changing fortunes, usually negative. Whereas the religious person understands the gods as powerful yet nurturing, firm yet forgiving, the superstitious person sees them as "rash, vengeful, cruel, and easily offended; as a result, the superstitious man is bound to hate and fear the gods . . . and yet, though he dreads them, he worships them" (Plutarch [c. 100 CE] 2002:489). Fear forces the superstitious person to comply: "The atheist thinks there are no gods; the superstitious man wishes there were none, but believes in them against his will" (p. 491). In sociological terms, religion inspires a person to understand, to strive toward improvement in all parts of life in which a person can have an impact. Superstition isolates the individual and causes a person to tremble in fear of the gods and of the world, all of which appear as overwhelmingly mysterious and threatening.

Plutarch's point is imperative for understanding the power of superstition compared to religion. The religious person loves God; the superstitious person fears God. The superstitious person hates the uncertainty of signs and portents, and all the meaningless rituals, magic charms (like a rabbit's foot), spells, gestures (such as knocking on wood), and the petty beliefs (that, for example, breaking a mirror brings 7 years of bad luck). They are annoying and petty and endless, and of little effect, but necessary for the superstitious person. Driven by fear, the superstitious person believes in God (or the gods) not for active improvement, "but because he is afraid not to believe" (Plutarch [c. 100 CE] 2002:491). Consequently, the fearful superstitious person runs amok, always on guard against transgressions large and small, but always uncertain as to outcome. Without the social integration that religion provides, the superstitious person never faces the vicissitudes of life, but constantly runs away from problems, large and small, real and imagined. The superstitious individual stands alone, powerless, ignorant, and afraid.

In contrast, the religious person knows that, whatever may happen in life, there is divine purpose involved and further, that faith connects people and provides the hope that we can know, we can understand, and we can work toward something better. The devout stand together. Plutarch's stance is strongly sociological—that religion and superstition are issues of the degree and type of social integration, not primarily of the content of beliefs.

In the sections that follow, we will see how this conceptualization applies to events in different times and places, and how superstition contrasts with religion. As always, we will not judge the value of one belief compared to others, but rather attempt to assess the outcome of different types of belief—both religious and superstitious—in social circumstances.

Sparta and Athens

Among the ancient Greek city-states, Sparta stood alone, with a social order and way of life that differed starkly from the others. Although we may think fondly of the Spartans for their valiant stand against the Persians at the battle of Thermopylae in 380 BCE, the full story of the Spartans is considerably less honorable. At Thermopylae, 300 Spartans, and other Greek allies, namely, 700 Thespians and 400 Thebans, stood against the Persian army, some 180,000–250,000 strong. The Greeks were cut down to the last man. However, they held out for 3 days, and this allowed the Athenian navy to move into position and obliterate the Persian fleet at sea. Dispossessed of supplies, the Persian army could not fight effectively against the Greek land army, which forced the Persian King Xerxes to withdraw from Greece.

Other than this shining moment of unity among the Greek city-states, Sparta otherwise was most incompatible with Thebes, Corinth, Athens, and the others. In

Spartans: Reality Versus Hollywood

The recent movie *300*, based on the battle of Thermopylae, is factually wrong at nearly every point. Indeed, the only historical accuracy seems to be the number of Spartans present.

As discussed in the main text, the Spartans were basically Greek-speaking barbarians. While true that the other Greek soldiers, generally known as *hoplites,* were usually not full-time warriors, they were nevertheless well-trained and often experienced in battle. Unlike the Spartans, who relied on the brutal oppression of the *helots* (collective term for local non-Spartans stripped of all rights) to produce food and perform manual labor, soldiers from the other Greek city-states lived as farmers or skilled workers who performed their own labor and provided their own support. In peacetime, they farmed the land, but skilled workers also quarried stone, built roads and aqueducts, and sometimes wrote literature and philosophy. Socrates, for example, served as a hoplite in three major campaigns, and the famous Athenian general and politician Alcibiades (450–404 BCE) writes in his *Symposium* that Socrates exhibited great bravery and saved his life at the battle of Potidaea.

The movie depicts the Persians as horrible savages. It portrays King Xerxes as a bizarre, apparently hermaphroditic pervert with an insatiable lust to dominate and destroy. His entourage and army include mutants and other depraved maniacs like himself. In reality, Xerxes, like all Eastern despots, maintained control through a complex arrangement of patronage and alliances—necessary preconditions to raise such a massive army. His personal manner would be cool and composed, his appearance traditional and dignified. This would include close-cropped hair and a long but highly stylized beard, which symbolized his authority and civilized sense of law and justice.

Athens, where democracy flourished, as well as art, sculpture, architecture, engineering, literature, commerce, and philosophy, Sparta was little more than an armed camp. It consisted mostly of tents and primitive wooden buildings—large huts that exhibited no style, engineering expertise, or artistic renderings. Far from a democracy, Spartans was a despotic kingdom that ruled over and ruthlessly exploited its conquered neighbors, Laconia and Messenia. These areas provided slave labor and free food for the Spartan military elite. Collectively, these enslaved people were known as helots.

At birth, the ruling Spartan elders examined every child. Anyone found to have obvious defects, or who appeared weak in any way, was immediately cast off the cliff known as the Apothetae. Male children grew up with constant physical exercises until the age of 13, when they were sent naked without possessions into the countryside, to survive on their own using any means possible. This included theft and murder. If caught, they would be severely flogged, not for committing theft or murder, but because they were caught. This coming-of-age ritual for males also required that they kill one helot male, and violently rape one helot female. This would harden them for battle and teach them to show no mercy toward their enemies.

Furthermore, about 8,000 Spartan elites oppressed about 250,000 helot slaves. The Spartans maintained control by terrorizing the helots, both in Spartan coming-of-age rituals and in the yearly ritual murder of random helots, perpetrated by the highly secretive *krypteia*, an elite fraternity based on ritualistic murder. All warrior males learned to live without comfort or luxury, and to engage tirelessly in physical training and skill of arms. Except on special occasions, their food consisted of gruel, made from some sort of grain, and roasted meat, but only from religious sacrifices.

As for females, they were judged solely on the basis of their sexual attractiveness. Spartan warrior males shared everything in common and renounced all private possessions, including women as wives. Instead, any woman must have sex with any male warrior who desired her.

The Spartans were also devout, as Plutarch conceptualizes it—devoutly superstitious. Illiterate, violent, brutal, and cruel, hostile to the arts and philosophy, the Spartans did not seek to understand the gods; they feared them. They adhered rigidly to their sacred rituals, of which there were many, and which must be performed at particular sacred sites in Sparta at the exact appointed time. Any mistake of place or delay of time would anger the gods and invite their wrath. In part due to the ongoing possibility of a helot uprising, the Spartans never ventured outside their homeland in the southern corner of Greece. Strict adherence to sacred ritual dictated events for the Spartans, which left very few days available for fighting or other activities. Consequently, they could not travel far, nor engage in protracted wars. They performed the sacred rituals as tradition dictated. Just as their hierarchical society maintained itself through fear, so the Spartan elite submitted to superstitious tradition out of fear.

In Athens, life was very different. With a vibrant philosophical tradition and democratic government, Athens thrived on public discourse, art, theater, and commerce. Athenian and other merchants from as far as China traded throughout Europe and Asia, and they filled the streets of Athens with all manner of goods and exotica. Silk and other fabrics, rare spices, animals, fruits, pottery, jewelry, and anything else that could be bought and sold passed through the *Agora,* or marketplace. The people of Athens indulged in culinary delights, and they passionately embraced the mysteries of excellent wine, music, and poetry. Philosophers conferred in the streets and in the schools, and artists and playwrights sold their skills to numerous patrons and public venues. Life in Athens was prosperous, diverse, and democratic. The other city-states were similar, but smaller.

Likewise, religion in Athens reflected the structure and values of the society. Priests tended to the rites of the various gods, and all citizens worshipped a patron deity at home. Working within the highly advanced philosophical tradition, Athenians sought ever higher and more sophisticated understanding of the gods and the nature of existence. Socrates (470–399 BCE), whom Plato (427–347 BCE) represented in writing, argued that only one true god existed, and Aristotle (384–322 BCE), Plato's student, developed an early scientific perspective. Although sometimes empirically inaccurate, he reasoned that thought and observable phenomenon must be brought in accordance. In other words, theory must fit the data. This included knowledge of the gods. Whether through Plato's idealism or Aristotle's materialism, the Athenians strived for higher understanding and a morally superior way of life.

The beliefs and practices of Athenians fulfill Plutarch's criteria for religion, compared to Spartans, whose practices constitute superstition. The Athenians devoted time and energy not only to worshipping the gods, but just as importantly, to understanding the gods and in the process, understanding human potential as well. The Spartans only feared their gods, and surrendered utterly to their power, especially their whims. Since the Spartans had no clear understanding of the gods, the gods thus could only appear as whimsical—sometimes beneficent, sometimes cruel, but never intelligible. Where the Spartans could feel only fear, the Athenians found inspiration for ever-greater achievement. As their understanding grew, so their society improved, and their gods became greater to reflect the advance of society. In contrast, fear imprisoned the Spartans and stagnated their culture.

The Virgin Mary in a Small German Village

In 1876, three young girls from a small Prussian village named Marpingen were out picking berries, when a woman dressed in all white approached and identified herself as "The Immaculately Conceived." By itself, this was not unusual. Over the centuries, many people in central Europe had reported contact from Mary and less frequently from Jesus. More generally, many people believed that ghosts walked the earth, clad in all white, and mostly female. Furthermore, many people in Germany and France believed that supernatural powers inhabited certain places, rocks, rivers, trees, and other natural elements. For example, Lourdes, France, was already a well-established site of miracles and Catholic pilgrimage. In 1858, the Virgin Mary appeared to a 14-year-old girl named Bernadette Soubirous (now St. Bernadette) in the remote Grotto of Massabielle. A statue of Mary was erected at the site in 1864. Soon, the previous chapel structure was replaced with a pilgrimage basilica. Bernadette Soubirous entered the Monastery of Nevers in 1866, and she died in 1879. She was canonized and became Saint Bernadette in 1933. Since that time, Lourdes has remained both a popular religious pilgrimage destination, not only for Catholics but people of many religions, as well as a secular tourist attraction.

Before Lourdes, the less famous Rocamadour, a commune in southwestern France, became an official Catholic holy site in 1005 CE, recognized in a bull (document of the Catholic Church) by Pope Pascal II. The preserved body of a male was found buried on the site, whom the Church later dubbed Saint Amadour. Like other such sites, Rocamadour is known for appearances of the Virgin Mary and healing miracles for the faithful, who have pilgrimaged to Rocamadour even before 1105 (Weibel 2005). For both Rocamadour and Lourdes, local belief and common pilgrimage established the sites as holy before and independently of official recognition.

Yet from the start, Marpingen was quite different. Following our usual sociological perspective, we should note the date. In 1876, the leading politicians in Prussia and the other German states fought for control of the emerging German national state. The aristocratic Otto von Bismarck had recently unified Germany, in 1871, under a combination of monarchy and socialism, but the exact power relations were far from settled. This fairly unusual political alliance allowed the old noble class to retain considerable power with support from the urban working class and

---

Rocamadour: The Virgin Mary Versus the Monkeys

(Deena Weibel, 2005)

In addition to visions of the Virgin Mary and miraculous healing, Rocamadour, France, also harbors a large troop of Barbary Macaques, an endangered monkey from northern Africa. Introduced in 1974, the monkeys are now a major tourist attraction. Alongside the monkeys, tourists can also visit the mechanical toy museum, and a large community of honeybees who supply honey for sale or prepared in cakes, cookies, and confectionary. Interestingly, the tourists and pilgrims remain mostly separate groups. Sometimes, people invent their own connections, and imagine, for example, that the bees are holy and the honey, rather than the sacred shrine, performs the healing miracles. Most of the 1.5 million visitors come to Rocamadour for the medieval atmosphere and to feed the monkeys, whom many imagine are somehow sacred. Most learn that the site is also a sacred shrine to the Virgin Mary after they arrive. This free association between the secular and religious approach now attracts mostly New Age pilgrims, not traditional Catholics.

the industrialists, over and against the parliamentarians and the Catholic parties, many of whom favored unification with Catholic Austria rather than Protestant Prussia. As a strict pragmatist, Bismarck regarded religion only as a tool, not as an important end in itself. Similarly, his socialist allies favored a secular state. Consequently, modern Germany emerged as a secular nation, yet with long and strong religious traditions in both Catholicism and Protestantism.

The economic and political success of the capitalists and the working class meant the demise of the landed gentry and the peasants, both economic decline and drastic changes in lifestyle. A process common throughout Europe, in the case of Germany the transition to modernism occurred as a top-down revolution. The ruling landed *Junkers* managed to assimilate the emerging capitalist class to produce a combination of parliamentary and imperial government that preserved hereditary noble privilege yet also promoted modern industrialization. Basically, two elite groups, the feudal nobility and the modern capitalists, united. In contrast, Britain and especially France entered the modern era through violent revolution as middle-class merchants and other small businesses overthrew the nobility (Moore [1966] 1993; Skocpol 1979). Either way, the rural villages that most people had inhabited for generations were no longer viable. As agriculture consolidated, the peasants became increasingly impoverished and forced into the cities. This process of urbanization has occurred and occurs today wherever modern capitalism develops. As we have seen elsewhere, social disruption produces religious disruption. The more desperate social disruption becomes, the more radical religious disruption will be. Marpingen follows the sociological prediction.

Regarding Marpingen, David Blackbourn (1993) concludes, "the movement of itinerant workers . . . brought contact with a much larger world, even if that contact was not always happy. If we interrogate the cliché of the remote apparition site, we find that they were not so remote after all, but had been at least partially penetrated by the forces of change" (p. 363). Thus, the cliché that apparitions (whether the Virgin Mary or Elvis) occur in remote places to illiterate rubes is degrading and overly simplistic. These places are in fact not remote, as in isolated, but rather recently drawn into contact with a much larger, more complex, and often very different world.

Blackbourn (1993) draws an important distinction that we should add to Plutarch, that "their problem was not that they were isolated, but that they were marginal. That is what fuelled the sense of being overshadowed by neighbors who were richer or more powerful" (p. 363). The world was changing, and life no longer seemed centered in the close-knit village. Even worse, the village seemed to lack any importance whatsoever. Poor, uneducated, ignored by a rapidly advancing nation and economy, the outside world penetrated places like Marpingen just enough to wreck the traditional economy and expropriate and exploit its land and people, but had not penetrated enough to offer social mobility. Blackbourn documents many such cases, demonstrating that apparitions of the Marpingen sort, where unremarkable people receive remarkable supernatural visitations, occurred overwhelmingly in small villages undergoing rapid transition from traditional to modern ways of life and livelihood. This transition destroyed the village's social networks.

Peasants sought work in far-off and often dangerous settings, such as coal mines and factories, which dispersed once close-knit populations around the country.

Those who remained, typically women of poor health or other attributes considered unattractive for marriage, faced the bleakest prospects. In the case of Soubirous in Lourdes, she suffered from what was likely tuberculosis, was the daughter of a bankrupt miller imprisoned for theft, and was regularly mistreated by a vicious foster mother. Similarly, Margaretha Kunz, Katharina Hubertus, and Susanna Leist, the Marpingen visionaries, were all from families with absent fathers and brothers, and mothers and sisters reduced to demeaning labor. Whether through death or far-off jobs, the men were often gone for long periods, and the women, once proud matrons of the household, were forced into maid services or in many cases, prostitution.

Blackbourn (1993) thus discerns another extremely important conceptual point. The problem is not primarily a decline in monetary fortunes, because visionaries almost always come from poor backgrounds, or in the case of nineteenth-century Europe, from peasant villages where livelihood depended on harvests and community production of clothes, tools, and so on. The standard of living was low, but stable and reliable. The peasants never had expectations of advanced education or manufactured luxuries, but they did expect a traditional level of status and respect in the community, and the stability of the often harsh and limited but certain way of life tradition provided.

Thus, Blackbourn (1993)—and Moore ([1966] 1993) and Skocpol (1979)— contend that material decline is only significant if it produces changes in lifestyle and especially, status decline. Material prosperity comes and goes but is always relatively marginal. Status is all-important, the living embodiment of tradition. This change disrupts established social relations, including religion, and thus provokes a superstitious rather than religious response. When material changes also produce changes in status and life expectations, especially the annihilation of the accustomed life course—when the observable world has failed—people are much more likely to rely on superstitious solutions.

As the community of Marpingen and then broader Germany came to accept the visions as valid, the girls and their families enjoyed a dramatic status elevation, since God and the Virgin Mary had apparently chosen them for a very special purpose. However, the status success could only occur with social recognition. As we have seen, status depends on how others see you, not on how you see yourself. It is likely that family members and others in the village assisted the girls in clarifying their experience, given that they were only 8 years old when it occurred. They could not have sustained such a vision without adult assistance. Similarly, the family could not enjoy status elevation without recognition from the village, nor the village without broader Germany.

Unfortunately, this broader status elevation and the potential for political influence it represents marked Marpingen as a target for the ruling monarchy–socialist alliance still in the process of power consolidation. Rural Catholic visionaries, whether intentionally or not, lent support to the opposing parties—especially in Bavaria, the single most populous state, which favored unification with Catholic Austria. Blackbourn (1993) records that the vast majority of pilgrims who accepted the vision as legitimate were tradespeople and former rural peasants. Pilgrims almost never included the professional classes and urban wage workers (p. 368). With Bismarck and his allies intent on creating a strong centralized government, fully committed to modernism, Marpingen represented everything they opposed, both politically and culturally—"backwardness, superstition, disorder, the power of the priest, and the rule of the ignorant mob" (p. 371). Whereas the Catholic Church officially recognized Lourdes as a place of legitimate visions, it never recognized Marpingen, even at the height if its popularity. The central government had no choice but to suppress the Marpingen visionaries and the movement they inspired, a movement that called for a return to small-town ways, strong controls on industry, and the repartition of Germany into the numerous small states, each with its own independent noble family and loyal peasant villages. The government suppressed the movement on the grounds that it disturbed the peace and threatened the stability of the nation. By the 1960s, Marpingen had once again become an unremarkable little town of marginal interest and little opportunity.

For a while at least, in the village of Marpingen, we can say that a religious movement formed. Soon after, however, the movement devolved into superstition as a result of interference and suppression from the central German government, and the fact that the increasingly urban population related less and less to the visions of rural girls promoting rural values. Their vision became local and eventually, personal and superstitious—the beliefs of local girls (and their parents) and an expression of their personal fear of the future.

Such visions confer status only to the extent other people accept the claim that God has chosen a person or group for some special recognition or mission. Such selection confers the highest status of all (among the believers). Empirical cases testify that public recognition is essential, that without the sense of legitimacy that public acknowledgment confers, the vision even becomes a liability and further lowers the visionaries' status. They are not recognized as visionaries, but rather, as ignorant simpletons or even mentally disturbed lunatics.

Witches and the Devil in Salem

As we saw in the previous chapter, witches in various forms such as goddess-worshippers, wise women, herbalists, seers, and midwives, as well as modern (neo)pagans, have been and are real. They existed over the centuries, and many claim today that the old traditions never totally died, although we may never know exactly what they were like in premodern times. In this section, we will consider an example of superstitious witchcraft, or more exactly, the transformation of superstition from imagination into action. The people of Salem, Massachusetts, like their counterparts in Europe, did not see witches as nature-based healers and wise women, but rather, as evil hags, as vile creatures in league with Satan who devour infants, spoil crops, and fornicate with animals and demons. Such evildoers, the *maleficarii*, did not actually exist, and therein lies the interest in Salem and the larger witchcraze in Europe.

That people could torture and execute other people for purely imaginary transgressions fascinates us still. The events in Salem (1692–1694) occurred at the end of

Witches and the Supernatural in the Bible

Exodus 22 covers various laws. Among them are

(line 18) Do not allow a sorceress to live.

Also see Deuteronomy 18:

(lines 10–14) Let no one be found among you who sacrifices his son or daughter in the fire, who practices divination or sorcery, interprets omens, engages in witchcraft, or casts spells, or who is a medium or spiritist or who consults the dead. Anyone who does these things is detestable to the Lord, and because of these detestable practices the Lord your God will drive out those nations before you. You must be blameless before the Lord your God.

The nations you will dispossess listen to those who practice sorcery or divination. But as for you, the Lord your God has not permitted you to do so. (New International Version)

However, in 1 Samuel 28, King Saul, in great distress at the sight of the massive Philistine army, decides to break his own law that does not permit a sorceress to live. Desperate, he consults with one, the Sorceress of Endor:

(lines 4–15) The Philistines assembled and came and set up camp at Shunem, while Saul gathered all the Israelites and set up camp at Gilboa. When Saul saw the Philistine army, he was afraid; terror filled his heart. He inquired of the Lord, but the Lord did not answer him by dreams or Urim or prophets. Saul then said to his attendants, "Find me a woman who is a medium, so I may go and inquire of her."

"There is one in Endor," they said.

So Saul disguised himself, putting on other clothes, and at night he and two men went to the woman. "Consult a spirit for me," he said, "and bring up for me the one I name."

But the woman said to him, "Surely you know what Saul has done. He has cut off the mediums and spiritists from the land. Why have you set a trap for my life to bring about my death?"

Saul swore to her by the Lord, "As surely as the Lord lives, you will not be punished for this."

(Continued)

the witch-burning period, and slightly outside the time frame in Europe (1450–1650). Prior to the 1400s, witch persecutions were rare and scattered. Sustained witch hunts did not occur at any particular time or place. Although King Saul in the Bible, for example, bans all contact with those who do magic, he nevertheless consults with the Sorceress of Endor when the need for information becomes desperate (see sidebar). Yet the Sorceress of Endor and her ilk in ancient times occupied a very different social status from the witches of the burning times. In Europe between 1450 and 1650, and Salem in 1692, the witch became a superstitious vision of pure evil, and thus became a supernatural monster far removed from the wise women and seers of ancient times.

Although the learned men of Salem (and in Europe) used the Bible as justification for their persecution and often execution of witches, the Bible never actually mentions witches. Rather, it refers to *mekhashshepheh*, best translated as sorceress (Exodus 22:18 and 1 Samuel 28:4–15). The masculine equivalent, mentioned in Deuteronomy 18:10, is *mekhashshepheth*, or sorcerer (both are Persian words). Such people practiced various forms of magic, which from a modern perspective blended folk medicine, mysticism, traditional knowledge, and experimental methods in animal husbandry, herbology, astronomy, and astrology. Their practices resemble the functions of the priestess at the Temple of Apollo in Delphi, and other temples throughout the Mediterranean in ancient times. The term witch actually derives from the Anglo-Saxon *wicca* (masculine) and *wicce* (feminine), which according to both Julius Caesar and Tacitus, refer to some sort of seer or prophet (see Caesar [c. 50 BCE] 2006 and Tacitus [c. 98 CE] 1999).

With an uncertain basis in scripture, no basis in history, and no factual evidence, the witch trials and executions in Salem (and Europe) proceeded on the basis of invented superstition. Just as the sense of special divine selection can empower people to deliver God-given prophesy to inspire a declining community as we saw in Marpingen, it can also work negatively. In Salem, the visions of evil that a few girls claimed to have had involving other members of the community were just as superstitious. However, in the case of Marpingen, the visions became a rallying cry to preserve a dying community and its traditional way of life. In the case of Salem, active imaginations worked not to preserve traditional society, but to escape oppressive social customs. As the persecutions progressed, acts committed in the name of God and Christianity were actually negations of Christianity—an abandonment of established social relations in favor of the personal pronouncements of a group of girls. It negated their faith, heightened their fear, and ultimately brought ruin to the community.

Salem, Massachusetts, was really two communities. The larger was Salem Town, a prosperous seaport on the coast. Salem Village (now the town of Danvers) was an inland community that depended on farming in the generally poor and rocky New England soil. The settlers here had never achieved much beyond subsistence, and in some years suffered from scarcity. Although both the town and the village were Puritan, Salem Town was far more open and relaxed. In contrast, Salem Village adhered

(Continued)

Then the woman asked, "Whom shall I bring up for you?"

"Bring up Samuel," he said.

When the woman saw Samuel, she cried out at the top of her voice and said to Saul, "Why have you deceived me? You are Saul!"

The king said to her, "Don't be afraid. What do you see?"

The woman said, "I see a spirit coming up out of the ground."

"What does he look like?" he asked.

"An old man wearing a robe is coming up," she said.

Then Saul knew it was Samuel, and he bowed down and prostrated himself with his face to the ground.

Samuel said to Saul, "Why have you disturbed me by bringing me up?"

"I am in great distress," Saul said. "The Philistines are fighting against me, and God has turned away from me. He no longer answers me, either by prophets or by dreams. So I have called on you to tell me what to do." (New International Version)

strictly to Calvinist-Puritan doctrine, which produced a very suspicious population constantly on guard against evil influences and moral violations. In strict Puritan doctrine, much as Weber described in an earlier chapter, people worked hard with few moments of respite, avoided all pleasures, and struggled for salvation in a religion that allowed no degree of certainty or forgiveness. In short, people worked very hard and without much joy for a most uncertain outcome. From here on in this book, "Salem" shall refer to Salem Village unless otherwise indicated. This discussion also applies only to the initial accusations in Salem Village that arose from popular fears and superstitions. It does not apply generally to later accusations that clearly became increasingly political calculations.

Of all the places where witch hunts occurred in New England, Salem ranks among the most famous. The events in Salem occurred after Europe had mostly abandoned witch hunting and embraced the Enlightenment. In 1692, eight young women—teenagers—complained that a witch inflicted torments on them, which included nightmares, convulsions, horrific images, pinching, and other tortures. These accusations, directed initially at three women—a house slave named Tituba whom the Reverend Samuel Parris owned, Sarah Good, and Sarah Osborne—would later spread throughout New England. Good was impoverished and survived as a beggar, and Osborne was elderly and frail, apparently disfigured by some previous disease as well. Tituba was of Carib descent, a tribe native to the island of Barbados.

Several sociologists and social historians have examined Salem closely. Of course, each has his or her own particular theory and consequently emphasizes certain detailed aspects over others. Yet collectively, they all highlight certain social factors in common, and the points of concurrence most concern us here.

John Demos (1982) finds that social disparities existed between the accusers and the accused. The accusers were young women—teenage girls, really—from families that possessed either wealth or high status. The accused, the alleged witches, were all women in midlife, with the eventual exception of one man, John Proctor, and one 4-year-old girl, Dorothy Good, the daughter of Sarah Good. The initial accusers—Elizabeth Parris, Ann Putnam, Elizabeth Howell, Elizabeth Knapp, Sarah Churchill, Mary Walcott, and Abigail Williams—were young friends who lived a life of boredom and leisure, until such time as their families would choose husbands for them and compel them to marry. The girls had few liberties in life, as they were expected to uphold the family honor at all times as daughters of leading citizens. In contrast, the accused were women overwhelmingly in the range of 41–60 years old, as John Demos (p. 65) shows, and at the margins of Salem society. As middle-aged women living either alone or with female children, they occupied a place of mystery in village life.

The girls often socialized at the Parris house, where the slave Tituba was herself an exotic artifact for the New England Puritans who owned her. She often entertained the girls with tales of legend and magic from her native Barbados, and taught the girls how to divinate the future and use magic themselves. As far as the people of Salem were concerned, her association with the occult and her obviously non-Christian ways openly displayed her guilt. The other women in the first group of accused, as well as the many women and a few men accused later as the girls pressed their accusations throughout New England, followed the same pattern: middle-aged women who were on the margins of society, and who were involved in certain trades or practices or of low status.

Certain trades were long associated with women since ancient times, and until the 1600s, viewed as sacred trusts essential to the community—especially midwifery and healing. In Salem, childbirth was entirely within the female domain (Demos 1982), and healing involved diverse knowledge, both practical and arcane. Herbology, cooling and sweating, as well as spells and chants constituted the healer's ensemble. The women likely gained this knowledge across centuries of time, as it was handed down through the women in their families as secret and sacred knowledge (Barstow 1994). They would have sought to protect this knowledge in any case, but the fact that they were now accused of witchcraft was a stunner, given the traditional importance of their services. Like many people with secret and powerful knowledge, these women lived their middle and later years on the edge of the village in secluded houses. In Europe, the women who possessed this knowledge were known as wise women, and men who possessed the secret knowledge of animal husbandry—the breeding and care of livestock—were known as cunning men. The latter practice could also improve crop yield and was therefore highly valued. Like the women, their knowledge was mysterious and sacred, not just a collection of trade secrets accumulated over centuries of time, but special and powerful knowledge that they believed could prove dangerous in the wrong hands. Both the wise women and cunning men viewed their knowledge as a sacred trust (Barstow 1994).

For the Salem accused, their status as outsiders increased suspicions, and the fact that some of the women ultimately accused were somehow financially stable, even prosperous, further increased suspicion. To people in strongly patriarchal New England, how could women possibly survive, and even prosper, without a man? This question arose in Europe as well (recall the discussion in Chapter 2), and we will consider the answer in the Salem context shortly. Suffice it to say for now that the women, whether wise women or lone women of other backgrounds such as a common widow, lived on the fringe of Salem Village (Boyer and Nissenbaum 1974:190–191).

In Salem, as in Europe, an accused witch must be physically examined, and then tested, if the physical exam results confirmed her status as a witch. The physical examination required that she be stripped naked, and her body examined for strange moles that might be a devil's teat, on which imps and other types of demons would suckle. In order to verify the growth as an evil teat, a man, trained as a witch pricker, would stick the woman's growth with a sharp object. If this produced no pain or blood, or produced what the pricker considered inadequate pain or blood, it was concluded to be a devil's teat. In Europe, witch pricking became so widespread that the practice terrorized women in general (Barstow 1994:130). However, it appears that Salem had no professional witch prickers, so a local clergyman, Cotton Mather (mentioned in the previous chapter), advised the two magistrates appointed to investigate, John Hathorne and Jonathan Corwin. It is not known if they followed the European tradition of naked exams and pricking, but at least they spared the women the humiliation of a naked exam in public (Reis 1997). In both Europe and America, the witch persecutions quickly became a persecution of not only women, but of the feminine, since the accused men shared the same supposed womanly failings as their female counterparts. In essence, women were thought to have inherently evil natures, whereas men succumb to evil desires.

Carol Karlsen (1987) delivers another foundational work. She develops a gender focus, following the Puritan gender-dichotomous worldview: If the soul of man is inherently good, since men are made in the image of God, then the soul of a woman is inherently inferior and evil. As we have seen with the *Malleus Maleficarum*, women's souls produce an insatiable sexual desire, and in general an insatiable desire for physical pleasure. Yet the problem according to New England clergy was not that women would commit sins of the flesh, as men could do this as well, but that women threatened to undermine all of creation (p. 119).

Building on Karlsen's specifically gender perspective, Elizabeth Reis (1997) further elaborates that "a woman's feminine soul, jeopardized in a woman's feminine body, was frail, submissive, and passive—qualities that most New Englanders thought would allow her to become either a wife to Christ or a drudge to Satan." However, unlike common sinners, the witch "took a further damning step. Their feminine souls made an explicit and aggressive choice to conjoin with the devil" (p. 94). Their evil souls threatened the entire order that God had created.

Examined sociologically, this belief means that women threatened the male social order, or more specifically, the social order that men dominated. In this regard, some men, like women, could be allies of the devil if they, like women, also threatened the established social order. Common brigands (robbers or bandits), for example, who steal property only violate earthly law, but women who fornicate with the devil break God's entire moral order of existence. Men can also commit sins of the flesh, but such is only a temptation, not an inherent evilness as with women.

Prosecution of the alleged witches, like the accusation, relied entirely on the word of the accuser, at first. Surely—it was believed—these young, innocent girls of good families would never invent something as drastic as accusations of witchcraft, and certainly, they could not fake the obvious symptoms that arose whenever they were in the presence of the accused. These strange, sometimes cantankerous older women lived suspicious lives on the fringe of village life; the accusers and the accused both from the outset seemingly fit naturally into their roles. In order to prosecute and render a verdict, however, authorities required more than accusation. Cotton Mather supplied the requisite examination, after which followed the most important evidence of all—the confession. Tituba, accustomed to following her owner's orders, confessed quickly to everything, and possibly did not understand the gravity of the charges against her. Spells, divination, and other arcane magical practices were not evil in her culture, and thus confessing to them carried no special significance for Tituba. For the authorities, it proved her guilt. She was imprisoned and later exiled.

As the trials continued, the girls broadened their accusations and named many more people, about 80 altogether. Following Tituba's confession, the witch hunts expanded with great zeal, just as in Europe, and many more women faced pricking and torture in order to extract the all-important confession. Without the confession, no evidence existed, and there could be none—the women did not actually commit any of the crimes they were charged with. There were no nocturnal Sabbaths with Satan, no fornication with the devil or eating of human flesh. Reis views the process of interrogation and confession as one of social negotiation between those in power and those accused of witchcraft, or in other words, those supposedly trying to undermine that power. The process of torture applies the power of society so as to break the will of the accused and force her to submit to society's power. She not only confesses her guilt, but also declares, in effect, that society was right all along. Through the confession, the woman legitimates established power relations, its methods of control, and the subservience of women to men. The confession also serves to warn all women that they should not expect to survive and prosper without the guidance and protection of men (see Reis 1997:136–163).

This also explains the power the teenage girls enjoyed for a year or so. It would seem at first that if Reis is correct, the entire process of accusation, interrogation, confession, and trial is a process of social control through which men perpetuate their dominance over women, just as male authority figures imposed control over the teenage girls in Salem. Perhaps the process is also more subtle. That is, the girls in effect become willing servants of established power, and lend even greater legitimization by accusing other, older, and marginal women. As firm insiders from families of quality, they are in fact part of the established order, a kind of informant against other women who would flaunt the system, so to speak. What we might call an alternative lifestyle of the healers and midwives could not be tolerated, especially given the already economically precarious position of Salem Village. The village was not economically or socially secure enough to incorporate diversity. Power will not tolerate the presence of its own undoing.

For a while, the girls enjoyed tremendous power, which would never come to them again. Once married, they became the virtual property of their husbands. Their sudden elevated status as witch victims and accusers brought them much positive attention, and invested them with great power. In effect, they commanded the powerful men of the community—clergy, judges, constables, and jailers.

As for the accused women, what of their marginal existence? Living alone, how did they survive? A few inherited some measure of wealth. Others, namely midwives and healers, received compensation for their services (Karlsen 1987). And some simply performed the same domestic labor that women had performed for centuries. They baked bread, brewed beer, and weaved and sewed fabric. By itself, this was entirely customary. Yet how did they prosper from age-old traditional domestic labor? The answer is capitalism. Always controversial, capitalism played a distinctly progressive role in this time period. As discussed in Chapter 2, its emergence as the dominant economic system during and after the late 1400s coincided with the return of the bubonic plague (mid-1500s), as well as the emergence of Protestantism, the Thirty Years' War (1618–1648), and general social chaos, all of which wreaked havoc with traditions and created social pandemonium.

As it emerged, capitalism replaced feudalism, and in so doing, changed the way people made a living and related to each other. In feudalism, goods changed hands according to relations established by tradition. In capitalism, goods trade hands according to negotiated market relations. These relations change according to the needs of the buyer and seller, and thus may change often. The individuals do not matter; they are simply buyer and seller. Exchange in capitalism takes place through an anonymous market. Women living alone, with no man to support them, took advantage of these markets by offering their bread, beer, fabrics, and services for sale. They received money as payment, which they used to buy other things, anything they desired. Feudalism, which typically involved the exchange of goods through barter, allowed no such flexibility or opportunity for individual improvement.

These features of capitalism seem commonplace to us today. Since we are all born and raised within a long-established capitalist system, we all understand the logic of its basic principles. Money is invested in materials and labor to produce a product or service, which is then sold in the market and turned into money. The business reinvests this money in order to make more money. The process repeats as often as desired. In Salem Village in 1692, where life was still centered on agriculture and village self-sufficiency, few people understood the logic or process of capitalism. Most people saw their lives changing, often for the worse, and all the familiar traditions, religious and otherwise, seemed useless, even counterproductive. While most people struggled to earn a living in a society that appeared increasingly chaotic and unintelligible, a few people prospered, including some women living alone.

With no concept of capitalism, such a thing seemed unimaginable. Certainly, some evil force must be at work, for how else could a lone woman survive, let alone prosper? Today, with the advantage of hindsight and sociology, the answer seems comprehensible.

The people of Salem Village and other rural locations at the time of the persecutions eked out a marginal existence close to the prosperous seaport of Salem Town. Decidedly less religiously devout than Salem Village, the town followed the logic of capitalism—merchant capitalism, specifically. In contrast, Salem Village struggled on the edge of the wilderness and followed the traditional farming system of feudal Europe. Although Salem Village was not feudal economically, most people lived on independent and mostly self-sufficient farms that conducted trade locally through barter. In contrast, Salem Town traded globally—the seaport opened Salem Town to Europe and the Caribbean. Thus, there was a decisive contrast: Salem Village, strictly devout yet struggling, and Salem Town, increasingly liberalized and prospering. How could Salem Village be so religiously devout yet still only be scraping by?

At that time, the social forces at work were unfamiliar and frightening, complicated by wars, plagues, and famines. Science and the Age of Enlightenment had not yet arrived, but the social forces of emerging capitalism, rational inquiry, and individual liberty were already transforming the social landscape omnipresently but behind the scenes. Science, capitalism, and personal freedom constituted a new worldview that simply didn't make sense according to the values and standards of feudal Europe. (See the discussion in Chapter 2 for more details on the transition from premodern to modern society.)

Furthermore, the girls who became the Salem accusers found their traditional roles increasingly unappealing. Their families would have few choices of men for arranged marriages, and certainly, there must be better places than Salem Village to live. Yet as members of leading families, they must uphold obligations to the village.

Once the persecutions began, with trials and executions, the fear of superstition intensified as people began to see evil everywhere. Neighbor turned against neighbor. Rather than embrace the faith and community of their Christian religion, they embraced the fear and isolation of superstition.

Right-Wing Nativism and White Supremacy

It may seem that this topic belongs in the chapter on intolerance and violence, or perhaps is not part of religion at all. While nativism and white supremacy are certainly intolerant views and often violent, they are at the same time laden with religious imagery and they weave religious references into their rhetoric. Yet without hesitation, it can be stated sociologically that nativism and white supremacy are not religious, but in fact superstitious.

Historically related and often interwoven, the past with the present, nativists believe that the only true and legitimate Americans are certain types of white, Anglo-Saxon Protestants. White supremacy, often indistinguishable from nativism in practice, approaches religion and race from a larger, global perspective, in that the issues here are found elsewhere as well. As we will see, the white supremacist movement in recent years has reached out to similar-minded people in Britain and Germany, as well as other countries. Other variations include the militia movements, Christian Identity (a specifically racist sect; see previous chapter for more on this movement), and Christian Reconstructionism, also known as Dominionism. Most of the time, though, we will discuss all of these as variations of the same movement, a view that I will justify through sociological commonalties, even though the particular ideologies differ on some points.

Nativism does not include Native Americans or Native American movements such as AIM (American Indian Movement), because they are not white or Anglo-Saxon, and they are only sometimes Protestant. Most important, they did not build the United States, according to nativist leaders, and neither did black people or any other people of color, the movement contends. True, they may have performed the tough, manual labor, but they provided none of the intellectual and technical know-how, nor could they; they are supposedly inferior in the higher functions that produce civilization. This attitude appeared shortly after the original thirteen colonies were settled, but mostly in a paternal form. That is, Native Americans and others may be inferior, but the white man should nurture them, help them develop their full potential. The so-called "White Man's Burden," taken from the title of a poem by Rudyard Kipling, captures the notion of the powerful yet benevolent white man who, through imperialist conquest, brings civilization to the backward and ignorant "half-devil and half-child" races around the world.

Without summarizing the different interpretations of this poem, what do you think? Suppose a person who was part of your study passed you this and said, "This is what I believe." What do you make of it? In actual research, this scenario commonly occurs. When sociologist James Aho (1990) studied the Christian Nativist Patriot movement in Hayden Lake, Idaho, one of the local members passed him a copy of the *Protocols of the Elders of Zion*. The *Protocols* are supposedly a manual smuggled out of a

---

"The White Man's Burden"

Rudyard Kipling (1899)

Take up the White Man's burden—
Send forth the best ye breed—
Go bind your sons to exile
To serve your captives' need;
To wait in heavy harness,
On fluttered folk and wild—
Your new-caught, sullen peoples,
Half-devil and half-child.

Take up the White Man's burden—
In patience to abide,
To veil the threat of terror
And check the show of pride;
By open speech and simple,
An hundred times made plain
To seek another's profit,
And work another's gain.

Take up the White Man's burden—
The savage wars of peace—
Fill full the mouth of Famine
And bid the sickness cease;
And when your goal is nearest
The end for others sought,
Watch sloth and heathen Folly
Bring all your hopes to nought.

Take up the White Man's burden—
No tawdry rule of kings,
But toil of serf and sweeper—
The tale of common things.
The ports ye shall not enter,
The roads ye shall not tread,
Go mark them with your living,
And mark them with your dead.

Take up the White Man's burden—
And reap his old reward:
The blame of those ye better,
The hate of those ye guard—
The cry of hosts ye humour
(Ah, slowly!) toward the light: —
"Why brought he us from bondage,
Our loved Egyptian night?"

Take up the White Man's burden—
Ye dare not stoop to less—

(Continued)

(Continued)

Nor call too loud on Freedom
To cloke your weariness;
By all ye cry or whisper,
By all ye leave or do,
The silent, sullen peoples
Shall weigh your gods and you.

Take up the White Man's burden—
Have done with childish days—
The lightly proferred laurel,
The easy, ungrudged praise.
Comes now, to search your manhood
Through all the thankless years
Cold, edged with dear-bought wisdom,
The judgment of your peers!

secret meeting, of which there have been many, during which Jews conspired to achieve world domination. By using capitalism, communism, religion, and atheism, they will manipulate world politics and economics. If successful, they will annihilate most Christians, and enslave the rest. The person confided to Aho that this book depicts factual knowledge and is a source of great inspiration to fight the evil Jewish global conspiracy. Like Aho (and myself, while studying the Promise Keepers), people will give you all kinds of things. You will need to interpret them.

Suffice it to say that in the late nineteenth and early twentieth centuries, most white people in Europe and the United States applauded imperialism. Not everyone benefited equally, of course. The working class and working poor suffered the casualties in combat to which the poem refers, and the capitalist class accumulated most of the profits. Yet rich and middle- and working-class white people in the industrialized countries all increasingly enjoyed access to cheap resources from other parts of the world and the rapidly expanding economy and quality of life they afforded. Whether one benefited directly or not, this did not change the widely accepted notion that nonwhites were primitive and inferior. This was about 150 years after the original colonies were founded. What began as paternalistic superiority had advanced through systematic enslavement of black people into ruthless exploitation by the end of the nineteenth century.

Here enters nativism and white supremacy as populist movements just prior to the twentieth century. Intertwined with religion, it would rise and fall rapidly from time to time and place to place. As with the earlier examples of ancient Greece and nineteenth-century Germany, the social conditions of time and place are decisive. In the United States, the very notion of a conservative or far-right populism seemed oxymoronic. As Michael Kazin (1995) observes, "conservatism had always supported unregulated capitalism and private riches, honestly obtained. For Americans who cherished property rights and the maintenance of public order, rebellions from below were to be feared, discouraged, and if necessary, put down by force" (pp. 165–166). Although some groups such as the Ku Klux Klan achieved national notoriety and influence in the 1920s, it was short lived, and by the early 1930s, the group had devolved into local infighting and national ridicule. Although racism still existed, once society in general sees a particular group as once part of the mainstream but now part of the lunatic fringe, the group almost never recovers mainstream credibility. As we will see, however, the story is different for groups that begin on the fringe, then move to the center.

In the 1860s, a self-educated son of an Irish weaver named John Wilson seized on an idea from the 1660s—that the British are the direct descendants of the lost Thirteenth Tribe of Israel. Wilson also entertained the idea that certain Germans, namely the Saxons of northern Germany, were also related. He concluded that the true descendants of the covenant are, and can only be, white Anglo-Saxon

Christians (Barkun 1997:8). Disillusioned with the loss of his father's small business, which he could no longer inherit, Wilson wrote mainly for himself. Edward Hine picked up Wilson's work and turned it into a British-Israelism movement.

Edward Hine believed that both Britain, a longstanding imperial power, and the emerging upstart, Germany, were chosen by God to deliver white civilization from racial corruption. God clearly favored both countries, as He now opened up possibilities for both nations to expand. Although by the 1890s the two nations were clearly moving toward open conflict with each other, Hine explained that Wilson erred in his acclamation of Germany. Not Germany, but the United States was the appropriate brother country. In the United States, the nativist movement gained increasing credibility in the 1880s (Bennett 1995), as Asian immigrants arrived on the West Coast and European immigrants on the East Coast. Whether Chinese on the one side of the country, or Poles, Italians, and Irish on the other, they were either Catholic, which was bad enough, or not Christian at all. They spoke foreign languages, they ate strange foods, and they sometimes looked white but were not really. The apprehension and unease that accompanied the new arrivals, and the concurrent changes after the Civil War and the rise of the great industrial centers, shifted the center of American life from the small town to the ever-larger big cities, especially New York, Chicago, and Detroit, where industry and immigration in collusion seemed to marginalize the native Protestant white man.

Once British-Israelism arrived in the United States, it transformed into Anglo-Israelism. This belief influenced many religious innovators, including Charles Fox Parham, whom we met in the previous chapter; Reuben H. Sawyer, a prominent leader in the Ku Klux Klan; and Henry Ford, founder of the Ford Motor Company. Sawyer is most important sociologically. He led two lives. In one life, he orated as an advocate of Anglo-Israelism; in his other life, he organized for the Ku Klux Klan. Although he did not conceal his Klan affiliation, he usually kept the two movements separate, and never advocated one when representing the other. The Klan enjoyed a widespread revival immediately after World War I, when social conditions in the United States changed drastically as the economy advanced furiously, and like in Germany, rural towns, once the mainstay of American life, became increasingly marginalized outposts of American life. Sawyer attacked not only black people, but also labor unions and big capitalists who rampaged through the countryside, stealing what they wanted and destroying the rest (the so-called robber barons)—a common image at this time that many speakers on both the left and the right used extensively. Yet one more element was so far missing—an enemy that the common person could recognize. Black people were easy to identify by skin color, and when the average white person of modest rural background looked to the centers of sin in financial hubs like New York City and manufacturing centers like Chicago and Detroit, it was clear that only white people were rich and in charge. Moreover, many were devout Christians. There must be some other type of person, someone not so obvious but no less virulent, and it would take William J. Cameron and Henry Ford to identify it—the Jew.

Cameron worked as Henry Ford's personal press secretary from 1925 to 1942 or 1943 (Barkun 1997:31). Ford rarely spoke in public, and his precise views on the Jews remain ambiguous. Not so for Cameron, who argued that the Jews constituted an enemy race, and that the white race—not a particular nation or state, but the whole race—was true descendants of the Israelites. Cameron, however, a longtime alcoholic, repented late in life and died as a member of the Unity Church, a fairly mainline Protestant church, having renounced his earlier anti-Semitism (Barkun 1997:43). With Cameron's renunciation, the decline of the evangelical preachers in the Midwest, and the collapse of the Klan after 1941 (when the United States went to war against Germany, the supposed master white race), the center of Anglo-Israelism shifted to California, where it would transform into the contemporary Christian Identity and white power movements.

Yet one formidable proponent remained in the Midwest. Father Charles Coughlin (a Catholic priest) became the most prominent midcentury political agitator in the white supremacy movement. Prior to this stage, the Anglo-Israel movement had been predominantly a very intellectual movement without a particular center or political orientation (Barkun 1997:47). If anything, the movement lacked any political goals, but mostly sought to develop a religious doctrine that correctly understood the true meaning of scripture and the people to whom it was truly directed (white people). With the exception of the Ku Klux Klan, Anglo-Israelism remained fairly innocuous on the margin of American society. Racism was not marginal, but most racists rarely attempt an intellectual or organized approach. Coughlin brought the movement to the common people—the working class and small farmer and others in small towns. He also solidified a superstitious aspect to the movement, which it retains to the present day.

Couglin's supporters were overwhelmingly the working-class elite, who had suffered recent wage cutbacks or reduced work opportunities, which threatened their elite status. Demographic analysis reveals his strongest support among "carpenters, electricians, plumbers, postal workers, bricklayers, railroad workers, as well as clerks, and small farmers" (Bennett 1995:258). Coughlin's popularity increased greatly and rapidly during the Depression years, and his radio show from Detroit, Michigan, generated about $5 million a year in revenue by 1936, a huge amount for that time. Immensely popular, Coughlin became the foremost critic of President Roosevelt, whom he believed had sold the country to foreigners and Jews, and allowed the immigrant factory worker and other unskilled workers to run the country through unions and collusion with big business. Sociologically, we can readily understand Coughlin's appeal among the aforementioned types of people, who regarded themselves as the working-class skilled elite, and nativist Americans who, as self-reliant individuals, lacked the support of unions and ethnic neighborhood enclaves. Although he was a Catholic priest, most of Coughlin's supporters were conservative Protestants (Bennett 1995).

Although his basic rhetoric was not new, Coughlin incorporated an additional aspect, which he borrowed from West Coast activist Gerald L. K. Smith, who until his death in 1976 was the most prominent anti-Semite in the United States. For Smith, the problem was not only that non-Protestant immigrants had inundated the United States, but also that they had masters who, using the banks and big business, controlled the economy and manipulated the government from behind the scenes. Smith and Coughlin did not oppose capitalism or profit per se, only profit which, in their minds, was unjustly gained rather than honestly earned. Coughlin campaigned against the "nonproducers: bankers, businessmen, and bond traders, parasites who grew nothing and made nothing except money.... [I]t was the specter of unearned, unfair profits acquired by guile and deceit, the corruption of the traditional American dream of achievement through hard work" (Bennett 1995:246). Coughlin's association with Smith and other anti-Semites would prove to be his downfall, however, after 1941 when the United States entered World War II against Hitler's anti-Semitic Nazism. However, anti-Semitism and the more significant sociological artifact it represents—a superstitious belief in unseen, mysterious, and sinister forces—endured long beyond the fall of Coughlin and Smith.

Superstitious anti-Semitism and its parallel, antiblack racism, continued through far-right literature and social networks, much of the time out of the mainstream spotlight. Only during the civil rights activism of the 1960s did racism starkly surface; as long as the nativist hegemony was apparently maintained, racism need not take an overtly belligerent form. Eventually, superstitious anti-Semitism would fade, as would the hysterical anticommunism of the 1950s, but antiblack racism endured. The specter of unearned wealth and privilege, achieved through conspiratorial domination, and the corruption of the American Dream, shifted from Jews to blacks. Consistently, however, superstition prevailed.

Just as Jews were supposedly the specter behind the scenes, the mysterious "master" manipulators who ruled through deceit and gained wealth through nonproductive investment, now the specter became the black who was seen as a welfare cheat, the lazy inner-city slumdweller who accumulated immense welfare checks and rather than work, indulged in all manner of vice and endless procreation. Soon, it was feared, lazy welfare cheats would overrun the honest, hardworking white person whose paycheck the government would appropriate and turn over to these lazy, nonworking, promiscuous blacks. This is not the place to examine the myths about welfare recipients, but suffice it to say that the superstitious perception described here is entirely false, and the truth quite different; for example, most welfare recipients are in fact white and rural, and the majority of people who receive some form of assistance work at least part-time (see DiNitto and Cummins 2006; Gilens 2000; Neubeck and Cazenave 2001; Quadagno 1996).

After the civil rights movement, politicians and other public figures could not articulate this vision openly. Social circumstances now required greater sophistication, and likely most politicians realized the claim was false and readily disproven. Coded racism garners votes more effectively than open declarations, and it allows constituents to indulge the fantasy without reflection. Wielding superstitious notions of an enemy among us, far-right politicians and activists appealed to an imprecisely defined "silent majority" who cherished traditional American values of hard work, monogamous and heterosexual self-discipline, and moral piety (Kazin 1995:247). This new message emerged in the 1970s, arguably the most liberal decade in U.S. history, and therefore fertile ground for backlash conservative views.

We should note that many conservatives hold well-reasoned, rational, and intelligent views on many issues. They are not the focus here. Rather, our focus is the use of superstition to justify attitudes and policies that discriminate against or preclude social opportunity for certain social groups. As in the 1970s, the strongest supporters for politicians who seek to dismantle welfare, Medicare, social security, and public education come not from the rich, but from the working class. As sociologist Arlie Hochschild (2005) discovered, 56% of men who earn wages of less than $30,000 a year strongly support Bush's plan to greatly reduce or eliminate all of these forms of assistance, and give tax breaks to the rich. In comparison, only 35% of those who earn salaries greater than $75,000 support reducing or eliminating these forms of assistance (Hochschild 2005).

Here is the part that is most important for us. Of those who mostly or strongly support dismantling public assistance, 36% believe the world will end in their lifetime. Moreover, whether millennialist or not, the vast majority belong to non-mainline evangelical churches (Hochschild 2005). The people who benefit the least from tax cuts and benefit the most from public services and assistance most strongly support dismantling them. Hochschild concludes that such people face a powerful dilemma. Suffering job loss or downgrades themselves, they can fight for worker's rights and decent pay, or divert their energy somewhere else. Expressed differently, they can join together with other people in similar situations, which includes people of various religious beliefs, orientations, and races, or retreat into a small and homogeneous community, no larger than the church congregation. As Hochschild argues, "he localizes empathy. . . . Pay for a tax to help a homeless mother in another city? Forget it. Charity begins at home" (p. 23). Thus we see the effect of superstitious racism: It reduces one's capacity for empathy. Remember that Plutarch argued that superstition isolates a person from other people and the real world. The welfare mother doesn't deserve help, and neither does any other supposedly lazy and most likely black welfare cheat, nor do any of the minorities who supposedly receive special grants and privileges from colleges and businesses. No, my money will stay with people like myself—hardworking, wage-earning, and white. Personal piety and donations at church take the place of collective social action.

Sociologically, the new far-right message would only carry weight if a person believed that something threatened such values of hard work, moral piety, and so on. Superstitious acceptance of the welfare cheat and whatever other fictitious stereotypes inhibits empathy by creating perceived inherent differences of superiority and inferiority. Just as in earlier times, the myth relies on feeling, not on fact. Jews no more controlled government and business in Coughlin's day than black people and other ethnic minorities receive special privileges and consume economic surplus today. Yet the Jew of yesterday and the black person of today, in their role of superstitious malefactor, both receive, in the mind of the superstitious believer, illegitimate and unearned gains.

In today's society, there are also people who seem to lack a meaningful community at all. Although they may live and work among other people, they feel no connection. Instead of marginalized communities, we see increasingly more often today the marginalized individual. Without the anchor of family, friends, and other associations, such people more willingly embrace superstition to explain—and as they hope, to overcome—their isolation and their social and emotional problems. As an example, we now turn to one of the fastest growing experiences in the United States—exorcism.

Deliverance in the United States

Once marginal and rarely seen, deliverance, also known as exorcism, finds dramatically increasing popularity today in the United States. What had been a very infrequent practice found only in the Catholic Church, now finds its greatest growth among evangelical Protestants. When Protestantism first emerged, the vast majority of the new sects specifically renounced all magical powers and supernatural occurrences as ignorant vestiges of the medieval church, but whereas exorcism remains marginal in Catholicism, it has spread throughout the United States among Protestant exorcists and faith healers.

Exorcism developed as a specific church practice in the Catholic Church of the Middle Ages (e.g., in Image 3.1). The idea that Satan or a minion could possess a person only became popularly held in the two centuries prior to the Enlightenment, about 1450–1650, the age of the witch persecutions. In the supposedly darkest period of the Middle Ages, long after the collapse of the Roman Empire in the West and long before the rise of the Renaissance, the emperor Charlemagne, crowned in 800 CE, declared that possession was impossible and he would tolerate no talk about witches or demonic possession (Trevor-Roper 1969). Without recounting the long history of Catholic theology and practice, suffice it to say here that exorcism never became widespread in Catholicism, even during the height of the witch hunts.

All through Catholic history, people could choose to associate with the devil, but the Church regarded unwilling possession as extremely rare and would treat cases as such only when all other explanations had been exhausted. In modern times, this meant that all social-psychological, neurological, and other explanations must first be exhausted—a requirement that involves extensive investigation and expertise (Wilkins 2007).

Far from the official and technical approach the Catholic Church employs today, various Protestant denominations, mostly evangelical and without national affiliation, practice exorcism in a manner comparable to their method of founding as a denomination in the first place—informal, non-erudite, and fully attuned to popular culture. Regarding the latter, very few people ever complained of demonic possession prior to the widespread popularity of *The Exorcist,* the book by William Peter Blatty published in 1971, and the subsequent movie by the same name released in 1973. In this book and film, the devil possesses a

Image 3.1   St. Michael Subduing Satan

young girl named Regan. During the course of the possession, among other things her skin turns sickly white and putrid; cuts and slashes appear on her body; she speaks in various languages, known and unknown, and speaks Anglo-Saxon backwards and she hurls profane insults, moves heavy objects telekinetically, and vomits copious amounts of green bile (see Image 3.2).

Although supposedly based on a real-life case, no reliable proof has ever surfaced, and these images remain the expression of Blatty's and film director William Friedkin's creative if somewhat demented imaginations.

Despite the fictional nature of the story, a number of people around the United States suddenly started to complain of possession symptoms. Although no documented cases of physical transformation exist to rival those the film depicts, some people seemed to speak in tongues, and strange, erratic behavior was clearly observable. Unlike Regan in the movie, people today seem to find that the demon they claim possesses them offers no resistance as they calmly attend deliverance services and calmly wait for their turn before the deliverance expert (Cuneo 2001). Only when they are front and center does the demon object.

One of today's foremost deliverance experts is Bob Larson, who expels demons both in person and over the radio. Larson sees his deliverance ministry as part of modern psychological treatments and counseling for emotional and other personal problems. Larson says that "psychotherapy helps people recognize their issues. But what if their issue is traumatized further by a demon?" (*Deliver Us From Evil*, 2003). Although Larson attributes some credibility to traditional psychotherapy, Larson also believes that demons and other supernatural forces are real. He says that "the first time I saw a demon look at me, evil look at me . . . was while I was traveling overseas in Asia, and I saw a Hindu ritual. . . . [T]he look would come into their eyes, a vacancy of the soul. I never anticipated that I would see that look in America" (*Deliver Us From Evil*, 2003). For Larson, Hinduism is not only non-Christian, but foreign and evil. Larson apparently equates America with ultimate good, and foreign countries and religions with something less than good. In his ministry, Larson scans the audience for "the look" of vacancy that betrays the presence of a demon.

Larson follows an American Protestant tradition of deliverance. In the 1960s, a Texas minister named Win Worley began doing exorcisms at his church in Texas. The Southern Baptist Convention soon rescinded Worley's charter, but his ministry enjoyed dramatic growth over the next several decades, until his death in 1991. After losing his Southern Baptist affiliation, Worley's church continued as a nonaffiliated congregation, ordaining its own ministers over the years. Worley also moved the church to Indiana, where one of the pastors he ordained took over his ministry in 1991 following his death. As Worley's successor, Mike Thierer feels that deliverance saved him from drugs and alcohol. Today, Thierer has developed his own method of exorcism. He "calls out" demons at each service, most of which enter people through very common means. Among other evils, Thierer calls out demons from ouija boards, sorcery, witchcraft, paganism, biorhythms, yoga, and many other items and practices from popular culture and alternative religions (*Deliver Us From Evil*, 2003).

Like Bob Larson, Thierer embraces a kind of folk-American outlook, that anything mystical or foreign poses a threat of demonic possession. While not overtly

Image 3.2   A Famous Movie Moment: Father Merrin Looking Up at Regan's
Window in *The Exorcist*

Source: Copyright © Bettman/CORBIS.

racist or xenophobic, contemporary exorcism ministries, both in terms of the
church itself and the people who attend, are overwhelmingly white, conservative,
lower-middle to working class, and less than college-educated.

Another disciple that Worley ordained, Pastor Monty Mulkey, presides over the
West Coast Church of Deliverance (WCCD) in Thousand Oaks, California. Worley
published Mulkey's various papers and books on deliverance-related topics, such as
"Alcoholic Patterns, Arrested Development, Shame, Slothfulness, Abuse, Mental
Illness, in His Hosts of Hell series" (WCCD Web site, www.wccd.com). In addition
to deliverance, Pastor Mulkey also receives frequent prophesies from God, which
are also available on the Web site. These are not just sermons or variations of Pastor
Mulkey's expository writings, but are presented as prophesies delivered directly
from God.

Believers in demonic possession and deliverance think that the problems
people face in terms of emotional disturbances or even more severe mental disor-
ders, derive not from lived experience or psychological trauma, but most importantly from intrusive demons that possess a person and force them to behave
aberrantly. In the early days of Pentecostalism, believers viewed demonic possession and sickness as interrelated—that sickness of any kind, whether of the body,
the mind, or the soul, was a demonic assault. Sociologist Michael Cuneo (2001)
notes, in his 2-year study of exorcism, that as Pentecostals moved from rural

meetings in open fields to urban churches with upwardly mobile congregates, they consigned exorcism and demons to infrequent backroom encounters (pp. 88–89). As we have seen throughout this textbook, religious beliefs relate directly to social position in terms of economic class, culture, status, education, and other sociological variables.

Cuneo (2001) argues that exorcism functions as a psychotherapy for people who, for economic or cultural reasons, cannot or will not consult a trained psychological or medical professional. However, Cuneo's research also confirms the sociological trepidation that exorcism allows people to "avoid responsibility for their own shortcomings by blaming them on demons" (p. 279). Moreover, we see that exorcism resonates with a generally conservative, white, uneducated ethos in which people do not distinguish between an internal and external locus of control, or distinguish empirical fact from belief. That is, people who feel afflicted by demons fail to realize that much of what they imagine as external demons who forcibly possess them are from a social-psychological perspective a manifestation of their own internal insecurities and conflicts. While the feelings of insecurity and conflict are real and can incapacitate a person, they are nevertheless internal, and not impositions from outside demonic forces.

For example, one of Bob Larson's devotees claimed that all her life, she felt like something was holding her back, talking to her, and filling her with feelings of guilt and anguish. Karen Miller realized, after several sessions with Larson, that her problems began when she witnessed the neighbor's house burning down when she was a child. She says that in flames, she clearly saw the face of Satan, and now believes that Satan or another demon entered her at this time (*Deliver Us From Evil,* 2003). In other cases as well, people believe that by whatever means, demons enter them through some traumatic event. Many of these events may be quite real, especially abuse parents inflicted on them as children, or traumatic events during adulthood, such as divorce or hitting rock bottom through drugs or alcohol. Others claim recovered memories, such as that as children, adults forced them to undergo Satanic rituals that involved grotesque sexual exploitation or human sacrifice. To date, no evidence exists to support even one such claim about ritual sexual abuse or murder as part of an underground organization (Frankfurter 2006) or the alleged day-care scares of the 1980s (M. McGrath 2002).

The desire to eradicate evil within a person can sometimes result in permanent injury or death. Cuneo (2001) documents several cases in which exorcism resulted in death. Typical of the process is the case of 17-year-old Charity Miranda, who died in 1998 as the result of an exorcism. Convinced that a demon possessed her child, Charity's mother, Vivian, as court testimony revealed, ordered Charity to blow into her mother's mouth and thereby expel the demon so that her mother could swallow and kill it. When this failed to produce the desired result, her mother and several other adults smothered Charity with a plastic bag (279–280). While the vast majority of exorcisms are not fatal, Cuneo accurately notes that when people substitute exorcism for genuine psychological treatment, or use exorcism to avoid an honest look at their emotional problems or other failings in life, then exorcism can only intensify, not diminish, a person's problems.

Discussion

So now we return to the theoretical points in the beginning of this chapter. As Plutarch argued, the superstitious person does not embrace self-improvement through education, understanding, and accomplishment, but rather, submission through fear and ignorance. Superstitious people believe superstitious falsehoods because they are afraid not to. Without the presence of a cheater and manipulator to blame, the superstitious person would need to face reality—a most frightful place for someone, for example, who is laid off from work, made redundant by machines or outsourcing, or with little education and with feeble or nonexistent family relationships and friendships. With diminished prospects, the comfort of the local congregation, the most welcoming of places, proves far more attractive than the foreboding and hated reality of higher education—the key to greater employment quality and prospects—or the ominous prospect of engaging in new social relationships. It also relieves the person from associating, directly or indirectly, with different and therefore undesirable types of people. It is always easier to associate with people just like oneself. This is not to blame the church congregation; they provide a welcoming community. Rather, the superstitious person hides within the church community, and because it is the church—the house of God—one feels completely justified in commitment to this sanctuary, and therefore justified in abnegating broader social responsibility. The vast majority of churches of whatever denomination do not intentionally promote superstition, but the social effect, regardless of doctrine, allows a person to accept superstition in place of genuine religion. Just as Durkheim argues that religion promotes or restrains suicide, regardless of doctrine, so churches today promote or restrain superstition, regardless of doctrine. It is not the church itself, but the social function of the church within the context of economic, political, and personal forces in which superstition increasingly substitutes for genuine religious commitment. The person need only commit to a stand-alone ritual, not to a new way of life.

We thus see that superstition, using the sociological conceptualization presented here, has the veneer of religious devotion. In practice, however, it occurs outside of established churches and other religious institutions and traditions. It appears as the result of status downturn, which itself occurs as an outcome of material downturn. The sudden shift of life opportunity and expectations, and the corresponding status demotion, inspires a desperation from which supernatural visions and other claims arise. They are, in sociological perspective, an attempt to regain some degree of status and sense of dignity. Superstition grants a false sense of empowerment, because it does not change the social conditions, but allows a person to feel more powerful, more influential. Suddenly, declassed and declining people feel empowered by supernatural forces that, in social context, prove that the little person matters. When articulated as a God-given vision or devil-inflicted torment, superstition reverses social roles. Suddenly, the teenage girl in a society ruled by male elders, and which grants women little respect and minimal autonomy, forces the elders to listen. In places like Marpingen and Salem, the young girls do the talking and the senior men do the listening. The girls, for a time, wield power and influence that would normally be well beyond attainment.

Today in the United States, there are declassed workers with declining wages who invent or accept superstitious notions of the Other, of people who are not worthy of money, attention, or even compassion. They submerge in a community of conformity that requires no thought or action, just an appearance on Sundays. Superstition shelters them from the forces outside, which they see as unknowable and all-powerful, from which they can only hide. Divorced, laid off, and otherwise dejected people of modest education and means find themselves alone and without prospects. With declining self-esteem and few friends, the possibility that demons, and not they themselves, account for their declining fortunes and dejection comforts otherwise forlorn individuals. Like religion in general, the deliverance congregation provides a welcoming haven that immediately and unequivocally accepts a person, and immediately displaces any possible blame and accountability from the individual to nefarious and external demons. This simple and immediate transferal provides instant relief. Also like religion in general, however, the palliative effects must be reaffirmed every so often, and the person must remain a member of the community. As Michael Cuneo observed, this relieves the individual of some apprehension, but simultaneously perpetuates the person's emotional difficulties because it does not address the objective causes. Exorcism only offers a substitute explanation for the individual's psychological discomfort, not a solution for it.

Superstition, to the extent it overcomes both reason and faith, must occur as a social process of claim and acclaim—the charismatic relationship—and in this way it also resembles religion. The significant difference lies not in the supernatural aspect of superstition, which it shares with religion, but in the social process. In religion, people celebrate community, a collective identity. In superstition, people celebrate personal reality that supersedes the community. In other words, people embrace individual differences and individual claims to truth. Though the community grants strength to the superstitious claim, the community dissolves itself in the process, because it elevates individual fear and despair over and against the collective well-being of the community as a whole. As Plutarch argued at the beginning of this chapter, the religious person awakes each day to a reality shared in common, which the individual strives to better understand and improve. The superstitious person shares no world in common with others. As we saw with many contemporary wage-earners, their world is getting smaller, and they deny their common concerns about work and family, separated by the superstitions of race and prejudice.

Devotion to superstition occurs outside established traditions and signifies the decline and dissolution of a community, not the celebration of a rising, or at least stable and viable, community as does devotion to religion. Whereas religious devotion requires the sacrifices of faith and also the development of the intellect in order to solidify collective association, superstition negates both. Religion empowers people to seek truth, justice, and virtue, and it reassures people that life matters. Superstition disempowers people and imposes the tyranny of fear and ignorance.

What about supernatural occurrences? Are they never real, but instead only the outcome of ignorant and fearful beliefs? Sociology cannot address this issue entirely because it does involve an element of faith, that supernatural occurrences—those which transcend reason and empirical laws—in the form of miracles, for example, really do happen. In addition to miracles, prophecy, divination, omens, communion with the divine, and other supernatural occurrences exist in many of the world's religions. It becomes absurd to conclude that nearly everyone is ignorant and fearful. Rather, perhaps a more useful and insightful conclusion would be to consider the ramifications of the supernatural. Does it replace real-life experiences and become an obstacle to education and progress? The Spartans clearly suffered from this; they constantly awaited omens and other messages from the gods that never arrived, or which arrived in very uncertain ways that effectively steered Spartan society into inaction and a rigid adherence to tradition that inhibited progress.

What of today? Is there room for belief in the supernatural, or is it inherently inimical to modern life? That depends on how far one concludes that modernity alone can explain the world, and to what extent a life without mystery can be fulfilling. The supernatural, like faith, requires a tolerance of mystery.

And what of something like love? Is it simply a conditioned response, as a behaviorist would argue? Is it simply a desire to fulfill incompleteness of the self, as a psychoanalyst might argue? Is it simply the expression of a genetic code that prompts us to become intimate in order to reproduce the species? A survival instinct? Or is it something more, much more? Something that requires expression of feelings and desires that have no other equivalent? For centuries, poets have searched for the words and metaphors to express the profound qualities of love, but the fact that love requires poetry suggests some elements of mystery, that the essence of love and all that it inspires in people lies somewhere beyond empirical thought and the theory built from it, that love can be something so powerful that we would die to protect what we love. If love is both mysterious and transcendent, can we perhaps call it supernatural?

4

Religious Adaptation

Introduction

This chapter builds on concepts from Robert K. Merton in order to understand alternative religious movements in comparison to established religion as a process of adaptation. Alternative religion occurs in a multitude of contexts, whether in the creation of evil, or during economic decline, or as a result of other major events that transform society and the corresponding religious beliefs. Just as tradition constitutes one essential aspect of religion, and we have seen examples of tradition at work, so alternative religion constitutes a decisive aspect of religion. Any religion that cannot change with the times and make sense of social change in the surrounding world will not survive. Religion not only responds to social events, but often actively shapes them as well.

Alternative religion refers to a movement that seeks to adapt itself to the dominant culture (see Table 4.1). As we will see, this takes a variety of forms, but all comprise the general concept of Alternative Religious Movement (ARM). We will examine two ARMs in a later chapter.

Therefore, this replaces the often used New Religious Movement (NRM) concept, a very broad term that usually includes cults and many other movements that are in fact not new. As Barrett (2001) notes, many place the Haré Krishna movement in the NRM category. Yet the Haré Krishnas are far from new. As a variation of Hinduism that started in India, they are over 100 years old and based on a trend that is over 600 years old. Alternative Religious Movement (ARM) thus proves more useful analytically, and it also makes better sense because it accounts for both new and old movements based on their relationship to society, not simply based on age or the crude discernment that a group has suddenly gained media attention.

Alternative religion does not always create enduring social change, although its ongoing presence, even if dispersed among many different religious groups,

Table 4.1   Conceptual Clarification: Empirical Manifestations of Adaptation

Cult	Alternative Religion	Emergent Religion
Separated from the society around it	Conformity	A general term usually applied to a group or movement that is still shaping definitive parameters, especially the following:
In conflict with the society around it	Innovation	
Apocalyptic doctrine	Ritualism	
Absolute devotion from the followers	Retreatism	
	Rebellion	
Premised on the mind, and/or perceived essential divinity of, the leader		Membership criteria
		Beliefs
Devoted to the leader's personal reality		Rituals
		Collective identity
Usually organized on the fringes of society in secluded or remote locations. Membership involves often severe degradation rituals. Strictly homogeneous	Wide variety of beliefs, rituals, and lifestyles. Particular groups may be homogeneous or heterogeneous. Degree of mainstream association varies	Broadly descriptive term that applies to groups in a state of transition, or newly existing but not yet fully formed

suggests that modern society contains ongoing discontent, and this discontent takes various forms, as we will conceptualize below. To differentiate, alternative religion pertains to any group or movement that invents a new belief system or way of life as a sacred obligation and successfully establishes a degree of permanence. In contrast, emergent religion refers to groups or trends still taking shape that may or may not establish a degree of permanence or sacred obligation.

If ARMs form in relation to an established religion, let us remember that the established religion need not be the most common or politically dominant religion, but it must be compatible with mainstream society in a way that does not require change. Alternative religion thus seeks beliefs or lifestyle changes that differ significantly from the original beliefs or practices of the group, as a result of conflict with the mainstream in some way or another. This conflict may be moral, economic, behavioral, theological, or any number of other possibilities that draw negative attention and even persecution. Unlike cults, alternative religions are not inherently closed to outsiders, nor premised on the will of a charismatic leader, and they often become compatible with, or at least nonoffensive to, the mainstream as a result of adaptation.

To be sure, difference does not constitute alternative status. For example, Dearborn, Michigan, has the second-largest Arab population in the United States, about 29,000 out of 98,000 residents. Long a white working-class stronghold, home to Ford Motors, Dearborn has suffered an extended period of decline as factory-wage jobs leave the area and strand the traditional working class with ever-fewer employment opportunities. Arab Americans share the values of the community—most significantly, that America is a land of opportunity where people are free to improve their place in life. They also accept the means of achieving self-improvement, that each individual must work hard to earn a better life; nothing comes for free.

At the same time, they retain the religion of Islam, which divides them from most working-class whites, some of whom see their presence as a type of invasion. From a sociological standpoint, the Muslim population accepts the essential elements of mainstream American life, and thus does not constitute a deviant subgroup. In fact, the vast majority consider themselves American and embrace American values of work, education, and government (Shryock 2002). Society in Dearborn has two foundational aspects: one is working class and law-abiding; the other is white and Christian. Being white and Christian, or Arab and Muslim, has no impact on economic life, a necessary element of all communities. Sociologically, Muslims in Dearborn conform to the dominant social standards of achievement—honest pay for honest work. Their religion is also mainstream—mostly Shiite Islam with some enclaves of Sunnis, not breakaway sects. We observe that in Dearborn, not all whites are racist or actively Christian, nor are all Arabs actively Muslim. But all residents of Dearborn must actively work within the established economic system; each individual must actively work in order to achieve any quality of life.

The mere fact that Muslims move to Dearborn does not by itself prove socially salient and transform society in Dearborn. It may add ethnic flavor, but the essential structure remains intact. The type of social change that concerns us takes four basic forms, as discussed below. Not all change is sociologically important. Some indigenous residents of Dearborn may feel suspicious toward the new Arab-Muslim residents, but this racial or cultural clash has been overplayed in the media. The greatest divisions arise within the Muslim community, based on class position and degree of cultural assimilation (Rignall 1997). As Belton (2003) concludes, relations have been overwhelmingly cordial, except immediately after September 11, when storefronts were broken. Still, Arab residents remain optimistic, and "Dearborn's Muslims continue to shift focus from their countries of birth towards a distinctly Arab, but very much American, civil society in their new home—an assimilated political stance directed not towards Lebanon but to Dearborn city hall, Lansing, and Washington" (Belton 2003). In this case, Muslims and Christians in Dearborn support the religion of their birth and of their respective communities, which are becoming increasingly intertwined economically and culturally. Both are mainstream religions tied directly to their cultural and historical past. There is nothing new, innovative, or alternative, other than a gradual process of adaptation as Muslims settle in their new country and local Christians acclimatize, if sometimes grudgingly, to their new neighbors (see sidebar).

Globalization started decades ago, and interestingly, religious globalization goes back much farther than modern capitalism. By the time modern capitalism and modern society emerged to any important degree in the late 1700s, Christianity and Islam had already become global religions in the full sense. Although each professes certain core beliefs that distinguish it from other religions, each also exhibits diverse local variations that depend on local customs and traditions that existed before, often long before Christianity and Islam appeared. In Africa, Asia, and South America, as well as in Europe and North America, both of these major religions incorporate variations and influences from local cultures, languages, geography,

Discrimination Against Islamic Americans

Despite their best efforts to live as Americans, even the most patriotic metro-Detroit Muslims face discrimination. Though not constant, such discrimination, when it strikes, still grabs attention.

Several Lebanese American Shiites were returning from a pilgrimage to Saudi Arabia on January 7, 2007, when Northwest Airlines refused to let them board their flight. The airline claimed the passengers arrived at the gate just minutes before the flight was to leave, and regulations require passengers to be at the gate at least 45 minutes before departure. The passengers said they were waiting at the gate for nearly 2 hours before departure (Worikoo 2007). On January 18, Northwest Airlines issued a formal apology and agreed to reimburse for hotel rooms, replacement flights, and any additional costs incurred. Ironically, some of the men denied boarding are in fact members of the Council on American–Islamic Relations, a mainstream organization that seeks, among other things, to integrate Muslim immigrants into mainstream American society.

and often, from other religions that still exist alongside. As this is far too extensive to address in one chapter in one book, we will focus on the religious innovation in the United States primarily, but occasionally with examples from other parts of the world as well.

The United States has, for legal, cultural, and demographic reasons, created an environment ideally suited for religious innovation. Although the United States still ranks as one of the most religiously devout nations in the world, it is also one of the most diverse. As we saw in an earlier chapter, however, the numbers of non-Christians is very small. A simple measure like the percentage of the population that believes in God (90.7%) is by itself very misleading. Liberal Christians believe in God, and so do conservative fundamentalists, as well as Muslims, Hindus, and many others, some of whom we will now consider. Noting that both liberal and conservative Christians believe in the same God (as do Jews and Muslims), they still disagree strongly on numerous social and political issues. Just because someone devoutly believes in God does not mean the person supports prayer in public schools, for example. Likewise, not all "alternative" religions are radical, or radical in the same way.

Misunderstandings About Functionalism Dispelled

The theoretical perspective that informs this chapter comes primarily from a theoretical tradition known as functionalism. However, let us briefly elaborate on this before readers embrace or vilify the word "functionalism." Conventionally, sociologists often interpret functionalism as a conservative theory, compatible generally with conservative social and political views. Functionalism is furthermore compatible with other conservative theories such as rational choice theory, conventional thinking goes, and incompatible with liberal, leftist, or generally critical theories. As this book suggested earlier, aligning social scientific theory with political orientations confuses two different things. Science attempts to understand the world, and while this always involves a bias in perspective, it is not the same as a political orientation that seeks to control social institutions, public opinion, and exert decision-making power. Although science can provide insight upon which political platforms may be based, science—whether natural or social science—is not a political platform. It is an analytical system, not a system of management and political control. In our effort to understand religion, sociology studies religion critically, but at the same time cannot draw conclusions about the merit of particular religious beliefs or practice.

From a scientific perspective, functionalism can be just as critical of taken-for-granted notions, of facile explanations, of unsupported conclusions. As one of its greatest proponents, Robert Merton ([1949] 1967) argues that functionalism and other critical, namely, Marxist and other historical-materialist perspectives share certain things in common. They are not completely nor automatically opposed. Marxists and functionalists both regard religion as "social mechanisms," which results from a formalistic aspect of their respective theories. In other words, both see religion as a formal process defined conceptually, and as an institution with established laws, procedures, and other more or less consistent patterns of belief, administration, and other attributes. Both sides take this as a starting point, as an assumption that requires no further proof. As Merton puts it,

> The functionalists, with their emphasis on religion as a social mechanism for reinforcing the sentiments most essential to the institutional integration of society, do not differ materially in their analytical framework from the Marxists . . . who also assert that religion operates as a social mechanism for reinforcing certain secular as well as sacred sentiments among its believers. (p. 44)

Both approaches apply a formal theoretical framework, and each respective framework views religion as an institution that serves to integrate members of society into a collective identity. So far, both sides agree on these basic sociological points.

There are differences, of course. As Merton ([1949] 1967) explains, "the point of difference occurs only when evaluations of this commonly accepted fact come into question" (p. 45). Religion may integrate people in a variety of ways, into very different types of societies. A society may be relatively free and open, or it may consist of strict groups and hierarchy, premised on race, class, gender, age, caste, or any number of other inequalities. Where the functionalist considers the degree of integration and the ability of religion as a social institution to function effectively as a system of integration, the Marxist challenges the outcome. That is, the Marxist challenges the desirability of a given religion and the social relations it supports. Thus, Merton concludes that "it is in the evaluation of the function of religion" in terms of the type of society it reinforces, "rather than in the logic of analysis, then, that the functionalists and the Marxists part company" (p. 45). Functionalism in essence thus compares any given religion to the established relations in society, and analyzes the extent to which it integrates people into established society, or into some other type of society. A Marxist goes one step farther, to assess whether a religion and the society it supports encourage freedom or legitimate oppression. In other words, the disagreement is not about understanding of the truth, but value judgments about the desirability of the truth as it currently stands.

Some sociologists regard functionalism as a consensus theory, in the sense that society is based on the values and practices that hold society together, and whenever conflict exists, society will encourage or impose consensus. This is not what Merton means. While consensus may result in some cases, conflict may intensify and social collapse may result and produce various forms of rebellion, anything from mob uprisings to organized civil war. Functionalism does not deny this, and in fact seeks to explain such occurrences as much as Marxism. As commonly believed, functionalism does not focus solely on institutions or "structure," but equally on agency and subjective states of mind. In fact, Talcott Parsons ([1937] 2002), Merton's mentor, lamented the sad state of American social science in his day, that

> behaviorism was so rampant that anyone who believed in the scientific validity of the interpretation of subjective states of mind was often held to be fatuously naive. Also rampant was what I called "empiricism," namely the idea that scientific knowledge was a total reflection of the "reality out there" and even selection was alleged to be illegitimate. (p. 37)

Far more dynamic than often depicted, Parsons and the functionalist school he helped to found (along with Pitrim Sorokin) reject crude and reductionist approaches like behaviorism (that all behavior is learned through positive or negative feedback) and crude empiricism (that the facts, especially statistics, speak for themselves). Parsons calls for analysis of subjective states of mind, as well as a theoretical perspective that is sophisticated and dynamic enough to account for subjective aspects of humanity, such as emotion, spirituality, and belief—certainly all vital aspects of religion.

In contrast, some identify Marxist and other theories as conflict theories. Allegedly, they focus on the social forces that drive society apart, whereas consensus theories focus on the forces that hold society together.

Clearly, the reason that an institution, religious or otherwise, engages in one or more modes of social adaptation is because conflict has arisen between institutions. Consensus occurs when institutions and people reach some sort of mutually agreeable accommodation, whether the consensus is relatively momentary or enduring. Thus, the distinction between conflict and consensus theories does not make sense in this application, and it does not provide a useful conceptual framework. Conflict and consensus are simply two sides of the same coin, that is, two parts of any social system. Rather than address them as abstract concepts with or without merit as ideas in their own right, Merton and others instead focus on substantive issues. The words we assign as names for substantive issues are not important; they are just a way to standardize vocabulary so we can further discuss substantive issues in greater detail. Just as Marx saw religion as partly a consensus-building institution, so Merton sees religion as partly divisive. The issue is not conflict versus consensus, but the ability to explain observable facts. Every society consists of both conflict and consensus elements. As Merton argued above, the difference lies not in the analysis of facts, but the value judgments made about the conclusions—whether a religion is desirable, not what it is and what it does in society. As always, we will avoid value judgments to the greatest extent possible. Let us instead turn to analysis.

Analytical Concepts

Regarding religion, Merton ([1949] 1967) specifies that functionalist theory explains "modes of adaptation to contradictions in the cultural and social structure" (p. 152) and not variations in character or personality types. This does not negate the importance of subjective modes of thought, but rather, it asserts that given any specific religion or congregation, any number of personality variations may be found. The Modes of Adaptation scheme that Merton developed, and the concepts that comprise it, have a technical sociological meaning. We will cover each in turn. The broader Modes of Adaptation scheme refers to the way in which groups adapt to conflict. When the values or behavior of a group are in conflict with the society around it, the group engages in one or more of the various modes of adaptation. As we will see, this is not always free of conflict, coercion, or violence.

Conformity describes a group that initially comes into conflict with the dominant society around it, and adapts by changing in ways to make it compatible with, and therefore conform to, the values and way of life of the surrounding society. Remember that this applies to a group that at some point does in fact conflict with the surrounding society. It does not apply to institutions or groups that are already constitutive elements of society. From its founding, for example, Congress has always been part of the U.S. government. It was never an external institution that demanded access to the system—it was always part of the system. In contrast, the Environmental Protection Agency (EPA) did not always exist, but because people agitated for such an office, the government incorporated (at least some) environmental values and established a new office, the EPA. In other words, the government *conformed* to demands from its citizenry and *adapted* to accommodate their views.

Innovation is an attempt to achieve the dominant goal in a society outside of the established institutional means. In other words, innovative religion accepts the values of society, but either rejects or lacks access to the established institutional means of achievement. For example, parents who home-school their children accept the value of education, but reject the school as an institution as a means to achieve an education. Home-schooling is thus an innovation in the sociological sense. In addition to innovation, there are four other categories of adaptation (see Table 4.2).

With innovation, a religion accepts the values of society, which includes life goals, such as earning money and accumulating property. Merton emphasizes

Table 4.2   Modes of Adaptation and Examples in This Chapter

Mode	Concept	Example
Conformity	Value changes that produce compatibility—the changing ideas approach	The Latter-Day Churches, especially the Mormon Church
Innovation	Actions that derive from similar values but differing opportunity—the new ways of acting approach	Unitarian Universalism
Ritualism	Compulsive adherence to norms—the going through the motions without meaning approach	Roman Catholic Traditionalism Movement
Retreatism	Embracing of replacement reality; usually personal or small enclaves—the escapist approach	Voudou in the New World
Rebellion	Attempts to overthrow or replace dominant values or customs—the rise-up approach	Native American Resistance

monetary success as the driving force of innovation, because few other aspects of life exert pressure to succeed as strongly as economic pressure. Still, Merton intended his theory to apply to broader social phenomena, and in this case, innovative religions seek the same things that all religious communities seek—meaningful belonging. Innovation thus exhibits two salient features. As Merton ([1949] 1967) explains, "First, incentives for success are provided by the established values of the culture, and second, the avenues available for moving toward this goal are largely limited" (p. 145). Merton specifies "class structure" as the decisive limit on the avenue of success, but Merton here speaks to criminal behavior for financial gain. Applied to religion, the innovative person seeks a meaningful community, but social circumstances block the person's access. We have seen recently how the Catholic Church seeks to purge gay men from the ranks of the clergy, and many other churches condemn homosexuality. Yet gay people have the same spiritual needs as non-gays. The more they are excluded from mainstream churches, the greater the tendency toward innovation will be.

However, a gay person may choose not to innovate, and instead will conform outwardly to acceptable codes of conduct. The individual will hide his or her homosexuality, or even deny its existence altogether. Merton would term this *ritualism*. Although one defines his or her own values, "one continues to abide almost compulsively by institutional norms" (p. 150). In this case, one's internal orientation changes to whatever the individual prefers, and here we see the importance of subjective states of mind that Parsons highlighted. The fact that people can think, feel, and believe one way but live a completely contrary outward life in order to blend in creates tremendous psychological conflict. In terms of behavior, this sort of person lives ritualistically, that is, devoted to rituals without an underlying meaning or sense of connection or one that is disconnected from the required behavior. Outward appearance replaces all internal commitment.

In retreatism, a person or group rejects both the values and the means of society, and retreats to an alternative reality. Retreatist religions incur a certain amount of persecution, because society cannot allow open violation of its values unless it acknowledges that its values are open to question. Nearly every society has at least some values that it thinks of as beyond question.

For Merton ([1949] 1967), this sort of adaptation usually takes a personal rather than a social form, but in the case of religion, groups can and do separate themselves morally and materially from mainstream society. Merton distinguishes retreatism from rebellion, by stipulating that

> although people exhibiting this deviant behavior may gravitate toward centers where they come in contact with other deviants and although they may come to share in the subculture of these deviant groups, their adaptations are largely private and isolated rather than unified under a new cultural code. (p. 155)

We should modify Merton somewhat in this case, because cults clearly do organize an alternative value system and way of life, but they do not rebel against mainstream society. They only separate from—that is, retreat from—the mainstream.

Consistent with Merton, cults remain small if not quite personal; they are the expression of the leader's personal beliefs, hopes, and often, psychopathology.

Rebellion, or revolution, also potentially rejects both the values and the means of mainstream society, but such groups do so selectively, in contrast with retreatism, which rejects both entirely. The rebellious sect actively creates a new value system and way of life, which may incorporate some existing values and behaviors and reject others. The goal is not to drop out, but to actively replace the current standard with new standards. Compared to retreatism, "rebellion . . . involves a genuine transvaluation." Furthermore, "the revolutionary not only puts the values into question, but he signifies that the unity of the group is broken" (Merton [1949] 1967:156–157). The rebellious types seek to reestablish the links of the group, yet with new and different values.

So as groups break away to varying degrees from the mainstream, they must establish some sort of alternative social connection between individual breakaway members, or they become simply a collection of disparate individuals. This also can happen, of course, as we noted in Chapter 1, in the case of a society composed of consumers who have no deeper connection with the people and society around them. They need not concern us for the moment, however, because a collection of disparate individuals will not form new religious movements.

What happens, in any case, when a nonconformist group achieves some degree of separation? Whether through innovation, ritualism, retreatism, or rebellion, how do they maintain their alternative religion? This is an empirical question, and to answer it, we must study relevant empirical examples.

We have seen examples of this, as for example when Christianity replaced paganism. This process did not occur all at once, but over a period of time as Christianity retained certain beliefs and practices and modified or discarded others. We often associate revolution with one decisive date or battle, when in reality revolution is a social process that typically occurs over extended periods of time. The pace of change varies, and not all aspects of society change dramatically, if at all. The mere presence of deviant groups is an important indicator of disenfranchisement, but by itself does not indicate a revolutionary situation. Most of the time, especially in modern pluralist society, the established order can accommodate many deviant beliefs and ways of life. Only those that actively and directly threaten the established order receive punitive action, such as Al-Qaeda terror cells within the United States, or groups such as the Branch Davidians who stockpiled weapons and explosives. Whether legally justified and necessary remains debatable, but the government lay siege to the Branch Davidian compound in Waco to preempt impending violence.

In cases where deviant groups establish some degree of alternative religion, what do they actually accomplish, in a sociological sense? They establish an alternative reference group, and more specifically, an alternative membership group. Reference groups are necessary for the individual to exist at all. In order to have a sense of self, an individual must receive validation from an established reference group, and a reference group to which the person actually belongs as a mutually recognized member—a membership group—exerts the greatest influence of all. People can imagine they belong to groups that do not actually accept them as members—for example, the Muslim in Dearborn who genuinely feels American, watches American television, goes to work every day, and eats at restaurants that serve steak and beer. From time to time, such a person discovers that the restaurant seats him in back and provides bad service, or people at work will never eat lunch with their Arab coworker who does the same job for the same pay. Similarly, a white person receives the same treatment when she shops at an Arab market in Dearborn, innocently curious about the ethnic foods and hopeful to meet new people. She finds that the proprietors speak only Arabic when she is in the store, and they never quite seem to wait on her. Both imagine they share some camaraderie with the other group, but find the other group does not accept them as members.

Of course, society in general is not this simple. People live in and among many reference groups, both in actuality and in their imagination. Some people actively select their reference groups, and some have their references forced upon them. To the extent people find a meaningful place in life, they do not concern us here. Of greater concern are those who cannot navigate competing claims placed upon them by membership in multiple and competing groups, or those people who have no consistent membership groups at all. For the classical theorists and most of the others we have discussed in this book, attention focuses on the problematic people, the ones who are neither entirely in nor entirely out of the mainstream ideal. Their social identity is ambiguous and their personal identity ambivalent. In social psychology, ambivalence refers to the tension that arises from competing commitments; it describes a heightened and agitated emotional state. We should not confuse this with apathy, which describes a state of nonemotion; the person has no particular commitments and generally lacks passion about anything.

On the Ambiguity, Ambivalence, and Vacancy of the Self in Modern Life

At times, such a state of self-ambiguity and ambivalence may describe the majority of people in any given society. Many have argued that such a state characterizes the typical condition of life in modern times. The literature on this is voluminous, and regardless of perspective—Marxist, feminist, functionalist, structural, social-psychological—the conclusions remain consistent, so consistent, in fact, that we should probably consider it as a given. We should not be surprised to find the various modes of adaptation all around us and in abundance.

Alternative religion may soon become more common than mainline religion.

The conclusions are that the socially ambiguous and emotionally ambivalent person in fact holds certain values, but these values carry no meaning and thus confer no particular code or standard for living. They provide no meaningful parameters to guide a person, which sociologically means to connect a person to society through genuine recognition in a membership group. We are forever searching for meaning and meaningful standards of life, but the choices are endless and many seem equally fair, just, and practical. This perpetual uncertainty compels people to constantly seek social relationships and groups, but in order to join them, we must malleably adapt and often to different groups at different times. All social relations in modern society are basically negotiated, and therefore inherently superficial and transient. In short, the more people seek social belonging, the more energy they must commit to negotiation, and thus the more alone they feel. The isolation of modern life is intolerable and inspires a quest for social belonging, but the negotiated boundaries of social life temporarily satisfy the need for belonging and simultaneously create new insecurity as the vast majority of possible relationships are temporary.

Consequently, as Merton ([1949] 1967) correctly notes, people can identify with groups to which they do not really belong, but such an orientation ultimately increases alienation and anomie. In order to have meaning, people must live within "patterned expectations of forms of interaction which are morally binding on them and the other members" (p. 286). While groups may have different levels of commitment among their members, the key in any religious community is that the patterned forms of interaction are *morally binding*. Without this aspect, the group will not connect to the individual with sufficient strength. Unless morally binding, the individual will feel the connection as trivial, something that can be disregarded whenever convenient. One of the great strengths of a free and open society is that people are free to pursue a life different from the one they were born into, but then they also face the simultaneous problem of anomie—one of the greatest weaknesses of a free society. When they decline membership in the groups of their birth, they may not find meaningful replacements.

> ## Resources on the Ambiguity, Ambivalence, and Vacancy of the Self in Modern Life: Many Perspectives, Similar Conclusions
>
> Bell, Daniel. [1976] 1996. *The Cultural Contradictions of Capitalism.*
> Bellah, Robert N. [1985] 1996. *Habits of the Heart: Individualism and Commitment in American Life.*
> Hochschild, Arlie. [1983] 2003. *The Managed Heart: Commercialization of Human Feeling*, Twentieth Anniversary Edition.
> Jenks, Chris. 2004. *Subculture: The Fragmentation of the Social.*
> Lasch, Christopher. [1978] 1991. *Culture of Narcissism: American Life in an Age of Diminishing Expectations.*
> Riesman, David. [1961] 2001. *The Lonely Crowd, Revised Edition: A Study of the Changing American Character.*
> Seligman, Adam B. 2003. *Modernity's Wager: Authority, the Self, and Transcendence.*
>
> NOTE: See References and Further Reading for complete bibliographic information.

Yet actual membership in a group is vital for religious identity. Alternative religions come into existence and thrive because they provide what the seeker is most lacking—actual reference group membership. Cults also provide this, but premised on a different agenda—the will of the leader, for the leader's benefit. In alternative religions, the potential member is someone who, in sociological terms, is a marginal person—someone who is neither entirely in nor out of any and often many different groups. Based on what Merton ([1949] 1967) terms "anticipatory socialization," that a person expects or anticipates acceptance in a group but fails to achieve it, "this type of case will be recognized as that of the marginal man, poised on the edge of several groups but fully accepted by none of them" (p. 265). This person therefore becomes the seeker—a person who actively seeks social membership, but whom groups never fully accept or entirely reject. This person is perpetually on the margins of all groups, the outsider who lingers at the edge. He or she is not the forever downtrodden and rejected, who tends to give up all hope (Durkheim's fatalism), but rather, the forever hopeful and the forever disappointed at the same time. This produces powerful, even desperate feelings of anomie. The hopeful desperation makes the person willing to assume the greater likelihood of association with alternative religions, and also cults.

We may now render some overall conclusions to create a degree of conceptual unity. Of all the nonconforming types outlined earlier, the one that generates the most alternative forms of religion and thus contributes most strongly to social change is the rebellious type. Although such types do not necessarily seek to overthrow mainstream society, they do seek to actively create a replacement community. In sociological terms, the revolutionary "appeals to a past or future reference group. He reactivates a forgotten set of values, standards, and practices, or activates a set which is not blemished by existing concessions and expedient compromises with current realities" (Merton [1949] 1967:363). In this regard, the revolutionary constitutes an exact opposite of the individual who rejects mainstream values and standards for purely personal gain in money, power, notoriety, or other things. This distinction is important sociologically in that it allows us to distinguish, among other things, the difference between a cult, discussed in Chapter 7, from an alternative religious group. Cults form around a leader who, above all else, seeks personal aggrandizement. In alternative religious groups, there may be the one leader, but the goal is to establish an alternative community with meaningful values that legitimate an alternative way of life. The interests of the group supersede the interest of any one member, including the leader.

We now possess adequate theoretical equipment to analyze representative examples.

Conformity: The Case of the Latter-Day Churches

At first glance, it might seem conceptually incorrect to place the Latter-Day churches in any of the adaptation categories. Famously known for their polygamy in the early years, such practices obviously differ from the mainstream. Yet such a conclusion pertains to the early years of the Church, and it has changed considerably since that time. Furthermore, the Church today exhibits a value system that, when excluding polygamy, places it very close to the center of American society. In its present form, the Latter-Day churches are conformist—they formerly rejected both the values and means of society, but now conform to the established values and institutions, in which they now participate fully.

Most people think of the Latter-Day Church as the Mormon Church, with its headquarters in Salt Lake City, Utah. Known commonly as the Mormon Church or the LDS, this moniker properly stands for the Church of Jesus Christ of Latter-Day Saints. There are numerous other denominations of the Latter-Day faith, although the size of the Mormon Church in Salt Lake City by itself dwarfs the others combined, and hence, this section refers only to the Mormon Church unless otherwise indicated. The Mormon Church reports 12.5 million members worldwide, with about 6.5 million in the United States.

Joseph Smith (Image 4.1) founded the Mormon Church on April 6, 1830. Smith claimed that an angel named Moroni had visited him beginning when Smith was 15. The visions took the form of lessons in a previously unknown ancient language, and several history lessons about a previously unknown group of Native Americans who were descended from one of the tribes of Israel. The visions concluded when Moroni directed Smith to a hilltop near where he lived in upstate New York, and revealed to Smith a set of gold tablets, written in the ancient language in which Moroni had tutored Smith. These tablets contained another Gospel of Jesus Christ, and revealed that Christ had appeared to this Native American tribe, just as he had appeared to the ancient Jews. Smith translated and published the Gospel as the Book of Mormon.

Smith viewed himself and his followers as restorers, not as revolutionaries (Arrington and Bitton 1992). Smith believed that the visions directed him to restore ancient Christianity, and in this sense, Mormonism in its early years resembles the broader reconstructionist movement of the period, associated with people such as Thomas Campbell, Barton W. Stone, and Walter Scott. Although these leaders vehemently denied any resemblance to the Mormons, in historical retrospect they quite clearly held many of

Image 4.1   Joseph Smith

the same principles—namely, that the modern world had become corrupt, and the Second Coming would not occur until humans had refashioned the earth to make it acceptable to God. This would, through action, prove to God that we are ready to receive the Second Coming. Yet the Second Coming was not so far off, either, and present-day actions would determine its exact timing, as well as exactly who would be saved—typical millenarian thought of the day (Underwood 1999).

With few allies and many critics, Smith led the early congregation from Fayette, New York, where it started, through various sites in Ohio, to settle in Independence, Missouri. Conflict arose with the local militia, which included the infamous Missouri Border Ruffians and Quantrill's Raiders, which was led by the ruthless William C. Quantrill and included Frank and Jesse James. They were a collection of mercenaries who hired themselves to proslavery groups to fight against free-state groups, located mostly in Illinois and Kansas. Quantrill led a raid against a free-state stronghold—the town of Lawrence, Kansas—and killed 164 people. Guilty of other bloody raids and numerous other armed criminal activities, the Missouri militia operated outside of the law, but also with its complicity.

Needless to say, the militia treated the Mormons harshly for their clearly deviant way of life, and threatened to kill all of them (about 250 at this time). On October 27, 1838, the governor of Missouri, Lilburn Boggs, issued the famous Extermination Order, which stated that for "open and avowed defiance of the laws, and . . . having made war upon the

Image 4.2 Brigham Young

people of this State . . . the Mormons must be treated as enemies, and must be exterminated or driven from the State if necessary for the public peace—their outrages are beyond all description" (excerpted from Hartley 2001). The congregation fled to Illinois and established a community at a town they called Nauvoo. However, they received a hostile reception in Illinois as well, and a mob killed Joseph Smith in 1844. Brigham Young (Image 4.2) emerged as the new leader, and proved to be a powerful speaker and skilled organizer.

Throughout most of 1847, Young led the congregation westward, where they settled on the banks of the Great Salt Lake, the last remnants of what was once a vast inland sea. They suffered no further persecution (for a while) in this remote place, and dedicated themselves to building the type of community they had long sought. Having suffered such ongoing trials and tribulations, their beliefs changed over time, and in order to become compatible with the nation as Utah became a state, they outlawed their most famous practice—polygamy. This did not bring immediate acceptance, of course, but it opened the door to a much more amenable relationship with mainstream society, and especially, the modern world.

The Mormon Church was one of the fastest growing churches throughout the twentieth century and now has connections throughout government and business. Although the Church still emphasizes its reconstructionist doctrine, many other denominations in the United States share this belief. Also, the Mormon Church has no doctrinal points to inhibit full participation in politics or business, both of which it pursues fervently. George Romney, a successful CEO of American Motors from 1954 to 1962, served as a Republican governor of Michigan from 1963 to 1969, a position from which he resigned to join the Nixon administration as Secretary of Housing and Urban Development. His son Mitt Romney, also a Mormon, recently (in 2006) retired as Republican governor of Massachusetts and was a candidate for the U.S. presidency in 2008.

Today, the Church has some doctrinal points that differ from mainline Christianity, such as the Book of Mormon and certain beliefs based on it, but these factors do not define the Church's socially relevant values and behavior, according to sociological theory. Although mainline Christians might consider Mormons to be revolutionary and perhaps theologically dangerous, their differences in beliefs

created an institutional structure, the Mormon Church, which today follows the established values of U.S. society. As shareholders in many large corporations, as executives and wage workers, as professionals in many fields, and as skilled trade workers, the Mormons participate in and contribute to most aspects of social life. As an institution, the Church functions with great organizational efficiency, and all together, the Church and its members share the values of American society and practice a lifestyle that is fully compatible—in fact, fully promoting—of traditional American values. Once outsiders, they are now to a great extent upholders of traditional U.S. values and lifestyle. They condemn homosexuality and sex outside of marriage, and they strongly advocate for monogamous heterosexual marriage, self-reliance, and hard work.

Here we see how a sociological analysis differs from a theological one. Clearly, their beliefs differ from most Christian churches. Yet the actual life they lead and their thorough integration into mainstream politics and business render them conformist; they adapted through conformity to make themselves compatible with the surrounding society. With a brief look at their history, we saw that clearly they once stood outside of and in opposition to mainstream values and lifestyles, and that practices such as polygamy and the blasphemy of the Book of Mormon evoked great social hostility. However, by moving doctrine to a background position, and removing in particular the offensive practices, they conformed to mainstream values. With doctrine in the background, they outwardly emphasize a clean-cut, hardworking life that allows them to fit in almost anywhere. They gain converts by examples of success, not by preaching.

On most issues, the Mormons are overwhelmingly conservative. In a recent study of all Christian-based affiliation in the United States, the research team found that Mormons believe decisively that "the U.S. has a special role in the world" and that the "U.S. should go it alone" wherever and whenever its interests are threatened, including in Iraq (Guth et al. 2005:5–6). Although the Mormons are almost always the most conservative across a variety of issues, they are definitely not alone, but rather are always on the majority side. The United States is generally conservative on issues such as war, poverty, AIDS, and disaster relief, with the Mormons as the most conservative in a country where conservatives predominate.

The Mormons have moved from the margins to the mainstream over the past 150 years. They are well-known today for their clean-cut appearance and their avoidance of alcohol and caffeine drinks. Although most people do imbibe, the Mormons emphasize healthy living, not simply the avoidance of temptation, and in this way, they partake of the fitness movement. Although the underlying motivation is religious observance rather than a desire for six-pack abs and a sexy body, the result is a socially compatible lifestyle. Similarly, the Mormons conform to conventional business practices and strive for economic success within legal parameters. The Church uses all means of modern technology in business and supports higher education—certainly a laudable goal that most people support. Once rebellious, the Mormon Church now conforms to, and in many ways actively maintains, mainstream society.

Innovation: The Case of Unitarian Universalism

In a sense, all Protestant denominations could be thought of as innovative. Although they accepted the basic beliefs of the Roman Catholic Church, they rejected its formality, both in terms of doctrine and its institutional structure. For each church that broke away from its parent institution, whether Catholic or a subsequent Protestant church, the various denominations accepted most of the beliefs, but rejected the means of fulfilling or living in accordance with those beliefs.

This discussion depends greatly on what we consider to be the essential beliefs that define Christianity, and what we consider auxiliary. For conceptual purposes, let us agree that Christianity is the acceptance that Jesus is the son of God, and that he came to earth to deliver a message. If followed, this message leads to salvation. This conceptualization purposely does not specify the content of the message, nor the nature of Christ himself—two issues that have separated Christians since the religion's inception. Basically, Christianity is a religion based on the life and teachings of Jesus Christ. Expressed sociologically, we would say that the teachings of Christ are normative values for all Christians. With this in mind, Unitarian Universalism is a Christian faith. It accepts the decisive beliefs of Christianity in general. Yet it also innovates regarding practice, and thus becomes an example of sociological innovation.

As the name suggests, Unitarian Universalism is a union of once institutionally separate churches. Both started on the East Coast in the late 1700s, as products of the Enlightenment (May 1976) and a time when reason and science asserted greater influence on religious thought. In 1787, King's Chapel, part of Harvard College, converted to the Unitarian moral theology (although it remained officially Episcopal), and in 1796, Joseph Priestly and others founded the First Unitarian Church in Philadelphia. During the same years, various itinerant preachers spread the view that all people of good faith would be saved, regardless of which church they attended. Decidedly populist, Universalism spread along the East Coast and then westward as the country expanded. Thus, Unitarianism developed as an enlightened doctrine of the educated elite, whereas Universalism developed as a popular doctrine among many different preachers. Although theologically compatible from the beginning, each belief system had to traverse strong class and status divides to unite with its counterpart.

Despite the class, status, and educational differences of Unitarianism and Universalism, they shared a common perspective that God's word and the life of Jesus are ultimately positive and uplifting messages. Consequently, people should experience joy rather than gloom, and hopeful optimism rather than bitter pessimism about the world and about each other. Perhaps most decisively, though, they agreed that faith must be compatible with reason (Olds 1995:88–89). There are different ways to understand truth, but truth is always compatible with other truth. Reason and faith provide two equal and essential sides of the complete picture of existence. They must be united, not one subordinated to the other.

American society at this time consisted of strong divisions between urban and rural, rich and poor, educated and uneducated. The Unitarian side formulated sophisticated doctrine through a combination of scripture, philosophy, and science—it was one of the most literate and intellectual beliefs in its day. It also developed within the church establishment (mostly Episcopal) in Boston and other cities on the East Coast. In contrast, the Universalists were mostly farmers and laborers, rural and uneducated. Individual preachers outside the establishment purveyed universalism as they traveled. With such completely different demographic foundations, the two churches did not officially unite until May 11, 1961.

The decisive factor, however, does not reside in doctrine. The Unitarian Universalists believe in universal salvation of all people of good faith, all those who strive to live a good life. While they accept the central importance of Jesus, they believe that God dwelt in Jesus in a unique way; he was not God *as* man but God *in* man. Unitarians view spirituality as a lifelong quest, not as assent to or affirmation of a preconceived and fixed doctrine. In this regard, they became the primary founders and promoters of liberal Christianity.

Brian Mountford (2003), an Anglican and the Vicar of the University Church of St. Mary the Virgin, at Oxford University, explains the basic premises of liberal Christianity. Contrary to popular belief, liberal Christianity does not reject the Bible, nor advocate an "anything goes" attitude toward morality. Rather, liberal Christians "read the Bible creatively and critically." They believe that Jesus provides us with a basic guideline of "the most selflessly loving action in any particular circumstances" and in general teaches us "to be compassionate and humane in moral matters" (p. 6). Each individual must search his or her thoughts and feelings, and actively decide on a moral course of action. Liberal Christianity does not exempt the individual from moral behavior; it makes the individual absolutely responsible for his or her own moral behavior.

Unitarian Universalism thus varies from some conservative Christian churches theologically. However, the core elements of Christianity remain intact. We find the innovative difference in terms of the church's organization; it is entirely democratic. Each local congregation retains full administrative control over its operations and full intellectual control over its doctrines and rituals. Some of these decisions may be passed up to the national assembly, but this happens democratically, each step of the way. Other denominations use democratic decision making as well, but arguably none as completely as the Unitarian Universalists (Olds 1995). As one Unitarian Universalist stated, "our faith is built on deeds, not creeds" (Buehrens and Church 1991:41). Unitarian Universalists seek moral action in the world, not debate about metaphysics. Again, many Christian denominations share this view, but arguably none practice it first and foremost. Since there is no hierarchy, there are no inactive administrative positions. Everyone works for the common good of humanity in a direct and participatory way—the same values as Christianity in general, but innovative in practice.

Ritualism: The Case of Roman Catholic Traditionalism

Upon first consideration, it might seem nonsensical for a religion to embrace a set of rituals without a corresponding set of beliefs, the very beliefs that the ritual supposedly expresses in the first place. The example of Catholic traditionalism offers an illustrative, but by no means pure, example. Often in the social sciences, one fails to find a pure example of any given concept. In addition to being a rough fit, rather than a perfect fit, this example offers great potential to offend Catholics who regard themselves as "traditional." However, let us clarify what this means.

The established Catholic Church, centered in Vatican City, Rome, is not part of this movement. In fact, Catholic traditionalism formed in opposition to the established church, especially after the reforms of the Vatican II Council in 1962. Traditionalists regard these reforms as a liberal betrayal of core Catholic beliefs and practices. Many Catholics regard themselves as "traditional" in a number of ways, but Catholic traditionalism refers to a specific movement outside of and in opposition to the established Church.

Traditionalists oppose the *aggiornamento,* or updating of the Catholic Church to make it more compatible with modern society. In the mid-twentieth century, many in the Church leadership felt that the Church had become mired in the Middle Ages, with such conventions as saying the Mass only in Latin, a very formal process of confession, and a strict and hierarchical separation of laity and clergy. Many felt that such medievalry would make the Church less and less relevant to real life today, and would reduce Catholicism to no more than an abstract and empty ritual on Sunday. The Church would lose moral relevance in everyday life and in terms of vital issues of the day. The Church would eventually become a quaint anachronism.

The Catholic traditionalist movement has denounced Vatican II as "heretical" and as "false theology" (Dinges 1995:101) that betrays the true foundations of the Church, going back to St. Peter. Traditionalists follow the pre-Vatican II Tridentine Mass and dogma, which refers to the official liturgical and theological decisions made at the Council of Trent, held at various meetings between 1545 and 1563. Among its most significant decisions, the Council of Trent established the standards for the sacraments and the celebration of Mass, which it declared must be conducted in Latin only. It also clarified the doctrine of salvation, and standardized the Biblical canon for the Catholic Church. In addition, the Council of Trent condemned Protestantism in any form. The doctrinal and liturgical standards the Council of Trent established remained more or less consistent until the Vatican II Council, opened under Pope John XXIII in 1962 and closed under Pope Paul VI in 1965.

Vatican II, the common name for the Second Ecumenical Council of the Vatican, was not just an intellectual and theological exercise, nor primarily a power battle between elites in the Catholic hierarchy. Rather, Vatican II addressed the concerns of clergy at lower levels worldwide, many of whom worked in third world countries where government-sponsored violence, corruption, and war ran amok. Especially in Central and South America, local clergy faced issues of poverty, death squads, and brutal oppression as facts of everyday life. As moral agents, local clergy looked to the Church to become a more active moral force and a voice for the oppressed. In other words, the reality of modern life included great poverty and widespread injustice, and Vatican II attempted to move the Church out of its theological isolation and to bring its moral authority into the struggle for human rights and emancipation.

Traditionalists object both to the progressive theological changes that Vatican II introduced, as well as to the Church's more active role in local politics, especially in freedom movements on the side of the oppressed. Vatican II also legitimated progressive Catholic lay organizations that opposed the death penalty, and supported environmental protection, civil rights, and groups that oppose war. Catholic traditionalists oppose these efforts, as well as the liberalization of Catholic doctrine and liturgy (Dinges 1995). They strongly oppose celebration of the Mass in any language other than Latin. After Vatican II, most clergy celebrated the Mass in the local languages of their congregation. Traditionalists align their interest with conservative politics and religious-right causes in general, often finding much greater common ground with conservative Protestants than with their more centrist and liberal Catholic cohorts.

Of particular note for our discussion here is the traditionalist call for greater supernaturalism and traditional Catholic symbolism. Supernaturalism refers to the mysteries of the Church—that for example the trinity is a mystery, as the saying goes, "that never could, cannot be, and never will be understood." Similarly, the Tridentine Mass specifies the exact words (in Latin) and the exact order the celebrant must follow for every Mass. It is believed that any deviation greatly displeases God. Also, traditionalists believe in literal transubstantiation—that the bread and wine in communion does in fact turn into the body and blood of Christ. From a sociological standpoint, these mysteries constitute examples of ritualism, because they embrace the ritual as an end in itself, with little concern for the underlying reasons. For example, a liberal Catholic might ask, Why does any deviation inherently displease God? What if conditions do not permit a full Mass? Why must the celebrant speak only in Latin? Where does scripture demand this? How does bread and wine turn into flesh and blood? Isn't such a notion appalling, a clear case of cannibalism? Sociologically, traditionalism places ritual over meaning and content. It names itself—ritualism. Traditionalists obediently submit to traditional ritual, which for them supersedes all other concerns, including the ability of the Tridentine Mass to reach the congregation or a belief like transubstantiation to make sense in a scientific world.

Just as important, the traditionalist movement aligns itself with non-Catholic and secular political interests, which offers no further justification for devotion to ritual, but explains sociologically why they prefer traditional dogma to contemporary updates. Traditional dogma relates to the movement's own worldview and political orientation. Whereas the Church leadership and most mainline Catholics identify with the oppressed and support human rights movements, traditionalist Catholics favor established powers and their established order, both within the Catholic Church and in social relations generally. Just as mainline Catholicism moved decisively to the side of the poor and oppressed, so the traditionalists moved decisively to the side of established power. Not an ideological move, traditionalism longs for a nostalgic return of the moral absolutism of the Council of Trent, and the medieval Church hierarchy that equated the levels of clergy with the levels of the secular nobility, that the Church might once again share in the status of royal grandeur and political power.

Retreatism: Voudou in the New World

Spelled various ways, Voudou (from the French) or Voodoo (popular Anglo-American) designates a religion that traveled to the United States among slaves from Africa in the sixteenth century. On their way from Africa, traditional African religions transformed upon contact with Christianity as well as the different cultures established on the Caribbean islands, especially Spanish, English, French, and Dutch. Voudou emerges as a distinct religion, as a syncretic blend of African tribal religions and the attendant cultures, as well as Christianity, island cultures, and the slave experience.

We should note from the outset that retreatism does not signify failure or inferiority, but rather, a particular relationship to the dominant culture. In the quest for survival, especially under the most oppressive conditions such as slavery, people adapt strategies appropriate for their conditions. If anything, retreatism signifies a refusal to surrender, that it is better to live on the margins than to collaborate through conformity in order to more closely resemble the dominant culture. Retreatism signifies a moving away from, not a capitulation. This tactic allowed Voudou to survive to the present day, which with greater freedom, even allows it to flourish. As we will see, though, retreatism tends to greatly particularize an institution, including or perhaps especially religion, and thus even today Voudou pertains to a relatively narrow demographic segment.

In New Orleans among slaves and free black people, for example, Voudou developed in almost parallel fashion to the Christian beliefs of the slave owners and the white community in general. With its own beliefs and rituals, Voudou developed from disparate beliefs drawn from all over Africa, and coalesced in New Orleans into an organized and complex culture of its own, distinct from both white religion and its African origins and Caribbean influences.

In contrast to Christianity, women played a much more prominent and often leadership role. Among the most famous of the Voudou priestesses was Marie Laveau. She was born in the French Quarter, also known as the Vieux Carré, the old square, in 1794. It is believed that her father was Charles Laveau, a wealthy white farmer, and her mother was Darcantel Marguerite, described as a mulatto (part white, part black) with a strain of Indian blood. Little is known about Darcantel, except that she was possibly a prostitute, or the victim of rape. White masters often forced sex upon their black female slaves, which was not considered a crime and indeed, was regarded as an act of male virility (Long 2005). Alternatively, however, she may have been a part of the Quadroon Ball.

The Quadroon Ball was a New Orleans tradition in which wealthy white men, especially from rural areas where women were scarce, would come into the city for the occasion. Quadroons were one-quarter black, and as such were considered black. However, their generally lighter complexion made them acceptable as wives for white men, and at the Quadroon Ball, white men would meet these women under proper circumstances, and court them as they would court any other proper lady. The quadroon women were reportedly extremely beautiful, well-educated, and socially sophisticated (Berlin 2000). In contrast to the rest of the South, slavery and race in New Orleans were far more complex institutions, such that black families could rise to elite status, and many blacks, especially women, gained a degree of public status as caterers to the interests of rich whites, either through services that included medicine, fashion, and prophesy (Hanger 1997), or through entertainment (Brooks 2006). However, such status and greater freedom did not extend beyond New Orleans, nor to unskilled free black workers (Arnesen 1994).

Image 4.3   The Tomb of Marie Laveau

Marie married Jacques Paris, a free black man, on August 4, 1819, in St. Louis Cathedral, the main cathedral in New Orleans. This setting suggests that they were of respectable social standing. Both were also practicing Catholics, and they received communion, which signifies their good standing with the Church as well. Jacques Paris seems to have disappeared a few years later, and Marie began to call herself the Widow Paris, although Jacques' death was not confirmed. In his stead, she began a relationship with Louis Christophe Duminy de Glapion, a quadroon from Santo Domingo. They also married, and they produced 15 children. He was also Catholic, but it is during this time that Marie began to practice Voudou. No reliably factual evidence exists to explain why or exactly when this happened. We know only that, by 1830, many people both white and black in the greater New Orleans community were asking Marie for special help and guidance (Ward 2004). Not only a Voudou high priestess, she also became a figure of public note.

We know almost nothing about her religious Voudou practices, because they were secret and entirely separate from the white community as well as the free and slave black community. Despite her relatively high social standing among whites (she worked as an expensive hairdresser for the wealthiest women in New Orleans), her Voudou religion remained secret and separate from mainstream society. As such, it became a cultural retreat from the mainstream. Marie Laveau did not invent Voudou, which was long established as secret and separate from the mainstream, but she likely incorporated aspects from Roman Catholicism, which she never renounced. Clearly however, she found greater meaning in Voudou, as an authentic religion of oppressed people of color. American Voudou in its original period thus remains a mystery, even when associated with such a notable public figure as Marie Laveau.

The essential elements of Voudou originated in West Africa, mostly among the Foon, Ewe, and Yoruba people (Metraux 1989). The word *vodun* is the Fon-Ewe word for spirit, and Voudou in general is an animistic religion, professing that all things, living and otherwise, possess varying degrees of vodun (spirit). This is the same as *mana* among the Polynesian people, and in general, animistic beliefs of Africa resemble animistic beliefs throughout the world, including among the Celtic people of Western Europe. The African religions that contributed to Voudou were likely polytheistic, but Voudou as such, after mixing with Catholicism, became *henotheistic,* another term for inclusive monotheism. However, Voudou has always remained outside of mainstream society, even among large ethnic Caribbean island enclaves in New York City and Chicago. Also, the one god of Voudou traditions is not interchangeable with the Abrahamic God, but is a more generalized notion of a supreme deity who takes many different forms.

New Orleans in the mid-nineteenth century represents only one expression of Voudou, but today, most of the old rituals have survived only in the form of folk medicine—potions, elixirs, herbal remedies—and charms meant to influence events. The tourist trade has also assimilated the symbols of New Orleans Voudou, such as alligator heads and *gris gris,* a bundle of herbs and other personal items that confers a protective charm on the wearer. Once the expression of sacred belief and practice, these and other symbols of Voudou now sell to tourists, devoid of meaning and mass produced in China.

Caribbean Variations

Properly applied, Voudou applies only to traditions established in or descended from Haiti or Creole and Patois-speaking people in the greater Caribbean region. Still, other similar traditions, surveyed below, share the essential basis that they developed as a fusion of colonial and African influences. Specifically, Spanish and French colonialism contributed Catholicism, which blended with African animistic traditions within the social context of slavery and plantation exploitation.

Cuba

Contrary to popular belief, the Castro regime in Cuba changed relatively little about daily life and village beliefs and Havana remains one of the most exciting cities in the Americas. In the Cuban countryside, Voudou practitioners continue the religion that developed there, a synthesis of African tribal religions and Catholicism. As in most of the Caribbean colonies, Voudou developed through the main institutions of colonialism where African and Spanish culture mixed. In Cuba, slaves worked sugar plantations, which dominated the economic and social life of the island. Spain had exploited the Caribbean islands longer than the other European powers that eventually moved into the region—namely England, France, and Holland—and like its competitors, Spain devoted its energy to economic exploitation. Catholic

missionaries spent little time in the countryside with the slaves of the sugar plantations, and many plantation owners outright refused Catholic rites and services for the slaves, for fear it would reduce production (Perez 1994). As a result, African slaves never received formal indoctrination in Catholicism, so they simply borrowed what seemed meaningful to them and integrated it with their preexisting African beliefs.

In the cities in the late 1500s, former slaves and other impoverished people, such as remaining Indians and stranded merchants, formed *cabildos,* a sort of mutual aid society in which people shared their resources and provided each other with religious and whatever other services the members might have. Cabildos also became social centers, and many cabildos sponsored public celebrations, parades, and musical gatherings. This should not be confused with administrative cabildos, found throughout Spanish possessions in the Americas. Used mostly in regard to Cuba (but sometimes elsewhere), the cabildo is not an administrative body, but actually a kind of people's collective. In the forum of the cabildo, Catholicism mixed with African traditions to create a new and unique religious expression. In this process of creation, "the Saints, Jesus Christ, and the Virgin Mary were identified with African gods or ancestors who, in return for sacrifices" (Olmos and Paravisini-Gebert 2003:29); would render various benefits, which included protection and—of great importance to a slave—security that the family would be kept together. This urban syncretism produced *Regla de Ocha,* more commonly known as *Santeria.*

In addition to Catholicism's influence, Santeria developed from the tribal religions of the Yoruba people of West Africa, which includes many different cultures united by the one Yoruba language. Like many African religions, the Yoruba religions involved complex cosmologies, and this dynamism permitted the incorporation of new beliefs without disrupting the long-established traditions. In this way, Santeria retained the beliefs of its African origins, and yet admitted Catholicism once it arrived in the New World. Furthermore, Santeria, like its African antecedents, is not only an institution associated with the divine, but a comprehensive social system of extensive types of knowledge, including pharmacology, art, music, and oral history (Olmos and Paravisini-Gebert 2003:30). Upon its incorporation, Catholicism augmented the existing beliefs and cultural body of knowledge. Santeria fused the celebration of African deities with feasts of the saints and other Catholic holidays.

Like most of the Caribbean religions, Santeria practices divination, animal sacrifice, and charismatic possession. These beliefs descended from African origins, and like animal sacrifice that occurs in a religious context all over the world, the practical side is that poor people in a tropical climate who lack refrigeration facilities must kill and immediately eat their meat while it is fresh. The religious context sanctifies the practice and connects it with the broader collection of knowledge about life and death, as well as the immediate dietary needs. In other words, it unites the spiritual and practical aspects of life. Santeria also worships ancestors and the *orisha,* who are personified natural forces that interact with human beings (Olmos and Paravisini-Gebert 2003:33). Fully polytheistic, Santeria integrates Jesus and other Christian elements alongside the orishas. Santeria accepts the recent arrivals as part of the larger cultural experience—that the Yoruba traditions now reside in Cuba, and must therefore acclimate to the new environment. Santeria, like other Caribbean religions, proves quite dynamic and adaptable because the religious aspect is only one part of a much larger system of knowledge, history, and meaning.

Haiti

Like New Orleans, Haiti was first a Spanish possession and was later taken by the French. Both cultures influenced Haiti's development and imparted both a generalized Christian and European element, as well as elements specific to Spanish and French heritage.

Haiti is actually the western half of Hispaniola, with the Spanish Dominican Republic occupying the other half. Columbus first landed in the New World at Hispaniola in 1493, a cruel misfortune that befell the Arawak Indians who originally lived on the island. Like other explorers and the later Conquistadors, Columbus left Europe in search of the three G's—Gold, Glory, and God. Unfortunately, Hispaniola offered none of these things, as the island had very little gold, the Arawaks were a peaceful people and thus deprived Columbus of conquest, and Columbus had little genuine interest in God without the first two G's. The Catholic priest Bartholome de Las Casas arrived in Hispaniola as a devout missionary, but his experiences quickly changed his perspective. His journal remains as a detailed eyewitness account of Spanish brutality toward the Arawaks, whom they eventually exterminated.

With the Arawaks gone, the Spanish, and later the French, imported many slaves to both sides of Hispaniola. The brutal exploitation of people continued as plantation owners literally worked the slaves to death, finding it cheaper to import fresh slaves rather than maintain the existing stock (Olmos and Paravisini-Gebert 2003:101). Hispaniola, and the French side of Haiti especially, had the highest mortality rate of all the Caribbean colonies. It is within the violent and oppressive history of Haiti that Voudou arose.

Like Santeria, the Voudou world is inhabited by natural spirits that can take human form and communicate with humans. Known as *loa* or *lwa*, these spirits, properly approached and appeased, offer protection, knowledge, assistance, and comfort. The loa inhabit a living human body, a state known as spirit possession. Although the loa are not gods as such, they are extremely long-lived, virtually immortal, and behave according to the quality of devotion among believers. They do not inflict evil on their devotees in the sense of malicious or capricious harm, but they will ignore the supplications of those who fail to cherish their beneficence appropriately (Deren 1983). Voudou depends on the relationship between the loa and the community of believers, which often makes Haitian Voudou practitioners in particular rather indifferent to the outside world. With its origins amid the suffering and struggle of slaves on sugar plantations, Voudou coalesced during the Haitian Revolution of 1791–1803, their war for independence (Hurston [1938] 1990). Voudou emerged as the religion of the freedom fighters against the French masters, and became not just the religion of the oppressed, but of the oppressed who were essentially different from the masters. The people of Voudou could not join the Christian church, just as the masters could not join the Voudou community—their respective religions derived from and legitimated two very different social orders.

The Voudou community exists in a reciprocal relationship with their loa. Humans and spirits mutually choose each other, and loa bestow benefits as humans demonstrate appropriate and sincere devotion. Devotion involves first and foremost dancing, through which a person invokes the loa and invites them to inhabit his or her body for a time (Deren 1983). Voudou dancing is very energetic and crescendos as it proceeds. On the surface, many outsiders view this as wild, orgiastic excitement and loss of control. On the contrary, however, the dance involves complex steps and patterns that must be performed in the correct order and in conjunction with the right incantations. Early witnesses saw the dances as backward and savage indulgences, but in fact, Voudou ritual dancing reinforces civilized community; it does not negate or suspend control and self-discipline, but intensifies it. As Joan Dayan (1997) concludes, "the possessed gives herself up to become an instrument in a social and collective drama" (p. 19). Ritual dancing, which reaches ecstatic intensity of the individual, reinforces collective identity for the group.

To the extent Voudou contributed to the revolutionary uprising of slaves against their owners, it became momentarily a revolutionary religion, rather than a retreatist religion. As Leslie Desmangles (1992) argues, "Voudou meetings had often been converted into offensive mechanisms for violent raids against the planters, some costly in human lives and materials" (p. 27). In times of crisis, political agitators converted Voudou into a more aggressive and defiant stance toward the Catholic Europeans owners, but this was not the essence of Voudou. As mentioned, sociologically, Voudou mostly preserves traditional African beliefs, blended with Catholicism. With the planters gone after 1803, Voudou lost its political agenda and continued as a kind of folk religion. Today in Haiti, Voudou and Catholicism flow in and out of each other (Desmangles 1992), with uncertain lines of demarcation, which Voudou practitioners regard as an unnecessary distinction. Nearly 80% of the population of Haiti claims both Catholic and Voudou affiliation (Olmos and Paravisini-Gebert 2003:105).

Even today, Voudou retains Spanish, French, Creole, or Patois (a combination of French, Spanish, English, and Native American languages) as the sacred languages of religious ritual. After centuries of contact with white and non-Voudou social influences, Voudou has remained retreatist, a haven for marginal and excluded people of color. Importantly, Voudou does not exclude whites on a racial basis, nor for that matter mainstream black people and others of color. Voudou has also become more mainstream as many middle-class whites have assimilated elements of Voudou into their own belief system.

However, authentic Voudou as a living culture and religion lives in particular social conditions—marginalized urban communities, and nearly forgotten rural enclaves in the Louisiana bayous. It thrives among poor people of Haiti and other Caribbean islands, as well as among poor people in Brazil, and in enclaves in London, Chicago, New York, and possibly elsewhere (Black and Hyatt 1993). In all cases, we should note that authentic Voudou that continues in direct descent from its sixteenth-century origins continues in poor and otherwise marginalized communities. Voudou also has no central organizational structure, and its beliefs and rituals pass down orally or through experience, not in written form. Consequently, Voudou varies from one enclave to another, each with features particular to the traditions and conditions of that locale. The effect is to greatly particularize Voudou enclaves, such that outsiders, even from nearby villages, do not fit the local traditions and history of the group. Very few people in the United States, for example, would intentionally impoverish themselves and renounce all affiliation with mainstream society in order to become more compatible with poor ethnic communities on the margins of mainstream culture and economic life. In the case of Voudou in particular, membership often depends on lineage and history as well, such that Voudou in each enclave serves as the beliefs and practices of an extended family.

It is possible that Marie Laveau learned of Voudou through her marriage to Glapion and that she thereafter embraced it as her heartfelt religion. Voudou is a *gemeinschaft* (community) tradition, and as such does not recruit new members, but rather, upholds traditions, which also constitute the collective identity of the community. It is a part of the community, not a stand-alone institution. Voudou and the community to which it belongs are the same reference group.

The people who first brought Voudou traditions from Africa and those who later blended it with Catholicism lived for the most part as slaves, indentured servants, or impoverished agricultural workers. For most of them, social advancement, or even basic freedom, was a lost hope. Voudou, as a remnant of their culture in Africa, brought together and sustained a culture and identity otherwise broken by slavery and imperial colonization. Voudou was the religion of a people who had little to no hope of ever becoming part of the mainstream and thereby striving for a better life. Voudou and the people it served had only one choice—retreat or die. They could either surrender their beliefs and the collective identity they reinforced, and allow mainstream society to assimilate them, or they could retreat into Voudou, one of the few things that was authentically their own. Many chose retreat, and in doing so, created a haven in which, for a time, they need not face the institutional racism and ruthless exploitation of mainstream society.

Revolution: The Case of Native American Resistance

When the white man arrived in North America and established a permanent settlement at Jamestown in 1607, Native American tribes filled the continent. There were many different linguistic and cultural types. White European culture and religion greatly impacted Native American civilization, and the Europeans introduced many diseases against which Native Americans had no natural resistance, such as smallpox, scarlet fever, typhus, and measles. These diseases rampaged through Indian villages and sometimes wiped out entire tribes (Loewen 1996). The natural environment suffered as well. Approximately 80 million American bison (buffalo) lived

Image 4.4   Bison Skulls, c. 1870s

in North America in 1800. By 1900, only 750 of those 80 million remained, and only about 20 in the United States (Dary [1974] 1989). Not only a food source, the buffalo were sacred to many Native American tribes, including the Sioux and the Paiute. The annihilation of the American bison not only destroyed a way of life; it destroyed the meaning of life for many Native Americans of the Great Plains.

To be sure, not all Native Americans advocated resistance to the white invaders and plunderers. Some, notably the Iroquois called Handsome Lake, claimed visions that promoted peace with the whites and sanctioned a transition from beliefs that sanctified a hunting lifestyle to those that sanctified a farming lifestyle (Lewis 1995:381). Among the Iroquois, men had always served in the Great Hunt, an annual and highly organized expedition that brought back game for the community to collectively share and store for the winter. This tradition rested on strong mythological tales of men as comrades in arms, united in warrior bands committed to heroic deeds. Handsome Lake introduced new myths to legitimate an agrarian lifestyle, and thus to position Iroquois society more amicably with the new white political, economic, and military reality.

Others advocated a more militant, defiant, and resistant orientation, also based on religious visions. Among the most sociologically significant was Wovoka, a Paiute, who received a vision that the white man was really a bad dream, and a Great Void would open in the desert and swallow the white man and his civilization. After this, all the buffalo, horses, and great open expanses would return and a new Indian paradise would ensue. Merging traditional Paiute beliefs with apocalyptic visions from Christianity, Wovoka formulated the Ghost Dance as a means to bring about the end of the white man. Wovoka said that when he fell into a state of near death during a solar eclipse, he saw many Indian souls tormented as a result of the failures of Indians in this life to reclaim their land and their heritage (Lewis 1995:382). Known as the Ghost Dance of 1890, it caught on initially among the Paiute of northern Arizona, Wovoka's home tribe, and spread among the Shoshoni, Arapaho, Crow, Cheyenne, Pawnee, Kiowa, Comanche, and Sioux who accepted it with great enthusiasm. The Ghost Dance bridged both great distances and significant cultural differences and forged a new unity among these and other tribes—many of whom otherwise shared little in common. Based on the Paiute Circle Dance, the Ghost Dance became a sort of pan-Indian celebration that rejected the cold, static, and passionless versions of Christianity that missionaries and settlers brought to the plains, and replaced it with what Wovoka said was a devout and authentic Indian ritual. Wovoka instructed his followers to perform the Ghost Dance for 5 straight days at a time, during which people would achieve ecstatic states and receive visions themselves. The Ghost Dance united Wovoka's revolutionary vision of a Native American Shangri-La with passionate ritual that defied the Christian Puritanism of the white invaders.

For a while, it appeared that Wovoka might unite the tribes and achieve his dream of ousting the white man from Indian territory and restoring the mythical past of a Native American utopia. In restoring the past, Wovoka promised that in the new Eden, true Native Americans would enjoy immortality, that cataclysm would destroy the white man and his Indian collaborators, and the Great Void would consume the rubble of their society. Although Wovoka's vision and his Ghost Dance were revolutionary, he taught followers to embrace peaceful observance of true Indian ways, rather than violent wars of aggression.

For the most part, Native Americans followed Wovoka's peaceful advocations. Some, however, did not. As much by choice as in response to white aggression, the Lakota—a member of the Sioux nation—developed a more militant version, and used the Ghost Dance to inspire greater and defiant resistance to white encroachment on their territory, which the whites had already violated many times (Yenne 2005). The Bureau of Indian Affairs (BIA) arrested a prominent Indian leader named Sitting Bull, chief of the Hunkpapa Sioux, and he died mysteriously while in captivity. Enraged by this unprovoked aggression and murder, the Sioux attempted a kind of civil disobedience in cooperation with Red Cloud, who led the Lakota, another tribe of Sioux. In peaceful defiance of the U.S. government, the Hunkpapa and Lakota Sioux refused to move any farther, having already ceded much of their traditional homeland to the whites (Utley 2003). After the murder of Sitting Bull, the Hunkpapa chose Big Foot as their new chief. The United States dispatched Samuel Whitside and the 7th Cavalry to disarm the Sioux and force them to retreat farther away from their ancestral homelands and deeper into Indian reservations. However, Big Foot and fellow chief Red Cloud would move no farther.

The 7th Cavalry rounded up Big Foot and the Lakotas at Wounded Knee, South Dakota, now with Colonel James W. Forsyth in command. Forsyth had moved

many Hotchkiss guns (a revolving cannon) into position on a ridge overlooking the Sioux encampment. Forsyth ordered his men to disarm the Sioux, which they did. Accounts at this point vary, but the fact remains that Forsyth ordered his men to open fire, and the Hotchkiss guns blazed away at close range, firing the new explosive shells, each gun at 43 rounds per minute. Recorded today as the Wounded Knee Massacre, Forsyth and his men killed Chief Big Foot and at least 300 Lakota, with approximately 150 more Lakota unaccounted for, most likely blown to pieces by the exploding Hotchkiss rounds. The 7th Cavalry did not bother to pick up the pieces strewn about the frozen ground, but did pursue fleeing women and children, some as far as 3 miles, in order to shoot them (Wilson 1975:305).

This massacre ended the popularity of the Ghost Dance, as well as open Native American resistance to U.S. aggression (Brown 1970). Native American spirituality in this revolutionary form lost it credibility at Wounded Knee. In contrast to retreatism, revolutionary religion seeks to alter the conditions or the social relations that afflict the activist religion. It seeks both to maintain itself and to challenge its oppressor for the right of self-determination. In other cases, whether through conformity, innovation, ritualism, or retreatism, the religion in question does not resist the contesting influence, but acclimatizes itself through varying strategies. In the revolutionary case, the religion adapts not primarily by changing itself, but by changing its rival. The attempt failed, and revolution turned to other modes of adaptation.

Since the 1890s, much has obviously changed in the American West. The landscape has indeed changed radically, but not as Wovoka hoped. The buffalo have not returned. Suburban sprawl, toxic waste dumps, addiction, violence, and tourist-trap simulations cover the countryside as the ecosystem of the Great Plains and the desert Southwest strains under the load of ever-expanding and demanding industrial development. As social historian Mike Davis (2002) argues, Wovoka offered a way, in retrospect, to judge our own progress, to see that the critical apocalyptic visions of the Ghost Dance did not come to pass in the late nineteenth century, but they have today (p. 31). The apocalypse is here—not the destruction as Wovoka envisioned in the form of a divine retribution, but in the form of Euro-American capitalist self-destruction. Whether Wovoka had a divinely inspired vision is impossible to say sociologically, but as Davis argues, contemporary sociology can, in retrospect, reconsider Wovoka's visions as a theory tested by history, that white development is not sustainable.

The same ethic of exploitation and immediate economic gain that exterminated the buffalo and massacred the Indians has, in the intervening 100 years, produced an overall ethic of ecocide in the West. That is, the environment has become a huge waste depository, resource mine, and experimental proving ground. Throughout the 1950s, for example, the U.S. government allowed unrestricted dumping of toxic waste, and tested the effects of nuclear fallout on unsuspecting populations in small towns such as St. George, Utah, where still today all manner of genetic mutation appears in the population. Several women have also produced "jellyfish babies" (Davis 2002), so-called because the arms and legs of the miscarried fetuses look like tentacles, and the heads look like the mushroom cap body of a jellyfish.

Davis (2002) concludes that in retrospect, Wovoka sought to recapture and instill a sense of the sacred to the West, that in order to maintain a sustainable society, people must have a moral framework that draws a line and restricts human expansion and exploitation. Although developed in the form of the mystical Ghost Dance, Davis argues that Wovoka's effort was quite empirical, in the sense that he witnessed rampant environmental destruction and social annihilation and realized that only moral forces could halt the destruction in the long term. Such a force never took hold, and large areas today have become, as even the Pentagon calls them, "national sacrifice zones" (Davis 2002:40).

The revolutionary religions, while often noble and empirical in their resistance to oppression or other forces of the present, evoke a longing for either a romanticized past or a romanticized future. Some call for a revolution that will bring down the present society and replace it with a radically different and better one, in which all the problems of today cease to exist and all conflicts are perfectly reconciled. On the other hand, groups that call for a return to the past likewise envision a revolution, but salvation lies in the ways that have been lost. Contemporary Islamic and Christian millennialism strives for the former, and movements like Wovoka's invoke the past. Either way, both reject the present as well as conventional means to both formulate and achieve change. Their romantic longings inspire through faith, and in this way typically rely on religious visions and teachings to encourage support. As Bryan Wilson (1975) shows across a wide variety of times, places, and cultures, revolutionary movements, often millennial, are usually short-lived, and all the shorter if they fail to achieve any measurable success in the present. People will not wait forever, and if life does not improve at least minimally, if the millennial moment seems no closer, then support wanes. The revolutionary movement must succeed, or change into one of the other forms of adaptation, or die.

CHAPTER 5

Religious Intolerance and Aggression

Introduction

In the world today, violence associated with religion, whether on a small or large scale, seems almost like a normal part of life. However, this was not always the case. Conventionally, we believe that the Romans persecuted Christians for their faith, but such is not exactly correct. Rather, the Romans perceived the Christians as a threat to their political hegemony, because the Christians refused to acknowledge the emperors (usually when deceased) as gods. Although it is true that the Christians did refuse to acknowledge the emperors as gods, they were not any more or less disloyal than their pagan contemporaries. By the fourth century, Christians served ably in the imperial legions, and eventually, as presented in Chapter 2, Christianity became the religion of the empire and thereafter reshaped Western civilization.

Yet today, we find that religious intolerance and aggression have become part of every major religion. Although a small part, intolerance and violence influence religion beyond their prevalence because they often produce dramatic and horrific acts, such as the destruction of the Murrah Federal Building in Oklahoma City on April 19, 1995 (Image 5.1) and the destruction of the World Trade Center towers on September 11, 2001. These are among the most infamous events, but there have been many others. We should also not imagine that religious violence takes the form only of terrorism, or that terrorism only takes the form of a quick, one-time event. Like war, terrorism can occur over long periods of time—sometimes spontaneously, sometimes systematically.

While intolerance may seem more the outcome of monotheism in that the one god tolerates no others, recent history shows that polytheistic Hinduism can produce intolerance and violence, and so can nondeistic religions like Buddhism.

Image 5.1   The Bombing of the Murrah Federal Building in Oklahoma City, April 19, 1995

Source: U.S. Department of Defense, Staff Sgt. Preston Chasteen.

If Hinduism allows for innumerable gods, and Buddhism has no god, why do they sometimes develop forms based on intolerance? As always, we must think sociologically. Religion is far more than just a set of beliefs; it is also a lifestyle, a worldview, and a culture, and is often connected to political and economic interests. As we will see with the example of "Hindutva" (Hinduness) movements, polytheism can produce intolerance and violence if supporters understand their religion in cultural, political, and patriotic terms.

In this chapter, we will first trace the origins of religious violence in Western civilization, and then consider contemporary Western and non-Western examples, including the attacks of September 11 (see Table 5.1).

Exclusive Monotheism

With the rise of Christianity and its concurrent grip on political power, the one God, or at least His representatives on earth, could not tolerate dissension. Whereas the paganism indigenous to Europe and the Mediterranean celebrated polytheistic plurality, the universe was no longer big enough for multiple gods. The one God expects one set of beliefs and one manner of worship. All competing approaches are heresy. Thus, the political and religious struggle began to define and enforce an official and exclusive version of Christianity. In 451 CE, the Council of Chalcedon, named after the city in Asia Minor where it took place, set forth various foundations of Christian doctrine, and in so doing, established the official basis of Christianity until the Great Schism of 1054, when Pope Leo IX and Michael I, Patriarch of Constantinople, excommunicated each other. This mutual excommunication established their respective Western Church and Eastern Church, both known officially as the One Holy and Apostolic Church, but commonly differentiated as the Roman Catholic Church and the Eastern Orthodox Church, respectively.

Yet controversy began much earlier. At the Council of Nicaea in 325 CE, as mentioned earlier, church scholars wrote the official statement of faith, now known as the Nicene Creed. It was revised in 381. In the original 325 and 381 versions, it stated that the Holy Spirit "proceeds from the Father." Over the years, however, the Western Church began to insert *"and from the Son,"* which placed Jesus as separate and equal to God the Father. This is known as the filioque clause, and it constituted an unacceptable change of doctrine to the patriarchs of the Eastern Church. In an attempt to

Table 5.1   Religious Intolerance and Violence: Selected Examples

Event	Religion(s) Involved	Outcome
1095–1272, the Crusades—European invasion of the Middle East	Christianity and Islam	Exact death toll unknown, but at least 1 million Destruction of several centers of civilization, including Antioch, Alexandria, Constantinople, Edessa, and Jerusalem Radicalization of Christianity and Islam
1618–1648, Thirty Years' War, Western Europe	Christianity—Internecine conflict Catholic side—Austria, Bavaria, Spain, Holy Roman Empire, Prussia Protestant side—Bohemia, Denmark, Sweden, England, Flanders (afterward Holland and Belgium), France (although a Catholic state)	Exact death toll unknown, but at least 1 million Widespread disease and famine Mass persecutions, including the Inquisition and the witch burnings
1983–2005, Civil War, Sudan, Africa	Islam in the North against Christianity and Indigenous Animism in the South	1.9 million people killed 4 million refugees
March 20, 1995, Sarin nerve gas attack, Tokyo subway	Buddhism, with elements of Christianity and Science Fiction	12 people killed 54 seriously injured. thousands with injured eyesight
April 19, 1995, Bombing of Murrah Federal Building, Oklahoma City	Christianity—White Supremacist variant	168 people killed 800 injured
September 11, 2001, destruction of the World Trade Center, New York City	Islam	2,749 people killed Thousands injured Extensive and obdurate environmental contamination
February–May 2002, Hindu–Muslim conflict, Gujarat State, India	Hinduism and Islam	790 Muslims killed 254 Hindus 2548 injured

reunite the increasingly divergent East and West, the Council of Chalcedon developed the Creed of Chalcedon in 451.

Theologically, the Eastern Church never fully accepted the Creed of Chalcedon. Although it seemed to resolve the filioque issue, the key phrase, "in two natures," recognized the *duophysite* belief over and against the *monophysite* belief. The

---

Nicene Creed, 381 CE

We believe in one God, the Father Almighty, maker of heaven and earth, and of all things visible and invisible.

And in one Lord Jesus Christ, the only begotten Son of God, and born of the Father before all ages. God of God, light of light, true God of true God. Begotten not made, consubstantial to the Father, by whom all things were made.

Who for us men and for our salvation came down from heaven. And was incarnate of the Holy Ghost and of the Virgin Mary and was made man; was crucified also for us under Pontius Pilate, suffered and was buried; and the third day rose again according to the Scriptures. And ascended into heaven, sits at the right hand of the Father, and shall come again with glory to judge the living and the dead, of whose Kingdom there shall be no end.

We believe in the Holy Spirit, the Lord and Giver of life, who proceeds from the Father, *and from the son*, who together with the Father and the Son is to be adored and glorified, who spoke by the Prophets. And one holy, catholic, and apostolic Church. We confess one baptism for the forgiveness of sins. And we look for the resurrection of the dead and the life of the world to come. Amen. [italics added]

---

former term is the belief that Christ consisted of two complete natures, one wholly divine, the other wholly human, and both resided in Christ totally and perfectly. He was both divine and human, equally. The monophysite tradition held that Christ was of one nature only—purely divine—with no human essence. Monophysites believed that there is only one God, who exists in three forms—God the father, the Son (Jesus), and the Holy Spirit. The Chalcedon Creed states that Jesus is consubstantial with the father (which Monophysites could accept) yet also says, "consubstantial with us," as consistent with his human aspect. Monophysites could not accept this. While both sides accepted the notion of the Trinity, the issue of Christ's humanity still divided the Church. The disagreement over the nature of Christ fomented centuries of conflict.

Of course, the battle was as much political as theological, with the various popes in the West and patriarchs in the East fighting for supremacy. Each side commanded great resources, though of different types. In the East, the orthodox patriarchs stood as office holders within the unified and centralized Byzantine state. As such, they worked cooperatively and with great cohesion with the emperors, using a combination of money—as the Byzantine Empire generated vast amounts of wealth for most of its history—and the professional military of the Byzantine state.

In the West, the pope and the church hierarchy stood outside and separately from the numerous and constantly changing, constantly fighting feudal lords and their estates. The Western Church relied principally on force of arms to conquer and then convert new territories. Divided into innumerable feudal states, the economy in the West rarely rose above subsistence levels, and the vast majority of people, including the nobility, were unwashed, illiterate, and superstitious. Consequently, they lacked the means to effectively manage conquered territory. Whereas the Byzantines extended their governmental administration and their culture, the West looted and moved on. The Eastern Church spread more readily and established itself more thoroughly in Bulgaria, Yugoslavia, the Levant, and Russia by introducing economic opportunity as well as the organization of advanced civilization. From 476 CE (the fall of the Roman Empire in the West), the Eastern Church remained ascendant until the decline of the Byzantine state following their monumental defeat at the battle of Manzikert in 1071.

Despite the political, economic, and cultural differences between East and West, the greatest religiously motivated violence occurred within each church, not between them.

In the East, one of the most intense conflicts concerned iconoclasm. Literally, iconoclasts seek to "smash the idols" because the Bible clearly prohibits their use. However, Byzantine culture was the continuous and direct descendent of ancient Roman civilization, which the even earlier Greek civilization greatly influenced. As a result, Byzantine culture embraced centuries of artistic development, which featured quite famously sculptures and other physical representations of divinity, first in the long pagan period beginning around 480 BCE, and then in the Christian period, especially after the fall of the West in 476 CE.

Icons: Intolerance of Religious Images

Byzantine civilization produced churches of magnificent grandeur and impressive magnitude, the greatest of which—Saint Sofia—still stands in Constantinople, now known as Istanbul, although as a mosque after the Turkish conquest of 1453, and now as a museum. Throughout the Byzantine world, which for centuries encompassed most of the eastern Mediterranean, devout Christians built lavish churches adorned with gold, silver, precious gems, intricate carvings, fine metalwork, statues, tapestries, mosaics, and icons. The icons in particular served as the focus of devotion, and Christians in the East customarily kiss the icons and direct their prayers to them. The icons always depicted religious scenes, often Jesus, but also martyrs, disciples, apostles, and—especially in Constantinople—Mary, the mother of Jesus. Emperors also appear in icons as God's sacred representative on earth.

Orthodox and Islamic historians throughout the Middle Ages describe great multitudes of icons and other religious representations, but most have since been destroyed. In the medieval period, iconoclasts considered them to be blasphemous, and destroyed them whenever possible. Between 740 and 842 CE, the Orthodox Church, united with competing factions within the Byzantine Empire, fought over the issue of iconography. When the iconoclasts gained power during this period, the first iconoclast emperor, Leo III, issued a decree that all icons in his empire should be destroyed. After his death, his son, the emperor Constantine V, continued his aggressive program of destruction, and killed anyone suspected of iconodule (pro-icon) sympathy as well. Although the icon-venerating Nikephoros I reigned briefly,

---

Chalcedonian Creed, 451 CE

We, then, following the holy Fathers, all with one consent, teach men to confess one and the same Son, our Lord Jesus Christ, the same perfect in Godhead and also perfect in manhood;

truly God and truly man, of a reasonable soul and body;

consubstantial with the Father according to the Godhead, and consubstantial with us according to the Manhood;

in all things like unto us, without sin;

begotten before all ages of the Father according to the Godhead, and in these latter days, for us and for our salvation, born of the Virgin Mary, the Mother of God, according to the Manhood;

one and the same Christ, Son, Lord, only begotten, to be acknowledged in two natures, inconfusedly, unchangeably, indivisibly, inseparably;

the distinction of natures being by no means taken away by the union, but rather the property of each nature being preserved, and concurring in one Person and one Subsistence, not parted or divided into two persons, but one and the same Son, and only begotten, God the Word, the Lord Jesus Christ;

as the prophets from the beginning concerning Him, and the Lord Jesus Christ Himself has taught us, and the Creed of the holy Fathers has handed down to us.

Image 5.2   One of the Most Famous Icons, the Theotokos of Vladimir, c. 1131

from 802 to 811, the subsequent emperors, Leo V, Michael II, and Theophilos, continued the icon-bashing until Michael III restored the icons in 843. From that point on, the iconoclasts never regained significant power.

Sociologically, important forces underlie the icon controversy. First, conflict with the Western Church intensified during this time, and iconoclasm clearly demarcated the Eastern Church theologically from the icon-loving West (Barraclough [1968] 1979:36). Second, the Byzantine Empire faced increasingly strong challenges from Islam, which also prohibits icons, and thus iconoclasm within Christianity pacified the various and diverse cultural groups within the Empire, both Christian and Islamic, that rejected icon veneration. In other words, it diffused an issue that might have otherwise contributed to greater rebellion from within as Islam pressed in from the East. Despite these rather practical political and cultural effects, the energy and enthusiasm that powered the leaders and armies on both sides arose from devout, perhaps even fanatical devotion, especially on the iconoclast side. Theological commitment is one thing, but it requires far more commitment to fight great battles over belief. Although politics clearly played a part, iconoclasm represented the battle over something far greater—salvation. Icon veneration was finally triumphant, but the struggle had killed thousands in battle, disrupted populations, destroyed centuries of religious art, and depleted the treasury.

As with most issues prior to modern times, it is difficult to ascertain how the common people felt about the icon issue. Likely, it made little difference to them (Norwich 1989). As a type of high art, icons represented the views and especially the tastes of elite strata, both religious and secular. Icons and other impressive works such as major buildings represented the power of the ruling class, and as such, common people had little say about them. By tradition, armies fought for the commitments of their leaders; individual soldiers were not expected to commit their loyalty to a cause, but rather to their commander. For this reason, Christians fought loyally for pagan commanders, as in the case of Julian, the last pagan emperor (Murdoch 2004). One of his most able and trusted commanders—Jovian—was a devout Christian who would ascend to the throne after Julian's death in battle. As emperor, Jovian restored Christianity as the favored religion of the empire.

In conclusion, numerous and sometimes conflicting loyalties inspired many sides in the icon wars. While religion was always central, personal loyalty, political rivalries, cultural hegemony, and money also contributed. Nevertheless, virtually every war in the Middle Ages included religion; no one could conduct a campaign of any kind without church endorsement and a religious purpose, even if somewhat specious, to all endeavors—especially those that required battle against a supposedly evil enemy in the form of heresy.

The Cathars: Intolerance of Heresy

In the West, about the same time the East battled iconoclasm, the Catholic Church warred against and typically crushed numerous heresies as well. Among the more notable heretics were the Cathars, also known as Albigensians. The Cathars originated in southern France sometime around 950 CE and gained converts rapidly. They eventually attracted the attention of the Catholic hierarchy at the Synod of Toulouse in 1056, which officially condemned the Cathars.

Beliefs

The Cathars believed that Satan, not God, created the earth, and thus the god of the Old Testament was actually Satan, and the world he created is inherently evil. They taught that all physical objects are inherently tainted by evil, a theological view called *diocetism*. Furthermore, they believed that Jesus was of one nature, entirely divine, because the human essence, being of this world, is inherently evil. Similarly, Jesus appeared to us in spectral form, with no physical substance at all. Therefore, they believed that the soul was the only spiritually important aspect of human existence, and that the physical body was irrelevant. The body not only contained the soul, but for the Cathars, the body also imprisoned the soul. They believed that the soul reincarnates forever, and thus remains forever imprisoned, unless the individual can break the cycle by achieving perfection. One achieves perfection by renouncing the physical world entirely—a belief that often manifests in religion, including Christianity, Islam, paganism, Hinduism, Taoism, Shintoism, Confucianism, and others. In practice, denial of the world is called asceticism, and also sometimes Puritanism. Beyond simply a denial of pleasure, full asceticism condemns anything that produces sensory stimulation or emotional excitement. An ascetic repudiates as much of the world as possible in order to avoid excitement in all its forms, including pleasure, but also surprise, tragedy, and anything else that might excite an emotional reaction of any kind. The Cathars taught and practiced this total form of asceticism.

Practices

The particular Cathar theological beliefs inspired certain unique social practices. First, since the body is irrelevant, the Cathars adopted the radical notion that women and men are entirely equal in all spiritual matters. Second, they expected everyone in their communities to strive for perfection, that is, a fully ascetic lifestyle. Those most successful in their ascetic pursuits became leaders in the Cathar sect, known as Perfects. They corresponded more or less to priests in

Catholicism and orthodoxy. Perfects lived an extremely frugal and ascetic lifestyle, often subsisting on nothing more than gruel (a thick mash of wheat or barley and water). Perfects performed the one and only sacrament, called *consolamentum,* or the wiping away of sins (Weis 2002). A person received this just before the moment of death. Cathars also practiced vegetarianism, as a result of the belief that plants contained less life force, and Cathars particularly avoided anything perceived as the result of or pertaining to sexuality, especially eggs and milk (Markale 2003). They did, however, eat fish, which they believed Jesus had blessed.

Perhaps most strangely, and what must have seemed especially appalling to non-Cathars, they advocated nonprocreative sex, conducted through nonintercourse techniques. If a person could not refrain from temptation, at least the individual would not imprison another soul in a physical body by bringing a child into the world. Abdication of life force was commendable, and when a person believed himself or herself ready, the person would starve himself or herself to death. All of these practices destabilized established feudal society, and thus the Cathars constituted not only a theological challenge, but a social one as well. The Cathar beliefs and practices destabilized society in that they rejected most systems of hierarchy that ruled throughout feudal Europe. Not only did the Cathars ignore the secular nobility, but they also ignored the theological hierarchy of the Catholic Church. As we have seen, the Cathars held to a very simple theology of purity as one worked toward perfection. All other concerns—indeed, the world in general—represented a corrupted and evil influence that would only pollute the individual with lust, greed, power, and craving of all sorts. There was no time or justification for noble privilege, feudal servitude, or Church dogma.

Intolerance and Conflict

Of course, the Catholic hierarchy regarded all of these beliefs as heretical. Over time, the established Catholic Church and the Cathars faced each other on the battlefield. Just like the iconoclasm issue in the East, various power interests within Western society joined one side or the other for reasons other than religious devotion. Northern nobles and the Church fought the Cathars and the nobles of southern France who were trying to maintain independent estates. By the time Innocent III became pope in 1198, he resolved to annihilate the Cathars once and for all. With the First Crusade already under way, which his predecessor Urban II had declared in 1095, Innocent III found that he lacked substantial military resources, as most of the knights were now in the Levant, having just captured Jerusalem. So at first he reluctantly attempted diplomatic means and appointed several legates (ecclesiastical emissaries) to meet with and bring Cathar leaders back to the Church. The Cathars, as well as sympathetic nobles, and even many local Catholic clergy opposed the pope's entreaties. Despite the fact that most nobles regarded themselves as devout Catholics, they also regarded themselves as autonomous nobles who could freely offer and freely withdraw their loyalty as they saw fit. They resented the attempts of the Church and the most powerful nobles to impose their will. Local church officials saw the decline of their own authority should the Church tolerate any degree of Cathar legitimacy.

With the failure of diplomacy, Innocent III resorted to the tried-and-true means of direct military attack. This led to several more battles throughout France, with the Catholic nobles of the North pitted against the Cathars and their noble sympathizers in the South. In 1209, Catholic forces achieved a major victory and slaughtered the defeated Cathar army and their towns (O'Shea 2001). When the victorious Catholic knights asked Arnaud Amalric, the Abbot of Citeaux, how to distinguish between the Catholics and Cathars after the siege of Beziers, he allegedly answered, "Kill them all; God will know his own" (S. Martin 2005). Although broken militarily and politically, the Cathar movement survived and after only a short time seemed to prosper once again.

In 1229, the Church brought the dreaded Inquisition to France, which exterminated the remaining Cathar towns using the most vicious and cruel methods of torture and execution. One particularly horrible event occurred on March 16, 1244, when the Inquisition built a massive fire pit near the town of Montségur and tossed several hundred Cathars into it, who died in a grisly tumult of fire, blood, and mayhem. The slaughter continued, with thousands more burned alive, until the last Cathar Perfect, Guillaume Bélibaste, was executed in 1321 (Barber 2000; Weis 2002).

Discussion

The story of the Cathars thus poses important and fascinating sociological questions. Why did the movement persist so vehemently, even under the most violent and persistent persecution? Why did people find the religion so compelling, given its strict asceticism and morbid view on life? We might readily explain the political interest among lesser nobles of southern France of using a breakaway sect as a reason to defy rival political authority, but how do we explain the strong popular support?

As usual, let us consider the material factors. We can assume that people found this unusual doctrine compelling, but why did it speak to them so powerfully? Why sacrifice their lives for it? If we consider the time in which they lived, and their location in southern France, we find that they had little to live for in the first place. Exploited by ruthless feudal obligations and with no prospects for improvement, Catharism offered salvation—an escape from the oppressive and miserable material conditions in which most people lived. Again, this was not a democratic society, nor one with a dynamic economy that offered opportunities beyond where one was born. Tradition ruled, and tradition dictated that people maintain their place in life—at least in this life—and fulfill their obligations to serve the nobles above them. Given that the nobles were engaged in more or less constant warfare, they drained the region of its produce and of its people. Those who survived found compensation in commitment to the unusual doctrines of Catharism, which exalted not only poverty, but also intentional deprivation as the holy and the only path to salvation. Of course, Christianity historically offered a better life in the beyond, in the Kingdom of Heaven, but the path to the Kingdom of Heaven has differed historically as well, even in Christian times (McDannell and Lang 2001; A. McGrath 2003). Now, only the lowest of the low, and especially those with nearly nothing in this world and who then intentionally rejected even minimal existence, would receive salvation.

Needless to say, few nobles ever converted to Catharism (Sumption 2000). Although they used it as a political tool against the Catholic Church and its allied monarchies elsewhere in France, the wars and other social disruptions generated a large class of disenfranchised peasants who already had nothing, and nothing to live for. Wealthy nobles ruled the church, and many church officials lived quite opulently. Seemingly, they had long ago stretched their vows of poverty to include ease and luxury. In this social and economic context—grand opulence next to grinding poverty—and a bleak perception of the future, the people who embraced Catharism had nothing left to lose. Compared to this life, death was welcome. Desperate people will fight tenaciously for something, for anything that offers some degree of consolation, perhaps even the possibility of triumph in the next life. We will see this in modern times as well.

Let us consider the concept of compensation. Developed by rational choice theory, it argues that the revealed religions in particular offer compensatory rather than direct benefits from one's investment in the religion in terms of time, money, devotion, and other forms of personal sacrifice. For example, salvation promises a future with the divine—in the next life, not in this life. Although religion can improve a person's earthly life, the main draw is the compensatory promise of salvation after death. This also tends to mitigate the likelihood and impact of free riders, who seek the benefits of a collective group without devoting their time, effort, and so on. In other words, they want the benefits without the costs. In the case of Catharism, the personal sacrifice was great, which the circumstances of life forced most of the members to make anyway. Thus, a person either lived the life already, or stayed away from Catharism entirely. As we will see throughout this chapter, extremist forms of religion typically have an inherent means of reducing free riders, because these forms require great personal sacrifice and offer little in return—in this life, that is (see Figure 5.1).

However, there is more to religion than materiality. As Yuri Stoyanov (2000) argues, beliefs also matter, and as he traces throughout history, wherever dualism develops in a religion, it almost always results in violence. In this case, the Cathars represented the Other, the exact opposite of the "good" Church in Rome. They were perceived as not just different, but a directly opposite and evil manifestation of Christianity that threatened the Church. Evil must be eliminated at all costs. Although the Church annihilated the leadership and thousands of members, Stoyanov argues that the Church assimilated, rather than obliterated, the so-called Cathar heresy—specifically, the demonization of the Cathars and the assimilation of their clear division of good and evil. "Cathar dualism was to play an important role in the very shaping of the medieval concept of witchcraft, as charges brought against the heretics were to be transferred to the alleged devil-worshipping witches" (p. 220). Malcolm Barber (2000) and Otto Rahn (2006) make the same

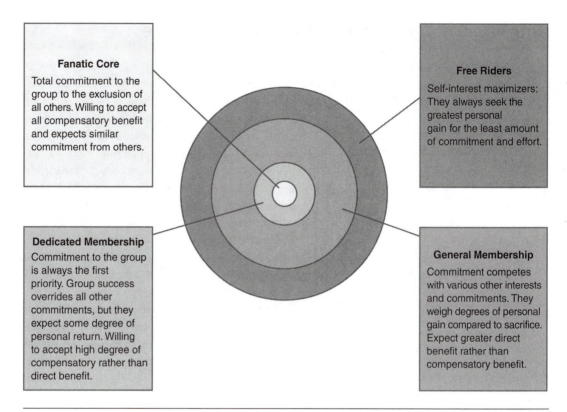

Fanatic Core
Total commitment to the group to the exclusion of all others. Willing to accept all compensatory benefit and expects similar commitment from others.

Free Riders
Self-interest maximizers: They always seek the greatest personal gain for the least amount of commitment and effort.

Dedicated Membership
Commitment to the group is always the first priority. Group success overrides all other commitments, but they expect some degree of personal return. Willing to accept high degree of compensatory rather than direct benefit.

General Membership
Commitment competes with various other interests and commitments. They weigh degrees of personal gain compared to sacrifice. Expect greater direct benefit rather than compensatory benefit.

Figure 5.1   Rational Choice Theory and Group Commitment

conclusions, that dualistic notions of pure good versus pure evil shaped the Cathar crusades, as well as the crusades against Islam, and nearly every other mass persecution of the Middle Ages. Thus, dualism played a double role. First, the Cathars' dualistic theology on one side and the Catholic Church's dualism on the other segregated all aspects of the world into clearly defined categories of good and evil. This brought both sides into irreconcilable conflict. Second, the basic existence of the Cathars constituted a challenge to the social and political authority of the Church in Rome. As inherent oppositions, the existence of one necessitates the demise of the other.

The extermination of the Cathars is just one example of religious intolerance prior to modern times. We could have considered many others. In each case, though, it was the established authorities who exercised intolerance against otherwise peaceful groups who sought merely to live their lives, however unusual their lives might appear to outsiders. In the case of the Cathars, as well as Lutherans, Puritans, and other Protestants, as well as Muslims and Jews, the established religious authority, often in conjunction with the secular nobility, enacted laws against, and often actively persecuted, denominations they considered heretical, which from a sociological perspective means precisely any beliefs or practices that challenged the established hierarchy or hegemony.

Intolerance and Aggression in Modern Times

In this section, we will look at some religious groups who not only differ from mainstream versions of their own faith, but actively seek to harm others, for purposes related to their beliefs. Arguably, *essentialism* stands as the basis of all religious violence and terrorism in modern times, which often takes the form of fundamentalism—a modern expression of dualism. Essentialism refers to any belief system that declares a basic, irreducible essence—a basic property that cannot be broken down into smaller pieces. Essentialism can sometimes be prosocial, as for example in the Declaration of Independence: All people have certain essential rights, which are self-evident, and the belief that we all share an essential humanity becomes the basis of unity and of liberation. These essential rights are "unalienable"; they cannot be taken away. However, essentialism can also establish clear demarcations between essentially "good" and "bad" people. In such cases, essentialist belief becomes the basis of intolerance and violence. Fundamentalism is one type of religious essentialism. Before we proceed with case examples, let us clearly conceptualize fundamentalism.

Fundamentalism

Fundamentalism can mean many things and carry many connotations in common usage. The exact conceptualization is important, however, and warrants a discussion. Imprecision has resulted in vague analysis concerning religious movements and beliefs.

Broadly, fundamentalism refers to a perspective that reads sacred texts (scripture) word for word, literally, and accepts them as inerrant. Although this may seem like an ancient view of scripture and belief, it is in fact a specifically modern perspective, as we saw in Chapter 2.

Declaration of Independence

(First several sections)

In CONGRESS, July 4, 1776.

The unanimous Declaration of the thirteen united States of America,

When, in the Course of human Events, it becomes necessary for one People to dissolve the Political bands which have connected them with another, and to assume, among the Powers of the Earth, the separate and equal Station to which the Laws of Nature and of Nature's God entitle them, a decent Respect to the Opinions of Mankind requires that they should declare the Causes which impel them to the Separation.

We hold these Truths to be self-evident: that all Men are created equal, that they are endowed, by their Creator, with certain unalienable Rights, that among these are Life, Liberty, and the Pursuit of Happiness.

That to secure these Rights, Governments are instituted among Men, deriving their just Powers from the Consent of the Governed, that whenever any Form of Government becomes destructive of these Ends, it is the Right of the People to alter or abolish it, and to institute new Government, laying its Foundation on such Principles, and organizing its Powers in such form, as to them shall seem most likely to effect their Safety and Happiness.

If we can agree as stated above that a sociological perspective considers more than just belief, we must do so here as well. All reading involves interpretation, in that any given word, phrase, image, reference, and so on, can mean many things, and we could reduce nearly any text to lesser and lesser degrees of complexity, or expand indefinitely. Sociologically, we must conceptualize fundamentalism within its context of occurrence. In this regard, Riesbrodt (1990) offers the clearest and most analytically discerning view.

Specifically, fundamentalism consists of universal and statutory truth, supported by textual literalism (Riesbrodt 1990:16). Given that this truth is not only universal but ordained by a universal higher power that claims dominion over all (typically God), the statutory truth and its law applies to all, willing or not. Fundamentalism thus claims authority over all people, times, and places. The fundamentalist individual or group sees itself as the exclusive holder of truth. Riesebrodt thus defines fundamentalism as a social process, dependent on time and place (p. 19), in that social conditions determine the type of truth (for example, that creationism is true) and the extent to which people or institutions violate the divine truth (for example, why is homosexuality seen as such a dire threat today, but not greed?). In any case, fundamentalism allows no room for negotiation or compromise. God's law is viewed as absolute. We can, of course, argue intellectually about what the proper "literal" reading of scripture would be. In the book of Genesis, for example, does God create Eve as Adam's equal companion, or as a subordinate? It doesn't

> ### Sociological Conceptualization of Fundamentalism
>
> - Scriptural literalism
> - Absolute devotion to absolute truth, which clearly demarcates pure good and pure evil
> - Tireless efforts to enforce divine truth, without negotiation or compromise
> - Eradication of evil
> - Culture based on a cosmic battle, in which particular issues of the present become moments in the larger battle between pure good and pure evil
> - The temporal world becomes a battleground, not meaningful in itself. Success is measured not in practical terms, but in terms of emotional gratification.
> - Restoration of a glorious past

actually say that she is created as a lesser human; one must look at the imagery, not simply the word-for-word denotation, to interpret that a human created from a rib is a lesser being than one who is created from earth. Indeed, the first creation story says they were both created in the image of God. Only later as punishment does God declare that woman shall be subordinate to man. Her subordination then seems more the consequence of action than of essence, and this raises the issue of original sin, also not mentioned as such. Must women still suffer for Eve's mistake?

Building on Riesbrodt (1990), literalism only justifies what a person or group has already constructed as truth from its social context, and the veracity of the truth claim depends on high levels of religious commitment (religiosity) and emotional commitment, in particular over processes of reason and empirical reality. Although the origins are individually emotional and a reaction to particular sociohistorical circumstances, the application is almost always socially reactionary—an attempt to use the word of God to prevent progressive social change, or on the other hand to actively steer society toward institutions and policies that appeal to people with the same emotional orientation. In other words, the goal is to feel morally righteous about society, not primarily to create a functional society in practical terms.

Fundamentalism differs from one religion to another, and one time and place to another. In all cases, though, it is a response to contemporary (and specifically modern) social conditions, and thus fundamentalist movements selectively cultivate some aspects from the past (whether real or imagined) and disregard others. This strategic selectivity proves true in research regarding Christianity (Ammerman 1987), Judaism (Shalvi 2002), Islam (An-Na'im 2002; Hassan 2002), Buddhism (Seneviratne 2002), and Hinduism (Ram-Prasad 2002; Udayakumar 2005). Sociologically, fundamentalist movements are a response to modernity, not the descendant of once-great theocratic civilizations or the rediscovery of universal divine truth (Haar 2002).

With this conceptualization, religious devotion as such (religiosity), no matter how strong, does not indicate fundamentalism; neither does textual literalism by itself indicate fundamentalism. Rather, all seven factors (listed in the sidebar) together indicate a type of religiosity premised on the exalted fundamentalist view. Any one factor may be significantly stronger than the others, but all are usually present to some degree.

In this way, science and reason in particular become enemies because they prove utterly useless in recognizing or serving the divine truth, and indeed lead people astray. More broadly still, secularism in general, which includes anything not specifically dedicated to the Divine Plan, constitutes a sacrilegious defiance of Divine Order. For strong fundamentalists, something is either part of God's plan or against it; there is no neutral ground. In terms of institutions such as education and government, fundamentalism embraces faith-based policies and programs, and specifically rejects scientific and secular forms. It is in its foundation antimodern, although it may use modern technology to further its cause. Nevertheless, fundamentalism premises restoration of an idealized past rather than forward progress (Khan and Langman 2005; Marty et al. 1997; McCarthy 2005).

Also, this is a sociological conceptualization, and any particular person or group may or may not acknowledge one or more of these factors. They are analytical concepts, not simply a description of what fundamentalists consciously believe. Lastly, this conceptualization applies to fundamentalism in all religions, not just Christianity and Islam, the two religions most commonly covered in the news media.

Islam

In reference to Islam, scholars usually refer to fundamentalist versions as Islamism or political Islam. Notice that this corresponds to the conceptualization of fundamentalism developed above. Fundamentalism includes an entire worldview and a way of life, not just for oneself or one particular group, but for everyone. Hence, in Islam as in other religions, fundamentalism often takes on political agendas.

As is well known, Islamicist terrorists destroyed the World Trade Center towers on September 11, 2001, hereafter referred to as 9/11. Nineteen hijackers commandeered four commercial passenger aircraft—two were flown into the World Trade Center towers in New York City, one hit the Pentagon in Washington, D.C., and one crashed in a field in Shanksville, Pennsylvania. The operation was planned and executed by Al Qaeda, which means "the base" in Arabic, and its leader, Osama bin Laden. According to a high-ranking Al Qaeda leader now in custody, Khalid Sheik Muhammad (KSM), the fourth plane was targeted at the Capitol building in Washington, D.C., and not the White House. The official *9/11 Commission Report* (2004) says that passengers on the fourth plane fought the hijackers for control, and consequently, the hijackers crashed the plane rather than surrender control. The two towers in New York collapsed completely, which caused fires and damage to nearby buildings, such that five buildings all together collapsed.

As of this writing, there is still considerable confusion about the hijackers' identities. Of the alleged nineteen, at least four have been discovered alive—meaning false identities were used by the actual hijackers, all of whom perished in the attacks. According to the BBC World News Service ("Hijack 'Suspects' Alive and Well" 2001), Waleed Al Shehri, purportedly the pilot on American Airlines Flight 11 (*9/11 Commission Report* 2004), which hit the World Trade Center's north tower, was in Casablanca, Morocco, at the time of the attacks, where he lives permanently. Also, Abdulaziz Al Omari, another named hijacker, lost his passport while a student in Denver, according to the BBC report, and at least four from Saudi Arabia used stolen identities (Maier 2003). As of 2006, the identity of hijackers "Al Shehri" and "Al Omari" remain uncertain, although the FBI believes it has positively identified all 19 (Herrmann 2006). The FBI may be correct, given that the two men still in question have relatively common names in the Arabic-speaking world. Interestingly, this uncertainty has led some people to posit various conspiracy theories that the U.S. government, Israel, or both were behind 9/11. No hard evidence supports this, however.

Contrary to popular belief in the United States, none of the hijackers were from or had ever trained in Iraq. The majority—15—were from Saudi Arabia. This is crucial if we are to sociologically understand the events of 9/11, especially the religious elements.

People in rural areas of Saudi Arabia are descended from communities that were nomadic until the early twentieth century. Now agriculturally bound, primarily around animal herding, they are impoverished. Islam arose in these regions around Mecca (where the prophet Muhammad was born) and Medina (where he died), and other places within the Hejaz region in modern-day Saudi Arabia. It was here that Muhammad received the word of God during the years 610 CE until his death in 632. Today, the main city in the region, Jeddah, is a center of cultural life in the Arab world and internationally. It contains the largest total collection of open-air public art displays in the world. As a center of international business and commerce, people from all over the world and from many different cultures populate its streets. Jeddah enjoys general economic prosperity that results from its integration in the world economy and cosmopolitan culture, and has become a focus for Saudis who favor a more modern and secular state (Al Rasheed 2007). The rest of the Hejaz region, however, still endures grinding poverty, like much of rural Saudi Arabia. The most ardent terrorists in Islam come from such areas, in Saudi Arabia and elsewhere.

Saudi Arabia provides a more intense atmosphere to foster violent versions of Islam than most other impoverished areas. In addition to religious fundamentalism (discussed below), the kingdom faces many internal conflicts, each represented by various competing factions: religion versus modernism, wealth versus poverty, and the legitimacy of its hereditary monarchy (Abukhalil 2004). On the religion front, not only is the Hejaz region the birthplace of Islam and the center of some of its most sacred sites, but Saudi Arabia furthermore practices Wahhabism, an especially strict and ascetic form of Islam. Named after Muhammad ibn Abd al Wahhab (1703–1792), the movement, now the official version of Islam in the Kingdom of Saudi Arabia and Qatar, seeks to reestablish traditional Islam—that is, what Wahhabist authorities see as the high form of Islam from the sixteenth century. Many proponents prefer to call it Salafism, after the Arabic word *Salaf,* which means "predecessors," a name that suggests an invocation of the ways of the ancestors. Among other things, they require men to wear beards and traditional

Islamic/Arabic clothing, and they enforce bans on modern entertainment, nontraditional education, and the knowledge that arises from it. Women are strictly second-class and must remain covered in public at all times. They may not work outside the home, operate machinery, or engage in public conversation (Commins 2006). These restrictions have been consistent since the inception of Islam, and likely derive from earlier Arab culture (Buergenthal and Howland 2001). Other than in Jeddah, Saudis adhere strictly to Wahhabist stipulations.

For example, 15 girls died in a fire at a school in Mecca in 2002, because the Mutawaa'in (religious police) officers refused to let them leave the burning building without proper headcover (Bradley 2006). Charged with enforcing Islamic standards, the Mutawaa'in are officially known as the Committee for Propagating Virtue and Preventing Vice. They operate separately from but alongside secular criminal police units.

In addition to specifically religious stipulations, Wahhabism represents a particular cultural order that rejects most things that are products of the modern world, or more specifically, the Western modern world. Wahhabism demonizes such things as secular education and cosmopolitan attitudes, viewing them as corrupt and irreligious. Whatever a person needs to know is in the Quran, and whatever a person needs to live day to day should be found in one's local and devout community. Thus, rural Saudis, especially, interpret the world through their localized Wahhabist perspective, which valorizes their own devout if impoverished way of life, and demonizes the foreign, especially the Western, way of life—the strongest embodiment of modernity and the version that most ominously threatens the Arab-Islamic Middle East.

Certain events in particular produce uniquely hostile reactions from severe and devout Wahhabists. Many in the Arab world, and throughout much of the developed world as well—such as in Western Europe, for that matter—find U.S. politics and actions in the Middle East to be problematic. Unwavering and often unqualified support for Israel over and against the Palestinians, as well as support for the central Saudi government—seen as corrupt by Wahhabist purists—and support for other corrupt governments in oil-rich states, such as Kuwait, enrage people of devout Wahhabist commitment. U.S. military bases in Saudi Arabia, Kuwait, and now Iraq portend even greater intrusions from the fundamentalist Islamic perspective. These intrusions are not just military, but strike at the very essence of Arab-Islamic existence.

Furthermore, the Wahhabists in Saudi Arabia are not the only fundamentalist version of Islam. In fact, we may speak generally of extreme Islamic fundamentalism that consists of influences from a variety of founders and promoters. In addition to Wahhab, most scholars agree that Sayyid Qutb (1906–1966), an Egyptian, founded the notion of modern Islamic fundamentalism. Working with the writings of Wahhab and others, Qutb formulated a doctrine that closely mirrors a fundamentalist version of Christianity, as we will see. Yet Qutb might never have become radicalized had he not visited the United States in the 1950s. During this time, Qutb attended Colorado State College (now the University of Northern Colorado) and traveled widely.

Two things horrified Qutb on his travels. The first was American racism, which he saw as systematic, widespread, and vicious. Numerous lynchings, for example, took place during and just prior to his years in the United States, many of which appeared on popular postcards (see Image 5.3).

The second was the emancipation of women, and in particular the mixing of the sexes in public, such as at movie theaters and sock hops (high school dances), popular at the time.

Considering these factors, Qutb concluded that the modern world was morally corrupt and devoid of God's influence. Even worse, he saw it as contrary to God's will (Moussalli 1993). At the time, these and other Western influences, namely sec-ularism, were exported around the world, including to the Middle East and his

Image 5.3   A postcard showing the burned and lynched body of Jesse Washington, Waco, Texas, 1916. Washington was a 17-year-old mentally impaired farmhand who had confessed to raping and killing a white woman. It is not known if he understood the charges, or if he actually committed the crime as there was no trial. He was castrated, mutilated, and burned alive, in that order, by a cheering mob that included the mayor and the chief of police. A newspaper account stated that "Washington was beaten with shovels and bricks. . .[he] was castrated, and his ears were cut off....Wailing, the boy attempted to climb up the skillet hot chain. For this, the men cut off his fingers."

The person who mailed this postcard wrote on the back: "This is the barbeque we had last night. My picture is to the left with a cross over it. Your son, Joe" (Wikipedia.org).

native Egypt. At the time, Gamel Abdel Nasser had established the modern and secular nation of Egypt.

Generally, the Middle East has assimilated the negative aspects of modern society without the positive benefits. Namely, the various totalitarian kingdoms have imported modern wage relations and foreign capital investment, which benefit the elites. As in the West, the transition from traditional feudal obligations and village life to modern wage employment and cosmopolitan (global) culture and trade destroyed the personal sense of community in the Middle East. At the same time, the moral suppression of consumerism, democratic culture, and gender liberation prevents many of the key benefits of modern life—a higher standard of living, social mobility, and individual freedoms. In other words, the Middle East has imported many of the oppressive and exploitive elements of modernism, such as low wages and the destruction of tradition, without the benefits, such as consumer goods, social mobility, and democratic political systems (Langman and Morris 2002). Thus, the conflict with the United States and the West is far more complex than a so-called clash of civilizations (An-Na'im 2002), and is rather a conflict over the ways and means by which the Islamic Middle East will fully enter the modern global system. It is, at the local level, about who benefits and who suffers.

In response, Qutb and contemporary Islamic fundamentalists argue that Muslims must protect themselves from Western and modern corruption. The evils of racism and secularism, as well as the most foul mixing of sexes, personal liberties, and open discourse must be prevented. Qutb argued that Nasser's secular state was evil and thus must fail, but likely, Muslims of true faith will require aggression and violence to stop it. Furthermore, Muslims must adopt a strict interpretation of scripture and implement it directly and completely, leaving no trace of modern civilization behind. Qutb argued that the Islamic world reached its zenith in the 1500s–1600s, a time during which Islamic civilization enjoyed great economic prosperity and political power (Musallam 2005). Improvement, he believed, lies in the past, not in the future. In the United States, Qutb had seen all he needed to see of Western modernity.

However, Qutb explained that the fall of the Islamic caliphate (a ruling council of clerics) and the Islamic civilization over which it presided did not result from the economic transformation of the West into modern capitalism, as sociologists argue, but rather, because Muslims turned away from the true path of God. Only intense devotion to a pure form of Islam could restore Arabic prosperity and greatness. Qutb applied the ancient concept of *Jahiliyyah*—which refers to a pre-Muslim state of ignorance, before God revealed the final revelation to Muhammad—to modern Islamic-Arabic societies (Khatab 2006). They had fallen from grace into a new state of ignorance, away from the glorious Islamic civilization of the past, which only a fundamentalist adherence to Islam could restore.

Modern fundamentalist Islam began with Wahhab, and continued through Sayyid Qutb, and his brother Muhammad Qutb, who became professor of Islamic studies in Saudi Arabia and theological mentor to Ayman al-Zawahiri. He in turn became mentor to Osama bin Laden (Al Zayyat et al. 2004), which brings us to the present day. Al-Zawahiri and bin Laden met in Afghanistan in the 1980s, as both men went there to fight against the Soviet invasion. Both served under Abdullah

Yusef Azzam, and bin Laden, using his wealth from the family's construction business, established a base for the various fighters—the Makhtab al Khadamat or Bureau of Services—for whom the battle against the Soviet invasion had become a holy war (*jihad*) (Coll 2004). The fighters, known as the *Mujahadeen* (holy warriors) came from throughout the Islamic and especially the Arab world. The war lasted from 1979–1988, and at least 1 million Mujahadeen died, but they were ultimately successful in ousting the Soviet invasion and its puppet government. After the war, al-Zawahiri and bin Laden determined to hold the vast Mujahadeen army together, along with other financial supporters and political sympathizers, in order to oppose anti-Islamic forces elsewhere in the region. To do this, they established a database, known simply as The Base—or in Arabic, Al Qaeda.

Many of those in The Base were former Mujahadeen from the Afghanistan war, who came of age during the long campaign against the Soviet invasion and thus knew nothing else except the life of the battlefield. Others were new ideologues, anxious to strike against the enemies of Islam as the movement expanded both in ambition and power (Coll 2004). We should note that the leadership, such as bin Laden, al-Zawahiri, and others—like 9/11 hijacker mastermind KSM and ringleader Muhammad Atta—all come from educated and prosperous backgrounds, but the rank-and-file fighters do not. Atta's father, for example, is a lawyer, and Atta himself studied architecture in Germany. Bin Laden's family, who owns the Bin Laden Construction Group, is among the wealthiest families in the world. But the rank and file come from the previously discussed rural areas (or urban slums) of Saudi Arabia and elsewhere in the Islamic world—men and some women committed to strict fundamentalist versions of Islam, from tough rural backgrounds of grinding poverty and bitter resentment toward the West and its illicit prosperity. Despite the existence of an extremely wealthy few, the economic conditions of the Islamic world are sobering: the GDP of the world's 57 Muslim-majority countries combined is less than that of France (Haqqani 2005).

In the teachings of bin Laden, al-Zawahiri, and others, common fighters find God and the strength and certainty of fighting a righteous cause on a cosmic scale. Through Al Qaeda, their lives transform from impoverished insignificance to divine significance. Yet economics alone does not explain religious extremism in Islam or other religions. Also at stake is existential significance, and this explains the attraction of Islamism for educated Muslims and those with professional prospects. Those 57 countries are home to about 500 universities, compared to more than 5,000 in the United States and 8,000 in India. Fewer new book titles are published each year in Arabic, the language of 300 million people, than in Greek, spoken by only 15 million. More books are translated into Spanish each year than have been translated into Arabic in the last century (Haqqani 2005). Indeed, research shows that the vast majority of reforms in the Islamic world, especially the Arab world, are purely superficial and have only intensified economic, political, and cultural conflict (Ottaway and Choucair-Vizoso 2008).

This lack of economic, intellectual, cultural, and technological progress in the Islamic world has left a vacuum that has been filled by "a culture of political anger . . . that keeps Muslims in a constant state of fear that Islam and Islamic culture are in danger of being snuffed out . . . by both external and sectarian enemies"

(Haqqani 2007–2008:19). This fear and anger pervades Muslims from all walks of life—the sense that one has no meaningful place in this world, whether in one's home country or, like Atta and others, abroad in modern countries. They feel like strangers in a strange land at home, and those living abroad feel as if they were forced into exile for purposes of education or career. These social forces and feelings are not unique to Muslims, as we will see.

Women seem to have the same capacity for extremism and violence as men, whether in a religious context or not (Bachetta and Power 2002). In the Moscow Theater takeover on October 23, 2002, women constituted 19 of the 41 terrorists. In the school hostage takeover at Middle School #1 in Beslan, Russia, in September 2004, at least 10 women joined approximately 30 men and eventually blew up the school, killing 250 people (Chivers and Myers 2004b). The day before, an unknown female suicide terrorist detonated a bomb that killed 13 other people (Chivers and Myers 2004a). Although very little literature exists that documents the role of women in religiously motivated terrorist attacks, a recent book by Jessica Stern (2003) finds that women conduct at least 30%–40% of all suicide attacks, and that groups like Hamas no longer recruit women because they are swamped with female volunteers that require no indoctrination (p. 52). Working independently, Juergensmeyer (2003) estimates the same frequency of female suicide attacks, and further notes the peculiar gender roles in Islamic terrorism—that is, women commit their actions primarily to inspire men to greater courage, not to serve God directly (pp. 199–200). Despite such active participation, their motivation derives directly from a religious worldview that regards men as decisive and their own female actions as auxiliary.

> From CNN, September 14, 2001, 2:55 AM
>
> On the broadcast of the Christian television program *The 700 Club,* Jerry Falwell made the following statement:
>
> "I really believe that the pagans, and the abortionists, and the feminists, and the gays and the lesbians who are actively trying to make that an alternative lifestyle, the ACLU, People for the American Way, all of them who have tried to secularize America. I point the finger in their face and say 'you helped this [9/11 attack] happen.'
>
> "I do believe, as a theologian, based upon many scriptures and particularly Proverbs 14:23, which says 'living by God's principles promotes a nation to greatness; violating those principles brings a nation to shame,'" he said.
>
> **Proverbs 14:23:** In all labor there is profit: but the talk of the lips tendeth only to penury (King James Version of the Bible—Author's Note: This is the version Falwell used.)

Stern and Juergensmeyer say little more than this in their respective books, both of which are otherwise theoretically and empirically well argued and supported. Moreover, neither draws connections between militant women in American fundamentalist Christianity, violent or not, and larger social issues. Although Juergensmeyer discusses abortion clinic bombings and shootings in the United States, he sees this violence as separate from nonviolent militancy. Yet the beliefs are basically identical, and Christian fundamentalist militants share the same goals—the unification of the fundamentalist church with the state.

Christianity

Certainly, Islamic radicals destroyed the World Trade Center in New York on September 11, 2001. Their motivations were religious, and their goals both religious and political. In response, far-right American evangelical Jerry Falwell (1933–2007) blamed our internal evil enemies for the tragedy (see text box).

Recently, many fundamentalist leaders, including Timothy and Beverly LaHaye, James Kennedy, the late Jerry Falwell (died in 2007), Pat Robertson, and others, have rallied around a central dogma, called *dominionism.* Presently, dominionism is becoming the unifying theology and agenda of the fundamentalist movement. It is also known as dominion theology and Christian reconstructionism, the latter based on the belief that the United States was once a true Christian theocracy, and has since fallen from grace. Prominent theologians include the late Roushas John (R. J.) Rushdoony (died in 2001) and Gary North. Prominent activists include Gary Bauer and Pat Robertson, and prominent organizations include Concerned Women For America, the Family Research Council, and the Institute for Christian Economics. The goal is to convert the United States into a fully theocratic state, according to the model shown in Figure 5.2.

As Katherine Yurica (2005) chronicles in great detail, theocracy under dominionism would use the Bible for the basis of all law and all conduct in general. Blasphemy, adultery, homosexuality, and heresy would receive the death penalty. All other crimes would be subject either to the death penalty or to restitution, depending on the motive. As the model illustrates, society would consist of three main institutions, which the church encompasses. The patriarchal family and the state, although to some degree autonomous, must at all times conform to religious law. Religious law derives from correct reading of the Bible, such that the only issue in law is reading the Bible correctly.

Some institutions, long since outlawed, would be reestablished according to biblical law, as dominionist theologian David Chilton explains about slavery (see sidebar).

Slavery in Dominionist Theology

The Bible permits slavery. . . . But the biblical laws concerning slavery are among the most beneficent in all the Bible. . . .

1. *Obtaining slaves.* Kidnapping is forbidden as a method of acquiring slaves, and deserves capital punishment (Exodus 21:16). Basically, there are only four legal ways to get slaves. They may be purchased (Leviticus 25:44–46), captured in war (Numbers 31:32–35; Deuteronomy 21:10–14), enslaved as punishment for theft (Exodus 22:1–3), or enslaved to pay off debts (Leviticus 25:39; Exodus 21:7). We should especially note God's merciful justice here. Heathen slaves who were purchased or captured in war were actually favored by this law, since it placed them in contact with believers. They received the relatively lenient treatment of the biblical slavery regulations, and they were also able to hear the liberating message of the gospel. . . .

2. *The care of slaves.* Slaves have no economic incentive to work, since they cannot improve their situation regardless of how hard they labor. Therefore the master is allowed to provide that incentive by beating them (Exodus 21:20–27). Obviously, the slave is not regarded as having equal rights as a free man. . . . Slavery has certain benefits (job security, etc.), but it has serious drawbacks as well. Slavery was not allowed to become irresponsible welfare or paternalism. The law limited the master, however. If he murdered his slave, he was executed (Exodus 21:20). On the other hand, if the slave survived a beating and died a day or two later, there was no punishment (Exodus 21:21); there was no evidence that the master had actually intended to murder him. Again, this risk was a serious incentive against enslaving oneself. God did not want men to heedlessly abandon their freedom, and this law would tend to keep men working hard and living responsibly in order to avoid the threat of losing their liberty and civil rights. Relatively minor but permanent injuries (such as the loss of an eye or a tooth) resulted in the slave's freedom (Exodus 21:26–27). This was also an economic incentive to keep the master from hitting the slave in the face, since a heavy blow could mean the loss of his "investment." (Chilton 1981:61–62)

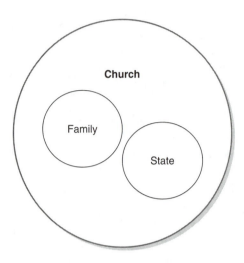

Figure 5.2   Model of Theocratic Society

Once in power, Rushdoony maintains that the righteous Christian government, now anointed by God, has the full right and obligation to annihilate competing religions, including other Christian denominations, and their members. There can be no mercy for this, since "by His birth of God, and of the Virgin Mary, Jesus Christ is head of the new race, as the new Adam, to provide earth with a new seed to supplant the old Adamic race" (Rushdoony 1973:210), and "as the second and last Adam, Christ undoes the work of the first Adam and begins the dispossession of the fallen race from the world and the re-establishment of the earth as the Kingdom of God under His new race" (Rushdoony 1983:287). As the mainline Presbyterian scholar Bruce Prescott notes, some elected officials openly eulogize Rushdoony and embrace dominionism, such as U.S. Representative Bill Graves from Oklahoma, and dominionist John Whitehead serves as official religious advisor to President George Bush (Prescott 2002). Alabama Supreme Court Justice Roy Moore, in the news for placing the Ten Commandments in the statehouse and refusing a court order to remove them, also embraces dominionism. Senators from Oklahoma—Don Nickles (1981–2005), Tom Coburn (2005–present), and James Inhofe (1994–present)— publicly declared their support for Moore.

In addition to political views and aspirations, these beliefs underlie the political goals, but also the culture, of the Christian right in the United States. The work of Timothy LaHaye provides an illustrative example. LaHaye cofounded the Moral Majority with Jerry Falwell in 1978, and in the 1990s began and continues to write an extremely popular series called *Left Behind*. This series, although often sold as science fiction, draws nothing from science, and LaHaye intends it as a vision of reality, not of fiction. The premise is that the Rapture has just occurred, an event in which fundamentalists believe God immediately takes the righteous up to heaven. These people will simply disappear from whatever they are doing and ascend to heaven. Everyone else remains on earth for a period of tribulation, in which they must earn their worthiness for heaven while in battle against the forces of Satan. Among the forces of evil, LaHaye includes the International Monetary Fund, the World Bank, and the United Nations. Indeed, the last of these becomes the center of power for the Antichrist. The series collectively has sold nearly 20 million copies.

Other notable dominionists include Bob Riley, governor of Alabama (2002–present); Ellen Sauerbrey, the chair of the United States Department of State Bureau of Population, Refugees, and Migration; Phill Kline, the current district attorney for Johnson County, Kansas (terms ends 2009) and former Kansas attorney general (2003–2007); and Janet Parshall—far-right Christian broadcaster, popularly known for her rallying cry, "Take up your spiritual bayonet and take this country back for God!" (Pollitt 2005:11).

Nowhere else in the West does Christian fundamentalism enjoy such widespread popularity as in the United States. The Christian right refers collectively to many different organizations, churches, and individuals who work toward a legal system based in scriptural law and an American culture premised on conservative Christian religion, to the exclusion or at least subordination of others. Although notable organizations beginning in the 1970s such as the Moral Majority, the Christian Coalition, Focus on the Family, the Family Research Council, the Eagle Forum, and the 700 Club are all male-dominated, women have found ample voice and power in female auxiliary organizations, many of which have become powerful in their own right. These and other faith-based organizations have received about $500 million in funds between 2002 and 2006 (U.S. Government Accountability Office 2006:11). The Office of Faith-Based and Community Initiatives (OFBCI) distributes money through many federal agencies, including the Agency for International Development, Department of Agriculture, Department of Commerce, Department of Education, Department of Health and Human Services, Department of Homeland Security, Dept of Housing and Urban Development, Department of Justice, Department of Labor, Small Business Administration, and Department of Veterans Affairs (OFBCI Web site).

As in the Middle East, women play a significant role. Among the leading organizations, Concerned Women For America (CWFA), founded in 1978 by Beverly LaHaye (wife of Moral Majority cofounder Timothy LaHaye) as a women's auxiliary to the Moral Majority (Diamond 1998), has since long outlasted that organization, which officially disbanded in 1986. At its founding, CWFA joined the battle against the Equal Rights Amendment for women (the ERA), which in 1981 failed to garner the three-fourths state ratification necessary to become a U.S. constitutional amendment.

Since then, the CWFA organization has grown from a few volunteers to a staff of several hundred, with 500,000 members and a self-generated budget of $14 million in 2004. The organization also receives $38 million in direct grant money from the United States government, under President George Bush's Faith-Based Initiatives. In 2001, CWFA created a spin-off organization, the Culture and Family Institute, which gives out grant money for research on "cutting-edge social issues with particular emphasis on the homosexual activist movement and other forces that threaten to undermine marriage, family and religious freedom," as stated on their Web site.

However, CWFA is not the only fundamentalist Christian organization to receive such money and power in the Bush administration. Others, such as Family Life, Focus on the Family, Family Policy Network, the Traditional Values Coalition, and others received a total of nearly $80 million in direct federal money in 2003, all of which pertain to reproductive issues, family planning, and sexuality. All the afore-mentioned organizations operate as 501(c)3 tax-exempt nonprofit organizations.

This current surge in fundamentalist resources and power arrived only recently, with the election of George W. Bush as the decisive factor. Yet fundamentalists had been organizing for decades, contributing to a culture in which an agenda that seeks to explicitly blend religion and politics becomes viable, and representatives are able to move such legislation through Congress. I have traced the rise of the religious right in American politics and culture elsewhere (see Lundskow 2002), but suffice it to say that their ascent developed over decades of time since World War II. Contrary to their claims, they are not rediscovering America's religious heritage, but have in fact created something new in the late twentieth century.

To be sure, the founding fathers were religious, but not in the way that some imag-ine. For example, Thomas Jefferson edited his own version of the Bible to make it more compatible with Enlightenment values (Prothero 2003), and James Madison dismissed the Bible almost entirely (Ketcham 1990). Though a Deist, Madison regarded most of scripture simply as ancient text that reflected the values of the people who wrote it. No religious representative of any kind attended George Washington on his deathbed. Washington asked for no prayers, nor spoke any himself. Rather, he took his own pulse, and sighed that the end was drawing near (Ellis 2004). All three founders celebrated the Enlightenment spirit that energized their life and times.

The success of the Christian right, and especially its women's organizations, might seem at first glance oxymoronic. On the one hand, their primary goal is to ultimately remove women from being in public life, which they feel threatens every-thing else about Christian society. Yet on the other hand, women like Beverly LaHaye play an increasingly assertive role in public life; they manage large organizations and now influence political decisions directly at the highest levels. Their own answer is that they must commit a lesser evil to combat a greater evil, and their own intentions are pure and motivated to please God. In contrast, they see feminists and secularists as being motivated only by evil—and not even a motivation of self-interest, accord-ing to fundamentalists (Almond, Appleby, and Sivan 2003), but the total destruction of Christian America and Christianity in general. Thus, women fundamentalists jus-tify their own participation in public life in that good people may commit a lesser evil in order to prevent a greater evil and serve the greater glory of God.

Since the stakes are so high, in their view—the survival of correct Christian civ-ilization (Buss and Herman 2003)—nearly any means are appropriate. Although CWFA is not associated directly with committing violence in pursuit of their goals, the organization, along with Operation Rescue president Randall Terry, refused to condemn Michael Griffin in 1993, and Paul Hill in 1994, for murdering abortion doctors in Pensacola, Florida (Kaczor 2003; Royse 2003). Thus, although funda-mentalist Christian organizations have not engaged in violence, individuals allied in terms of belief have.

It is important to realize, however, that although violent acts and sensationalist statements garner far more media attention, most fundamentalist women apply themselves to local groups and politics on a less sensational basis. Notably, most curriculum movements that seek to marginalize or replace evolution with creationism in the schools engage in battle through local PTAs. Recently, for example, several public school districts in suburban Birmingham, Alabama, have shifted curriculum to creationism by utilizing PTA networks to establish "review boards" to actively intimidate science teachers (Dean 2005). Biology teachers at the primary and secondary levels often avoid even mentioning evolution, as the PTA has proven that it can influence retention and promotion decisions.

Local networks persevere toward a faith-based system, as evidenced recently in several public school districts that now openly defy the long-established separation of church and state. In Kansas, Pennsylvania, Mississippi, Georgia, Ohio, and other states, school boards have placed warning stickers on biology textbooks that teach evolution, and some require creation theory to be taught alongside evolution, or else the latter cannot be taught at all ("2 School Boards Push on Against Evolution" 2005). In other cases, the fundamentalist group Focus on the Family publicly argued in 2004 in front of the assembled leaders of the Republican Party that the cartoon *SpongeBob SquarePants* is an insidious and covert attempt to corrupt children by teaching pro-gay, evolutionary, and anti-Christian values (Kirkpatrick 2005). If one can see such agendas in SpongeBob, presumably one can see them anywhere and everywhere.

Yet the Christian right is not estranged from popular culture; it functions much more seamlessly within mainstream culture now than in the 1950s and 60s, and effectively uses the rhetoric of the left to serve its own agenda. Indeed, many far-right fundamentalists self-identify as hippies, radicals, punks, metalheads, and countercultural activists (Shires 2007). Regarding women specifically, Brasher (1998) finds, in her ethnography of women in a fundamentalist congregation, that none of them oppose feminism in general, and they are certainly not antiwoman. The issue is rather the roles that women play and their position in society. As Buss and Herman (2003) note, as well as Diamond (1998), far-right evangelical women distinguish what they call "radical" or "antifamily" feminism from "godly" women. Thus, fundamentalist women do not contest women's rights, but rather, what they see as a specifically anti-Christian women's agenda, that is, the sinful and ungodly aspects—in particular, abortion and lesbianism. Rather than argue against women's rights, they argue in favor of truly moral and godly women over and against evil women, who deserve no quarter.

Furthermore, Brooks and Manza (2004) find that the religious right has exerted increasing influence on Republican Party politics over the past 30 years. Within the context of the wider history of this time period (Eisgruber and Sager 2007; Lundskow 2002), the religious right has moved from the margins to the mainstream of American politics and social life. This reduces the need for radical, militant, or terrorist action, given that the religious right exerts sufficient political and cultural capital to achieve its goals through established institutions. Let us be clear that the religious right remains highly active politically, and their quest for control of American society undiminished (Rudin 2006); rather, their success in the mainstream supersedes the need to act illegally and violently.

Overall, evangelicals have become far more consistently conservative in voting trends over the past 20 years (Brooks and Manza 2004), even as their denominations remain unchanged and roughly equally divided between religious and secular perspectives in politics. As a bloc, evangelicals vote primarily on moral issues, and they accept only those candidates who sincerely represent those views, which includes faith-based education and biblical foundations for law. The success of the religious right arose from local grassroots movements. If the Bush administration, like many politicians, is beholden to major corporations, especially oil, utilities, the defense industry, the insurance industry, and banks, the capitalists only supply money; common people supply the votes, and fundamentalists strongly support Bush and other discernably authentic religious conservatives. In other words, their success is not an aberration, but a predictable outcome of social change over the past several decades that has, at least for the present, allied Christian conservatives and fundamentalists with big business (Wallis 2008; Wilcox and Larson 2006).

Christian Violence

On September 11, 2006, the fifth anniversary of the terror attacks that devastated the United States, a man crashed his car into a building in Davenport, Iowa, hoping to blow it up and kill himself in the fire. Except for Keith Olbermann on MSNBC, no other national newspaper, magazine, or network newscast reported this attempted suicide bombing, though it was sent out on the Associated Press newswire (Pozner 2006). According to the local newspaper, *The Des Moines Register,* David Robert McMenemy, 45, of Sterling Heights, Michigan, was charged with second-degree arson. He was accused of driving his car into the Edgerton Women's Health Center at about 4:30 AM.

The center does not perform abortions and does not provide abortion referrals, said Tom Fedje, the president of the clinic. He said the clinic does advise pregnant women on the various options available to them (Pozner 2006).

Since 1977, casualties from such attacks have included 7 murders, 17 attempted murders, 3 kidnappings, 152 assaults, 305 completed or attempted bombings and arsons, 375 invasions, 482 stalking incidents, 380 death threats, 618 bomb threats, 100 acid attacks, and 1,254 acts of vandalism, according to the National Abortion Federation (cited in Pozner 2006). Abortion providers and activists received 77 letters threatening anthrax attacks before 9/11, and since then, Planned Parenthood and abortion rights groups have received 554 envelopes containing white powder and messages like this one: "You have been exposed to anthrax. . . . We are going to kill all of you." They were signed by the Army of God, a group that hosts scripture-filled Web pages for "Anti-Abortion Heroes of the Faith," including minister Paul Hill, Michael Griffin, and James Kopp, all convicted of murdering abortion providers, and a convicted clinic bomber, the Reverend Michael Bray (Pozner 2006).

Another of their members (or martyrs, as they call themselves) is Clayton Waagner, who mailed anthrax letters while a fugitive on the FBI's 10 Most Wanted list for antiabortion-related crimes. "I am a terrorist," Waagner declared on the

Army of God's Web site. Boasting that God "freed me to make war on his enemy," he went on to say, "It doesn't matter to me if you're a nurse, receptionist, bookkeeper, or janitor, if you work for the murderous abortionist, I'm going to kill you" (www.armyofgod.com).

In addition to Paul Hill and Michael Griffin, the movement has produced violent women activists as well. Perhaps foremost among these is Rachelle Shannon, who participated in numerous abortion clinic blockades until November 17, 1992, when she decided to take more direct action. Beginning the next day, Shannon started firebombing clinics. She credits God with giving her the knowledge necessary to make firebombs:

> God, if you really want me to do this, you're gonna have to show me how, because I can't even get the fire started in my fireplace. The ideas kept coming, including thoughts from people who had accomplished Big Rescue. My plan was to fill five plastic milk cartons (the kind with the pop-off tops) with gasoline, throw them through the window, throw in a lit torch (a stick with oil-soaked rags tied on the end), and scram. I had to know for sure I had God's how, when, and where before I would act. If I was going to spend what's left of my life in prison or die in an explosion, I was at least going to do so in the will of God! (www.armyofgod.com)

The logic is similar to that of all terrorists, in that the faithful may commit violent acts provided it serves the greater will of God. Indeed, Shannon rejoiced when she heard that Griffin, and later Hill, had each killed an abortion doctor. In retrospect, today, she remains fully unrepentant:

> He [Griffin] didn't shoot Mother Teresa, he shot a mass murderer such as Saddam Hussein or Hitler. I don't even think it is accurately termed "murder." God is the only one who knows whether Gunn would ever have repented or if he would have killed another 5,000 babies and probably 3 or 4 more women who probably weren't Christians either. (www.armyofgod.com)

Shannon decided to imitate Griffin and Hill's example, and in December of 1994, the state of Kansas convicted Shannon of the attempted murder of George Tiller, an abortion doctor. She was sentenced to 11 years in prison, and in 1995, to another 20 years for several counts of arson.

Shannon is not the only woman in the United States to commit violence in the name of God. Others include Brenda K. Phillips, who opened fire with a shotgun in 2003 at the Femcare Women's Clinic in Asheville, North Carolina. Fortunately, no one was injured.

Hinduism

Like Muslims and Christians, the vast majority of Hindus favor peaceful coexistence with people of other faiths. Also like Islam and Christianity, however, the Hindutva (Hinduness) movement assumes an essential Hindu foundation to people and living, and like their essentialist counterparts in other religions, Hindutva activists equate Hinduness with broader cultural factors beyond just belief. Although polytheistic, Hindutvas assume a fundamental essence that true Hindus possess inherently, compared to pretenders and non-Hindus. Many in India regard the Hindutva movement as a nationalist movement rather than a strictly religious movement.

In 1925, the Hindutva perspective first appeared as Rashtriya Swayamsevak Sangh (RSS)—the National Volunteers Union—founded by Keshava Baliram Hedgewar. Founded in 1980, the Bharatiya Janata Party (BJP)—the Indian People's Party—is one of two major parties in India today and is closely associated with the RSS, as are the Vishva Hindu Parishad (World Hindu Council), the Akhil Bharatiya Vidyarthi Parishad (All India Students Council), and other Hindutva organizations. The BJP recently held power, from 1998 to 2004, and is now the main opposition party.

Hindutva parties and organizations see themselves as great nation builders, but they exclude Muslims and Christians, who are inherently anathema to Hinduness. Secular democracy, the current system in India, implies pluralistic tolerance of all religions, languages, and cultures, and thus Hindutvas oppose it in favor of a true Hindu system. As the RSS motto states, "Sangathit Hindu, Samartha Bharat," that is, "United Hindus, capable India." The RSS worldview holds that human civilization began in India, which in turn created the great civilizations of Mesopotamia and the Far East, including China. While India certainly influenced these civilizations, the human species did not originate in India as Hindutvas contend (Elst 2001), and as civilization advanced, each influenced the others (Thapar 2004). China is not Indo-European, for example, and indeed the Indo-Europeans, as we saw in Chapter 2, section I, were not indigenous to India. Consequently, the Hindu language, religion, and civilization are themselves the result of invasion and blending (Basham 1999). Like its Christian counterparts, Hindutva challenges many contemporary historical and anthropological theories about migration, language, and culture. Mainstream scholars in India, however, find little or no evidence to support Hindutva claims, and point out that such views derive from ethnocentric and nationalistic sentiment, not scientific fact (Sharma 2004; Udayakumar 2005). In reaction, Hindutva supporters counter that the educational establishment betrays a Western and foreign bias, with further anti-Hindu influences from Islam, as Arun Shourie (1999, 2005) argues. We see a counterargument in the sociological and social historical approaches of Robert Stern (2003) and Romila Thapar (2004), that Hindutva support derives from opposition to capitalist invasion, with Western culture tagging along behind. While India has long assimilated various cultural influences, Hindutva ethnocentrism and nationalism respond to modern economic forces, which entered with British imperialism, and which tend to destroy cultural distinctiveness entirely. In this regard, Hindutva resembles fundamentalism everywhere.

Hindutva influences have contributed to Hindu violence against Muslims, the religion of India's greatest rival—Pakistan. Muslims constitute about 15% of the population of India, and relations with Hindus have generally been peaceful. Notable outbreaks of violence have accelerated in recent years, however. In 1992, Hindus razed the Babri Mosque in Ayodhya. Muslims retaliated with bombings in Mumbai and Calcutta in 1993, which killed 317 and wounded over 1,400. With tensions simmering for the next 10 years, any innocuous scuffle would set off more violence.

On February 27, 2002, a train carrying Hindus was returning from a convention to raise money to build a temple at the site of the Babri Mosque—a highly inflammatory goal. While stopped at a station in Godhra—a city in Gujarat State that has a size-able Muslim population—a scuffle started between some Hindu passengers and Muslim vendors. At this point, the confrontation amounted to only name-calling and some minor jostling. The station master decided to depart the train early in order to avoid any escalation. As the train slowed at a signal a ways down the track, it caught fire. Some claimed that Muslim militants hurled Molotov cocktails at the train, while others claim the militants actually boarded the train as it slowed and ignited the fire from inside. Either way, 59 Hindus died. Images of the gutted train appeared throughout India.

In response, various Hindutva-inspired groups rampaged through Muslim neighborhoods in the Gujarat State in February and March 2002. Their purpose was clear: to kill Muslims. Muslims also organized to defend themselves and then retaliate. When the rioting finally ended, official sources declared 790 Muslims and 254 Hindus were killed, 223 people missing, 2,548 injured, 919 widowed, and 606 children orphaned ("Gujarat Riot Death Toll Revealed" 2005). Most of the Muslims were killed in the manner of the train deaths. They were barricaded in their homes, which were then doused with gasoline, and set alight.

Parliament empowered A. C. Bannerjee (an Indian Supreme Court justice) to lead a committee to investigate the Godhra train incident. The Bannerjee Report concluded that, while the fire definitely started from the inside, the conflagration most likely resulted from attempts to cook food in passenger compartments. There was no evidence of malicious incendiary devices ("India Train Fire Not Mob Attack" 2005). The BJP and its Hindutva allies declared the report "a disgrace" and insisted that Muslims had perpetrated a premeditated terrorist act.

Discussion and Analysis

We are here concerned with the worldview and social psychology of religious intolerance. We are also concerned with the perpetrators of religious violence who set their beliefs above all other concerns, and who act on these beliefs at all possible moments, by force and violence if necessary, but always aggressively.

In fundamentalism, belief transcends this reality, which also means that conventionality and traditions can be legitimately, and not just opportunistically, suspended. Desperate times call for desperate measures, and even apparently routine times in this reality are vital moments in the larger cosmic struggle. All traditions, laws, customs, worldly values, reason, logic, and even gender roles may be sacrificed. In sociological terms, Max Weber identifies this power as "charismatic authority," a concept he borrows from Rudolf Sohm (Weber 1978:216), such that charisma represents the belief in a power or force, and hence authority, that transcends and supersedes this reality—usually understood as God, nature, the nation, and so forth. Using the concept of charisma, Weber juxtaposes it with reason, its exact opposite. Although both seek to change the world, and both hold the necessary authority to render change in established systems or to create order from social breakdown, the means are opposite. Specifically, "reason works from without: by altering the situations of life and hence its problems, finally in this way changing attitudes towards them" (p. 245). In contrast, charisma seeks to "effect a subjective or internal reorientation born out of suffering, conflicts, or enthusiasm" (p. 245). In other words, reason seeks to understand the world in objective (that is, logical-empirical) terms, whereas charisma seeks to reorient the person or group based on perception of the world, primarily through emotional perception and reaction. Both affect and guide behavior, but reason seeks to alter the conditions of life, whereas charisma seeks to make a person feel a certain way about the world.

With the destruction of the Taliban regime in Afghanistan, Saudi Arabia remains as an illustrative example of a scripture-based and routinized charismatic state system—it has created a faith-based society in terms of social hierarchy and education. We know this system as Wahhabism, a fundamentalist version of Islam discussed earlier. Scripture is the sacred (charismatic) guide to all things, such that if something does not appear in the Bible or the Quran, then it is not necessary to know. Although such a system achieves emotional fulfillment for the devout, it also renders Saudi Arabia especially incompatible with global culture and economy. The nation imports the vast majority of its technical experts because its educational system teaches Islamic studies and little else (Khan and Langman 2005; Langman and Morris 2002, 2004). However satisfyingly self-righteous Saudi faith-based society may feel, it is inherently impractical in the modern global world.

For Christian fundamentalists, the daily battles over particular issues are only instances of a much larger battle between ultimate good and ultimate evil on a cosmic scale. Mark Juergensmeyer (2003:150–151) finds that fundamentalist activists view the cosmic war quite literally, and given the good-versus-evil perspective, no compromise is ever possible or desirable—the true believer must be forever willing to do anything to defeat ultimate evil. Extremists find in the Book of Genesis, from the beginning of creation (Pagels 1988), a battle between good and evil that is repeated throughout the Bible, including in the Gospels, where the life of Jesus is part of the larger cosmic battle (Pagels 1995). Specifically, the Gospel of Luke suppresses all Roman initiative and even interest in prosecuting Jesus, and instead depicts the Jews not only as unjust and corrupt, but as essentially evil (Pagels 1995:94–98). The Gospel of John goes further still to portray the Jews as the active servants of Satan. As Pagels (1995) explains, John's frame of reference in the struggle of Light and Dark from Genesis "informs the reader that both Jesus' coming and all his human relationships are elements played out in a supernatural drama between the forces of good and evil" (p. 100). In John, we see both the ultimate good (Jesus, the son of God) and the ultimate evil (the Jews as the children and servants of Satan). This view constitutes the original model for the social process of demonization, and has persisted, against Jews and others, for 2,000 years.

Yet it would be a mistake to conclude that fundamentalist extremists have no sense of real time or history. On the contrary, the leadership and most rank and file are keenly aware of historical and ongoing policies, injustices, and wars. They do not grow up in isolation, in closed communities in which one particular extreme religious view dominates and stands in isolation from larger national or global forces. Indeed, as Burgat (2003) finds in a recent empirical study, fundamentalist organizations have a keen sense of factual history, both in terms of military events, but also moments of great injustice that define the battle between good and evil. For fundamentalists, the enemy takes many forms, and Juergensmeyer is instructive here. The conflict rages eternally. Particular issues may come and go, various real people live and die, but the struggle continues. In this perspective, "the war cannot be won in real time" (Juergensmeyer 2003:165). Rather, the religious extremist fights in cosmic time, simply as one true believer in a vast, ongoing battle for all of existence. Yet at any given moment, real people, practices, organizations, governments, or lifestyles—nearly anything—can acquire the status of Enemy. When this happens, all available means must be applied to defeat it, with no exceptions.

Michel Wieviorka (1993) glimpses the central significance of this social-psychological orientation, in that religious violence occurs when the group subconsciously perceives, but cannot admit, that the cause is already lost in this reality, and they have in fact abandoned their religious beliefs, such that transcendence "has become a substitute for a movement which has either become imaginary or incapable of achieving the goals pinned on it" (p. 291). I would specify that this applies to achieving the goals *in this reality*. Fundamentalists are not insane, but rather, they willfully choose a substitute reality, one measured in cosmic time, and one in which acts in this world are really measured by their contribution to the eternal struggle of good versus evil, and not in terms of their ability to achieve measurable political or cultural goals.

Learning creationism rather than evolution does not prepare a person for a career in the global economy, but it might make a person feel more existentially secure, and certainly provides the authority of self-righteousness. The increasing popularity of fundamentalism arises from personal insecurity, which results from social decline—both economic and status decline. Fundamentalist movements, especially at the grassroots level (creationism in schools, for example), has nothing to do with facts or logic, but with power. The believer willfully disregards logic and evidence, and instead embraces a belief, which he or she then attempts to force on the school board. The believer receives emotional gratification from this, because it feels good to force the school board, and the intelligentsia more generally, to submit. It provides emotional gratification in place of real personal and social improvement. Creationism in science classes will not improve education, but it will make some parents feel more important.

Furthermore, Mike Davis (2002) identifies a central aspect of American culture—the tendency to negate reason and embrace what he calls "uncanniness." As the World Trade Center (WTC) towers fell, for example, they signified that the American quest for "a bourgeois utopia of a totally calculable and safe environment has paradoxically created great insecurity" (p. 8). The perfection Americans seek is inherently impossible, and thus creates dissatisfaction and ongoing disappointment. Extraordinary events thus trigger a panic, which arises from the inherent and underlying insecurity, which in turn feeds feelings of uncanniness. This orientation defines the world in terms of the extraordinary, rather than the ordinary. The facts and dangers (and the joys) of the mundane give way to transcendent myths. The spectacular attack on September 11, 2001, killed 2,752 people (New York City District Attorney's Office, www.manhattanda.org). That same year, 42,900 people died in common car crashes (National Highway Transportation Safety Administration data, www.nhtsa.gov); there were also 15,980 murders and 1,436,611 total violent crimes (FBI Uniform Crime Report, www.fbi.gov). Yet the WTC attack received all the media attention, and it captured the public imagination.

Perception of the world based on the extraordinary allows people to abandon reason in favor of emotional gratification. The solutions to mundane crime, for example, are complex and require careful study and policy formation that must be implemented within competing political interests. Comparatively, the extraordinary event has a simple solution—attack and destroy the enemy. Above all, then, the transcendent worldview requires an enemy that embodies all that threatens the perfection of the dream. That is, a world constituted by the designs of an extraordinary authority (namely, God) requires an extraordinary enemy—a Great Evil. As Sartre ([1948] 1976) argues, this has historically taken the shape of the Jew, which the anti-Semite conjures from his own imagination: "Far from experience producing his idea of the Jew, it was the latter which explained his experience. If the Jew did not exist, the anti-Semite would invent him" (p. 13). This does not refer to real-life Jews, but rather, a transcendent Jew, as depicted for example in the *Left Behind* series (the apocalyptic fiction series by Tim LaHaye and Jerry Jenkins)—an enemy of extraordinary evil that is everywhere yet nowhere specifically, embodied as any one person, but essentially a great cosmic entity. Gavin Langmuir (1990) conceptualizes this fantastical social-psychological creation as a chimera, a monstrous beast constructed from real-life creatures (a lion, a goat, and a snake), but which in combination is impossible. Such is the Jew that the anti-Semite imagines. Today, fundamentalists conjure terrorists, homosexuals, Christians, Muslims, Jews, Hindus, Americans, Arabs, and science as among the great chimerical evils. All exist, but not in combination as embodiments of a great evil conspiracy that is at all times both obvious and devious, evil and powerful, yet perverse and weak, crude yet sophisticated, intelligent yet bestial, and virtually any manner of impossible dualistic combinations.

The supremely righteous require a supremely evil enemy, and we have seen various enemies in this chapter—Cathars, Muslims, Christians, Jews. Indeed, the in-group identity can exist without a productive element, but not without a nihilistic evil enemy that demands eternal vigilance and often eternal battle (Adorno et al. 1950; Worrell 2005). The fundamentalist right, in fact, has a long history of charismatic motivation, typically expressed as attacks on the Great Evils of modern times, including rock music, homosexuality, feminism, and anything secular. This is well-documented elsewhere. In charismatic fashion, their zealous, faith-based worldview and prescriptions create an inner emotional satisfaction. Substantive changes in society, or actual social improvement on a variety of issues, is irrelevant except to the extent that policy change, curriculum change, and so on demonstrate fulfillment of faith-based (charismatic) direction. In the simplest terms, it feels good to throw out evolution in favor of creationism. It replaces the cold, dispassionate, and secular views of human biology with an intense, passionate, and religious fervor premised on the directives of a loving but also harshly judgmental God.

Faced with a relentlessly evil enemy, marginalized men (and sometimes women) take on the role of holy warrior, and with it "the grand spiritual and political struggles in which their movements envision themselves . . . [which] impart a sense of importance and destiny to men who find the modern world to be stifling, chaotic, and dangerously out of control" (Juergensmeyer 2003:193). For religious radicals of any denomination, an otherworldly battle supplants this-worldly advancement.

Yet how can self-imposed denial, rejection of the world, and sacrifice of one's life create emotional satisfaction? A theory of charismatic rationality cannot fully answer this. We must turn to a correlate, suggested by Weber but developed fully by critical theory—the concept of the authoritarian personality.

Authoritarianism

On of the most thoroughly researched but also widely misunderstood concepts, authoritarianism means simply the desire to submit to anyone or anything perceived as superior, and it also refers to the desire to dominate anyone or anything perceived as inferior. The authoritarian accepts authority uncritically, including all manner of illogical and impossible notions, provided that such surrender of the intellect produces emotional satisfaction. Developed initially by Erich Fromm (1936), the concept of authoritarianism received extensive empirical research in the mid-twentieth century (Adorno et al. 1950; Bettelheim and Janovitch 1950; and Massing 1949, among others). Altemeyer (1997) counts at least 744 separate published studies between 1950 and 1974, followed by many in the late twentieth century including his own quantitative studies throughout the 1980s and 1990s (with a sample of nearly 50,000) that finds religious fundamentalism as the strongest predictor of authoritarian aggression. Hunsberger (1995, 1996), using similar analytical statistics, finds that religious fundamentalism is the strongest predictor of authoritarian submission and aggression among fundamentalist Christians, as do Tsang and Rowatt (2007) and Watson et al. (2003), both in cross-cultural (non-Christian) contexts. On the qualitative side, social-historical research by Zafirovsky (2007) also confirms this connection.

In essence, authoritarianism intensifies when people feel insecure—not in a vague or transitory sense but insecure regarding the great existential issues: Who am I? Why am I here? How should I live? What happens when I die? (P. Berger [1967] 1990). As Peter Berger (1999) has discovered recently, however, secularism in whatever form has difficulty in answering these questions. More profoundly, Fromm ([1955] 1990) argued that a *nomos*—a worldview that explains the meaning of life—must connect emotional fulfillment with material fulfillment and reality in general. People and civilizations cannot prosper if beliefs and feelings exist separately from actual lived experience. As Fromm and Maccoby ([1970] 1996) discovered empirically in a study of a Mexican village that was rapidly transforming from a local and traditional-based community to a modern industrial economy, the destruction of tradition often includes the destruction of the meaning of life. They found that the destruction of tradition also replaced cooperation with competition as a virtue, and also rewarded aggressiveness with social prestige and rescinded prestige from friendliness.

Similarly, economic modernization and Western cultural influx into the local and traditional communities of the Islamic Middle East are not inherently perceived as evil. In India as well as Western society, modernism brings prosperity, and also existential crisis. Yet this predates modern society, in that the Cathars appealed to disenfranchised peasants who had little hope for a better future. To the extent social forces destroy the accepted nomos, they not only disrupt established ways of life (even if it means greater economic opportunity and political freedom), but in the transition, destroy the meaning of life as well. Under such circumstances, the most disrupted members of society establish and submit to authoritarian promises of eternal life, eternal righteousness, and eternal meaning in the eternal struggle against eternal evil. The Great Evil has arrived at the godly societies of the Middle East and of the United States, and only submission in service of an even Greater Good can save us. In exchange for total and eternal meaning and purpose, one need only surrender to the leader and the cause. Yet authoritarian submission requires negation of the self. In this way, the individual thinks and feels as he or she is told, and thereby gains a feeling of security and purpose, but only so long as reality can be ignored, avoided, or manipulated, and crucially, only so long as the leader–follower relationship enthralls the person emotionally.

In the Middle East, the Islamic world has been struggling with the forces of modernization for 100 years. As modern forces marginalize and discredit Islamic tradition, especially regarding the subordination of women, only the fundamentalists offer a powerful replacement vision premised on religious intensity and the glories of the fifteenth- to sixteenth-century caliphate. If women are the last and most oppressed group in Islam, then their emancipation, which modernism promises, must be opposed. Such emancipation would signify the final fall of the fundamentalist vision.

This applies equally to the United States, where it is no coincidence that religious conservatism and fundamentalism thrive in the so-called red (Republican and conservative) states, as opposed to the blue (Democratic and more liberal) states. Modernization has completely disenchanted the world and destroyed our traditions. Modern developments such as women's freedom and equality signify the death of tradition, including moral and religious tradition—the old nomos. What shall replace it?

And what of the position of women? Consider Table 5.2. In terms of their decision-making power, how do women in the United States compare to other first world countries and the Islamic Middle East?

Table 5.2 Percent of Public Offices Held by Women: Top Ten Middle Eastern Islamic and Non-Islamic Countries

Non-Islamic Countries	Percentage	Islamic Countries	Percentage
Sweden	45.3	Pakistan	21.6
Denmark	38.0	Uzbekistan	7.2
Finland	37.5	Iran	4.5
Netherlands	36.7	Turkey	4.4
Norway	36.4	Egypt	2.4
Cuba	36.0	Kuwait	0.0
Spain	36.0	Saudi Arabia	0.0
Argentina	34.0	Oman	0.0
South Africa	32.8	United Arab Emirates	0.0
Germany	32.2	Bahrain	0.0
United States	14.3		
Average (non-USA)	36.49	Average	4.01

Source: "Where Women Rule." Ode Magazine, September 2004:36.

As the chart indicates, there are substantial differences between Middle Eastern Islamic countries and Western countries, with the obvious exception of Pakistan.

Yet just as clearly, the United States is far behind several major Western countries, although in no country in the world have women yet breached the 50% mark. Still, the United States is the only Western country with a significant and politically salient fundamentalist and reactionary movement that seeks to reduce women's rights and sociopolitical power. Since the bottom five countries on the Islamic side provide no legal basis to protect women's rights, no particular freedom thus exists for women, and consequently, women have no legal recourse or independent means of income, so they engage in activism at great risk. Yet of the top five Middle Eastern countries, all exhibit strong fundamentalist reactionary movements, just like the United States.

And what of opportunity and quality of life? We would perhaps not lament the loss of tradition if rational modernity delivered a stable quality of life. Is life more uncertain in the conservative states? Consider this: the highest rates of personal bankruptcy claims in the United States—90% of which result from only two sources: unexpected major medical bills, or unexpected job loss—are (in order) in the following states: Utah, Tennessee, Georgia, Nevada, Indiana, Alabama, Arkansas, Ohio, Mississippi, and Idaho (Labaton 2005)—all politically or culturally conservative states. Except for Ohio, these are the same states with the lowest standard of living; the lowest rates of college attendance; the least amount of welfare, educational, and Medicaid support; the highest rates of teen pregnancy; and the lowest literacy rates (U.S. Census Bureau, www.census.gov). Does religious extremism promise a better life, or instead a psychological reorientation, as social-scientific research on authoritarianism over the last 58 years concludes?

Conclusions

Certainly, the situation requires more study to prove a connection between social uncertainty and authoritarian versions of religion. Yet also clearly, it is a worthwhile direction in which to proceed. Today's global world requires advanced education, broad knowledge, and critical thinking skills to advance beyond low-wage slavery, frequent job changes, and layoffs. Even the educated classes experience increasing disillusionment and uncertainty (Mishel, Bernstein, and Allegretto 2005). Yet most of the American South since the Civil War and the Midwest since the 1970s have experienced consistently uncertain opportunity, especially in the South, with only the bare minimum levels of institutional support in health and education. The only consistent opportunity is ideological and faith-based, not economically based. The illusion of charisma and authoritarianism cannot long endure without real accomplishment, but it can inflict significant social and psychological harm in the meantime.

As Wieviorka (1993) argues, this is really a last stand, a final attempt to retain the familiar and strict traditional worldview and anti-intellectual simplicity that has already passed. The modern age has long since triumphed.

Or has it? Rejection of scientific cosmology, especially regarding the origin of the universe and subsequently the origin of species, seeks to replace evolution with creationism. Now in its early stages, this antiscientism will likely expand to challenge such basic theories as plate tectonics and glaciation with creationist beliefs that the continents do not move, and assert instead that large geological change occurred only during Noah's flood. Ultimately, if it's not in the Bible, or the Quran, or any other scripture, then you don't need to know it. This sentiment is popular and gaining official legitimacy through local and state school boards in the United States, and already official in Saudi Arabia and elsewhere.

To what extent fundamentalism will transform American education and government requires empirical research to predict. Can individuals, families, and social networks survive under perpetually uncertain social forces? Yes. Can they live fulfilling lives, and even more, develop as free-thinking, critically aware, creative, and compassionate individuals under perpetual uncertainty? Past research says decisively no, but we need to research these questions. Authoritarian submission to charismatic figures is one way to address insecurity, but an ultimately futile way, because it cannot produce real material changes or reinstate values that have already lost their meaning. Other ways exist, but American culture includes a powerful dislike and distrust of intellectualism and reason, which are arguably necessary prerequisites to realistically address today's social problems.

Yet neither reason alone nor the expanded opportunities of social mobility have brought peace and prosperity to all. However much one may disagree with Qutb's response to the problems of modernity, the racist violence he observed was real, and poverty remains a significant problem. Modernity has also failed to produce a new system of meaning, and although idealized visions of a supposedly religious past may not be the answer, neither does the course of the present suggest likely existential improvement, however much we may manage to redistribute wealth or guarantee just enforcement of civil rights. Although not a solution, religious intolerance and violence may be a harbinger of changes yet to come.

CHAPTER 6

Evil

Introduction

As we saw earlier, some devout believers view difference as evil. Although not limited to any particular religion, it does tend to occur most frequently in the monotheistic traditions, beginning with Zoroastrianism and continuing in the Judeo-Christian-Islamic tradition. Indeed, the concept of evil varies considerably from one religion to another, each conceptualization arising from the antisocial threats as perceived and experienced by each culture.

Most religions have some concept of evil. The Judeo-Christian-Islamic tradition teaches a particular concept of evil with which we are most familiar. Whatever the exact notion, evil only becomes real within a social context. Without real-life referents, ideas remain vague and mysterious shades that never quite take material form. In order for evil to have meaning, it must be attached to empirical manifestations; it must be attached to real-life people and things. As sociologists, we should keep in mind that, as C. Wright Mills hoped in the introduction, we will use theory as a tool to understand the real world, and not speculate endlessly about concepts. Evil becomes a sociological issue to the extent it shapes social action.

The social basis of evil, as we will see, means that nearly anything can become an embodiment of evil and therefore an object of exclusion, persecution, or extermination.

We glimpsed the importance of evil, in the form of an evil enemy, in the previous chapter on religious intolerance and violence, and now in this chapter, we will explore the concept of evil more thoroughly and sociologically. As we will see, the belief in a pure, ultimate evil (such as Satan) is far from universal.

Evil Around the World

Polynesia

Let us begin with notions other than the Judeo-Christian-Islamic concept. Among Pacific Islanders, which includes many different cultures and languages, most of the people are descended from the ancient Polynesians, a seafaring civilization with advanced navigational skills that allowed them to reliably find tiny islands throughout the vast Pacific Ocean. The settlement period was long, starting around 1600 BCE and concluding around 1000 CE. They settled throughout the region now known as Oceania (the islands and archipelagos of the central and south Pacific Ocean [see Image 6.1]). During this period, Europeans, as a comparison, were unable to navigate open water, and in any case, European ships could not withstand rough seas. In places such as Samoa, Fiji, Hawaii, Tahiti, Tonga, New Zealand, and over 1,000 others, the Polynesians established advanced civilizations, and although they would gradually diverge over centuries in terms of language and culture, a basic core set of religious beliefs remained as testimony to their common heritage. In these beliefs, we find no notion of pure evil.

Evil does exist in these cultures, but not as a pure, omnipresent evil of ultimate and transcendent proportions. Rather, evil takes the form of various intelligent entities that are not human or animal, but nevertheless exist as living beings. The *Taura'u* (the apostrophe indicates a syllable break) are spirits who manifest as animals. Although they look like the animal they portray, they have a much higher order of intelligence and various supernatural powers. At times, they may cause problems for humans— sometimes serious problems, such as driving off schools of fish or eating stored food. Similarly, the *Tokway* are a kind of imp or sprite that most of the time is simply mischievous and at worst annoying, but if angered, can cause minor illnesses and a great deal of mischief. Humans can appease both entities by offering gifts of food or providing a more comfortable habitat. This usually means that part of an area developed for human use must be turned back to the Taura'u or the Tokway.

On a more serious and potentially malevolent level, the *Bwaga'u* and the *Mulukwausi*—male sorcerers and female witches, respectively—are also supernatural beings, except they manifest in human rather than animal form. Both can inflict potentially devastating harm on individual people or entire villages. In addition, the Mulukwausi may steal organs from the living, and thereby inflict great pain and suffering until appeased. They can also rob people of their senses and steal a person's memory. Like the Taura'u and the Tokway, they are not gods, but rather, beings that developed (evolved) alongside humanity. They share the world with us; they are not transcendent beings, although they possess very long life spans that make them virtually immortal (Messadié 1996). However, the Polynesian people believe they can be imprisoned or killed, which requires certain knowledge and magic to accomplish, and which invites their kind to exact revenge.

None of these beings inspires worship. Although they sometimes require appeasement, they are not gods.

Most Polynesian religions emphasize a harmony with nature, and thus their gods are neither evil nor good, but very powerful beings like the forces of nature they represent, that both provide sustenance to humans and sometimes do harm.

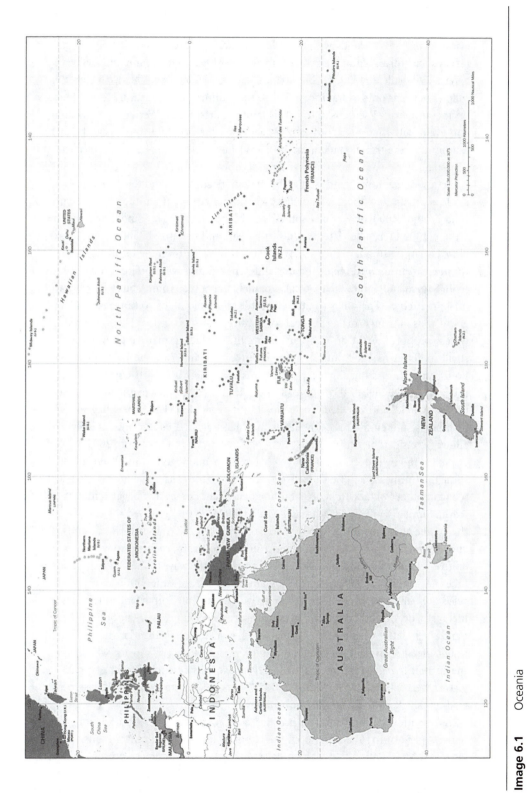

Image 6.1   Oceania

Source: University of Texas Libraries, University of Texas–Austin.

Although likely descendent from one original seafaring people, the Polynesian islands manifest diverse cultures today, each with somewhat different beliefs. We also see that those islands with abundant natural resources tended to favor egalitarian social forms, compared to resource-poor islands, where more internally and externally hostile and harshly hierarchical societies developed. The discussion that follows pertains only to traditional Polynesian culture, not the culture found today on the numerous Pacific Islands. Christianity, tourism, war, Western colonization, and eventually Islam have radically transformed the people of these islands, such that little of the traditional culture remains. They have all long since converted to Christianity (and a few to Islam) and modern ways of life.

Let us look at four islands settled by the same people around the same time and in close proximity—the Lapita people, who migrated out of Southeast Asia beginning around 4000 BCE. They settled the islands of Tonga, Samoa, and Fiji by around 1300 BCE. They later sailed farther east and colonized Tahiti, Hawaii, and New Zealand. Although once a more or less unified culture, the local island environments transformed the Lapita into different cultures with different ways of life.

In Samoa and Tahiti, the tropical climate is warm year-round, but with pleasant offshore breezes. The soil is a naturally fertile combination of volcanic ash and layers of topsoil, which makes it ideal for a variety of food crops. The surrounding waters support a great diversity of marine life, including many types of fish and shellfish. Tahiti is agriculturally very resource rich. In 1768, the French explorer Louis Antoine de Bougainville visited the island, and his reports contributed significantly to the idea of the "noble savage." He viewed the people of Tahiti as beautiful to behold, and intelligent in manner and expression. They knew little of war, he reports, and enjoyed an easy life as the island yielded its resources readily and allowed considerable leisure time (de Bougainville, cited in Dunmore 2005).

As we might expect, the Tahitians believed in many gods, but all represented some nurturing aspect of nature. They were not angry gods or war gods, as we will see with other Polynesian people, but the beneficent deities of a beneficent natural world. Similarly in Samoa, Margaret Mead ([1928] 2001) observed the routines of the people at a time just before Western influences began to transform the culture, and although there is an obvious gender division of labor, each group works cooperatively. Older men and women respectively teach the ways to the new generation. Like the Tahitians, the Samoans enjoy abundant leisure time; numerous festivals celebrate Samoan culture, and religious rituals mark the important milestones in life. Birth, death, and everything in between are all public events. The Samoans recognize very little of the private time we cherish today. With everything part of public life, it is difficult for people to exploit one another, and anyone who dislikes the current living arrangements may freely move in with a relative. This applies to girls as well as boys, starting around 11–12 years old, although the Samoans do not traditionally keep track of years or birthdays.

As mentioned, the Samoans practice a clear gender division of labor, with females performing the usual domestic labors while men concentrate on fishing. However, Mead argues that women have nearly as much influence on social life as men; that the Samoans value both forms of labor; and their overall culture emphasizes cooperation as a moral value, over and against competition. Men who brag about

the excellent fish they have caught are not heroes or hard workers, but moral violators. Although Mead has been criticized for her idealization of traditional Samoan
society, we should note that, for example, the !Kung (The ! represents a clicking
sound) Bushpeople of the Kalahari Desert in South Africa hold similar values
(E. Thomas [1958] 1989). The Samoans show a relaxed attitude about nearly everything, including sexuality. Girls and boys, before they come of age, are allowed to
engage in exploratory behavior, both heterosexual and homosexual. There is no
concept of sin or evil in traditional Samoa, only a concept of antisocial attitudes
and behavior. The Samoans value cooperation and social interaction highly. They
celebrate festivals throughout the year that serve to reinforce a high degree of integration and interaction. Through dancing and feasting, the Samoans reinforce their
mutual respect and integration. Whenever hostile emotions arise, people actively
seek out more pleasant interaction with different people. Rarely do Samoans confront each other in anger (Mead [1928] 2001).

This contrasts starkly with the numerous small islands of New Guinea. Although
the main island of New Guinea is large and includes several different climatic zones,
there are many small islands that are all resource poor. Not only do the islands provide little land-based sustenance, but the close proximity of many small islands creates conflicts between them as each vies for control over the best fishing areas. Many
of the islands consist of hard and often razor-sharp volcanic rock with few fresh-
water sources and minimal fertile areas suited to food production. Even on the large
island, mountains, flood plains, arid regions, and other difficult terrain divide the
island into small sections, such that any one way of life is not compatible with ways
of life in other sections. This produces many different cultures, each of which corresponds to a survival strategy appropriate to that zone.

Consequently, many of these people lived traditionally in harsh forms of social organization. Even on the main island, some people, such as the Korowai, segregated the
men from the women and children and created all-male warrior groups. These warrior
groups preyed upon weaker neighbors, but also on their own women. The men of the
warrior caste held all rights and privileges, while the women amounted to little more
than chattel, which the men traded amongst themselves. Unlike the Tahitians and
Samoans, the people of New Guinea cherish individual displays of power and achievement, especially in war. They interact relatively little with each other, and adults talk as
little as possible. They show considerable suspicion and mistrust, often confront each
other in anger, and perpetrate violent acts frequently (Benedict [1934] 1989). According
to Ruth Benedict, the Dobu (New Guinea Islanders) are among the most suspicious
and hostile people on the planet. Compare her description below of the Dobu to de
Bougainville's description of the Tahitians or Mead's of the Samoans:

> All existence appears to the Dobu as a cutthroat struggle in which deadly
> antagonists are pitted against one another in a contest for each one of the
> goods of life. Suspicion and cruelty are his trusted weapons in the strife and he
> gives no mercy, as he asks none. (p. 160)

The Korowai of West New Guinea allowed only the men to participate in religious ceremonies, as they regarded women as inferior and subhuman. Their gods

were angry and hostile gods of war, who demanded harsh tests of manhood and human sacrifices. Like animal sacrifices found throughout the world in many traditional religions, the Korowai, like the Fijians and others, ate their human sacrifices. Although Western accounts typically exaggerated the frequency of cannibalism among traditional Pacific Islanders, the practice did in fact occur, and was a crucial part of their traditional religion. Various peoples of New Guinea and nearby islands, such as the Dobu and the Fijians, practiced cannibalism as a devout religious ceremony, and in many cases, the cruelty that pervaded their worldview became starkly manifest in cannibalistic ritual. Enemies captured in battle faced an extended period of torture, in which the entire male population partakes as a form of entertainment. The men acquired pride and earned status for particularly effective torture. Following the torture ritual, the women joined the men for a gruesome vivisection ritual that not only celebrated the gods, but provided one of the few collective joys for the community gathered to partake in the event (Lindenbaum 1978; Zigas 1990). As Ruth Benedict documented decades earlier, the people of resource-poor areas of Oceania face a daily struggle for survival, and consequently, their religious beliefs legitimate an internal social hostility and worldview premised on cruelty that the gods not only permit, but require.

However, not all cannibalism results from cruelty. Another people in New Guinea, the Foré, also practiced cannibalism, but of their own dead, not the corpses of their enemies (Gajdusek 1981). When one of the Foré died, the women dismembered the body, stripped away its soft tissue, and removed the internal organs. Anthropologists and medical workers studied the Foré because a kuru epidemic was sweeping through their community (Daniel Carleton Gajdusek and Baruch S. Blumberg won the Nobel Prize for Medicine in 1976 for their work on kuru.). Also known as laughing sickness, kuru was discovered by Gajdusek and Blumberg to be an untreatable spongiform brain disease associated with cannibalism, caused by prions—proteins that replicate without DNA or RNA. It is similar to mad cow disease (now called Creutzfeldt-Jakob disease when it occurs in humans). Kuru disappeared entirely from the Foré in one generation when they stopped practicing cannibalism. This occurred only after they revised their religious beliefs so that an unstripped body is not believed to attract evil spirits and may in fact be cremated or buried with no spiritual ill effects.

Of course, cannibalism has been documented in the West as well, such as among the Donner party, a group of settlers bound for California whom heavy snows trapped in the Sierra Nevada Mountains in the winter of 1846–1847. As is well-known, they were forced to resort to eating their dead. Cannibalism as an act of survival occurred fairly often on sailing ships as well as European navies exploring the world from the 1500s to the early 1800s (Askenasy 1994). However, these are acts of momentary desperation, not the ritual and organized sacrifice of people to appease malevolent gods or to humiliate opponents. Ritual cannibalism typically occurs in societies that face social and military pressure from without, and live under conditions of limited resources and strict hierarchical social arrangements. The Aztecs in Mexico, for example, practiced ritual human sacrifice and cannibalism, and they were a violent warrior society under a strict combination of theocracy and warrior kings (Donnelly 2006). One never finds religious torture and cannibalism in peaceful and cooperative communities, but rather, in communities that have elevated violence, greed, cruelty, and exploitation to the highest degree (Benedict [1934] 1989; Donnelly 2006; Fromm [1973] 1994). In all cases that involve faith and worship in a religious (sacred) context, Sanday (1986) argues that cannibalism as a religious ceremony serves to transmit cultural identity across generations. As such, it transmits values and worldviews as well, and thereby perpetuates the social orientation of hostility and cruelty.

Despite such violent practices, none of these religions involves evil gods as such. Although the gods might be harsh, unforgiving, and demanding, they were not evil in the sense that they represented the antithesis or negation of human society. Rather, they reflected and thus legitimated the nature of the society that created them. Oppressive and desperate societies envision harsh gods.

What is the ideal-type concept of evil in such societies? Evil is anything that saps strength, whether of human, natural, or supernatural origin. Evil surrounds and also penetrates the social world, ready at any moment of weakness to strike a man down (often in the form of women, whom such societies regard as inferior). Only through harsh warrior discipline and open cruelty can a man resist evil. One must regard weakness in all forms suspiciously at all times, especially in the form of women, enemies, and even one's sickened or aging warrior comrades. In the desperate struggle for survival, only the strong prevail.

Vedism

Vedism originated somewhere in the Middle East or northern India, premised on the truths of existence as explained in the Vedas, the sacred texts. They have no named author, but like the later Upanishads, which are commentaries on the Vedas, they are perceived as timeless and universal truths about life and the afterlife. The Vedas were written sometime around 1500 BCE, but they almost certainly existed as oral traditions long before. Sanskrit is the language of the earliest known manuscripts. It is not known if the original creators of the Vedas in oral form and the religion based on them were Indo-European, like Hindi- and Bengali-speaking people today, or Asian.

Although the original religion is lost to history, the Vedas became the basis of both Hinduism and Buddhism, with great influence on Confucianism and Taoism.

The Upanishads (or more formally, the Upanishad Vedanta) form the textual basis of Hinduism, which, like the Vedas on which they are based, have no named author. The Upanishads were clearly composed after the Vedas, although a clear distinction may not have developed until 1656 CE, when Emperor Dara Shikoh ordered they be written in a clear and complete form. This official written form gives the Upanishad Vedanta its name, which would translate as "the conclusion of the Vedas" (Easwaran [1987] 2000). The earliest versions of the Upanishads also predate Siddhartha Gautama (623–543 BCE), known as the Buddha, which means "enlightened one." Although he was the founder of what we know today as Buddhism, the title of Buddha refers to anyone who has discovered true enlightenment. Siddhartha taught that anyone has the potential to discover enlightenment, which varies from one person to another, but which always involves a type of spiritual purity, uncluttered with the mundane concerns of the material world. Much of his teaching draws from his interpretation of the Upanishads.

The Upanishads and the Vedic texts upon which they are based do not provide answers or doctrine. Instead, they ask questions about the nature of existence, in order to direct the reader to find the right type of answer that leads to enlightenment. They direct the person to the worthwhile places to look, and the worthwhile things to concentrate on. The Upanishads are based on the basic question, Who knows . . . ? Collectively, they are a kind of poetic liturgy, a long testimonial to the many gods and their powers. They combine prayers to various pantheonic deities with magic incantations and instructions for living, especially in terms of rituals and spiritual purity. At the same time, they serve to inspire the individual to actively seek divine knowledge and improvement through self-discipline in both body and mind. This basic theme runs throughout the Eastern religions based on Vedism.

At the same time, the Upanishads form the basis of Hinduism, both in terms of beliefs and rituals. Vedism exhibits no particular concept of evil, and definitely no embodied evil. Typical of Eastern religions, there is one "evil" that leads to all others—ignorance (McEvilley 2002).

Hinduism

Much disagreement exists as to whether Hinduism is an inclusive monotheism (also called henotheism) or a polytheism. Without engaging centuries of theological discussion, let us consider the matter sociologically. From this vantage point, we see that in fact both views are accurate, that Hinduism is both an inclusive monotheism and a polytheistic religion. Like Christianity, Hinduism exists in various denominations, and some—most notably, Swaminarayanism—view the Hindu gods as separate, pantheonic deities. Other denominations, especially Smartism (also known as Brahmanism), hold that the one God, Brahman, is the origin of all things, and the other deities are manifestations of or differing names for the one God. Smartism dominates Hinduism in Western Europe and the United States, as well as the upper classes in India, mostly because it has become the religion of Hindu business executives (Albertson 2007) and intellectuals (Subramuniya 2001) and now teaches the concept of "one humanity, one god," which makes it more readily compatible with Western monotheism (Beyer 2006).

Class provides decisive insight into the monotheism/polytheism controversy. Monotheistic Smartism predominates in the West, where monotheistic Christianity sets the hegemonic standard, and Smartism allows Hindus to assimilate more readily without renouncing Hinduism. The three other major denominations—Vaishnavism, Shaivism, and Shaktism—each emphasize one ruling deity, Vishnu (Image 6.2), Shiva (Image 6.3), and Lakshmi (Image 6.4), respectively. Yet each also acknowledges that other, separate gods exist. In this view, the many gods exist as manifestations of existence; they are not arrayed hierarchically any more than, for example, trees are more important than or superior to rivers, or mountains matter more than the ocean. Of the three, Lakshmi is female, although Shiva may appear as female, male, both, or as androgynous.

Among the agrarian peasants, rural populations, and uneducated laborers in India, beliefs are clearly polytheistic, or at least devoted to one particular god among many gods (C. J. Fuller 1992). In this case, it appears that class corresponds to the

Image 6.2   Vishnu Riding Garuda, 9th Century CE

Image 6.3   Lord Shiva

Image 6.4   Lakshmi

degree of Westernization. Moreover, Hinduism has no formal or official central hierarchy or authority, and rather consists of numerous individual gurus, each of whom may or may not subscribe to an established school of thought, of which there are many. Over the centuries, Hinduism has developed into a great many and diverse perspectives, some of which are really more philosophical than religious, in the sense that they are not concerned mainly with the divine, but rather, with understanding the nature and meaning of existence, of which the divine is one particular aspect.

In such a diverse and complex religion, there is no central notion of evil, and none of the various subgroups speaks of a notion of pure evil. Often, Westerners mistake the goddess Kali—the Destroyer—as equivalent to Satan, but this comparison is not accurate. Kali (Image 6.5), is the consort of Shiva, lord of creation, and she can never act independently from him, just as Shiva cannot act independently of Kali. Life and death are inseparable. Although the image might look somewhat horrific to Westerners, the symbolism is not nearly so frightful. The garland of heads represents the letters of Sanskrit, the ancient language from which Hindi, Urdu, and others evolved. The garland of letters, depicted as a string of heads, represents awareness—the idea that thought as language originates in the head. The trident symbolizes justice, and many major Hindu deities carry it. The sword represents death, as does the severed head. Kali stands on the body of Shiva, who is not dead, but momentarily subdued, as all living things must eventually bow to death. Yet as Shiva rises again, so Kali must stand aside as life begins anew (Kinsley 2000). Life and death are part of the same cycle of existence. Kali is not Satan—the Great Destroyer—who represents the complete negation of existence. Rather, the symbolism is clear—Kali is the consort of Shiva; she brings death so that Shiva may bring new life.

Hinduism sees existence in terms of cycles, both within the natural world and in the spiritual realm. Hence, Hindus believe in reincarnation—the idea that a person is reborn depending on the quality of his or her previous life. Eventually, a person may attain *moksha*, a state of ultimate enlightenment or goodness, and thus dwell in heaven forever. Yet the Hindus do not have a corresponding opposite for moksha; there is no concept of eternal damnation where one resides forever with evil. Rather, Kali represents part of the cycle of life—the concept that all living things must die in order to sustain new living things, and all living things feed on death. Death, like life, is part of an eternal cycle of existence. For some, Kali represents the untamed forces of nature, or unbridled passion, and some contemporary Hindus embrace Kali as a force of feminism (Mokerjee 1988). Beyond the cycle of life and death, she is the force that keeps the cycle moving, including the changing of the seasons. Spiritually, she prevents stagnation by challenging people to always improve, to remain aware of their actions and the ramifications of them. She is the force of change, the movement toward death as a necessary precursor to life.

Lastly, what about the part human, part elephant Ganesha (Image 6.6)? Is this god some sort of monster—a human and demon hybrid?

Absolutely not. From a Western perspective, we may conclude sinister things about Ganesha, but this is not the case for Hindus. Many myths account for Ganesha's elephant head (Krishan 1999), but suffice it to say that, whatever the origin, the elephant in Indian culture symbolizes wisdom. Like many Hindu gods, Ganesha has more than two arms, and this simply testifies to his divinity. In

Image 6.5   Kali

Source: Balaji Viswanathan.

this depiction, Ganesha holds various items typical of Hindu deities. The trident, as mentioned, symbolizes justice. The large object resting on the ground is an incense burner, which symbolizes purity; incense is necessary to cleanse the air in many Eastern religions, including Orthodox Christianity. The axe represents the ability to remove obstacles, one of Ganesha's key aspects. The open hand with palm facing forward is a gesture of peace, as in "I come in peace with nothing to hide" (Pal 1995). Often shown with a rat or shrew-like animal at his feet, this shows the triumph of wisdom over pettiness. Overall, Ganesha is a sort of companion god who walks with a person through life (Courtwright 1985), removing obstacles but also placing them as necessary in order to help a person overcome pettiness, greed, and ignorance as necessary accomplishments on the path toward enlightenment (Krishan 1999; Ramanchandra Rao 1992). In more recent times, business people have modified Ganesha into a patron of commerce and the attainment of wealth, but this is a late twentieth-century invention (R. Brown 1991; Khokar and Saraswati 2005), and quite at odds with Ganesha's ancient traditions.

Image 6.6   Ganesha

China and Japan

One common element that all Far Eastern religions share is the emphasis on mind–body harmony. As the native religion of Japan, Shinto shares certain similarities with the Polynesian beliefs discussed earlier. Shinto likely arose as a collection or pantheon of deities, in a way very similar to the rise of polytheism in the West, as discussed in Chapter 2. That is, innumerable gods began as local tribal deities, with no particular affiliation with the tribal deities of other villages. As travel and commerce increased, local gods became regional gods, and some eventually became gods of monarchies and the state. It is not known what people first settled on the island of Japan, whether the Ainu—now a population that suffers status inequality in contemporary Japan—or the ancestors of the modern Japanese arrived first. In all likelihood, they arrived more or less simultaneously and settled in different areas of Japan (Morton, Olenik, and Lewis 2005), and conflict arose after their respective societies began to expand.

The earliest known accounts of Shinto, the Kojiki or Furukotofumi, or Record of Ancient Things, was presented to the emperor in 712 CE. It chronicles the mytho-religious origins of Japan and its people. According to the Kojiki, the gods Izanagi and Izanami—husband and wife, respectively (Image 6.7)—created the heavens, the earth, and the underworld. After that, they created all life, including humans. The elements of the Shinto creation story closely resemble that in Greco-Roman, Norse, and other traditions, which may suggest a common origin in central Asia in the mesolithic period (18,000–9000 BCE) (Kitagawa 1987). The second-oldest document, the Nihon shoki, also begins with ancient myths about the creation of humans, but continues to events that were present-day when it was completed in 720 CE. Among other things, it seems to accurately cover the history of several real emperors, and includes commentary on their virtues and flaws, and the successes and failures of their reign.

Among other things, these documents establish the fully polytheistic nature of Shinto, and specify that the *kami* (translated as gods, but also as spirits) are part of the cosmic cycle of birth, death, and rebirth, but unlike humans, they retain all the knowledge and experience of their past lives, and their full identity. Among the most important are the sun goddess *Amaterasu,* from whom the royal family of ancient Japan claimed lineage. Like other polytheistic religions, there is no purely evil deity

(Messadié 1996). Some deities are more favorable than others, and sometimes a community may earn the gratitude and protection of one or more deities, as well as the wrath of others, but like the ancient Greek gods, they behave more or less like immortal people, such that each god possesses a mixture of qualities. In some local versions of Shinto, people believe only in spirits rather than clearly articulated deities (Yamakage 2006), which makes the concept of pure evil even less sensible.

Given the foundational influence of Vedism, and the subsequent spread of Buddhism, it is difficult to determine uniquely Chinese religions. This becomes even more difficult, given that Chinese civilization has always had contact with many other cultures, some with advanced civilizations like China, and some violent and barbaric. Nevertheless, Taoism and Confucianism typify Eastern mystic religions, which, like Buddhism, a religion of India, are essentially atheistic (Coogan 2005).

The Yin–Yang symbol of Taoism (Image 6.8) is recognizable around the world and encountered in innumerable variations. The Tao means "the Way" in Chinese, and the philosopher Lao Tsu expanded many of the basic beliefs in writing around 600 BCE. His work, called *The Way,* is likely an interpretation of much earlier beliefs from Chinese prehistory, and is written as a lyrical poem.

Image 6.7   Izanagi and Izanami, the Divine Husband and Wife Who Created All of Existence in Shintoism

Eastern mystery religions differ from those of the West because there is no god to understand, and no god to reveal the mysteries of existence. Rather, the Eastern religions teach a method of discovery that a person may use to understand himself or herself and the world. The answers differ for each person, and hence the

Image 6.8   The Yin–Yang Symbol

enlightenment of one remains a mystery for others. Yet Taoism specifies certain beliefs that function as preconditions to enlightenment. Contrary to popular belief as Eastern religions enter the West, the teachings of Lao Tsu, the Buddha, and others are not the words of enlightenment, but only explain the necessary preconditions for beginning one's own journey.

Also contrary to Western assimilation of Buddhism and Taoism, enlightenment does not premise the centrality or importance of the individual, but rather, the utter insignificance of the individual (Bruce 2002). Westernized versions of Eastern religions emphasize individual and self-centered interests, motivations that Eastern religions traditionally considered completely contrary to enlightenment. Knowledge and then wisdom can be gained only through discipline, asceticism, and humility of the self, not through self-aggrandizement.

In Taoism, Lao Tsu rejected the animistic beliefs of primitive people, which suggest that the Chinese once held polytheistic beliefs closely connected to nature (Fowler and Fowler 2008). Some versions of Taoism today accept the existence of gods, ghosts, and other supernatural beings, but whether this remains from the original ancient Chinese beliefs or entered into Taoism more recently is unknown (Robinet and Brooks 1997). Like many Eastern religions, most of which have no central doctrine or creed, Taoism is readily syncretic and adaptive.

In place of animistic polytheism, Lao Tsu argues for the need to develop the intellect, because only through the intellect can a person truly understand. The mind alone can exert discipline over the body, and also discipline over thoughts and emotions. In the Tao, one applies the intellect to comprehend the complexity of existence, and especially, to understand the complex interaction and interconnectedness of all things (hence the Yin–Yang symbol). Moreover, existence is not just interactive and interconnected, but also occurs in definite ways. Only the intellect can understand these ways. In Taoism, then, misunderstanding and ignorance are the enemy, because they produce faulty behavior and disorder. Those people who perform evil actions are not in any way evil in essence, but they are instead ignorant. When people become educated and learn the discipline that only intellectual development can bring, then people begin to see their inherent relationship with other people and with nature. Taoism thus emphasizes balance and harmony. This harmony does not happen automatically, but only when people guide their actions with intelligence.

Confucianism began with the teachings of its founder Kung Fu Tsu (551–479 BCE). It shares many characteristics with Taoism, and some believe that Confucius may in fact have been a student of Lao Tsu (Ames 1999). However, Confucius wrote considerably more than Lao Tsu, and elaborates the way to enlightenment in great detail. Like Taoism and Buddhism, these details are mostly the means to begin one's own journey, the necessary preparation for success. As Kung Fu Tsu says, "I am only a guide; I have invented nothing" ([c. 500 BCE] 1998). Also like Lao Tsu, Kung Fu Tsu taught the methods to understand the vital life force, or ch'i. As it flows through the body, one can learn to direct and control it, so as to produce various desired outcomes. Medical practices such as acupuncture and other holistic methods use the concept of ch'i. One must learn to master ch'i both for physical health as well as intellectual excellence.

Kung Fu Tsu taught that the goal of life is self-improvement in a spiritual sense. As mentioned, in Eastern religions this takes the form of humility in the fact of the greatness and expansiveness of existence, not the expansion of individuality as Westerners increasingly value. Confucianism is no exception. Kung Fu Tsu's own life exemplifies the Eastern way.

Like many great religious leaders in many different traditions, Kung Fu Tsu was born into a life that seemed quite far from spirituality. Showing great promise, he became an imperial civil servant, that is, a bureaucrat. Dissatisfied with this way of life, he began a journey of discovery around China, and in the process, came to understand himself. This process of self-discovery occurred in stages—one cannot skip from basic worldly education up to the meaning of life. Enlightenment consists of many aspects, and one must pursue them all. A controversial figure, Kung Fu Tsu concluded that, as each person gains enlightenment and self-mastery, "the emperor will become as useless as a clod of earth" ([c. 500 BCE] 1998). This does not mean the rise of individual autonomy in place of the emperor's power, but rather that the affairs of this world are trivial, and the life of any one person—whether emperor, peasant, or anyone in between—is in itself insignificant.

Above all, one must remember that "goodness is acquired" and each of us, without well-developed intellectual ability and education, inherently wallows in ignorance and chaos, which is the natural condition of humanity. As in Taoism, there is no evil entity, only ignorance and chaos. This results from human failure, not from the machinations of a malevolent deity.

> **The Four Problems of the World**
>
> 1. Dukkha: All worldly life is unsatisfactory, disjointed, containing suffering.
>
> 2. Samudaya: There is a cause of suffering, which is attachment or desire (tanha) rooted in ignorance.
>
> 3. Nirodha: There is an end of suffering, which is Nirvana.
>
> 4. Maggo: There is a path that leads out of suffering, known as the Noble Eightfold Path.

Buddhism

Now a worldwide religion, Buddhism is based on the teachings of the Buddha (the Enlightened One)—Siddhartha Gautama (566–482 BCE). Born into a wealthy and royal family in the town of Kapilavastu, which is now in Nepal, Siddhartha's father groomed him to become the next king. One day, as a young man, he ventured outside the castle and observed the Four Sights. Having grown up in luxury and privilege, he now saw the reality beyond the castle walls—an old crippled man, a diseased man, a decaying corpse, and an ascetic—and it changed his life

---

Wisdom (The Noble Eightfold Path)

1. Right Understanding (or Right View, or Right Perspective): samma ditthi—the knowledge of sadness (or suffering) and how to stop it

2. Right Thought (or Right Intention, or Right Resolve): samma sankappa—resolved to commit no harm

3. Right Speech: samma vaca—abstinence from lying, discord, and abuse

4. Right Action: samma kammanta

5. Right Livelihood: samma ajiva—striving to stay on the path

6. Right Effort (or Right Endeavor): samma vayama—persistence toward good; attainment of skills and ability

7. Right Mindfulness: samma sati—refusal of greed and self-centeredness

8. Right Concentration: samma samadhi—abstinence from killing, stealing, and sexuality

---

forever. He abdicated his position as heir to the throne and began a spiritual journey. Eventually, he attained wisdom and insight that created a feeling of great joy and contentment; he reached enlightenment. Like the other Eastern religions, the Buddha offers means, not doctrine.

Presented as dialogues with students, much as Plato presents Socrates, the major beliefs begin with the problems in this world, of which there are four. As a solution, the Buddha offers an eightfold path.

As we saw also in Taoism and Confucianism, Buddhism seeks a harmony and balance. Siddhartha looked outside one day and saw suffering, and thereafter the images of suffering preoccupied his thoughts. Buddhism holds that suffering, the extent of evil in the world, results from ignorance and the inaction of people—the failure of people to do the right thing. There is no transcendent evil and certainly no evil being to corrupt the will of people and lead them astray. Rather, we are born ignorant and primitive, and must actively elevate ourselves and one another into the realm of civilization, and from there to spiritual enlightenment through right understanding and right action. Although the Buddha is famous for leaving civilization and meditating in the mountains as an ascetic monk, he also contends that a person must first know civilization in order to transcend it. He does not accept the idea of a noble primitive, and indeed rejects tribal animistic beliefs as superstition (Armstrong 2001).

Eastern mystical traditions, some of them lacking a notion of divine beings at all, inherently exclude the concept of transcendent and eternal evil. With no such concept, one need not become eternally vigilant for the rise of some supernatural evil, and instead can concentrate on observable suffering. The fault lies in ourselves, our ignorance and inaction, rather than with some omnipresent evil that tempts us from some other realm of existence.

Native Americans

There are hundreds of Native American cultures and civilizations—far too many to discuss here, and far too diverse to generalize about. White Europeans destroyed many of them, and their indigenous beliefs are lost. Therefore, let us focus on a particular people and the narrative of historical events that are known to us. These events reveal a dramatic change in their way of life, and a corresponding change in their religious beliefs. It is the story of the decline and fall of a great civilization.

Commonly known as the Anasazi, their descendants today—the Pueblo and Hopi Native Americans—prefer to call them "ancestral Puebloans" or "ancient Pueblos." The name Anasazi is actually a Navajo word that means "ancient enemy," although today many scholars and others prefer to say "ancient people." It should be mentioned that "Navajo" is a Spanish name for a people who call themselves the Diné. However, it was not the Navajo who introduced the concept of evil to the ancient Pueblos. They discovered this notion on their own. Famous for the cliff dwellings they constructed throughout the Four Corners region of the American Southwest, the ancient Pueblos were not initially cliff dwellers. In fact, the cliff-dwelling period represents the decline and ultimate fall of their civilization.

During the period 850 BCE to around 1250 CE, the ancient Pueblos, known during this period as the Chacoans, built a large and thriving civilization in what we now call Chaco Canyon, which is today a national park (Image 6.9). This group was part of a much larger population of Chaco people who inhabited much of Central and South America as well, known as the Gran Chaco (E. Miller 2001). Chaco Canyon was once a major city, with as many as 50,000–80,000 inhabitants in the greater Chaco area. The city itself consisted of many large pueblos, or buildings constructed of stones or adobe clay, with an interior and below-ground circular chamber. Many of the pueblos were multistoried, and the largest one—Pueblo Bonito—was a multipurpose building that included 700 units. Other buildings were purpose-built for government, commerce, and religious devotion (Fagan 1996, 2005). Chaco Canyon was the center of Chacoan civilization, with roads and marked trails that connected it with smaller cities and settlements. Many of the buildings rivaled ancient Greek and Egyptian structures in terms of size and sophistication.

Around 1140 CE, something happened. Recent evidence strongly suggests that drought struck the region suddenly and for several years (Akins et al. 2006). Local agriculture likely suffered immediately, given that few water sources exist in Chaco Canyon without rain. The large population likely consumed stores of corn, beans, and squash saved for just such an emergency, but the drought's persistence outlasted the stores. The drought thus forced the people to seek other places to live (Fagan 2005; Noble 2004), and numerous symbols survive today that indicate a great migration from Chaco Canyon (Rohn and Ferguson 2006). Likely traveling in extended families or tribes (also known as clans—people related by spiritual affiliation), each group migrated

Image 6.9   Its original name unknown, the great structure known as Pueblo Bonito is the largest in Chaco Canyon. Much like modern urban buildings today, Pueblo Bonito included housing, commerce, administrative, and religious functions. The scale becomes apparent with the doorways in the wall in the foreground, center.

Source: National Park Service, Russ Bodnar.

north and settled on mesas—the flat areas atop and surrounding canyons (Kantner 2004). From here, they could take advantage of any rain, and the flat mesa could be farmed. Also, caves under the mesas offered groundwater springs near the surface, as they still do today, and this attracted settlement as well.

However, as the drought persisted, lasting 10 years or more, some of the mesa communities began to fail. Unable to sustain themselves by peaceful farming and trade, as their civilization had done for centuries, the depleted communities began to prey on the others. This forced the others to move from the mesas into the cliff-side caves. The most famous and one of the best preserved is Mesa Verde, in what is now Colorado. Images 6.10a and 6.10b show Gila Cliffs, another major dwelling site, and one that is typical of ancient Puebloan cliff dwellings. It shows the remoteness and inaccessibility, and the favorable defensive position. With numerous caves, the residents would have ladders to gain access, which they would pull up during an attack.

The community likely farmed on top of the mesa, and then moved within the cliff for defend against marauders. Many of these sites still possess seep water that flows through the stone. As more and more communities failed and turned to marauding out of desperation, the cliff dwelling became increasingly defense oriented, with living space, watchtowers, and stone quarry sites in ever more precarious locations.

The marauding eventually became quite violent and bitter, with the marauders apparently eating their victims. Cannibalism was never part of Chaco culture, but in the extreme desperation brought about by drought and the collapse of civilization, a new and violent culture emerged, which eventually destroyed the last living remnants of Chacoan civilization. By the time the Navajo people arrived in the region in the late 1500s, the Chacoans were reduced to a few isolated settlements, while others had assimilated into various other Native American cultures.

The Chacoans had destroyed themselves. Their cave art depicts symbols of diaspora (such as lines with a marked endpoint) and violent struggles with raiders (Muench and Schaafsma 1995), and archaeological evidence clearly shows cannibalism (White 1992), which apparently occurred after violent struggles in which the cliff-dwelling inhabitants were killed. The killers apparently devoured their victims with great ritualistic zeal, and often left pits filled with flayed and cooked human bones (Debra Martin and Frayer 1998; Ortner 2002), known to archaeologists as charnel pits. The marauders also consumed whatever other grains and livestock they found, and then moved on. A debate continues among scholars as to whether cannibalism among cliff dwellers was of the survival type, or practiced as aggressive social exploitation (Kantner 2004). As Pringle (1996) and Sebastian (1996) separately argue, the struggle between the cliff dwellers and the marauders led to the demise of both, such that the once-great Chacoan civilization nearly passed into oblivion, and survived only in isolated folklore among some contemporary Native Americans. The violent confrontations and battles do not suggest cannibalism simply as a means of survival.

Although the Chacoans left no written records of their struggles other than the cave art, research shows that their lives became based on defense against a recurring enemy, an evil enemy who brought only death and destruction. Their entire way of life changed from a peaceful agricultural and commercial civilization, in grand

Image 6.10a   Gila Cliffs on Approach

Image 6.10b   Gila Cliffs From Within

buildings in wide-open areas, to one of closed and fearful cliffside enclaves, isolated and ever guarding against attack from marauding bands of their own people.

In response to the cataclysmic changes in their social structure and way of life, a notion of evil enters into Chacoan awareness. In their paintings, they depict the marauders as monsters, a type of image that does not appear in Chacoan art prior to the great diaspora, and indicates a radical shift in Chacoan culture (Sebastian 1996). As their life conditions collapsed, so their perception of the world shifted from comforting traditions and complex social organization and a world once filled with bountiful nurturing, to a world that now appeared to be filled with dangerous deprivation and daily struggles simply to survive. Still, we see no concept of transcendent evil, but rather, a notion of evil attached to very real and material marauders who engaged in ruthless and ultimately cannibalistic plunder of fellow Chacoans.

The Persians

Unlike the Chacoans, whose concept of evil arose from a great fall as their once settled and sophisticated civilization declined into anarchy and war, the ancient Persians developed a notion of evil through the daily difficulties of living nomadically in a desert environment. The Persians migrated into what is now Iran and the Tigris-Euphrates river valleys in Iraq sometime around 1500 BCE, as part of the larger Indo-European migration to the Middle East and then on to Europe. They were not the first people in the region by a long shot, with the earlier and far more advanced Sumerian civilization dating to around 5500 BCE, and the earliest known written language to 3500 BCE. The early Sumerians, known as the Ubaid, established cities at Eridu and 7 miles away at Ur, which originally stood at the mouth of the Tigris and Euphrates near present-day Basra, but which are now well inland. In what were possibly the first cities in the world, the massive ziggurat temples still survive. The temple at Eridu is dedicated to Enki, a water god, and the temple at Ur is dedicated to Nanna, also known as Inanna and Ishtar, goddess of the moon and generally equivalent to Eos, mentioned in Chapter 2. The Ubaid either evolved into or succumbed to the Uruk civilization around 3500 BCE, when Enmerkar established a new dynasty. It is during the Uruk period around 2000 BCE that the *Epic of Gilgamesh* appears, although the surviving written versions today come from Babylon, in the 600s BCE.

The Sumerians relied on advanced irrigation to maintain crop yields, both in terms of quality and diversity. Their primary staple, barley, was equally important for bread and for beer. They also cultivated lentils, chickpeas, dates, lettuce, leeks, onions, garlic, and mustard. The last three are not essentials, which indicates an advanced society that appreciates culinary sophistication. They also raised goats, cattle, and various types of fowl. Their engineering and hydrological skills produced a vast network of dykes, levees, and reservoirs, which rival contemporary irrigation in complexity.

The Persians were very different. Upon arrival, the Persians generally maintained their seminomadic way of life, centered primarily around goat herding, although they did cultivate the fertile river valleys during the growing season before moving the herds to higher ground in the winter when the rivers expand across vast flood plains. Given the environment, the Persian life centered around the stark contrasts of day and night, summer and winter. In the desert, in Iran and elsewhere, temperatures often soar during the day under the direct sun, which heats the ground quickly, and then cools dramatically at night, with temperatures over 100° F during the day and below freezing at night. Numerous predators—human and nonhuman—prowl the darkness. Sudden windstorms can strike anytime and drive sand and dust into great clouds that can quickly separate an individual from the group.

Unlike the Sumer, Elamite, Ubaid, and other people indigenous to the region, the ancient Persian religion reflects this day–night dichotomy. The day, as the source of light, becomes all good, and the night, with its various dangers, becomes all evil. Life takes place during the day, when productive activity is possible, and night becomes a time to secure within tents and buildings and await the sunrise. Like all ancient people, the Persians were polytheistic, but unlike the Greeks, for example, the gods of the light were good and friends of humankind, whereas the gods of the night were malevolent threats.

Initially, the Hebrews were also polytheistic (Dever 2003)—their god YHVH (Hebrew does not include vowels; this word is pronounced variously as Yahweh, Yehovah, and Jehovah) was the patron and tribal god of Abraham and his people, and only later became the one true God. He also had a wife, and there were many other female (and male) deities (Dever 2005). YHVH is likely a local variation of Yaw or Yahu, the god of thunder and storms (similar to Thor in Norse mythology) among many people of the Levant (C. Smith 2002), and God's (Yahweh's) behavior in the Old Testament would be consistent with this derivation. Babylonian texts from the same period as the Old Testament state that El, the sky god (similar to Zeus), assigns Yahweh to be the patron of the Israelites, who are the Elohim (children of El) (Albright 1990). This will be important, as we will see. The concepts of pure good (the One God) and pure evil (Satan) result from the syncretic mixture of Abrahamic monotheism and Persian dualism. To understand the latter, we must turn to Zarathustra.

Zarathustra

Zarathustra, also known as Zoroaster among the ancient Greeks, which also names the religion—Zoroastrianism—was most likely born around 1200 BCE (Boyce [1979] 2001), although dates range as far back as 10,000 BCE, and contemporary Zoroastrians believe it to be about 6500 BCE. As a historian, Boyce's estimation is likely correct, as we will see, in that it adheres to our sociological theory that religions reflect the social order and way of life of which they are a part. 1200 BCE places his life about 300 years after the Persians arrived in Mesopotamia, which would have placed them in contact with settled and much more advanced civilizations. Zarathustra likely came from a seminomadic Persian tribe in northeastern Iran who, in this remote area of deserts and mountains, would have had the least contact with the Sumerians and other advanced people, and thus maintained their nomadic traditions. His teachings reflect the values of desert nomads, especially the elements that he declares sacred (water and light) and those he declares evil (cold and darkness).

Zarathustra brought his message to the urban rulers of the region, and found the willing ear of a powerful king, Vishtaspa. We don't know who this man was, and he should not be confused with the later Vishtaspa, father of Darius I of Persia (549–486 BCE), who waged war against the Greeks. In Persian, Vishtaspa means "poet-leader" and could be a title rather than a name. In any case, Zoroastrianism spread quickly throughout the Persian world, which itself increased rapidly in power and sophistication, such that by the time of Darius I, the Greeks were quite familiar with the people, their culture, and their unusual religion. Once dominant in the Middle East, Zoroastrians live today in relatively small enclaves in India, with some congregations still in Iran.

Zoroastrianism holds that the one true God, Ahura Mazda, reigns supreme, and although there are other gods, they are always subordinate to Ormazd (another name for Ahura Mazda), and have no power separate from him. Furthermore, there is a being of pure evil, known as Ahriman, who exists only to destroy existence. He lives in an underground abyss, in which wicked souls are tortured forever. Ahura Mazda rules the heavens and is the source of everlasting life. In some traditions, the *ahura*— a general terms for gods—overthrew the *daevas,* the forces of nature, and established themselves as the new pantheon, in what for us is a familiar story. The daevas thus become evil entities, the primordial enemy of the ahura. Daeva is likely the origin of the word daemon as adopted by the Greeks, for whom it retained its traditional meaning as a force of nature, but the Christians later acquire the Zoroastrian meaning—likely from a movement inspired by the teachings of a Zoroastrian priest named Mani, whose variant we now known as Manichaeism. We return to Mani below.

In Zoroastrianism, the actions of humans become decisive. It is humans who will turn the battle one way or the other in favor of Ahura Mazda or Ahriman. While Zoroastrian scripture says that Ahura Mazda will eventually triumph, this will only happen after the great and final battle, with the forces of good arrayed against the forces of evil, each person on one side or the other, with no neutral ground and no way to avoid making the choice. Each individual must choose good or evil.

Light is the symbol of Ormazd, and darkness represents Ahriman. Zoroastrians wear white robes during worship and other sacred times, and view the night as a time when the daevas (in the evil sense) can run amok. A person of Ormazd should not venture out at night unless absolutely necessary. The sacred elements for Zoroastrians are fire and water. Their beliefs require that a priest maintain an eternal flame in a temple, and thus their sacred shrines are often called fire temples. The flame must be maintained with only pure, dry wood, of which sandalwood, an aromatic wood in the Middle East, is preferred. Under no circumstances can the fire be corrupted with impure wood or other material—it is an atrocity to burn refuse or cook food with the sacred fire.

Water is also sacred, and Zoroastrians regard the pollution of any flowing or still body of water as a mortal sin. In Images 6.11 and 6.12, we see an ancient and a contemporary fire temple. With these and all others, Zoroastrianism unites fire and water; the fire temples are always located next to a body of water (Stausberg 2004). Zoroastrians believe in three levels of flame, and this temple held one of the few third-level fires—the victorious fire. It consists of 16 different kinds of fire, gathered from 16 different sources, including lightning, a cremation pyre, a forge, and other sources. Each of these is then subject to a purification ritual before it joins the others. Thirty-two priests are required for the consecration ceremony, which can take up to a year to complete (Boyce 1975). In Image 6.11, we see the remains of an ancient fire temple on a lake formed by a large meteor crater.

In both the ancient and contemporary example, we see the fire temple built next to water, as all Zoroastrian temples maintain this symbolic physical dualism between fire and water as the two sacraments of the one true God, Ahura Mazda.

Sociologically, we can see the underlying logic of Zarathustra's teaching. Fire and water are essential for nomadic desert people. Both represent life, and fire in particular shields the people against the cold and dangers of the night. With scarce sources and often limited quantity, water is also held sacred—the corruption of a water source could threaten the survivability of the entire community and its flocks. Overall, the tenuous living conditions of the desert nomads encouraged the worship of the one strong and entirely good Ormazd, and the fear and loathing of his counterpart, the entirely evil Ahriman. Just as the boundaries of life and death of the community were clear and tenuous, so was the boundary between good and evil, dependent on careful human action, just as in life.

A Zoroastrian priest named Mani (which is a title of respect that, like "Vishtaspa," replaced his name) lived from 210 to 276 CE, and claimed that an angel visited him and provided him with a revelation. This revelation said that everything exists as either light or dark, and everything in existence is either of the light and good, or of the darkness and evil. No person or thing is neutral, and the divine follows the same dichotomy. Zoroastrianism had already invented angels (the Amesha Spenta—divine beings of good) and also devils (the Angra Mainyu—divine beings of evil). Mani carried the Zoroastrian dichotomy to its greatest extent and

Image 6.11   The Ancient Fire Temple of Adur Gushnasp, at Takht i Suleiman (the Throne of Solomon) Near Takab, Iran

Image 6.12 Contemporary Fire Temple in Yazd, Iran

produced a completely dualistic concept of existence. The religion, called Manichaeism after its founder, holds that good and evil are perfectly equal and opposite. The challenge for people is to overcome their own inherent good/evil dualism—the soul is good; the body is evil. Manichaeism spread rapidly throughout the Persian and Roman world. Although Christianity was a rival religion, many notable Christians—including Paul of Tarsus and St. Augustine, who was in fact originally a Manichaean—clearly held to dualistic beliefs, which they emphasized in Christianity. The Zoroastrian imagery of light and dark, and the deistic concept of one good God and an evil counterpart, in combination with eternal dualistic separation of good and evil, created the Christian notion of the devil. Thus, evil had finally become embodied in a pure form (Messadié 1996).

Introduced early in Christianity, the dualistic notion still shapes much of Christian belief today. It found ready acceptance in the turmoil of the late Roman Empire, and even more so in the tumult of the early Renaissance. Still, Satan's power varies greatly during the Christian period. In the 1700s, the Age of Enlightenment, Satan reached the nadir of his power and became a small old man. In popular awareness, he acquired nicknames like "Old Nick," "Little Nick," and "the Dickens," names for a wizened, crotchety old man who is sometimes interesting, sometimes annoying, but always harmless (Muchembled 2003). Pure evil tends to become more prominent as social conditions become uncertain and people feel afraid, and it then dissipates as conditions stabilize. In its worst form— such as the Inquisition and the witch-hunting craze, or in modern times, the

Holocaust and contemporary terrorism—dualism produces the worst kind of oppression and violence. If one believes that pure evil has become manifest, even if that manifestation is human, one must destroy such evil utterly, using whatever means are necessary.

Discussion

Let's have sociologist Mark Worrell begin the discussion, and then we will elaborate with more of his work and that of others.

Gods and Devils

By Mark P. Worrell

Society is a compression chamber. From our earliest moments as infants to our last day on earth, we are under constant pressure from other people and institutions. Social life is, in short, a vast system of interlocking forces. Some forces are small and comprehensible—e.g., the pressure friends place on us to use drugs or have sex when we might not want to. We know these simple forces as peer pressure. Other forces are larger and more complex. As people become integrated into society, they face the pressures of bills, jobs, racism, sexism, terrorism, wars, illness, and so on. Still, most people, in most cases, can grasp that these forces are financial, political, biological, etc. Everyday, mundane powers are not enough to inspire in people the belief in something like a god, the Almighty Power. The belief in Almighty Power needs an education in Almighty Power. This educational process is the special role of collective religious conduct.

Periodically, people are expected to convene to perform rituals, ceremonies, and participate in celebrations of various kinds. Getting married, graduation, initiations, sporting events, concerts, rallies of this, that, and the other kind are all group events where people congregate and get excited. There are other rare cases like massive antiwar riots and revolutions where people get really excited to the point where they may kill others or die for a cause. All these events are unique in their ability to produce what sociologists call "collective effervescence," a phrase from Durkheim. Collective effervescence is the shared excitement and electric-like energy produced at mass events. The most intense gatherings can affect people such that they feel as if a tidal wave of power breaks over them. They can be literally "raised up" by this tremendous power and transformed form their normal, everyday selves into "super-humans"—capable of withstanding pain they would normally not be able to endure; running faster, jumping higher, or throwing farther than normal; and acting in the most outlandish manner in public in ways they would never dream of doing in "everyday" reality.

Experiencing collective effervescence as a member of a group awakens in us the feeling of external forces. And these forces are real. They are not natural forces like, say, gravity or electricity; rather, they are social or moral forces—different but still very real or, as we would say, "objective." To have a lasting effect, collective moral energies must not be allowed to drain away after a gathering has come to an end. In other words, social energies must assume some kind of crystallized, external, social form—special words and

(Continued)

(Continued)

phrases, bodily gestures, images, symbols, and holy places. These forms are what sociologists call "collective representations" insofar as they literally represent the group, embody shared meanings, and evoke strong emotions in us.

One way to think about collective representations is to view them as "mirrors" or reflectors of energies. If you, a mere individual, look at yourself in a full-length mirror, you see a reflection of "just you"—the image is basically of some person with average capacities. Now, imagine instead of just one person seeing [his or her] reflection in a mirror, a whole group or even an entire society seeing a reflection of itself in a mirror. Now this is obviously impossible, a whole society or moral community cannot stand in front of a mirror, and this is where a god or some other sacred representation or symbol is necessary. Gods are simply the symbolic reflection of a group—a kind of composite, perfected reflection: When you look in the mirror, you see a reflection of yourself. When a society "looks in a mirror," it sees a god.

The symbol, whatever it may look like (and it can look like almost anything), is the moral energy and power of the group in an objective form. Literally, collective representations represent a group: the object of devotion, say, the image of Christ, is merely the group in its transfigured, social form. From this, it is easy to see, now, that the symbol represents not only the god but the group as well; the god and the group are *identical*. Sacred objects and symbols are the outward, visible form of the group's own feeling and self-consciousness.

If the sacred object or symbol takes the form of a god, then

God = group

If a god is the visible and outward form of a group, then the sum total of all groups who worship the same god form a moral community or society:

God = society

In monotheism, God represents the most valued attributes and characteristics of a group, condensed into one image; the one God possesses (at least) the combined strength of the entire group, and embodies (at least) the combined capacities of the entire group. Modern gods are free from the petty weaknesses, frailties, and imperfections of the people who create their god. But since society is a mixture of not only the good but also the bad, both aspects are necessarily represented. Anywhere you find the one God, a devil can't be far behind.

Just as a god represents the condensed virtues of a group, all the imperfections, evil, corruption, deformities, greed, hatred, etc., are embodied in a devil—a negative god. We can see here that both gods and devils are sacred:

God = the "sacred pure," or Good

Devil = "the sacred impure," or Evil

The Devil is merely God's (society's) alter ego or other self. If God has divine minions such as angels, then the Evil One will have opposite minions as well. Collectively, devils represent those aspects of life that we would like to suppress and, as such, religious practices are crucial to social control and the maintenance of order.

Devils were an important historical development because not only do they give folks an explanation for why bad things happen, but we can also blame our misfortunes on devilish others and punish them by killing them either individually or exterminating the whole lot of them at once. As is often the case in history, "devilish others" have been known to possess things that we would like to have for ourselves such as land, oil, diamonds, minerals, and other valuable resources. Often, the coveted resources are entirely social, such as money, power, and prestige. If self-described "good people" can deprive "evil people" of their resources, the possibility for mass violence and large-scale death is heightened. But people are not inherently "good" or "evil"—these moral statuses are socially constructed.

Rituals are very useful in transforming people into devil helpers. That's right, "the forces of Evil" don't exist independently but have to be constructed through collective processes and manipulation of one form or another. As sociologists have learned, others are not objects of negative worship because they are hated; they are hated *because* they are objects of negative worship. While gods tend to be relatively stable objects, they do change over time, may disappear from history altogether, or be transformed into devils. Added to this, every god has what appear to be multiple personalities.

The more complex a society, the more complex the god(s): for example, all Christians worship what appears to be the same God. But upon closer inspection, we find that each flavor of Christianity worships a very different deity: some Christians are devoted to a New Testament, laid-back buddy that easily forgives when you sin. Other brands of Christianity worship an Old Testament authoritarian tyrant who dishes out rough justice at the slightest infraction. If a god is easy-going, it is because the group who worships it is also easy-going; likewise, if a god is a monster, it is because the group that worships it is monstrous.

Religious indoctrination provides people with a set of concepts for thinking about their lives and the course of society. Religion is rooted in reality, but religion offers a distorted and distorting perspective on the world. In short, religion is ideological: an upside-down form of thinking whereby people construct, from their own energies, the objects and institutions of their own domination. It would seem obvious, then, if all this were true, that people could be educated to think non-ideologically. If god is just society in a symbolic, transfigured shape, then wouldn't it be easy to see gods for what they are and "get over it"? Perhaps you've heard somebody claim that belief in gods is as infantile as believing in the Tooth Fairy. It's not that simple, though.

The Tooth Fairy, the Easter Bunny, and Santa Claus are transfigured symbols of Mom and Dad—they're like little, family-level magical beings or gods. As children, we are convinced of their existence. And they do exist insofar as your family (a micro society) exists. Of course, once you reach a certain age, you realize that the Tooth Fairy is really just a family member who secretly exchanges your teeth for dimes (Fairies seldom consider inflation). When you were a believer in the Tooth Fairy, you experienced her effects (teeth were magically replaced with money), but you did not see the causes (because it happened at night, when you were asleep). The same sort of thing goes on with big gods. We feel the effects of social structures and processes but do not see the causes (because you're metaphorically asleep, i.e., unenlightened).

By a certain age, believing in the Tooth Fairy is impossible unless you want to be labeled an imbecile. But regardless of your age, you are still expected to have faith in some kind of Almighty God. Why? It is difficult to get behind the symbol and grasp the social origins of any given deity. To "get behind" a god would mean to have a firm grasp on the way society and history function.

Not comprehending how or why things happen the way they do, we are left with few alternatives to thinking in terms of gods and devils. And most educational programs don't put a dent in this magical way of thinking. All the natural science training in the world does *not* convert people into "atheists" as theologians and moralists often fear. One would expect science to strip away superstition. But consider

(Continued)

(Continued)

this: gods and devils are not natural facts. Therefore, learning all the natural science we care to will not help solve the mysterious and social origins of gods.

Gods and related beings are *social* realities and, since few people are social scientists, and since a lot of social scientists aren't even that good at their jobs, the overwhelming majority of people persist in experiencing and explaining abstract and impersonal social processes and forces in a "primitive" or pre-modern, traditional fashion. Funny, [but] despite being so "modern," we have, as one famous sociologist put it, "the mindset of primitives."

Well, if all this is true, then where will I go when I die? Is there an afterlife? The sociology of religion is not exactly the atheistic perspective you might imagine. As we have seen, gods are real: real to the extent that society is real. And the afterlife is a reality as well—it's not a physical place but a moral and symbolic place.

When you die, you're not just tossed in the ground and forgotten about. No. Quite literally, you live on in your creative products and in the lives of other people: children, stories, photographs, books, music, values, and so on. The whole purpose of the funeral rite, for example, is to convert dead bodies into purified signifiers that "go to Heaven" (or Hell, the negative Heaven)—society's sacred symbolic and cultural matrix. What happens at a funeral is that the dead and impure person is converted into a living, purified, public object worthy of memory and respect. It is true that most of us, given enough time, will fade from collective memory and even our monuments *(reminders)* will crumble into dust. Others, though, will live on, seemingly, for all eternity; could Elvis, for example, ever *really* die? I think not. Hail to the King!

Evil (and good) can thus be understood sociologically, without resorting to metaphysics or the supernatural. It is quite real, and quite empirical. We have seen empirical examples in this chapter, from different times and places, of how beliefs about good and evil arise from reality. As Worrell argues elsewhere, evil, as well as good are the union of socially dominant forces—the forces that determine class especially, but other forms of rank, privilege, prosperity, and threat as well. Worrell argues that the classic sociological texts on religion, taken together, offer a coherent conceptual framework to understand the concept of evil. With Marx, Weber, and Durkheim, the confluence occurs with the concepts of value, charisma, and mana, respectively (Worrell 2005:12). Each of these items represents something both concrete and perceived. This latter aspect in particular depends, as always, on the subjective reaction of people within a social context. Perception in this sense is at once a personal and psychological reaction, but also a collective and social reaction.

Value seems at first thought to be something different from charisma and mana, which are typically associated with magic and intangible aspects of life, as we have seen with charisma in a previous chapter. Likewise, we also examined the status of the enemy in the chapter on violence and intolerance. In the context of religious violence and terrorism, the enemy becomes something more than a concrete foe, but acquires supernatural negativity which, in religious terms, usually becomes the embodiment of evil—a supernatural and eternal foe. From this perspective, the concept of value seems especially inappropriate, because normally we associate value as something positive, desirable, and used specifically in an economic sense. Economically, value refers to either use-value—the degree of utility—or exchange-value, also known as market value. Either way, value constitutes something positive and embodies the ability of a society to construct its livelihood and increase the standard of living.

Commodities and services of value mean that a society can build objects or organize services beyond naturally occurring value. For example, consider how much value human thought and labor adds to materials such as iron, aluminum, glass, and plastic when they take the shape of a car. The end product is worth far more than the sum-total of its constituent materials, as well as the labor required to produce the final product. Although iron, glass, and so on have value separately from each other, the form they take in the car increases their value as constituents of a finished product in which we have invested substantially more labor time to shape the various parts and assemble them. A car window, for example, holds more value than a random piece of glass of the same size. As we invest more labor time in the object, it holds more value. A person can find iron ore in a hillside (or as I did once, in an iron meteorite), but it requires substantial investments of time and energy to forge it into a car body.

How, then, does value resemble the perceived properties of charisma and mana? As we saw in an earlier chapter, Weber quite clearly juxtaposes charisma as an emotional force, and rational organization as a material force. Both seek change, but in fundamentally different ways—charisma changes how we perceive material conditions, whereas rationalism changes the material conditions directly. Here stands Worrell's great insight. First, we must separate value from price. The latter is simply, as nearly everyone knows, whatever the market will bear. Whatever people are willing to pay for something is how much it costs, relative to its availability. Collectively, in economic terms, we call this supply and demand.

Yet for Worrell, drawing from Marx, this is entirely superficial; it is only the final stage of a much more complex and social process. Price often becomes free-floating from value, because price is relevant only when commodities are exchanged. Value goes far deeper, and this is where emotional and symbolic elements become relevant. Worrell argues that we are greatly mistaken to assume that the death of gods or a collectively shared divine religion means that the supernatural has left society. Today, instead of God, we worship the all-powerful market and the commodities it displays for consumption. As Worrell (2005) asks, "does not the labor product bearing a price tag, a commodity, enjoy the same protective moral force of any other sacred object?" (p. 18). The underlying logic of sacredness and worship are the same, whether the object of devotion is a transcendent and disembodied god or a worldly commodity; the social orientation to the object is the same.

As Worrell (2005) argues, "Gods and demons come and go, but society is never without its gods and demons because it never lacks the ability in one way or another to externalize, fetishize, and organize people around the enjoyment of their own collective energies" (p. 18).

Thus, the creation of value, which always requires human labor, is a process that transfers human ingenuity and labor into a material object, and that object often signifies far more than simple utility or price-value. Cars, whether powerful and impressive or feeble and nondescript, symbolize many things beyond their usefulness as transportation. Some cars, for example, project an ostentatious display of wealth, while others signify a more European attitude, and still others suggest the driver is just another mindless sheep following the herd. We buy cars not only for the solemn and serious aspects of mileage, reliability, and price, but just as much for the way they look, and the way we think they make us look.

Many things have such multiple levels of value beyond market price. Cars also illustrate Worrell's further insight, that the special or perceived qualities in a car transcend the ability of most people to understand the power of the object. Few people understand how cars work, and they know equally little about how they are made. Perception and belief replace rational knowledge of production and mechanical function. Thus, we celebrate value as a mysterious property, more akin to charisma and mana than to the rational forces that produced the car in the first place. Designers and engineers use math and science, not arcane ritual and mysticism, to produce functioning automobiles. Marketing experts use quantitative and qualitative methods to gather and analyze data, and companies hire creative artists to portray their vehicles with style and existential significance, all designed to develop an emotional connection between the buyer and the product. The car is not just a car; it's also an attitude, a lifestyle, and an object of veneration.

The car, or whatever the commodity of desire, becomes a transcendent object that therefore deserves sanctity and worship no less than any other god. And the key to access any desired commodity is money. As Worrell (2005) concludes, "the point is not that money has pushed out the moral or the sacred, but rather, purely economic and mundane activities take on a sacred, ritualized hue" (p. 20).

Money is not only a sacred object in this case, but a universal exchange equivalent; it becomes the means to acquire anything and everything else, and thus becomes the object of universal desire. Our desire and devotion deify money, and just like religion in earlier times, they make money the universal bond between people. Value appears to be an independent force, which, like any other omnipotent god, manifests in various forms, yet maintains the underlying and inherent divinity. Whether as money, cars, clothes, popularity, or any other form, value remains value, mystical and existing in and of itself. Cars and other commodities are the magical and glittering manifestations of value, just as charisma and mana exist as independent powers, which may manifest in any given person or thing. Value, charisma, and mana thus describe the same social relationship between the individual and society—that the social world still appears magical and glittering in its power. Whether in the form of money, or the God of Abraham, Jesus, and Muhammad, the divine still exists and still impresses and inspires the believer. If people were willing to give their life for God, are they no less willing to do anything today in the name of money?

Like charisma and mana, value in its magical form refers both to good magic and evil magic, the eternal good and the eternal evil. Just as God and Satan eternally oppose each other, so money may be both good and evil, depending on whom and what it serves. Remember, value in this sense is a universal truth, and value as the essence of eternity may be both essentially good and essentially evil, depending on its particular manifestation. God and Satan are, in essence, eternal supernatural beings. This leads sociologist James Aho (1994) to imagine a "thing of darkness," the idea that evil, like good, transcends ordinary understanding. It is not just opposition on particular issues or courses of action. For example, some people believe their computer is evil and "out to get them." The computer may cause great frustration and anger, but sociologically speaking, evil is an entirely different negative force, and of a different magnitude. It is qualitatively and quantitatively different.

Evil and the various enemies people believe it produces are not the result of stupidity or insanity. In the *Malleus Maleficarum,* for example, which we saw excerpts from in Chapter 2, a random selection of any part of it demonstrates how intellectually sophisticated Kramer and Sprenger were. They cite scripture and ancient philosophy, and discuss the synthesis with great detail and vigor. They are not stupid, and they possess an impressive education. However "crazy" some notions of evil may appear—whether Kramer and Sprenger's witches, Hitler's Jews, McCarthy and Hoover's communists, or Falwell's pagans, abortionists, feminists, and others—these notions are not delusions, any more than sincere devotion to religion is a delusion. As we have seen, religious devotion is devotion to an idealized social order and a celebration of human potential and achievement, sociologically speaking. If so, then evil is the inversion of the good, an inversion of the idealized society and its hopes and achievements.

The evil that Jews, communists, and so on present is not their overt qualities, real or imagined. In other words, it is not the observable characteristics or stereotypes applied to groups. The construction of evil does not come from the observation of reality, but from belief about the essence and presumed existence of evil in the first place. Evil is always some sort of impurity, perversion, and corruption of good and right. It is the opposite of morality and order, and exists as an opposite of good, whether big or small. Most important, evil cannot be redeemed, only controlled or exterminated. The same applies to any people who bear the essence of evil.

For this reason, evil becomes an issue when some group of people perceives it to exist in others and acts accordingly. Whatever people believe constitutes evil depends on the social context as we have seen. Sometimes the notion of evil is small. When applied to people, the outcome is always similar—persecution and extermination. Therefore, Ervin Staub (1989) concludes that evil cannot be separated (at least in the social sciences) from its manifestations. Just as positive value, charisma, and mana cannot be separated from their manifestations as commodities or great leaders, so negative value, charisma, and mana cannot be separated from the enemy, and those who embody evil are inherently enemies; their mere existence is the inherent negation of good. Staub argues that we cannot define evil by the intentions of the perpetrators, because they always believe that they are perpetrating good, and that their actions, even if they involve killing, derive from the desire to do good. In the case of the ancient Puebloans, the marauders attacked the cliff dwellers in a desperate attempt to survive; likewise, religious terrorists believe they are serving God's will, or at least the survival of their people. The Cathars saw the Catholic establishment as evil, and the Catholic Church saw the Cathars as an evil heresy. The people and the cause become one and the same thing.

Worrell's sociological theory argues that the confluence of social forces of production and exchange with culture creates relations of power. Those who have it are good, as are the people who identify with established power (whether they benefit much or not), and those who are outsiders become the Other that threatens the established social relations and thus constitute evil. The evil ones are pretenders—weaker and polluted but aggressive imposters who will wreck the establishment and reduce it to a grotesque perversion of its once-divine perfection. To fully function as an evil enemy, the carrier groups must look like the righteous person, but have some superficially minor but transcendentally major distinguishing characteristic. This one apparently minor difference betrays their existentially essential difference. Sometimes we know what the perpetrators of persecution think about their victims, and vice versa. In the case of the ancient Puebloans, did the cliff dwellers see their adversaries as monsters, or as victims of misfortune? Did the marauders detest the cliff dwellers as weak? Did they respect them in some way? Did they see them simply as a means of survival?

Historically, Jews have borne this role in European society. Long since assimilated into Europe, Jews physically resemble their fellow non-Jewish citizens. Only their religion differs. The fact that anti-Semitism emerged most virulently in Germany illustrates the sociological concepts at work, that the more closely the supposed out-group resembles the in-group, the greater their evil status becomes. In Eastern Europe, Jews lived a forcibly separate existence from non-Jews and occupied distinctive urban ghettos, such as in Warsaw, and their own rural villages. In Germany, Jews and non-Jews alike were becoming increasingly secular, and few traditional differences remained. Attempts in Germany to distinguish Jews physiologically failed, before and during the Nazi period (Langmuir 1990a). Instead, the Nazis and their predecessors, going back centuries, attributed various evil but hidden characteristics and practices to the Jews. That it was "a camouflaged conspiracy was very old. It had appeared with the first chimerical fantasy about Jewish ritual murder in 1150" (Langmuir 1990a:341) and persisted until the late nineteenth century.

Europe had long marginalized Jews as contrary to Christianity, but this marginalization was only anti-Jewish, not anti-Semitic. The first term refers to basic bigotry and prejudice, the belief that Jews are different and adhere to false beliefs that fail to accept Christ as the savior, and on that basis they should be shunned. Not until the twentieth century did anti-Judaism become anti-Semitism, the belief that the Jews are part of a race of evil subhumans. Their evil transgresses a misguided religion, and their essential difference reveals their inherent evil. Yet by the twentieth century, Jews in Germany had long since assimilated into European society, and they physically and culturally resembled non-Jews. This presented Hitler and other virulent anti-Semites with the greatest problem, in that real Jews disproved their belief that Jews represented a grave and omnipresent threat to Germany (Langmuir 1990a:345). Real Jews just did not fit the evil chimera monstrosity, the concept of which was introduced in Chapter 1. The chimera—a goat, a snake, and a lion, all in one animal—can only exist as an imaginary, mythical being. Each animal is real separately, but not in combination with the others.

But why this monstrosity? Why something that requires faith in such an imaginative vision? Worrell (2005) answers that the complexity of social confluences—economics, culture, and personal experience—requires a careful and rational analysis to understand. Chimerical beliefs in the popular imagination simplify this confluence in mystical terms, that rather than delineate the various factors that configure life in modern times (or any time), chimerical beliefs reduce this to the mystical enemy, the evil Other that stands at the center of decay and from whom all suffering flows. This enemy is more than a scapegoat, which receives blame for real problems; rather, it is the imaginary source of imaginary wrongs—the very existence of the evil group undoes the fabric of moral order. The fact that they live denies us our livelihood. The exact mechanisms by which this happens do not matter, only the belief that they make us suffer. Without knowledge of the exact mechanisms, the intersection of social forces and institutions that create social problems and personal dissatisfaction, the chimerical view allows people to project their worst fears onto others. It also allows them to imagine whatever feels comforting, because they need never compare their sentiments to reality, nor wrestle with the complexities of social, economic, political, and cultural conflict.

In conclusion, we may say sociologically that the chimerical evil enemy corresponds to the greatest fears of the society that imagines it, and the fantasy enemy "is like any other god or demon: it is a form of consciousness and logic of representation, peculiar to some segment of society, devoted to explaining authority, wealth, and the working of transcendental forces" (Worrell 2005:33), the unity of which would remain otherwise unfathomable. People may not understand politics, economics, cultural differences, or psychological ambivalence, but they feel like they understand "evil." Thus, evil brings together in a neat little package all the fears a person and community hold, and seemingly exalts otherwise unknowable forces, without clarifying any of the parts that constitute the neat little package. As Arlie Hochschild (2005) argues, this not only obscures the true relationship of social forces to each other and their impact on the individual, it also renders the individual powerless through a kind of willful ignorance, because it requires the individual to accept the chimerical reality in place of observable reality. Once disempowered, the individual becomes susceptible to whatever his or her favorite authority figure decides to instill. In her analysis of the American working class and its support for the policies of George W. Bush, Hochschild sees a contradiction—the people who suffer the most support Bush most ardently. Bush does not provide them with a better life, but he does provide a target for their frustration—Muslims, the French, intellectuals, liberals, immigrants, and others—which corresponds to a chimerical worldview. In simplest terms, Bush explains their problems as the result of too many of the wrong kind of people in the world.

In the history of the West, Jews have been the most consistently demonized people, but today in the United States, various others have joined them. In a detailed historical study, Robert Fuller (1995) traces the American obsession, as he sees it, with "naming the anti-Christ," a pastime that has become primetime. Fuller argues that demonization of any particular group occurs when the group making the accusation rejects inclusiveness and strives for exclusiveness. The reasons for this goal may vary, but as we have seen in historical examples, demonization usually occurs when people feel overwhelmed by forces they do not understand, and they feel their life is veering out of control. Again, the practice surpasses simple scapegoating and constitutes a distinctly chimerical image—an image of an evil other that can only exist in the imagination and cannot exist in reality. Based on his historical analysis, Fuller concludes that it is sufficiently clear that apocalyptic name-calling has served decidedly nativistic and tribalistic functions. The "labeling of witches, Catholics, Jews, Masons, Deists, modernists, socialists, feminists . . . functioned not to promote more inclusive wholes but to strengthen separatism and tribalism" (p. 195). As you may recall from Chapter 1, the tribe constitutes an entirely homogeneous group of one language, one lifestyle, one race, and one religion. There can be no deviation, no divergence. Differences must be prevented or, if they already exist, eradicated.

As we saw in the beginning of this chapter, Jerry Falwell and Pat Robertson name many of the "demons" that Robert Fuller (1995) documents in the history of the United States, plus a couple of new ones. On the surface, it appears that Falwell and Robertson share a concern for the United States, but Fuller finds that history consistently shows that the naming of demons corresponds to calls for exclusive, homogeneous groups—a concern only for people exactly like oneself—not a pluralistic and collective solidarity or society in general. History shows that an obsession with identifying evil and naming the Antichrist develops among people who are on the way out, whose lifestyle and place in society have already suffered a long period of decline, and which the future now threatens to eclipse entirely. Naming the Antichrist, the evil Other, is not the call of hope, but the cry of desperation as the end approaches and a different world supersedes fading traditions.

CHAPTER 7

Cults

Introduction

As mentioned in Chapter 2, "cult" has two meanings in the sociology of religion. When applied to the ancient world, it describes an exclusive group of devotees, committed to a particular god or particular temple. Especially in the later Greco-Roman world, membership in these temples often involved rites of passage, which were sometimes quite demanding physically and mentally. The rites also involved secret knowledge about the deity and other things as well, so that in general these exclusive groups became a cult in the sense that membership required a high order of personal devotion and absolute commitment to keeping the rites and the mysteries of the group secret. In short, ancient cults were exclusive and secret groups dedicated to a particular deity.

In modern times, the specific time and place determines the cult status of a particular group. As the mainstream changes, so the status of a group may move from the margins to something closer to the mainstream, as we will see. Conflict with the mainstream need not take an open and combative form; more often, it involves the values or lifestyle of the cult compared to the larger society.

Yet lifestyle and collective identity do not define cults. Local friendship networks centered on "goth," for example, or on heavy metal music and culture, or sports teams, or the math club, are not cults. They

---

Cults Today . . .

Are separated from the society around them.

Are in conflict with the society around them.

Preach an apocalyptic doctrine.

Require absolute devotion from their followers.

Are premised on the mind of the leader.

Live the leader's unique reality.

Often, popular usage applies the term "cult" to any group that some people don't like, especially if the group is involved with some sort of death or destruction. Al Qaeda does not constitute a cult because they are very much engaged in the issues of the world, and although we may condemn their goals and tactics, they are not living their own reality.

have no absolute leadership or organization, and they are not out of touch with reality. They are just peer groups—a collection of friends who share similar views, emotions, interests, and place in life.

In academia, no consistent definition or practical usage of the term cult prevails. Some reject the term entirely, and Catherine Wessinger (2000) raises a valid point in this regard, that in popular usage, "the word *cult* dehumanizes the religion's members and their children. It strongly implies that these people are deviants; they are seen as crazy, brainwashed, duped by their leader." Wessinger is correct, that most people use the term in this manner, and as we will see, most people are therefore mistaken about cults. We are not interested in the popular notion of cult, but in a sociological conceptualization. If we reject the word cult, then we simply choose another word. What matters is the conceptualization attached to the word.

For our purposes, we will distinguish a cult as different from other alternative religious movements (ARMs), which often share some of the specified characteristics (sidebar), as well as public derision and scorn. Specifically, a cult also requires devotion to the pronouncements and worship of one leader, for purposes of serving the leader's personal interests (whether the leader or the followers consciously recognize this or not). It also requires that the leader's vision constitutes a substitute reality that does not just interpret the world, but actively replaces it. Although alternative religious movements may form around a particular leader, ARMs do not serve the leader over and against the members and do not reject the real world in favor of an imagined reality. Indeed, they adapt themselves in direct relation to the dominant culture, as discussed in Chapter 4. We are also not interested here in the popular derision and scorn that ARMs and cults often receive. The topic of religious intolerance was covered in Chapter 5. Our interest here is not why outsiders (society) dislike cults, but why some people enthusiastically embrace them.

Stated sociologically, an ARM integrates the individual into the group collective, yet allows the individual to retain his or her own sense of self and to maintain a degree of independent thought, as well as some degree of integration with the larger society (Daschke and Ashcraft 2005; Melton and Partridge 2004). The group also maintains some contact with the mainstream. However, many scholars do not conceptually distinguish new religious movements (NRM), some of which are quite old, from alternative religious movements, which makes analysis difficult because it subsumes new, old, schismatic sects, and cultic groups under one vague category. As specified in Chapter 4, we will favor ARM over NRM, a conceptual necessity that Stein (2003) also stipulates in his analysis of (alternative) religious movements.

The cult thus becomes an analytical subtype of ARMs, because cults involve a distinctive social-psychological aspect not found in ARMs generally. Whereas ARMs allow some degree of individuality and broader social integration, the cult demands unquestioning submission to the leader, such that the individual must negate his or her independent sense of self and thereby become totally dependent on the leader. Not only does such a person obediently submit his or her behavior to the leader, but the person's emotions as well. The cult leader tells the person how to behave, how to think, how to feel, and even whether to live or die.

For many nonscholars, a "cult" in the modern sense evokes great concern, and often a hostility that arises from fear. Many believe that cults are dangerous, and that they kidnap and brainwash innocent victims, especially teenagers. Many believe that cults practice bizarre, obscene, and evil rites, which may involve human sacrifice or wild, orgiastic sex. Basically, people project their worst fears, the worst images their mind can conceive, onto any mysterious group in their midst, or often not in their midst, or often one that does not exist at all.

In the 1980s, for example, many people believed that satanic cults were forming secretly throughout the country, in search of "blond-haired, blue-eyed virgin girls" to sacrifice to Satan. In the 1990s, ritual abuse scares ran amok, such that people believed day-care workers used the innocent children in their care for horrific sex and murder rituals as part of satanic worship (Victor 1993). The press greatly fomented this by presenting unsubstantiated testimonials of ritual abuse and satanic sacrifices as authentic, with no fact checking (Ellis 2000). Several people were actually prosecuted, although no evidence was ever introduced beyond professionally manipulated testimony from children (Nathan and Snedeker 2001). In popular usage, a cult may be any closely knit group that people find they dislike and that they blame for secret and horrific practices. The fear of unseen forces that negatively influence life may be real, but satanic conspiracies are not. Job loss, divorce, and death are real, but predatory sacrificial cults are not. Religious cults sometimes perpetrate violence against themselves (i.e., suicide) or against others, but this is overt; there is no evidence of conspiratorial cult murders, rape, or abductions (Bromley and Melton 2002; Dawson 2003; J. Hall 2002).

With this in mind, the sociological conception extends, but also challenges, the popular conception that the reason people find a group unappealing or even appalling results from a fear not of the unknown, but of the known. As sociologist Eileen Barker ([1984] 1993) argues, the people who feel most threatened by cults actually react to the familiar, not the unfamiliar. Cults remind people, even if subconsciously, of the things they like least about their own lives or fear about their prospects in life. Yet public response is not decisive. As sociologists, critical of what we observe and what people claim, drawing on research and theory, we have one more criterion: In order to be a true cult, the group must objectively contradict some central aspect of mainstream society, not merely seem distasteful to some individuals.

Let us consider three examples of cults in the modern sense, all of which resulted in death. All began peacefully, but later turned apocalyptic and violent. They are not the only such examples, but they are typical of contemporary cults. Although most groups that fit our definition of a cult do not turn violent, either against themselves or against others, the possibility exists so long as the leader requires absolute submission of the followers. That is, the followers must negate their independent sense of self and become an extension of the leader's will. So long as this particular social-psychological relationship exists, the followers will uncritically, even gleefully, do whatever the leader orders. Let us start with a unique group that, although it faded away, became a kind of template for later groups, both ARMS and cults—the Millerites.

Millerites

The Millerites from the nineteenth-century United States preconfigured the present-day cult in structure and beliefs. The group was founded by William Miller, a farmer who studiously read the Bible in order to interpret it. Miller typified the everyday Bible reader during the democratization of religion in the United States in the late 1880s as described in Chapter 2. While few readers ever sought to establish new denominations, Miller's analysis of the Bible founded an apocalyptic movement. Applying what Miller saw as scientific methods, he devised a means to determine when the end of the world would occur, based on the assumptions that the world began in 4004 BCE, as James Ussher calculated in 1650, and that in Biblical prophecy, one day always equals one year. He further argued that Daniel 8:14 and 9:24 offer the key to the time line encoded in the Bible. Once decoded, one may calculate from the beginning of creation to the end of the world. Miller concluded that the apocalypse would arrive on October 22, 1844 (Stein 2003).

> ### Miller's Scriptural Apocalypticism
>
> Daniel 8:14
>
> He said to me, "It will take 2,300 evenings and mornings; then the sanctuary will be reconsecrated."
>
> Daniel 9:24
>
> "Seventy 'sevens' are decreed for your people and your holy city to put an end to transgression, to put an end to sin, to atone for wickedness, to bring in everlasting righteousness, to seal up vision and prophecy and to anoint the most holy place [or one]" (New International Version)

By itself, this prediction was not unusual. Throughout the Christian era, people have predicted various dates as the end of the world, including December 31, 1000 CE; December 31, 2000 CE; and many other dates. Apocalyptic visionaries typically do not specify technical details, such as the time zone of the apocalypse, or which version of the Bible is correct, and why. As with Miller, the end never arrives. The Millerites termed October 22, 1844, as the Great Disappointment. Miller attempted to recalculate, and other members since Miller's death offer various explanations. One of Miller's devout followers, Jonas Wendell—now known as a Seventh-Day Adventist—became a traveling preacher who sermonized Charles Taze Russell, who in turn founded the Bible Student Movement, which later became the Jehovah's Witnesses. Seventh-Day Adventists and Jehovah's Witnesses are the two largest descendents of the Millerites and retain the emphasis on the apocalypse, but are much less specific with the date. Rather, they emphasize the need for constant preparedness through purity of body and mind. The Adventists in particular emphasize physical health and intellectual development through education, and accept worldly success through productive work as part of healthy living (Bull and Lockhart [1989] 2007). They practice vegetarianism (as meat is pleasurable) and also avoid alcohol, tobacco, and caffeine. In 1894, an Adventist named John Harvey Kellogg—a doctor who supervised a health spa in Battle Creek, Michigan—invented Corn Flakes as a perfect food for Adventists. They contain all necessary nutrients and, he believed, their blandness also serves to suppress sexual desire. By 1900, the Adventists and other Millerite derivatives had become, at least in parts of the country, mainstream.

In their own day, the Millerites manifested some aspects of contemporary cults. Members were required to give up all money and property (to charity, not to Miller), which would serve no purpose in the coming and imminent apocalypse. They also devoted themselves entirely to Miller, who represented the only and absolute source of truth regarding the end of the world. Lastly, the Millerites generated considerable controversy, and thus lived in their own communities that were separate from, and in conflict with, mainstream society. Unlike contemporary cults, however, the Millerite vision of the apocalypse never included violence against oneself or others, nor wealth-gathering for Miller. Given that Miller did not command people and did not use his authority to carry out nefarious purposes using religious beliefs as a cover, we may term the Millerites an alternative religious movement. Nevertheless, the breakaway manner of Miller's movement set a precedent for many alternative movements in the twentieth century, including cults.

For most Millerites, the Great Disappointment ended Miller's singular prophetic role, and most people returned to the mainstream to earn a living and continue their lives since the apocalypse now appeared to be further off. However, as indicated, many retained apocalyptic beliefs, which not only shaped direct descendents like the Adventists and the Witnesses, but also contributed significantly to broader evangelical versions of Christianity. To a great extent, apocalypticism is increasingly mainstream (Newport and Gribben 2006), based primarily on popular readings of the book of Revelation, which appears in some versions of the Bible (but not in the Orthodox version, for example).

To the extent apocalypticism becomes mainstream, the notion of the end times and imminent judgment resonates with wider segments of the population, even those who are not conservative evangelicals or descendents of the Millerites. Even in secular and atheistic traditions such as Marxism (Lundskow 2005), the notion of a final battle—whether Jesus against Satan or the proletariat against the bourgeoisie—promises perfect justice, redemption, and utopia.

Let us now consider the recent example of the Branch Davidians, who split from the mainstream Adventists and in so doing, acquired the characteristics of a cult.

Branch Davidians: From Alternative Religion to Cult

The Branch Davidians are a religious group that splintered off from the Seventh-Day Adventist Church. From its inception, the group shared the apocalyptic beliefs of the Adventists, in that they believed themselves to be living in a time when Christian prophecies of a final divine judgment were coming to pass. They became famous in 1993 when the FBI, Bureau of Alcohol, Tobacco, and Firearms (ATF), Texas State Police, and other law enforcement agencies lay siege to their Mt. Carmel compound near Waco, Texas. The siege resulted in the deaths of 82 of the church's members, including David Koresh. However, by the time of the siege, Koresh had encouraged his followers to think of themselves as "students of the Seven Seals" (Thibodeau and Whiteson 1999) rather than Branch Davidians, while other Branch Davidian factions never accepted his leadership (Kerstetter 2004). Both of these factors—the changing belief identity centered on Koresh's personal pronouncements and the group's renegade status among Davidians in general—positioned the Waco community as a breakaway movement. In the Koresh period, it would become a cult.

Foundational Davidian Scripture

Ezekiel 9

(3–4) Now the glory of the God of Israel went up from above the cherubim, where it had been, and moved to the threshold of the temple. Then the LORD called to the man clothed in linen who had the writing kit at his side and said to him, "Go throughout the city of Jerusalem and put a mark on the foreheads of those who grieve and lament over all the detestable things that are done in it."

(5–6) As I listened, he said to the others, "Follow him through the city and kill, without showing pity or compassion. Slaughter old men, young men and maidens, women and children, but do not touch anyone who has the mark. Begin at my sanctuary." So they began with the elders who were in front of the temple. (New International Version)

The Branch Davidians began in 1929 when Victor Houteff (1885–1955), a Bulgarian immigrant, claimed that he had a new message for the Seventh-Day Adventist Church. Influenced greatly by Miller and Ellen White, a later Adventist teacher, Houteff wrote a book entitled *The Shepherd's Rod,* which became the original name of the group, in which he presented the elements of his new message. His theology uses his own concepts of type and antitype. Rather than contradictions, as the terms imply, a type foreshadows some later person or event, and the antitype fulfills the type. For example, drawing from Ezekiel 9 (see text box), he argued that rampant sin (the type) calls forth its antitype—redemption. These are not, however, prophesies, but as Houteff saw it, a religious analysis of history (Newport 2006). Yet Houteff's analysis does not produce a rational analysis of history as a historian or sociologist would develop. Rather, Houteff sought to describe the mystery of existence, the paradoxes of religious history that require faith rather than logic to accept. For example, the Jewish and pagan temples were a type; Jesus is the antitype. The system of animal sacrifices was a type, the sacrifice of Jesus on the cross the antitype. The former calls forth the latter.

One of Houteff's most crucial teachings relates to Ezekiel 9, which describes a bloody purification of Jerusalem by angels. He believed this prophesied the purification of the Seventh-Day Adventist church, which would leave alive the 144,000 as specified in the Book of Revelations, although more conventional evangelical belief holds that this number refers to the number of "good" Jews who will convert to Christianity as part of the end times. Houteff argued that particular events would precede the end times, which included a German victory in World War II. The Germans would become the forces of the Antichrist, and they would slaughter the people of God until only 144,000 remained, who would ascend into heaven (Newport 2006).

When Houteff established the Mt. Carmel community near Waco, Texas, in 1935, one reason for selecting the location was that it was out of town. Davidians attempted to make Mt. Carmel as self-sufficient as possible, growing their own food and sharing necessities. Community leaders decided what news from the outside world to tell residents. Mt. Carmel had its own currency and its own schools, and Davidian children pledged allegiance to the Davidian flag "and to the theocracy for which it stands" alongside the American flag.

While residents of Mt. Carmel dedicated all their energy to spreading the word, the majority of Davidians continued to live in the outside world, supporting the work with tithes. In 1942, the name of the organization was changed to the General Association of Davidian Seventh-Day Adventists because of an alignment of ideas with the Seventh-Day Adventists on conscientious objector status during WWII. Houteff objected to fighting the war because a German victory was necessary to bring about the end times. Up to 1942, his movement was known as the Shepherd's Rod, but when Houteff found it necessary to formally incorporate and clearly associate with an established denomination so members could claim conscientious objector status, he changed the name from the Shepherd's Rod to the Davidian Seventh-Day Adventists. The term "Davidian" refers to the restoration of the Davidic kingdom, also called the Kingdom of David. Houteff directed Davidians to focus exclusively on converting Adventists. Under Houteff's typological system described earlier, Davidians believed in a cyclical series of events, which Houteff described as a spiral, such that historical events foretell future events, yet at the same time history advances in terms of cosmological progress (Newport 2006). In other words, history repeats itself according to a pattern of type and antitype, but this mundane cycle indicates a transcendent and divine progress toward the end times. Believers must therefore seek to identify the types and antitypes in order to correctly understand history and the progression of events toward the Second Coming.

After Houteff died in 1955, a crisis ensued because Houteff was considered to be the "Elijah" (the herald) announcing the Second Coming. Germany clearly lost the war, and in any case the herald of the Second Coming was dead. His wife, Florence, assumed the leadership and declared the Second Coming would occur on April 22, 1959. In anticipation of the event, members were urged to gather at Mt. Carmel and to sell their houses and businesses. Over 800 came, but like the Millerites and many other end-time believers over the centuries, they suffered yet another Disappointment.

As Florence took over one group, another of Houteff's followers named Ben Roden organized another splinter group known as the Branch Davidians. Roden led the group from 1955 to 1978, succeeded by Lois Roden (1978–1985), George Roden (1985–1987), and finally by Vernon Howell (1987–1993), later known as David Koresh (Newport 2006). After Florence Houteff's disastrous prophesy of the Second Coming, she and the other leaders eventually resigned in 1962, declared the Davidian Seventh-Day Adventists dissolved, and sold the Mt. Carmel property.

Shortly after Florence and the other leaders resigned, Ben Roden bought the property at Mt. Carmel in 1965. The Roden family remained in control until 1987, when George Roden was jailed for 6 months for contempt of court. Vernon Howell came on the scene in 1981, working at Mt. Carmel as a handyman. He soon became a favorite of Lois Roden, and she declared him to be the next prophet of the end times. A power struggle occurred involving Howell and Lois Roden on the one side, and George, her son, on the other. Eventually, Vernon and Lois gained control and quickly moved to establish a unique identity. Lois Roden apparently allowed Howell to play an unfettered leadership role (Faubion 2001). Howell immediately made himself the center of the Church, and placed himself as spiritually equivalent to Victor Houteff, the founder.

Howell began taking "spiritual wives" from among the young unmarried women in the group. Later, this practice included married members among the flock. Howell had justified this latter inclusion in a new teaching introduced in 1989 known as the "New Light," which revealed that all female members of the Branch Davidians were his spiritual wives. Another purpose of the teaching was to produce a new lineage of God's children (Haldeman and Wessinger 2007).

Koresh's Foundational Scripture

Revelation 6

(1–2) I watched as the Lamb opened the first of the seven seals. Then I heard one of the four living creatures say in a voice like thunder, "Come!" I looked, and there before me was a white horse! Its rider held a bow, and he was given a crown, and he rode out as a conqueror bent on conquest.

Revelation 19

(11–16) I saw heaven standing open and there before me was a white horse, whose rider is called Faithful and True. With justice he judges and makes war. His eyes are like blazing fire, and on his head are many crowns. He has a name written on him that no one knows but he himself. He is dressed in a robe dipped in blood, and his name is the Word of God. The armies of heaven were following him, riding on white horses and dressed in fine linen, white and clean. Out of his mouth comes a sharp sword with which to strike down the nations. "He will rule them with an iron scepter." He treads the winepress of the fury of the wrath of God Almighty. On his robe and on his thigh he has this name written: King of Kings and Lord of Lords.

(17–18) And I saw an angel standing in the sun, who cried in a loud voice to all the birds flying in midair, "Come, gather together for the great supper of God, so that you may eat the flesh of kings, generals, and mighty men, of horses and their riders, and the flesh of all people, free and slave, small and great."

(19–21) Then I saw the beast and the kings of the earth and their armies gathered together to make war against the rider on the horse and his army. But the beast was captured, and with him the false prophet who had performed the miraculous signs on his behalf. With these signs he had deluded those who had received the mark of the beast and worshiped his image. The two of them were thrown alive into the fiery lake of burning sulfur. The rest of them were killed with the sword that came out of the mouth of the rider on the horse, and all the birds gorged themselves on their flesh. (New International Version)

In 1990, Howell took the name of David Koresh—the name "David" from King David, successor to King Saul in the Bible, and from whom Howell said he was descended, and the latter name a form of Cyrus, the only non-Israelite to be given

the title of "messiah." As a messiah, Koresh viewed himself as the lamb mentioned in Revelation, whom Koresh viewed as a prophet who announces the Second Coming of Jesus—the rider of the white horse. At this point, Koresh moved from cult leader to apocalyptic leader, a common progression in charismatic groups in American religious history (Kerstetter 2004).

By 1992, Koresh had declared that the apocalypse would occur in the United States and not in Israel, so the group took a survivalist stance and became self-sufficient. They grew basic foods on the compound, as well as operated an auto repair business.

As the group closed itself off from the outside world, allegations of misconduct soon circulated among anticult groups, including child abuse and the illegal possession of firearms. There was, however, no decisive evidence uncovered relating to child abuse. Regarding illegal gun possession, a search-and-arrest warrant was issued on February 25, 1993, by the Bureau of Alcohol, Tobacco, and Firearms.

An internal split had also developed between the dedicated minority living at Mt. Carmel and the majority living on the outside who still paid tithes to the Mt. Carmel community. In 1992, David Koresh called for an in-gathering of believers at Waco. Still officially a part of the Seventh-Day Adventist Church, the wider Adventist leadership condemned Koresh's claims of divinity and other departures from basic church teachings and standards. Therefore, he was disfellowshipped (excommunicated) (Linedecker 1993).

Following disfellowship and the failure of the in-dwelling to significantly increase the ranks of those living at the compound, Koresh became increasingly apocalyptic. He predicted that agents of the Antichrist (the False Prophet in Revelation) would come for him, and in order to fulfill God's word, all loyal members should resist their incursions, by violence if necessary. As ATF agents attempted to serve the warrants against Koresh on February 28, 1993, gunfire erupted from within the compound, apparently from a 50-caliber machine gun. Four agents and nine Branch Davidians were killed. After the initial gunfire, Koresh talked with an FBI agent by phone over a period of several weeks, in a long verbal dissertation about his theology. Some suggest (see Lewis 1994 and S. Wright 1995) that Koresh would have surrendered if the government had allowed him to finish his lengthy discourse because he saw himself as a prophet bringing the Word of the Second Coming, not as Jesus himself. Once pronounced, Koresh may have regarded his mission as complete. In any case, understanding Koresh's theology was crucial to any potentially peaceful resolution (Docherty 2001).

On April 19, 1993, after 51 days, Attorney General Janet Reno, on recommendations from the FBI, authorized agents to storm the compound. They attempted to ram through the outer walls with urban assault vehicles. In the process, a fire started and immolated the compound in only a few minutes. While some claim the FBI used incendiary devices, the subsequent investigation conducted by the State of Texas, known as the Danforth Report, found no evidence to support that claim. Rather, the report found that the Davidians had intentionally started the fire (Danforth 2000). Eighty-two Branch Davidians died, including 17 under the age of 12. During the siege, the FBI asked Koresh to release the children, but he refused.

Discussion

Koresh's teachings were definitely apocalyptic, and evidence indicates that the Davidians, and not the federal government, were responsible for the fire. Importantly, none of the charges of child abuse was ever confirmed. These accusations arose from outside the compound, by outsiders who were never part of the Branch Davidians. Although Koresh apparently had several sexual partners, none were children. In many respects, the Davidians in the Mt. Carmel compound lived typically austere and ascetic lives, like many devoutly religious people in many faiths. As with other cults, accusations of bizarre and grotesque rituals and practices came from outside the group. As we will see with our next case study, whether a group lives an austere monastic lifestyle or an extremely indulgent one is not a decisive factor in cult life.

The Branch Davidians established Koresh as a divine figure, and as such, a common person can only submit utterly. In this frame of mind, a person thinks only to please the leader, not to question. Regardless of the details of the belief system and the lifestyle that ensues, cults distinguish themselves through a particular social-psychological relationship between the leader and the followers. We will cover this particular relationship at the end of this chapter.

Charles Manson and the Family

The man who would order several people to kill for him as a means to start a race war to spark Armageddon seemed an unlikely candidate for a position of such power. Born in Cincinnati, Ohio, on November 12, 1934, Charles Milles Manson never knew his father, and lived for a few years with his mother, who was a drug addict and prostitute. Having no desire from the beginning to raise Charles, she attempted to place him in a foster home at age 13, but unable to do so, she abandoned him at the Gibault School for Boys in Terre Haute, Indiana. Soon after, Charles ran away and went back home, but his mother rejected him, and he lived thereafter on the streets in a life of crime to support himself, when not doing prison time.

On March 21, 1967, Charles Manson was released on parole. Only 33 years old, he had numerous convictions, including fraud, grand theft auto, and pimping. Manson pleaded not to be released, on the grounds that he knew no other life and was unfit to live in normal society. The prison psychologist doubted that his motives were as altruistic as they appeared, and stated in 1966,

> He hides his resentment and hostility behind a mask of superficial ingratiation. . . . [E]ven his cries for help represent a desire for attention with only superficial meaning; pattern of instability continues . . . [has an] intense need to call attention to himself . . . [he] manifests fanatical interests; Manson is about to complete his ten-year term. He has a pattern of criminal behavior and confinement that dates to his teen years. . . . [L]ittle can be expected in the way of change. (cited in George 1998)

This observation would prove very prescient, and it explains in essence the basis of Manson's behavior over the next 2 years. Here was a man who, utterly rejected by his parents, grew up on the streets and spent more than half his life in reform schools, juvenile facilities, and state penitentiaries. At only 5'3" and of small build, we can only imagine how Manson fared in prison.

Upon his release, Manson moved to the Haight-Ashbury district in San Francisco, named after the intersection of the two streets. The summer of 1967 is now known as the Summer of Love, and it marked the national emergence of the hippie movement as a spin-off of the antiwar movement and the more general youth movement. The hippie movement was part of a larger countercultural movement that included an environmental movement, a women's movement, and—most relevant for our purposes—a religious-spiritual movement. This latter aspect included conservative movements as well as more experimental and radical movements. For example, the so-called Jesus movement also arose in California, in which primarily young people sought to live the life of Jesus. Consistent with the hippie uniform of long hair, comfortable and well-worn clothes, and peace signs and love beads, the enthusiasts who embraced the Jesus movement had the appearance of typical hippies, except that they were also enthusiastic evangelicals who sought to spread the word of God. This earned them the epithet "Jesus Freaks," although this was not derogatory. Rather, a hippie in general was often popularly called a "freak," which hippies wore as a mark of pride and thus converted into a positive title. Similarly, those hippies who committed their lives to Jesus were still, and proudly, "freaks."

Of course, Manson was not interested in peace and love. He sensed that these teenagers and young adults who walked the streets wearing love beads, passing out flowers, and talking about free love were at the same time quite innocent, and ready marks for an experienced con like Manson. At this point, however, his interest was not primarily criminal, but social-psychological. As the prison psychiatrist recognized, Manson's overtly good-natured displays in fact evidenced an underlying hostility—a demand for attention and a commitment to fanaticism and other forms of extreme thought and behavior. Unlike his past, Manson now realized that he was an older, wiser, and far more cunning person. In prison and before, Manson found meaning in stories about Adolf Hitler from *Life* magazine (whether he read Hitler's book, *Mein Kampf,* is unknown). Manson also held strong racist attitudes, and believed that a race war between black and white people loomed on the horizon (Bugliosi [1974] 2001). Yet Manson also realized that he no longer needed to play the secretive, scheming criminal. The Summer of Love offered new possibilities in which Manson could finally have both the attention and the power he craved.

Still ambivalent, Manson attempted twice more to establish genuine involvement in society, and in the process achieve some measure of self-validation. First, Manson met Dennis Wilson of the Beach Boys, and eventually the band recorded one of Manson's songs. However, this failed to produce any success for Manson, who longed for a career in music. Second, Manson visited the Esalen Institute in Big Sur, California, on August 5, 1969. The Esalen Institute explores alternative learning through experience and altered states of consciousness. The institute functions as a retreat center where residents live communally and explore new possibilities in massage, yoga, psychology, ecology, spirituality, art, music, and all manner of alternative education. According to Vincent Bugliosi ([1974] 2001), the prosecutor for the Manson murders, Esalen rejected Manson's audition to join and he argues that this final rejection resolved Manson's ambivalence. From now on, Manson would fully indulge his intense hatred for the world. After returning from Esalen, Manson told Linda Kasabian, one of his devotees, "now is the time for Helter Skelter" (Bugliosi [1974] 2001).

From the beginning, after his release from prison in 1967, Manson recruited mostly women, and he had the ability to tell them exactly what an alienated middle-class girl wanted to hear. Some felt stifled by pointless rules and sterile routines. Some felt dominated and set up as marriage fodder for successful men. These girls sought escape. Others already felt ostracized and tossed away. These girls sought connection and regulation.

Manson's first convert was Mary Brunner, a recent community college graduate who worked as a librarian. Manson quickly realized how dissatisfied she was in her life. In place of the workday routine of getting up, going to work, going home, going to sleep, getting up, going to work, and so on, Manson offered a life of apparent freedom—first on the road, and eventually at the Spahn Ranch, an abandoned movie set in the desert outside Los Angeles. Shortly after Brunner, Manson recruited his other core followers who would commit murder for him: Patricia Krenwinkel, Leslie van Houten, Susan Atkins, and Charles "Tex" Watson. There were about 100 other followers who eventually joined the Family (as they were called) at the Spahn Ranch, but according to prosecutor Bugliosi, only about 15–20 people constituted the core of fanatically devoted followers. The core followers who did not participate in the murders include Lynette "Squeaky" Fromme, who later attempted to assassinate President Gerald Ford. Another is Ruth Ann "Ouish" Moorehouse, who on Charles's orders attempted to murder Barbara Hoyt, a 17-year-old runaway who fled the Family after she heard Susan Atkins brag about killing Sharon Tate.

It is important to understand that the followers did not immediately cease to be simply alienated suburban or marginalized youth and suddenly become murderers at Manson's command. The conversion process required time and certain steps that all such processes follow. Several Family members not implicated in the murders, such as Paul Watkins and Barbara Hoyt, have confirmed that the various "family" members felt real love for each other before Manson became obsessed with power and death. Remember that Manson vacillated between legitimate success through art and music on one side and authoritarian domination on the other. After the failure to gain entrance to the Esalen institute, he embraced authoritarianism. Let us examine the backgrounds of some of the core Family members.

Patricia Krenwinkel was, in her childhood, well-behaved and intelligent. She was a Bible student, and a good student in general. She was not very social and had few friends; her peers considered her "uncool." Her parents divorced when she was in high school; Pat turned to marijuana and her grades suffered, but she graduated nevertheless, uncertain about her personal and professional future. She met Charles Manson at the party of a friend, who told her that Manson was a musician and a kind of spiritual guru. This combination of attributes was common and appealing to young people in the late 1960s in California. Krenwinkel says they made love that night, and Manson made her feel beautiful for the first time in her life (Sawyer 1994).

Leslie van Houten was a straight-A student who was very attractive and voted prom queen. She was also athletic and good at everything she tried. In contrast to

Krenwinkel, she was very popular and definitely considered "cool" among her peers. Still, as she explained to Diane Sawyer (1994), she wanted more from life than was expected from a suburban, middle-class girl at that time. While her peers went to college, mainly to find a quality husband, Leslie met Charles Manson and joined him on the road, and then at Spahn Ranch. From her perspective, he seemed to offer perfect freedom—freedom from prohibitive and irrational morality and gender restrictions, and freedom from the pressure to conform, at least to mainstream banality.

Charles Watson similarly was a high school star in Texas, where he was captain of both the baseball and football teams, and his classmates voted him "most likely to succeed." He started college at North Texas University as a business major, but never finished. Watson today explains that he, like van Houten, wanted more from life; he couldn't see himself sitting behind a desk in an office. He spent his whole life through high school fulfilling the expectations of his parents, teachers, and peers, and now Charles Manson seemed to offer freedom from all that, a new and much more exciting and vital life. In prison, Watson says he was "born again," and founded the Abounding Love Ministry in 1980, whose Web site also includes his autobiography (aboundinglove.org).

Susan Atkins was the only core follower who grew up in material deprivation. Forced to leave home as a teenager, she earned a living on the margins of society as a stripper and possibly as a prostitute after her mother died. This loss affected her deeply. She harbored the same if less intense hostility toward life as Manson did. After meeting Charles Manson, he offered her what she most wanted—a sense of purpose and belonging. She didn't want to escape the restrictions of mainstream life; she wanted to embrace a life with boundaries and control.

The same is true of Lynette Fromme, who was very popular in high school, but who lived under bizarre circumstances at home. Her father, for unknown reasons, simply stopped speaking to her for 3 years, although they lived under the same roof (Bravin 1997). As Bravin recounts, Lynette was very popular, but also troubled. Perhaps abused by her father, she once took a stapler and proceeded to inject staples up her arm. Like Susan, she sought a life with meaningful boundaries. This Charles offered in abundance.

Degradation Rituals— The Process of Cult Initiation

With his group of core followers and various others, Manson settled the group at the Spahn Ranch. Once there, the degradation ritual began. This type of ritual functions specifically to break down certain key elements of a person's identity, which makes it possible to rebuild them according to the designs of the group, or in the case of cults, the one leader. Moreover, it makes the individual especially dependent on the group, as the person now lacks key elements of the sense of self that have been removed. The formation and maintenance of the self is diagrammed in Figure 7.1.

With this model in mind, the degradation ritual seeks to break the individual loose from his or her familiar reference groups. Notable reference groups include family, friends, peers, and others whom the person trusts and whom in popular language we may say the person "identifies with." The individual identity thus depends on

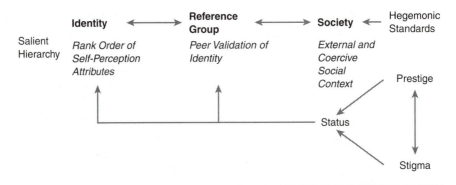

Figure 7.1   Individual and Social Formation of the Self

reinforcement from the reference group, and the reference group exists for the individual to the extent he or she contributes to its collective set of ideas, values, behavior, and so on. The degradation ritual also seeks to separate the individual from society, as shown in the model, which exerts order and regulation on the individual, whether the person likes it or not. In the contemporary United States, this control often takes an anonymous form, as social standards of public behavior, manners of speech, degree of formality, and the language that people expect as customary. In short, society exerts regulation and control most of the time not through force, but through conventionality. Society also determines the quality of any given reference group, and likewise of the associated individuals. Status exists as a continuum between positive status, or prestige, and negative status, or stigma. It is important to keep in mind that no person determines his or her own status—it depends entirely on how others perceive the person. Based on reaction from the reference group and society, one's sense of self, that is, one's identity, consists of a rank order of attributes, according to their dearness to the individual, with the most self-defining attributes at the top. We call this in sociology a "salient hierarchy," a concept developed by Aaron Cicourel (1974).

Once broken, the individual exists in the cult only as a subordinate who depends entirely on the leader for a sense of self. The other subordinates serve as the reference group, but they likewise lack autonomy. The cult social-psychological model may be diagrammed thus:

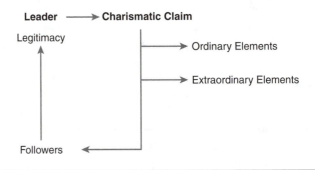

Figure 7.2   The Cult Social-Psychological Model

In this case, the leader singly replaces any other possible reference groups, and society disappears completely. If legitimacy in the wider social world depends on conventionality, what forms the basis of legitimacy in the cult, since it rejects conventionality? In the cult, the world exists only according to the leader, who has power and legitimacy to the extent the followers accept the leader's vision. This vision, this claim to authority, is called a charismatic claim, as discussed in Chapter 1. Yet the leader has no real supernatural power; the leader wields no genuine ability to work miracles, see the future, or control destiny. Yet the leader's power is real, just as the power of society is real. If mainstream society grants power based on established, conventional social relations, then the cult leader receives power from the followers. In short, the followers hand power and legitimacy to the leader. Everyday people submit to conventionality because it allows them to participate in society; whether that society is free and open or oppressive and closed, it offers life through relations with others. In the cult, people submit to the leader for the same reasons.

Remember that in sociology, charisma, as discussed in Chapter 1, has a specific meaning. It is the belief that a person or thing possesses supernatural powers. A would-be leader makes a charismatic claim, which typically includes both ordinary elements, with which the prospective follower is already familiar, and also *extraordinary* elements, which only the leader can provide. These extraordinary elements can take nearly any form.

Let us first consider the degradation aspects of the Manson Family. Prospective members endured various treatment to break their sense of self utterly. As general principles of life at Spahn Ranch, Manson forbade all references to one's past, including family and friends. He forbade anyone to keep track of time in any way—no watches or calendars—or even track the changing of the seasons. No one was allowed to recall his or her birthday or any events from the person's past. In addition to these general prohibitions, each new member underwent specific degradation experiences. Manson required that all new males engage in all manner of sexual activity with men, and all women engage in all manner of sexual activity with women. This broke down their most deeply held moral values, but also effectively transferred control of their bodies to Manson. Everyone was required to have sex with whomever Manson directed, often under the influence of LSD, while Manson orchestrated the nightly group sex (Sawyer 1994). Thus, what might appear to be free love was actually controlled by Manson.

Stripped of external references and shamed into reliance on the group through regular destruction of moral boundaries and self-autonomy, each person now relied increasingly on the group. The longer a person conforms to the reality of the cult, the more distant the external world seems (Dawson 2006). Degradation rituals negate the old self, such that the core members became more devoutly committed to Manson than the others who lived at the ranch. Once initiated, Manson gave new names to each member, and he prohibited the use of their former names. Manson kept the Family busy with all sorts of activities that included mundane functions like acquiring food and money, often through sexual favors to store managers. The Family would also reenact the crucifixion on a regular basis, before which Manson would pass out LSD to everyone present (Sawyer 1994). With Manson as Jesus, they simulated the scourging and the subsequent nailing to the cross.

The Leader and the Message

As stated, the charismatic claim consists of both ordinary and readily familiar elements, and also extraordinary elements that are unique to each particular leader. In the case of Manson, the ordinary elements included the Beatles, and in particular, the *White Album*. One of the best-selling records of all time, this album was well-known and thus Manson need only refer to it; he didn't need to explain its existence or who the Beatles were. Manson also talked about the race riots in Detroit, Los Angeles, and elsewhere that shook the United States in 1967. The news featured stories about these events prominently, and thus they were also a part of public awareness.

The extraordinary elements build on the ordinary. Manson identified the Beatles as prophets, and the *White Album* as not just a popular record, but as a sacred text. Most important, only Manson could understand and correctly interpret the divine messages in the *White Album*. The popular listener heard only rock music. Also, Manson revealed that he was Jesus and that the Second Coming had arrived. In themselves, such claims are not inherently malevolent. Many people make extraordinary claims about themselves and very few commit or inspire violence.

Manson's Foundational Scripture

Isaiah 66

(22–24) "As the new heavens and the new earth that I make will endure before me," declares the LORD, "so will your name and descendants endure. From one New Moon to another and from one Sabbath to another, all mankind will come and bow down before me," says the Lord. "And they will go out and look upon the dead bodies of those who rebelled against me; their worm will not die, nor will their fire be quenched, and they will be loathsome to all mankind."

Revelation 21

(1–4) Then I saw a new heaven and a new earth, for the first heaven and the first earth had passed away, and there was no longer any sea. I saw the Holy City, the new Jerusalem, coming down out of heaven from God, prepared as a bride beautifully dressed for her husband. And I heard a loud voice from the throne saying, "Now the dwelling of God is with men, and he will live with them. They will be his people, and God himself will be with them and be their God. He will wipe every tear from their eyes. There will be no more death or mourning or crying or pain, for the old order of things has passed away." (New International Version)

In the case of Manson, however, we saw from his psychological report that he exhibited an underlying hostility and that he craved attention. His new followers supplied the attention, and likewise enabled him to express his hostility in overt and real ways. Known by their Manson-endowed nicknames, "Tex" Watson, "Katie" Krenwinkel, "Lulu" van Houten, and "Sadie" Atkins—the murderers—became an extension of Manson's will, which included an extension of his hatred for life and his own personal insecurity. The unloved child finally found unquestioning acceptance and even exaltation. He could now act on his deepest and most violent fantasies, created during years of abandonment, abuse, desperation, incarceration, and humiliation.

With a core group of members fully committed to him, Manson articulated his vision for them and the world, which he called Helter Skelter, after the song of the same name on the *White Album*. Manson declared, as mentioned, that a race war was coming, and that black people would win. This would be the Battle of Armageddon as described in the Book of Revelation in the Bible. However, they would have no experience with government, so they would be unable to control the country after their victory. To remedy this, Manson and his followers would come out of the desert and, as the only white people left, would take control. This would be the beginning of a new earth as the Bible prophesizes, especially in Isaiah and Revelation.

Yet in order to fulfill prophesy, Manson said that he and his family must spark the war. This spark would take the form of murder. It must appear that black people committed the crimes, so the white establishment would take revenge on the black community, who in turn would retaliate, and eventually a full-scale war would ensue.

The first planned victims would be Sharon Tate, wife of director Roman Polanski, and several houseguests who were staying with her while Roman was abroad working on a film. Manson apparently chose this particular house because he had once attended a party there, invited by Terry Melcher, son of Doris Day and a record producer who was friends with Dennis Wilson of the Beach Boys.

The first to die that night of August 9, 1969, was Stephen Parent, a 19-year-old who was on his way off the Polanski property after visiting with his friend who was the groundskeeper. Charles Watson shot Parent at close range. In addition to Watson, Manson selected Krenwinkel and Atkins as his most loyal followers, and also Linda "Yana the Witch" Kasabian, because she had the only valid driver's license. Testimony at the trial revealed that the murder of Parent had horrified Kasabian, who was clearly not committed to Manson in the same manner as the others present that night.

They proceeded up the long curving driveway and left Kasabian in the car while the others entered the house. Watson shot and stabbed Wojciech Frykowski, a friend of Polanski. This frightened the other residents, who fled in various directions while Jay Sebring, a well-known Hollywood hairstylist, attempted to protect Tate, who was nearly 9 months pregnant. Abigail Folger, heiress to the Folger coffee fortune, spent most of her time in the Watts neighborhood, a mostly poor black area of Los Angeles, where she tutored schoolchildren. She ran outside to the back lawn, where Krenwinkel chased her down and stabbed her to death. Meanwhile, Atkins stabbed Sharon Tate to death, after Sharon pleaded for her life. Watson shot and stabbed Sebring to death. Afterward, the group snacked on milk and cheese from the refrigerator, then returned to the ranch. Manson instructed the group to "leave something witchy" at the scene of the crime (Sawyer 1994), so Krenwinkel wrote various words in blood, which included "Rise," "Death to Pigs," and "Healter Skealter" [*sic*]. Since they neglected to check the groundskeeper's cottage, he survived.

The next night, Manson selected a house owned by Leno and Rosemary LaBianca, who owned a chain of supermarkets. Why he chose this house is uncertain. Manson apparently recognized that Kasabian was not devoted to him or his vision of Helter Skelter, so he drove the car himself the second night. He also selected van Houten to join the others from the first night. Van Houten recounted later that she enthusiastically sought out Manson with the hope that he would choose her for the second night. Although she never asked to participate (that would be presumptuous, she felt), she says that everything on her face begged to be included (Sawyer 1994).

With van Houten now included, and Manson driving the car, they approached and entered the LaBianca home. After Tex tied up Leno, Manson left without explanation. The girls took Rosemary to a back bedroom while Watson stabbed Leno to death. Tex ordered the girls to kill Rosemary, which Krenwinkel and Van Houten did. The coroner's report stated that they stabbed Rosemary at least 30 times. The group again wrote similar words on the walls in blood, and Krenwinkel jabbed a fork into Leno's abdomen and left it there, as another "witchy" sign.

So far, we have examined how the relationship between the leader and followers forms, and all cults, properly conceptualized, have this feature. While most are not violent, the relationship between the leader and the followers defines a cult as much as the relationship between the cult and the surrounding society. We will analyze the leader–follower dimension and the role of religious sentiment much more fully at the end of the chapter. Before that, let us consider one more example.

Heaven's Gate

This group made the headlines not by killing other people, but by killing themselves. Thirty-nine people committed suicide on March 26, 1997. About half were men and half women. The people had ingested alcohol and barbiturates, and they died in their bunk beds in a large house in an upscale neighborhood in San Diego.

The Heaven's Gate cult started in the mid-1970s, and it gained some media attention at that time when they declared that UFOs would pick them up (and in this manner they would ascend to heaven, or as they called it, the "Next Level"). This of course did not happen, but the media attention brought more people into the group. The founders were Marshall Applewhite and Bonnie Nettles. They shortly thereafter took the names Do and Ti, respectively.

Applewhite was a choir and band professor at the University of Alabama in the 1950s, and colleagues recount that he was extremely skilled in identifying talent and turning incoherent ensembles into impressive orchestral accomplishment. Although married to an attractive and popular wife, Applewhite was in fact gay. Alabama did not tolerate homosexuality in the 1950s, and the university fired Applewhite upon learning his secret. His marriage subsequently collapsed. Applewhite confided to a friend that sexuality completely perplexed him, and that he feared he would never understand his own feelings or discover personal intimate happiness.

In 1974, Applewhite met Nettles, who had recently gone through a divorce, and the two became platonic friends. They traveled around the country for several months and decided to found the group that would take the name Heaven's Gate. Their doctrine, like Manson's, includes both ordinary and extraordinary elements. On the ordinary side, the pair taught that the various *Star Trek* television series (the original ran 1966–1969 and *The Next Generation* aired from 1987–1994) and movies offered valuable and insightful lessons about life and death. Moreover, the doctrine put forth that people could find themselves and the meaning of life by traveling on the open road, and thus invoked a powerful image from American culture—the road trip. In numerous books and movies, the open road has become part of the American cultural psyche, a place where a person might find himself or herself, escape the past, start a new life, find the meaning of life, overcome fears, recognize dreams, and perhaps even find salvation. Ti and Do thus equated their own trials and tribulations on the road with a powerful and pervasive aspect of American culture.

On the extraordinary side, the pair taught that Jesus would come again, and that Ti and Do were prophets sent to prepare people for His arrival. In addition to this, the pair also revealed unique visions that only they knew—namely, that Jesus was in fact an alien from a higher level of existence, which they called "The Level Above Human." At this higher level, people are freed from physical bodies, which they called "vehicles," and exist only as beings of pure and eternal energy (*Star Trek* episodes often feature aliens that exist as pure energy beings). This corresponds to the more primitive notion of a soul and salvation, which the pair said the Next Level instructed them to modify through teaching. People must therefore enter into a process of education, which Heaven's Gate called the "class." The entire group comprised the one class, which was in fact a lifetime process of lessons, and required that a person go through the full initiation, or as we say in sociology, degradation rituals. Like the Manson Family, Applewhite and Nettles kept people busy with both mundane and sacred activities to reinforce their commitment to the group.

The degradation rituals required first that people be paired, one male and one female. Just as Ti and Do had traveled around the country in a platonic male–female relationship, which eventually led to contact from the Next Level, so each pair of initiates had to follow their example. The group gave each pair a small amount of money and told them to return after a certain length of time. Upon return, they would recount their experiences and any insight they gained. Often, the group sent them to prearranged destinations to pick up packages, which included food or other items. They were supposed to contemplate the meaning of the items, which in retrospect appear to have been meaningless. Such exercises were to keep the pairs focused on Ti and Do's teaching.

After a pair returned from this initial ritual, they were required to turn over all their money and property to the group, and from that point on abstain from any further contact with family or friends who would not join the group. Furthermore, members had to de-sex themselves, and commit to a nonsexual and nongendered lifestyle. Members adopted short, bowl-shaped haircuts, imitating Vulcan haircuts from *Star Trek*. Members also were required to wear gender-neutral and sex-concealing clothing. Each person must face the others and reveal every hidden thought, desire, fear, and so on. Ti and Do taught the members how to recognize their spirit influence, which is the source of all negative feeling toward oneself and toward others. They were taught that every soul is pure, so members would talk about negative emotions (such as hate, jealousy, and fear) in terms of their spirit influence, and also in terms of the frailties of the body, which was simply a vehicle that carried the soul.

This seems very different from the sex and drug orgies of the Manson family, and in fact, the aforementioned Puritan lifestyle of Heaven's Gate is far more typical of cults than Manson's rituals of extreme indulgences. However, we must think sociologically. In both cases, members must submit to the leader(s), who make all the decisions and require total conformity. Both also require that each person separate from outside influences, especially the intimate ones such as family and friends, as well as reveal all their innermost feelings and fears, so that nothing remains personal and private. Each person ceases to be an individual and becomes a member, a unit identical to the others.

Also, the only purpose for members is that of fulfilling the leader's goals, and in so doing, making the leader happy. Remember that the sex and drugs were not spontaneous expressions of freedom or love in the Manson family, but rather, rituals that Manson orchestrated to create and reinforce his control over people. Ti and Do similarly orchestrated their followers' lives, which were focused entirely on fulfilling Ti and Do's directives and thereby making them happy. In such situations, the greatest fear becomes a fear of displeasing the leader, from whom all purpose, meaning, and happiness flow. As we saw, Leslie van Houten recounted how she actively sought to please Manson, and that her devotion to please the leader consumed her, such that on the night of the murders she thought of nothing else and nothing else mattered.

So with the "class" established, Ti and Do taught that the messiah would not come until the class was ready, which they would announce when the time arrived. However, something unexpected happened. In 1985, Nettles died of cancer. Applewhite (Do) nevertheless explained that Nettles (Ti) had moved to the Next Level, that her mission on earth was finished. Applewhite further detailed and consolidated the beliefs, explaining that "the vehicle" not only carries the soul, but imprisons it. The vehicle contains all manner of frailty and destructive desires, especially sexual desires and negative emotions like jealousy, hate, and so on. Each person must strive to "exit" the vehicle, which, however, must occur at the right time, and the right time would be when the spaceship from the Next Level arrives. In order to exit the vehicle, a person must kill the vehicle, or in other words, commit suicide. Otherwise, the soul would simply be reborn in another vehicle. Applewhite also revealed that he was, in fact, Jesus Christ, the same Jesus who died on the cross in ancient times. At the crucifixion, people were not yet ready to ascend to the Next Level, because they were not capable of understanding the true message. Hence, Jesus died violently for the truth of existence.

Since the time to exit had not yet arrived, the group must endeavor to recruit new members—or in their terms, to educate more people for the final harvest. Only those properly prepared can be beamed up to the spaceship and live in the Next Level—The Level Above Human. From 1985 to 1997, the group traveled on and off around the country in search of new members. In 1997, the Hale-Bopp comet appeared (readily viewable at night with the naked eye), which Applewhite said concealed the spaceship. The time had arrived. The group had always made films and videos of their time together over the years, and some members had been in the group since the 1970s. Applewhite filmed a final farewell video, and divulged the finer points of his theology before the Exit. Each member also filmed a farewell statement, and one of the most interesting aspects is the members' apparent joy as the end approached. They happily looked forward to the Exit, and hoped that people would celebrate rather than mourn their ascendance, for which they had prepared over many years. The next day, 38 people plus Applewhite committed suicide. Two other members, Charles Humphrey (known as Rikkody) and Wayne Cooke (Justody), attempted suicide 2 months later. Cooke succeeded, and Humphrey recovered but then later succeeded on his second attempt.

Discussion: What Cults Really Are

One popular myth about cults is that they trick, kidnap, or brainwash their members. Although the meaning of such terms in their popular usage remains unclear, none of them accurately captures the reality we have reviewed. Members seek out groups to which they can belong, and the groups they choose to join offer them the one thing they want most of all—unequivocal acceptance. People who join cults—or at least those who become core members—willingly surrender their sense of self because in exchange they receive total acceptance. They also gain a clear sense of purpose and meaning. Thus, cults do not and need not brainwash people, in the sense of coercive changes to their identity, because members make such changes willingly. The degradation rituals are a small price to pay for total acceptance—and in the case of cults, the certainty of salvation.

In fact, empirical evidence rejects the brainwashing thesis. In notable research over decades of time, from Eileen Barker ([1984] 1993), Barker and Warburg (2000), Bromley and Melton (2002), Philip Jenkins (2000), Melton and Moore (1982), Victor Turner (1995), and Bryan Wilson (1999), it is clear that both cults and alternative religious movements mobilize a stifled passion, a longing to break free and find one's true self. Far from coercively brainwashing a person, they bring out what the person already felt and longed to express. As Turner concludes, "the proponents of brainwashing have not produced evidence to support their position. . . . [T]he burden of proof is on those who proffer the brainwashing hypothesis. Until such evidence is forthcoming" (p. 6), we should commit ourselves to more dynamic theories that, if less astounding, are factually accurate—hence, our discussion here.

Cult core membership thus consist of seekers, people who are in transition between major moments in their lives, the kind of moments or events that define who we are (our identity) and how we see the world. In the case of the Manson Family, the core members had recently graduated high school or college, and they wondered what to do next. In the case of Heaven's Gate, members were somewhat older, but had recently been laid off from work or gone through a divorce. Similarly, they were looking for new directions. In both examples, the members were also intelligent and critical of mainstream society (the United States), and were already marginalized and seeking something other than conventional, mainstream life courses. For the Branch Davidians, by the time Koresh changed the group from an ARM to a cult, most of the members had been in the group for more than 10 years, and some for a second generation. They knew no other life. Cults thus do not kidnap or trick people, because the members are already seekers looking for something different and challenging; the degradation rituals that initiate people into a state of total acceptance are not easy and require a strong desire to belong. In some cases, people are born into the group or are in so long that they cannot even contemplate a different way of life, much less function in mainstream society (Palmer and Hardman 1999).

Once initiation occurs, especially when the rituals and other requirements destroy the old identity and connections to one's past, the individual becomes entirely dependent on the group. Not only do they not want to go back (leave the group), but they also can't leave; they can no longer function according to established conventions. The cult does not force them to stay, but it makes it nearly impossible on a practical level to leave, given that they now have no money, no job, no property, and an unusual view of reality that makes socialization difficult with anyone other than a cult member. They become accustomed to their own terms, expressions, and assumptions. The longer a person stays in, the more difficult it is to regain the necessary elements of a mainstream life. The person is unwilling to leave because he or she has negated an independent sense of self.

Now, the members' identity exists only in relationship to the leader, who supplants the reference groups that keep other people connected to society. In the case of cults, the outside world, the larger society, also ceases to exist except as an omnipresent threat—something that should only be avoided.

The religious aspects of cults play a decisive role, because they transform ideas into transcendent truth, which a person must accept without question. No matter how brilliant a philosopher or professor might be, he or she is still only a person. In the case of the charismatic leader, the good ideas are divine ideas, and a human individual can only bow to divine truth. A regular person does not debate Manson, Applewhite, or Koresh, nor does the person expect to. Rather, a common person who believes must submit and surrender one's own thoughts and feelings and replace them with the thoughts and feelings of the divine leader.

Why are some people so eager to join a cult? Why are they so desperate to negate their sense of self in favor of absolute submission, even to the point of death, to achieve absolute belonging? We might ask the same of terrorists from Chapter 5, and the answer is related. As we saw with terrorist recruits, both the rank and file as well as the educated and professional members, conditions of deprivation, a lack of hope about the future, or both compel them to take desperate action. Death becomes preferable to hopelessness. Cults rely on similar longings. Although the Manson and Heaven's Gate members did not come from poverty, they did reach a state of despair, of hopelessness. Circumstances did not force them into any one particular and unappealing fate, but they did cause them to founder rudderless in a sea of innumerable possibilities with no way to judge one over and against the others. This uncertainty creates just as much hopelessness as having few or no choices. This further intensifies the power of the religious aspect of the cult, because only something of a religious nature, something divine, allows the individual to abdicate decision-making power and uncritically embrace a higher power. Other people may provide sound advice, but they are still just people who suffer from the same flaws as anyone else. They are just part of the Man, as Manson would say, or just another vehicle, as Ti and Do would say, or not of the Covenant, as Koresh would say. Instead, a cult offers divine guidance, which is infallible and absolute.

As we saw in Chapter 1, Émile Durkheim developed useful concepts about suicide that apply here. Remember that Durkheim saw homicide as simply the inverse of suicide; in the latter, one directs the violence toward other people, and in the former, toward oneself. Yet the motivations remain the same. People seek out cults because they experience anomie or fatalism. In the case of anomie, people feel lost in an ocean of possibilities, none clearly better than or even clearly different from the others. Should I take this job or that job? Should I get married again or not? Should I attend this church or that church? Do any of these decisions matter one way or the other, and how would I know? Without a system of values that defines the meaning of life, and thereby places meaningful limits on a person, anomie results. Others, especially younger people in the Manson example, experience fatalism. Given their youth, they could not imagine how their life could ever improve. They all felt forever trapped fulfilling the dreams of parents or the directives of teachers, and unable to live their own life. A few, like Mary Brunner, felt trapped by a dead-end job. Manson offered a release from such mundane, dreary, and hopeless conformity. Both anomie and its opposite, fatalism, create a seeker orientation. To remedy this, cults offer altruism, in Durkheim's terms (see Chapter 1). The person must fully and completely surrender to the leader, and just like the terrorist, become a nameless, faceless part of a larger whole. As O'Brien, the inner party member in George Orwell's *1984*, explains, the individual is finite and meaningless; only the Party is infinite and important. Similarly, an individual only matters so long as he or she is part of a chosen group—the cult. Only the cult and the leader matter, and the members only matter to the extent they fulfill the leader's wishes.

The leader cannot relinquish power once he or she has obtained it. The charismatic illusion lasts only so long as the people fulfill it. Cult leaders do not seize power or brainwash the followers. Rather, the followers must first be seekers, and second, possess issues of ego weakness. Many people are seekers at different points in their lives, searching for meaning. However, only some people suffer from ego weakness—the notion that the self is not sufficiently established to draw boundaries and hold to them. Such people often hold conflicting values they cannot resolve—for example, the desire to do good and cause no harm, but also the desire to break rules and indulge in taboo sensations, especially drugs and experimental sexuality. Most of the time, these conflicts produce no serious or long-term harm. Many people simply live out their lives without ever finding resolution to internal emotional conflicts. However, this can deprive them of some degree of happiness. Most likely, the conflict is rarely pathological, that is, severe enough to disable their performance in other social roles, such as work, family, and friendship.

For some people, however, the desire to break away from an unsatisfying life overpowers other conflicting values, especially moral values. They are willing to suffer any humiliation in order to achieve harmony, even if that harmony, as in the case of a cult, requires negation of the self. This point is crucial, because cults do not resolve emotional conflicts; they only eliminate one side of the conflict. Manson, Applewhite, and Koresh all developed means to negate conventional morality, and all cults develop means to separate people from their past lives and their past identity. In sociological terms, self-negation occurs when the self no longer connects to meaningful reference groups that we all require in order to validate who we think we are. As the early symbolic interactionist Charles Horton Cooley (1864–1929) conceptualized it, the looking-glass self is how we think other people see us, as if looking into a mirror. But this self-image depends on reference-group validation; whether we like or dislike the face in the mirror depends on social acceptance. Erving Goffman (1922–1982), in *Stigma: Notes on the Management of Spoiled Identity* ([1963] 1986), elaborates more extensively, noting that people can imagine nearly anything about themselves, but only those images that other people recognize and legitimate will have any meaning.

Thus, the cult, through the degradation ritual and various reinforcements afterward, separates the person from his or her old reference groups, and binds the person to only one—the cult. Still, such separation and transference would not be possible unless the person lacked a suitably strong identity in the first place. In Goffman's *Asylums* (1961), he studies the ways that people adapt to and cope with the separation from mainstream life and the replacement structure that "total institutions" instill. Although Goffman studied mental institutions, the social aspect of structure and control is similar. The total institution, whether a mental health facility or religious cult, represents a "total" world, one that is self-contained and that manages every aspect of the members' lives. Neither allows any private time, and the individual must conform to the institution's agenda. Everyone conforms to the same agenda—there is no personalization. In this sort of environment, which is its own social world with its own social laws, the inmates become fundamentally different people from who they would be if they lived in mainstream society. In their sociological aspects, total institutions are nearly identical to each other, even if the particular agenda—mental health versus religious devotion—differs. As an undergraduate when I read *Asylums* for the first time, I decided, along with my classmates, that Boston University was almost a total institution. In addition to offering classes, the campus made it possible to never leave. The dorms provided living space—with at least one roommate for each of us, which limited privacy—and all the necessities of life: dining halls, movie theaters, laundry, and—before the drinking age increased from 18 to 21—in-house pubs. The point is that a concept is an analytical tool that can be applied to many different cases that, although different in many regards, share the same underlying conceptual elements. As mentioned in Chapter 1, sociology orders the world through concepts. Goffman did not study cults, but the concept of the total institution and its observed effects on the individual are similar, if not identical, to the way cults govern the individual. Such institutions not only regulate a person's life, but in the process also require the person to internalize the system of control and not just submit, but actively create his or her own regulation. In other words, a person must willfully commit to the institution, not just follow the routines. Is perhaps the military also a total institution? What about prisons? By the way, I thoroughly enjoyed my 4 years at Boston University, and found both my formal education and social experiences enlightening and empowering, so total institutions should not be thought of as inherently disabling or oppressive.

Despite the high degree of control that a total institution like a cult can exert, not everyone responds the same way and becomes a devoted follower. In *Asylums,* Goffman (1961) notes that many patients become dependent on the institution, so much so that they become unable to leave, even when they have mastered their psychological problems or completed their physical therapy. They simply no longer know how to live without the structure and the corresponding roles the total institution provides. In the case of Manson, several hundred people moved through the Spahn Ranch, and several dozen lived there in the months of the murders, but only 8–10 were devoted to Manson sufficiently to follow his every command with great enthusiasm. The others retained enough of their old identity to refuse, and many fled the Family after the murders. A few devoutly stood vigil outside the courthouse throughout the trial, but these eventually dispersed without incident after the verdict and the realization that Manson would be in prison for life.

In the cases of the Branch Davidians and Heaven's Gate, there could be no hangers-on. A person was either in or out, with no in-between ground to think it over. The Branch Davidians lived in a self-contained community in Waco, Texas, outside town, and Heaven's Gate members lived in their own house, but spent much of their time on the road, traveling only with each other. They rarely interacted with anyone outside the cult, and both groups required that new members immediately relinquish money, property, and all ties to past friends and family. This initial separation, even before the degradation rituals, limited the size of the group, but also filtered out insufficiently devoted people. Sociologically, it barred those who were not willing to negate their sense of self.

The cult does not maintain devotion through force or coercion, but more subtly, through desperation. People already desperate for belonging and an end to emotional conflict join a cult and in so doing, become more desperate as it renders them even less able to deal with issues and the vicissitudes of life on their own. They become dependent on the cult, finding they cannot live without the highly structured life a cult provides, and cannot navigate through life's complexities as a free-thinking human being. The cult provides a place in life, and as long as the person maintains that place, he or she feels secure, but the person can never leave. If a devoted member leaves, the person must, from his or her perspective, give up everything the individual has been searching for and start over with no coping skills or frame of reference. The person must turn away from his or her god on earth and return to the world from which they fled in the first place. What would it take for any of us to turn away from our god, and from everyone we have ever loved and who has loved us in return? Would rational realizations about a group and leader provide enough personal strength to stand alone?

CHAPTER **8**

Emergent Religion

The Examples of Neopaganism and New Evangelicalism

Introduction

Much of this book addresses the antisocial side of religion—intolerance, oppression, persecution, and war. In this chapter, we will look at one of the prosocial aspects of religion, through which people find meaning and inspiration. The study of emergent religion is the study of people actively and positively shaping their lives in conjunction with other people, with a hope for a better and more meaningful future. Although emergent religion can include the formation of intolerant beliefs and oppressive dogmas, here we will examine emergent religion as a prosocial response to life's vicissitudes.

An emergent religion differs from an alternative religion in that it is still in the process of taking shape. Specifically, emergent religions have no central organization, no consistent tradition, and unclear types and degrees of commitment. Long-established religions may enter emergent periods now and then, and many religions lack any one of the above criteria. Hinduism has no central organization, for example, but it does have ancient and well-established traditions, each with clear forms and degrees of commitment. Similarly, an alternative religion may be undergoing change, but it will exhibit some established and more or less certain aspects. Voudou, for example, has very clear, established rituals and other modes of devotion.

It is possible that some religions are forever emergent, that they are developed by and exist for people at the individual level, and thus may be whatever the individual desires. As a collective social movement, they never develop consistent beliefs or practices that endure for discernable lengths of time. In this chapter, we discuss one emergent religion (Neopaganism) that has yet to settle down, so to speak, and another (New Evangelicalism) that arose from well-established evangelical congregations and traditions, but which since the late 1970s has become an emergent religion, distinctive from established Evangelicalism. Neopaganism and New Evangelicalism are obviously not similar in beliefs, practices, or political orientation. It is rather their emergent quality that concerns us. Moreover, they are both part of an ongoing tradition of religious innovation and revival that pervades the history of religion in the United States.

Revival and Emergence

Religious revival in the United States since 1990 compares in magnitude to the most intense periods of revival in American history (Finke and Stark 1992; Jenkins 2002). The vast majority of this growth has been conservative and sometimes fundamentalist in the form of New Evangelicalism (discussed below) at the expense of mainline churches (Perrin, Kennedy, and Miller 1997). However, measurable growth has occurred in other, progressive new religions, specifically in Neopaganism (Jorgensen and Russell 1999), and evangelicalism includes less conservative and progressive elements as well. As John Bartkowski (2004) and I (Lundskow 2002) both argue about the Promise Keepers, for example, they constitute in many ways a progressive movement in a very conservative evangelical culture. For both New Evangelicalism and Neopaganism, the vast majority of enthusiasts consciously choose their new faith as a result of dissatisfaction with their mainline beliefs, or dissatisfaction with life in general (Zinnbauer and Pergament 1998). For enthusiasts, discontent in the spiritual side of life results directly from the dissatisfaction and spiritual vacancy that characterizes modern social relations (Dawson 1998a).

Both Neopaganism and New Evangelicalism are modern creations in response to disenchantment within modern society. Neither completely rejects the modern world, and both seek to instill purpose and meaning in life through spirituality coupled with varying types and degrees of criticism about modern life. Although both also express concern for social issues and develop a relevant theology, the movements differ decisively in the culture of the communities they form. The respective belief systems arise from their preferred form of social interaction—as we have already seen throughout history—their preferred form of society. In this sense, both therefore pose a vision of the future because their present orientation takes a highly critical stance toward established social relations. Neither accepts the status quo, and contrary to popular belief, Christian New Evangelicals, even in their most conservative form, grant only tentative allegiance to conservative political leaders, only if and so long as they appear to be authentic conservative Christians. Likewise, Neopagans are politically aware and often engaged in politics, but they also support candidates selectively, and like their conservative counterparts, have no consistent party allegiance.

Thus, both movements constitute a contemporary religious revival. Contemporary revivalists maintain that humans cannot live without some higher and better purpose, some transcendent sense of meaning, nor can they long tolerate a society that functions on empty routine, regardless of the social benefits one accrues in terms of money, fame, power, and so forth. Since both Neopaganism (Jorgensen and Russell 1999) and New Evangelicalism (D. Miller 1997; Perrin, Kennedy, and Miller 1997) consist primarily of educated and middle-income people—neither the lowest members of the economic order nor high enough to assume economic certainty—uncertainty, rather than direct deprivation, defines their social life, which in turn feeds their discontentment about the quality of life and existential issues of meaning.

Neopagans and New Evangelicals both turn to religion of their own choosing in the search for meaning in a world in which economic vicissitude and injustice dominate. Both groups draw members from disaffected members of other religions or the ranks of the nonreligious who purposely seek new alternatives (Gee and Veevers 1990; Jorgensen and Russell 1999; Perrin, Kennedy, and Miller 1997), and both rely primarily on friendship networks rather than intentional proselytizing for recruitment (Raphael 1996; Zinnbauer and Pergament 1998). This has become especially true in the last few years, as megachurches in particular have grown exponentially (C. Smith 2002). Furthermore, of those churches that increased enrollment in the 1990s, face-to-face interaction and friendship networks most strongly influenced new members, regardless of the particular orientation (Roof 1996; Zinnbauer and Pergament 1998). The more personal the interaction, the more successfully new religions bring in new members. In other words, the hunger for real and sincere connections with other people concerning ultimate existential questions inspires people more than any other factor. Stark (1996) contends (in my view, correctly) that the extent to which a religion accommodates the search for meaning, in combination with practical concerns about such things as health, livelihood, and family life, predicts the success or failure of the religion. Stark correctly points out the necessity to theoretically unify idealism and materialism in order to understand new religious appeal in practice.

As we saw in the theory chapter (Chapter 1), religions typically function as a system of social control because religion connects the individual with society by transforming the dominant social values into an apparently transcendent and eternal form. In this way, religion regulates the way and extent to which people feel connected to society and, therefore, to meaning and purpose beyond their own individual existence. If a society is oppressive, then its dominant religion(s) will likely reinforce (or ignore) inequality. Religion and spirituality sometimes coincide, but the presence of one in no way necessitates the existence of the other, particularly in alienated society in which social life becomes a relationship of commodities, and likewise, religion becomes another commodity for sale, void of meaning (Kintz 1997; Ott 2001).

New Evangelicalism and Neopaganism both rebel against precisely this commodification of spirituality, and they seek spontaneity and autonomy in place of religious routinization. Sociologically, both reject religion as simply a routinization of life. In place of religion in the oppressive sense, they seek spontaneous spirituality that expresses their personal and collective hopes, allays their fears, and provides meaning to their lives beyond the daily drudgery of routine functionality.

Neopaganism

The origin of the Witch's Rede or Wiccan Rede is unknown. Although some claim prehistoric origins, it may only date to the following poem published in 1974 in *Green Egg* magazine. Lady Gwen Thompson attributes this poem to her grandmother, Adriana Porter, and claims that it has been passed down through the women of her family for millennia.

Rede of the Wiccae

Being known as the counsel of the Wise Ones:
Bide the Wiccan Laws ye must In Perfect Love and Perfect Trust.
Live an' let live—Fairly take an' fairly give.
Cast the Circle thrice about To keep all evil spirits out.
To bind the spell every time—Let the spell be spake in rhyme.
Soft of eye an' light of touch—Speak little, listen much.
Deosil go by the waxing Moon—Sing and dance the Wiccan rune.
Widdershins go when the Moon doth wane, An' the Werewolf howls by the dread Wolfsbane.
When the Lady's Moon is new, Kiss thy hand to Her times two.
When the Moon rides at Her peak Then your heart's desire seek.
Heed the Northwind's mighty gale—Lock the door and drop the sail.
When the wind comes from the South, Love will kiss thee on the mouth.
When the wind blows from the East, Expect the new and set the feast.
When the West wind blows o'er thee, Departed spirits restless be.
Nine woods in the Cauldron go—Burn them quick an' burn them slow.
Elder be ye Lady's tree—Burn it not or cursed ye'll be.
When the Wheel begins to turn—Let the Beltane fires burn.
When the Wheel has turned a Yule, Light the Log an' let Pan rule.
Heed ye flower bush an' tree—By the Lady Blessèd Be.
Where the rippling waters go, Cast a stone an' truth ye'll know.
When ye have need, Hearken not to others greed.
With the fool no season spend Or be counted as his friend.
Merry meet an' merry part—Bright the cheeks an' warm the heart.
Mind the Threefold Law ye should—Three times bad an' three times good.
When misfortune is enow, Wear the Blue Star on thy brow.
True in love ever be Unless thy lover's false to thee.
Eight words ye Wiccan Rede fulfill—An' it harm none, Do what ye will.

One of the fastest growing and most misunderstood religions today is Neopaganism. This term—used more by scholars than by practitioners—covers any of various earth- or nature-based religions. Much of the controversy surrounding Neopaganism results from the common perception that it equates with Satanism, and that Satanism is itself not just the worship of evil, but the living embodiment of every evil and horror a person can imagine. Mostly, the controversy arises when some people brand Neopagans as evil in order to scapegoat them for all manner of personal and social problems, including delinquency, petty crime, drug and alcohol abuse, failing grades, rape, and murder. Some even claim that Neopagans commit human sacrifice. Such outlandish claims persist despite the fact that the FBI has never documented even one case of ritual rape or murder. In fact, Neopaganism differs completely from Satanism. They represent completely different beliefs and demographic constituents (H. Berger, Leach, and Shaffer 2003; Jorgensen and Russell 1999).

As shown in Figures 8.1–8.3, Neopagans tend to be young, white, and well-educated. Other findings from the Pagan Census (H. Berger et al. 2003) reveal a propensity to accept supernatural occurrences as valid, including

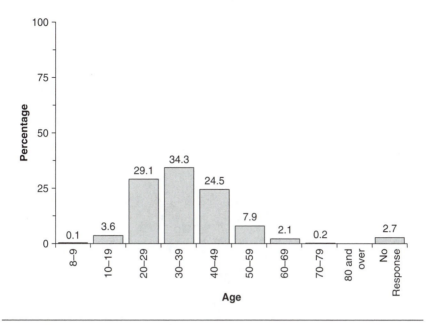

Figure 8.1   Age Breakdown of Neopagans

Source: H. Berger et al. 2003.

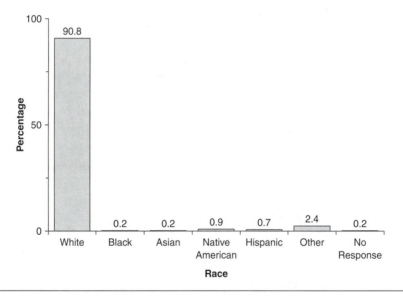

Figure 8.2   Race of Neopagans

Source: H. Berger et al. 2003.

interaction with spirits, supernatural beings, and portents. Moreover, Neopagans hold liberal-leftist political views and, in general, favor moral freedom so long as one's activity does not harm others. This follows from the witches' creed: Do What You Will, but Harm None (see sidebar). See H. Berger et al. for a complete statistical analysis.

Like all living religions, Neopaganism corresponds to the social reality in which the practitioners live. It reflects their desire for community, as well as their political

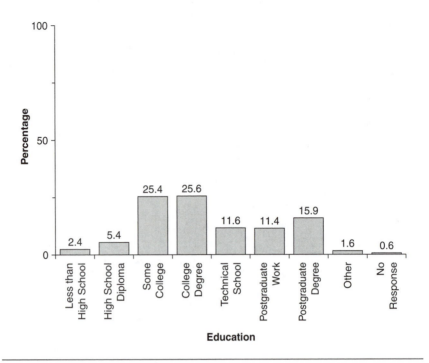

Figure 8.3 Educational Level of Neopagans

Source: H. Berger et al. 2003.

views and overall worldview. Interestingly, political orientation and worldview differ somewhat for practitioners in the United States compared to those in Britain— the home of Celtic culture that inspires Americans and Europeans alike. Despite this common source of inspiration, Britain and the United States are not identical cultures, and correspondingly, American and British Neopaganisms reflect the respective cultural differences and the history of the Neopagan movements.

In both cases, though, practitioners are still constructing a new religion, which they hope will take them beyond the present. Like many religions, it not only sanctifies the present, but also inspires the future.

As mentioned, Neopaganism finds inspiration and spiritual solace in nature. It is also a good example of an emergent religion, that is, a religion that is still in the process of forming its essential characteristics. Although nearly 80% of Neopagans agree that practitioners should have some type of formal training and education about their beliefs, they disagree strongly about how to implement such training and education. Practitioners are more or less equally divided among formal schools, networking, and mentoring relations as the best ways to train and transmit beliefs and practices (H. Berger et al. 2003). This corresponds roughly to differing views on the role of hierarchy and formality, with Neopagans divided among high, middle, and low levels of hierarchy and formality.

The emergent designation refers primarily to beliefs and practices, which are not yet decisively determined, and given the structure of the religion, they may never be. We may also witness the emergence of several different denominations or sects. Certain differences already exist, but none consistently enough to establish clear demarcations. For the most part, scholars discuss one Neopaganism, which consists of different types, yet these are types that have not yet become patterned denominations. In other words, the religion has not developed institutional subgroups.

Ronald Hutton (1999), in his excellent social history of Neopaganism, notes that Neopaganism has become far more diverse in America than in Britain, and Americans actually founded the first Neopagan organization, the Church of Aphrodite, in 1938 (p. 340). Furthermore, some of the diverse American traditions may be entirely separate from those in Britain, as an early study by Vance Randolph (1947) uncovered pagan traditions in the Ozark Mountains, and New Orleans has many pre-Christian traditions and a cultural history that varies greatly from the rest of the country. Yet, Hutton honestly admits that "proper treatment of pagan witchcraft in America . . . far outruns my capabilities and probably would that of any British academic" (p. 340). In the United States, Neopaganism remains for the most part undocumented, a haphazard mélange of competent academic treatises and popular folkloric reconstruction of pagan traditions. The Church of Aphrodite and its West Coast counterpart—the Bohemian Grove—differ significantly from what scholars now call Neopaganism. These two groups are private clubs for wealthy people from certain families. The pagan veneer provides cover for licentiousness and debauchery, a hedonistic escape from their otherwise upstanding and proper public personas, mostly in the business world. In short, the paganistic aspects provide an excuse to party hearty.

As in many religions, Neopagans debate the criteria that constitute authentic practice and distinguish it from superficial and imposter forms. As for authentically spiritual and earth-based practitioners, no one knows for sure, or even with any particular degree of accuracy, how many people in the United States today profess Neopagan spirituality. For various reasons, the number has been difficult to count despite the Pagan Census cited earlier. The reasons appear to be definitional—what constitutes a Neopagan?—and also methodological.

The methodological problems relate directly to definitional problems, in that Neopagans, unlike the

Some Common Types of Neopaganism

Wicca (Witch): Wiccans worship a goddess and a god; they observe the festivals of the eight Sabbats of the year and the full-moon Esbats. Wicca incorporates a specific form of witchcraft, with particular ritual forms involving the casting of spells, herbalism, divination, and other forms of magic.

Alexandrian Wicca: Emphasis on ceremonial magic and gender polarity. High priest and priestess with equal but gender-differentiated power.

Dianic Wicca: A feminist variation in which devotees perceive the goddess as complete by herself; they do not worship the god at all.

Shamanism: Animistic beliefs and focus on transcendent realms of perception and experience

Druidism: Premised on communion with nature. Holds living (e.g., animals, plants) and nonliving (e.g., rocks, rivers) natural forms as sacred. Centered on a formally trained caste of priests

Hellenic Revivalism: Reveres the ancient Greco-Roman pantheon. Also embraces the ancient philosophic and artistic tradition. Offers sacrifices in the form of libations and feasts; does not practice blood sacrifice

Kemetic Orthodoxy: Named after Kemet, the name of Egypt in the ancient language, practitioners revere the Egyptian pantheon.

Unitarian-Universalist (UU) Pagan: Relatively few UU's are pagan, but those who are integrate paganism (especially Wicca) with Christianity and sometimes Judaism, based on 1 Samuel 28, in which King Saul consults the Witch of Endor, who summons the ghost of the prophet Samuel. Other passages, however, condemn mysticism and witchcraft, such as Leviticus 20:27, which says that any who consult with or practice witchcraft shall be stoned to death.

scholars who study them (who agree on the term Neopagan), differ on their definition. Many people whom scholars would identify as Neopagan would not ordinarily recognize that designation. In addition to the many particular identities—Wiccan, Dianic, and so on—which some see as only remotely if at all related, others might acknowledge a Neopagan spirituality as such, yet within the bounds of an established faith, and not as a separate religion. Thus, they identify, for example, as Unitarian-Universalist or as Buddhist rather than as Neopagan. Others profess no group affiliation, but see themselves as self-taught witches, druids, and so forth. Some are simply suspicious of any attempts to ascertain Neopagan affiliation, given the sometimes hostile atmosphere they encounter, while others intentionally thwart quantitative assessment—always a problem in survey research. As one pagan male stated in an interview with the Berger team, "It seems like you are trying to get data to create a general picture of pagans—that's bullshit!" (H. Berger et al. 2003). The mere desire to conceptualize neopaganism sometimes generates hostility.

Many pagans also fear persecution, and thus are reluctant to publicly declare their faith. Sampling becomes much more effective if a researcher gains inside access and face-to-face credibility as part of the survey process. For most surveys about most topics, mail forms usually suffice, sent to a randomly selected sample. Such anonymous methods prove much less effective if the survey requires a person to declare something that might arouse public stigma, even if the researchers keep the respondent's identity secret. In addition to problems of nomenclature, researchers also need to establish a rapport with potential respondents to achieve a representative sample.

Thus, as a result of all these factors, numerical estimates of Neopagan affiliation in the United States range from 100,000 to over a million. One scientific study estimates 250,000–500,000 (Jorgensen and Russell 1999), but the anti-authoritarian nature of most Neopagans and the diverse fluidity of Neopagan identity make more exact determinations difficult. A more recent study (Magliocco 2004) concludes that there are about 700,000 Neopagans. The Pagan Census attempts no total number of pagans, but instead reports on attitudes about a variety of issues. However, the report also focuses on official pagan organizations, such as the Covenant of the Unitarian-Universalist Pagans, the Elflore Family, and others. While certainly these groups are important to the movement, the majority of pagans do not belong to such groups, and instead favor local organizations, groups formed from friendship networks, or solitary practice (Jorgensen and Russell 1999; Pike 2001). Indeed, Sarah Pike discovered that pagan festivals draw many solitary practitioners who find special meaning and religious revival at these events. They depend on these extraordinary moments to maintain exuberance in their pagan religion, for which they otherwise have no shared experience.

No absolute line exists between superficial or New Age practitioners and "authentic" or lifestyle practitioners. "Authentic" Neopagans contend that New Age pagans randomly and nonchalantly blend various influences, mostly at a superficial level, and lack a deeper emotional and intellectual (lifestyle) commitment. As one pagan argues, New Age is "a very shallow approach to everything, taken without any real context or understanding. . . . [I]t also seems to have been stripped of anything that might really challenge people or make them uncomfortable—yes, you too can achieve total enlightenment in about an hour!" (quoted in Pike 2001:145). As Sarah

Pike concludes in her analysis, New Agers pursue "worry-free knowledge" (p. 145) that does not require them to take a moral position on anything, nor reflect on their own behavior. As Pike found in her studies of Neopagan festivals, pagans struggle over many issues, including authority, alcohol, drugs, social justice, and the environment, as well as their own conduct at festivals. Although moral codes differ, everyone agrees that Paganism requires the practice of morality (H. Berger et al. 2003).

Beliefs and History

Table 8.1 illustrates the major holidays that Neopagans celebrate, although we should remember that the concept of Neopagan is academic and includes many different beliefs and practices.

The beliefs among American Neopagans are diverse and currently undocumented in a scholarly fashion. However, all three communities in this study (introduced below) draw much of their theology from a particular tradition of feminist and green spirituality. Arguably, the strong green and feminist elements with a generally progressive political stance distinguish American Neopaganism from its mainly British antecedents, which have often been nationalistic and politically conservative (see Hutton 1999 for an exhaustive treatment of British Neopaganism).

Generally, contemporary Neopagans construct their beliefs as rediscoveries of lost beliefs. However, Neopagans such as Margot Adler ([1979] 2006) and Starhawk ([1982] 1997) contend that Neopaganism did not die, nor was it destroyed by zealous Christians (although they continue to try), but in fact it has survived to the present in rural areas of Britain, continental Europe, and now in the United States. Starhawk in particular argues that Christianity and capitalism together negated Neopagan spiritual values of tolerance, sharing, balance, and especially harmony with nature and nonhuman species. As we saw in Chapter 2, there is some scholarly support for this thesis. But whatever the particular beliefs, the general point remains that Neopagans today emphasize that their beliefs are ancient—descended from an earlier and better form of social organization. In this section, I do not

Table 8.1 Neopagan Holidays

Fall	Winter	Spring	Summer
Fall Equinox (around September 21) Also called Michaelmas.	Winter Solstice (around December 21) Also called Christmas, Yule.	Spring Equinox (around March 21) Also called Ostara. Sometimes celebrated with Easter, St. Patrick's Day.	Summer Solstice (around June 21)
Samhain (October 31–early November) Also called Halloween, All Hallow's Eve, All Saint's Day, Day of the Dead.	Candlemas (Early-mid-February) Also called Imbolc. Sometimes celebrated with Mardi Gras, Lent.	Beltane (late April–early May) Also called Walpurgis Night. This is the celebration that features the famous Maypole dancing.	Lammas (early August)

attempt to comprehensively catalog the details of Neopagan beliefs. Rather, I will briefly cover the features that most distinguish it from other religions.

Magic, as described earlier, is an essential element of pagan religions today. For most, magic is both an intuitive and objectively rational process of influencing events. Just as understanding can occur on different levels and from different perspectives, so magic, found in many cultures, exists both as a real force, and as a symbolic representation of a larger and complex process of interconnectedness.

Like almost all communities, Neopagans celebrate certain holidays, although given the nonhierarchical nature of the religion, the particular names and dates vary tremendously. Neopagan traditions are nature-based, and thus holidays correspond to changes in nature. The major holidays fall on summer and winter solstices, the fall and spring equinoxes, and the midpoints in between these events.

Central to Neopagan spirituality is the justification of the belief that, although ancient, prehistoric pagans recognized essential truths about life and existence that we have since lost and ought to rediscover. Once people realize the basic truth of interconnectedness, then they will realize that cooperation and equality are not only morally superior, but also more practical than hierarchical forms of social organization, because cooperation is more in accordance with the natural order and interconnectedness of things. Yet Neopagans do not reject science or modern ways of thinking; rather, they believe that people should not commit exclusively to one way and neglect all others.

American Neopaganism typically holds nature-goddess worship and nonhierarchy as sacred notions, handed down or rediscovered from prehistoric times. My purpose here is not to challenge the validity or accuracy of Neopagan beliefs, except to say that paganism today is contemporary, not ancient (see Hutton 1991, 1999 for a very detailed discussion). It is today constructed as a living, vital spirituality that corresponds to the lives of real people, to their jobs, their families, their thoughts, dreams, and feelings. In other words, Neopaganism, as distinct from ancient paganism, is a contemporary social construction that continues to unfold and develop; it is not an archaeological relic.

Neopaganism is not just new paganism; it is *very* new. Hutton (1999) places its advent in the mid-twentieth century, the outcome of writings by Aleister Crowley, Robert Graves, and especially the organizing activities of Gerald Gardner (1950s and 1960s). Gardner presented the term "Wica" in his 1954 book *Witchcraft Today,* which set forth many of the common features of Neopaganism (Hutton 1999:241) and became a sort of standard guideline for later authors in the "Wicca" tradition as it is known today. However, all of these people (and others) drew their imagery and mythology from earlier cultural traditions and events going backward through consecutive events to the Middle Ages, to organizations that had nothing to do with paganism or religion (see Hutton 1999 for a an extremely detailed historical treatise). Gerald Gardner invented much of the ritual that characterizes Neopaganism generally. As mentioned, Neopagans in the British Isles were, in contrast to later American versions, often patriotic and capitalist—sentiments that derive from two powerful hierarchies.

In the United States, fictional and theological works would reshape Neopaganism at its core into an antihierarchical, pro-environmental, and feminist spirituality (Eller 1993), which now finds equal appeal among men and women. However, as I found in my own interviews, most enthusiasts learned about Neopaganism through friendship networks, and only later began reading about newfound spirituality that already appealed to them. In other words, most people do not convert in the sense of changing their views, but rather, find that Neopaganism corresponds to or affirms feelings and views they already have. Thus, the two American Neopagan theologians I will cover in detail, Margot Adler and Starhawk, are significant here because they have exerted by far the greatest influence on American Neopaganism (Pike 2005).

The overall coherence among Neopagans on two major points—feminist and nature-centered spirituality (both expressions of interconnectedness)—is not coincidental. Neopagans often share ideas through friendship networks, and especially now through the Internet. They tend to read far more than the general public and treasure knowledge in diverse areas (Matthews 1995). Moreover, women's issues and the environment are typically important for anyone who considers himself or herself progressive or alternative in one way or another. In the 1980s and 1990s, Neopagan novelists and theologians presented a general but coherent vision of Neopagan spirituality, which in America centered on notions of nature, the goddess, awareness of social issues, and progressive social change. This latter aspect in particular distinguishes American from British Neopaganism, and arguably marks a decisive separation between the two.

Adler and Starhawk draw on other writers, both Neopagan authors (especially Gardner) and social theorists and critics. Moreover, they add a spiritual element to existing social criticism, documented history, and folklore. Both continue to update their most important books and to represent the sentiments of Neopagans generally. Thus, they are not authoritative leaders so much as published Neopagan theologians and social critics of modern society. Let us look at them each more closely.

Margot Adler

One of the first and most influential attempts to map the Neopagan landscape was Margot Adler's ([1979] 2006) *Drawing Down the Moon*. Through personal experience, anecdotes, and survey research, Adler identifies various versions of Neopaganism and offers examples of actual practice—chants, poems, incantations, and descriptions of rites and rituals. Her compilation, though relatively thorough, nevertheless constructs a particular perspective on Neopaganism. Specifically, she places it within an urban, educated, white, liberal or progressive culture, which contemporary research confirms (H. Berger 2003; Jorgensen and Russell 1999). She excludes Caribbean and African traditions that include animal sacrifice, such as Santeria and Voudou, or other faiths that rely upon patriarchal values and hierarchical domination of the strong and privileged over the weak, such as ancient Central and South American traditions. The Aztecs, as is well-known, conducted human sacrifice.

Thus, Adler's early work promotes a progressive version of Neopaganism that decisively breaks from indigenous American and folk traditions, and precludes paganistic but reactionary groups such as Odinism. Although it sometimes draws on the symbolism of past societies, including ancient Britain, Egypt, Greece, and

Rome, Adler's depiction becomes typically modern—an intentionally constructed set of beliefs to support a particular political or social agenda. As she says, most people come to Neopaganism because it "confirms some original, private experience" (Adler [1979] 2006:14) and corroborates attitudes and hopes they have felt all along. In short, it provides a name and social context for preconceived attitudes that arise from personal experience.

Moreover, Adler displays typically modern rationality. Neopaganism becomes a conscious and rational tool to facilitate change, whether personal or social. In this way, she engineers the deities of Neopaganism into metaphors, whereas folk beliefs like Santeria worship actual and very materially real gods and goddesses. Voudou accepts that gods can literally possess people, speak through them, and control their actions, and that possession can occur malevolently as well as by invitation from the possessed. In Adler's and also in Starhawk's Neopaganism, the material existence of deities is indeterminate at best, and few of the Neopagans I have interviewed believe that the Goddess (or any number of named gods and goddesses) are actual, coherent, and autonomous beings.

Finally, Adler ([1979] 2006) cites creativity as the essential element to Neopaganism. Consistent with her rationalist approach, that "most revivalist witches in North America accept the universal Old Religion more as metaphor than as a literal reality—a spiritual truth more than a geographic one" (p. 86), she further emphasizes that Neopagans of her own ilk reject dogmatic beliefs and routinized practice. In short, they reject tradition in the sociological sense, that is, the institutionalization of spirituality—religion. Tradition is, by definition, the practice of doing things the way they have always been done, without question. Most Neopagans reject unquestioning obedience, replacing it with living, dynamic, and creative beliefs, tailored to contemporary issues and daily life.

Whether a person ought to be a traditionalist or a creativist is an issue for the individual, not a sociologist. Rather, sociological significance depends on the exact type of social relationship that beliefs and practice establish and legitimate. Below, we will examine living Neopagan communities.

In conclusion, Adler outlines the general beliefs and practices of Neopagans and establishes what does and does not constitute Neopaganism. Most important, she establishes American Neopaganism as progressive, creative, and nonhierarchical, all of which contrast sharply with its British antecedents, which in both the Gardnerian and Alexandrian variations reaffirm mostly mainstream or conservative politics (or avoid politics altogether) and practice their faith through religious hierarchy. Adler moves away from this model, and Starhawk, whom I will discuss next, moves still farther toward the progressive and nonhierarchical, activist orientation as she develops a much more concise and detailed Neopagan theology.

Starhawk

Among Neopagan theologians, Starhawk (real name, Miriam Simos) is probably foremost. Through a series of books, she draws connections between environmental and social issues, in combination with feminist activism and even classical social theorists such as Karl Marx, Herbert Marcuse, Max Weber, and Simone de Beauvoir.

A very talented, intellectual, and passionate writer, knowledgeable in a range of areas, Starhawk nevertheless constructs an accessible, intriguing, and practical spirituality. Often very eloquent and stirring, Starhawk combines social criticism with self-reflection, science with emotion, reason with passion. In her view, Neopaganism became a means to add spirituality to her Marxist-feminist commitments, and in the process, I suggest, she invented a unique version that decisively distinguishes American Neopaganism from its British antecedents and other contemporary spiritual movements.

Sociologically, Starhawk exemplifies the social construction of belief; by integrating elements from existing perspectives through her own creativity, Starhawk has devised a sophisticated spirituality to address vital issues of the modern age—inequality, poverty, pollution, and especially alienation. For those who find no solace in established churches and in general feel like outsiders in their own society, Starhawk's Neopaganism offers a spirituality that comforts and empowers the individual through a criticism of the society that rejects sensitivity and diversity. From the outset, she frames social alienation in terms of spirituality:

> Even the small acts that ordinarily bring us pleasure or comfort become tinged at moments with horror. There are time when I walk down the street, and smile at the man who sits on his front stoop playing the radio, and the kids laying pennies on the streetcar tracks, and the woman whose dog plays with my dogs, but in between the blinks they are gone. I see the flash, and then nothing is left—of these charmingly painted Victorian houses, of these ordinary people, or the features of the earth beneath the streets. Nothing—but ashes and a scorched, black void.
>
> I know that I am not alone in being overwhelmed at times by hopelessness and despair. . . . Everybody's personal pain is touched by this greater uncertainty: we are no longer confident of leaving a better world, of leaving a *living* world, to our children.
>
> Yet the children must be fed, the dogs must be walked, the work must go on, so we raise the barriers that defend us from unbearable pain, and in a state of numbness and denial we go on. The work may seem flat, but we carefully avoid questioning its meaning and usefulness, even though we sense that something deep and sweet is missing from our lives, our families, our friendships; some sense of purpose and power is gone. (Starhawk [1982] 1997:2–3)

In subsequent sections of the book quoted above, Starhawk ([1982] 1997) challenges the mechanistic worldview that each person and thing is a separate and isolated entity, available for use and manipulation. Furthermore, the power to isolate and alienate—or as she says, to estrange people from each other and from nature—is "power over," a type of domination that is "ultimately, the power of the gun and the bomb" (p. 3). In its place, Starhawk calls for power from within—not the ability to dominate and control, but the power to be able to do things: "The power we feel writing, weaving, working, creating, making choices, has nothing to do with threats of annihilation" (p. 3). Thus, she condemns the mechanistic worldview that inherently negates spiritual feeling because it privileges separation and isolation and the idea that difference is always a matter of better and worse. This in turn supports domination—men over women, white over black, industry over nature and each against all—the essence of modern society. Although people still work and live in social relationships, they are relationships of inequality in which the many serve the interests of the few, in which people work according to the designs of others, and in which people lose a sense of meaning.

In its place, Starhawk proposes a worldview of immanence—that meaning and the ability to do things reside in each person, yet each person requires cooperation with others in order to realize his or her unique and collective potential. Clearly influenced by Marx, Starhawk is both an idealist and a materialist—individual and social problems derive from both the way people think and the way people actually live. For example, she writes,

> The split between culture and nature determines the character of work itself. It is no coincidence that so-called industrial discipline began to be imposed on labor in the late sixteenth and seventeenth centuries when the workplace began to be split from the home, when women were gradually driven out of many types of productive work, and when the revenge against nature was played out in the Witchburnings. In a mechanistic society, whether capitalist or communist, our underlying conception of work is that mothering, nurturing, feeling should be excluded. (Starhawk [1982] 1997:77)

Furthermore, in our mechanistic world, everything that makes us unique individuals and human beings should be excised. Domination becomes increasingly complete and secure to the extent that it becomes impersonal and unfeeling. Yet to the extent we deny our emotions and the ability to feel the condition of others, we negate and disempower our own self, and in the extreme forms become simply a tool of outside forces—the employer; the pursuit of wealth, power, and profit; popularity; or even a tool of the Holocaust. In short, we become alienated. As Starhawk ([1982] 1997) elaborates:

> This alienation is no accident. Our economic and political systems, our science and technology, are rooted in our alienation from our own bodies and from the realms of deep feeling. The imposition of the puritan ethic in the seventeenth century and the denigration of sexuality that accompanied the Witchburnings created conditions in which capitalism was fostered and peasant classes were forced into alienating wage labor. Today, as long as we remain cut off from the sources of deep feeling in our lives, we remain avid consumers of packaged substitutes for feeling that can be sold at a profit to a mass market. (p. 137)

Thus, the domination of women, the exploitation of nature, and other consequences of mechanism result from both ideology, the belief that women should be restricted to domestic labor, and material interests, that workers must discipline themselves according to the directives and priorities of the employer's need for profit, and as consumers we must conform to the calculated sentimentality of mass market culture. In order to create change, people must recognize the power from within—the ability to accomplish things as free thinkers who willingly accept responsibility, not just conform to external authority. This recognition requires a spiritual sensibility of self-empowerment. Since Starhawk draws a direct connection between all types of exploitation, she similarly creates a spirituality that challenges all forms of exploitation—the domination of man over man and man over woman (and nature). In other words, she creates a feminist and socialist spirituality. In another book, *The Spiral Dance* ([1979] 1999), Starhawk uses "the dance" as a metaphorical expression and celebration of the unity between masculine and feminine, mind and body, civilization and nature. As a metaphor, it refers both to personal lifestyle, as well as collective values that govern association and interaction.

But why pagan? She doesn't exclude the possibility of reform within Christianity, and in reality, some Christian denominations accept and even embrace Neopaganism—the Unitarian-Universalists in particular—as a productive form of spirituality. But Starhawk requires more than spiritual reform, because she links oppressive social reality with spiritual malaise. Consequently, her spirituality includes an inherent social activism, and in order to change society, in which privileged groups will not willingly relinquish power, something stronger than reform is required.

Two aspects emerge. First, people must rediscover authentic passion, the power of true love, and the spontaneous emotions that arise within each of us in relationship to other people. Although hierarchical society allows and even promotes feelings associated with domination, such as anger, hatred, and the corresponding action necessary to maintain inequality—violence—progressive change requires that we rediscover the unity of passion and physical sensuality. Specifically,

> Sexuality is the way we, as adults, experience this particular dance, deep in the caves of the body. For in sex we merge, give way, become one with another, allow ourselves to be caressed, pleasured, enfolded, allow our sense of separation to dissolve. But in sex we also feel our impact on another, see our own faces reflected in another's eyes, feel ourselves confirmed, and sense our power, as separate human beings, to make another feel. (Starhawk [1982] 1997:138)

If passion and sexuality are separated—that is, alienated—then people reduce each other to simply sexual objects, such that we dehumanize each other and in so doing, lose the feeling of reciprocation. Sex then becomes an empty act, or even worse, an act of selfish domination premised on separate and private rather than mutual and collective satisfaction and joining together.

For Starhawk, sexuality represents a special kind of power because it is potentially the most intimate and most gratifying aspect of human existence. In true sexuality as she describes above, people find their own complete selves as well as find others as complete human beings; they share an intensely spiritual moment. If people begin to work for true sexuality rather than superficial sex, they will work toward and demand authenticity in other aspects of life. In the language of feminism, the personal becomes the basis of political action.

Essential Characteristics of Neopaganism in the United States

- Worship of nature, either directly or through representative symbols, often in the form of deities
- The belief in magic as a practical and symbolic means of effecting change and influencing events, based on the real and symbolic concept of interconnectedness
- Progressive social politics, focused primarily but not exclusively on women's issues, the environment, and social justice

In addition, Starhawk contends that our current culture and economic system reinforce each other, and that our spiritual system, namely Christianity, supports patriarchy, domination, and "power over." Reforming Christianity cannot take us far enough, because it would leave the essence of the system intact. Starhawk basically calls for a social revolution, of which spiritual revolution is one aspect. In contrast to the familiar and comfortable Christian symbols (Jesus on the cross, the halo, the Bible), paganism offers familiar but discomforting symbols (magic, the coven, the Goddess, the Horned God). Symbols are also concepts and representations of ideology that govern identity, and in turn govern social relations and behavior. Thus, to embrace and reclaim pagan symbols means to challenge the established order, to say in effect that I choose something different, something contrary to conventional beliefs, and I will not submit to externally imposed meaning, but rather will create my own meaning and my own spirituality. With this, we will create a new community. And I'm not the only one; there are others with me.

The problem still remains: How does Neopaganism so constructed integrate free-thinking individuals who do not submit to external authority? The answer becomes relatively simple. People always need other people; it is an essential fact of being human. Points of contention concern the terms on which people will interact. Neopaganism, with an absence of formal doctrine, requires the active participation of individual practitioners and the active construction of belief. Given the possibility of free association premised on collective respect, people will endeavor to support the group, which includes compromise and tolerance, because their individual identity depends to a great extent on continued free association. In short, people learn and practice self-control from within, rather than through submission to an external authority.

For Neopagans, all things, including people, are part of and dependent upon the natural world. Thus, the "worship" of nature becomes a life practice and not an isolated or abstract event. The worship of nature is a spiritual practice that influences daily living, not a religious ritual. Concern for nature is a moral issue, and thus is both a spiritual and practical concern because Neopagan spirituality unites values and actual behavior. To worship nature is to worship the social world as a constituent of the natural world, but Neopagans also celebrate the diversity of existence, in that existence consists not only of society and nature in broad terms, but also the individuals that populate it.

Ethnographic Testimonies—Original Research

Published here for the first time are ethnographic examples I have collected over the last several years. They illustrate the Neopagan worldview, as well as views about particular issues and attempts to live according to pagan beliefs. All the names are changed, and some people are represented here as amalgams of several people, all in order to preserve anonymity and ensure a fully representative depiction. All of the quoted interview material, however, is presented as recorded. In one community, people live in a collective household, meant to serve as a working model of an urban pagan community. Although the interviews were gathered in three different cities, they are presented here collectively.

Balthasar strikes one as the classic—and quite intentional—dark, mysterious, Neopagan stereotype. With naturally pale skin, he wears only black clothes, except on special occasions he also wears red and purple, and he has numerous gothic tattoos. His views in general represent the foundations of the community. The exact beliefs are, for the most part, unimportant. Rather, the community identifies itself according to a few general principles, as Balthasar explained:

> Probably the most basic point is "do what you will, but harm no one." This is the essence of life, the essence of being human. Most religions place formal restrictions on actions. In Christianity, for example, most, and I might even say all of the doctrine is based on "thou shalt not do this, thou shalt not do that," and so on. But how do you live under that system? Under a system that is based on denying everything? On condemning everything in thought, word, and deed as they say. Well, it makes people very unhappy, to say the least. So instead, paganism celebrates life, and all the things that people can do with other people: talk, travel, argue, enjoy meals, have sex, make music, whatever. For me, and for most of the people I would consider part of the community, music, good music, is always spiritual. It is one of the most powerful things that people can do together, even if one person plays and only one person listens, they are still making music together. For me, my music only means something because other people hear it. And that's why it's so important to "harm no one," because we need other people to complete ourselves. I think, needless to say, if you do harm to others, you drive people away, and then you will never get the acknowledgment that I matter to someone; they want to be with me. It's very chilling if you think about [it], to be alone.

The particular rituals are not very noteworthy either, and most respondents practice rituals described generally by Adler, Starhawk, and other writers.

Of all the ritual practices that might distinguish Neopaganism from other religions, perhaps no single practice captures the attention of outsiders more than that of nudity. Outsiders tend to focus on (and often misunderstand) the role of nudity in Neopaganism. Balthasar explained that

> it's a lot more important to some people than others. I was really into it at one time, because it seemed like one of the most radical things to do if you want to offend conservatives or your parents or whoever. Over several years, though, I still practice it once and a while [sic], and I know a lot of groups still premise a lot of their ritual on being naked, but my attitude now is completely indifferent,

unless nudity itself becomes a focus, and that's not what Wicca is about for me. I think sometimes that younger practitioners become too focused on nudity, and they lose track of the more important spiritual aspects. I think people eventually outgrow being naked as a main feature of their ritual.

Ashur, a 27-year-old woman with jet black hair and porcelain white skin, says,

Nudity is important for me because it does set us apart from other religions. But by itself it doesn't really mean anything. I think it feels really good to be outside and naked under the night sky, with a soft wind, surrounded by your coven. Sensuality is a big part of being a witch for me, and it's important to celebrate the fact that we're sensual and sexual beings. Nudity is always optional with us, though, because not everyone is comfortable being naked, for different reasons. A lot of women especially have major issues with their bodies, and I know at least one man who was afraid he would get an erection in front of everyone, and he didn't want to make us uncomfortable. One girl who has been in the coven for a while now, is 25 I think and absolutely gorgeous, but she has a problem with her body and her self-image so she keeps her clothes on, and I mean all the way on—jeans, top, boots, everything. Some people just go topless. We have 13 members right now, and no, that's not intentional, and usually about 10 go naked, two are topless and the one I said stays fully dressed. One of the topless women thinks she's overweight and ugly, but I think she's really curvy and beautiful. Anyway, I think she also still buys into the mainstream idea that sex organs are dirty, but that's her thing. For any of us to get hung up on "nudity" is to miss the point of being a witch.

Which is?

To explore the mysteries [birth, death, love] of life. I know that's an official kind of answer, but a person can make it as simple or as complex as they want. For me, and for everyone in my coven, it's a life journey that occupies everything we do. To explore the meaning of existence, which is really what the mysteries are about, is the essence of witchcraft. We have traditions and rituals and things passed down through the ages, but each witch still has to explore life for herself, or himself, to turn tradition into investigation and action. One thing I want to say is that it's more than reading, even though education is a big part of it. It's just as much about experience and living all aspects of life—mental, physical, sexual, spiritual. And having fun is a necessary part of it. There's no reason why life should be drudgery, and if it is drudgery then that really limits what a person can achieve because they don't have the freedom to discover the mysteries of life. Learning magic is important, too.

Do you believe in magic as a real force that can change reality?

Yes, but not in the way I think you mean. Is there magic that can turn a car into a horse by waving a magic wand and saying the magic words? Of course not. Magic is a power to inspire people to do things with the belief that change is possible, that we can actually accomplish something. Spells and incantations are a way to focus the mind and raise energy levels.

Regarding nudity, some take a more practical approach. One respondent said, "There's no way I'm going to stand naked out there on the shores of the North Atlantic at night. Even in summer it's chilly at night."

Tall and muscular, Nightshade is one of the most intellectual and outspoken pagans I interviewed. She offers some thoughts about the healing power of pagan spirituality, which for her is also specifically feminist:

> Some women are just so fucked up they can't see things clearly. I mean, when you've been abused all your life or enough that you are traumatized, and this goes for men too, you feel so shitty about yourself that you start looking for people to go on treating you like shit. What can you do? I think all we can do is welcome them into our hearts, even though you know they're going to fuck up again, and in the same way, again and again. I think S&M [sado-masochism], or sleeping around, or any degrading thing is the kind of thing that people do when they have low self-esteem and aren't able to accept someone as a real person, only as an object for some empty thrill. They especially can't accept themselves.

What, then, is the solution? What do you think can help them?

> Love. I know that sounds really flaky, but there is a lot of risk and responsibility in that. It means you care about somebody enough to forgive them, and to have the patience that they may *never* change, but that you hope they will. They might disappoint you a hundred times, but they deserve one more chance, and then one more. . . . [E]verybody has the potential to be a unique person, and every time we as a society lose someone, that is one more person who never lived.

Is there ever a point where you say, enough?

> Well, you shouldn't let someone drag you down and wreck your life. It depends on each person, how strong you are and what you can handle. A couple of these girls that live here now are still basically fucked up, but I think they are a lot better than they would be somewhere else. They are something this house can handle, and they are responding. I mean, they're a lot more interesting than having some conventional square live here who never causes trouble but never says anything interesting either. . . . Basically, every individual matters, and we— everyone collectively—has a responsibility to reach out. Love is also about a lot more than sexuality or even intimacy. I don't let Tara walk on me, but I love her enough to want her to stay here, and she can actually be a blast sometimes. People and relationships are messy and difficult, but they can also be exciting.

Overall, the community strongly supports the notion of free individuals who unify around shared values of respect and mutual affirmation through collective living. In a Neopagan community, the interests of the individual and the interests of the collective mutually reinforce each other, yet the community does not subsume the individual, but rather, creates the opportunity to explore one's individuality by freeing the person from privation, whether material or emotional.

Since community members cherish their alternative spiritual identity as the source and inspiration for alternative living, politics, and so on, many are sensitive to outside distortion of or attack on their beliefs. In regards to the notion that Neopagans promote devil worship, or conduct ritual abuse or human sacrifice, Nightshade says,

> Do I really need to say anything about it? Human sacrifice?! Give me a fucking break! When I see that kind of crap, I can't believe it. The people here are the sweetest, most loving people I have ever known, and some of them don't care about Pat Robertson or Jack Chick or whoever says shit like that, but it makes me really angry. They can't stand it that some people have discovered a better way to live, that Christianity is bullshit and has been oppressing people for hundreds of years. I think on some level that conservative Christians do realize the travesty of their own lives and the emptiness of their faith, but they're afraid to move beyond it, so they attack us, or anything they don't understand or are afraid of. They imagine all these bizarre images, which I think are really their own repressed fantasies, I mean, right-wing Christians aren't known for their relaxed, tolerant lifestyle, so they have all this repressed sexual energy which they vent as hate.

One couple showed me into their apartment, which, although nearly empty of furniture, was filled with knives, swords, armor, and other metal works. "Have you ever met real Smiths before?" SunBlaze asked, a short, 30-something woman with bright red hair, freckled skin, and taught, sinewy muscles. She and her partner, Hephaistos (Heffy to friends), married in an Alexandrian pagan ceremony, which as they explained, is actually recognized by law because it was performed by a legally recognized Unitarian-Universalist minister. Heffy is tall and lanky, with brown hair tied back in a long ponytail, overalls, and heavy work boots. His hands are toughened from his work, yet his manner is very refined and soft-spoken. SunBlaze chose her name because she likes to celebrate the sun, and light, and warmth. "I hate the cold, and I don't really like the feel of night air," she says.

The couple makes custom weapons, armor, and other pieces that range in price from about $300 for high-quality but unadorned items, to over $5000 for intricate items. A full suit of handmade plate armor can be $30,000. All are unique and are made to the specifications of the buyer. They own a real, hand-bellowed forge and a small house in a small bayou town in southern Louisiana in a Native American community. Heffy says, "The Indians understand our beliefs better than most people. We share a lot in our respect for nature, the continuity of all things."

SunBlaze explains that

> we try to live as much outside the system as possible. Beliefs don't mean anything if you don't live by them. I was one of those D&D [Dungeons and Dragons] geeks in high school, and then I read [Margot] Adler and a few other

people, and wished I could make swords and worship nature and not contribute to the capitalist system. So I studied with Heffy and we got married, and well, here we are. It's not always easy, because sometimes we sell a lot of pieces and sometimes we don't sell as many, but we've never gone hungry.

How does your lifestyle represent your beliefs?

Heffy: It's freedom, as free as anyone can be. We have the community here in New Orleans [Gaia Spirit] and the community in [bayou town] and we know people all over the country.

SunBlaze: Nobody can be totally free in the sense that they have no commitments or obligations. It is never possible to live in total freedom unless you prey on other people, you know, make a living by appropriating from others. For us, our work is as direct as you can get, as direct as a farmer. Paganism is all about self-expression, living on your own terms but respectful of others. Whenever we hire other people, they get a share of the profits, not just some meager wage. In our household, and among most of the people we know, everything is split evenly, or according to need. The master and slave relationship is the worst there is, and it comes in many forms, like the capitalist and the worker, like the man and the woman in a patriarchal marriage, like the Christian God and his worshippers. It's all basic submission and domination.

Heffy: And it's not easy to get away from, especially if your society is based inherently on one or more of those master/slave relationships, like the U.S. is. But the point is not just to escape things you don't like, but to be something, and for us, smithing is a way to be individual, to be creative, and to work for ourselves. If you do it the way we do, it's also a way to get in touch with Gaia [the earth goddess] . . . [T]he forge is stone, with a hand bellows. Different combinations of coal, wood, herbs . . . give you different types of flames. It's all very earthy and heavy and woody and dirty, but rewarding.

SunBlaze: But it's not as crunchy-granola either as he's making it out to be. It is definitely spiritual, but you have to know a lot about metallurgy and alloys and other things. The type of alloys we use were unknown in medieval times. They would just freak out over the quality of metal we work with today.

Is your life pagan in particular?

SunBlaze: Totally. We aren't just Smiths; it's being Smiths in relationship to cycles of the season, to particular festivals and celebrations—all things, like rhythms of life that a pagan observes. Mardi Gras is one of the most important spiritually, and New Orleans is one of the most important and intense spiritual centers on earth. It is a mixing pot of different traditions, and I think it's a center of Gaia energy.

Heffy: Now who's being crunchy? Gaia energy? . . . But seriously, Mardi Gras was a pagan festival of rebirth long before it was taken over by the Catholic Church. It was originally a celebration of people and the earth, of the two living together, of life returning after winter. It's no coincidence that Jesus supposedly rose from the dead in the spring, now part of Easter from the pagan Astarte. Spring is rebirth, part of the natural cycle of the seasons and of life in general. Paganism is much more in touch with that, because it recognizes and celebrates the importance of [the] natural cycle and rhythms. We try to live within that. We basically take winters off because as a season it's not conducive to work. Christianity lost touch with natural cycles, and now we live in a Christian-capitalist society that forces people to work all year, which is completely unnatural.

SunBlaze: That's why paganism in all its different traditions is the only way to achieve justice, and the only way to save the planet. It teaches individuality, but also limits and you can't just walk all over people or expect people to be happy if they live in submission, and that the earth has limits, and if we go beyond them, then we die. . . . We want children someday, to whom we can pass on our trade as in earlier times, and all the beliefs that go with it, because that's really what it is, paganism in practice.

SunBlaze and Hephaistos integrate Neopagan thought with other issues—in this case, with socialism and environmentalism. Similarly, Neopagans pride themselves on a wide range of knowledge, including scientific, spiritual, and practical, which altogether contribute to rational choices in combination with moral values and compassion. Like their appreciation for all types of knowledge, Neopagans strive for awareness on all possible levels—self, social, cultural, historical—and seek to create life practices that embody their beliefs and strong sense of awareness.

Nightshade also looks forward to an alternative and, as she sees it, feminist witch career. She is studying to be a midwife:

Midwifery was the standard before the modern medical establishment, which, I might add, is dominated by men and cold, abstract ways of doing things. With childbirthing especially, it's supposed to be this totally nonsexual, cold, detached thing, as if the doctor and the patient were two machines or something. In the age of the midwife, many people helped with the birth, and it wasn't shameful to see a woman give birth, or to stimulate her body sexually to help her relax and to make the birth easier. When I gave birth to Aura, several members of the coven I was in at the time helped, and delivered at home. The midwife was really cool; she said I should move around however I felt, whatever was most comfortable, and to trust the sensations in my body. I was a little scared at first, but with the love of my friends and the midwife's compassion and sensitivity, I relaxed a lot and the birth wasn't so bad.

Is modern birthing procedure bad from a functional standpoint, or do you see more to it?

It's definitely bad functionally—strapping a woman's legs into stirrups and forcing her to stay on her back is the worst position. But what it's really about, and this is true I think of modern medicine in general, is to disempower the patient, and women especially are treated as objects in the whole process, not as living beings. I want to be a midwife not just because it's the pagan way, but because it empowers the mother and women in general. But it's definitely part of my pagan sensibilities—always go with natural rhythms and feelings. Let your body speak to you, and trust your friends. When it was over, I felt so close to everyone who was there, I understood what community really means. Modern doctors aren't usually part of your life; they're not part of your intimate circle or even your daily routine. The midwife isn't always either because there are so few so most towns don't have one. Most covens don't even have one. But the good ones definitely have a spiritual side, which was very important for me.

Do you reject all of modern medicine?

No, but we need to think about what we want to keep, and what to use when. Take antibiotics, for example. Only antibiotics can cure certain things, but they're way overprescribed, because the medical establishment dictates they should be used all the time, and I guess it's really the drug companies that push them. But the whole medical establishment tends to think very one-dimensionally, that there is only one way to cure something, and it should be fast and if necessary, harsh. The problem is not any one specific procedure or type of drug, it's the mentality that the body is an object to control, and that nature is a problem we need to control with technology. I'm not against technology or science, but it becomes a problem when we try to reduce everything to scientific variables, and the miracle of birth is one thing that is more than just a biological process. It should be a very spiritual moment, and a very social moment, but I would say that about almost everything people do. Life is best when shared.

The members see their political activities as an expression of their personal lives; just as they work toward a more fulfilling personal life in the community, so they imagine social change in a context of intimate, personal relationships. They all believe essentially that it would be hypocritical to advocate some sort of progressive political platform or work relations, and then at the end of the day go home to living arrangements that contradict the supposed possibilities that one advocates in the public arena. In other words, the revolution, so to speak, starts locally, one person at a time, with working models of alternative society.

New Evangelicalism

New Evangelicalism, also known as what Donald Miller (1997) identifies as New Paradigm churches, offers emotionally powerful theology that turns everyday routine into a sacred obligation. For evangelical revivalists, humans who would receive salvation must serve God, who is a superior power. The obligation of service and the benefit of salvation are handed down from God, and an individual can choose to follow and thereby submit to God's designs and receive His grace, or choose to reject God, for which the outcome is eternal damnation. There are no other possibilities.

In earlier times (such as the First and Second Great Awakenings), Evangelicalism confronted issues such as the role of emotion in religious life (Noll 1994) and the relationship between Protestantism and Catholicism (Wolffe 1994). New Evangelicalism, born in the late 1960s as described in Chapter 2, thus faces long-standing as well as more recently conceived contradictions. In general terms, contradiction arises as (1) the tension between adherence to established doctrine, and the call for reform. This relates directly to (2) the tension between a religious life that occurs essentially separate from society in general, and the call to participate more directly in everyday issues as part of religious devotion.

Historically in the United States, Evangelicalism has faced numerous issues in the secular world for which religious belief provided no clear position, and thus New Evangelicals today increasingly appear on both sides of major social conflicts. In the past, such divisive issues have included slavery (Carwardine 1994; Hill 1994) and prohibition (Gusfield [1963] 1986). Both of these issues ignited controversy over the proper role of the true Christian. Prohibition and slavery also marked the first divisions between those who believed the Bible was a guide for life and decisions about social issues, a view known in the 1920s as progressivism, and those who believed the Bible to be an infallible mandate to rule over society, a view we now know as fundamentalism.

Today, fundamentalism greatly influences New Evangelicalism (Alexander-Moegerle 1997; Diamond 1998; Georgianna 1989; Lundskow 2002; D. Miller 1997; Noll and Kellstedt 1995; Wilcox and Larson 2006). Fundamentalism typically correlates with conservative political agendas (Noll, Bebbington,

---

Two Creation Stories in the Bible

As we see in the following, there are actually two creation stories, one that portrays both men and women as made in the image of God, and the other which portrays women as made from part of the man (the rib). Both versions express creation in terms of days, although the definition of a day is unclear—just as we would say, for example, "back in the day . . ." when we don't mean one exact day, but a period of time in the past.

Genesis 1:

(26) Then God said, "Let us make man in our image, in our likeness, and let them rule over the fish of the sea and the birds of the air, over the livestock, over all the earth, and over all the creatures that move along the ground."

(27) So God created man in his own image, in the image of God he created him; male and female he created them.

The second version is expressed in Genesis 2:

(7) [T]he LORD God formed the man from the dust of the ground and breathed into his nostrils the breath of life, and the man became a living being.

(20–22) But for Adam no suitable helper was found. So the LORD God caused the man to fall into a deep sleep; and while he was sleeping, he took one of the man's ribs and closed up the place with flesh. Then the LORD God made a woman from the rib he had taken out of the man, and he brought her to the man. (New International Version)

and Rawlyk 1994; Shibley 1996) and a preference for charismatic candidates (Diamond 1998; Guth et al. 1996b; Hunt 1998), but not always. As Gerson (2006) and L. Miller (2006) both document, even fundamentalists—often regarded as inherently part of the Christian right—sometimes advocate for social justice and poverty issues, combined with an antiwar stance (Gerson 2006).

However, fundamentalism is not the only force in New Evangelical Christianity. While still mostly conservative in politics and attitudes, many New Evangelicals also embrace a more open and vibrant view of life and religion, a view based on tolerance and enlightenment rather than intolerance and fear. Indeed, Curtis Hutson (1984), writing as a fundamentalist, sees New Evangelicalism as the direct opponent of fundamentalism. Scholarly authors such as Mark Noll (1995) and James Sire (2000) lament the decline of serious evangelical thought in favor of emotional fervor and conservative politics, and call for a dynamic intellectualism as a legitimate calling and as a means to strengthen faith.

As the recent 2006 U.S. elections show, New Evangelical support for neoconservative policies and politicians is not automatic (see Figure 8.4). Of those who voted, 71% of white Evangelical born-again Christians (the most conservative) voted for Republicans, but relatively few such New Evangelicals even voted. They constituted only 24% of voters in this election, and would normally be about 35% of voters. Religion in general favored the Democrats. As New Evangelical leaders commented

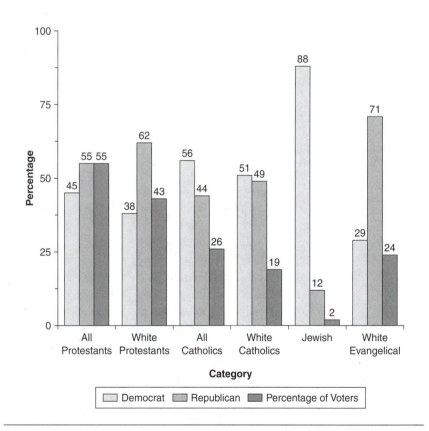

Figure 8.4   Religion and Voting in the 2006 Midterm Election

afterward, New Evangelical Christians are "fed up with the Republican leadership, particularly in the House," said the Reverend Richard Land, head of the public policy arm of the Southern Baptist Convention, which has 16 million members. "They're disgusted that Republicans came to Washington and failed to behave any better than Democrats once they got their snouts in the trough." Roberta Combs, chair of the Christian Coalition, said responsibility for the Republican loss of the House and Senate "goes right back to the leadership, the corruption among Republicans." James Dobson, founder of Focus on the Family, issued a statement saying that "many of the Values Voters of '04 simply stayed at home this year" because the Republican Party has "consistently ignored the constituency that put them in power" (Cooperman 2006). As longtime political analyst David Gergen commented, "The New Evangelical vote cannot be taken for granted now. Republicans are going to have to earn it back" (interviewed in Wenner 2006).

Middle-class New Evangelicals feel the contradictions of fundamentalism more strongly, because certain tenets directly condemn affluent lifestyles, such as prohibitions against the enjoyment of wealth; the call to abstain from secular, especially political issues; the subordination of women; and commitment to church service over career. In middle-class New Evangelicalism, Lundskow (2002) and Bartkowski (2004) found among the Promise Keepers, and D. Miller (1997) found among various conservative congregations, that strong contradictions exist between, on one hand, the desire to serve one's family over career and to reinstate traditional gender roles—the subordination of the woman as homemaker—and on the other hand, the fact that New Evangelicals cherish their lifestyle of suburban leisure and privilege. For example, few are willing to hold their daughters out of college and marry them off early, even though they believe that a woman's first and best calling in life is always to bear and raise children. As we saw in the sidebar, however, the Bible contains two creation stories, which seem to present a contradictory view of women. In one, God creates men and women together. In the second, the woman could be interpreted as subordinate to the man. Research shows that as education increases, fundamentalism decreases (Pascarella et al. 2004) unless students attend specifically fundamentalist schools (Hood, Hill, and Williamson 2005). Biblical fundamentalism has an especially negative impact on the educational attainment of women (Sherkat and Darnell 1999; Glass and Jacobs 2005). For such reasons, tensions exist within New Evangelicalism, and consequently the movement is not a unified totality.

Servant-Leadership

This passage has formed the basis of Christian evangelism for nearly 2,000 years. The present-day servant-leadership concept is thus both new and a development from earlier doctrine.

1 Corinthians 9

(1–2) Am I not free? Am I not an apostle? Have I not seen Jesus our Lord? Are you not the result of my work in the Lord? Even though I may not be an apostle to others, surely I am to you! For you are the seal of my apostleship in the Lord.

(19–23) Though I am free and belong to no man, I make myself a slave to everyone, to win as many as possible. To the Jews I became like a Jew, to win the Jews. To those under the law I became like one under the law (though I myself am not under the law), so as to win those under the law. To those not having the law I became like one not having the law (though I am not free from God's law but am under Christ's law), so as to win those not having the law. To the weak I became weak, to win the weak. I have become all things to all men so that by all possible means I might save some. I do all this for the sake of the gospel, that I may share in its blessings. (New International Version)

In the present day, then, New Evangelicals—especially the more affluent New Evangelicals—face material contradictions in addition to spiritual contradictions and uncertainty. The modern world offers opportunity, yet also temptation to sin. Many New Evangelicals address theological issues only during the church service, and move difficult issues aside during the daily routine (Ammerman 1987; C. Smith 2002). The resolution, so to speak, between conservative religious values and the reality of modern life is to separate aspects of their religion that require critical thought from those aspects that may be applied in ritual fashion in daily routine. For example, a person may say his or her prayers every night without ever considering critically why many prayers are never fulfilled. A person can speak of a just and forgiving God who nevertheless brings suffering (such as a natural disaster) without ever confronting the obvious contradiction that good people suffer alongside the wicked. Also known as the problem of theodicy, how can evil exist if God is all-knowing, all-powerful, and cares about humanity? The resolution arguably lies in the concept of slavery and the more contemporary version—servant-leadership—which is both an ancient and modern concept.

In ancient times, the concept of slavery contributed to the core of Christian leadership principles, and it can be found throughout the Bible in the form of slavery metaphors (Dale Martin 1990), which later became the justification for actual slavery in the late ancient Christian world and until the end of the U.S. Civil War (Glancy 2006). However, the status and material position of slaves in ancient times was a complex and highly variable designation, and to understand the slavery-leadership concept as the basis of contemporary servant-leadership and its significance to contemporary American culture, we must first understand its significance to ancient society and the foundation of Christian thought.

Central to servant-leadership is the use of the slavery metaphors. New Evangelicals have adopted the concept more or less unchanged, except to change *slavery* into *servant* because some people might object to the former term—especially black people, given the history of race in the United States.

Slavery was central and primary to the labor process in ancient societies. Yet the position of slaves was complex. For example, in Rome, slaves held nearly every type of job, and those who held managerial positions often became wealthy and influential (Dale Martin 1990:15–22). Although slaves were not free in the sense we understand freedom today, the patrimonial (patron–client) system allowed managerial slaves to exercise considerable authority and leeway, and as the representatives of wealthy and powerful Romans, they shared in the same prestige (Dale Martin 1990:29). Wealthy slaves often owned slaves themselves (Bradley 1987). Clearly, the life of common slaves was difficult and short, but managerial positions meant that "being connected to someone in power, even if only a slave, was the next best thing to being in power oneself" (Dale Martin 1990:30).

Although the designation of *slave* carried generally negative associations, the fact that many slaves occupied important positions in the power hierarchy made Greco-Roman slavery an ambiguous institution. Since nearly everyone except the highest noble patrician citizens was beholden to someone, according to traditional patrimonial obligation, the mere fact of serving someone higher while at the same time controlling those of lower status and privilege was typical and expected (Bradley

1987). This shaped a worldview for the ancients around everyday obligations, pre-scribed by tradition. Therefore, a concept that originated in such a culture, *slave of Christ,* is not a radical idea of zealots, but a typical relationship that most people in the ancient world would readily understand. Likewise, a slave of Christ carries both deference to and reverence for a higher authority, and at the same time the right to dominate those of lower rank. Moreover, reverence for and deference to the higher authority also meant that the subordinate shared in the power and prestige of the master as the master's representative.

In the Bible, Paul elaborates on the slavery-leadership concept. In 1 Corinthians 9, he argues that one's legal status as slave or any other status does not matter, because one's relationship to God supersedes earthly obligations. Only the divine obligation really matters, but the relationship of the believer to God mirrors the dominant social structure. Overall, Paul's rhetoric allows a certain amount of free-dom to the slave of God (the believer); however, this is not personal freedom as we understand it today, but freedom as an increase in status, whereby the slave, though still an earthly slave, gains higher status in the House of the Lord God (Dale Martin 1990:65–66). Paul's rhetoric thus does not challenge patrimonial obligation, as at first it might seem. Rather, he compares two different hierarchies and assesses the relative obligation that early Christians have toward each. That is, he separates divine status—the important one, which is eternal—from earthly status, which is transient. Ultimately, the foundation of servant-leadership is internal conviction, which the external church and, for contemporary New Evangelicals, the family reflect in practice. The male-headed nuclear family is servant-leadership in actual practice. It is a gender-based form of the patrimonial patron–client relationship.

The basic patrimonial relationship that configured nearly all social relations endured from ancient times through the fall of the Roman Empire and continued through the Middle Ages. It reinforced medieval feudal relations and, following the collapse of feudal society, persisted as the central principle of Christian life. This ethic continued into modern times, and the pilgrims carried it to the American colonies where it flourished alongside the many emerging sects and breakaway denomina-tions. Today, the servant-leader concept in Christianity is already 2,000 years old—a remnant of a patrimonial society long since gone. Although long separated from the social form that created it, the servant-leader ethic lives on as the guiding principle of New Evangelical life, as the living model of devotion in action, but transformed into the nuclear family, which corresponds to the rise of modern capitalism.

In modern times, the patriarchal nuclear family maintains a type of patrimonial order in modern Christian life, and among the most conservative New Evangelicals in particular, it unifies the congregation in common status—men collectively as servants of God, leaders of their families, and their wives at their side. Although everyone of good faith shares in God's glory and grace, men in a patriarchal reli-gion (as reflective of a patriarchal culture) share somewhat more. Thus, they also gain a sense of empowerment through closer association with God and in turn a higher status over their family.

In this way, New Evangelicals gain a sense of collective empowerment through servant-leadership, a sense that they are not isolated units in a vast social system, but in fact share a close relationship with a powerful God. Service to the Lord raises up the Christian man and woman, each in his or her proper place. A man leads his family and thereby becomes lord of the household. Their position is—like the Lord God over them, and like the Roman patrician—a status that subordinates can never attain; they can only share by association the status of the superior partner.

But if this moral system is so old and people still embrace it so enthusiastically, why is there a crisis? Why do contemporary New Evangelicals have identity problems, as documented in various sociological studies (Gibbs and Bolger 2005; C. Smith 2002)? In order to understand the present crisis in identity, we must think sociologically. Because a meaningful identity must be socially constructed, not idiosyncratically constructed, New Evangelical identity, as in Neopaganism, is not a central ideology, but a more generalized and flexible cultural identity, and configurable at the individual level. This would explain why the New Evangelical movement draws across denominational lines. It speaks to familiar beliefs that transcend denominations. Specifically, its members exalt not only New Evangelical identity, but a larger culture of which their religious beliefs are a part, coupled with an actual or aspirational middle-class lifestyle (Shibley 1996). However, the dominant culture they exalt is not a pure and old-fashioned patriarchy of domination. Their goals are not primarily organized on a large-scale political level, to reassert a conservative New Evangelical identity as a dominant one in society (C. Smith 2002), but instead, they seek approval of their peers, that is, other New Evangelicals face to face, and approval from their superior—God.

Approval (salvation) ultimately descends from God; it is not created or attained through human effort. God's standards are transcendent standards of perfection, not earthly standards. Nevertheless, in New Evangelicalism, one's relationship with God is always personal. The truly faithful will hear His voice within. Similar to their Neopagan counterparts, the values and identity New Evangelicals build are just as much personal as social and religious. Thus, religion is not the only salient force for New Evangelicals. Their collective identity depends equally on their success in the secular realm, but in an emergent way. New Evangelicals accept that less in the career realm is more in the personal realm. Still imbued with a notion of the calling (as discussed in Chapter 1), the true path to salvation is not through property and money, but rather a sincere, powerful, inner commitment to God. Like their pagan counterparts, New Evangelicals sociologically experience dissatisfaction with their religion, careers, and family and feel that none of them offers fulfillment because they have become routinized, their own participation reduced to mechanical compliance.

Foundations of New Evangelical Belief

Men and women have separate and distinct gender roles. To cross over violates an eternal and unquestionable order ordained by God.

Living in a godly manner is primarily an internal conversion and intensity of faith. Salvation is thus measured not by works, but by internal commitment and sincerity—to hold the Lord in one's heart.

The exact content of faith is personal and cannot be obtained externally through sermons, education, literature, or social experience.

New Evangelical Social Values

- Middle-class and conventional status, regardless of income
- Demeanor of quiet accomplishment and well-mannered behavior
- Leisure success enjoyed in careful moderation

New Evangelicals are not suffering from anomie, but rather what William James ([1901] 2007) long ago identified as a central attribute of the Protestant tempera-ment—the melancholic soul. Applying the concept figuratively, James argues that the melancholic soul feels a constant weight and burden of morality and spiritual obligation to uphold God's purpose, yet without fanfare. The result is an ongoing suppression of emotion and passion, which produces a reserved disposition. Interestingly, those denominations most prone to sudden emotional outbursts dur-ing a service, which includes speaking in tongues, revelations, convulsions, and so on, are those that outside of church service practice the greatest degree of emo-tional suppression, in particular the charismatic sects.

New Evangelicals seek fulfillment through religious experience, which they hope will lighten their "melancholic soul" and provide the certainty of fulfilling divine standards in place of the uncertainty of inadequacy. In this way, the movement pro-vides what Donald Meyer (1966) calls "positive thinking," a long-standing aspect of American evangelicalism. In reaction to the fragmentation, moral relativism, and declining opportunity of late capitalism, New Evangelicalism offers a revival expe-rience that encourages emotion, provides reassurance, and instills an ethic of commitment—that devout Christians should accept the path Christ has chosen for them, which they believe will simultaneously increase their happiness. Thus, they should learn to positively attempt to overcome burdens and tribulations, drawing on faith as inspiration, a decisive break with old-school evangelicalism.

Thus, as Christian Smith (2002) concludes, New Evangelicals are not the mono-lithic automatons that leaders on the far right (and liberal critics) assume, but nuanced, sometimes contradictory, sometimes innovative people who struggle to reconcile faith, modernity, and pluralist democracy. We have already seen some of the thoughts of conservative evangelical leaders in Chapter 5 regarding religious intolerance. In contrast, New Evangelicals at times exhibit an uplifting and fun-lov-ing side, as we see for example in one of the most popular New Evangelical books, *Velvet Elvis*, by Rob Bell (2005).

Far from a dogmatic treatise on faith or aggressive, fire-and-brimstone threats of damnation, Rob Bell (2005) writes that "[t]imes change. God doesn't, but times do. We learn and grow, and the world around us shifts, and the Christian Faith is alive and listening, morphing, innovating, letting go of whatever has gotten in the way of Jesus and embracing whatever will help us be more and more the people God wants us to be" (p. 11).

In this introductory statement, Bell frames a dynamic and active Christianity, not one bogged down in the past or forever fearful of change that results from uncritical acceptance of tradition. Similar to Neopaganism, the Christianity that Bell envisions is one that fully engages modern times and looks to the future.

Bell (2005) describes an enlightened, compassionate faith that embraces education, community, friendship, and optimism. Fear, anger, and violence are for the unenlight-ened and unbelieving. Bell's Christianity is not at war with the secular world, but rather seeks to maintain the relevance of scripture and tradition within the context of modern times. He draws from evangelical tradition, with special emphasis on disci-pleship and servant-leadership. He cites the Bible, Protestant theologians, important moments in Christian (mostly Protestant) history, and even popular culture.

Bell (2005) articulates an open and forgiving church that serves a loving God, not a harshly judgmental one:

> God blesses everybody. People who don't believe in God. People who are opposed to God. People who do violent, evil things. God's intentions are to bless everybody. . . . The best and greatest and most important are the people who humble themselves, set their needs and desires aside, and selflessly serve others. (p. 165)

For Bell, these good people are the church. The church is not a bricks-and-mortar edifice, but a living community of believers who actively serve others in the real world. Life will not always be easy and pleasant, and many will live through more than their share of suffering and death. What Christianity offers overall is not a belief system or dogma, but a moral code based on service to others in need, and above all, it offers hope. This hope, which arises from sincere faith in God, allows Christians to endeavor on, with the comfort that one's actions matter, and death is not the end. Bell's New Evangelicalism is life-affirming, not death-centered. It is not about personal happiness or redemption in an abstract sense, but through active, real-world engagement.

In a further decisive break from fundamentalism, Bell (2005) views the Bible as a guide, not because tradition or a church hierarchy dictates it is so, but because "through the centuries God's children have heard the voice of the Father speaking in these books" (p. 185). In this view, sacredness arises from the people, in that some parts of scripture inform the times better than other parts, and the meaning may change as people read it differently. Bell's view is increasingly popular compared to fundamentalist readings of the Bible, and his own "megachurch" (a phenomenon addressed later in this book) named Mars Hill is one of the fastest growing churches in the country.

Discussion

Neopaganism and New Evangelicalism are two of the fastest growing religions in the United States. From a demographic standpoint, the two are quite similar. Both derive from the middle to upper-middle class. Practitioners of both religions value college education, often including advanced degrees; they engage social issues; and they seek emotionally gratifying religious experience. All came to their religion feeling alienated, fragmented, and without direction or enthusiasm in life. Of course, the particular doctrines and rituals are very different, but this is not the decisive difference from a sociological standpoint.

Stated succinctly, Neopaganism and New Evangelicalism alleviate alienation not with exact answers about life, but rather by offering a means, in close association with other people, to seek answers. Both celebrate a creative renewal of one's faith. We should not confuse a sociological analysis with an emphasis on political orientation, which is only one aspect of a much larger social process of faith and living. While New Evangelicals tend toward more conservative views and conventional lifestyles, they seek vital experience no less than Neopagans. They seek this vitality outside of established institutions—whether religious or not—and view individuality as central. As we saw in Chapter 2 and above, New Evangelical and Neopagans hold that faith and practice extend from the free association of free individuals, and not from routinized institutions. This leads to a particular process of socialization, which both movements also share.

The process of socialization instills a structure of feeling and tendencies that shapes the way practitioners approach situations and experience in general, according to the values that dominate the group. It guides their actions, whether cautious, suspicious, bold, courageous, selfish, or selfless. As people grow, they develop character traits that become the basis of how they interact with other people. In this way, we may think of these traits as their social character. In close friendships, family life, or romantic interests, character perhaps becomes most manifest, as the person drops pretensions and whatever other façade he or she may project to a more anonymous relation. As studies have found consistently, attachment between people at intimate levels depends on character orientation, not on abstract principles or rational choice from one moment to the next (Percy 1996). Whether a person is aggressive, manipulative, and cold, or on the other hand cooperative, considerate, and warm "are not merely abstract philosophical preferences. Rather, they reflect a key dimension of the personality—the way people characteristically relate to others and their sense of commitment to them" (Oliner and Oliner 1992:171).

New Evangelicalism and Neopaganism are both, as social movements, forms of religious revival. The former is one of several variations of Christian revival in the United States, the latter one of several progressive forms of revival, although none prior to the 1960s has been "pagan." In the United States, revival since the First Awakening (late eighteenth to early nineteenth centuries) has crossed denominational lines, with new alliances forming along lines other than particularities in denominational doctrine. A basic "conservative" compared to "liberal" orientation now distinguishes movements that doctrinal differences previously separated, such that, for example, Catholics with conservative social values find more in common with conservative Baptists than with other Catholics. Similarly, previously "alternative" practices, such as Neopaganism or American versions of Buddhism, find enthusiasts among mainline Christian churches, such as among Catholics and Protestants. Given the inclusive nature of Neopaganism and Buddhism, a person can be pagan or Buddhist (or both) and still remain faithful to mainline Christianity.

As I have shown (Lundskow 2002), the Promise Keepers, Calvary, and similar New Evangelical revival ministries have minimalist doctrines that consist of general yet typically fundamentalist and emotionally forceful statements of belief. Within this general framework, enthusiasts are free to fill in the specifics, just as Neopagans emphasize personal and local construction of belief and practice. New Evangelical churches offer exuberant and contemporary services: sermons in common language with contemporary references; Christian rock and rap music; extensive casual conversation; and individual worship that may take many forms, from charismatic speaking in tongues to group prayer to quiet personal prayer. Many such churches are thoroughly enmeshed in popular culture, and parishes are often found in strip malls and suburban commercial thoroughfares. They also offer exciting and energetic Sunday services.

Aside from overt differences in belief and style, Neopaganism and New Evangelicalism differ sociologically. In particular, the concept of "freedom" requires careful specification.

For New Evangelicals, humans who would receive salvation must serve God, who is a superior power. The obligation is handed down from God—God calls everyone to fulfill particular tasks—and an individual can choose to accept his or her calling, and thereby submit to God's designs, or choose to reject it. Very differently, Neopagan revival holds that obligation arises from mutually recognized responsibility, and a more dynamic sensibility that individuals face a series of choices that have both personal and social impact. Decisions and actions are good or bad depending both on intention and effect on others, and not on whether an action offends a higher power, that is, God. Thus, religious belief and practice are not simply a matter of accepting and submitting to a higher power, but rather choosing a path in relation to others. Humans can approach spiritual issues better when in conjunction with each other as dynamic, thinking, and interactive individuals who are also part of a community of their own making.

This difference in belief and practice points to a crucial difference that emerges at the social-psychological level. As with any religion, both movements reinforce the dominant values of the society in which the members live; as Durkheim discovered long ago, to celebrate religion is to celebrate the idealized social order. Thus, it should not be surprising that New Evangelicals generally embrace conservative political platforms, and Neopagans embrace more progressive platforms.

But these two different revivals indicate a more profound difference; both movements emphasize religious exuberance, but in different ways. New Evangelicalism requires a degree of submission, whereas Neopaganism requires self-affirmation. The former calls for self-limitation in the service of others and the priorities of an outside and superior presence (in this case, God) and whatever the person perceives to be God's earthly intentions. Neopaganism, on the other hand, calls for and reinforces self-affirmation—that beliefs are created by and in the service of the human members; they are negotiated, and thus in turn, the terms of social life and the ideal order are likewise a process of negotiation in which all voices are relevant. This inherently produces a social ethic premised on diversity and pluralism. Even for someone like Rob Bell, pluralism remains somewhat ambiguous.

Furthermore, the need for spiritual meaning in both movements arises from social conditions, yet the particular approach—self-limitation or self-affirmation—results from a particular social character orientation. This is, to be sure, not a psychological theory, but a social theory premised on commonly shared values and experience, which altogether produce a particular outlook or worldview that similar people share in common. Thus, social character overlaps with other collective variables such as gender, ethnicity, class, and many others. These collective variables represent social roles, and each of us plays any number and combination of roles.

Let's add a further element of sociological refinement. Daniel Bell ([1976] 1996) proposes that, to fully understand the disjunction of modern society (which emergent religion seeks to overcome), we must distinguish the social role from the individual. That is, in modern society people are for the first time viewed as developing differently as individuals, compared to their place in society—their role. An individual can have many roles (parent, supervisor, friend, worker, etc.), which may or may not correlate with his or her personal sense of identity. A person may fill any given role in a more or less mechanical manner; the person invests no emotion and derives no sense of self from that role—it holds no meaning for the individual other than practical necessity. Thus, the sense of self develops separately from, and sometimes in conflict with, a social role. After all, roles are determined by society, and we conform to some of them willingly, while others are thrust upon us. In contrast, personal development usually results from conscious choices—how to dress, where to vacation, what sort of friends to have, what movies to see, what to read, what political positions to hold, how to treat others, and a wide, nearly infinite array of consumer choices through which, based on the commodities we buy, we hope to create a unique definition of who we are as individuals. It is precisely this separation of person and role that will serve as the basis to understand contemporary religious revival, which is an attempt to create a meaningful sense of self, in contrast to increasingly meaningless social roles that people find thrust upon them.

In response, religion seeks to mend this disjuncture, to offer a unity of belief and practice or, in sociological terms, to create continuity among person, role, and society. Yet disjuncture requires free individuals with the capacity to imagine life differently from how they currently live it. In other words, people must exist who feel unfulfilled as a result of separation from their individual selves and the social world around them. Both movements assert that the self must be made stronger, more dynamic, and more resilient, but this requires the support of nothing less than a free and diverse community in which people continually question the answers, yet nevertheless maintain social cohesion by recognizing the inherent right and necessity to remain critically aware of one's own life and the lives of others in society. In the case of Neopaganism, society often includes nature as well. Self-affirmation consists not only of individual critical awareness, but also active participation in a community that affirms the individual self as a vital part of a collective identity.

As stated, neither movement depends to any great extent on complex doctrine for most enthusiasts. While most read the Bible or various pagan authors, most embrace what they like and readily understand, and set aside the rest. The issue is instead the way in which a person embraces the doctrine, whether it be simple or detailed. As Helen Berger (1995) found, Neopaganism can succumb to routinization and dogmatism as much as the most vibrant and exuberant New Evangelical sects (B. Wright and Rawls 2006). Usually, the degree of fervency responds to the perceived level of external threat, as Bonnie Wright (2005), for example, found with race and religion in two New Evangelical churches.

The more threats or challenges, in general, the more duress a person perceives, whether real or imaginary, the more fervently the person embraces the faith (Beit-Hallahmi and Argyle 1997). The threats are typically, as Batson, Schoenrade, and Ventis (1993) term it, extrinsic—that is, social in the form of economic pressure, changing cultural norms, or within one's significant others, such as death of a loved one, or personal, such as one's own illness. The fervent embrace of faith in times of duress constitutes an "intrinsic" response, because it emanates from the person's inner psychic state, and because it settles many existential fears (such as the fear of death) or fear of self-destructive behavior (depression, drinking, etc.), the person values his or her beliefs highly. As Batson et al. (1993) find, though, "the freedom obtained by devout, intrinsic belief is obtained at a high price; it is freedom with bondage, bondage to the belief system itself" (p. 224). However, from the perspective of neorevivalists, both pagans and Christians, they interpret the threat as equally intrinsic—that they have personally strayed from God's (or nature's) intentions. Thus, enthusiasts of both persuasions believe that the solution is just as much internal as it is external and political. It involves personal orientation as much as social organization and action. It also involves surrender, in the sense that a person socially and psychologically resigns himself or herself to circumstances that the individual—accurately or not—perceives as beyond his or her control.

Although this tendency of psychological resignation is weaker in Neopaganism, many still resort to solitary practice and nonsocial commitment. As Sabina Magliocco (2004) argues, "the process of becoming a Witch or a Pagan is essentially a process of training the imagination" (p. 100). This explains why pagans draw significantly from popular culture, especially fantasy movies and literature. *The Lord of the Rings, Harry Potter, Buffy the Vampire Slayer,* and *Charmed,* among others, figure prominently. Similarly, New Evangelical culture draws from and contributes to popular culture. In music and literature, rock and rap artists promote Christian themes (such as in Christian heavy metal) and writers, like Rob Bell, speak in the language of the times. The book title *Velvet Elvis* refers to a black velvet painting of Elvis that Bell owns—an authentic work of art from the 1970s. Bell's point is that black velvet paintings (which glow in groovy colors under a black light) were once very cool. Now, they are, well, something else. Christianity must also change with the times. God does not change, but our perception does.

On the subject of religious personalization, Kintz (1997) and Ott (2001) emphasize the consumerist aspect of contemporary religion—that each individual may construct his or her own beliefs, but only from those offered in the spiritual marketplace. Moreover, both movements include their own specialty religious stores where one can purchase all the accoutrements of faith and practice.

Overall, neorevival movements of both types considered here offer some degree of spontaneity and a semblance of shared meaning, but in substance offer also commodified belief, contradiction, isolation, and submission to abstract authority. In other words, commodified faith depends on spectacle—an exciting composite of socially recognizable symbols that each individual may interpret to suit his or her personal preferences, which inherently deprives the symbols of socially recognizable meaning (DeBord [1967] 1995). In turn, this vacancy deprives the group of shared meaning, and thus of community.

If neorevivalism offered nothing new to its enthusiasts, it would not exhibit its current and rising popularity. If New Evangelicalism were nothing but oppressive or abstract ideology, it would not speak to the troubles of real people living in the United States today. New Evangelicalism arises from the very same material and cultural deprivations and uncertainties out of which Neopaganism emerges. Both to an extent legitimate social identity in a spectacle world—a world that simulates yet remains separate from daily life. Both movements call for involvement in the world—New Evangelicalism through service to others and Neopaganism through antiwar and pro-environment causes—and both posit individuality at the center. Thus, we may see New Evangelicalism and Neopaganism on a continuum.

Neopaganism emphasizes self-affirmation, as does New Evangelicalism to a somewhat lesser degree. Thus, they are not either/or contrasts, but different degrees of individuality.

The resulting individualistic (more or less) identity does not challenge either cultural or economic hegemony, and consequently, the new collective identity the enthusiasts seek remains the character of spectacle—the experience and identity of isolated individualism. More than anything else, spectacle constitutes the "new" in new-revival movements. If so, then this poses a challenge to both movements, and any other emergent religious movements, rather than a final judgment about their success or failure at creating social change and constructing community. It also poses an important question: Is modern culture, as a celebration of individuality, capable of also constructing existentially meaningful communities? Or is it a dead end, a failed attempt at liberation?

CHAPTER 9

Religion and the Forces of Globalization

Introduction

Prior to the twentieth century, the concept of globalization made little sense. Although various countries had been drawing resources and labor from outside their borders for centuries, each country did this in its own way, only for certain segments of its economy, and inconsistently. Today, nearly every country, state, province, city, town, and village feels the impact of globalization. This does not simply mean that each is connected to the others, but more exactly, that the same economic system—namely, capitalism—governs economic exchange at all levels, and similarly, cultural exchange occurs interactively. Although local and regional markets still exhibit particular preferences, commerce meets market demands through a worldwide, that is, global system of resources, production, and distribution. In so doing, each region comes to depend on the others, and this over time integrates systems of communication, transportation, and even government. For example, the euro has become the common currency of the European Union, which established a European parliament as well. Similarly, Peru and El Salvador have adopted the U.S. dollar as their official currency. As the dollar and the euro spread, it will gradually integrate fiscal and monetary policy decisions. This is only the beginning.

In addition to opening economic markets, cultural markets have opened as well, and religion, as a cultural commodity, now flows increasingly freely. In modern society, nearly everything becomes a commodity—anything that is bought and sold in a marketplace. Regarding religion, the United States set the standard, as discussed in Chapter 2, by establishing an open and democratic forum in which all religions (or at least a multitude of variations within Christianity) freely develop and associate in society. Not all survive and prosper, of course, but each large, medium, or small denomination exists without official interference or promotion.

Consequently, we may tend to think that other nations—especially those that impose one version of one religion as the official religion—lack an open forum for the free exchange of ideas and beliefs. While exchange is often not free, exchange nevertheless exists, as we will see. Moreover, not all deviations from the official standard constitute a necessary threat to the established order, and thus incur no particular suppression attempt. Such would be the case for Zoroastrians in Iran and India, for example. Although such small minorities may differ greatly from many of the precepts of the established religions—Islam in Iran and Hinduism in India—they do not face consistent persecution, or at least not severe enough to extinguish the religion. It is true that Iran formally bars non-Muslims from certain positions, and India does the same informally with non-Hindus, yet Zoroastrian communities endure in both countries. Whatever the particular status of a religion, we will see that in a global age—perhaps in any age—it must be part of a functioning community and contribute a nomos (meaning of life): a set of beliefs, values, and codes of behavior. Yet the global marketplace adds another challenge for religion, in that not only must it sustain the identity of a community in a meaningful way, it must also not hinder the community in relation to the entire global system. Thus, Zoroastrianism survives because it is still permitted to form its own communities, and still permitted to participate in most, if not all, aspects of social life. In short, it remains a living if not entirely equal religion in Iran and India.

As we will see below, globalization is the latest phase in capitalism. As it draws economies and people together, people bring their culture—religion included—into larger forums of interaction.

Capitalism

Economics refers to the system by which a society produces and distributes resources to meet the needs and wants of the society. Historically, there have been different ways of doing this, or in some cases, failing to do this. As mentioned, the present global system is a type or phase of *capitalism,* which is a system by which money is invested to make more money (see Figure 9.1). This might seem like a natural process today, but the concept of systematic monetary investment to achieve a more or less predictable profit is a uniquely modern concept. Globalization expands the capitalist economic system worldwide, and in the process it replaces local and premodern systems.

In 1999, for the first time in the history of the world, more people worked as wage laborers than in any other capacity (McMichael 2000; Mishel, Bernstein, and Allegretto 2005). Prior to modern times universally, and until 1999, most

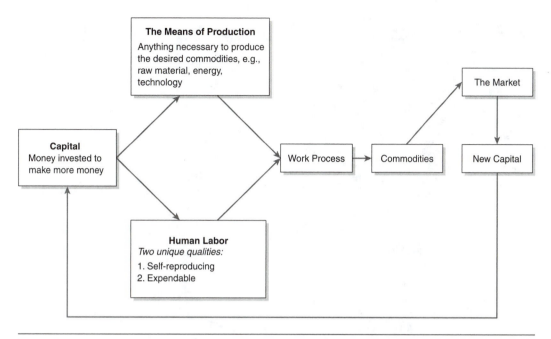

Figure 9.1   The Production of Capital—How Capitalism Functions

people worked under traditional obligations, typically at peasant farming. Under such a system, the extended family does not own the land or the farm, but rather, works a plot of land at the discretion of the owner. The peasants pay rent, sometimes in money (tenant farming), or sometimes in produce (sharecropping), and then consume the surplus or trade it for other goods or services (barter). Liberalization, the name given to the often forceful opening of markets and assimilation of localities into global capitalism, creates its own opposite. The cultural implications of global liberalization inspire resistance in the form of environmentalism, nationalism, religion, and sometimes all three together (McMichael 2000).

Globalization differs from multinationalism. The latter refers to a situation where large companies have offices and other facilities in multiple countries, yet each location functions more or less autonomously, and develops goods or services for each specific country or region. In globalization, each local or regional facility is integrated into a total worldwide system, such that work is allocated based on the greatest efficiency (Sklair 2001). For example, it is more efficient (i.e., cheaper) for General Motors to build its small-block V-8 engine in Michigan, and ship it to Australia, where workers assemble the engine with other parts from China, Thailand, and elsewhere, to produce the new Pontiac G8 sedan (a.k.a. the Chevy Caprice in the Middle East, the Buick Park Avenue in China, and the Holden Commodore in Australia), and then ship the finished car back to the United States (and elsewhere)—one car,

Image 9.1a   The Chalice of Romanos II tells us much about Byzantine culture. This item was made to impress, to exalt the divine status of the emperor. It is one of a kind, made of gold with hand-painted ceramic inlaid. This signifies a rich and powerful society that confers special privileges on the elite, and on The One. Although functional, it was used to serve wine only at the highest functions of state, and only the emperor was allowed to drink from it.

Image 9.1b   Similarly, the Styrofoam cup tells us much about the culture that produced it. It requires certain advanced chemical technology, yet the cup carries little value. Although functional, it has minimal lasting quality and when produced by the millions, signifies a throwaway attitude. Accessible to everyone, what kind of people would imbibe from such a coarse, unpleasant substance and discard it with such reckless abandon?

several names, with parts sourced from many locations and the car sent to market in many places.

In addition to economic globalization, culture has also gone global, and religion is part of culture. Culture refers to shared symbolic meaning. This can take physical or tangible form, for example, as pottery, clothing, music, and other artifacts. It also includes ideas and beliefs, or ideas and tangible artifacts in combination. Yet it is not the functional aspect of clothes, music, and so on that constitutes culture, but the particular style and the meaning or statement about life that they impart. Images 9.1a & b considers the culture encoded into the chalice of Romanos II, Byzantine emperor (chalice was made about 960 CE), and a Styrofoam cup.

Religion typically occurs as a set of beliefs and as a way of life, with a particular lifestyle and other practices. Like economics, culture in all its forms permeates the global system, and thus people can exchange cultural ideas and practices in much the same way as business transactions exchange goods and services for money. For example, body tattoos and piercing, both of which express specific religious meaning in their original cultures, have become popular forms of symbolic expression in Western societies. Although many tattooing and piercing aficionados (body modification or "body-mod" enthusiasts) declare their religious or spiritual affiliation or solidarity with the indigenous peoples with whom the body-mod practices originated, the meaning of these practices changes in the process of exchange. Tattoos and some forms of piercing have been common in the West for decades or even centuries, such as ear piercing, or associated with certain populations, such as tattoos among convicts and sailors. In the 1990s, tattoos became mainstream, as did more exotic forms of piercing.

In their cultures of origin, such as the tattoos of the Maori in New Zealand, or the nostril piercing among Hindu women in India, body modification conveys specific, socially recognized meaning. It means one thing to everyone, whether that meaning relates to power, status, wealth, age, or any number of other elements, separately or in combination. It is not a choice, nor is its meaning open to individual interpretation. For the Maori in New Zealand, men earn tattoos both through age and accomplishment, typically success in battle. Traditional Hindu women pierce the left nostril, guided by the Ayurvedic belief that it will make childbearing easier as it affects an important energy conduit in the body. In both examples, the practice corresponds directly with socially acknowledged rites of passage, status, or practical affairs, which collectively identify the individual—to himself or herself and to others—as someone who in fact belongs to a community, occupies a certain status location, and accepts the foundational beliefs of that community. In short, religion and social practice are united.

In contrast, tattooing and piercing are marginal when part of a subculture, and superficial types of consumption when mainstream. In their culture of origin, these body-mod practices are not choices that an individual makes, but rather, a status placed upon the individual by the community. In sociology, as mentioned in Chapter 1, individuals do not choose their own status; that depends on how other people perceive you. When reproduced in a global market, traditional symbols and practices lose part of their significance—the commonly accepted meaning—and thus lose their ability to define a group, even if the beliefs or practices are commonly acknowledged among members of a particular subgroup. Unless the larger society acknowledges the same meaning, tattoos, piercing, styles of dress, speech, and whatever else are simply differences, but not in themselves meaningful. To the extent they have meaning between different subgroups or between a subgroup and the hegemonic standard, each person or group is free to apply its own interpretation. For example, some contemporary people who identify themselves as witches wear a pentagram, which can be drawn two ways:

One is a symbol of existence, and the five points stand for the five elements: earth, air, fire, water, and spirit. The other is a symbol of evil and stands for domination. Can you tell the difference? Most people do not make a distinction, and if they think about it at all, assume that both represent evil—namely, Satan. However, for members of the Wicca subculture, the differences of course are vital. For the record, the first is Wiccan; the second, with the star pointing down, is a symbol of domination usually associated with Satanism. Since only members of the subculture would recognize such distinctions, or even care to, the image's value as a social or even personal statement is limited. In other words, the identity that the group claims for itself is not the identity that others recognize and therefore validate. Anyone who watches *Miami Ink* or *LA Ink*, two TV shows about tattoo shops, can readily see how intensely personal tattoos are. In highly stylized and artistic fashion, tattoos typically represent deaths of loved ones, personal interests, or abstract concepts such as salvation, enlightenment, or transformation. While interesting and compelling for the individual, they cannot convey social meaning without familiarity with the individual's life history.

The globalization of religion thus offers two competing potentials. On one hand, it offers an open exchange of ideas, beliefs, and practices, which people in some-times distant cultures might find meaningful. On the other hand, though, this tends to dilute or confuse the meaning of these beliefs and practices, which renders them much less effective in creating group cohesion and distinction compared to other groups in a pluralistic society. Depending on how the larger society perceives any given symbol, it may in fact construct an identity quite different from what the believers intend or what the symbol meant originally.

Haré Krishna: Indian Religion Arrives in the United States

Yet issues go well beyond symbols. In the 1970s in the United States, people suddenly became fearful of small groups who practiced strange rituals that many people regarded as suspicious, and even dangerous. Americans came to know these groups as religious cults. As we saw in Chapter 7, the label *cult* should be carefully adjudicated from *alternative religion* and other modes of social adaptation. In a few cases, as Chapter 7 illustrated, they did prove dangerous and even fatal. However, the vast majority of so-called cults are not dangerous, but rather, simply a religious import. As such, they appear strange and threatening to many Americans, but in their countries of origin, they are quite normal, even routine (Lewis 2001). In a sociological conceptualization, they are properly understood as alternative religions, not cults. For example, the Haré Krishna movement arrived from India as an alternative religious movement.

Properly known as the International Society for Krishna Consciousness (ISKCON), the group was founded in 1966 by an elderly Indian monk called Abhay Charan De Bhaktivedanta Swami (or Sri) Prabhupada (Image 9.3) (1896–1977). Abhay Charan De Prabhupada is his birth name, and his full name includes the titles of Bhakti-Vedanta

Image 9.3   Swami Prabhupada

(Devotion-Ultimate Knowledge), and Swami (or Sri), a term that indicates mastery of a spiritual discipline.

A variation of mainstream Hinduism in India, the core philosophy is based on scriptures such as the Bhagavad Gita and Srimad Bhagavatam, both of which date back centuries into antiquity. The distinctive appearance of the movement, with robes of yellow, pink, and other bright colors, and its culture derive from the Gaudiya Vaishnavism tradition, which has had adherents in India ever since the late 1400s. In the United States, ISKCON formed to help spread the practice of bhakti yoga (the yoga of devotion). Bhaktas, or devotees, dedicate their devotion to Krishna, whom they call "The Supreme Lord." They also celebrate Radha, who is Krishna's divine consort, and many other manifestations of Krishna, such as Sita and Rama. In traditional Hinduism, there is no formal hierarchy or organizational body, only the authority of individual gurus, who attract followers based on their ability to deliver gratifying teachings and other guidance to the seekers. Sometimes they are simply the elders in a local community.

The Maha Mantra

Haré Krishna Haré Krishna

Krishna Krishna Haré Haré

Haré Rama Haré Rama

Rama Rama Haré Haré

The mantra, or chant, of the members of the International Society for Krishna Consciousness (ISKCON), celebrates the aspects of God—Haré, Krishna, and Rama. Devotees believe that this chant invokes the rhythm or "transcendental vibration" of life energy that flows from the divine. As Swami Prabhupada explains,

> Krishna consciousness is not an artificial imposition on the mind; this consciousness is the original energy of the living entity. When we hear the transcendental vibration, this consciousness is revived. . . . This chanting of "Haré Krishna, Haré Krishna, Krishna Krishna, Haré Haré/Haré Rama, Haré Rama, Rama Rama, Haré Haré" is directly enacted from the spiritual platform, and thus this sound vibration surpasses all lower strata of consciousness—namely sensual, mental, and intellectual. . . . There is no need, therefore, to understand the language of the mantra, nor is there any need of any mental speculation or intellectual adjustment for chanting this maha-mantra. It springs automatically from the spiritual platform, and thus anyone can take part in the chanting without any previous qualification. (Prabhupada 1973)

Compared to the U.S. mainstream, the dress and practices of the Haré Krishna, such as meditation, vegetarianism, and commitment to poverty (all typical of monastic orders throughout the world's many religions), became fodder for active American imaginations. All sorts of lurid tales abounded about this entirely peaceful and spiritual group, such that the resulting hysteria led to cult deprogrammers who would kidnap people away from Krishna communes and force them to divest of all Krishna influence. This was often a traumatic process, as Bromley and Melton (2002) document. Parents decided, upon advice from professional "deprogrammers," that their perfectly normal and well-adjusted 18- to 20-somethings had been seduced and brainwashed by bizarre cults. The possibility that some alternative religious groups actually offered a preferable way of life seemed inconceivable (Dawson 1998b). These imports were viewed as not only strange, but subversive, and possibly evil. However, the features of Haré Krishna are entirely mainstream in India—asceticism, vegetarianism, meditation, inner harmony—and they are also features of monastic life found in many major religions, including Christianity. In short, Haré Krishna is basically an import, part of an established religious tradition in India that was then transplanted to the United States and, like in India, is premised on the teaching of a guru (Bryant and Ekstrand 2004; Tucker 2004). Regardless of its noncontroversial status in India, many of its precepts do not transplant to the different culture of the United States without controversy and conflict.

Such confrontations result from the multiculturalism that globalization produces. As local and regional religions traverse the globe, they come into contact with other local and regional religions. Often, some sort of conflict results, especially if the presence of a different religion provokes a legitimation crisis (Kurtz 1995:168–69). In the case of the Haré Krishna, the beliefs and values of ancient and traditional Hinduism and Indian culture challenged the legitimacy of the modern consumerist United States. The practices of a modest peasant culture—vegetarianism, meditation, and renunciation of material goods—not only differed from the American consumer mentality, but also challenged its very precepts and prompted questions: Could meaning and happiness really be found in a much simpler mode of life? In the global world, people must reconcile their familiar beliefs with the strangeness of recent imports, and in the process, reassess the legitimacy of their previously held beliefs in light of these new ones. While a new transglobal belief system may yet develop—a religion that carries some sort of global meaning and legitimacy but also legitimates local variations—it just as likely may fail to. The success of community over chaos depends on the ability and willingness of people to transcend their familiar provincialism and engage a larger and more complex world. As the local gives way to the cosmopolitan, a new system of meaning must make sense from a cosmopolitan worldview, rather than a strictly local one.

Overall, people in the modern age strive for meaning—specifically, for a nomos that both holds emotional content and facilitates a unique but practical lifestyle. What people seek in a world that has become increasingly commodified, homogenized, sterilized, genericized, and superficial, is authenticity in belief and practice—authentic experience. Let us now examine various types of religious experience and their likely outcomes.

Pentecostalism

Syncretism refers to a blend of two or more initially separate and different influences, which blend together and create a new form. This new form is not just the combination of the original influences, but a new form with fundamentally different attributes that differentiate it from any of the facets that created it. This has occurred throughout the history of Christianity, from ancient times to the present, and these influences have originated from Christian as well as non-Christian sources (Walls 2002). As Riley (2003) shows, Christianity arose from Jewish, Greco-Roman pagan, and Middle Eastern sources.

On January 1, 1901, a woman named Agnes Ozman began speaking in tongues during a service at the Bethel Bible College in Topeka, Kansas, led by Charles Fox Parham, a Methodist minister by training. Parham interpreted this as a sign from God, and shortly thereafter declared that speaking in tongues, called *glossolalia,* was the definitive proof that a person had received God's grace. So began Pentecostalism.

In those early years, Pentecostal services were often interracial, but by 1948, two denominations formed. One, the Pentecostal Fellowship of North America, determined that whites and blacks—indeed, all races—must remain separate according to God's will. The other denomination, the United Pentecostal Church, embraced interracial services. The two would unite in 1998 to form the Pentecostal-Charismatic Churches of North America.

In this context, "charismatic" refers to the belief that the Holy Spirit can and will possess people of true faith. A person so possessed will then be able to speak in tongues, and may manifest other behavior as well, such as writhing on the ground and experiencing various manner of convulsions.

Parham himself was greatly influenced by the British-Israelism movement (Barkun 1997), which believed that Anglo-Saxon Britons were the only true descendants of Adam. Using various linguistic conveniences, Parham argues, for example, that the Anglo-Saxons were descendants of the Tribe of Dan, the lost 13th tribe of Israel. Everywhere they went, they left behind names that include the D*N sequence. Since Hebrew does not write vowels, the middle letter can be any vowel. Thus, the river DANube (or *DONau* in German) in present-day Germany may indicate that the tribe passed through this region. Eventually, they settled in the British Isles, with their primary settlement in LonDON. No scientific evidence supports such linguistical claims, however. History tells us that the Romans founded London, which they called Londinium, and overall, linguistical similarity proves nothing. For example, the word *gift* exists in German, but it means "poison." Two words that happen to resemble each other often have completely different origins and meanings. The British-Israelists offered no physical evidence nor ancient written texts to support their claims.

Yet many like Parham accepted their claims, as well as their beliefs. One core belief was that only white people of Anglo-Saxon descent could be saved. Since God made a covenant with the people of Israel, not people in general, and since the Anglo-Saxons were the only supposed survivors, only they inherit the covenant and the potential for salvation. Thus in the United States, where race, especially black–white relations, is already a prominent feature of religion and politics, Pentecostalism syncretically arises from British-Israelism; American democratization of religion; and a desire for vital, powerful, emotional and religious experience. By itself, British-Israelism reflected the dominant version of British culture at the time—conservative and emotionally restricted public behavior. This contrasted sharply with Pentecostalism.

Rather, Pentecostalism revived the earlier Methodist charismatic tradition, yet in combination with the other influences, it becomes something unique, with unique beliefs and practices (David Martin 2001). One unique belief is that all people of true faith will eventually manifest glossolalia and other charismatic signs, and those who don't have not yet been saved. This alone demarcates Pentecostalism from mainline churches and from other charismatic churches, most of which, such as the Assemblies of God, believe that the Holy Spirit will possess only certain people, and that by itself possession does not indicate salvation, and therefore not all of those possessed will be saved. In comparison, Pentecostalism evidences a much greater democratic ethos—especially today after relinquishing racial segregation—in that all can be saved regardless of background or any other preceding factor (Cox 2001), and all will receive the Holy Spirit with outward manifestations.

When it started, Pentecostalism appealed mostly to poor people, both whites and blacks, and during Parham's lifetime congregations remained mostly segregated and confined to rural areas. At the time, rural life revolved around strict family and community obligations, with little free time and little individual opportunity for expression. The success of a farm, often relying on slim margins, depended on hard work for most of the year. Belief and lifestyle were not choices, but stipulations that family and community imposed. Pentecostalism allowed poor people in such circumstances a legitimate means to release suppressed emotions within a context that did not threaten the otherwise strict and staid social order.

Today, Pentecostalism has a much broader appeal that now draws from the middle class as well. Attendees are expected to dress well—usually suits and ties for men, and suits or dresses for women. Interestingly, Pentecostal churches in the poorest villages in Africa also uphold the standard of suits and ties, the purchase of which is a major investment for villagers (Anderson 2004). Pentecostals, in accordance with their roots in very controlled communities, expect their members to behave with utmost good manners and proper demeanor at all times—except, of course, during the service when the Holy Spirit may take over. Even when it does not, Pentecostals energetically, even ecstatically, participate in the service, with enthusiastic and boisterous singing and dancing. Such services typify the spectacle religions, in that each member must actively participate in the service, and the more the congregation takes part, the less formal and more energetic the service becomes. Possession by the Holy Spirit always takes precedence over any official itinerary.

Of all the versions of Christianity today, Pentecostalism is among the fastest growing, globally, and increasingly displaces Islam in parts of Africa and the Far East (Cox 2001; Jenkins 2003). This has produced extensive controversy and violence as aggressive Pentecostal missionaries penetrate traditional Muslim enclaves, especially for purposes of conversion. Although missionary work includes care for the poor, Pentecostalism is not primarily oriented toward social services, but is rather a ministerial denomination; it preaches salvation through inner spiritual healing, rather than worldy wealth or medical health (Synon 1997). In third world countries, Pentecostal churches do often improve the standard of living, but only to the extent that a person participates in the church and contributes directly to the church's development as an institution. There is little if any outreach, and little charity for nonmembers. The Church improves peasant housing, for example, but retains ownership of it as investment property. Like its U.S. progenitors, global versions of Pentecostalism in the third world and elsewhere, especially in Eastern Europe and Asia, operate like businesses (Cox 2001).

In fact, Pentecostalism in the third world grows fastest where poverty is the most entrenched. Whereas the largest first world cities, such as London, Paris, and New York, have populations of 7–10 million, comparable cities in the third world and developing countries are much larger, such as Seoul (23 million), Mexico City (20 million), and Mumbai, India, and São Paolo, Brazil, at 18 million each. All but 3 of the top 30 largest cities in the world are in poor or developing nations. In all cases, the majority of the population lives in abject poverty—miles and miles of slums. As Devisch (1995) and Nlandu (1998) found in Africa, or as Portes and Hoffman (2003) found in Latin America, Pentecostalism arises from many sources but always as a response to hopeless poverty. Such churches become quite lucrative, and they capitalize on the meager money of people who live 300 per toilet and who forage for food as often as they purchase it. What food might be available through foraging in an urban environment does not invite close scrutiny. Rats, dogs, pigeons, insects, and garbage offer the obvious possibilities. Amidst political incompetence, corruption, and foreign exploitation, Pentecostal revival in the third world "corresponds to grassroots spiritual renewal—a reenchantment of a catastrophic modernity" (Davis 2006:195) where faith healing, trances, prophetic dreams, and celestial tongues replace any hope of modern medicine, nutrition, and sanitation.

In conclusion, Pentecostalism allows people from conservative cultural backgrounds or economically depressed conditions to fully indulge and express powerful emotions, with glossolalia, singing, dancing, writhing, and convulsing all perfectly permitted—and indeed, the more powerful the manifestations of possession, the more respect the person receives from the congregation.

Yet as B. Wright and Rawls (2005) and Mike Davis (2002) found, the type and degree of spontaneity often correlates with race and class. Basically, the more white and/or wealthy a congregation becomes, the more the institution exerts managerial control, such that only certain officially approved forms of spontaneity are acceptable. Both traditionally spontaneous and managed types of Pentecostal congregations seek emotional outlet, but for different reasons. Low-income and ethnic minority congregations seek a reprieve from the bleakness of low-wage employment, while wealthy or white congregations seek release from emotionally stifling regimens of corporate and professional life, or from the stifling confines of emotionally repressed cultural standards. To the extent that Pentecostal services practice the style of spontaneity but without the actual unpredictable substance, they become increasingly *carnivalized*. The theory argues that this does not transcend ethnic or class differences, but rather, pretends that such differences do not exist at all (Kellner 2003). This may perhaps be true, but only within the walls of the church. The real world beyond the walls operates quite differently, where race and class inequality still dominate social life. As an example of the changing dynamics of race and class in the context of globalization, we now turn to original research by Melissa Guzman.

Nuestra Identidad: Identity Construction in a Latino Pentecostal Congregation

By Melissa Guzman

What if we suspect that some local religious movements constitute something new or different from what we already know? Can a survey help us if we don't know what questions to ask? Clearly, no. How do we determine what the important variables are? How do we interpret survey results without context? We can't, at least not meaningfully. Religious change is nothing abstract; it is beliefs, emotions, and spiritual identities in the process of social construction. I suggest that qualitative research is a necessary precursor to quantitative survey research, and context can only be discovered through ethnographic methods.

Thus, I developed a conceptual model to examine the process of collective identity construction in a local Latino Pentecostal congregation with a focus on gender, language, culture, and tradition. My goal is to suggest that beneath the assertion of a Pentecostal identity—in this local context—is the integration of specific culturally and institutionally created images, meanings, sentiments, and practices. Try measuring that quantitatively without knowing what questions to ask people! I attended a Latino Pentecostal church in a medium-sized Midwestern city, known historically for furniture and automobile manufacturing, and more recently as a medical research and delivery center and as a city with a rapidly growing university presence.

Pentecostalism has been able to successfully provide meaningful subcultures and collective identities to its adherents. Developing from Methodist and Baptist branches of Christianity at the end of the nineteenth century, Pentecostalism was concerned with adjusting rural migrants to city life in the United States. Moreover, since the concepts and practices of this religious movement have been considerably influenced by issues of culture and race, let me mention a couple of relevant points.

The general Pentecostal model is distinguished from other versions of Christianity by the diminishment of formal hierarchical distinctions through practice rather than through theology and is premised on the free expression of emotion. My study on the dynamics of Pentecostalism from the perspective of Latino immigrants demonstrates its ability to combine religious and secular matters in the construction of identity. Pentecostalism is a discourse of emotion, intertwining mind, body, and spirit—a fusion that diminishes the significance of formal leadership and theology and allows great flexibility.

To better understand the type and extent of influence that Latino culture exerts on the general Pentecostal model, my ethnographic analysis considered the language, traditions, concepts, and practices of a local congregation in the Midwestern United States, mostly composed of first-generation immigrants from Guatemala, Mexico, and lesser numbers from other Spanish-speaking nations. Specifically, I discovered that the notion of Pentecostal identity was influenced by Mexican cultural expectations more than other Spanish-speaking cultures. Why is Mexican culture so salient?

Pentecostalism has had a substantial impact among Spanish-speaking Latinos in the United States, precisely because it has employed vernacular language in the evangelization of recent immigrants. Latino Pentecostalism is linked to a search for community and equally to the creation of a unique identity. Since this church reaches out to adherents not just as Pentecostals, but also as Latino Spanish-speaking immigrants, I suggest that the construction of a Pentecostal religious identity accompanies the creation of an immigrant identity.

Along with culture, concepts about sex and gender were significant in the construction of a Pentecostal identity. Previous works examining the role and definition of gender among immigrant Pentecostal congregations have yielded ambiguous conclusions, proposing that Pentecostalism both prevents and allows for the maintenance of traditional gender attitudes and roles. These paradoxical conclusions make it necessary to question more carefully how gender relations were unfolding in this particular church; I focused on the subtle ways that women redefined traditional gender concepts. For instance, the section about the weekly *tamaladas* [group cooking Mexican-style corn-meal pies] shows how a uniquely Mexican socio-cultural practice integrates gendered metaphors and actions with Pentecostal demands for church women. The tamalada was a social event for the women, symbolizing how they subtly reclaimed their position in the congregation's spiritual identity. The tamalada organizes women congregants on a regular basis, and maintains a reliable financial source for the church institution.

As a result, Mexican traditions shape the social interaction outside of services, and this makes it an informal agenda-setting standard for church-related activities. It sets the Mexican way as the way to integrate Pentecostal and immigrant identities.

This makes Pentecostalism an actual response to the reality of a Latino community situated in a specific social world. It means that Mexican culture defines the way

(Continued)

(Continued)

to be an immigrant Latino/a Pentecostal, even if someone is not Mexican. It establishes linguistic, emotional, behavioral, and political stances that also define the religious stance. My ethnography allowed me to see that the emotional and spiritual judgments and attitudes of the congregation propel their actions within the church, interpreted through a Mexican lens. Yet the Mexican influence is informal and far from total, while outside forces such as the local educational system are formal but also far from total. The growing Latino influence is changing city institutions even as the Spanish-speaking community continues to evolve.

The Spanish language in Mexican dialect, Latino traditions and culture, immigrant status, and a shared understanding of certain gender and sex concepts were crucial elements in the construction and enactment of a Pentecostal identity for this congregation. The actions of this church were formulated by a particular context: a diverse Latino community thriving within a Pentecostal religious structure. Yet Pentecostalism has become a Latino institution only in the last 20 years at most. The Pentecostalism practiced in this congregation allowed the congregants to be socialized into a unique type of religious practice and belief, through which they could still readily design and perform their Latino identity along with the demands of the general Pentecostal identity model.

From my analysis, the practices of religion and identity construction are formed in relation to the demands of particular environments. The congregants of this Latino Pentecostal church gradually developed a Latino Pentecostal identity only after they actively integrated into a more institutionalized religious structure the realms of their spoken language, tradition and cultural practice, and beliefs about sex and gender.

Although my study resulted from years of concern with the experiences of Latinas in the United States, [and I am] a native Spanish speaker, I faced a few challenges. I must first acknowledge that the women in this congregation were a crucial source for my interpretations, and as a Latina myself, it allowed for close, intensive interaction. Second, engaging with the congregants in Spanish enabled me to examine the language and imagery as actually thought and spoken in a religious setting. Even so, reconciling different stances on religion and identity into an objective sociological model required a degree of analytical distance. Lastly, the reciprocity of my relationships with church members required a certain responsibility when interviewing and collecting data.

As a qualitative researcher, I seek the subtle underpinnings of my analyses—the up close and personal within the actual context of life. My ethnography took place in a real community of which I was not a member. Yet, closely analyzing theory and field data, while employing my sociological imagination, helped me establish key guidelines that I will likely embrace in future ethnographic projects.

I found that the location and demographic makeup of this church provided the right conditions for the creation of a Latino Pentecostal identity, as well as the construction of unique concepts of gender, language, and Latino culture, that was influenced by certain Mexican cultural standards. In particular, my findings suggest that the respective institutions and communities in which the congregants lived limited the potential explanations, interpretations, emotional responses, and metaphors about their own religious identities. The congregants constructed identities gradually as they responded to real-life conditions bounded by migrant status, religion, and language. At the same time, they evaluated collectively through the demands instilled by Anglo-Pentecostal traditions. The result—Nuestra Identidad. Latino immigrants are reshaping religion as well as politics and economics.

Roman Catholicism

Far older than Pentecostalism, the Roman Catholic Church has survived numerous wars, schisms, and splinter groups, mainly through syncretic assimilation and sometimes annihilation of local heretical movements and secular trends. The Roman Catholic Church was the first church of the late Roman Empire, after Constantine embraced Christianity and his successors made it the official religion of the empire. After the fall of the empire in the West in 476 CE, the Catholic Church continued through the Middle Ages as a more or less autonomous institution, with the pope, cardinals, bishops, priests, and brothers serving as a corollary to the secular nobles.

As Catholicism spread throughout Western Europe, it assimilated local pagan beliefs and symbols, such that the Saxon Winter Solstice Tree, for example, became the Christmas tree, and the pagan fall equinox festival, Halloween, became All Saint's Day and Day of the Dead, which Mexican Catholics still practice. Easter, based on the pagan Ostara, celebrates the rebirth of Jesus who rises from the dead and ascends to heaven, a belief that closely resembles the pagan rites of spring, when the gods return from the underworld and ascend back to their celestial homes. Giving them new names, the Catholic Church not only assimilated pagan symbols, but in the process, created a distinct version of Christianity, replete with extensive symbolism, lengthy rituals, and formal hierarchies. Furthermore, Catholic theology and doctrine follows the seasons and includes patron saints for all days and purposes. Saint Christopher, for example, protects travelers; Saint Crispin is the patron of cobblers and tanners; and Saint Martin is the patron of winemakers. Catholicism also celebrates numerous feasts in honor of saints, martyrs, and important events. All of this follows pagan customs.

In modern times, science presented a new type of challenge. Religions not only confronted other religions, but must additionally confront science as it impinged on issues once regarded as central to a religious worldview and the meaning of life. Whereas in ancient and medieval times the Church faced various religious challenges, both as it converted new territories and from within, in the form of heresies, it now faced a secular challenge. In the early days, the Church attempted to suppress scientific discovery, such as forcing Copernicus in 1497 to deny his discovery that the sun was the center of the solar system and that the earth rotated around it. The Church held to a geocentric view, that the earth was the center of the solar system and indeed of all creation, as the Bible seemingly indicates in Joshua 10:12–13 (see sidebar). He would not publish the

---

The Sun and the Moon Stand Still Around the Earth

The following biblical text has been used to claim that a day is missing from the cosmic record, and also that the earth is the center of the solar system, with the sun in orbit around the earth. Hence, the sun stops moving for a day.

Joshua 10:

(12–13) On the day the LORD gave the Amorites over to Israel, Joshua said to the LORD in the presence of Israel:

"O sun, stand still over Gibeon,

O moon, over the Valley of Aijalon."

So the sun stood still, and the moon stopped, till the nation avenged itself on its enemies, as it is written in the Book of Jashar. (New International Version)

theory until 1543 in his now famous *De revolutionibus orbium coelestium (On the Revolutions of the Heavenly Spheres)*.

Later, the church threatened Galileo with torture both for his experimental methods and for various specific discoveries. Among these, he identified four of Jupiter's moons in 1610—which he named Ganymede, Callisto, Io, and Europa, the names they still carry today. This also conflicted with the aforementioned geocentric theory, as it indicated that not only did Galileo support the heliocentric theory, but he also now claimed that other bodies had their own satellites, making the earth one planet among many, and not really the center of anything.

Many church fathers attacked Galileo for impiety, heresy, and atheism. In 1633, Galileo faced the Inquisition, an institution that Ferdinand and Isabella of Spain created in 1481, and appointed Tomás de Torquemada as Grand Inquisitor. Initially founded to persecute Jews and Muslims, its mandate had since expanded to include all manner of heresy and *maleficium*—evil deeds. Charged with heresy, Galileo was sentenced to life imprisonment. As Galileo was then 69 and in poor health, the Church commuted the sentence to house arrest. It would not lift the ban on his major contribution to science, the *Dialogo sopra i due massimi sistemi del mondo (Dialogue Concerning the Two Chief World Systems)* until 1822.

Since the time of the Inquisition, the Catholic Church has greatly changed its stance toward science. In 1962, The Vatican II Council reconsidered and reformulated much of Catholic doctrine, and officially changed the Church's position on various controversial scientific theories. Perhaps most controversial, the church developed an innovative approach to the theory of evolution. Concluding that the creation story in Genesis should be read metaphorically, not literally, the Council determined that Genesis teaches a moral lesson, not a literal history lesson. Consequently, the Church could accept evolution conceptualized as mitigated evolution. This holds that evolution occurs exactly as science argues, with the additional doctrine that God's hand guides it every step of the way. The Catholic Church could thus step confidently and without apologies into modern times. Science is correct, and so is belief. Science tells us *what* and *how* something happens, and faith—in this case, Genesis—tells us *why* it happens. As we will see, the concept of mitigated evolution actually differs considerably from "intelligent design" beliefs, that God created everything in its present form. The Catholic concept of mitigated evolution accepts that different types of phenomena require different approaches—science addresses empirical questions, and religion addresses the meaning and purpose of life. Stephen Jay Gould (2002), an evolutionary biologist, makes an identical argument. In contrast, intelligent design, creationism, and other beliefs associated with contemporary fundamentalism do not hold science and religious belief to be either different or equally valid, but rather, they attempt to subsume science within religion.

For Catholicism, syncretism takes two forms. In the older form, the Church assimilated existing beliefs within its own Christian and ecclesiastical framework. In the modern era, the Church adapts doctrine in order to make it compatible with different types of knowledge. In other words, it does not seek to refute the theory of evolution, which as a theory of science draws on different criteria of proof—logic and observable evidence. Neither does the Church deny its own moral framework, history, or rituals. Instead, it acknowledges that science pertains to observable phenomena, and the Church pertains to existential issues, the four great questions that Peter Berger posited in Chapter 1. The Catholic Church thus emerged from Vatican II in a new form—not just updated, but essentially different in its relationship to science. Catholic doctrine and traditions considerably predated modernism and the emerging global system, but changed as the world changed. Rife with conflict, this change occurred over centuries. By 1962, however, the Church could no longer deny the forces of modernism and globalization. The reality of the world system in terms of culture and political conflict was reshaping the world with irresistible force.

Global Clashes

Russia

Not all syncretic developments lead to positive effects that inform new and progressive social and religious change. Often, the cultural sharing that characterizes globalization collides with long-established traditions. Let us start with American Pentecostalism as it spreads today in Russia and conflicts with the Russian Orthodox Church.

In the period of the Soviet Union, 1917–1989, the government officially disallowed all religious observation, including the historic church of Russia, the Orthodox Church. The Church was founded in 988 when the Prince of Kiev, Vladimir I, converted to the religion of the Byzantine Empire, known properly as the One Holy and Apostolic Church, which today we commonly refer to as the Eastern Orthodox Church. The Russian Church grew in power and prestige and became independent of the Patriarch of Constantinople in 1448, and after the fall of Constantinople in 1453, the Russian Orthodox Church under the Patriarch of Moscow became the center of Orthodoxy. Just as Constantinople had become the Second Rome, Moscow was now called the Third Rome, which signified its position as the new center of the Eastern Church.

With such a long and exclusive history, the Church today faces recent imports, foremost among which stands Pentecostalism. The fall of communism not only freed the Russian Orthodox Church from state suppression under communism, but freed people to consider other faiths as well. As in the United States, Pentecostalism offers exciting new possibilities in terms of belief and services. It suggests a connection to the future, compared to the medieval culture of the Orthodox Church. The Patriarch still wears traditional regalia from the Middle Ages, and the Church still practices the lengthy rituals, thus seeming quite anachronistic to many Russians. In contrast, Pentecostalism offers contemporary styles, and with an emphasis on proper attire, connects Russians culturally to fashions of the West. The emotionally charged services offer a release from daily drudgery and integrate Russians with the thriving culture of the West. Since 2004, the Russian economy has entered a great boom period, and is now grouped with other large, rapidly developing economies, namely, the BRIC countries (Brazil, Russia, India, China). Communism and medievalism are gone, and the future looks much brighter than it has in decades.

Image 9.4   Alexei II, Patriarch of Russia, and President Vladimir Putin. The Patriarch presided over Putin's inauguration, and the two often appear together in public, each in his official role. This follows Russian tradition, itself descended from Byzantine tradition, that the head of state and the head of the Church embody the entirety of Russian civilization and its people.

Source: Copyright © Getty Images.

Why should all of this cause conflict? Many see Pentecostalism as a foreign and un-Russian version of Christianity. The Orthodox Church is not only old, but it is also specifically Russian, a part of Russian cultural and national identity. As Filatov (1999) finds, various alternative religions have inundated Russia, in addition to various mainline churches. It seems that the greater the difference between an imported religion and Russian Orthodoxy, the more popular the import becomes. In addition to Pentecostalism, evangelical fundamentalism in general is also among the most popular (Elliott and Deyneka 1999). Although Putin will step down as president in 2009, his hand-picked successor will be Dimitri Medvedev, and Putin will remain in government as prime minister (Rodgers 2008). During his time as president, Putin removed many of Russia's democratic reforms and centralized his own power. The Orthodox Church entered into a tenuous alliance with Putin in order to maintain its own position over and against foreign imports, and in turn, offered Putin some measure of legitimacy (Warhola 2007). Although he has been dismantling Russian democracy, the Church blessed him as a "true" Russian (Politkovskya 2004). So long as the economy continues to climb, people will likely tolerate the decline of democracy (Shevtsova and Bouis 2005). Perhaps Putin's faith is genuine, but even so, the Orthodox Church makes a powerful political ally, and the Church in turn benefits as the ethnonationalist (the patriotic church) of Mother Russia compared to the so-called foreign invaders.

Poland

Poland and Russia are both Slavic cultures, but the Catholic Church dominates Poland, compared to the Eastern Orthodox Church in Russia. Over the centuries from the Middle Ages to the present, Eastern and Western forces fought for political influence and religious dominance in lesser developed or nonaligned countries. Like the Orthodox Church in Russia, the Catholic Church in Poland is intricately woven into cultural life and awareness. For many, being Polish inherently means being part of the Polish Catholic Church. Just as Russian nationalism includes the Orthodox Church, so Polish nationalism includes the Catholic Church.

Also like in Russia, globalization has brought new versions of Christianity and many religious products to Poland. Outside Soviet domination since about 1980, even while it remained officially part of the Eastern Bloc, Poland has imported Western culture for decades longer than Russia has. In addition to Pentecostalism and Western Protestantism in general, New Age religions also flourish in Poland. Historically monolithic, even the Polish Catholic Church now produces internal divisions, many of which follow a tradition of Catholic visionaries in Poland, but some others exhibit a more globalized synthesis of traditional Polish religious culture and New Age commercialism that challenges not only Church leadership, but also the position of the Church in Poland. Many see such blends as foreign incursions, as a corruption of the Church and Polish culture (Koscianska 2005). New Age religions are collections of beliefs, drawn from many different religions, and assembled as any one individual prefers. New Age beliefs emphasize a self-centered approach to spirituality, and reject any form or organization. They also reject collective responsibility and morality, which frees the individual to pursue his or her own moral path, or no particular moral path at all. It is the religion of extreme individuality.

Yet these incursions are not new in this part of the world. New Ageism, of course, is new, a product of the late twentieth century, but unofficial visionaries have been common in Poland. One of the most celebrated was Faustina Kowalska, now Saint Faustina. Born in 1905 in Glogowiec, Faustina entered the Congregation of the Sisters of our Lady of Mercy, a convent, sometimes in her 20s. Shortly thereafter, she began to experience visions. Over time, these events included physical convulsions, trances, and extended periods of isolation in her convent cell. As Catholic canonical law requires, the Church conducted an official investigation to determine the veracity of her visions and other symptoms of experience with the divine. Using the formal standards of proof as established in Church law, the appointed committee determined that

Image 9.5   Jesus, as he appeared to Sister Faustina

her experiences were not authentic, that Faustina was mistaken in the nature and significance of her visions and other manifestations (Koscianska 2005). Official condemnation did not deter sister Faustina, and her visions inspired a new form of devotion within the Church, the Divine Mercy (see Image 9.5).

Tolerated as a fringe movement—not quite sufficiently contrary to official doctrine to formally be expelled and not quite acceptable enough to be officially recognized—the Divine Mercy movement has endured since Faustina's time at a consistent but low level of popularity. The Divine Mercy is only one of several such small populist movements, and the Church historically prefers to tolerate them rather than make an issue of any particular group, which might inspire more vehement resistance to the official hierarchy and generate greater popularity for such movements. However, the Divine Mercy would gain more attention beginning in the late 1990s, when a new woman appeared, claiming visions from St. Faustina.

Sister Zofia, like Faustina, is an uneducated rural woman of poor and ordinary upbringing. Zofia leads a devoted group, calling themselves the Legion of Small Knights, within the Divine Mercy tradition. As it is widely held in Polish culture and Catholicism that dead Saints and martyrs share visions with people like themselves, Zofia's claim that St. Faustina delivers visions to her makes sense to religious Poles. At this level, Zofia resembles many such visionaries from poor and uneducated backgrounds who gain momentary notoriety and then slide back to anonymity. Zofia's visions have proven far more resilient however, because her visions not only follow the Divine Mercy traditions of St. Faustina, but incorporate global New Age elements as well.

As Victor Turner (1974) argues, populist movements within established religious traditions often become *liminal,* that is, they reaffirm an antistructuralist association between members, that relations should be "undifferentiated, egalitarian, direct, extant, non-rational, existential" (p. 274). In sociological terms, the liminal religious community mirrors the characteristics of its populist constituents, in that formal rituals, hierarchies, and structure do not interfere with the simple and direct relations between people. To a great extent, the Legion of Small Knights is a liminal community of believers. They attest to the special spiritual status of Sister Zofia, who in turn proclaims her humility to other people and to God, and also to the Polish Catholic Church. Although she has no official status in the Church, and the Church in fact denies her any religious authority, Zofia nevertheless declares her unfailing and eternal devotion to the Church as a common member (Koscianska 1995).

The most controversial aspects of Zofia's claims transgress not only official Catholic doctrine, but Polish religious culture more generally. Sister Zofia teaches that each person must harness his or her own spiritual energy. Her use of this concept closely resembles the Human Energy Field (HEF) idea common to New Age beliefs. The HEF is a potential within each person, and in order to achieve health, success, psychological stability, or anything else, a person must learn to harness and control this energy. While it's true that New Agers borrow freely from all religions, the more sophisticated argue that many religions teach HEF manipulation, especially the meditative traditions, and of these, especially Buddhism (Bowman and Sutcliffe 2000, Sutcliffe 2003). However, where meditation in Buddhism pertains traditionally to spiritual enlightenment by settling the mind and removing distractions, New Agers use mediation primarily for personal gratification or material accumulation (Heelas 1996; Possamai 2005; Rothstein 2002; Sutcliffe 2003). Similarly in Poland, New Age religion "assembles people based on an individualistic self-development and personality transformation, within a mystical, transcendent social cultural context" (Dorota Hall 2005:271). As Hall notes about Poland, New Age religion assimilates local elements as it does elsewhere, and in the case of Poland, this means it assimilates elements of Catholicism.

In sharp contrast to New Age beliefs that seek to privilege the individual over any collective responsibility, Sister Zofia professes total devotion to the Catholic Church and that only through submissive and humble devotion to God, through Catholicism, can a person gain healing, salvation, and so on. In contrast, new Age religions place the individual above and beyond all moral codes and collective responsibility (Hedges and Beckford 2000; Heelas 1996; Rothstein 2002). Zofia rejects this kind of individualism. On a conscious level, then, Zofia poses no challenge to traditional Catholicism.

Sociologically, however, her position is not so simple. Regardless of conscious intent, the fact that Zofia incorporates contemporary notions of human energy that closely resemble New Age beliefs makes her movement not only nontraditional, but secular as well. At best, she dilutes Catholicism by according secular beliefs equal status with traditional doctrine. In addition, Zofia detracts from formal Church authority, in that she teaches each individual to recognize the power of God within himself or herself, and that God works independently of the Church. More exactly, an individual does not require the formal Church to achieve health or salvation. This suggests that the Church is just a rubber stamp on personal devotion.

Despite her declarations of Catholic piety, the functional outcome of her movement is to detour around Church hierarchy, not pass through it. As sociologist Agnieszka Koscianska (2005) argues, the Legion of Small Knights constitutes a clear divergence from official Catholicism, and is rather "Polish ethnocentric Catholicism" (p. 171). Whatever her conscious intentions, Zofia understands Catholicism from the perspective of an illiterate rural person who conflates

Catholicism with the Polish language and culture. Zofia's notion of a perfect world, so to speak, is a restored rural primacy that has long passed from existence. As in the West, small towns in Poland are rapidly dying, having lost economic salience long ago. As a grassroots mystic, Zofia's Catholicism is nationalistic and discriminatory. Furthermore, she counsels women to defend the traditional moral values and way of life. With little knowledge of or even exposure to contemporary urban and cosmopolitan life in Poland's major cities, Zofia seeks a return to a rural idealism, with the Church as the uncontested moral center and authority. Zofia's beliefs contain a clear contradiction, that on one hand the church is the absolute moral authority of Polish society, and on the other hand, that each individual must find his or her own moral values through direct communication with Christ or their patron saint. In this way, the Legion contains elements of contemporary fundamentalism, imported from the West. Everyone must learn and remain in their proper God-given place, always submissive to religious authority and the straightforward Word of God. At the same time, each individual must find for himself or herself the correct path in life and the correct code to follow. A person is thus at once a stand-alone individual with the personal authority to seek his or her own path, and an anonymous member among many who submits to a higher authority.

Koscianska concludes that the Legion of Small Knights thus constitutes a Polish version of religious fundamentalism and conservatism. It syncretically joins traditional Catholicism with Polish nationalism and New Age beliefs and fundamentalism imported from the West. Such populist movements are not new in Poland, as Zofia herself follows in the tradition of the Divine Mercy movement that St. Faustina inspired. Once viewed as heretical, Faustina now holds official recognition as a saint. However, Faustina and other populists led very localized movements that conformed to local customs and thus rarely found appeal beyond their place of origin. In contrast, the broader influences in the Legion demonstrate larger connections to the world, despite the fact that Zofia rejects or seems oblivious to global influences. The fact that she unknowingly incorporates such elements testifies to their pervasiveness: global forces have even reached an illiterate peasant woman in Poland. Contrary to her intentions, Zofia has created a global movement—a movement that at once contests the globalization of Poland, and is itself globalized. New Age influences surround the Legion of Small Knights and subject them to global influences, whether they realize it or not. They are a reaction to globalization, but in their resistance, they ironically expand the forces of globalization they oppose, and, under the guise of rural tradition, infuse the olish Catholic Church with the modern and cosmopolitan forces they seek to exclude.

The Russian case is not so clear, however. As we have seen, Vladimir Putin, a former KGB operative, has joined with the Russian Orthodox Church to create a Russian ethnocentric orthodoxy. This union both resonates with centuries-old tradition, demarcates Russian culture from outside imports, and also hints at a new partnership. Like the great tsars of old, the State and the Church will once again lead the people to greatness. Yet this is not the hereditary monarchy of the past, but a forward-looking and fully modern government ready to move Russia into the global arena. At least, this is the image that Putin would like to cultivate. Strategic and shrewd, Putin does not devote his time to trivial or whimsical actions. Whatever his vision of the future, he hopes to achieve a new Russian nationalism by invoking the ethnic and religious sentiments of the past.

As in the United States, the established religion of Poland—Catholicism—has a faction aligned with the far right. Koscianska provides the discussion that follows.

Mohair Berets: The Development of Fundamentalism Within the Catholic Church in Poland

By Agnieszka Koscianska

The death of the Pope John Paul II (April 2, 2005) created in Poland a deep mourning combined with various spontaneous expressions of commitment to the pope. For the entire week between the pope's death and his funeral, followers prayed together not only in churches but also on the squares and in the streets. Advertisements disappeared from the media and people turned off the lights in their apartments at 9:37PM (the moment of his death). Commentators, both scholars and journalists, stressed that Polish society was experiencing a true religious revival. Young participants were crowned "generation JP2." However, those who were not religious complained that they felt excluded from the community or pressured to participate in the national sorrow.

At the same time, the death of the Polish pope facilitated an internal division of the Polish Roman Catholic Church, which had existed for a long time. Fundamentalists of Radio Maryja—a Catholic radio station established in 1991—have gained enormous influence. The presidential and parliamentary elections held in the fall of 2005 were won by candidates supported by Radio Maryja. The charismatic leader of Radio Maryja, Father Rydzyk, is a Redemptorist—part of an ecclesiastical order that calls people to closely imitate the life of Christ. They believe that religious teaching should be simple, direct, and powerful. His media company now includes not only Radio Maryja but also a TV station, a daily newspaper, and a school of journalism.

Radio Maryja represents the fundamentalist wing in the Polish Roman Catholic Church. Radio Maryja commentators tout a conspiracy theory: the Polish nation is in danger due to Jews and Freemasons, the main rulers of global capitalism. This worldview is a mixture of historical Polish anti-Semitism and nationalism, the latter now supposedly under threat from modern phenomena such as globalization and the transnational flow of ideas. At the same time, Radio Maryja itself obviously uses modern technology. Therefore it should be understood as a reaction to modernity and postsocialist transformation, and thus as a reaction to social change, and not as an antitechnological or anti–mass media movement.

As Radio Maryja and other media belonging to Father Rydzyk have been criticized for being anti-Semitic and crudely nationalistic, the Polish episcopate has tried to exert some control. However, those efforts have not brought any results. Radio Maryja is an influential radio station and members of parliament as well as ministers of the Polish government, including the prime minister, are very often guest speakers on it.

During political broadcasts on Radio Maryja, politicians combine religion and politics, and religious language thus becomes a language of politics. This tendency dominates the public discourse in contemporary Poland. Although in Poland there is an official separation of Church and state, many religious issues became the main concern of the ruling elites. Issues discussed by the politicians consist of a wide range of topics central to the interest of the Church in general, not only of the fundamentalist wing.

(Continued)

(Continued)

Promotion of family values constitutes an important element of the government's policy. From the conservative perspective, the family is understood as a union of man and wife who have a lot of children. Women are supposed to stay at home while men work outside the home. At the same time, pro-family politics is part of the fight against gay rights and feminist postulates. The fight against abortion and contraception is also a focal point. Right-wing politicians attempted to change the Polish Constitution in order to introduce further restrictions to the anti-abortion law, the most restrictive in Europe. The same group also tried to propose a law that would require contraceptives to have the same kind of warning labels as cigarettes, saying that usage is a threat to women's health and life. Those two legislative initiatives eventually failed, but they were seriously considered and found support among Church officials and many members of parliament. It is worth adding that anti-abortion activists collaborate with pro-life movements from abroad, mostly the United States (see Włodarczyk 2005).

Church involvement in the political sphere is not a new phenomenon in Poland; for instance, during Communist rule, the Church supported the Solidarity movement in the 1980s. At the same time, however, the Church also advocated for the dignity and rights of Polish citizens. Catholic intellectuals, who are open to dialogues with other social groups and worldviews, were the most visible group in the Church (see, for example, Casanova 1994), whereas now the fundamentalist extremists are highly influential.

What are the social and cultural mechanisms that contribute to the popularity of Radio Maryja and the success of the radical right in the 2006 elections? Who are the supporters?

Supporters of the political right are usually people without higher education, representing older generations, living in small towns and in the countryside, and having smaller incomes. I would like to emphasize that the Polish right is nationalistic, religious, and conservative in moral terms. At the same time, it puts a stress on values such as social solidarity and at least declares the [need for] maintenance of the welfare system.

An active group of supporters of Radio Maryja (and the political right) consists of elderly women. They organize parish associations of Radio Maryja listeners and participate in pro-life marches. Moreover, they are linked by informal networks led by visionaries, lay persons (mostly elderly women) who claim revelations from God and the Virgin Mary—revelations that are hardly ever officially recognized by the Church (see Koscianska 2005).

These women are disrespectfully called "mohair berets," as woolen or mohair berets are popular among elderly women in Poland. At the same time, this expression has military references in Polish (e.g., Green Berets). However, the disrespect expressed by the politicians and journalists who use this expression is also an important factor contributing to the popularity of the radical right and the development of religious fundamentalism. The more that intellectual elites and the liberal media ridicule these "common" women, the more popular the women become. These women (though not only women) represent a social group excluded from the advantages of the postsocialist transformation, not only economically but also in that their problems have been marginalized within neoliberal discourse that dominates political-economic discourse in Poland (Buchowski 2006).

For these women, religion combined with nationalistic ideology often remains the only space for activity in the contemporary world, and the only support for dealing with life problems such as poverty or lack of health care. This also relates to a Polish model of womanhood, which requires women to take care of their families and the national community, and allows them (and sometime requires them) to act in the public sphere. Furthermore, this concept of womanhood stands in opposition to new images and identities that became visible with the postsocialist transformation. Within this model, women's agency is not always defined as a capacity for autonomous action, but rather is relational, based on commitment to God and to community (the family, the nation, etc.). Fundamentalist movements allow religious elderly women, as well as others who are excluded from the advantages of post–Cold War restructuring, to participate in defending their nation and their families, though leaders often manipulate them and use them nefariously to achieve their own political goals.

Queer Islam in the United States

Not all developments within globalization need inspire conflict, or even if they do, they may include prosocial developments as well. Indeed, as transplanted religions interact with the local culture, they not only inject their own elements into multiculturalism, but also change in accordance with the local culture. In this example from Mahruq Khan, Islam in the United States has developed a public aspect—a viable openly gay constituency. Legally prohibited and often staunchly punished in Islamic nations, Muslim homosexuality in the United States finds a much more open and tolerant culture.

"I'm Gay by God's Grace" and "I'm Muslim by God's Grace": Reconciling a Queer Muslim Identity in America

By Mahruq Khan

What images come to mind when you think of Muslims? If you are like many Americans, you might think of Arabs, terrorists, and oppressed women in headscarves or burqas. These and other stereotypes have historically constrained our knowledge of Muslims. As the religious landscape of the United States continues to become more complex, and international conflict between the United States and the Middle East intensifies, such stereotypes can have wide-reaching consequences.

However, there are additional layers of stereotypes that exist within minority groups. For instance, when Muslim leaders teach their followers that homosexuality is a sin in Islam, many heterosexual Muslims develop hostile feelings towards lesbian, gay, bisexual, transgendered, and queer (LGBTQ) persons. As a result, many Muslims (and non-Muslims) think the "queer Muslim" identity is a paradox. But queer Muslims do exist, and they face multiple oppressions based on their faith, sexual orientation, race, and sometimes even their gender status. Despite these obstacles, a growing number of queer Muslims are reconciling their religious and sexual identities and struggling for greater acceptance and equality, and in doing so, they are working to make faith communities more inclusive.

Since many queer Muslims are first- or second-generation Americans, they are embedded within immigrant faith communities that emphasize the importance of maintaining group solidarity and a distinct identity in their host society. One way they do this is by emphasizing specific family and gender roles (Denton 2004; Nichols 1996). Religious leaders uphold sexual taboos against conduct they see as threatening family structure, community stability, and even the survival of their faith itself. The

(Continued)

(Continued)

maintenance of these established gender and sexual categories, however, relies in part on continuous condemnation of any sexual behavior that contradicts these fixed roles (Davies 1982). This condemnation, often with the additional backing of scripture or divine law, results in queer Muslims being ostracized by their faith communities.

In my ethnographic research of Muslims in the United States, heterosexual Muslims expressed homophobia based both on Muslim religious rhetoric and on preexisting homophobia in American culture. All of the queer Muslims I interviewed heard Sunday school teachers, mosque imams, family members, and friends describe homosexuality as "wrong," "sinful," and "unacceptable." The cultural (nonreligious) homophobia that heterosexual Muslims propagate includes ridiculing, criminalizing, and fearing queer persons. Drawing from American culture, some heterosexual believers employ terms such as "sick," "faggots," and "disgusting" to describe queers in general and queer Muslims in particular.

Rejection of homosexuality is a common family experience for queer Muslims as well. Many religious families refuse to accept their son/daughter's dual identity as both Muslim and gay. Especially after they "come out," some queer Muslims' families and friends react with blame, guilt, denigration, and emotional disconnection. Some parents also threaten to rescind financial support for their children and try to "cure" their homosexuality through psychological counseling or religious healing. As a result, many queer Muslims find their relationships with Muslim relatives and friends strained, and they choose to avoid emotionally detrimental relationships. Others opt not to come out because they fear it would dishonor, disrespect, or emotionally burden their families, and especially their parents. This distress that queer Muslims experience results in dissociation from their mainstream faith communities, self-loathing, suicide attempts, and attempts to cure their sexual orientation. As Boisvert (2000) notes, marginality and exile have clearly emerged as two central images in gay believers' lives.

While many queer Muslims in the United States and around the world still struggle with their sexuality, there are shifting social forces within the American context that are enabling some to slowly start accepting their sexual orientation, come out to their family members and friends, and even create networks to support struggling queer Muslims. While some, including fundamentalists, react to a pluralistic environment by seeking a return to an idealized vision of the past, progressive and queer Muslims draw strength from the interaction of secular and religious ideologies and the fading of distinct cultural boundaries and social roles in societies such as the United States. Facilitated by easy access to alternative perspectives and lifestyles via the Internet, believers are inspired and empowered to contest commonly held beliefs and generate newer, more inclusive interpretations of religious doctrine. As more Muslims gravitate toward culturally diverse universities and large cities, and pursue careers outside their ethno-religious enclaves, they interact more frequently with queer neighbors, colleagues, and religious community members. In addition, the anti-Muslim sentiments generated by the September 11 attacks have led many heterosexual Muslims to become more sensitive to the need and rights of other minority groups.

The depiction of Islam as the enemy of freedom and democracy, and the continued association of Muslims with terrorism by the U.S. mainstream media and government officials, affect how queer Muslims are treated by the broader queer community. Queer Muslims feel excluded by non-Muslim or secular queer circles due to their racial, ethnic, or religious minority status, and many choose to hide their religious affiliation in these contexts. They lead refracted lives in many different contexts; they hide their sexual orientation from other Muslims and they hide their religious identity from other queers, fearing persecution of one form or another.

The disconnection that they experience from the broader queer community leads many queer Muslims to seek support from each other. They have formed their own organizations like al-Fatiha and Salaam Canada to offer a safe physical and emotional space for queer Muslims, allowing them to meet other queer Muslims and share their practice of faith with one another. These organizations, and the networks they foster, influence how queer Muslims frame their religious and sexual identities. The Internet has further facilitated religious community development through e-mail groups for queer, gay, lesbian, bisexual, intersexed, and transgendered Muslims. Through electronic communication, queer Muslims are able to maintain contact and foster mutually supportive relationships in a space that allows for flexible communication, sexual diversity, and collective discussions over religious matters.

These developing communities are playing a key role in addressing the cognitive dissonance associated with being queer and also being a religious adherent. The shared experiences of gay believers and their efforts to reform religious doctrine (Mahaffy 1996) enable the reconciliation of religious and sexual identity. In addition, the increasing visibility of queer persons in the media also contributes to Muslims' belief in their right to a queer identity.

Muslims also learn to accept themselves as queer by emphasizing traditional Islamic concepts such as God's love and mercy for all peoples, by accepting their sexual orientation as more permanent than temporary, and by not singling out Islam as uniquely homophobic compared to other monotheistic faiths. As queer Muslims recognize how their own religious beliefs and practices have traditionally reflected the standpoint of heterosexist men, a theological space has emerged for their own counterarguments, perspectives, and alternative practices. Dialogues online, at conferences, or in local meetings show gay believers that they do not need to resign themselves to marginalization and social labeling (Buchanan et al. 2001).

As this queer faith community is becoming more diverse, members are providing religious advice and support to one another that is ethnically, racially, and sexually specific. Interestingly, white, queer Muslim converts are actively helping immigrant and second-generation Muslims reconcile their sexual identities with their faith. By using their cultural capital as whites and their greater familiarity with secular queer rights groups, converts are uniquely equipped to bridge social divides, not only between Muslim and non-Muslim queers but also between American Muslims and the society at large.

My research found that queer Muslims are defying narrow conceptions of faith and sexuality. These individuals continue to pray, fast, read the Quran, and perform other religious rituals despite isolation from their religious communities. Access to secular civil and human rights discourse in the United States, combined with an emphasis on scriptural passages that focus on God's love and mercy, enables queer Muslims to accept their sexuality, reject male/female gender binaries, and transcend gender-based limitations on worship. If current trends are any indication, this diversity will increase as the community's gender, sexual, and racial differences become more variant and as believers find their social or spiritual needs unmet by existing institutions. Though the religious marketplace of the United States definitely facilities pluralism and competition, the queer Muslims that I interviewed for my research have not chosen to leave Islam to join Protestant, Catholic, or Jewish congregations. Instead, they have remained committed to their faith and have injected critical doubt and the discourse of civil, sexual, and human rights in order to create space for themselves within Islam. The establishment of openly queer Muslim identities and communities is creating interpretations and practices of Islam that place respect, dignity, and justice at the core of belief.

Types of Religious Experience

The global and religious marketplace did not arise overnight, and neither has all religious experience become commodified. The increasing exchange of beliefs and practices suggests that people are searching for new and authentic experience—not mass-produced tokens of identity, but something they find to be real and genuine that corresponds to lived experience and education. Many also feel their culture and people face assimilation or extinction unless they can maintain some sort of unique identity. In this context, religion requires experience as well as belief that affirms one's place in the world. Still, membership in any given religious community is not automatic in the global context, and each of the following types has different requirements for participation, that is, to become and be recognized as a legitimate member. Furthermore, each type below represents a different social configuration, which may or may not be possible in the contemporary world (see Table 9.1).

Folk religion is the oldest type of religious experience. In this type, the beliefs and practices are particular to a given, usually very small locale; as we saw with the gods of polytheism, each village had its own deity. The folk—the one people—hold one set of beliefs and practices that correspond directly to daily living and to the events that define a person's life, ascension to adulthood, marriage, childbirth, and death being among the most common of such events. Everyone participates in worship, in celebration, and in nearly all events of the community. Everyone has a particular place in life; religion in this context reinforces the specific roles of the individual, and therefore the relationship of the individual to the community. There are no choices to make, no different or competing beliefs or lifestyles to consider. Tradition governs all aspects of life, including religion.

Popular religion broadens the size of the world, so to speak, in which beliefs and practices reside. No longer limited to a small and immediate locale, popular religion

Table 9.1   Types of Religious Experience

Folk Religion	Localized and homogeneous. Membership is compulsory and tradition governs all aspects of life. Religion and daily life coincide. Unity depends on upholding and enforcing tradition.
Popular Religion	Various religions coexist as they spread beyond their locale of origin, but the underlying patterns of life coincide with each religion. Unity arises from shared experience rather than belief.
Mass Religion	Unique to modern society, it standardizes doctrine and practice, but along very general guidelines that can be adapted to correspond with life in different locales. Unity depends on shared if very general beliefs.
Spectacle Religion	Also unique to modern society, it retains the generalized aspects of mass religion, but allows even greater adjustment, even to the individual level of preferences. Unity depends on feeling, not correspondence between belief and practice with actual ways of life.

arises when differing cultures interact. Different beliefs and practices coexist, but the underlying way of life matches closely enough that people recognize the essential elements of this coexistence as more or less equivalent. For example, the Greek god Zeus corresponds to the Roman god Jupiter, each the king of his respective pantheon. Popular religion is a collection of beliefs, all mingling together such that sometimes they exist alongside each other and sometimes blend together. Popular religion describes how the population understands religion, and it occurs when somewhat different communities interact but remain basically compatible because of similar lifestyles, hierarchies, economies, and so on.

However, not all communities are compatible. When incompatibility occurs, two basic outcomes are possible. First, they may remain in ongoing conflict, each seeking advantages over and against the other(s). Second, they may combine, syncretically, and generate a new form that is more than just a blend of the parts, but something entirely different. However, in order for the new form to be meaningful, it must correspond to actual lived experience, as we have seen. If it appears as abstract, it becomes a form without substance, without relevance to the real world. As an abstraction, such a religion requires force to establish itself as part of the social order. In order to challenge and eventually supersede established traditions, some powerful group or class must promote the new religion, using whatever wealth, mass communication, force of arms, or other means of coercion they possess. A third outcome would be the solution in the Greco-Roman world—create a new order at a higher level. Polytheism of the ancient Mediterranean world allowed virtually unlimited deities to coexist as part of the larger pantheonic assembly of gods. As the empire expanded, the universe expanded also to accommodate more deities that conquest assimilated or commerce proliferated.

Mass religion constitutes the first unique form of modern times. In Chapter 1, the classical theorists in general, and Karl Marx in particular, referred mostly to this type, although not by name. Before modern times, powerful empires attempted to create mass religions, but their authority in this regard was fairly limited, because they depended on the cooperation of local authorities and lacked the centralized power that we associate with government today.

In fact, mass culture is less the outcome of centralized authority as such, and more the outcome of a far more pervasive yet uncentered power—commodification. As an uncentered social force that permeates nearly all of modern life, commodification applies to most everything, yet operates unnoticed precisely because it has no particular manifestation to distinguish it from other social forces and facts. For example, if I say "shalom," that greeting pertains specifically to Judaism, just as "Allah Akhbar" (God is great) pertains to Islam. Commodification is a social force that has no particular identifier. Rather, it occurs as a process whenever something loses its particular identifier and becomes a generalized social fact. For example, if I build my own motorcycle like on the show *American Chopper,* I have a bike that is one of a kind. It reflects my particular taste, style, and ability. If I develop a pattern and use machines to manufacture many bikes following the same pattern, then I have a commodity that happens to be a motorcycle. They are not unique and they are not for me, but rather, they are standardized and for sale, just like any other mass-produced item. As commodities, they lack personal attributes like my one-of-a-kind motorcycle.

Just as music, clothing, motorcycles, and many other cultural expressions can be mass produced to a particular standard, so too can religion. For example, Christian culture has existed for centuries, but today, we see the rise of a Christian culture industry that exists alongside the mainstream popular culture industry and increasingly resembles it. Given nearly any form of popular culture, whether movies, books, or music, various Christian producers, publishers, and record companies seek to establish a Christian counterpart (C. Brown 2002, 2003b, 2003c). In music alone, there is Christian top 40, Christian country, and even Christian heavy metal. In each case, the economic success depends on the ability of the companies to market a predictable, standardized Christian product. However, the relationship between the faith and the market is often not entirely amicable, because many Christians find the profit motive distasteful, if not offensive. While few believers reject the Christian commodity industry completely, most producers and vendors employ various strategies to maintain a sense of authentic devotion to faith even as they pursue profit—a requirement of all businesses (C. Brown 2002). The same can be said for Wicca, Islam, Hinduism, and many others. It remains to be seen to what extent such commodified versions retain their authenticity, and therefore meaning, for the consumers.

Spectacle religion draws from a concept by Mikhail Bakhtin ([1918] 1984), Guy DeBord ([1967] 1995), and others. Bakhtin originated a concept called *carnivalization* to describe an apparently real but ultimately illusory inversion of values, authority, and other manifestations of power and domination. More specifically, Lauren Langman (2005) focuses this concept on religion, to argue that religion has become a public spectacle, much as the spectacle of the carnival, with fools parading around as the king and the customary standards of public decency suspended. Religion in its spectacle or carnivalized form has become an artificial world, a place separated from society and the usual laws, power relations, and economic realities. In contrast to mass-produced religion, people do not buy and consume it as a product, but rather participate within its illusory confines. This allows them to feel like active participants in making a better world, and to build their self-esteem, but only—and this is crucial—within the boundaries of the spectacle space. In the words of Shakespeare in *Macbeth*, "It is a tale told by an idiot, full of sound and fury, signifying nothing." Each individual may freely construct and believe whatever strikes his or her fancy, and no matter how sincerely heartfelt, it remains idiosyncratic and personal.

Like the medieval spectacle, the contemporary spectacle involves and indeed relies on crowd participation. Not only do the people attending such a religious service participate, but they also make the event. Spectacle services have very little formal organization. Rather, anyone who wants to read from the Bible, deliver a sermon, play music, and so on may do so, such that readers and performers vary from one service to another. However, it would be wrong to conclude that such services, and the congregations they serve, have no particular identity, doctrine, or order. In fact, research shows that many apparently spontaneous services, even those that involve speaking in tongues and other charismatic displays, also enforce, overtly and covertly, codes of conduct and means to marginalize unapproved spontaneity (B. Wright and Rawls 2005). Wright and Rawls studied Pentecostal and Assembly of God congregations that had moved from inner-city to exurban locations. The urban neighborhoods they left, like the congregations, were originally white, but as the racial composition of the neighborhood became increasingly black, churches moved to the white suburbs or exurbs. As Wright and Rawls conclude, the informal codes that marginalize or restrict unapproved spontaneity enforce white cultural norms over and against black norms.

Thus, the once genuine spontaneous expressions of the Holy Spirit have become the following, as Mike Davis (2002) writes below. Sundays in churches that once fired the soul with mystery and magic now entertain the crowd with big-money stage shows. As he observed at a Pentecostal church in California,

> Angels soar seventy feet above the congregation on invisible wires; mega-choirs, often led by country music celebrities, stamp out gospel hits. . . . There are no seizures, balls of fire, dancing in the aisles, or speaking in tongues. Everything is responsibly staged, without a hint of spontaneity, danger, or shamanism. The largely affluent congregation of six thousand just had a wholesome good time and then adjourns to the gift shop to purchase . . . holy knickknacks for the entire family. (p. 124)

Of the same type but on a larger scale, the Promise Keepers (PK) rose to prominence in the late 1990s, with peak attendance of 1.2 million in 1996, and 700,000 to 1 million in a gathering on the Mall in Washington, D.C., in 1997. Although the PK organization arranges for speakers at their mass rallies, called conferences, each speaker delivers a rousing but very general sermon on some aspect of religion and life, almost always about personal moral choices. Although emotionally powerful, the sermons advocate many commonly accepted principles, many of which are not particular to a Christian life: self-control, devotion to family, care for the downtrodden, and devotion to God. Conference attendees must fill in the details themselves (Lundskow 2002). Regarding self-control, for example, often centered on control of one's sexual activity, one may assume that they advocate fidelity in marriage. But it is not made clear whether all sexual practices are considered properly Christian, so long as they are practiced only within marriage.

One famous PK teaching is servant-leadership, as discussed in detail in Chapter 8. A man should be a servant to God and a leader to his family, yet he must be a benevolent leader, dedicated to his family's well-being, and selflessly committed to his wife and children. One is free to interpret this conservatively, that a man is the master of the household, or more progressively, that the man is one person, in partnership with his wife, and the two together govern family affairs, or even that the man should, as the leader, place the interests of his family above his own. In any case, he plays a leadership role and assumes responsibility for his actions and the well-being of his family.

At the PK spectacles across the country in the 1990s, speakers of all ethnic groups dressed in contemporary sport clothes and stylish haircuts exhorted men to embrace Jesus and each other. Between speakers, the Maranatha! band played a mix of Christian traditionals and their own compositions. Their style is a mixture of folk, rock, funk, blues, and jazz. The conferences were very high-energy affairs. At the Kansas City conference and the Million Man March in Washington, D.C., that I attended, Minivans, SUVs, and station wagons—family vehicles, overwhelmingly late models—filled the parking lots. There was considerable tailgating, as commonly occurs at football games, except at PK events there is no alcohol.

At both the Kansas City and Washington, D.C., events, many church groups were present, easily identified from their T-shirts, or often a vest that proclaimed their congregation. Most of the men were middle-aged, 30-something to 50-something, and many had sons along. The fathers dressed in stylish but conservative sports clothes, with fashionably short hair. The sons dressed in styles typical of high school or college age, with a mixture of conservative oxfords and topsiders, but also Birkenstocks, long hair, and alternative styles. Some wore rock T-shirts or jerseys, and many wore fashionably dark or retro clothes.

Outside stadiums throughout the country, volunteer workers (all women) in large tents sold official PK merchandise—everything from pens and appointment books to a full line of PK sports clothes. A man could buy a complete ensemble. They also sold PK publications that covered a broad range of topics, but mostly they centered on marriage, family, and personal commitment to Christ.

In services large and small, then, whether the local congregation or the stadium rally, the spectacle form lends the appearance of diversity, but the PK, just like the churches that B. Wright and Rawls studied, are overwhelmingly white, suburban, middle class, and moderately conservative. This cannot be a coincidence, but rather, is the outcome of common experience among participants who find comfort in familiar surroundings—a venue filled with people like themselves. Such an environment feels safe, and the men trust others like themselves as they talk about personal feelings they otherwise hide. Their moderately conservative backgrounds teach a notion of manhood that requires emotional control most of the time, especially regarding sensitive emotions, yet is just open enough that they may reveal their sensitive side in the proper setting. In this case, they feel proper amidst other men like themselves.

The Promise Keepers are but one version of the spectacle. Usually, sociologists apply this concept to entertainment, and that notion completes the concept. Regardless of content, religious or otherwise, the spectacle event must provide an interactive and entertaining experience. Learning about or singing about God is not enough; the spectacle must also entertain. If the medieval spectacle inverted the established social order in a symbolic way as Bakhtin ([1918] 1984) argues, the modern spectacle denies that any order exists at all. For an hour or two in church on Sunday, or during a football game, or at a rock concert, everyone is equal—each and all are part of a community of believers and fans. In contrast to premodern times, when the service and doctrine reflected the established social hierarchy, the modern spectacle pretends no hierarchy at all. Each person becomes one individual among others. From this perspective, then, spectacle separates religion from real life, because in the world outside the spectacle, hierarchy, privilege, and oppression clearly prevail. Religion in the spectacle form does not invert, challenge, or even replicate the real world. Instead, it offers an entirely different world as if the real world didn't exist at all. It offers total personal gratification without the responsibility of collective membership.

From another perspective, though, we have already seen how the classical theorists such as Marx and Durkheim see religion as the idealized social order. With this emphasis, the spectacle could be interpreted as forward-looking—that the illusion becomes an ideal of what could be, rather than simply reinforcing society as it is currently. In the case of the Promise Keepers, this seems accurate; the PK represent a progressive movement (in some ways) within an otherwise conservative evangelical culture. Men must be leaders in the family, but they must serve the interests of the family, rather than their own selfish interests. They are patriarchal, but it must be a benevolent patriarchy. Some PK men prefer to emphasize marriage as a partnership, thus further minimizing the patriarchal aspects, and certainly, exhorting men to embrace sensitive emotions and express them openly seems like an ennobling counterforce to heightened violence in video games, grisly scenes of mutilation and torture in horror films, and "sports" pastimes like the Ultimate Fighting Championship. Religion and masculine culture must be studied in context.

The point is that in sociology, terms such as conservative, liberal, progressive, reactionary, and so on only make sense in a comparative context. As we have seen in this chapter, religious clashes between long-established traditions and recent imports are at the same time liberal, conservative, traditional, and progressive as globalization forces a revaluation of values. Comparative standards require a global perspective, which means that cultures intersect at various levels and to varying degrees of contrast with each other. It also means that the old nomenclature becomes outdated as we compare things for the first time. For example, is charismatic religion that moves to Russia from the United States liberal or conservative compared to traditional rituals from Russian Orthodoxy? In the same way, critics who condemn the Promise Keepers for being "patriarchal" miss the point, that while the PK are obviously patriarchal, the more important question is, What does patriarchy mean in today's world? In a global context, it can mean many different things. Do the terms liberal, conservative, progressive, or reactionary even make sense when applied to comparisons for which the terms were never envisioned? In short, do we need a new language to talk about and understand the globalization of religion?

CHAPTER 10

Religion Beyond Religion

Sacredness, Mystery, and Faith in Other Contexts

Introduction

This chapter considers religion that is not religious. Even to enthusiasts, things such as popular music, sports, and TV shows are entertainment or some other pastime, but usually not religious, or at least not seriously religious. As sociologists, however, we might take a different perspective, that the religious quality of some person, thing, or activity depends not on the presence of a deity or acknowledged devotion, but rather, on the extent to which something answers the great existential questions posed in Chapter 1—in other words, the extent to which something provides meaningful boundaries to a person's life—a sense of the sacred. From this perspective, many things that are not religious institutions or activities on the surface in fact fulfill a religious purpose at both the social and psychological level. As I have tried to illustrate throughout this book, sociologists engage conceptual frameworks and theory, not simply one's perception or the perception of people under study, in order to generate insight.

Heavy Metal Hierophany

Hierophant is a term from ancient Greek that is commonly used with religion. Although there is no exact English translation, a hierophant is basically one who reveals sacred knowledge of the divine. Deena Weinstein (1991, 2000), a sociologist who has researched heavy metal music and its subculture, concludes that the concert

Image 10.1   Black Sabbath, 1970

Source: © Tony Frank/Sygma/Corbis

event consummates an overall experience with heavy metal. In a way directly analogous to religion, metal fans experience a revelation of the divine at the concert, which is a total emotional and sensory experience. The concert venue becomes a temple in which the fans worship and partake of the divine, and the artists serve as both priests and demigods. The concert is a hierophany, and the artists are the hierophants. To fully appreciate Weinstein's argument, we should look more closely at this subculture.

Heavy metal began with the band Black Sabbath in the early 1970s. Although other hard rock bands contributed vocal styles and wailing guitars, Black Sabbath set the dark, ominous tone with its thundering drums and bass and its lengthy songs with several key and tempo changes. Lyrical content emphasized death, dreariness, and generally forlorn and melancholic feelings. Just as important as mood and tone, the lyrics told stories of trials and tribulations, emotional turmoil, depression, mythical encounters, and always alienation. Growing up in the burned-out industrial wasteland of Birmingham, England, the band always played with a sense of urgency as well, that the alternative to music was the oil and grime of the steel mill or the black lung of the coal mine. Ozzy Osbourne, the original vocalist and lyricist (the others in the long history of the band were Ronnie James Dio and Ian Gillan, both established hard rock/metal vocalists), devoted great attention to mood and themes, and guitarist Tony Iommi played crunchy, dirge-like rhythms of power chords, bold yet sublime, which he accented with soaring leads. Drummer Bill Ward seemed to play with sledgehammers instead of drumsticks, and Geezer Butler's staccato bass permeated and extended the entire sound the way thunder projects the power of a storm. Although bands like Deep Purple and Led Zeppelin also featured heavy tones, darkly moody themes, and instrumental prowess, Black Sabbath used far more developed themes of death and destruction, rather than the party tone of their peers. Sabbath also set the "look" for metal artists. The early 1970s aesthetic displayed in the photo of the band

(Image 10.1) transcended the decade and became the standard appearance for heavy metal rockers, with a few modifications, up to the present day.

Later metal bands toward the end of the 1970s and into the early 1980s adopted the tone and style of Black Sabbath. British bands such as Iron Maiden, Fist, Motorhead, and Judas Priest continued the trends that Black Sabbath had founded, dressed in black and all manner of metal accoutrements, and in so doing, diverged from the emerging glitz and big-hair coifs of 1980s American "glam metal." Real metal sports long, natural hair, tattoos, jeans, boots, leather, and no makeup. Real metal also means more to the fans than just a catchy song. It is an attitude and a way of life, and for the true fan, a religious experience. True fans separate themselves from the posers through devotion to the history of the genre as well as the history of particular bands and artists. By the twenty-first century, metal had developed into numerous subgenres—opera, thrash, speed, doom, black, death, and many others.

More than anything else, heavy metal in all its forms is about alienation and community. Jeffrey Arnett, who has studied the heavy metal subculture closely, argues that alienation stands at the center. Arnett (1996) elaborates on the classical Marxist concept to say that alienation is "a sense of estrangement from one's culture, a deep loneliness arising from a lack of gratifying emotional connection to others, and cynicism about the ideals and possibilities for life offered by one's culture" (p. 17). Heavy metal responds to the condition of alienation and the feelings that arise from it. Although metal is not the only possible response—indeed, most of the theorists in Chapter 1 see alienation as a defining feature of modern life—heavy metal constitutes one possible outcome. But the appeal of the metal subculture involves far more than just alienation. It is the juncture of alienation, experience, and social position.

Arnett's (1996) study only considered adolescent metal fans, and he notes that much of their alienation arises from their social position as adolescents. In this stage, they face the responsibilities of adulthood without the privileges and respect, and without the possibility of self-sufficiency. Furthermore, Arnett argues that the major socializing institutions—the institutions that integrate the individual into society—have become dysfunctional. In particular, he notes seven key institutions that either fail to exert meaningful control, or in fact encourage and reward an antisocial ethic of selfish individualism. Namely, Arnett studies the impact of family, peers, school, neighborhood, the media, the legal system, and cultural values (p. 26). Dispersed among these categories is religion, which most of the youth in his study either reject outright or simply view indifferently.

Consequently, metal fans look to the subculture to replace the function of these other institutions. Thus, "Heavy Metal is not simply a musical preference . . . but something that both shapes and reflects their view of the world and themselves" (Arnett 1996:68–69). Above all else, what they expect is authenticity, and the way to "distinguish the authentic Heavy Metal performers from the imitators is that the authentic Metal performer loudly and vehemently spouts the ideology of alienation, whereas imitators, the poseurs, sing songs about frivolous topics such as partying and the joys of promiscuous sex" (p. 69). For the true fans of heavy metal, the stakes are very high. At stake is far more than just the integrity of the music—although this is important—but the music also speaks to larger issues, arguably, issues of community and of the soul. Fans look to metal for belonging, understanding, and the meaning of life.

One of the most common misperceptions about heavy metal is that it embraces Satanism, or at least celebrates Satan and demonic forces. In his interviews with metal fans, Arnett (1996) found that fans overwhelmingly laugh at this notion, because the music clearly has nothing to do with devil worship. As Arnett's quantitative analysis of metal lyrics shows, only about 9% of all metal songs include any mention of Satan, directly or obliquely (p. 46). Deena Weinstein (2000) argues that Satan represents power and defiance in heavy metal; he is not a literal being, but a symbolic representation of independent power. In other words, songs *about* Satan are not songs *in praise of* Satan.

Another misconception is that heavy metal is closely allied with the white power and white supremacy movements. Although these racist movements often include their own bands that perform in a heavy metal style, few fans listen to them outside of the white supremacy movement, and their themes do not resonate with metal fans in general. If anything, the metal subculture is increasingly open and diverse. Although still overwhelmingly white, fans have, for example, accepted Rob Halford's admission that he is gay; his comeback albums *Resurrection* (2000) and *Crucible* (2002) have outsold any of the albums he did in the 1970s and 1980s with Judas Priest, another classic metal band now effectively deified among the faithful fans. His homosexuality has not harmed his popularity in the least. Also, women musicians used to be virtually absent from heavy metal groups, but they now front or play in several up-and-coming bands, including Fireball Ministry, Otep (Image 10.2), Crisis, and Arch Enemy.

Image 10.2   Lead Singer of the Band Otep

Source: ©Hector Mata/AFP/Getty Images

In a discussion in one of my classes about the song "Dead Skin Mask" by Slayer, from their classic album *Seasons in the Abyss,* one of my students said that she didn't know what the song meant, but while scrutinizing the lyrics projected on the overhead, she commented that Slayer definitely has a much wider vocabulary than top-40 bands, with words such as "provocative," "placid," and "adulating." Expressed through metaphors, the song and the album address psychosis, depression, and other serious psychological maladies—all the result of social alienation rather than defects in the individual. Literally, the song refers to a corpse, but metaphorically "dead skin mask" refers to what people see when they genuinely look each other, and how people feel when they look at themselves in the mirror. In social interaction, we are "provocative, placid," and "adulating," but that is just superficial pretense to conceal the reality of the "dead skin mask." Underneath the pretense, we feel like the walking dead, animated zombies with no genuine life of our own. Other interpretations may be possible, which is the point: like any good art or literature, to intrigue fans and inspire interest in the material on a deeper level through sophistication and complexity.

Lyrical content also often draws from mythology, literature, and history to reenact moments of alienation, desperation, isolation, and cataclysm. For example, Therion's recent album, *Lemuria/Sirius-B* (2005), collects mythology from cultures around the world, especially Norse, Greek, and Hindu, and sets the stories to heavy metal music (using opera singers as the vocalists), presenting them as a musical tome. Likewise, Blind Guardian's album *Nightfall in Middle Earth* (1998) translates the story of *The Silmarillion* into a heavy metal opera. Each song narrates in succession the tales in the book. The story of *The Silmarillion,* a novel by J. R. R. Tolkien, precedes the events of *The Hobbit* and *The Lord of the Rings. The Silmarillion* covers the age of the Elves, who battled with Morgoth, a divine being who rebelled against his kindred gods and the supreme creator, Illuvatar. At that time, the evil one known later as Sauron was only a minion of Morgoth, one of few to survive his master's eventual downfall. In another example, the album *Dance of Death* (2003) from Iron Maiden includes the song "Paschendale" (the Flemish spelling "Passchendaele" is also common), about the World War I battle in which the Allied and German armies collectively lost approximately 550,000 soldiers, with about 45,000 bodies never recovered (Wolff 1958).

War, death, and destruction are not the focus of the songs in heavy metal, but rather, they provide a context for certain emotions and attitudes. Indeed, metal songs overwhelmingly oppose war. Considered an essential founder of the genre, Iron Maiden has several antiwar songs, including "Run to the Hills," which takes the side of the Native Americans as they valiantly but unsuccessfully oppose the marauding U.S. cavalry that destroys their villages and slaughters Indians and buffalo. "Two Minutes to Midnight" refers to the doomsday clock invented in 1947 by a group of atomic scientists at the University of Chicago, which for decades symbolically represented the world as 2 minutes away from midnight—from nuclear annihilation. The song "Trooper" tells the story of a common infantry soldier in the Crimean War.

Metallica's song "One," based on the antiwar novel *Johnny Got His Gun,* tells the story of a soldier from World War I who returns with no limbs and no face. Unable to communicate but with his mind still intact, he is trapped in a living hell. The land-mine has taken all possibility of connection to people outside himself; his world consists of just "one," forever condemned to isolation. In all of these songs and others, the bands do not present a political platform, but like Black Sabbath's "Warpigs" from 1970, heavy metal depicts the emotions of death and loss in an unjust, dehumanized, and violent world where a protagonist does his or her best to survive physically and mentally intact under circumstances beyond the individual's control.

Violence and mayhem, war and destruction are contexts, not ends in themselves, for emotions such as alienation, anger, and bleak expectations. In the antiwar songs of heavy metal, lyrics and music express the futility and arrogance of war, and the tragedy of lives lost for money, power, and dreams of rich people to rule the world.

Yet despite its consistently bleak outlook, on war or any other subject matter, heavy metal also holds out the possibility of transformation and salvation. Regardless of injustice or personal mistakes, metal promises more than the cold, hard reality of the mundane world, filled with petty little people bustling about and arrogant, condescending people in positions of power. Metal imagines a world where the deeply passionate and genuine person finds solace and reassurance that something more lies beyond this world, even if that something is beyond the veil—a conclusion that Natalie Purcell (2003) corroborates with her ethnography of the "death metal" subculture. Despite its dark and ominous imagery and tone, metal offers the possibility of personal and spiritual redemption. Partly real and partly perceived, heavy metal unites the genuine fan, as defined above, with a community of people who feel similarly.

If heavy metal builds a sense of community, even if most of one's comrades are relatively distant historical or mythological figures, anonymous, or dead, does it build a spiritual sense? So far, we have seen that metal draws inspiration from history and reinterprets mythology to invent a version that is relevant to contemporary feelings of alienation. Certainly, conventional religion depends considerably on ties to history in terms of events, heroic individuals, and narratives that reinforce a collective religious identity. Conventional religion also relies on scripture, which often depicts supernatural beings and events. Heavy metal does all of these things. Yet does it create a transcendent belief system, some sort of collective identity that connects the individual to something higher and eternal? No thorough study exists to either substantiate or deny this possibility.

However, some anecdotal evidence and ethnographic studies exist to suggest that in fact the heavy metal subculture does inspire a transcendent collectivity. Consider, for example, the song "Creek Mary's Blood," by Nightwish. The title suggests a religious association, as it draws Mary, the mother of Jesus, together with the Creek Indians. Blood in this context suggests suffering, as both Christ and the Indians suffered. The lyrics tell the story of the Native Americans generally, and the song concludes with a poem in the language of the Lakota, one of the Sioux peoples (as are the Creek). Translated in the liner notes, the song and the poem clearly express a strong spirituality, and the overall tone and content resonate with typical heavy metal mood and imagery. The Lakota storyteller's chanted vocals tell how the white man destroyed the Lakota people, their culture, their land, and their gods. Still, he remains defiant that the white man cannot touch him or his people in the afterlife.

The details may differ from one person to another, one band and song to another, but clearly, heavy metal as a subculture contains collectively shared normative values that reinforce individual membership and also set the boundaries between metal, other musical subcultures, and broader subcultures in general. True metal, as defined earlier, is not mainstream but neither is it entirely countercultural—its patterns follow the collective patterns of the mainstream even if the symbols and exact content differ. In other words, metal resembles mainstream religion in its dependence on ritual and symbolism, and its connections to the past and to mythical-transcendent identity.

Within this context, sociologist Donna Gaines (1991), in a genuinely interesting ethnography of heavy metal teenagers in a working-class town, discovers that the local metal subculture, often derided as the "burnouts" by nonmetal teens, parents, police, and nearly the whole town, intersects with local places and history. The burnout subculture, in which heavy metal is central, possesses its own lived history, "shared in places coded with secret meanings, on grounds that have been held so long they are sacred. Legends, tales of famous teenagers, preserved linguistic and spatial and sartorial practices, traditions carried over the decades, impenetrable to the outsider" (p. 47). These sacred grounds—mostly places where teenagers could party or just hang out, beyond the ready surveillance of adults and the establishment—were familiar to all in the burnout subculture, and notorious to other kids: an abandoned baseball field, a broken-down factory, a forgotten old house, an overgrown public park.

No matter how many times police broke up parties, the kids would return to these places, the hallowed ground of the marginalized teenagers, whom the community called burnouts. Parties, sexual encounters, simply time free from surveillance and peer humiliation, even suicides happened in these secluded places, where the marginalized teenagers experienced life—and death—on the edges and in the darkness. Gaines uncovered the allure of these locations. With so many memories and legends, and with nowhere else to go, local teenagers could never abandon these places.

Gaines (2007) discovers similar patterns in other suburban and urban communities as well, and a related study by Duany, Plater-Zyberk, and Speck (2000) confirm the suburban and gentrified small towns to be the center of heavy metal and alienation. Gaines finds that urban youth are no less alienated, but they turn more to rap/hip-hop or punk rather than metal. For a brilliant, funny, scathing, and very non-PC treatise on alienation in small towns, see *Deer Hunting With Jesus: Dispatches From America's Class War,* by Joe Bageant (2007). Among other things, Bageant draws out the connections among country music, religion, and class in Winchester, Virginia. Like in numerous towns across the country, everyone including corporate executives, local real-estate developers, and the professional gentry from nearby urban centers exploits the working class, uses them up, and then discards them saddled with debt, no retirement, and no health care. Country music and Christian fundamentalism are all many people in such a town have left when they die.

On the Road: A Journey of Discovery

Feeling trapped in a town or suburb that ostracizes them, some teenagers try to escape to the open highways, as the outsider has done since the advent of the train and especially the automobile. Joe Bageant, the author mentioned above, went on the road and is one of only a handful in his generation of native Winchester townsfolk to get a college education. With no less bohemian exuberance than Jack Kerouac in *On the Road* ([1957] 1991) but perhaps more akin to the critical cynicism of Hunter S. Thompson in *Fear and Loathing in Las Vegas: A Savage Journey to the Heart of the American Dream,* a young but not burned-out woman sets off in *Diary of a Redneck Vampire.* This book chronicles the journey of a female heavy metal drummer around the United States. Known only as Flo (2004), the author tells her own story through a collection of ragged notebooks filled with stories about the trials and tribulations of a metal band that earns just enough money at one show to afford food, gas, and vehicle maintenance to make it to the next show.

Through all the problems of the tour, with broken-down vehicles, dishonest club owners, an all-male environment, a boyfriend lost to drugs, and a friend's suicide, Flo discovers religion amidst intense feelings of alienation and isolation. Initially attracted to Wicca, she develops her own beliefs on tour, as the music, the subculture, and the overall experience move her away from the female-centered religion. If Wicca is too exclusively feminine, then Christianity is too rigidly masculine and patriarchal. In place of both, she invents a sense of the divine premised on a different but equal masculine–feminine duality. As Flo says,

> I always thought that God was above gender. . . . I definitely believe that God has both a masculine aspect and a feminine aspect, and I have identified them as the god and goddess present in Wicca. But Wicca is really feminine based, which is the opposite of Christianity, and I think that the goal should be balance of both. (p. 47)

Despite periodic uncertainty, the music and the subculture eventually encourage Flo to find greater certainty, and furthermore they convince her that it really matters to meaningfully understand the divine. Three years after she first joined the band, Flo (2004) experiences a kind of epiphany, that "now I realize that it's okay to define God however you want . . . and that definition will truly save your ass" (p. 203). By the end of the diary entries, Flo has matured into a self-confident rock drummer and human being. Her emergent religious beliefs contribute significantly to her confidence. In her final show with the Redneck Vampires, Flo says, "I played for every moment that I had ever spent in front of a stage as a teenager . . . dreaming to be up there. . . . I played for all the times I thought I could never do it. . . . I played for Flo . . . for the little girl that was scared she wasn't good enough . . . and for the woman that discovered she was" (p. 227). As Flo recognized and developed her ability as a musician, she also matured as a person and as a spiritual human being. Also common in the metal genre, but typical of youth (ages 13–25) today, her religion becomes something very personal. Her notion of God, and the manner in which she practices her faith, integrate an idiosyncratic blend that fulfills her on a personal level, yet which does not create routinized institutional relations. As we saw in Chapter 2, part II, an in-depth sociological study showed that youth in the contemporary United States construct their religious beliefs in the same manner—very idiosyncratically and very personally (C. Smith and Denton 2005).

Not everyone involved with the heavy metal scene finds God or religion or necessarily looks for it as such. But over the decades since Black Sabbath originated the look, the attitude, the emotions, and the sound that became heavy metal, the genre in its authentic form has always tried to make itself important. While this can sometimes become inept and comical, the best bands and the most dedicated fans find more than just the music. They find a community of the faithful who integrate mythology, history, literature, and experience into a composite that both celebrates alienation and brings people together at shows and in the privacy of the individual in his or her room. It unites the fans in a realm that mirrors and also transcends the mundane. Heavy metal builds a community that reminds the faithful that life matters, and that they are not alone.

Metal and Goth: Comparison and Contrast

It would be wrong to conclude that distinctive styles of dress, attitude, and music, or other subcultural trappings, inherently indicate a religious or spiritual commitment or sense of fulfillment. As two scholars of the goth subculture found, one remarkable feature is that its enthusiasts find no particular meaning at all in goth. For Hodkinson (2002) and Siegel (2005), the subculture exists overwhelmingly as a stylistic display, and indeed, "years of ethnographic research . . . have confirmed for me that there was no underlying shared structural, psychological, or political meaning to be discerned from the style" (Hodkinson 2002:62). Rather, the distinctive style imparts a sense of identity and exclusiveness. Furthermore, goths tend to be highly conventional most of the time, and typically quiet, reserved, and pacifistic. Contrary to popular misconceptions, goths rarely pose a threat to schoolmates, and are statistically far more likely to become the victims of violence than the perpetrators (Siegel 2005:137–138). Both authors find that goths celebrate sexual ambiguity and, as Siegel sees it, sexual self-determination as resistance to masculinist values and compulsory heterosexuality. Yet this resistance plays out on a personal and most often private level. Goths associate through friendship groups, not as a community, with often strict boundaries of insiders and outsiders set by the friend with

Table 10.1   Metal and Goth

	Metal	Goth
Dress	Anything black, especially leather, lace, and band t-shirts. Red is also common. Tight-fitting, revealing for men and women alike. Sexually alluring for women	Anything black, especially leather, lace, and band t-shirts. Purple and red are also common. Tight-fitting, revealing for men and women alike. Sexually alluring for both men and women, but often sexually ambiguous as well
Body Types	Distinctly masculine and feminine forms	Distinctly feminine for both women and men
General Themes	Focus on death, despair, the macabre. Possibility of redemption	Focus on death, despair, the macabre. Possibility of redemption
Musical Themes	Addiction, depression, anger, isolation, alienation, survivor identity, mytho-poetry, transcendence	Addiction, depression, isolation, alienation, survivor identity, mytho-poetry, transcendence
Socialization	1. Awareness of the subculture's history and past influences. Sense of historical periodicity of styles, e.g., classic, death metal, thrash, operatic, etc. 2. Association through friendship networks and shared concert/club experience. Antistatus in-group orientation. Celebrates marginal and defiant position with the mainstream	1. Awareness of the subculture's history and past influences. Sense of historical periodicity of styles, e.g., classic, techno, acoustic, operatic, etc. 2. Association through friendship networks and shared concert-club experience. Emphasizes accumulation of cultural capital as basis of in-group status hierarchy. Celebrates marginal and eccentric position with the mainstream

the greatest goth cultural capital (Hodkinson 2002:80–81). As other sociologists concur, an eccentric-styled subculture usually centers on shared tastes and the accumulation of cultural capital, often in the form of simple popularity (Jenks 2005).

Thus, we have an interesting comparison. Goth and metal share many similarities as Table 10.1 shows, but goth lacks one crucial element—spirituality. While many metal fans are oblivious to the spiritual aspects, many others find meaning, even perhaps salvation, in the volume and power of heavy metal. With similar styles of dress, exaltation of marginal status, and lyrical and musical overlap (yet with definite differences in this regard as well), goth and metal sometimes even blend together. Space concerns do not permit a full exegesis of musicological similarities and differences. However, in the aforementioned empirical studies by Hodkinson and Siegel, as well as another by Muggleton (2002) and one by Thornton (1996), virtually no goth enthusiasts mention anything that could be interpreted as spiritually significant. I can offer no explanation for this particularly clear and decisive contrast between metal and goth—both subcultures of alienation and marginalization. However, it would certainly make for an interesting research project.

Sports

> **Touchdown Jesus**
>
> One final thought to add to the ton of cyber-ink already spilled on the Super Bowl: Who says religion and football don't mix? As throngs of whooping and hollering Steelers fans flooded from Ford Field late Sunday, Kevin Farrer and fellow proselytizers from Bible Believers were there to heckle them. "Do you know why you're going to hell?" he yelled into a megaphone. "Because you love football more than Jesus." A young Steelers fan didn't miss a beat, shouting "But Jesus is a Steelers fan!"—Joel Kurth, *Detroit News*, Monday, Feb. 6, 2006

In this example, religion not so much appears in or alongside football as collides with it. The two massive spectacles compete for Sunday attention, and both receive similar types of reverence, both in the form of religious devotion and superstition. Of all the commonly experienced events of modern life, sports manifests innumerable superstitious practices. These include athletes who will not shave during a series, a superstition to which many hockey players subscribe as well as the famous tennis player Bjørn Borg, champion for much of the 1970s. Many golfers have a special club, usually a putter, which they employ only in the most desperate circumstances. Many fans have superstitious rituals as well, such as wearing a special hat during the game (and only during the game). Chicago Cubs fans throw back the baseballs from all home runs the opposing team hits. (At all other baseball parks, fans are free to keep any balls that fly into the stands.) One of my roommates in graduate school had a 5-year-old can of Classic Coke (20 years old as of 2008) he was saving until the Buffalo Bills won the Super Bowl (he is still waiting). He said that it would jinx the team to drink it otherwise, and to reveal why he had to wait to drink this particular can of soda would also jinx the team.

Like a church, sports venues often acquire a sacred reverence; the place itself becomes hallowed ground. Among the most famous that combine sports with the sacred is the Allen Fieldhouse, the men's and women's basketball arena at the University of Kansas (KU) (Image 10.3). Since 1990, the Jayhawks (men's team) have won 204 and lost only 17 games in the Allen Fieldhouse. Dedicated in 1955, the building is named after the legendary Forrest C. "Phog" Allen, who coached the men's team at Kansas for 37 years (1908–1909, 1920–1956) and for 49 years total, counting experience prior to Kansas. During his tenure at Kansas, Allen won a total of 590 games (771 total career), a record surpassed by only four other coaches as of this writing, two of whom learned the game as assistant coaches under Allen and became legendary coaches in their own right. They are Adolph Rupp at the University of Kentucky and Dean Smith at the University of North Carolina (UNC). The two other coaches not part of Allen's legacy are Bobby Knight and Eddie Sutton. Rupp and Smith each in turn produced protégés of great accomplishment, including former KU and current UNC coach Roy Williams and current KU coach Bill Self. In terms of both history and legacy, all roads lead to the Allen Fieldhouse in men's college basketball.

Image 10.3   The Allen Fieldhouse, Lawrence, Kansas

Today, Allen is known as the "grandfather of basketball coaches," and his first book, *My Basketball Bible,* explains his devotion to the game. Like Allen's mentor, James Naismith, the inventor of basketball, who founded the program at KU and served as the first coach, Allen regards basketball as a religious calling that builds moral character. In its original version, Naismith based the entire game on self-control and discipline. The game permitted no touching whatsoever among players; any contact at all was a foul. Naismith felt that physically demanding, noncontact team sports built character by teaching players to work together, yet with individual self-control. Players would develop skill and execute intelligent plays that required mind-over-body discipline, rather than simply muscle each other around the court. The game has obviously changed since the early days, but the moral quality as an aspect of spiritual commitment remains.

In the Allen Fieldhouse, a banner above the stands reads "Pay Heed, All Who Enter," an ominous reference to the inscription over the gates of hell in Dante's *Inferno,* "Abandon All Hope, Ye Who Enter Here." Just beneath, the facility accords reverence to the local demigod, Phog Allen, and warns the opposition, "Beware of the Phog." All colleges have chants and cheers associated with sports teams, but at KU, the legendary "Rock Chalk" chant distinguishes this university from all other schools. Simple and powerful, the chant starts as a slow, Gregorian monotone: "Rooock . . . chaaaalk . . . Jaaay-haaawk . . . K . . . U." The fans repeat this twice, and each syllable corresponds to specific arm and body motions. On the third time, the tempo increases to full speed, and a full-throated cheer replaces the chant— "Rock Chalk Jayhawk KU!"—shouted three times in rapid succession. In another collective ritual started at KU and now copied elsewhere, fans raise both arms straight overhead and sway back and forth, what KU fans call "waving the wheat." No one today recalls the origins of either the Rock Chalk chant or the waving of the wheat, but the eerie and Gregorian monotone resonance of the Rock Chalk chant truly makes the Allen Fieldhouse feel like a cathedral court.

Abounding in religious imagery, sounds, rituals, and traditions, student culture reaffirms one's commitment to the team, as students wait outside the fieldhouse for seats before each game. Many wait for several days, and students form teams, each of which provides a "roster" from which organizers take roll call. Since students must still attend classes, students may leave the line as long as at least one team member remains each hour when roll is taken. Any team for which no member is present loses its place in line. KU students have used this system for decades. Such dedication before, during, and after games at local student bars and in street parties might seems pointless to the outsider, but to the dedicated fan, to the believer, it's not just about the game, it's about the tradition, about being part of something old and filled with legends, about sharing in the collective identity that is KU basketball, and all the rituals and ceremonies that surround it. For a while at least, students belong to something sacred, where others have gone before them and where later generations of KU students will continue the reverence. No less than any formal religion, fans at KU worship something authentic—not gods, perhaps, but the community that is the university. Alumni share game moments for a lifetime, and often define their past in reference to the memorable moments in great games they witnessed.

Image 10.4   The Green Monster, Fenway Park, Boston, Massachusetts

Other colleges, other venues, other teams have devout followings as well. We could name Fenway Park in Boston, for example, which features the Green Monster (Image 10.4). Opened in 1912, Fenway is the oldest baseball park still in use. The massive green wall blocks many hits that would be home runs in most other baseball parks. In football, Lambeau Field in Green Bay, Wisconsin, holds great allure and mystery, and various university fields, such as The Big House at the University of Michigan and The Swamp at the University of Florida inspire memories and emotions. But among college football teams, perhaps none evokes more reverence than the Fighting Irish of Notre Dame. It was here that the legendary George Gipp played for the legendary coach Knute Rockne. Gipp was out past curfew one night, and unable to gain access to his dormitory, he slept outside, contracted pneumonia, and died soon after, on December 14, 1920. On his deathbed, Rockne claimed that Gipp's last words were

> I've got to go, Rock. It's all right. I'm not afraid. Some time, Rock, when the team is up against it, when things are wrong and the breaks are beating the boys, tell them to go in there with all they've got and win just one for the Gipper. I don't know where I'll be then, Rock. But I'll know about it, and I'll be happy. (quoted in Gekas 1988)

Although possibly fictional, such legends reinforce the sacredness of the game, which Notre Dame as a Catholic university further amplifies and brings into closer contact with religion. Although not intended as part of football, the large mural of Jesus on the side of Hesburgh Library overlooks the field. Entitled "The Word of Life," the mural depicts a resurrected Jesus with arms uplifted—a pose that looks very similar to the football sign for a touchdown, hence the nickname, Touchdown Jesus (see Image 10.5).

Image 10.5   The Word of Life, also known as Touchdown Jesus, Hesburgh Library Mural Overlooking Notre Dame Stadium

Most of the world does not play football, but rather soccer, which the rest of the world calls football. Yet the same religiosity exists outside the United States, where people worship soccer heroes with no less devotion than Americans worshipping their athletes. For example, the Argentine star Diego Maradona scored a goal in the 1986 World Cup Championship. Not in use at the time for officiating purposes, a replay clearly shows that Maradona hit the ball with his hand, a foul in soccer. Since the referees did not catch the foul, fans view it as divine intervention, and the "foul" is popularly called "la mano de Dios" or the Hand of God. British soccer fans rank among the world's most famous (or infamous), and they write their own legends as "hooligans" who routinely fight pitched battles with other hooligans and occasionally—though usually reluctantly—with the police. Mostly, they seek to vandalize property as they march through a town, a kind of pillaging as the conquering army.

Organized as clubs with their own home pubs, soccer fans—who call themselves "supporters"—follow their teams across Europe and around the world, if necessary, and few supporters can match the English in devotion and ferocity. Typically employed and civilized during the week, English soccer supporters often go berserk on weekends before and during the game. Following the traditional rituals, they consume massive amounts of lager (their favored type of beer), and any number of fatty meats deep fried, with plenty of chips (French fries). Tanked up and bloated, seething with rage, trans fats, and alcohol, they seek out rival clubs and sometimes the police for a knock-down, drag-out battle, often inflicting and receiving significant injuries (Buford 1992). Sometimes, innocent bystanders substitute if suitable opponents are not forthcoming and get pulled into the fray. English soccer hooligans follow a ritual like any other religious or semireligious organization, except that the sacraments are beer, batter, and fry-grease.

The violence provides a great catharsis for the (mostly) men who otherwise live without excitement in low- or medium-skill trades that are in slow decline in Britain (Buford 1992). They find the spice of life on the weekends like sports fans do all over the world, except the quiet desperation of their mundane lives explodes in debauchery and violence more intensely and more or less in proportion to the greater gloom they feel—a whole class slowly fading into oblivion. With little joy and few prospects, British soccer supporters seek greater sensation and thrills; they greatly amplify the intensity level to the point where only the truly dedicated remain, ready to sacrifice all in order to belong.

As Buford (1992) documents, club leaders sometimes must bring the supporters together at the stadium venue clandestinely and in small groups at a time to avoid police detection and interference. Often, tourists will attempt to partake in the festivities, to dabble in the delights of soccer hooliganism as part of their vacation. True supporters angrily reject such free riders, as supporting one's team is serious business, the only meaningful part of their lives (Buford 1992). Indeed, the violence actually goes back over a century, to at least 1900, when supporters rioted at cricket matches (Dunning 1989). Throughout the decades, angry, disillusioned working-class youth have sought meaning through supporter clubs, expressed through violence and other high-intensity, sensation-seeking indulgence, especially overeating and drinking (Dunning 1989).

Sociologically, analytical conclusions do not depend primarily on the exact activities, whether peaceful, violent, or otherwise. Rather, in both sports and music subcultures, the religious aspect enters through feelings of transcendence, a sense of being connected to something larger, more important, and more or less timeless. In order to achieve this feeling, the individual must experience excitement—some sort of sensation that one cannot or does not feel in everyday life. In their otherwise bland and hopeless lives, metal fans and soccer supporters find high sensation in the music and the weekend rituals. The fact that metal fans are not generally violent and British soccer supporters often are is secondary. At the center stands a fairly exclusive experience that requires rites of passage and conscious commitment in order to fully belong. Heavy metal does not appeal to just anyone, but the rage and alienation speaks especially to certain groups, who find solace in the volume and distortion and lyrics that transport the listener from this world of corruption and hypocrisy to a world of myth and mystery. Likewise, soccer supporters leave their mundane jobs and rush into the realm of mystery; they become knights on a holy quest to support their teams and vanquish their foes. From a world of mediocrity and bland shades of gray, they hurtle headlong into a world of risk and moral clarity.

Branding

Not all secular religious commitments involve disillusionment and the choked passions of fatalism. Some gleefully accept their designation. Unlike branded cattle, teenagers today do not have the symbols of the ranch owner burned into their flesh. Yet in a sense, they along with older age groups brand themselves with the symbols of self-declared loyalty—the trademark. Branding of this sort proves one's loyalty and reassures the wearer that he or she belongs to a community—at least a community of consumers, who stand in contrast to other consumers with other identities and communities. Companies have achieved a great breakthrough with decades of advertising, brand placement in films and TV shows, and direct marketing to teenagers. Although brand logos have been around for decades, such as the Munsingwear Penguin and the Izod Alligator, brands no longer serve as a visible identifier of status or quality, but of legitimacy.

In the early 1980s, a popular movie called *Fast Times at Ridgemont High* depicted teenagers in various coming-of-age situations, and often, the problems that resulted from them. Teen pregnancy, drugs, and other issues played out in a partly funny, partly serious way, centered around a suburban shopping mall. All the characters either worked in or hung around this mall. In *Fast Times,* however, the mall was not a home, but a dangerous place filled with unscrupulous retailers, ticket scalpers, predatory older men, and superficial, back-stabbing peers. As Naomi Klein (2002) argues, this depiction contrasts sharply with the early twenty-first century mall—prefigured in 1990s movies such as *Clueless* and TV shows such as *Beverly Hills 90210,* the shopping mall becomes a safe haven, a place where cool and beautiful people hang out, a place where teenagers are free to live on their own terms, unfettered by parents and other authority figures. Most important, the stores are the easiest places to fit in, where anyone can become a member—one simply need spend the right amount of money on the stores' latest styles. Parents don't get you and teachers are idiots; they don't love you or understand you. The store, on the other hand, loves you and understands you, the branding culture claims, and cares about your happiness (McChesney 1994). The mall becomes more than a compensatory family; it becomes the *real* family such that one's natural family by comparison is not really a family at all. The mall family becomes more real than the real family, and the media carries this message worldwide in search of new family members/customers (McChesney and Herman 1997). Retail space becomes family and sacred space where justice prevails and the tribulations of the outside world disappear behind corporate logos, waiting racks of clothes, and shelves of mass-produced commodities.

While perhaps overstated, the point remains that the malls, or other retail spaces, compete strongly for a new type of loyalty—a loyalty that involves not just adherence to the latest trends, but to an identity. In the same way, churches refashion themselves to function more like retail businesses, opening in malls as a vendor, or in the case of megachurches, enclosing businesses within their own walls. Entrepreneurial churches develop their own brand of religious "product," with the same branding techniques that clothing and other retailers employ. Known as *entrepreneurial spirituality,* one of the foremost examples is the Potter's House, a nondenominational church based on the Pentecostal charismatic tradition. The reverend T. D. Jakes, a son of black civil rights activists from the 1960s, presides over both the church and the multimedia corporation located next door—TDJ Enterprises (Pappu 2006:92). Jakes has built a substantial personal fortune; he drives to work in a Bentley and travels the country in a Lockheed Jetstar II. Dressed in the latest custom-made suit fashions, Jakes still delivers sermons with a down-home twang and colloquial manner of speech. The Potter's House currently boasts 30,000 members, and it regularly draws over 150,000 to services around the country whenever Jakes goes on the road.

As we saw in Chapter 2, megachurches offer a familiar message of personal improvement as the key to salvation. In the case of the Potter's House, this message is delivered in a 7,500-person auditorium fully outfitted with two jumbotrons, TV cameras on all sides, and an elaborate lighting and sound system. More like a rock concert than a religious service, Jakes preaches self-betterment through entrepreneurialism, and that making money in business is both spiritually righteous and its own reward as a means to character improvement. As sociologist Shayne Lee (2005) argues, materialism in the crude sense—that is, the accumulation of wealth and possessions—drives Jakes and his ministry. Unlike most of the black religious community in the United States, Jakes feels comfortable with the white establishment. For example, he refrained from condemning the Bush White House or the Federal Emergency Management Agency (FEMA) for its lack of appropriate action after Hurricane Katrina destroyed New Orleans (Pappu 2006:101), a city with a black majority population.

Jesus, CEO

T. D. Jakes isn't the only entrepreneurial preacher who blurs the lines between business and faith. Like the Potter's House, many evangelical churches collect revenue as nonprofit organizations—501(c)3 in the Internal Revenue Service category—tax exempt. Indeed, the most successful churches today, both in terms of attendance numbers and revenue, embrace the business model. One of the largest of the megachurches, Willow Creek Church in South Barrington, Illinois, dedicates itself to "total service excellence" ("Jesus, CEO: Churches as Businesses, 2005). Willow Creek offers a variety of services—not as charity like a traditional church, but as products and services like a business. The Second Baptist Church in Houston, Texas, has its own football field. The Phoenix First Assembly of God lends medical equipment. The World Changers Ministry in Georgia offers a wide range of professional services, including tax preparation, investment advising, mortgage brokers and real estate agents, and test-preparation services for the SAT and other standardized tests ("Jesus, CEO" 2005:42). The Willow Creek Association, a consulting business for Christian entrepreneurs, earned $20 million last year ("Jesus, CEO" 2005:44).

Ironically, "rather than making America more Christian, megachurches have simply succeeded in making Christianity more American" ("Jesus, CEO" 2005: 44). Gone are the passion and ecstasy of religious devotion, and in their place stands a suburban megaplex that transforms religion into simplistic slogans and product, devoid of inspiration or meaning.

Megachurches and smaller but no less entrepreneurial churches preach easy-to-understand doctrine that reflects the suspicion of the world that characterizes most of the devotees. The vast majority preach biblical literalism, a word-for-word interpretation (in English) of the Bible. Furthermore, entrepreneurial churches believe that the acquisition of wealth through the systematic accumulation of profit in business is the primary message of the Gospel. Rick Warren (2002), pastor, author, and unofficial theologian of entrepreneurial Christianity, argues in line with Bruce Barton, that Jesus was the first great entrepreneur, who recruited 12 businessmen (the 12 apostles) and molded them into an organization that conquered the world ("Jesus, CEO" 2005:44).

Not only do individual churches embrace marketing principles as well as the profit motive, but they also collectively contribute to and receive funds from organizations such as the National Christian Foundation (NCF), which serves both to distribute funds for church services and provide a tax shelter for the vast revenues that entrepreneurial churches generate. With personal, institutional, and ideological connections with the religious right, the NCF channels money into political campaigns as well, using techniques the IRS studied for several years to decide if they were legal (Reynolds 2005:43). The more an individual donates, the more influence he or she can buy through NCF with lobbyists and friendly politicians. NCF remains tax free, even though it receives money for services and contributes freely to political organizations—not directly, but through a complex network of organizations and board appointments whose members receive large compensation packages (Reynolds 2005:79). Still under investigation, NCF has so far avoided indictments, and operates through loopholes in the tax code and through new investment and money-management techniques for which no laws have yet been devised.

The people who mange entrepreneurial churches, large and small, as well as the people who manage Christian investment companies and other services, typically become very rich. The organizations and businesses they manage likewise accumulate and often wield great wealth for various social and political purposes, all the while operating tax free. The entrepreneurial spirit that drives these people and organizations not only uses management techniques from businesses, but engages fully in broader techniques, such as tax loopholes, shelters, political lobbyists, and networks to channel money as necessary to create social and political impact without the cost of taxes or governmental regulation that applies to most other businesses.

Moreover, many churches now sponsor personal and private entrepreneurial activity within their membership, as we see in the following study by Sadie Pendaz.

God the Economist?
Economics and Religion in an Inter-Faith Business Organization

By Sadie Pendaz

As central institutions of modern life, economics and religion play pivotal roles in how groups of people and individuals understand the world and their social locations within the world. Discussions of interconnections between religion and economics—public, private, and pulpit—are often awkward, tenuous, and controversial. As sociologists, we strive to understand how larger patterns of history and public life inform, contextualize, and ground the experiences of individuals. Here, I briefly examine three recent and varied examples of the interplay between religion and economics and then turn to how a small group manages an attempt to resolve the awkwardness, tenuousness, and controversy associated with this coupling of faith and business.

In the fall of 2006, *Time* magazine ran a cover story entitled, "Does God Want You to Be Rich?" where they tracked a burgeoning movement within American Evangelical Protestantism, dubbed "Prosperity." Proponents of Prosperity advance two important objectives:

God wants people to enjoy the material world, which involves being, at the very least, financially stable, if not prosperous; and

Christians should give to and take care of those less economically blessed, which requires first that they have something to give.

The Prosperity movement has as many detractors as supporters within Evangelical Protestantism, and those against Prosperity regard money as a false idol—note the tendency of the Biblical accounts of Jesus to highlight his time spent among the poor—and emphasize the importance of living a life of sacrifice and simplicity. Since Biblical scripture serves overwhelmingly as a model for action among Evangelicals, both supporters and detractors of Prosperity find support in the Bible, which makes mention of money several thousand times.

The interplay of the overlapping institutional mechanisms involved in joining economic and religious concerns has also recently generated political policy. For example, President George W. Bush made the charitable choice provision of the Personal Responsibility and Work Reconciliation Act of 1996 key to his campaign in 2000. The purpose of this provision was to maximize the economic role of religious charities through the allocation of national funds to be dispersed through the dual economic and religious institutional mechanisms of religious charities (Formicola and Seegers 2002).

In some cases, prominent individuals in particular denominations or congregations bring more public attention and discussion to the precepts of that particular church. For example, a June 2007 international episode involving the Church of Scientology and well-known American actor Tom Cruise attracted media attention. When Cruise planned to use German military sites for the filming of a Nazi-era film, the German government made threats to ban the filming because of Cruise's involvement with Scientology. The German government contends that Scientology is a for-profit business that masquerades as a religion to make money. Consequently, the German government does not recognize Scientology as a legitimate religion.

Showcased in the preceding examples—the Prosperity movement, Bush's charitable choice provision, and external claims regarding the economic intentions of the Church of Scientology—we see the ubiquity and integration of religious and economic institutions in American culture. These diverse examples illustrate how broad cultural patterns shape institutional behavior, as well as notions of institutional legitimacy. The United States readily accepts the religion–business union; Germany does not. To further understand the process of legitimation, we need to understand how individuals struggle with and make meaning of these patterns of influence. Legitimacy can only exist when people think it does, and in our context, the legitimacy of faith and business develops both from sociocultural acceptance and from individual decision-making and priorities.

Symbolic interactionism, as a sociological theory and method, allows an examination of how social location, patterns of cultural influence, and the subsequent decisions and actions of individuals are negotiated through a faith-based business organization. This approach enhances our ability to uncover how people create meaning in their relationship to religious and economic spheres of influence, how people interpret each other's actions and the social world around them, and how they fit together their own courses of action. This decision-making process occurs in accordance with the priorities of faith-based living within the larger social context of financial advancement and success.

In 2005, as part of the American Mosaic Project (the AMP), a large multimethod (national survey and field work) and multicity (Boston, Atlanta, Minneapolis-St. Paul,

(Continued)

(Continued)

and Los Angeles) initiative at the University of Minnesota, I interviewed several members of a faith-based business owners' group in the Minneapolis-St. Paul area. The result of these interviews provides a symbolic-interactionist attempt to understand just how they managed to negotiate meaning and action between their priorities of faith and their business interests.

At the time of the interviews, the faith-based business organization (called the "Business Owners' Group") had existed for a little over 3 years, was inter-faith (Protestant and Catholic), and resided in the home church of the founder. Membership had been fairly steady, as four of the five founding members were still in attendance. The current membership of five were all white males and in their mid-forties to mid-fifties. Over the course of the life of the group, two females, one of whom was African American, had also participated. The only requirement for participation was that members be business owners and comfortable with the group's emphasis on Christian values and Bible study.

The group met twice monthly for 2-hour stretches, during which they would spend the first hour engaged in Bible study. The second hour was often more ad hoc and pertained to particular problems, struggles, successes, and so forth that individuals were having in their particular businesses. One interviewee noted that as a result of these discussions, loose networks of affiliation arose that resulted in the hiring of or contracting of services to other Christian affiliates of fellow members of the Business Owners' Group.

Once each year, members rotated the presentation of vision statements for the future year, which included their prioritized (1) plans to walk with God, (2) family vision, and (3) business vision.

The ongoing purpose of the group was negotiated through the interactions of its members. These interactions centered on the two central tasks undertaken by the group: Bible study and goal setting/problem solving within their businesses. As one interviewee stated, "I guess what we're attempting to learn is how God would want us to live our lives and then secondly how he'd want us to conduct our businesses."

Several consequences follow from this collective vision. The group has a high level of social cohesion as a result of shared religious values and because they all own businesses. Regarding practical affairs, one interviewee noted that "when you own your own business, a lot of times you don't have a place to bounce a lot of your ideas against other people, you know." Another result of the group's shared meaning is a collective unification and legitimation of religious, personal, and business aspects of their lives. As such, the previously mentioned networks of affiliation that arise during meeting discussions, and which led to the employment of fellow Christians, were attributed to religious serendipity or direct intervention from God, rather than to other institutional or structural mechanisms or networks of affiliation. Members believe that faith and God's hand guided their business decisions.

The group also serves as an anchor to help ensure that religious influence holds primacy over business as well as other matters in their lives such as family. In addition, the shared meaning of the group shapes the way that members think about their place in a larger social context, such as American society. For example, when I asked one member how he saw the Business Owners' Group fitting into his overall vision of America, he responded with the following:

> Well they're people that had dreams and they're people that were able to live out those dreams, and they had the freedom to be able to do it. They had the ability to start at whatever level it was they were at; they had the ability to grow through . . . their knowledge. And they had the ability to kind of look and see what they thought they wanted out of their life, or where God was directing them to live their life and they had the ability to do that.

> The shared meanings developed through the small-group interactions of the Business Owners' Group allow the members to make sense of their lives of faith, their business lives, and their place in American society through the prioritizing of their adherence to God's direction. According to the collectively derived purpose of the group, they are successfully merging their religious and business interests.

Clearly a development of modern capitalist society, new issues arise that Max Weber envisioned long ago. Has Christianity become a business, and what impact does this have on its spiritual aspects? As we saw in Chapter 2, the recent study of religion among American teens shows that, overwhelmingly, they understand religion on an entirely personal level, and that God is a personal tool that people may use when and if they see fit. Whether to accomplish some task, to gain success in some endeavor, or to feel better, the research suggests that religion increasingly takes the form of *moral therapeutic deism* (C. Smith and Denton 2005). That is, Christians of all types today (who make up about 80% of the U.S. population) use religion as a personal tool to justify their personal moral beliefs. They use God and religion to assuage undesirable emotions—a self-administered therapy. Lastly, they view God however they want; that is, they are deists (believe in God), but each person holds a uniquely individual and idiosyncratic view, constructed for his or her own purposes (C. Smith and Denton 2005). At the same time, popular church leaders and managers generate tremendous revenue and draw substantial salaries in the millions, telling the devout what they want to hear. Is personal therapy and the accumulation of profit and wealth the message of Christianity today? From the perspective of a believer, the answer depends on, well, one's personal beliefs. Neither science nor a congregation can challenge the validity of personal beliefs.

Still, sociology as a science can address the changes that entrepreneurialism represents in contemporary American Christianity. The entire concept of entrepreneurial advancement is a modern one and represents a process of acquisition that is only possible in modern times. Specifically, capitalism as the systematic accumulation of profit is a modern development, and in this regard, the entrepreneurial churches of today are a product of this process of rationalization that long ago systematized industry and many other aspects of society, and which is now transforming religion.

Yet let us consider another issue. The systematic accumulation of wealth involves a particular value system, one that posits money as the primary goal of activity in life. General accumulation of wealth may happen at any time—for example, a person wins the lottery, inherits money, or saves up as best they can over time. Yet the systematic accumulation of wealth requires planning and projections, and the study and scrutiny of market forces and investment opportunities. This study and scrutiny further emphasizes the central significance of money and further directs the activity of life to its accomplishment. In other words, the acquisition of money in a systematic manner doesn't just happen; it is a way of life. What impact does this have on Christianity, or any other religion that embraces this specifically modern set of priorities as a form of spiritual and religious devotion? If Christianity, like all religions, reflects the values of the society that believes in it, what does that say about the type of society the United States has become?

References and Further Reading

"2 School Boards Push on Against Evolution." 2005. *New York Times,* January 19. Available at http://www.nytimes.com/2005/01/19/national/19evolution.html.

9/11 Commission Report: Final Report of the National Commission on Terrorist Attacks Upon the United States. 2004. New York: Norton. Available online at http://www.9-11commission.gov/report/index.htm.

Abukhalil, Asad. 2004. *The Battle for Saudi Arabia: Royalty, Fundamentalism, and Global Power.* New York: Seven Stories Press.

Adler, Margot. [1979] 2006. *Drawing Down the Moon: Witches, Druids, Goddess-Worshippers, and Other Pagans in America Today.* New York: Penguin Books.

Adorno, Theodor, Else Frenkel-Brunswik, Daniel J. Levinson, and R. Nevitt Sanford. [1950] 1982. *The Authoritarian Personality.* New York: Norton.

Ahlstrom, Sydney E. 1972. *A Religious History of the American People.* New Haven, CT: Yale University Press.

Aho, James. 1990. *The Politics of Righteousness: Idaho Christian Patriotism.* Seattle: University of Washington Press.

———. 1994. *This Thing of Darkness.* Seattle: University of Washington Press.

Akins, Nancy J., Linda S. Cordell, Jeffrey S. Dean, and Stephen H. Lekson. 2006. *Archaeology of Chaco Canyon: An Eleventh-Century Pueblo Regional Center.* Santa Fe, NM: School of American Research Press.

Albertson, Todd. 2007. *The Gods of Business.* Los Angeles: Trinity Alumni Press.

Albright, William. 1990. *Yahweh and the Gods of Canaan: An Historical Analysis of Two Contrasting Faiths.* Winona Lake, IN: Eisenbrauns.

Alexander-Moegerle, Gil. 1997. *James Dobson's War on America.* Amherst, NY: Prometheus Books.

Allen, Theodore W. 1994. *The Invention of the White Race: Racial Oppression and Social Control.* New York: Verso.

Almond, Gabriel A., R. Scott Appleby, and Emmanuel Sivan. 2003. *Strong Religion: The Rise of Fundamentalisms Around the World.* Chicago: University of Chicago Press.

Al Rasheed, Madawi. 2007. *Contesting the Saudi State: Islamic Voices From a New Generation.* New York: Cambridge University Press.

Altemeyer, Bob. 1997. *The Authoritarian Specter.* Cambridge, MA: Harvard University Press.

Al Zayyat, Montasser, Sarah Nimis, and Ahmed Fekry. 2004. *The Road to Al-Qaeda: The Story of Bin Laden's Right-Hand Man.* London: Pluto.

Ames, Robert T. 1999. *The Analects of Confucius: A Philosophical Translation.* New York: Ballantine Books.

Ammerman, Nancy Tatom. 1987. *Bible Believers: Fundamentalists in the Modern World.* New Brunswick, NJ: Rutgers University Press.

——. 1990. *Baptist Battles: Social Change and Religious Conflict in the Southern Baptist Convention.* New Brunswick, NJ: Rutgers University Press.

——. 2002. "Re-Awakening a Sleeping Giant: Christian Fundamentalists in the Late Twentieth-Century US Society." In *The Freedom to Do God's Will: Religious Fundamentalism and Social Change,* edited by Gerrie ter Haar and James J. Busuttil. New York: Routledge.

Anderson, Allan. 2004. *An Introduction to Pentecostalism: Global Charismatic Christianity.* New York: Cambridge University Press.

Angold, Michael. 2001. *Byzantium: The Bridge From Antiquity to the Middle Ages.* New York: St. Martin's Press.

Angus, Samuel. [1928] 1975. *The Mystery-Religions: A Study in the Religious Background of Early Christianity.* Mineola, NY: Dover.

An-Na'im, Abdullah Ahmed. 2002. "Islamic Fundamentalism and Social Change: Neither the End of History Nor a Clash of Civilizations." In *The Freedom to Do God's Will: Religious Fundamentalism and Social Change,* edited by Gerrie ter Haar and James J. Busuttil. New York: Routledge.

Antonio, Robert J. 1999. "After Postmodernism: Reactionary Tribalism." *American Journal of Sociology* 106:40–87.

Armstrong, Karen. 2001. *The Buddha.* New York: Penguin Books.

Arnesen, Eric. 1994. *Waterfront Workers of New Orleans: Race, Class, and Politics, 1863–1923.* Champaign-Urbana: University of Illinois Press.

Arnett, Jeffrey Jensen. 1996. *Metalheads: Heavy Metal Music and Adolescent Alienation.* Boulder, CO: Westview Press.

Arrington, Leonard J. and Davis Bitton. 1992. *The Mormon Experience: A History of the Latter-Day Saints.* New York: Knopf.

Askenasy, Hans. 1994. *Cannibalism: From Sacrifice to Survival.* New York: Prometheus Books.

Bachetta, Paola and Margaret Power. 2002. *Right-Wing Women: From Conservatives to Extremists Around the World.* New York: Routledge.

Bageant, Joe. 2007. *Deer Hunting With Jesus: Dispatches From America's Class War.* New York: Crown Publishing.

Bakhtin, Mikhail. [1918] 1984. *Rabelais and His World.* Bloomington: Indiana University Press.

Barber, Malcolm. 2000. *The Cathars: Dualist Heretics in Languedoc in the High Middle Ages.* New York: Longman.

Barker, Eileen. [1984] 1993. *The Making of a Moonie.* London: Ashgate.

Barker, Eileen and Margit Warburg. 2000. *New Religions and New Religiosity.* Aarhus, Denmark: Aarhus University Press.

Barkun, Michael. 1997. *Religion and the Racist Right: The Origins of the Christian Identity Movement.* Chapel Hill: University of North Carolina Press.

Barraclough, Geoffrey. 1976. *The Crucible of Europe.* Berkeley: University of California Press.

——. [1968] 1979. *The Medieval Papacy.* New York: Norton.

Barrett, David V. 2001. *The New Believers: Sects, Cults, and Alternative Religions.* New York: Sterling.

Barstow, Anne Llewellyn. 1994. *Witchcraze: A New History of the European Witch Hunts.* San Francisco: Pandora/HarperCollins.

Bartkowski, John P. 2004. *The Promise Keepers: Servants, Soldiers, and Godly Men.* New Brunswick, NJ: Rutgers University Press.

Basham, A. L. 1999. *A Cultural History of India.* New York: Oxford University Press.

Bates, Timothy. 1997. *Race, Self-Employment, and Upward Mobility: An Illusive American Dream.* Baltimore: Johns Hopkins University Press.

Batson, C. Daniel, Patricia Schoenrade, and W. Larry Ventis. 1993. *Religion and the Individual: A Social-Psychological Perspective.* New York: Oxford University Press.

Beall, Alyssa. 2005. "There's No Place Like Home.html: Neopaganism on the Internet." In *Religious Innovation in a Global Age. Essays on the Construction of Spirituality.* Jefferson, NC: McFarland.

Beit-Hallahmi, Benjamin and Michael Argyle. 1997. *The Psychology of Religious Behaviour, Belief, and Experience.* London: Routledge.

Bell, Daniel. [1976] 1996. *The Cultural Contradictions of Capitalism,* Twentieth Anniversary Edition. New York: Perseus/Basic Books.

Bell, Rob. 2005. *Velvet Elvis: Repainting the Christian Faith.* Grand Rapids, MI: Zondervan.

Bellah, Robert N. [1985] 1996. *Habits of the Heart: Individualism and Commitment in American Life.* Berkeley: University of California Press.

Belton, Patrick. 2003. "In the Way of the Prophet: Ideologies and Institutions in Dearborn, Michigan, America's Muslim Capitol." *The Next American City* 3 (Fall).

Benedict, Ruth. [1934] 1989. *Patterns of Culture.* New York: Mariner Books.

Benjamin, Walter. [c. 1927] 1999. *The Arcades Project.* Cambridge, MA: Harvard University Press.

Bennett, David H. 1995. *The Party of Fear: The American Far Right From Nativism to the Militia Movement.* New York: Vintage Books/Random House.

Berger, Helen A. 1995. "The Routinization of Spontaneity." *Sociology of Religion,* 56 (1) Spring:49–60.

Berger, Helen A., Evan A. Leach, and Leigh S. Shaffer. 2003. *Voices From the Pagan Census: A National Survey of Witches and Neo-Pagans in the United States.* Columbia: University of South Carolina Press.

Berger, Peter. [1967] 1990. *The Sacred Canopy. Elements of a Sociology of Religion.* New York: Anchor Books/Random House.

——. 1992. *A Far Glory: The Quest for Faith in an Age of Credulity.* New York: The Free Press.

—— (ed.). 1999. *The Desecularization of the World: Resurgent Religion and World Politics.* Grand Rapids, MI: Eerdmans.

Berlin, Ira. 2000. *Many Thousands Gone: The First Two Centuries of Slavery in North America.* Cambridge, MA: Belknap Press.

Bettelheim, Bruno and Morris Janowitz. 1950. *Dynamics of Prejudice: A Psychological and Sociological Study of Veterans.* New York: Norton.

Bettelheim, Bruno and Morris Janowitz. 1950. *The Dynamics of Prejudice.* New York: Harper.

Beyer, Peter. 2006. *Religion in a Global Society.* New York: Routledge.

Black, S. Jason and Christopher S. Hyatt. 1993. *Urban Voodoo: A Beginners Guide to Afro-Caribbean Magic.* Tempe, AZ: New Falcon Press.

Blackbourn, David. 1993. *Marpingen: Apparitions of the Virgin Mary in a Nineteenth-Century German Village.* New York: Vintage Books.

Boisvert, Donald. 2000. *Out on Holy Ground: Meditations on Gay Men's Spirituality.* Cleveland, OH: Pilgrim Press.

Boston, Robert. 1996. *The Most Dangerous Man in America? Pat Robertson and the Rise of the Christian Coalition.* Amherst, NY: Prometheus Books.

Bourdieu, Pierre, [1980] 1990. *The Logic of Practice.* Stanford, CA: Stanford University Press.

——. 1980. "The Production of Belief: Contribution to an Economy of Symbolic Goods." *Media, Culture, and Society* 2:261–293.

——. 1985. "The Market of Symbolic Goods." *Poetics* 14 (April): 13–44.

——. 1991. *Language and Symbolic Power.* Cambridge, MA: Harvard University Press.

——. 1993. *The Field of Cultural Production.* New York: Columbia University Press.

Bowman, Marion and Steven Sutcliffe. 2000. *Beyond New Age: Exploring Alternative Spirituality.* Edinburgh: Edinburgh University Press.

Boyce, Mary. 1975. "On the Zoroastrian Temple Cult of Fire." *Journal of the American Oriental Society,* 95 (3):454–465.

——. [1979] 2001. *Zoroastrians: Their Religious Beliefs and Practices.* London and New York: Routledge.

Boyer, Paul and Stephen Nissenbaum. 1974. *Salem Possessed: The Social Origins of Witchcraft.* Cambridge, MA: Harvard University Press.

Bradley, John R. 2006. *Saudi Arabia Exposed: Inside a Kingdom in Crisis,* Updated Edition. New York: Palgrave Macmillan.

Bradley, K. R. 1987. *Slaves and Masters in the Roman Empire: A Study in Social Control.* New York: Oxford University Press.

Brasher, Brenda. 1998. *Godly Women: Fundamentalism and Female Power.* New Brunswick, NJ: Rutgers University Press.

Bravin, Jess. 1997. *Squeaky: The Life and Times of Lynette Alice Fromme—Runaway.* New York: St. Martin's Press.

Brecht, Bertolt. [1943] 1999. *The Good Woman of Szechuan.* Minneapolis: University of Minnesota Press.

Bromley, David G. and Gordon J. Melton. 2002. *Cults, Religion, and Violence.* New York: Cambridge University Press.

Brooks, Clem and Jeff Manza. 2004. "A Great Divide? Religion and Political Change in U.S. National Elections, 1972–2000." *Sociological Quarterly* 45 (3) Summer:421–451.

Brooks, Daphne A. 2006. *Bodies in Dissent: Spectacular Performances of Race and Freedom, 1850–1910.* Durham, NC: Duke University Press.

Brown, Charles M. 2002. "Which Way Should I Go?: How Industry Members Address The Tension Between Artistic Expression and Traditional Ministry in the Christian Retailing and Entertainment Industry." Paper presented at the Midwest Sociological Society, Milwaukee, WI.

——. 2003a. "Enemy at the Gate: Gatekeeping and Censorship in the Christian Popular Culture Industry." Paper presented at the Society for the Scientific Study of Religion, Norfolk, VA.

——. 2003b. "Selling Faith: Marketing Christian Popular Culture to Christian and Non-Christian Audiences." Paper presented at the Eastern Sociological Society, Philadelphia.

——. 2003c. "Working for God: How Christian Faith Influences Work in the Christian Popular Culture Industry." Paper presented at the Midwest Sociological Society, Chicago.

Brown, Dee. 1970. *Bury My Heart at Wounded Knee: An Indian History of the American West.* New York: Owl Books.

Brown, Robert L. 1991. *Ganesh: Studies of an Asian God.* Albany: State University of New York Press.

Bruce, Steve. 1990. *The Rise and Fall of the New Christian Right: Conservative Protestant Politics in America, 1978–1988.* New York: Oxford University Press.

——. 2002. *God Is Dead: Secularization in the West.* Malden, MA: Blackwell.

Bruns, Roger A. 1992. *Preacher: Billy Sunday and Big-Time American Evangelism.* New York: Norton.

Bryant, Edwin and Maria Ekstrand. 2004. *The Haré Krishna Movement: The Postcharismatic Fate of a Religious Transplant.* New York: Columbia University Press.

Buchanan, James and Gordon Tullock. 1962. *The Calculus of Consent.* Ann Arbor: University of Michigan Press.

Buchanan, Melinda, Kristina Dzelme, Dale Harris, and Lorna Hecker. 2001. "Challenges of Being Simultaneously Gay or Lesbian and Spiritual and/or Religious: A Narrative Perspective." *American Journal of Family Therapy* 29:435–449.

Buchanan, Patrick J. 2007. *Day of Reckoning: How Hubris, Ideology, and Greed Are Tearing America Apart.* New York: Thomas Dunne Books.

Buchowski, M. 2006. "The Specter of Orientalism in Europe: From Exotic Other to Stigmatized Brother." *Anthropological Quarterly* 79 (3):463–482.

Buehrens, John A. and F. Forrester Church. 1991. *Our Chosen Faith.* Boston: Beacon Press.

Buergenthal, Thomas and Courtney W. Howland. 2001. *Religious Fundamentalisms and the Human Rights of Women.* New York: Palgrave.

Buford, Bill. 1992. *Among the Thugs.* New York: Norton.

Bugliosi, Vincent. [1974] 2001. *Helter Skelter: The True Story of the Manson Murders.* New York: Norton.

Bull, Malcolm and Keith Lockhart. [1989] 2007. *Seeking a Sanctuary: Seventh-Day Adventism and the American Dream.* Bloomington: Indiana University Press.

Burgat, Francois. 2003. *Face to Face With Political Islam.* New York: St. Martin's Press.

Burkert, Walter. 2005. *Ancient Mystery Cults.* Cambridge, MA: Harvard University Press.

Bushman, Richard L. [1970] 1989. *The Great Awakening: Documents of the Revival Religion, 1740–1745.* Chapel Hill: University of North Carolina Press.

Buss, Doris and Didi Herman. 2003. *Globalizing Family Values: The Christian Right in International Politics.* Minneapolis: University of Minnesota Press.

Caesar, Gaius Julius. [c. 50 BCE] 2006. *The Gallic War.* Mineola, NY: Dover.

Carroll, Jackson W. and Wade Clark Roof. 1993. *Beyond Establishment: Protestant Identity in a Postmodern Age.* Louisville, KY: Westminster/John Knox Press.

Carwardine, Richard. 1994. "New Evangelicals, Politics, and the Coming of the American Civil War." *New Evangelicalism: Comparative Studies of Popular Protestantism in North America, the British Isles, and Beyond.* New York: Oxford University Press.

Casanova, J. 1994. *Public Religions in the Modern World.* Chicago: University of Chicago Press.

Catholic Encyclopaedia, Vol. 3. 1908. New York: Robert Appleton.

Chadwick, Henry. [1967] 1993. *The Early Church,* Revised Edition. London: Penguin Classics.

Chandler, Timothy and John Nauright. 1996. "Rugby, Manhood, and Identity." In *Making Men: Rugby and Masculine Identity,* edited by John Nauright and Timothy Chandler. Portland, OR: Frank Kass.

Chilton, David. 1981. *Productive Christians in an Age of Guilt Manipulators.* Tyler, TX: Institute for Christian Economics.

Chitty, Susan. 1976. *Charles Kingsley's Landscape.* Newton Abbott, Devon, UK: David and Charles.

Chivers, C. J. and Steven Lee Myers. 2004a. "Insurgents Seize School in Russia and Hold Scores." *New York Times,* September 2, page A1.

——. 2004b. "Terror in Russia: Battle in Beslan: 250 Die as Siege at a Russian School Ends in Chaos." *New York Times,* September 4, page A1.

Chomsky, Noam. 1989. *Thought Control in Democratic Societies.* Boston: South End Press.

——. 1991. *Deterring Democracy.* New York: Hill and Wang.

Christ, Christina P. 1987. *Laughter of Aphrodite: Reflections on the Journey to the Goddess.* San Francisco: Harper & Row.

Cicero, Marcus Tullius. [c. 40 BCE] 1960. *Cicero: Selected Works.* New York: Penguin Classics.

Cicourel, Aaron. 1974. *Cognitive Sociology: Language and Meaning in Social Interaction.* New York: The Free Press.

Cohen, Jere. 2002. *Protestantism and Capitalism: The Mechanisms of Influence.* New York: Aldine de Gruyter.

Coleman, Simon. 1993. "Conservative Protestantism and the World Order: The Faith Movement in the United States and Sweden." *Sociology of Religion* 54 (4) Winter:54–65.

——. 1998. "Charismatic Christianity and the Dilemmas of Globalization." *Religion* 28:245–256.

Coleman, William S. E. 2000. *Voices of Wounded Knee.* Lincoln: University of Nebraska Press.

Coll, Steve. 2004. *Ghost Wars: The Secret History of the CIA, Afghanistan, and Bin Laden, From the Soviet Invasion to September 10, 2001.* New York: Penguin.

Commins, David. 2006. *The Wahhabi Mission and Saudi Arabia.* New York: I. B. Tauris.

Comnena, Anna. [1120] 1969. *The Alexiad.* New York: Penguin Books.

Compagna, Joel. 2006. "Princes, Clerics, and Censors." *Special Report, July 9.* New York: Committee to Protect Journalists.

Conn, Joseph L. 1992. "Apocalypse Now: Pat Robertson's New World Order and Your Place in It." *Church and State,* June.

Coogan, Michael D. 2005. *Eastern Religions: Hinduism, Buddism, Taoism, Confucianism, Shinto.* New York: Oxford University Press.

Cook, Karen S. (ed.). 2003. *Trust in Society.* Washington, DC: Russell Sage Foundation.

Coontz, Stephanie. 2000. *The Way We Never Were: American Families and the Nostalgia Trap.* New York: Basic Books.

Cooperman, Alan. 2006. "Democrats Win Bigger Share of Religious Vote." *Washington Post,* November 11, p. A1.

Courtright, Paul B. 1985. *Gaṇeśa: Lord of Obstacles, Lord of Beginnings.* New York: Oxford University Press.

Cox, Harvey. 2001. *Fire From Heaven: The Rise of Pentecostal Spirituality and the Reshaping of Religion in the 21st Century.* Cambridge, MA: Da Capo Press.

cummings, e. e. [1926] 1994. *Selected Poems.* New York: Liveright.

Cuneo, Michael. 2001. *American Exorcism: Expelling Demons in the Land of Plenty.* New York: Broadway Books.

Cunningham, Mary. 2002. *Faith in the Byzantine World.* Downer's Grove, IL: InterVarsity Press.

Curtis, Susan. 1991. *A Consuming Faith: The Social Gospel and Modern American Culture.* Baltimore: The Johns Hopkins University Press.

Danforth, John C. 2000. *Final Report to the Deputy Attorney General: Concerning the 1993 Confrontation at the Mt. Carmel Complex Waco, Texas.* Washington, DC: United States Department of Justice.

Dary, David E. [1974] 1989. *Buffalo Book: The Full Saga of the American Animal,* Revised Edition. Athens: Ohio University Press.

Daschke, Dereck and Michael Ashcraft. 2005. *New Religious Movements: A Documentary Reader.* New York: New York University Press.

Davies, Christie. 1982. "Sexual Taboos and Social Boundaries." *American Journal of Sociology* 87(5):1032–1063.

Davis, Mike. 2002. *Dead Cities and Other Tales.* New York: The New Press.

——. *Planet of Slums.* New York: Verso.

Dawkins, Richard. 2008. *The God Delusion.* New York: Mariner/Houghton Mifflin.

Dawson, Lorne L. 1998a. "Anti-Modernism, Modernism, and Postmodernism: Struggling with the Cultural Significance of New Religious Movements." *Sociology of Religion* 59 (2) Summer:131–156.

——. 1998b. *Cults: Understanding New Religious Movements.* New York: Oxford University Press.

——. 2003. *Cults and New Religious Movements: A Reader.* Malden, MA: Blackwell.

——. 2006. *Comprehending Cults: The Sociology of New Religious Movements,* Second Edition. New York: Oxford University Press.

Dayan, Joan. 1997. "Voudoun or the Voice of the Gods." *Sacred Possessions: Voudou, Santeria, Obeah, and the Caribbean.* New Brunswick, NJ: Rutgers University Press.

——. 2005. "Evolution Takes a Backseat in U.S. Classes." *New York Times,* February 1.

Dean, Cornelia. 2005. "Evolution Takes a Backseat in U.S. Classes." *New York Times,* February 1.

de Beauvoir, Simone. [1952] 1989. *The Second Sex.* New York: Vintage Books.

DeBord, Guy. [1967] 1995. *The Society of the Spectacle.* New York: Zone Books.

Deliver Us From Evil. 2003. The Learning Channel/Discovery Channel. Videocassette.

Demos, John. 1982. *Entertaining Satan: Witchcraft and the Culture of Early New England.* New York: Oxford University Press.

Denton, Melinda L. 2004. "Gender and Marital Decision Making: Negotiating Religious Ideology and Practice." *Social Forces* 82 (3).

Deren, Maya. 1983. *Divine Horsemen: The Living Gods of Haiti.* Weston, MO: McPherson.

Desmangles, Leslie. 1992. *The Faces of the Gods: Voudou and Roman Catholicism in Haiti.* Chapel Hill: University of North Carolina Press.

Dever, William G. 2003. *Who Were the Early Israelites, and Where Did They Come From?* Grand Rapids, MI: Eerdmans.

——. 2005. *Did God Have a Wife? Archaeology and Folk Religion in Ancient Israel.* Grand Rapids, MI: Eerdmans.

Devisch, René. 1995. "Frenzy, Violence, and Ethical Renewal in Kinshasa." *Public Culture* 7:3.

——.1995. *Roads to Dominion: Right-Wing Movements and Political Power in the United States.* New York: Guilford Press.

Diamond, Sara. 1995. *Roads to Domination: Right-Wing Movements and Political Power in the United States* New York: Guilford Press.

——. 1998. *Not by Politics Alone: The Enduring Influence of the Christian Right.* New York: Guilford Press.

Dinges, William. 1995. "Roman Catholic Traditionalism." *America's Alternative Religions.* Albany: State University of New York Press.

DiNitto, Diana M. and Linda K. Cummins. 2006. *Social Welfare: Politics and Public Policy,* Sixth Edition. Upper Saddle River, NJ: Allyn & Bacon.

Dinnerstein, Leonard. 1994. *Anti-Semitism in America.* New York: Oxford University Press.

Dio, Cassius. [c. 210 CE, 1905] 2006. *Dio's Rome,* Vol. 4. New York: BiblioBazaar.

Docherty, Jayne Seminare. 2001. *Learning Lessons From Waco: When the Parties Bring Their Gods to the Negotiation Table.* Syracuse, NY: Syracuse University Press.

Donnelly, Mark. 2006. *Eat Thy Neighbor: A History of Cannibalism.* Stroud, Gloucestershire, UK: Sutton Publishing.

Dorsett, Lyle W. 1991. *Billy Sunday and the Redemption of Urban America.* Grand Rapids, MI: Eerdmans.

Downs, Anthony. 1997. *An Economic Theory of Democracy.* New York: Addison-Wesley.

Duany, Andres, Elizabeth Plater-Zyberk, and Jeff Speck. 2000. *The Rise and Sprawl and the Decline of the American Dream.* New York: North Point Press.

Dunmore, John. 2005. *Storms and Dreams: Louis De Bougainville: Soldier, Explorer, Statesman.* London: Trafalgar Square.

Dunning, Eric. 1989. *The Roots of Football Hooliganism: An Historical and Sociological Study.* New York: Routledge.

Durkheim, Émile. [1893] 1984. *The Division of Labor in Society.* New York: The Free Press.

——. [1897] 1951. *Suicide: A Study in Sociology.* New York: The Free Press.

——. [1912] 1995. *Elementary Forms of the Religious Life.* Glencoe, IL: The Free Press.

——. [1915] 1965. *Elementary Forms of the Religious Life.* New York: The Free Press.

Easwaran, Eknath. [1987] 2000. *The Upanishads.* Tomales, CA: Nilgiri Press.

Eck, Diana L. 2002. *A New Religious America: How a "Christian Country" Has Become the World's Most Religiously Diverse Nation.* San Francisco: HarperSanFrancisco.

Eisgruber, Christopher L. and Lawrence G. Sager. 2007. *Religious Freedom and the Constitution.* Cambridge, MA: Harvard University Press.

Eisler, Riane. 1988. *The Chalice and the Blade: Our History, Our Future.* San Francisco: HarperSanFrancisco.

Eller, Cynthia. 1993. *Living in the Lap of the Goddess: The Feminist Spirituality Movement in America.* Boston: Beacon Press.

Elliott, Mark and Anita Deyneka. 1999. "Protestant Missionaries in the Former Soviet Union." *Proselytism and Orthodoxy in Russia: The New War for Souls,* edited by John Witte and Michael Bourdeaux. Maryknoll, NY: Orbis Books.

Ellis, Bill. 2000. *Raising the Devil: Satanism, New Religions, and the Media.* Lexington: University of Kentucky Press.

Ellis, Joseph J. 2004. *His Excellency: George Washington.* New York: Knopf.

Ellwood, Robert S. 1995. "Theosophy." In *Americas Alternative Religions,* edited by Timothy Miller. Albany: State University of New York Press.

Elst, Koenraad. 2001. *Decolonizing the Hindu Mind: Ideological Development of Hindu Revivalism.* New Delhi, India: Rupa.

Emerson, Michael O. and Christian Smith. 2000. *Divided by Faith: Evangelical Religion and the Problem of Race in America.* New York: Oxford University Press.

Essed, Philomena. 1990. Everyday Racism: Reports From Women of Two Cultures. Anaheim, CA: Hunter House.

Essed, Philomena and David Theo Goldberg. 2001. *Race Critical Theories: Text and Context.* London: Blackwell.

Fagan, Brian. 1996. *Time Detectives: How Archaeologists Use Technology to Recapture the Past.* New York: Simon & Schuster.

——. 2005. *Chaco Canyon: Archaeologists Explore the Lives of an Ancient Society.* New York: Oxford University Press.

Falwell, Jerry. 1981. *The Resurgence of Conservative Christianity.* Garden City, NY: Doubleday.

Fasick, Laura. 1994. "Charles Kingsley's Scientific Treatment of Gender." In *Muscular Christianity: Embodying the Victorian Age.* New York: Cambridge University Press.

Faubion, James D. 2001. *The Shadows and Lights of Waco: Millennialism Today.* Princeton, NJ: Princeton University Press.

Filatov, Sergei. 1999. "Sects and New Religious Movements in Post-Soviet Russia." In *Proselytism and Orthodoxy in Russia: The New War for Souls,* edited by John Witte and Michael Bourdeaux. Maryknoll, NY: Orbis Books.

Findlay, James F. 1969. *Dwight L. Moody: American Evangelist.* Foreword by Martin E. Marty. Chicago: University of Chicago Press.

Finke, Roger and Rodney Stark. 1992. *The Churching of America.* New Brunswick, NJ: Rutgers University Press.

Finkielkraut, Alain. [1980] 1997. *The Imaginary Jew.* Lincoln, NE: Bison Books.

Flo. 2004. *Diary of a Redneck Vampire: The True Story of a Rock and Roll Girl in a Boy's World.* Lincoln, NE: iUniverse Press.

Florida, Richard. 2004. *The Rise of the Creative Class: And How It's Transforming Work, Leisure, Community and Everyday Life.* New York: Basic Books.

Forbes, H. D. 1985. *Nationalism, Ethnocentrism, and Personality: Social Science and Critical Theory.* Chicago: University of Chicago Press.

Formicola, Jo Renee and Mary Seegers. 2002. "The Bush Faith-Based Initiative: The Catholic Response." *Journal of Church and State,* September:693–715.

Fowler, Jeaneane and Merv Fowler. 2008. *Chinese Religions: Beliefs and Practices.* Portland, OR: Sussex Academic Press.

Frank, Thomas. 2000. *One Market Under God: Extreme Capitalism, Market Populism, and the End of Economic Democracy.* New York: Anchor Books.

Frankfurter, David. 2006. *Evil Incarnate: Rumors of Demonic Conspiracy and Satanic Abuse in History.* Princeton, NJ: Princeton University Press.

Fraser, J. G. and Robert Fraser. [1890] 1994. *The Golden Bough: A Study in Magic and Religion.* New York: Oxford University Press.

Fraser, Robert. 1994. "Introduction." *The Golden Bough: A Study in Magic and Religion.* New York: Oxford University Press.

Fredrickson, George M. 1983. *White Supremacy: A Comparative Study of American and South African History.* New York: Oxford University Press.

——. 2002. *Racism: A Short History.* Princeton, NJ: Princeton University Press.

Frend, W. H. C. 1965. *Martyrdom and Persecution in the Early Church.* London: Basil Blackwell.

Fromm, Erich. 1936. "The Social-Psychology of Authoritarianism." *Studien Über Authorität und Familie.* Paris: Alcan.

——. [1941] 1994. *Escape From Freedom.* New York: Henry Holt.

——. [1947] 1990. *Man for Himself: An Inquiry Into the Psychology of Ethics.* New York: Henry Holt.

——. [1955] 1990. *The Sane Society.* New York: Henry Holt.

——. [1966] 1991. *You Shall Be as Gods.* New York: Henry Holt.

——. [1973] 1994. *The Anatomy of Human Destructiveness.* New York: Henry Holt.

——. [1984] *The Working Class in Weimar Germany: A Psychological and Sociological Study.* Cambridge, MA: Harvard University Press.

Fromm, Erich and Michael Maccoby. [1970] 1996. *Social Character in a Mexican Village.* Piscataway, NJ: Transaction.

Fukuyama, Francis. 1996. *Trust: Human Nature and the Reconstitution of Social Order.* New York: Touchstone Books.

Fuller, C. J. 1992. *The Camphor Flame: Popular Hinduism and Society in India.* Princeton, NJ: Princeton University Press.

Fuller, Robert C. 1995. *Naming the Antichrist: The History of an American Obsession.* New York: Oxford University Press.

Gaines, Donna. 1991. *Teenage Wasteland: Suburbia's Dead End Kids.* New York: HarperCollins.

——, Donna. 2007. *A Misfit's Manifesto: The Sociological Memoir of a Rock and Roll Heart.* New Brunswick, NJ: Rutgers University Press.

Gajdusek, Carleton D. 1981. *Kuru: Early Letters and Field-Notes From the Collection of D. Carleton Gajusek.* New York: Raven Press.

Galbraith, John Kenneth. [1958] 1998. *The Affluent Society.* Boston: Mariner/Houghton Mifflin.

Gallagher, Carole. 1993. *American Ground Zero: The Secret Nuclear War.* Cambridge, MA: MIT Press.

Gans, Herbert J. 1996. *The War Against the Poor: The Underclass and Antipoverty Policy.* New York: Basic Books.

Gauvreau, Michael. 1994. "The Empire of Evangelicalism: Varieties of Common Sense in Scotland, Canada, and the United States." *Evangelicalism: Comparative Studies of Popular Protestantism in North America, the British Isles, and Beyond.* New York: Oxford University Press.

Gee, Ellen and Jean E. Veevers. 1990. "Religious Involvement and Life Satisfaction in Canada." *Sociological Analysis* 51 (4) Winter:387–396.

Gekas, George. 1988. *The Life and Times of George Gipp.* South Bend, IN: And Books.

George, Edward. 1998. *Taming the Beast: Charles Manson's Life Behind Bars.* New York: St. Martin's Press.

Georgianna, Sharon. 1989. *The Moral Majority and Fundamentalism: Plausibility and Dissonance*. Lewiston, NJ: Edwin Mellen Press.

Gerson, Michael. 2006. "A New Faith-Based Agenda." *Newsweek*, November 13.

Gerth, H. H. and C. Wright Mills. (eds.). 1958. *From Max Weber: Essays in Sociology*. New York: Oxford University Press.

Gibbon, Edward. [1776] 1993. *The History of the Decline and Fall of the Roman Empire*, Vols. 1–3. New York: Knopf/Everyman's Library.

Gibbs, Eddie and Ryan K. Bolger. 2005. *Emerging Churches: Creating Christian Community in Postmodern Cultures*. Grand Rapids, MI: Baker Academic.

Gilens, Martin. 2000. *Why Americans Hate Welfare: Race, Media, and the Politics of Antipoverty Policy*. Chicago: University of Chicago Press.

Gimbutas, Marija. 2001. *The Living Goddesses*. Berkeley: University of California Press.

Glancy, Jennifer A. 2006. *Slavery in Early Christianity*. Minneapolis, MN: Augsburg Fortress Press.

Glass, Jennifer and Jerry Jacobs. 2005. "Childhood Religious Conservatism and Adult Attainment Among Black and White Women." *Social Forces* 84:555–579.

Goffman, Erving. 1961. *Asylums: Essays on the Social Situation of Mental Patients and Other Inmates*. San Francisco: Anchor Books.

——. [1963] 1986. *Stigma: Notes on the Management of Spoiled Identity*. Glencoe, IL: The Free Press.

Goldenberg, Nina. 1979. *Changing of the Gods: Feminism and the End of Traditional Religions*. Boston: Beacon Press.

Gould, Stephen Jay. 2002. *Rocks of Ages: Science and Religion in the Fullness of Life*. New York: Ballantine.

Grant, Michael. [1962] 1995. *Myths of the Greeks and Romans*. New York: Meridian/Penguin Group.

Greeley, Andrew and Michael Hout. 2006. *The Truth About Conservative Christians: What They Think and What They Believe*. Chicago: University of Chicago Press.

Greven, Philip J. [1977] 1988. *The Protestant Temperament: Patterns of Child-Rearing, Religious Experience, and the Self in Early America*. New York: Knopf.

"Gujarat Riot Death Toll Revealed." 2005. *BBC News*, May 11.

Gusfield, Joseph R. [1963] 1986. *Symbolic Crusade: Status Politics and the American Temperance Movement*, Second Edition. Urbana and Chicago: University of Illinois Press.

Guth, James L. 1996. "The Politics of the Christian Right." *Religion and the Culture Wars*. New York: Rowman & Littlefield.

Guth, James L. and John C. Green. 1996. "The Moralizing Minority: Christian Right Supporters Among Political Contributors." *Religion and the Culture Wars*. New York: Rowman & Littlefield.

Guth, James L., John C. Green, Lyman A. Kellstedt, and Corwin E. Smidt. 1996a. "Onward Christian Soldiers: Religious Activist Groups in American Politics." *Religion and the Culture Wars*. New York: Rowman & Littlefield.

——. 1996b. "The Political Relevance of Religion: The Correlates of Mobilization." *Religion and the Culture Wars*. New York: Rowman & Littlefield.

——. 2005. "Faith and Foreign Policy: A View from the Pews." *Review of Faith and International Affairs* 3, 1.

Haar, Gerrie ter. 2002. "Religious Fundamentalism and Social Change: A Comparative Inquiry." *The Freedom to Do God's Will: Religious Fundamentalism and Social Change*, edited by Gerrie ter Haar and James J. Busuttil. New York: Routledge.

Haldeman, Bonnie and Catherine Lowman Wessinger. 2007. *Memories of the Branch Davidians: Autobiography of David Koresh's Mother*. Waco, TX: Baylor University Press.

Hall, Donald F. 1994. "Muscular Christianity: Reading and Writing the Male Social Body." *Muscular Christianity: Embodying the Victorian Age.* New York: Cambridge University Press.

Hall, Dorota. 2005. "Catholicism Recycled: The New Age in Poland." In *Religious Innovation in a Global Age: Essays on the Construction of Spirituality.* Jefferson, NC: McFarland.

Hall, John R. 2002. *Apocalypse Observed: Religious Movements and Violence in North America, Europe, and Japan.* New York: Routledge.

Handley, Rod. 1995. *Character Counts.* Grand Island, NE: Cross Training.

Hanger, Kimberly S. 1997. *Bounded Lives, Bounded Places: Free Black Society in Colonial New Orleans, 1769–1803.* Durham, NC: Duke University Press.

Haqqani, Husain. 2005. *Pakistan: Between Mosque and Military.* Washington, DC: Carnegie Endowment for International Peace.

——. 2007–2008. "Why They Hate Us: The Long Answer." *Bostonia Magazine,* Winter.

Hartley, William G. 2001. "Missouri's 1838 Extermination Order and the Mormons' Forced Removal to Illinois." *Mormon Historical Studies* 2 (1): 5–27.

Hassan, Sharifah Zaleha Binti Syed. 2002. "Strategies for Public Participation: Women and Islamic Fundamentalism in Malaysia." In *The Freedom to Do God's Will: Religious Fundamentalism and Social Change,* edited by Gerrie ter Haar and James J. Busuttil. New York: Routledge.

Hatch, Nathan O. 1989. *The Democratization of American Christianity.* New Haven, CT: Yale University Press.

Hechter, Michael. 1987. *Principles of Group Solidarity.* Berkeley and Los Angeles: University of California Press.

Hedges, Ellie and James A. Beckford. 2000. "Holism, Healing, and the New Age." In *Beyond New Age: Exploring Alternative Spirituality.* Edinburgh, Scotland: Edinburgh University Press.

Heelas, Paul. 1996. *The New Age Movement: Religion, Culture and Society in the Age of Postmodernity.* Cambridge, MA: Blackwell.

Heelas, Paul and Linda Woodhead. 2005. *The Spiritual Revolution: Why Religion Is Giving Way to Spirituality.* Malden, MA: Blackwell.

Heertsgaard, Mark. 1988. *On Bended Knee: The Press and the Reagan Presidency.* New York: Farrar, Straus and Giroux.

Heilbrunn, Jacob. 1995. "On Pat Robertson: His Anti-Semitic Sources." *New York Review of Books,* April 20.

Herivel, Tara and Paul Wright. 2003. *Prison Nation: The Warehousing of America's Poor.* New York: Routledge.

Herman, Didi. 1997. *The Antigay Agenda: Orthodox Vision and the Christian Right.* Chicago: University of Chicago Press.

Herrmann, Steve. 2006. "9/11 Conspiracy Theory." *BBC World News,* October 27.

Hewitt, Glenn A. 1991. *Regeneration and Morality: A Study of Charles Finney, Charles Hodge, John W. Nevin, and Horace Bushnell.* New York: Carlson.

Heyrman, Christine Leigh. 1997. *Southern Cross: The Beginnings of the Bible Belt.* Chapel Hill: University of North Carolina Press.

"Hijack 'Suspects' Alive and Well." 2001. *BBC World News Service,* September 23.

Hill, Samuel. 1994. "Northern and Southern Varieties of American New Evangelicalism in the Nineteenth Century." *In New Evangelicalism: Comparative Studies of Popular Protestantism in North America, the British Isles, and Beyond.* New York: Oxford University Press.

Hirschman, Albert O. 1972. *Exit Voice and Loyalty: Exit Voice in Firms, Organizations, and States.* Cambridge, MA: Harvard University Press.

——. 1977. *The Passions and the Interests: Political Arguments for Capitalism Before Its Triumph*. Princeton, NJ: Princeton University Press.

Hitchens, Christopher. 2007. *God Is Not Great: How Religion Poisons Everything*. New York: Twelve/Hatchette Book Group.

Hochschild, Arlie. [1983] 2003. *The Managed Heart: Commercialization of Human Feeling*, Twentieth Anniversary Edition. Thousand Oaks, CA: Sage Publications.

——. 2005. "Bush's Empathy Shortage." *The American Prospect* 16, 7.

Hodge, Charles. 1866. "Commentary on the Epistle to the Romans." *Essays*. Philadelphia: James S. Claxton.

Hodkinson, Paul. 2002. *Goth: Identity, Style, and Subculture*. Oxford: Berg Publishers.

Hoffer, Eric. 1951. *The True Believer: Thoughts on the Nature of Mass Movements*. New York: Harper & Row.

Hood, Ralph W., Peter C. Hill, and Paul W. Williamson. 2005. *The Psychology of Religious Fundamentalism*. New York: Guilford Press.

Horkheimer, Max and Theodor Adorno. [1947] 1994. *The Dialectic of Enlightenment*. New York: Continuum Press.

Horkheimer, Max. (ed.). 1936. *Studien Über Authorität und Familie*. Paris: Alcan.

——. [1936] 1995. "Egoism and Freedom Movements: On the Anthropology of the Bourgeois Era." *In Between Philosophy and Social Science: Selected Early Writings*. Cambridge, MA: MIT Press.

——. [1946] 1974. *The Eclipse of Reason*. New York: Continuum Press.

Hunsberger, Bruce. 1995. "Religion and Prejudice: The Role of Religious Fundamentalism, Quest, and Right-Wing Authoritarianism." *Journal of Social Issues* 51: 113–129.

——. 1996. "Religious Fundamentalism, Right-Wing Authoritarianism, and Hostility Towards Homosexuals in Non-Christian Religious Groups." *International Journal for the Psychology of Religion* 6: 39–49.

Hunt, Stephen. 1998. "Magical Moments: An Intellectualist Approach to the Neo-Pentecostalist Faith Ministries." *Religion* 28:271–280.

Hurston, Zora Neale. [1938] 1990. *Tell My Horse: Voodoo and Life in Haiti and Jamaica*. New York: Harper Perennial.

Hutson, Curtis. 1984. *New Evangelicalism: The Enemy of Fundamentalism*. Murfreesboro, TN: Sword of the Lord Publishers.

Hutton, Ronald. 1991. *The Pagan Religions of the Ancient British Isles*. New York: Ballantine.

——. 1999. *The Triumph of the Moon: A History of Modern Pagan Witchcraft*. New York: Oxford University Press.

"India Train Fire Not Mob Attack." 2005. *BBC News*, January 17.

James, William. [1901] 2007. *Varieties of Religious Experience: A Study in Human Nature*. Charleston, SC: BiblioBazaar.

Jameson, Fredric. 1991. *Postmodernism, or the Cultural Logic of Late Capitalism*. Durham, NC: Duke University Press.

Jenkins, Philip. 2000. *Mystics and Messiahs: Cults and New Religions in American History*. New York: Oxford University Press.

——. 2003. *The Next Christendom: The Coming of Global Christianity*. New York: Oxford University Press.

Jenks, Chris. 2005. *Subculture: The Fragmentation of the Social*. Thousand Oaks, CA: Sage Publications.

"Jesus, CEO: Churches as Businesses." 2005. *The Economist*, December 20, pp. 41–44.

Jorgensen, Danny and Scott E. Russell. 1999. "American Neopaganism: The Participants' Identities." *Journal for the Scientific Study of Religion* 38 (3) September:325–338.

Juergensmeyer, Mark. 2003. *Terror in the Mind of God: The Global Rise of Religious Violence.* Berkeley, Los Angeles, London: University of California Press.

Kaczor, Bill. 2003. "Gov. Bush Signs Death Warrant for Pensacola Abortion Killer." *Tampa Tribune,* July 9.

Kamat, K. L. 2006. "Prehistoric Rock Paintings of Bhimabetaka." *Kamat's Potpourri.* Available at http://www.kamat.com.

Kantner, John. 2004. *Ancient Puebloan Southwest.* New York: Cambridge University Press.

Karlsen, Carol F. 1987. *The Devil in the Shape of a Woman: Witchcraft in Colonial New England.* New York: Norton.

Kasarda, John D. 1990. *Jobs, Earnings, and Employment Growth Policies in the United States.* New York: Springer.

Kazin, Michael. 1995. *The Populist Persuasion.* New York: Basic Books.

Kelley, Robin D.G. 1996. *Race Rebels: Culture, Politics, and the Black Working Class.* New York: Basic Books.

Kellner, Douglas. 2003. *Media Spectacle.* New York: Routledge.

Kerouac, Jack. [1957] 1991. *On the Road.* New York: Penguin Books.

Kerstetter, Todd. 2004. "That's Just the American Way: The Branch Davidian Tragedy and Western Religious History." *Western Historical Quarterly* 35 (4) Winter.

Ketcham, Ralph Louis. 1990. *James Madison: A Biography.* Charlotte: University Press of Virginia.

Khan, Maruq and Lauren Langman. 2005. "Islamic Fundamentalism, Modernity, and the Role of Women." *Religious Innovation in a Global Age: Essays on the Construction of Spirituality,* edited by George N. Lundskow. Jefferson, NC, and London: McFarland.

Khatab, Sayed. 2006. *The Political Thought of Sayyid Qutb: The Theory of Jahiliyyah.* New York: Routledge.

Khokar, Ashish and S. Saraswati. 2005. *Ganesha-Karttikeya.* New Delhi, India: Rupa.

Kidd, Thomas S. 2007. *The Great Awakening: The Roots of Evangelical Christianity in Colonial America.* New Haven, CT: Yale University Press.

Kieckhefer, Richard. 1989. *Magic in the Middle Ages.* Cambridge, UK: Cambridge University Press.

Kieckhefer, Richard. 1998. *Forbidden Rites: A Necromancer's Manual of the Fifteenth Century.* University Park: Pennsylvania State University Press.

Kinsley, David R. 2000. *The Sword and the Flute: Kali and Krsna,* Second Edition. Berkeley and Los Angeles: University of California Press.

Kintz, Linda. 1997. *Between Jesus and the Market.* Durham, NC: Duke University Press.

Kirkpatrick, David D. 2005. "Conservatives Pick a Soft Target: A Cartoon Sponge." *New York Times,* January 20.

Kitagawa, Joseph Mitsuo. 1987. *On Understanding Japanese Religion.* Princeton, NJ: Princeton University Press.

Klein, Naomi. 2002. *No Logo.* New York: St Martin's Press.

Koscianska, Agnieszka. 2005. "Legion of Small Knights: Informal Movements Within the Polish Catholic Church." In *Religious Innovation in a Global Age: Essays on the Construction of Spirituality.* Jefferson, NC: McFarland.

Kovel, Joel. [1970] 1984. *White Racism: A Psychohistory.* New York: Columbia University Press.

Krause, Neal and Christopher G. Ellison. 1998. "Church-Based Emotional Support, Negative Interaction, and Psychological Well-Being: Findings From a National Sample of Presbyterians." *Journal for the Scientific Study of Religion* 37 (4) December:725–741.

Krishan, Yuvraj. 1999. *Gaṇeśa: Unravelling an Enigma.* New Delhi, India: Motilal Banarsidass.

Kroll, Luisa and Allison Fass. 2007. "The World's Billionaires." *Forbes Magazine,* March.

Kung Fu Tsu. [c. 500 BCE] 1998. *The Analects,* translated by D. C. Lau. New York: Penguin Classics.

Kurtz, Lester. 1995. *Gods in the Global Village.* Thousand Oaks, CA: Pine Forge Press.

Labaton, Stephen. 2005. "Bankruptcy Bill Set for Passage; Victory for Bush." *New York Times,* March 9.

Lamy, Philip. 1996. *Millennium Rage: Survivalists, White Supremacists, and the Doomsday Prophesy.* New York: Plenum Press.

Langman, Lauren. 2005. *Trauma, Promise, and the Millennium: The Evolution of Alienation.* New York: Rowman & Littlefield.

Langman, Lauren and Douglas Morris. 2002. "Islamic Modernity: Barriers and Possibilities." *Logos* 1 (2):61–77.

——. 2004. "Islamic Terrorism: From Retrenchment to Ressentiment and Beyond." *In Essential Readings in Political Terrorism.* Lincoln: University of Nebraska Press.

Langmuir, Gavin. 1990a. *History, Religion, and Antisemitism.* Berkeley: University of California Press.

——. 1990b. *Toward a Definition of Antisemitism.* Berkeley: University of California Press.

Laquer, Walter. 1996. *Fascism: Past, Present, and Future.* New York: Oxford University Press.

Lasch, Christopher. [1978] 1991. *Culture of Narcissism: American Life in an Age of Diminishing Expectations.* New York: Norton.

Lederer, Gerda. 1993. "Authoritarianism in German Adolescents: Trends and Cross-Cultural Comparisons." *Strength and Weakness: The Authoritarian Personality Today.* New York: Springer-Verlag.

Lederer, Gerda and Angela Kindervater. 1995. "Internationale Vergleiche." *Authoritarismus und Gesellschaft: Trendanalysen und Vergleichende Jugenduntersuchungen, 1945–1993,* edited by Gerda Lederer and Peter Schmidt. Opladen, Germany: Leske and Budrich.

Lee, Shayne. 2005. *T. D. Jakes: America's New Preacher.* New York: New York University Press.

Levinson, Daniel J. [1950] 1982. "The Study of Ethnocentric Ideology." Pp. 102–145 in *The Authoritarian Personality,* edited by Theodor W. Adorno et al. New York: Norton.

Levi-Strauss, Claude. 1971. *Totemism.* Boston: Beacon Press.

Lewis, James R. (ed.). 1994. *From the Ashes: Making Sense of Waco.* Lanham, MD: Rowman & Littlefield.

——. 1995. "New Religions and American Indian Religions." *America's Alternative Religions.* Albany: State University of New York Press.

——. (ed.). 2001. *Odd Gods: New Religions and the Cult Controversy.* Amherst, NY: Prometheus Books.

Lewis, Napthali and Meyer Reinhold. (eds.). 1966. *Roman Civilization, Sourcebook 1: The Republic.* New York: Harper & Row.

Lincoln, Bruce. 2003. *Holy Terrors: Thinking About Religion After September 11.* Chicago: University of Chicago Press.

Lind, Michael. 1995. "Reverend Robertson's Grand International Conspiracy Theory." *New York Review of Books,* February 2.

Lindenbaum, Shirley. 1978. *Kuru Sorcery: Disease and Danger in the New Guinea Highland.* San Francisco: McGraw-Hill.

Lindsey, Hal and Charles Colson. (2005). "Religious Conservatives Claim Katrina Was God's Omen, Punishment for the United States." Retrieved September 13, 2005, from http://www.MediaMatters.org.

Linedecker, Clifford L. 1993. *Massacre at Waco, Texas: The Shocking Story of Cult Leader David Koresh and the Branch Davidians.* New York: St. Martin's Paperbacks.

Lippy, Charles H. 1997. "Miles to Go: Promise Keepers in Historical and Cultural Context." *Soundings* 80 (2–3):289–304.

Livius, Titus. [c. 12 CE] 2002. *The Early History of Rome,* Books I–V. New York: Penguin Classics.

Loewen, James W. 1995. *Lies My Teacher Told Me: Everything Your American History Textbook Got Wrong.* New York: Simon & Schuster.

——. 1996. *Lies My Teacher Told Me: Everything Your American History Textbook Got Wrong.* New York: Touchstone Books.

Long, Alecia P. 2005. *The Great Southern Babylon: Sex, Race, and Respectability in New Orleans, 1865–1920.* Baton Rouge: Louisiana State University Press.

Lowenthal, Leo and Norbert Guterman. [1949] 1970. *Prophets of Deceit: A Study of the Techniques of the American Agitator.* New York: Harper & Row.

Luce, R. Duncan and Howard Raiffa. [1957] 1985. *Games and Decisions: Introduction and Critical Survey.* New York: Dover.

Lucian of Samosata. [c. 170 CE] 2001. "The Passing of Peregrinus." *Loeb Classical Library: Lucian,* Vol. 5, edited by Jeffrey Henderson. Cambridge, MA: Harvard University Press.

Luidens, Donald A. 1993. "Between Myth and Hard Data: A Denomination Struggles With Identity." In *Beyond Establishment: Protestant Identity in a Postmodern Age,* edited by Jackson W. Carroll and Wade Clark Roof. Louisville, KY: Westminster/John Knox Press.

Lundskow, George N. 1998. "Smiles, Styles, and Profiles: Claim and Acclaim of Ronald Reagan as Charismatic Leader." *Social Thought and Research* 28 (1-2):158–192.

——. 2000. "Are Promises Enough? Promise Keeper Attitudes and Character in Intensive Interviews." *The Promise Keepers: Essays on Masculinity and Christianity.* Jefferson, NC: McFarland.

——. 2002. *Awakening to an Uncertain Future: A Case Study of the Promise Keepers.* New York: Peter Lang.

——. 2005. "Marxist Class-Cultural Spirituality in Theory and Practice." *Critical Sociology* 31, 1–2.

MacMullen, Ramsay. 1981. *Paganism in the Roman Empire.* New Haven, CT, and London: Yale University Press.

——. 1997. *Christianity and Paganism in the Fourth to Eighth Centuries.* New Haven, CT, and London: Yale University Press.

Magliocco, Sabina. 2004. *Witching Culture: Folklore and Neopaganism in America.* Philadelphia: University of Pennsylvania Press.

Mahaffy, Kimberly A. 1996. "Cognitive Dissonance and Its Resolution: A Study of Lesbian Christians." *Journal for the Scientific Study of Religion* 35 (4).

Maier, Timothy W. 2003. "FBI Denies Mix-Up of 9/11 Terrorists." *Insight on the News,* June 11.

Marable, Manning. [1984] 2007. *Race, Reform, and Rebellion: The Second Reconstruction and Beyond in Black America, 1945–2006,* Third Edition. Oxford: University Press of Mississippi.

——. 1999. *How Capitalism Underdeveloped Black America: Problems in Race, Political Economy, and Society.* Boston: South End Press.

Markale, Jean. 1999. *The Great Goddess: Reverence of the Divine Feminine from the Paleolithic to the Present.* Rochester, VT: Inner Traditions International.

——. 2003. *Montségur and the Mystery of the Cathars.* Rochester, VT: Inner Traditions.

Martens, James W. 1996. "Rugby, Class, Amateurism and Manliness: The Case of Rugby in Northern England, 1871–1895." In *Making Men: Rugby and Masculine Identity,* edited by John Nauright and Timothy Chandler. Portland, OR: Frank Kass.

Martin, Dale B. 1990. *Slavery as Salvation: The Metaphor of Slavery in Pauline Christianity.* New Haven, CT: Yale University Press.

Martin, David. 1999. "The New Evangelical Protestant Upsurge and Its Political Implications." In *The Desecularization of the World: Resurgent Religion and World Politics,* edited by Peter L. Berger. Grand Rapids, MI: Eerdmans.

——. 2001. *Pentecostalism: The World Their Parish.* New York: Blackwell.

Martin, Sean. 2005. *The Cathars: The Most Successful Heresy of the Middle Ages.* New York: Thunder's Mouth Press.

Martin, William. 1996. *With God on Our Side: The Rise of the Religious Right in America.* New York: Broadway Books.

Martin, Debra L. and David Frayer. 1998. *Troubled Times: Violence and Warfare in the Past.* New York: Routledge.

Marty, Martin E. 1970. *Righteous Empire: The Protestant Experience in America.* New York: Harper & Row.

——.1984. *Pilgrims in Their Own Land: 500 Years of Religion in America.* New York: Penguin Books.

Marty, Martin E. and R. Scott Appleby. 1992. *The Glory and the Power: The Fundamentalist Challenge to the Modern World.* Boston: Beacon Press.

Marty, Martin E., R. Scott Appleby, Helen Hardacre, and Everett Mendelsohn. (eds.). 1997. *Fundamentalisms and Society: Reclaiming the Sciences, the Family, and Education.* Chicago: University of Chicago Press.

Marx, Karl. [1844] 1978a. "Contribution to the Critique of Hegel's Philosophy of Right." *The Marx-Engels Reader,* Second Edition. New York: Norton.

Marx, Karl. [1844] 1978b. "Economic and Philosophic Manuscripts." *The Marx-Engels Reader,* Second Edition. New York: Norton.

Marx, Karl. [1845] 1978c. "Theses on Feuerbach." *The Marx-Engels Reader,* Second Edition. New York: Norton.

Massey, Douglas S. and Nancy A. Denton. 1998. *American Apartheid: Segregation and the Making of the Underclass.* Cambridge, MA: Harvard University Press.

Massing, Paul. 1949. *Rehearsal for Destruction.* New York: Harper & Row.

Matthews, Carol. 1995. "Neo-Paganism and Witchcraft." In *America's Alternative Religions,* edited by Timothy Miller. Albany: State University of New York Press.

May, Henry E. 1976. *The Enlightenment in America.* New York: Oxford University Press.

Mazlish, Bruce. 1990. *Leader, the Led, and the Psyche: Essays in Psychohistory.* Middleton, CT: Wesleyan University Press.

McBain, D. 1997. "Mainstream Charismatics: Some Observations of Baptist Renewal." *Charismatic Christianity: Sociological Perspectives.* London: Palgrave Macmillan.

McCarthy, Rory G. 2005. "Martyrdom and Violence in Sikhism: The Transfer of Embodied Experience Through Witnessing." In *Religious Innovation in a Global Age: Essays on the Construction of Spirituality,* edited by George N. Lundskow. Jefferson, NC: McFarland.

McCartney, Bill. 1995. *From Ashes to Glory.* New York: Thomas Nelson.

McChesney, Robert. 1994. *Telecommunications, Mass Media, and Democracy: The Battle for the Control of U.S. Broadcasting.* New York: Oxford University Press.

McChesney, Robert and Edward S. Herman. 1997. *The Global Media: The Missionaries of Global Capitalism.* London: Cassell.

McDannell, Colleen and Bernhard Lang. 2001. *Heaven: A History,* Second Edition. New Haven, CT: Yale University Press.

McEvilley, Thomas. 2002. *The Shape of Ancient Thought: Comparative Studies in Greek and Indian Philosophies.* New York: Allworth Press.

McGrath, Alister E. 2003. *A Brief History of Heaven.* Malden, MA: Blackwell.

McGrath, Malcolm. 2002. *Demons of the Modern World.* Amherst, NY: Prometheus Books.

McMichael, Philip. 2000. *Development and Social Change,* Second Edition. Thousand Oaks, CA: Pine Forge Press.

Mead, Margaret. [1928] 2001. *Coming of Age in Samoa: A Psychological Study of Primitive Youth for Western Civilization.* New York: Harper Perennial.

Meeks, Wayne A. 1993. *The Origins of Christian Morality: The First Two Centuries.* New Haven, CT: Yale University Press.

Meloen, Jos D. 1999. "Authoritarianism in the Netherlands: Mission Completed? Downward Trends of Authoritarianism in the Netherlands 1970–1992 With an International Comparison of World Data." *Social Thought and Research* 22 (1–2):45–95.

Melton, J. Gordon and Robert L. Moore. 1982. *The Cult Experience: Responding to the New Religious Pluralism.* New York: Pilgrim Press.

Melton, J. Gordon and Christopher Partridge. 2004. *New Religions: A Guide to New Religious Movements, Sects, and Alternative Spiritualities.* New York: Oxford University Press.

Merton, Robert K. [1949] 1967. *Social Theory and Social Structure.* New York: The Free Press.

Messadié, Gerald. 1996. *A History of the Devil.* New York: Kodansha International.

Metraux, Alfred. 1989. *Voodoo in Haiti.* New York: Pantheon.

Meyer, Donald. 1966. *The Positive Thinkers: A Study of the American Quest for Health, Wealth and Personal Power From Mary Baker Eddy to Norman Vincent Peale.* New York: Doubleday.

Meyer, Marvin W. [1987] 1999. *The Ancient Mysteries: A Sourcebook of Sacred Texts.* Philadelphia: University of Pennsylvania Press.

Miller, Donald E. 1997. *Reinventing American Protestantism: Christianity at the New Millennium.* Berkeley: University of California Press.

Miller, Elmer S. 2001. *Peoples of the Gran Chaco.* Westport, CT: Bergin & Garvey.

Miller, Lisa. 2006. "Sex vs. Social Justice: New Evangelicals at the Crossroads." *Newsweek,* November 13.

Miller, Timothy. (ed.). 1995. *America's Alternative Religions.* Albany: State University of New York Press.

——. 1999. *The 60's Communes: Hippies and Beyond.* Syracuse, NY: Syracuse University Press.

Mills, C. Wright. [1959] 2000. *The Sociological Imagination.* New York: Oxford University Press.

Mishel, Lawrence, Jared Bernstein, and Sylvia Allegretto. 2005. *The State of Working America, 2004–2005.* Philadelphia: ILR Press.

Misztal, Barbara A. 1996. *Trust in Modern Societies: The Search for the Bases of Social Order.* Polity Press.

Mokerjee, Ajit. 1988. *Kali: The Feminine Force.* Rochester, VT: Destiny/Inner Traditions.

Moore, Barrington. [1966] 1993. *Social Origins of Dictatorship and Democracy: Lord and Peasant in the Making of the Modern World.* Boston: Beacon Press.

Morone, James A. (2003). *Hellfire Nation: The Politics of Sin in American History.* New Haven, CT: Yale University Press.

Morton, W. Scott, J. Kenneth Olenik, and Charlton Lewis. 2005. *Japan: Its History and Culture,* Fourth Edition. New York: McGraw-Hill.

Mountford, Brian. 2003. *Perfect Freedom: Why Liberal Christianity Might Be the Faith You're Looking For.* Alresford, UK: John Hunt.

Moussalli, Ahmad. 1993. *Radical Islamic Fundamentalism: The Ideological and Political Discourse of Sayyid Qutb.* Syracuse, NY: Syracuse University Press.

Muchembled, Robert. 2003. *A History of the Devil: From the Middle Ages to the Present.* Malden, MA: Blackwell.

Muench, David and Polly Schaafsma. 1995. *Images in Stone: Southwest Rock Art.* San Francisco: Browntrout.

Muggleton, David. 2002. *Inside Subculture: The Postmodern Meaning of Style.* Oxford: Berg Publishers.

Murdoch, Adrian. 2004. *The Last Pagan: Julian the Apostate and the Death of the Ancient World.* Stroud, Gloucestershire, UK: Sutton.

Musallam, Adnan A. 2005. *From Secularism to Jihad: Sayyid Qutb and the Foundations of Radical Islamism.* Westport, CT: Praeger.

Nathan, Debbie and Michael R. Snedeker. 2001. *Satan's Silence: Ritual Abuse and the Making of a Modern American Witch Hunt.* New York: Authors Choice Press.

Neubeck, Kenneth and Noel Cazenave. 2001. *Welfare Racism: Playing the Race Card Against America's Poor.* New York: Routledge.

Neumann, Franz. [1944] 1966. *Behemoth: The Structure and Practice of National Socialism.* San Francisco: Harper Books.

Newman, Mark. 2001. *Getting Right With God: Southern Baptists and Desegregation, 1945–1995.* Tuscaloosa: University of Alabama Press.

Newport, Kenneth G. and Crawford Gribben. 2006. *Expecting the End: Millennialism in Social and Historical Context.* Waco, TX: Baylor University Press.

Newport, Kenneth G. C. 2006. *The Branch Davidians of Waco: The History and Beliefs of an Apocalyptic Sect.* New York: Oxford University Press.

Nichols, Jack. 1996. *The Gay Agenda: Talking Back to the Fundamentalists.* Amherst, NY: Prometheus Books.

Nicol, Donald M. [1972] 1993. *The Last Centuries of Byzantium, 1261–1453.* Cambridge, UK: Cambridge University Press.

Nigosian, Solomon A. 1993. *The Zoroastrian Faith.* Montreal, Quebec, Canada: McGill Queen's University Press.

Nlandu, Thierry Mayamba. 1998. "Kinshasa: Beyond Dichotomies." *African News Bulletin,* Issue 347.

Noble, David Grant. 2004. *In Search of Chaco: New Approaches to an Archaeological Enigma.* Santa Fe, NM: School of American Research Press.

Noël, Lise. [1989] 1994. *Intolerance: A General Survey.* Montreal, Quebec, Canada: McGill-Queens University Press.

Noll, Mark A. 1994. "Revolution and the Rise of New Evangelical Social Influence in North Atlantic Societies." *New Evangelicalism: Comparative Studies of Popular Protestantism in the North America, the British Isles, and Beyond.* New York: Oxford University Press.

——. 1995. *The Scandal of the Evangelical Mind.* Grand Rapids, MI: Eerdmans.

——. 2004. *The Rise of Evangelicalism: The Age of Edwards, Whitefield, and the Wesleys.* Downers Grove, IL: InterVarsity Press.

Noll, Mark A., David W. Bebbington, and George A. Rawlyk. 1994. *New Evangelicalism: Comparative Studies of Popular Protestantism in North America, the British Isles, and Beyond.* New York: Oxford University Press.

Noll, Mark A. and Lyman A. Kellstedt. 1995. "The Changing Face of Evangelicalism." *Ecclesia* 4:146–164.

Norwich, John Julius. 1989. *Byzantium, Vol. 1: The Early Centuries.* New York: Knopf.

——. 1992. *Byzantium, Vol. 2: The Apogee.* New York: Knopf.

——. 1995. *Byzantium, Vol. 3: The Decline and Fall.* New York: Knopf.

Obenhaus, Victor. 1963. *The Church and Faith in Mid-America.* Philadelphia: The Westminster Press.

Olds, Mason. 1995. "Unitarian Universalism: An Interpretation Through Its History." *America's Alternative Religions.* Albany: State University of New York Press.

Oliner, Samuel P. and Pearl M. Oliner. 1992. *The Altruistic Personality: Rescuers of Jews in Nazi Europe.* New York: The Free Press.

Olmos, Margarite Fernandez and Lizabeth Paravisini-Gebert. 2003. *Creole Religions of the Caribbean.* New York: New York University Press.

Olson, Mancur. [1964] 1971. *Logic of Collective Action: Public Goods and the Theory of Groups.* Cambridge, MA: Harvard University Press.

Ortner, Donald J. 2002. *Identification of Pathological Conditions in Human Skeletal Remains,* Second Edition. San Diego, CA: Academic Press.

O'Shea, Stephen. 2001. *The Perfect Heresy: The Revolutionary Life and Spectacular Death of the Medieval Cathars.* New York: Walker.

Ostrom, Elinor and James Walker. 2003. *Trust and Reciprocity: Interdisciplinary Lessons for Experimental Research.* Washington, DC: Russell Sage Foundation.

Ott, Michael. 2001. *Max Horkheimer's Critical Theory of Religion: The Meaning of Religion in the Struggle for Human Emancipation.* New York: Rowman & Littlefield.

Ottaway, Marina S. and Julia Choucair-Vizoso. 2008. *Beyond the Façade: Political Reform in the Arab World.* Washington, DC: Carnegie Endowment for International Peace.

Paczor, Bill. 2003. "Gov. Bush Signs Death Warrant for Pensacola Abortion Killer." *Tampa Tribune,* July 9.

Pagels, Elaine. 1979. *The Gnostic Gospels.* New York: Random House.

——. 1988. *Adam, Eve, and the Serpent.* New York: Random House.

——. 1989. *Adam, Eve, and the Serpent.* New York: Vintage Books.

——. 1995. *The Origin of Satan.* New York: Random House.

Pal, Pratapaditya. 1995. *Ganesh: The Benevolent.* Mumbai, India: Marg Publications.

Palmer, Susan J. and Charlotte E. Hardman. 1999. *Children in New Religions.* New Brunswick, NJ: Rutgers University Press.

Pappu, Sridhar. 2006. "The Preacher T. D. Jakes." *The Atlantic,* Vol. 297, 2:92–103.

Parenti, Michael. 1994. *Land of Idols: Political Mythology in America.* New York: St. Martin's Press.

Parsons, Talcott. [1937] 2002. *The Structure of Social Action,* Vol. 2. New York: The Free Press.

Pascarella, Ernest T., Christopher T. Pierson, Patrick T. Terenzini, and Gregory C. Wolniak. 2004. "First Generation College Students: Additional Evidence on College Experiences and Outcomes." *Journal of Higher Education* 75:249–284.

Pennington, John. 1994. "Muscular Spirituality in George MacDonald's Curdie Books." *Muscular Christianity: Embodying the Victorian Age.* New York: Cambridge University Press.

Percy, Martyn. 1996. *Words, Wonders, and Power: Understanding Contemporary Christian Fundamentalism and Revivalism.* London: Society for Promoting Christian Knowledge.

Perez, Lisandro. 1994. "The Catholic Church in Cuba: A Weak Institution." In *Puerto Rican and Cuban Catholics in the US, 1900–1965,* edited by Jay P. Nolan and Jamie R. Vidal. South Bend, IN: University of Notre Dame Press.

Perrin, Robin D., Paul Kennedy, and Donald E. Miller. 1997. "Examining the Sources of Conservative Church Growth: Where Are the New Evangelical Movements Getting Their Numbers?" *Journal for the Social Scientific Study of Religion* 36:71–80.

Pike, Sarah M. 2001. *Earthly Bodies, Magical Selves: Contemporary Pagans and the Search for Community.* Berkeley: University of California Press.

——. 2004. *New Age and Neopagan Religions in America* (Columbia Contemporary American Religion Series). New York: Columbia University Press.

——. 2005. *New Age and Neopagan Religions in America.* New York: Columbia University Press.

Plutarch. [c. 100 CE] 2002. "On Superstition." *Moralia,* Vol. 2. Cambridge, MA: Harvard University Press.

Politkovskaya, Anna. 2004. *Putin's Russia: Life in a Failing Democracy.* New York: Henry Holt.

Pollitt, Katha. 2005. "Subject to Debate: The Cheese Stands Alone." *The Nation,* March 21, p. 11.

Pollock, John Charles. 1963. *Moody: A Biographical Portrait of the Pacesetter in Modern Mass Evangelism.* New York: MacMillan.

Porpora, Douglas V. 2001. *Landscapes of the Soul: Loss of Moral Meaning in American Life.* New York: Oxford University Press.

Porterfield, Amanda. 2001. *The Transformation of American Religion: The Story of a Late Twentieth-Century Awakening.* New York: Oxford University Press.

Portes, Alejandro and Kelly Hoffman. 2003. "Latin American Class Structures: Their Composition and Change During the Neoliberal Era." *Latin American Research Review* 38 (1).

Possamai, Adam. 2005. *In Search of New Age Spiritualities.* Burlington, VT: Ashgate Publishing.

Pozner, Jennifer. 2006. "The Terrorists Who Aren't in the News." November 11. Available online at http://www.alternet.org/story/43182 (originally published in *Newsday*).

Prabhupada, A. C. Bhaktivedanta Swami. 1973. *Elevation to Krishna Consciousness.* Los Angeles: ISKCON Press.

Prescott, Bruce. 2002. "Christian Reconstructionism." *Interfaith Alliance Forum on Religious Extremism.* Norman, OK. Available online at http://www.mainstreambaptists.org/mob4/dominionism.htm.

Pringle, Heather. 1996. *In Search of Ancient North America: An Archaeological Journey to Forgotten Cultures.* Hoboken, NJ: Wiley.

Prothero, Stephen. 2003. *American Jesus: How the Son of God Became a National Icon.* New York: Farrar, Straus and Giroux.

Purcell, Natalie J. 2003. *Death Metal Music: The Passion and Politics of a Subculture.* Jefferson, NC: McFarland.

Quadagno, Jill. 1996. *The Color of Welfare: How Racism Undermined the War on Poverty.* New York: Oxford University Press.

Quinley, Harold E. 1974. *The Prophetic Clergy: Social Action Among Protestant Ministers.* New York: Wiley.

Rahn, Otto. 2006. *Crusade Against the Grail: The Struggle Between the Cathars, the Templars, and the Church of Rome.* Rochester, VT: Inner Traditions.

Ramachandra Rao, S. K. 1992. *The Compendium on Gaṇeśa.* New Delhi, India: Sri Satguru Publications.

Ram-Prasad, Chakravarthi. 2002. "Being Hindu and/or Governing India? Religion, Social Change, and the State." In *The Freedom to Do God's Will: Religious Fundamentalism and Social Change,* edited by Gerrie ter Haar and James J. Busuttil. New York: Routledge.

Randolph, Vance. 1947. *Ozark Superstition.* New York: Columbia University Press.

Raphael, Melissa. 1996. "Truth in Flux: Goddess Feminism as a Late Modern Religion." *Religion* 26:199–213.

Reavis, Dick J. 1995. *The Ashes of Waco: An Investigation.* New York: Simon & Schuster.

Reed, Kimberly. 1991. "Strength of Religious Affiliation and Life Satisfaction." *Sociological Analysis* 52 (2) Summer:52–61.

Reis, Elizabeth. 1997. *Damned Women: Sinners and Witches in Puritan New England.* Ithaca, NY: Cornell University Press.

Rennie, Ian S. 1994. "Fundamentalism and the Varieties of North Atlantic Evangelicalism." *Evangelicalism: Comparative Studies of Popular Protestantism in North America, the British Isles, and Beyond, 1700–1990.* New York: Oxford University Press.

Reynolds, Michael. 2005. "Rendering Unto God." *Mother Jones,* Vol. 30, 7.

Riesbrodt, Martin. 1990. *Pious Passion: The Emergence of Modern Fundamentalism in the United States and Iran.* Berkeley: University of California Press.

Riesman, David. [1961] 2001. *The Lonely Crowd, Revised Edition: A Study of the Changing American Character.* New Haven, CT: Yale University Press.

Rignall, Karen. 1997. "Building an Arab-American Community in Dearborn, MI." *Journal of the International Institute* 5 (1) Fall.

Riley, Gregory J. 2001. *The River of God: A New History of Christian Origins.* San Francisco: HarperCollins.

Robertson, Pat. 1991. *The New World Order.* Nashville, TN: Thomas Nelson.

Robinet, Isabelle and Phyllis Brooks. 1997. *Taoism: Growth of a Religion*. Stanford, CA: Stanford University Press.

Rodgers, James. 2008. "Moscow Diary: A Putin Puppet?" *BBC News*, February 5.

Roediger, David R. 1999. *The Wages of Whiteness: Race and the Making of the American Working Class*. New York: Verso.

Rohn, Arthur H. and William M. Ferguson. 2006. *Puebloan Ruins of the Southwest*. Albuquerque: University of New Mexico Press.

Roof, Wade Clark. 1996. "God in the Details: Reflections on Religion's Public Presence in the United States in the mid-1990s." *Sociology of Religion* 57 (2) Summer:149–159.

Roof, Wade Clark, Jackson W. Carroll, and David Roozen. 1995. "The Post-War Generation: Carriers of a New Spirituality." *The Post-War Generation and Establishment Religion: Cross-Cultural Perspectives*, edited by Wade Clark Roof, Jackson W. Carroll, and David Roozen. Boulder, CO: Westview Press.

Roof, Wade Clark and William McKinney. 1987. *American Mainline Religion*. New Brunswick, NJ: Rutgers University Press.

Rosen, David. 1994. "The Volcano and the Cathedral: Muscular Christianity and the Origins of Primal Manliness." *Muscular Christianity: Embodying the Victorian Age*. New York: Cambridge University Press.

Rosman, Doreen M. 1984. *Evangelicals and Culture*. London and Canberra, Australia: Croom Helm.

Rothstein, Mikael. 2002. *New Age Religion and Globalization*. Aarhus, Denmark: Aarhus University Press.

Royse, David. 2003. "First Abortion Clinic Murderer Scheduled to Die for Crime." *Naples Daily News*, August 31.

Rozell, Mark J. and Clyde Wilcox. 1995. "The Past as Prologue: The Christian Right in the 1996 Elections." *God at the Grassroots: The Christian Right in the 1994 Elections*, edited by Mark J. Rozell and Clyde Wilcox. Lanham, MD: Rowman & Littlefield.

Rudin, James. 2006. *The Baptizing of America: The Religious Right's Plans for the Rest of Us*. New York: Thunder's Mouth Press.

Runciman, Steven. 1982. *The Medieval Manichee: A Study of the Christian Dualist Heresy*. Cambridge, UK: Cambridge University Press.

——. 1987. *A History of the Crusades: Vol. 1: The First Crusade and the Foundation of the Kingdom of Jerusalem*. Cambridge, UK: Cambridge University Press.

——. 1990. *The Fall of Constantinople, 1453*. Cambridge, UK: Cambridge University Press.

Rushdoony, R. J. 1973. *The Institutes of Biblical Law*. Nutley, NJ: Craig Press.

——. 1983. *Salvation and Godly Rule*. Vallecito, CA: Ross House Books.

Ruthven, Malise. 1989. *The Divine Supermarket: Shopping for God in America*. New York: William Morrow.

Ryan, W. F. 1999. *The Bathhouse at Midnight: Magic in Russia*. University Park: Pennsylvania State University Press.

Sagan, Carl. [1985] 1997. *Contact*. New York: Pocket Books.

Samuel, Maurice. [1940] 1988. *The Great Hatred*. Lanham, MD: University Press of America.

Sanday, Peggy Reeves. 1986. *Divine Hunger: Cannibalism as a Cultural System*. New York: Cambridge University Press.

——. 1990. *Fraternity Gang Rape: Sex, Brotherhood, and Privilege on Campus*. New York: New York University Press.

——. 1997. *A Woman Scorned: Acquaintance Rape on Trial*. Berkeley: University of California Press.

——. 2004. *Women at the Center: Life in a Modern Matriarchy*. Ithaca, NY: Cornell University Press.

Sartre, Jean Paul. [1948] 1995. *Anti-Semite and Jew.* New York: Shocken Books.

Sawyer, Diane. 1994. "Interviews with Charles Manson, Patricia Krenwinkel, and Leslie Van Houten." *Turning Point* [TV news program]. New York: ABC News.

"School Boards Push on Against Evolution." 2005. *AP Newswire,* January 19.

Schultz, Ronald. 1994. "God and Workingmen: Popular Religion and the Formation of Philadelphia's Working Class." In *Religion in a Revolutionary Age,* edited by Ronald Hoffman and Peter J. Albert. Charlottesville: University of North Carolina Press.

Sebastian, Lynne. 1996. *The Chaco Anasazi: Sociopolitical Evolution in the Prehistoric Southwest.* New York: Cambridge University Press.

Seligman, Adam B. 2000. *The Problem of Trust.* Princeton, NJ: Princeton University Press.

——. 2003. *Modernity's Wager: Authority, the Self, and Transcendence.* Princeton, NJ: Princeton University Press.

Sellers, Charles. 1991. *The Market Revolution: Jacksonian America, 1815–1846.* New York: Oxford University Press.

Seneviratne, H. L. 2002. "The Monk's New Robes: Buddhist Fundamentalism and Social Change." In *The Freedom to Do God's Will: Religious Fundamentalism and Social Change,* edited by Gerrie ter Haar and James J. Busuttil. New York: Routledge.

Seznec, Jean. [1953] 1995. *The Survival of the Pagan Gods: The Mythological Tradition and Its Place in Renaissance Humanism and Art.* Princeton, NJ: Princeton University Press.

Shakespeare, William. [c. 1601] 1963. *The Tragedy of Hamlet, Prince of Denmark.* New York: Signet Classics.

Shalvi, Alice. 2002. "Renew Our Days of Old: Religious Fundamentalism and Social Change in the Modern Jewish State." In *The Freedom to Do God's Will: Religious Fundamentalism and Social Change,* edited by Gerrie ter Haar and James J. Busuttil. New York: Routledge.

Shannon, Rachelle. 1997. *Army of God Manual.* Reprinted in part in "The Threat From Within." In *The Future of Terrorism: Violence in the New Millennium,* edited by Harvey W. Kushner. Thousand Oaks, CA: Sage.

Sharma, Jyotirmay. 2004. *Hindutva: Exploring the Idea of Hindu Nationalism.* New York: Penguin International.

Sherkat, Darren E. and Alfred Darnell. 1999. "The Effect of Parents' Fundamentalism on Children's Educational Attainment: Examining Differences by Gender and Children's Fundamentalism." *Journal for the Scientific Study of Religion* 38:23–35.

Shevtsova, Lilia and Antonina W. Bouis. 2005. *Putin's Russia.* Washington, DC: Carnegie Endowment for International Peace.

Shibley, Mark A. 1996. *Resurgent Evangelicalism in the United States: Mapping Cultural Change Since 1970.* Columbia: University of South Carolina Press.

Shils, Edward. 1980. *The Calling of Sociology and Other Essays on the Pursuit of Learning.* Chicago: University of Chicago Press.

Shires, Preston. 2007. *Hippies of the Religious Right: From the Countercultures of Jerry Garcia to the Subculture of Jerry Falwell.* Waco, TX: Baylor University Press.

Shourie, Arun. 1999. *Eminent Historians: Their Technology, Their Line, Their Fraud.* New Delhi: HarperCollins India.

——. 2005. *Worshipping False Gods: Ambedkar and the Facts Which Have Been Erased.* New Delhi, India: Rupa.

Shryock, Andrew J. 2002. "New Images of Arab Detroit: Seeing Otherness and Identity Through the Lens of September 1." *American Anthropologist* 104 (3):917–922.

Shupe, Anson and William A. Stacey. 1982. *Born-Again Politics and the Moral Majority: What Social Surveys Really Show.* New York: Edwin Mellon Press.

Siebert, Rudolf. 1987. *Horkheimer's Critical Sociology of Religion: The Relative and the Transcendent.* New York: Edwin Mellen Press.

——. 2001. *The Critical Theory of Religion: The Frankfurt School.* New York: Scarecrow Press.

Siegel, Carol. 2005. *Goth's Dark Empire.* Bloomington: Indiana University Press.

Silberman, Neil A. and Israel Finkelstein. 2001. *The Bible Unearthed.* New York: Simon & Schuster.

Simpson, John H. 1984. "Support for the Moral Majority and Its Sociomoral Platform." In *New Christian Politics,* edited by David G. Bromley and Anson Shupe. Macon, GA: Mercer University Press.

Sire, James W. 2000. *Habits of the Mind: Intellectual Life as a Christian Calling.* Downer's Grove, IL: InterVarsity Press.

Sjoo, Monica and Barbara Mor. 1987. *The Great Cosmic Mother: Rediscovering the Religion of the Earth.* San Francisco: HarperSanFrancisco.

Sklair, Leslie. 2001. *The Transnational Capitalist Class.* Malden, MA: Blackwell.

Skocpol, Theda. 1979. *States and Social Revolutions: A Comparative Analysis of France, Russia and China.* New York: Cambridge University Press.

Smart, Ninian. 1987. "Three Forms of Religious Convergence." In *Religious Resurgence: Contemporary Cases in Islam, Christianity, and Judaism,* edited by Richard T. Antoun and Mary Elaine Hegland. Syracuse, NY: Syracuse University Press.

Smidt, Corwin, John C. Green, Lyman A. Kellstedt, and James L. Guth. 1996. "The Spirit-Filled Movements and American Politics." In *Religion and the Culture Wars.* New York: Rowman & Littlefield.

Smith, Christian. 2002. *Christian America? What Evangelicals Really Want.* Berkeley and Los Angeles: University of California Press.

Smith, Christian and Melinda Lundquist Denton. 2005. *Soul Searching: The Religious and Spiritual Lives of American Teenagers.* New York: Oxford University Press.

Smith, David N. 1996. "The Social Construction of Enemies: Jews and the Representation of Evil." *Sociological Theory* 14(3):203–40.

——. 1997. "Judeophobia, Myth, and Critique." Pp. 123–154 in *The Seductiveness of Jewish Myth,* edited by S. Daniel Breslauer. Albany: State University of New York Press.

——. 2001. "The Stigma of Reason." *After the Science Wars.* New York: Routledge.

Smith, Jonathan Z. 1990. *Drudgery Divine: On the Comparisons of Early Christianities and the Religions of Late Antiquity.* Chicago: University of Chicago Press.

Smith, Mark S. 2002. *The Early History of God: Yahweh and the Other Deities in Ancient Israel,* Second Edition. Grand Rapids, MI: Eerdmans.

Smith, Rex Alan. 1981. *Moon of Popping Trees.* Lincoln: University of Nebraska Press.

Smith, Timothy L. [1957] 1965. *Revivalism and Social Reform: American Protestantism on the Eve of the Civil War.* New York: Harper & Row.

Snowball, David. 1991. *Continuity and Change in the Rhetoric of the Moral Majority.* New York: Praeger Press.

Soucek, Priscilla. 1997. "Byzantium and the Islamic East." In *The Glory of Byzantium,* edited by Helen C. Evans and William D. Wixom. New York: The New York Metropolitan Museum of Art/Harry N. Abrams.

Spencer, Herbert. [1862] 2004. *Principles of Sociology,* Vol. 2. Honolulu, HI: University Press of the Pacific.

Spengler, Oswald. [1918] 1991. *Decline of the West,* Vol. I. New York: Oxford University Press.

Sprenger, Jacob and Heinrich Kramer. [1486] 2000. *Malleus Maleficarum.* Hyperscribe E-Books.

Starhawk. [1979] 1999. *The Spiral Dance: A Rebirth of the Ancient Religion of the Great Goddess.* New York: HarperCollins.

——. [1982] 1997. *Dreaming the Dark.* Boston: Beacon Press.

Stark, Rodney. 1997. *The Rise of Christianity.* San Francisco: HarperCollins.

Staub, Ervin. 1989. *The Roots of Evil*. Cambridge, UK: Cambridge University Press.

Stausberg, Michael. 2004. *Die Religion Zarathushtras (Band 3)*. Stuttgart, Germany: Kohlhammer.

Stein, Stephen J. 2003. *Communities of Dissent: A History of Alternative Religions in the United States*. New York: Oxford University Press.

Stern, Jessica. 2003. *Terror in the Name of God: Why Religious Militants Kill*. San Francisco: HarperCollins.

Stern, Robert W. 2003. *Changing India: Bourgeois Revolution on the Subcontinent*. New York: Cambridge University Press.

Stone, Merlin. 1978. *When God Was a Woman*. Fort Washington, PA: Harvest Books.

———. [1979] 1990. *Ancient Mirrors of Womanhood*. Boston: Beacon Press.

Stone, William F., Gerda Lederer, and Richard Christie. 1993. *Strength and Weakness: The Authoritarian Personality Today*. New York: Springer-Verlag.

Stoyanov, Yuri. 2000. *The Other God: Dualistic Religions From Antiquity to the Cathar Heresy*. New Haven, CT: Yale University Press.

Subrimunaya, Satguru Sivaya. 2001. *Living With Siva: Hinduism's Contemporary Culture*. Kapaa, HI: Himalayan Academy.

Sumption, Jonathan. 2000. *The Albigensian Crusade*. London: Faber & Faber.

Sunday, Billy. [1912] 1992. "Selected Sermons." *Preacher: Billy Sunday and Big-Time American Evangelicalism*, edited by Roger A. Bruns. New York: Norton.

Sutcliffe, Steve. 2003. *Children of the New Age: A History of Spiritual Practices*. New York: Routledge.

Swartz, David. 1996. "Bridging the Study of Culture and Religion: Pierre Bourdieu's Political Economy of Symbolic Power." *Sociology of Religion* 57 (1) Spring:71–81.

Sweeney, Douglas A. 2005. *The American Evangelical Story: A History of the Movement*. Ada, MI: Baker Academic.

Swift, Donald C. 1998. *Religion and the American Experience: A Social and Cultural History, 1765–1997*. Armonk, NY: M.E. Sharpe.

Synon, Vinson. 1997. *The Holiness-Pentecostal Tradition: Charismatic Movements in the Twentieth Century*. Grand Rapids, MI: Eerdmans.

Tabbaa, Yasser. 1986. "Bronze Shapes in Iranian Ceramics of the Twelfth and Thirteenth Centuries." *Muquarnas*, 4:98–113.

Tabor, James D. and Eugene V. Gallagher. 1995. *Why Waco? Cults and the Battle for Religious Freedom in America*. Berkeley: University of California Press.

Tacitus, Gaius Cornelius. [c. 98 CE] 1999. *Agricola and Germany*. New York: Oxford University Press.

Taylor, Eugene. 1995. "Swedenborgianism." In *America's Alternative Religions*, edited by Timothy Miller. Albany: State University of New York Press.

Taylor, Mark Lewis. 2005. *Religion, Politics, and the Christian Right: Post-9/11 Powers in American Empire*. Minneapolis, MN: Augsburg Fortress.

Thapar, Romila. 2004. *Early India: From the Origins to AD 1300*. Berkeley: University of California Press.

Thibodeau, David and Leon Whiteson. 1999. *A Place Called Waco: A Survivor's Story*. New York: Public Affairs.

Thomas, Elizabeth Marshall. [1958] 1989. *The Harmless People*. New York: Vintage.

Thomas, Thelma K. 1997. "Christians in the Islamic East." In *The Glory of Byzantium*, edited by Helen C. Evans and William D. Wixom. New York: New York Metropolitan Museum of Art/Harry N. Abrams.

Thompson, Hunter S. [1972]. 1998. *Fear and Loathing in Las Vegas: A Savage Journey to the Heart of the American Dream*. New York: Vintage Books.

Thomson, F. J. 1978. "The Nature of the Reception of Christian Byzantine Culture in Russia in the Tenth to Thirteenth Centuries and Its Implication for Russian Culture." *Slavica Gandensia* 5:107–139.

Thornton, Sarah. 1996. *Club Cultures: Music, Media, and Subcultural Capital.* Middletown, CT: Wesleyan University Press.

Titus Livius. [c. 12 CE] 2002. *The Early History of Rome,* Vols. 1–5. New York: Penguin Classics.

Toennies, Ferdinand. [1887] 2001. *Community and Civil Society.* New York: Cambridge University Press.

Tracy, Joseph. 1989. *Great Awakening: A History of the Revival of Religion in the Time of Edwards and Whitefield.* Carlisle, PA: Banner of Truth.

Trevor-Roper, H. R. 1969. "The European Witch Craze of the Sixteenth and Seventeenth Centuries." *Essays.* Oxford, UK: Oxford University Press.

Troeltsch, Ernst. [1912] 1960. *Social Teaching of the Christian Churches.* New York: MacMillan.

Tsang, Jo-Ann and Wade C. Rowatt. 2007. "The Relationship Between Religious Orientation, Right-Wing Authoritarianism, and Implicit Sexual Prejudice." *International Journal for the Psychology of Religion* 17 (2):99–120.

Tucker, Ruth A. 2004. *Another Gospel: Cults, Alternative Religions, and the New Age Movement.* Grand Rapids, MI: Zondervan Press.

Turcan, Robert. [1996] 2000. *The Cults of the Roman Empire.* Malden, MA: Blackwell.

Turner, Victor. 1974. *Dramas, Fields, and Metaphors.* Ithaca, NY: Cornell University Press.

——. 1995. "The Ritual Process: Structure and Anti-Structure." In *America's Alternative Religions,* edited by Timothy Miller. Albany: State University of New York Press.

U.S. Government Accountability Office Report. 2006. *Faith-Based and Community Initiative: Improvements in Monitoring Grantees and Measuring Performance Could Enhance Accountability.* [GAO-06-616]

Udayakumar, S. P. 2005. *"Presenting" the Past: Anxious History and Ancient Future in Hindutva India.* Westport, CT: Praeger.

Underwood, Gant. 1999. *The Millenarian World of Early Mormonism.* Champaign-Urbana: University of Illinois Press.

Utley, Robert. 2003. *The Indian Frontier 1846–1890.* Albuquerque: University of New Mexico Press.

Vaughan, Alden T. 1995. *Roots of American Racism: Essays on the Colonial Experience.* New York: Oxford University Press.

Veblen, Thorsten. [1899] 1994. *The Theory of the Leisure Class.* New York: Penguin Books.

Verden, Paul, Kathleen Dunleavy, and Charles H. Powers. 1989. "Heavy Metal Mania and Adolescent Delinquency." *Popular Music and Society* 13:73–82.

Victor, Jeffrey S. 1993. *Satanic Panic: The Creation of a Contemporary Legend.* Chicago: Open Court Press.

Vryonis, Speros. 1985. "The Impact of Hellenism: Greek Culture in the Moslem and Slav Worlds." In *The Greek World: Classical, Byzantine, and Modern,* edited by Robert Browning. London: Verso.

Vryonis, Speros P. 1997. "Byzantine Society and Civilization." In *The Glory of Byzantium,* edited by Helen C. Evans and William D. Wixom. New York: New York Metropolitan Museum of Art/Harry N. Abrams.

Waite, Gary K. 2003. *Heresy, Magic, and Witchcraft in Early Modern Europe.* New York: Palgrave MacMillan.

Wald, Kenneth D. 1987. *Religion and Politics in the United States.* New York: St. Martin's Press.

Wallis, Jim. 2008. *The Great Awakening: Reviving Faith & Politics in a Post-Religious Right America.* San Francisco: HarperOne.

Walls, Andrew F. 2002. *The Cross-Cultural Process in Christian History: Studies in the Transmission and Appropriation of Faith*. New York: Orbis Books.

Ward, Martha. 2004. *Voodoo Queen: The Spirited Lives of Marie Laveau*. Oxford: University of Mississippi Press.

Warhola, James W. 2007. "Religion and Politics Under the Putin Administration: Accommodation and Confrontation Within 'Managed Pluralism.'" *Journal of Church and State*, 49 (1):75–100.

Warren, Rick. 2002. *The Purpose Driven Life*. Grand Rapids, MI: Zondervan Books.

Watson, Justin. 1997. *The Christian Coalition: Dreams of Restoration, Demands for Recognition*. New York: St. Martin's Press.

Watson, Pauline Sawyers, Ronald J. Morris, Mark L. Carpenter, Rachel S. Jimenez, Katherine A. Jonas, and David L. Robinson. 2003. "Reanalysis Within a Christian Ideological Surround: Relationships of Intrinsic Religious Orientation With Fundamentalism and Right-Wing Authoritarianism." *Journal of Psychology and Theology* 31(4): 315–329.

Weber, Marianne. 1907. *Ehefrau und Mutter in der Rechtsentwicklung*. Tübingen, Germany: J. C. B. Mohr.

Weber, Max. [1905] 1998. *The Protestant Ethic and the Spirit of Capitalism*, translated by Talcott Parsons. Los Angeles: Roxbury.

——. [1905] 2002. *The Protestant Ethic and the Spirit of Capitalism*, translated by Stephen Kalberg. Los Angeles: Roxbury.

——. [1918] 1946. "Science as a Vocation." *From Max Weber*. New York: Oxford University Press.

——. [1918] 1958. *From Max Weber: Essays in Sociology*. New York: Oxford University Press.

——. [1919] 1952. *Ancient Judaism*. New York: The Free Press.

——. [1919] 1958. *From Max Weber: Essays in Sociology*. New York: Oxford University Press.

——. [1919] 1967. *Ancient Judaism*. New York: The Free Press.

——. [1920] 1958. *The Protestant Ethic and the Spirit of Capitalism*, translated by Talcott Parsons. Boston: Roxbury.

——. [1920] 2002. *The Protestant Ethic and the Spirit of Capitalism*, translated by Stephen Kalberg. Boston: Roxbury.

——. 1978. *Economy and Society*, Vols. 1 and 2. Berkeley and Los Angeles: University of California Press.

Wee, C. J. W. L. 1994. "Christian Manliness and National Identity: The Problematic Construction of a Racially Pure Nation." In *Muscular Christianity: Embodying the Victorian Age*. New York: Cambridge University Press.

Weeks, Louis B. 1993. "Presbyterian Culture: Views from 'the Edge.'" In *Beyond Establishment: Protestant Identity in a Postmodern Age*, edited by Jackson W. Carroll and Wade Clark Roof. Louisville, KY: Westminster/John Knox Press.

Weibel, Deana. 2005. "The Virgin Mary Versus the Monkeys." In *Religious Innovation in a Global Age*, edited by George N. Lundskow. Jefferson, NC: McFarland.

Weinstein, Deena. 1991. *Heavy Metal: A Cultural Sociology*. New York: MacMillan.

——. *Heavy Metal: The Music and Its Culture*. Cambridge, MA: Da Capo Press.

Weis, Rene. 2002. *The Yellow Cross: The Story of the Last Cathars' Rebellion Against the Inquisition, 1290–1329*. New York: Vintage Books.

Wenner, Jann S. 2006. "A Cleansing Election." *Rolling Stone*, November 30.

Wessinger, Catherine. 2000. *How the Millennium Comes Violently: From Jonestown to Heaven's Gate*. New York: Chatham House.

"Where Women Rule." 2004. *Ode Magazine*.

White, Tim D. 1992. *Prehistoric Cannibalism at Mancos 5Mtumr-2346*. Princeton, NJ: Princeton University Press.

Wieviorka, Michel. 1993. *The Making of Terrorism.* Chicago: University of Chicago Press.

——. *The Arena of Racism.* Thousand Oaks, CA: Sage Publications.

Wilcox, Clyde. 1988. "Seeing the Connection: Religion and Politics in the Ohio Moral Majority." *Review of Religious Research* 30 (1):47–58.

——. "Feminism and Anti-Feminism Among White Evangelical Women." *Western Political Quarterly* 42:147–160.

——. *God's Warriors: The Christian Right in Twentieth-Century America.* Baltimore: Johns Hopkins University Press.

Wilcox, Clyde and Elizabeth Cook. 1989. "Evangelical Women and Feminism: A Second Look." *Women and Politics* 9:27–50.

Wilcox, Clyde and Carin Larson. 2006. *Onward Christian Soldiers: The Religious Right in American Politics.* Boulder, CO: Westview Press.

Wilken, Robert Louis. 2003. *The Christians as the Romans Saw Them.* New Haven: Yale University Press.

Wilkins, Tracy. 2007. *The Vatican's Exorcists: Driving Out the Devil in the 21st Century.* New York: Warner Books/Hatchette Group.

Willner, Ann Ruth. 1984. *The Spellbinders: Charismatic Political Leadership.* New Haven, CT: Yale University Press.

Wilson, Bryan. 1975. *Magic and the Millennium.* St. Albans, UK: Paladin.

——. 1999. *New Religious Movements: Challenge and Response.* New York: Routledge.

Wilson, William Julius. 1997. *When Work Disappears: The World of the New Urban Poor.* New York: Vintage Press.

Witte, John and Michael Bourdeaux. (eds.). 1999. *Proselytism and Orthodoxy in Russia: The New War for Souls.* Maryknoll, NY: Orbis Books.

Włodarczyk, J. 2005. "Skąd się wziął syndrom." *Krytyka Polityczna* 4 (7/8):372–386.

Wolfe, Alan. 2003. *The Transformation of American Religion: How We Actually Live Our Faith.* New York: The Free Press.

Wolff, Leon. 1958. In *Flanders Fields.* New York: Viking Press.

Wolffe, John. 1994. "Anti-Catholicism and New Evangelical Identity in Britain and the United States, 1830–1860." *In New Evangelicalism: Comparative Studies of Popular Protestantism in the North America, the British Isles, and Beyond.* New York: Oxford University Press.

——. 2007. *The Expansion of Evangelicalism: The Age of Wilberforce, More, Chalmers and Finney.* Downers Grove, IL: Intervarsity Academic.

Worikoo, Niraj. 2007. "Northwest Plans to Pay Muslims Kept Off Flight." *Detroit Free Press,* January 18.

Worrell, Mark. P. 2005. "Surplus, Excess, Waste, Leftovers, and Remainders: The Dialectic of Productive Functions, Antisemitism, and the Vicissitudes of Social Forces." In *Religious Innovation in a Global Age,* edited by George N. Lundskow. Jefferson, NC: McFarland.

Wright, Bonnie. 2005. "Discerning the Spirit in the Context of Racial Integration and Conflict in Two Assemblies of God Churches." *Journal for the Theory of Social Behavior* 35 (4):413–435.

Wright, Bonnie and Anne Warfield Rawls. 2005. "The Dialectics of Belief and Practice: Religious Process as Praxis." *Critical Sociology* 31:1–2.

——. 2006. "Speaking in Tongues: A Dialectic of Faith and Practice." In *Marx, Critical Theory, and Religion: A Critique of Rational Choice,* edited by Warren S. Goldstein. Boston: Brill.

Wright, Stuart A. (ed.). 1995. *Armageddon in Waco: Critical Perspectives on the Branch Davidian Conflict.* Chicago: University of Chicago Press.

Wuthnow, Robert. 1998. *After Heaven: Spirituality in America Since the 1950s.* Berkeley: University of California Press.

Yamakage, Motohisa. 2006. *The Essence of Shinto: Japan's Spiritual Heart.* New York: Kodansa.

Yenne, Bill. 2005. *Indian Wars: The Campaign for the American West.* Yardley, PA: Westholme.

Yinger, Milton J. and Stephen J. Cutler. 1984. "The Moral Majority Viewed Sociologically." In *New Christian Politics,* edited by David G. Bromley and Anson Shupe. Macon, GA: Mercer University Press.

Yurica, Katherine. 2005. "The Despoiling of America: How George W. Bush Became the Head of the New American Dominionist Church/State." Available online at http://www.yuri careport.com/Dominionism/TheDespoilingOfAmerica.htm.

Zafirovsky, Milan. 2007. *The Protestant Ethic and the Spirit of Authoritarianism: Puritanism, Democracy, and Society.* New York: Springer.

Zigas, Vincent. 1990. *Laughing Death: The Untold Story of Kuru.* Totowa, NJ: Humana Press.

Zinnbauer, Brian J. and Kenneth I. Pergament. 1998. "Spiritual Conversion: A Study of Religious Change Among College Students." *Journal for the Scientific Study of Religion* 37 (1) March:161–180.

Index

About the Author

George N. Lundskow's long-standing interest in religion and social theory began academically at his Jesuit high school. Since then, Professor Lundskow has examined religion in the context of social change, both reactionary and progressive. Professor Lundskow also maintains that theory must always develop in conjunction with empirical observation. In this way, C. Wright Mills's *The Sociological Imagination* informs his general approach to sociology—that sociology should contribute to vital issues of the day.

In his own theoretical perspective, Lundskow draws mostly from Erich Fromm and Pierre Bourdieu. First-generation critical theorists with an empirical focus such as Paul Massing in *Rehearsal for Destruction,* contemporary scholars such as Daniel Bell in *The Cultural Contradictions of Capitalism,* and Peter Berger in *The Sacred Canopy* also inform his perspective. Like his predecessors, Lundskow rejects attempts to return to the past, but rather, like Mills, maintains that the sociological imagination requires passion and intellect, imagination and critical observation. In this direction, sociology offers much to help us understand the necessary social, psychological, and spiritual coherence that the human condition requires. Lundskow asks, How do we maintain individual initiative, insight, and passion and at the same time maintain a viable social character and civil society?

Presently, his research interests pertain to social change, and include alternative religious groups of the present, medieval demonology, and ancient class-cultural conflict. In particular, he is working on a sociological understanding of class and religion in the Greco-Roman and Byzantine world.

Marianne Weber's work, *Wife and Mother in the Development of Rights,* also inspires his interest in the possibility of Neolithic goddess-oriented civilizations that predated the arrival of patriarchal invaders. As this work has been available only in German, Professor Lundskow has started a translation of this 600-page volume with a colleague. Marija Gimbutas and others documented extensive archaeological evidence in the 1970s and 1980s beyond what was available in Marianne Weber's time, and Professor Lundskow would like to continue Marianne's sociological project.

Professor Lundskow is also currently working on a multimethod analysis of labor in the U.S. automobile industry, with several colleagues. This project also examines popular perceptions of the auto industry and attitudes about cars.